MUSIC IS THE DRUG

MUSIC IS THE DRUG

THE AUTHORISED BIOGRAPHY OF
COWBOY JUNKIES

DAVE BOWLER

OMNIBUS PRESS

London / New York / Paris / Sydney / Copenhagen / Berlin / Madrid / Tokyo

Dedicated to
A.L.B.
TIFM
D.W.B.

CONTENTS

AUTHOR'S NOTE

That this book came about at all says as much about Cowboy Junkies as the words contained in it. Catching them at the Liverpool Philharmonic Hall in October 2004, I was struck by Margo Timmins' comment from the stage that they were about to celebrate their twentieth anniversary. Seemed to me it was a good time to record that history, so I emailed them. Pretty much by return, Michael Timmins replied, and within a week had essentially given the green light, a remarkably open response, completely at odds with the secretive way in which most normal rock'n'roll bands operate.

You can tell from the music that the Junkies are anything but a "normal rock'n'roll band" and, as the research process for this book unfolded, that impression grew stronger, taking things in different and totally unexpected directions from those I originally had in mind.

This is not a biography in the classic sense – there's plenty of biographical information in here, but if you're looking for a simple chronological journey from A to B, this ain't it. Instead, as the hours of interview tape mounted, it became obvious that the story of Cowboy Junkies was far richer and far more complex than that, leaving me with a series of impressions of who they are, how they operate, where the music comes from and what impact it has on the musicians and on their audience. To try to make sense of it, the chronology is there as the backbone of the book, its chapters, but hanging off that, in between chapters are shorter tales, things that don't necessarily fit the business of recording the history, but which are, I hope, all the more illuminating for it. They're the "notes falling slow", if you like, that couldn't fit the main narrative but were worth saving.

Right from the outset, Mike made it clear that their twentieth anniversary was never simply an excuse for nostalgia, for it's as much a time for looking forward as back. Just as well given that, by the time this book was finished, the thirty-fifth anniversary was looming. As it always has been, maybe more so now than ever, Cowboy Junkies is an intellectually and emotionally ambitious, artistically driven unit which clearly believes that its best work is yet to be done. I can't think of another band, three decades in, where you would consider that possible. But the Junkies make believers of us all. That is their singular gift.

I'll come clean here. I'm a Junkies junkie, a believer. Given the chance, I'd be clocking up the miles in pursuit of more concerts just like Cookie Bob and Crazy Ed – if you haven't met them yet, don't worry, all will become clear. So much for objectivity, then, but let's be grown up about this. I've been on the fan side of the Cowboy Junkies equation since way back in 1988, a pretty thankless side of that equation if you happen to live in Junk-starved, junk-fuelled England. That makes you appreciate the records all the more, makes you devour them increasingly voraciously, instantly destroying your impartiality credentials. You either get it and live with it, or you move on to somebody you can see a little more often. And anyway, putting this kind of book together from five time zones away is hardly the work of the disinterested observer.

In this increasingly compartmentalized world, where every interest has its own TV channel, the idea of someone casually picking up a book about a band they've never heard of is, sadly, ever more absurd. So I think it's safe to say I'm preaching to the church here. And, like me, I guess most fans are pretty frustrated by the lack of recognition the band gets, despite creating a songbook as emotionally powerfully as anything created during their time as a band. They may not have changed the world the way The Beatles did, but for some of us Mike, Al, Pete and Margo make music that affects our personal universe every bit as much as did John, Paul, George and Ringo. That's no idle comparison, either, for, like the Fab Four, Cowboy Junkies is a band in the truest sense of the term, a unit where every member is important and valued, where each plays a part, obvious or otherwise, in holding it together, taking it forward and allowing it to create something which is a whole that far exceeds the sum of the individual parts.

It wasn't the intention, but as things turned out the interviews for this book were carried out over, oh, just the decade and a half.

In hindsight, it's as well it was for if it had been completed in those early days, we'd have missed *The Nomad Series* and *All That Reckoning*, which both play a huge part in the unfolding story. Equally, Cowboy Junkies of 2005 are not the same Cowboy Junkies of 2020: they write differently, record differently, tour differently. Those are developments wholly typical of them, a vital entity not afraid to question, to evolve, to change. If we revisit this thing in another ten years, there'll be new things to say by then, too, and that is an exciting prospect.

To give you some sense of how this was pieced together, the interviewing started in a snow-covered Montreal in February 2005 as *Early 21st Century Blues* was coming together in their Clubhouse studio, and then on the 'United States of Canada Blues States' tour, a blisteringly hot trek through the northeast United States in June of the same year – as the title of the tour suggests, it was hard then to conceive of a more divisive president than George W. Bush. Simpler days. I then went back to Toronto in November 2006 as the strings were being added to *At the End of Paths Taken* at Metal Works studio in Mississauga, tagged along with the electric and acoustic tours of the UK in early 2007, took in the June dates of that year back in the northeast USA, followed that up with the 'Trinity Revisited' tour of England that year and then hopped back over to the States to travel through Arizona, Texas and New Mexico in 2008. We added some more material on their brief jaunt to the UK in 2013 and finished it all off over the phone and then in Bristol and Holmfirth in 2019. They truly have the patience of saints.

Throughout that period, the band and those that work with them could not have been more helpful, open or welcoming. Whatever good there is in this book stems from a pretty admirable group of people who live a stranger professional existence than you might imagine. Whatever good there *isn't* … well, you'd be within your rights to shoot the messenger.

INTRODUCTION

Cowboy Junkies is a band that defies categorization, that refuses to be pinned down. You think you have a hold on them, their music, a heavy shot glass in which you swill life's golden liquid. Then, as you think you've got it taped, the tumbler tumbles, the whisky slips through a crack in the floorboards, and turns up behind you in a cocktail glass.

In years to come, the guy from 'Where Are You Tonight?' might still be you, someone like you, someone who was you, or will be you, but he won't be listening to 'Crazy' all night long. It'll be "Cause Cheap Is How I Feel' or 'Something More Besides You' or 'Notes Falling Slow'. And it'll still make the sound of a splintering life just the most beautiful, beguiling noise you ever heard. Because, somehow, in those slivers lie the hope that gets us all out of bed again to confront the next day. In *The Great Gatsby*, Nick Carraway speaks of Gatsby's "heightened sensitivity to the promises of life … an extraordinary gift for hope". He would have recognized that in Cowboy Junkies, too.

Wrap yourself in *The Trinity Session* or *At the End of Paths Taken*, and you'll be seduced and shocked, romanced and slapped across the face by reality, drawn in by emotions and by music that delivers on the duality that their name promises. Cowboys, junkies, lovers, losers, leavers, leavees, travellers, shysters, seers, searchers, scapegoats, bewildereds – they're all in these songs. *We're* all in these songs.

There's blood and soul in their music, purity and dust, loss and hope, humour and pain. Their music comes from Western rock'n'roll traditions, from American roots music, from European minimalism, from the folk idiom. But it draws from elsewhere, too, from a Zen tradition. Though not ascribing to the seventeen-syllable form, the ethos of the haiku is prevalent in Junkies music. That ancient form is all about opposites and the way in which they rub up against each other to give themselves sense, because one could not exist without the other. That is perhaps the central truth at the heart of their work; the heartbeat which gives it its sense of calm in the eye of the storm, its integrity, its reliability, its hope.

Another paradox. More duality. For all these most human elements, somehow, on record at least, Cowboy Junkies sometimes seem too fragile to exist. It's music that comes at you from some alien place, musicians insinuating themselves into the ether from the other side. Before you know it, they've put their hands over your eyes, their music in your ears and taken you someplace else, a place that is still your life, your world, but seen in half-light, in moonlight, in sunlight, in psychedelight, through the looking glass darkly. Put on that shiny compact disc and you can feel a scratchy 78 coming at you from tomorrow.

The music doesn't come from these people. Because they're open to it, it falls out of the sky, into them and then out of them. How could it be otherwise? These timeless twenty-first-century spirituals, written and recorded by people who are relentlessly normal, whose concerns are ours – did I turn the lights out, which school is the best for the kids, who's going to fix the roof, do these shoes look stupid?

And that's the other side of Cowboy Junkies, the band you get to see every year or so out on the road. The people who might have been sitting in the bar for an hour, who might have been in the pizza place or the coffee shop, or shopping at the local drugstore before realizing it's showtime. The people who get up on the stage, no fuss, no entourage, just getting up there, living and breathing the music before they work out where the hotel is that they're going to shower in afterwards, before getting back on the bus and heading off to another town.

Maybe it's those live shows that give you the closest idea of who and what Cowboy Junkies are. Where for some bands the audience sits there waiting to be impressed, the Junkies' audience wants them to do well. And, even if it's a rare night when they're not at their best, they accept that this is still the best show they're going to see this year and that the band has done everything it could to make it happen; that, to coin a phrase in a different context, the band "has kept it real". Because that's what a Junkies show is. Real.

They encompass the ends of their spectrum, where they can be as lost in a musical moment as we are, or where Margo might tell us about the vagaries of life lived out of a suitcase for weeks at a time, about missing home, bad hair days, a four-year-old who needs to know how he can pick his nose and climb the monkey bars at the same time, the joys or otherwise of your city. That too has its Zen roots, an egolessness that is completely alien to rock music. In the majority, you have Bono, Jagger, Madonna, Gaga, all screaming, "Look at me, listen to me!" That's fine, that's the way rock'n'roll operates. But then there's Cowboy Junkies saying, "We're playing here. You're welcome to come and be a part of it."

Yet another paradox, and one which songwriter and guitarist Michael Timmins acknowledges. "There is a real contradiction in our personalities. We don't court attention. I like being on my own. I don't like communal anything, really. I love the sense of being in a crowd and experiencing something as part of a whole, but I don't ever want to be the center of attention. I think we're all like that. But at the same time, we love having the music connect with people and this is the way you do it. We get a thrill out of the connection, not from being the ones doing the connecting. The energy is fun, it's exciting, it keeps us going. We love going onstage, but the thrill isn't 'See me!' It's more the potential of having one of those nights where you connect and that feels so amazing. That's what's always turned us on."

There is a live, vital connection between band and fans (the "llamas" who follow them so assiduously), and even those who tune in more casually. Maybe it's the bond of fellow travellers – for the music, even once it's recorded, continues to breathe, change, take on the experience of musicians and audience. The songbook grows older with us just as the ongoing additions to it reflect the distance they've come and how far we all still have to go.

For some – those outside the llama enclosure, those who buy their music solely from gas stations and supermarkets – it's possible to believe that Cowboy Junkies was born somewhere around 1988, lasted a couple of years, made *Trinity Session* and a couple more records, then burned out. These are the same people who believe that Cassius Clay and Muhammad Ali are two different people and that it's amazing that Jack Nicklaus won so many golf tournaments yet still had time to be so great in *One Flew Over the Cuckoo's Nest*. We need not concern ourselves with them.

Instead, let us concentrate on the band that shouldn't have made it, but did – and does – in an era of corporatism, of image, of lies, of no ethics. A band that is wholly about music, ethics, philosophy. A band that exists for the music in a time when the music industry seemingly exists solely to destroy it, to lowest-common-denominator it, to replace it with data, to create lower and lower attention thresholds so you're not satisfied by the album you just bought but have to go get, download or stream a new one.

Cowboy Junkies has its own heartbeat, its own internal logic, its own way of doing things. Most important, over thirty years into existence, Cowboy Junkies still has places to go, music to make. There ain't no turning back.

CHAPTER 1

Marching to the slow

You can't work out quite what that noise is. But then, you don't get time to process it before you're overwhelmed by a voluptuous tsunami of a sound. Which is ironic. So much of what is to come is about taking time, being given time. Time to let it breathe, to let it speak, to let it take hold. Time to be.

There's a silence, then a whoosh, like waves, but not. Back then, as the needle hit the groove for the first time, you had a split second to curse and think you'd got a faulty vinyl pressing, awash with surface noise. And then Margo Timmins opens her mouth. Then you get it. Even though it's a solitary voice, the band nowhere to be heard, not even in the building when the recording was made, a sound is being laid down. The sound of Cowboy Junkies.

Those few seconds are among the signal sounds of popular music, as devastating as the curl of feedback on 'I Feel Fine', as much a signature as Keef cranking out that riff at the start of 'Satisfaction'. A sound you can't ever forget. Nor would you want to. They are the opening moments of *The Trinity Session*, a recording that was to change the lives of siblings Michael, Margo and Peter Timmins and Alan Anton, a friend that all three had known pretty much forever. Change, but not transform. The change came with the possibility of a career as a professional band stretching into the future instead of as a quartet playing tiny bars and looking for floors to sleep on as they crisscrossed America.

These are not people to be transformed by the shallow nature of commercial success, nor people who would give themselves over to the industry at Robert Johnson's crossroads. To the music maybe, but not to the industry. More than thirty years on from that remarkable session in the Church of the Holy Trinity, Toronto, of course, they are all different people, just as every one of us who have lived those years are different. They have lived another 11,000 days or more since then. Who isn't going to evolve through experience? But, at the core, they are still the same. Cowboy Junkies still has the same ethos, the same principles, the same ideals that the band had when it first rumbled into life back in 1985. That's a rare achievement, certainly in the music business, but you can hear it's true just by listening to the recordings they've made along the way.

You can hear that it was always going to be that way in the couplet of songs that open *The Trinity Session*, their second album, but the one that launched them into a world beyond the Toronto club scene and the American bar circuit. From the purity of a solitary voice and into the mournful wail of the harmonica, another signature sound, the music is immediately about life and death, about relationships, emotion, hope, rare honesty rather than the glib cynicism that characterized the music of the 1980s, music that was processed to death in soulless recording studios, packed with more equipment than NASA. This was a sound unlike anything else, made by people who were happy to be not rock stars, but music fans, just like the people they were making the records for.

Being music fans and remaining music fans has been the central part of their story. It makes them fairly unusual. You'd be amazed how few people who actually work in the music business have anything other than a passing interest in the subject. If you sell engine bearings for a living, maybe you don't take your work home with you. But making a living from music should be about as good as it gets. Instead, too many, musicians included, don't have enough songs in their collection to discomfort the capacity of even the tiniest smartphone. Cowboy Junkies have collections that date back pretty much to kindergarten and which have been growing ever since.

Though Cowboy Junkies have come to be closely associated with Toronto, they all grew up in Montreal. As Alan recalls, they were exposed to an odd duality in that city, right from birth. "It was strange to grow up in a city with two distinct cultures, French and English, as we lived in a very English enclave and didn't interact much with French-speaking Montrealers until we were older and exploring the city. At 17 or 18 when you're looking for a job and realizing that you need to speak both languages to earn a living, you think maybe you should have paid more attention in French class."

By 1977, Montreal was behind them as they moved to Toronto. For Pete, the youngest in the family, it was a good place to escape to. "The Timmins name carried something in Montreal, that was always behind you. You'd meet people and they'd say, 'Oh, you're the Timminses of Montreal.' Not that we lived the lifestyle they were talking about, because Dad wasn't rich and he was very conservative with his money. He thinks we're nuts when we buy things!"

The town of Timmins in northeastern Ontario grew up around a goldmine in the early twentieth century, a claim partly developed by Mike, Margo and Pete's great-grandfather, a claim that made him and his brother wealthy and made the Timmins family local celebrities of sorts. But, as money has a habit of doing, it had long dried up by the time their musical descendants came on the scene. Mike explains that "Dad had left home when he was 16 and things were very arm's length with the Timmins 'legacy'. Our growing up was very normal. Dad worked like a dog to provide a very comfortable life for his six kids and never really got the credit, because most people outside the family probably thought that it was all handed to him."

A strong work ethic was one gift that the Timmins siblings received from their parents, something that has been an important component in their career. Equally as crucial was the ton of guts that appears to come with the birth certificate in this family. For all its gentle nature, this is a collective that has balls. Mike constantly opens himself up to scrutiny in his songs. Pete turned up with a drum kit as the Junkies were forming, ready to play despite never having hit a beat in anger before. Margo was equally untrained and then found herself singing a cappella to barrooms full of drunks. She traces that willingness to try back to her upbringing.

"I think our attitudes and our willingness to do things came from our parents. My dad always did what he wanted to do. He wasn't a rebel but he loved airplanes. He always stayed in that field, but when he felt it was time to switch jobs, he did. Even though he had six kids to feed, he felt he could manage it. If he wasn't happy, he went. He never collected the pension. He used to travel a lot when we were kids and he used to say, 'Rome is only as far as the airport.' And it is – you have to go get the money too, but that's a whole other problem!

"I think we were lucky that my mom always raised us as individuals. She never compared us. Some were better in school, some of us were better at swimming – I was good at swimming! – but that was OK, she never pushed us to be the same little peas in a pod. We were never brought up with the expectation that you should be a banker or a lawyer or a doctor, you could become whatever you wanted to become. That's not to say they didn't freak out when three of us formed a band and disappeared, because having half your kids join a band isn't something you want as a parent. I can see that now! But whatever courage we have is part of who we are. We just do it. It's not a 'look how brave I am' thing.

"None of us have ever cared much about our status, how cool or sexy or pretty we are or we aren't. It is what it is. If you start from there, if you can just get onstage and be comfortable in your flowing, flowery dress that's not in fashion any more, then it's easy. You do it. Same with our older brother John when he agreed to come and play guitar on tour with us after being out of the band for nearly twenty years. It's scary to start doing this for the first time at 50, God knows, but that's exciting. That's the fun part. He knew he didn't have to live up to any expectations except his and ours, and that's always been our way, in the band and at home.

"Maybe having six of us, we've always had a support group. We liked each other and our parents, so we've always had a security blanket. Doing whatever we were doing was easy because we knew we'd be supported – 'even if the rest of the world thinks I'm nuts, my sister will like it!' That's a gift my parents gave us. If my mom had married someone else, I guess it would have been different, because a lot of what people see as guts comes from my dad. He always gave us the idea that this was your life, you had to live it as you wanted, believe in what you're doing and just do it. If it works out, great; if not, move on. No big deal."

Oldest brother John Timmins picks up the theme. "What people might see as courage comes from our upbringing, from the world view we were given as kids by our parents. My father's modus operandi was 'Do what moves you.' Though he added a qualification to that: 'Make sure you make a lot of money!' He did teach that to us in the way he lived his life, that's the biggest example of having guts that you'd find. I edited his memoirs and you see it all the time in his life; he went through all sorts of changes. His passion was not music, it was aviation in the earliest days of commercial aviation in Canada, and you can see in his career the intelligent approach he took, seeing which way the wind was blowing, going with it, but always following his passion rather than mere opportunity. So what may look like a lot of guts, it's a lot easier if you have a love and a passion for what you're doing. You diminish the challenge. I think we all grew up with the feeling that if you love it, just get on and do it. It sounds like a simplistic approach, probably is, but I guess it gets results. Even in my non-music life, I've had a lot of stops and starts, changed direction, ignored some sound advice, all in favour of the voice within."

Pete is very much of the same opinion, adding, "I just like trying new things. I picked up the drums because I wanted to be involved in what Mike and Al were doing. I guess it does take balls but maybe it's more curiosity than anything. I started painting in the mid-1990s and I got really into that and then graphic design. It's just being willing to see if you can do something. Dad is a pretty strong character, Mom too, and coming from that has a lot to do with going out and trying things. It's kinda natural. My mother raised us that way, 'Just go give it your best shot.'"

Music was always around the Timmins household too, a host of it by the time Mike and Margo were old enough to pay attention. "At Christmas," recalls Margo, "records were always things you got as gifts. I'd get a Burl Ives children's record from somebody, a Moody Blues album from somebody else. It was pretty varied right from the start. That was normal to me. Every day, when my dad got home from work, he'd put on a big band record and so we were always listening to music. He'd been a drummer as a hobby when he was younger."

A different kind of music was also coming into the house from another source – John Timmins, the eldest of six siblings and perhaps the most fortunate of all when it came to the music of his time. "I'd turned 50 when I returned to work with the band on the *Early 21st Century Blues* record in 2005, so you can work out the years when I got into music. I was pretty lucky with that timing because I really started to absorb music in the mid-1960s. I was a very big Beatles fan as a

5

kid and I remember all those great summer album releases marked my childhood in a very big way. I could pretty much tell you what happened to me in each year according to which Beatle album was out at the time. *The White Album* is still an extraordinary record, still head and shoulders above anything that's out there today for its musicality, its timing, its cultural impact.

"As the older brother, I was bringing this music into the house and I didn't exclude my younger siblings any more than any other older brother would. They listened to my music with impunity when I was home – Mike was four years younger; Margo, five. Then a little later, I was playing with friends in bands and I think that came filtering down too, and showed the others, especially Mike, that it was something you could do."

Pete wasn't equipped to hear *The White Album* at the time. He was two. 'Revolution 9' is probably lost on you at that stage. But John's music was being voraciously consumed by another youngster, Alan Anton. Despite not being part of the Timmins family, Alan was in on the start of the Junkies even before his partner in the rhythm section. That's proved important as the years have gone on.

"I don't think it's ever really mattered that I'm not a Timmins, just because I've been there so long," he says. "Pete was just a baby when I really stated hanging out with Mike. We go back to kindergarten, so I've known Mike and Margo even longer than Pete has. I'd hang out there and John educated us in music. He was the guy who had all the records, going through the late 1960s, bringing home the Velvet Underground, The Beatles. 'You gotta hear this man, it's really great!' He was instrumental in getting us into music, and really cool music too, because he had such good taste."

"John was very important to us," agrees Mike. "In the late 1960s he was in his late teens so he brought all those Beatles, Stones, Doors records into the house. Everything that was happening then, commercial and non-commercial, I was getting to hear. At a very young age I was listening to weird music, not really understanding it but being fascinated by it. I hooked up with Al and we'd share records – we'd go to the record store and he'd buy one album and I'd get another so we could tape each other's, so we developed our tastes together. From a very early age I was obsessed by music, I was a fan, my world revolved around buying records, going to shows. Same with

Al, too – that's what bound us together, maybe the only thing in many ways, and it still is."

"We were the musicheads at school," continues Alan. "Buying records, reading the rock press, especially from England. There was no rock criticism in the States until *Rolling Stone* came out, in 1967. They missed the whole decade that really created the rock industry. There was some great rock writing in England, especially through the 1970s. I used to buy *NME* just for the writing. They were lucky to have Anton Corbijn doing a lot of photography, which was perfect for the time. I love his work. We did a shoot with him once – we were in awe of his style."

The Beatles cast a long shadow over rock music, even today. Closer to the fact, after their split in 1970, chronicled in the pages of that nascent *Rolling Stone* by Lennon's exorcism of an interview, their legacy coloured the early part of that decade, not only because of the music they made, but the way in which they'd made it. After they quit the stage at Candlestick Park in 1966, John, Paul, George and Ringo retreated to the studio to make a new kind of record, one only hinted at on *Rubber Soul*, the hints getting heavier on *Revolver*. Until then, recording had been about putting your live act down on tape. In the future, recording and performing would become very separate art forms. The expanding imagination of The Beatles – and many other acts, such as the Beach Boys, whose *Pet Sounds* was another landmark – demanded new sounds, sounds you couldn't get simply by strumming a guitar, thumping the drums or even by bringing in an orchestra. They forced producer George Martin and the recording engineers at Abbey Road to turn the studio into another instrument, to cobble together pieces of equipment to create hybrids and, above all, to link together recording consoles to give them more and more tracks to play with on every song. When *Sgt. Pepper* was finished in 1967, it represented a long journey from the two-track recordings of *Please Please Me* just four years before.

Technology continued to evolve ever more quickly and, by the mid-1970s, the major acts were routinely making their records on forty-eight-track desks, while musicians were becoming more and more technically proficient. As Alan says, "We grew up listening to classic rock. One of the hardest things was that rock music had become so sophisticated that you couldn't imagine yourself starting a band and competing with Pink Floyd. How would you do that? Everything was so layered in these huge studios. It was all so expensive, so technical, we could just never imagine playing music within the business. You listen to Steely Dan, you never think you can be in a band."

Mike agrees, remembering that the shows they went to as early teens were at once inspirational and restricting. "Toronto was a great town for concerts in the 1970s and we saw dozens and dozens of bands. One of the first big ones was Bowie on the 'Diamond Dogs' tour – we bought tickets from a scalper. We were fans, but for some reason we never thought we could do it too, maybe because that was the age of the rock star, Mick Jagger, David Bowie. We couldn't do that. We were supposed to sit back and listen."

And then things changed. The protagonists will argue forever over who started the ball rolling, but when Johnny Rotten roared that he was an antichrist, pop music shifted on its axis. Asked to select his ten favourite British punk songs for the *Independent* newspaper in 2004, Alan wrote, "'Anarchy in the UK' is the groundbreaker, the summation of an ethos, delivered with so much anger that there is no doubt about the message, nor any question of the messengers' commitment." With imported English punk records costing $15 each, Mike and Alan would pool their resources to buy three new ones a week to learn the ropes from this new blueprint that was constantly changing, however simple the ethos.

Music kept the two of them in touch, even as they grew up and could have grown apart, as Alan points out. "I was still in Montreal, a meter reader, checking the electricity meters in some really wealthy houses. One day I went into this huge living room with this huge painting above the fireplace, Chairman Mao, these bizarre colours. I'm 18, so I was, 'Wow, that's just amazing! What is it?' 'It's a Warhol my husband bought for $5,000.' Turns out that was a pretty good investment.

"Anyway, Mike had gone off to university and we were in touch, but we didn't see a lot of each other. I gave him a call and said we should think about getting a band together. Mike was interested, and he said that he wasn't really into his literature degree, that he didn't want to go on and use it as a career kind of thing, he wanted to be a jet pilot. His dad had got him an interview in Ottawa a few days later, and it happened there was a film festival on there, and we were really into film. They were screening this seven-hour German movie, *Our Hitler*, and we wanted to see it, so I drove Mike out there. He went into the interview and, pretty much as soon as he got through the door, they turned him down because he was too tall! We saw the movie, drove home and on the way pretty much decided to get a band together."

Mike's memory of it all is a little different: "I don't know if I wanted to be an airline pilot. I guess it was one of my early career choices – my dad was in aviation and, as a kid, I spent a lot of time going on business trips with him. Part of his career was selling business jets, those twelve-passenger type of things, Lears and de Havillands, and so he'd demonstrate them, maybe fly Toronto to Dallas, then turn round and come back the next day. I would quite often go with him, sit in the back if he felt the client wouldn't mind, and so I was really into planes. It was my father's life, so naturally it fascinated me. I learned to fly pretty young, I did a few interesting things – flew a small twin-engine plane across the Atlantic as a co-pilot, I flew in the Middle East as a co-pilot for three months. I guess my idea was that it was something I might do, but after I got a commercial licence I flew a bit as a commercial pilot and quickly realized I didn't like it. It was like driving a bus, just a bit more dangerous, so I stopped it.

"Music was becoming a bigger and bigger thing. Punk was a revelation for so many people. You didn't have to be a rock star, you could just play, be a musician, be a non-musician, just pick up a guitar, slam it around and express yourself. We totally bought into that. We were 17, 18, and it hit us really hard and set us off. We were lucky that there was a great punk scene in Toronto, very intense, The Edge was a great club where all the touring bands from London and New York played – Toronto had a couple of excellent promoters, so anybody coming to the US would usually come to Toronto as well. I remember we sat in there after a show one night and just said, 'Let's start a band.' This was 1979. A 'let's do the show right here!' thing, that was the way it affected us. We rented guitars and found a space and started trying to figure it out. We went from there, the DIY philosophy. Al and I both played guitar, we got a drummer in, a guy called Geoff Railton. He was the singer and bass player for the Popular Spies, who were pretty popular here, but he liked what we wanted to do and joined up with us. Then we started to look for a female singer."

They looked quite close to home, according to Margo. "I auditioned for the band, but thankfully I failed. It wasn't really my kind of band, I didn't have the attitude that it needed. Eventually the band broke up anyway, so later on I got a second chance!"

Liza Dawson-Whisker, later to be Alan's sister-in-law, got the gig in the end, and Hunger Project was formed. Prime inspirations were the Velvet Underground, Siouxsie and the Banshees and Joy Division, an influence that would endure. "We were huge Joy Division fans after *Unknown Pleasures* came out," says Alan. "We were just listening to that all the time. I'd say, if any one album defines the sound of Cowboy Junkies, it's that one. That whole idea of space. The sadness, the heaviness in the music. That record was mind-blowing for us. Mike and I had tickets to see them at The Edge, where I used to work as a bartender actually. They would always get bands on their first station-wagon tour, get them over after the first album. It held 200 people. Joy Division were due to fly out for their tour but, the night before, Ian Curtis killed himself. Pretty selfish, I know, but I was so pissed off. The other guys did a few of the dates where they were booked – New York, LA, the big towns – played as a three-piece, no singing, just the music as a kind of memorial service. That would have been real interesting to see."

With those influences working their way through a band whose sound was "mid-range and aggressive" according to Mike, where both guitarists would turn their backs on the audience and the singer would be happy to antagonize them, Hunger Project was an archetypal punk band. But the Toronto punk scene flared into life only briefly. Soon enough, it had burned out around them.

CHAPTER 2

Some time in New York City

If you were young and wanted to get a band, especially a punk band, off the ground in 1979, Toronto was not the place to do it. Nor Canada, period. There was almost no such thing as Canadian music then, the nation's most successful musical sons and daughters, such as Neil Young, Joni Mitchell, The Band and Leonard Cohen, all having flown to the United States to create their music, build their reputations. By the late 1970s – as far as the rest of the world was concerned, anyway – they were honorary Americans. Ask anyone beyond the border to name a Canadian band at the time and few would come up with much beyond hard-rock staples such as Rush, Triumph or Max Webster. *Have Not Been the Same*, the weighty volume devoted to the "CanRock renaissance" of the mid-1980s and beyond, concedes that any interesting music scene that there might have been earlier in the 1970s had pretty much reached the end of the road, with interest in punk and New Wave drying up after The Edge closed its doors and the Horseshoe Tavern reverted to the safer waters of country and western. Few were listening; there was no place to play even for bands who wanted to. But just a few hundred miles away was New Wave New York. The next step for Hunger Project didn't take much thinking about.

"It wasn't that big a deal at the time," remembers Mike. "Moving to New York wasn't a career thing. We were playing in Toronto and we got a certain amount of notoriety, but a few clubs started to close, the scene was shutting down a little bit so we figured we'd go to New York for a while. We used to go there all the time anyway, because it was the place to see the bands we were into. We'd get in a car and drive overnight, ten hours, see a show, sleep in the car, drive back. For us, New York wasn't that extreme, it was a place we knew as tourists. We knew the scene, we knew the clubs, we knew a few people. It was a magnet, as it still is, and always will be, I guess. I'd finished university, got a BA in history, so I wasn't tied down here. It was nothing more than me and Al sitting round saying, 'What do you wanna do?'

"'I don't know. Let's move to New York.'

"'OK.'

"Nothing more to it than that, literally. Just the same way we'd decided to form Hunger Project originally – no great plan behind it. A friend of ours drove us there in his station wagon, we went to the East Village, rented a place and that was it. We were still just doing what we wanted to do, looking for something we could connect to."

Hunger Project rented a place on the Lower East Side, on Avenue B, near 14th Street. It was cheap. No wonder. Alan gave John Timmins a guided tour of their old haunts when they were in town for a gig in June 2005. Writing the online tour diary for the Junkies, John noted that, twenty-five years earlier, it was "a neighbourhood that was so literally burned out, crime ridden and drug infested that the cops stayed away. Today, it has been painted and gentrified. There are dog runs in the park and it is a much happier place, or would appear to be." It's not so cheap any more, either.

Actually, even way back then, the cops didn't always stay away, according to Alan. "There used to be a club, after-hours bar called A7, the only bar within twenty blocks. The area was just a desert, a ghetto, and this was the only bar that stayed open late. It attracted all kinds of bad business, cops were always there and, somehow, Hunger Project got a gig there because it was a kind of hip place. Ten cop cars pulled up outside and they busted absolutely everybody in the whole place except us. We said, 'We're Canadian!' We showed them our driver's licences and that was OK, they let us go!

"One New Year's Eve, we were coming back from some party or something in the Village, it was snowing, so I said to Mike, 'It'll be OK tonight, it's snowing, New Year, the boys aren't going be on the streets tonight, we can just go straight back home.' So we went the direct way, which we would never do, because it was terrifying. You spend five minutes there and, normally, you'd be dead. I had my bike with me because I was a bike courier at the time. We turned the corner and, sure enough, there was a whole gang around some burning barrels. They looked over at us, 'Hey white boys!' I said, 'Oh fuck', dropped my bike and we just ran! That was the end of my bike courier career. It was a really scary neighbourhood. Greg Keelor from Blue Rodeo came to visit us one time and got mugged at gunpoint.

"We had our tourist moments, too; it was a cool place to be. One night, we went up to Radio City Music Hall for the premiere of a Coppola movie and he was there, wearing a parka for some reason, sitting in the aisle seat, and we were just looking at him, that was really cool. Great movie, *One from the Heart*. As we walked out into the lobby, up on the second level, the balcony, I looked up and saw this guy with a blond wig looking down. 'Holy fuck, that's Andy Warhol! Mike, look!' That made the night. Another time, Mike couldn't sleep, and at four in the morning he went out for a walk, ended up in Greenwich Village, Bleecker Street, and Bob Dylan was there, showing this pretty little girl around, taking her on his little tour, pointing out the spots where he'd started, that kind of thing. It was so weird, nobody out there except Bob and this girl."

In its run-down state, it was the perfect location for a group to learn how to play. Mike remembers that "We lived on the ground floor behind an empty storefront. We cut a hole in the floor of our apartment which got us into the rear of the cellar. We then built a cinder-block wall which cut off the front of the cellar. The only way in was through the hole in our floor. We rehearsed in that hole for hours every night for a year. Never a complaint from anyone in the building. It must have been loud as hell.

"It's easy to be an illegal in New York, there are lots of jobs you can do to make money, and we spent the rest of our time playing – Al worked as a courier at one time, then in a real high-end deli and, at the end of the day, he'd bring back fresh salads, bread, whatever they had left, that's what we lived on, so we ate pretty well at least. I worked in a dildo store. When we rehearsed, we were just kids who'd barely started to play. It took us a year to really work out how the equipment worked, real basic stuff like turning the amps on."

Later assessments have labelled Hunger Project as an art-rock outfit, an interesting indicator of where Mike and Alan would eventually end

13

up. Though Hunger Project was formed in the wake of the punk DIY ideal, it wasn't quite so instinctive or thoughtless as that suggests. Even then, there was a lot of conceptualizing going on in the background, a hallmark of Cowboy Junkies in due course. The very fact that they were such musical novices was crucial, as Alan points out. "We didn't really start to play until we were around 18, 19. That was a good thing in a lot of ways because we'd absorbed all this music, we'd got tons of influences, a pretty good knowledge of music and a lot of ideas to work with. We had enough musical education by then to work out a sound that we wanted to make, but we didn't have the technique to do too much because we couldn't really play. That narrowed the focus. Those limits made for more original music."

CBGB was the epicentre of the New Wave scene in New York, the setting for legendary gigs by Patti Smith, Television, Talking Heads, Blondie, the Ramones et al. But one club alone cannot sustain a movement and through those vibrant times New York had been full of punk clubs. "Had" being the operative word, because by the time Hunger Project pitched up in New York, CBGB was pretty well all that was left of it, as the rest of the city moved on to the next thing. Nothing stays still for long in New York, as Mike accepts. "Our timing was off. That whole New Wave thing was tailing off there. The same things started happening that we'd gone through in Toronto. The clubs started closing, and we never really did connect, we were outsiders. Maybe we just weren't there long enough, just a year I guess, but nothing was happening for us. But, while we were in the States, we thought we should make the most of it and we did some touring. We went through the Midwest, down to Texas, across to the West Coast, just literally picking up gigs as we went, making phone calls to try to find clubs. But, after we'd done that, again we were thinking, 'What next?'"

Just as New York had seemed the obvious destination when they were back in Toronto, the next move was just as inevitable. With The Cure, Joy Division and the Banshees as key influences, England was the place to be. The move across the Atlantic wasn't as daunting as it might have been, as Alan explains. "It wasn't happening for us as Hunger Project. We did tours out of here and the posters would say 'From New York', so people would come to check that out. But that music was dying in the States, so London seemed the place to try, that was where our influences were from. Liza's mother had a house in Notting Hill

Gate where we could live for free if we showed up." And, as Mike says, "I could sign on the dole straight away, too, because my grandmother was English. So we did – we showed up."

Less determined characters might have started to think they'd be better off going back to the day job, if they'd had one, because "We moved there just as the scene we loved ended," remembers Alan. "1982 wasn't a good year to get there. We had three years in London and it just became a horrible place for music. ABC was the biggest band. Just about the only good band around was The Birthday Party, who weren't even from England but were living there too, so we caught their gigs all the time, still some of the best shows I've ever seen, so intense. When they were all on the right drugs and they connected, they were amazing. Jesus and Mary Chain were around, maybe a couple of others, but it was mostly terrible. There was nowhere to play, you had to pay to play if you wanted to get a gig, put up £300 and they'd book you, so we ended up doing two gigs or something and the band finished really quickly. We were doing Siouxsie and the Banshees type material, but really slow, a lot like Cowboy Junkies in that sense. I played guitar as well, so we had two guitars, drums and voice. It had a New York-y kind of feel to it, like Bush Tetras maybe, a guitar-noise thing. Our big influences were The Cure, Joy Division for sure, Siouxsie, Killing Joke. We played loud and slow, kinda like The Swans. We even toured with them in the early days. They had two drummers playing the exact same beat and they were even louder and slower than us, pretty cool."

Hunger Project didn't survive for long in that London environment, but Mike, Alan and Geoff Railton continued to make music together, occasionally adding sax player Richard O'Callaghan to the fold. As Mike admits, the music scene they found turned out to be a blessing in disguise. "We hadn't really known where to take Hunger Project next, so it was just time to break that up. Musically, London was horrible, but it was good in a way because it totally made us rework our thinking. Pop music at that time was dead to us; we didn't want anything to do with Haircut 100 or ABC. So we went very internal, explored all these strange avenues in music, listened to a lot of jazz, a lot of improvisational stuff, went to a lot of experimental concerts, we really explored that and got into it. It opened up our ears." That improvisational approach would become a staple of the Junkies' live set in years to come.

15

Plenty of thought went into the ideas behind what was to become Germinal before a note was played – not least from Alan, who concluded it was time for a fresh challenge. "In Hunger Project I played guitar, but I really played it like a bass because the setup was two guitars, drums and a singer. So I started playing the low stuff, riffing away. It wasn't until that band broke up that I realized, I should probably get a bass now. Just like we'd had a lot of music in mind before Hunger Project, by the time I got a bass I had a whole bunch of really focused bass-playing listening to go back to. All my favourites are from that punk era really, because none of it was about technique. It was all about the sound, the attitude.

"Jean-Jacques Burnel is the God of it – his sound is so distinct, you hear the attitude in what he's playing, it's just so ferocious but interesting at the same time. The Stranglers was really the first band that took the guitar out of the melody mix and the bass became the melody instead. Later on, that was always our idea when we started Cowboy Junkies; it was an idea we'd loved for years and that was where we first got the opportunity to apply it. Burnel was the original guy and he influenced everyone else, like Peter Hook from Joy Division, Jah Wobble, Tracy Pew from The Birthday Party, all those bass players that went through The Cure; Robert Smith, as well. Cocteau Twins were that way too; I really liked that about them. John Peel's radio show was still pretty good. But that was it."

Synth-pop was everywhere in the UK in the early 1980s, ironically a return to the studio-tan days of a decade earlier when Steely Dan and Pink Floyd had frightened Mike and Alan off making music of their own. Haircut 100 and A Flock of Seagulls weren't in that league, but they were in the vanguard of the slick, processed, MIDIed-to-death material that slowly suffocated the life out of music. Many recordings from the 1980s were so drenched in polish that they were impenetrable. Good songs in a few cases, but encased in production techniques, like stuffed animals in a natural history diorama. Music made by robots, music with no need to breathe. Little wonder that Mike and Alan saw Germinal as a reaction to that.

"It was like some strange experiment," recalls Mike. "It wasn't anything that people would want to listen to maybe, but it was a really important period for us in the evolution of what we've done. We would just play and play, blowing our brains out with this free-jazz, noise thing. I think we wanted to play the most intense thing we possibly could, and to do that we got rid of all structures. Basically, we didn't want it to have any reference points at all. Maybe you wouldn't hear it in the music we made as Germinal, but I think it took us towards what Cowboy Junkies would be. My guitar playing really came from having no idea what I was doing. I didn't take any lessons, I couldn't just sit down and play something by somebody else on the spur of the moment, I'd need to work it out. Most people learn guitar because they want to play 'Stairway to Heaven', then they want to learn the solo from 'Layla'. I've never had any interest in that. I don't want to copy anything. But, as a form of expression, I love it. A lot of that came from that period in London where I was listening to a ton of jazz, a ton of improvisation. Not just guitar players, but sax players, piano players, people who use the instrument as a form of expression. There's no form, no structure, you use it rhythmically, sonically, melodically, however you want, and you combine all that."

Although Germinal has been pretty much dismissed as little but raw noise – even Margo has called it "the sound of Michael having a nervous breakdown", while his parents understandably began to fret about how he was ever going to make a decent living – that thrashing around served a purpose. Both Mike and Alan have described it as cathartic, perhaps extending punk to its logical conclusion, but there was some important R&D work going on here. In an era when pop music was desperately superficial, was being structured and polished to the nth degree, what other reaction could musically enquiring minds have than to head off in the opposite direction, away from Main Street, in an effort to inject a little humanity back into the mix?

Germinal never actually played live, but they released a cassette, *Germinal 1*, and then an album, *Din*, on their own Latent Recordings label. As Al remarked later, both "sold dozens". Just as Hunger Project had done, Germinal was beginning to run its course, not least because Mike was turning back towards more traditional music.

"I was working at Record & Tape Exchange in Notting Hill Gate, a huge used record store, with thousands and thousands of albums in there. It gave me this huge library of music to go through and, not just that, the people working there were very knowledgeable about music. I learned a ton from there, I picked their brains and their collections. By the time Germinal had flushed that stuff out of our system, suddenly the blues was there. One of the guys there was a real blues fan and he played me some Lightnin' Hopkins, John Lee Hooker, the classic stuff. It was just totally revelatory to me. That was the human element that was missing in the music of the time, especially the guitar playing. It was so simple, so basic, but you could hear everything there in the one note, especially Lightnin' Hopkins. That gave us an interest in a more traditional style again. We'd had three years of hearing music that was all about machines, but this was going back to people singing and playing instruments. It had the same kind of impact that punk had had on us. Things came back into focus."

CHAPTER 3

Four Timminses and an Anton

Never mind the music, the 1980s weren't a great time to live in England on pretty well every level. The politics were completely screwed – if you didn't like Blair, just remember Thatcher – the economy was going quickly down the toilet, there were riots on the streets, deaths at our football games, the country was getting divided up between the haves and the have-nots, the North and the South. Those of us who were born here were sick of the place, so it's no surprise that people who actually had somewhere else to go got out while the getting was good. After just over three years, both Mike and Alan had had their fill, their passage home being expedited by the fact that Mike contracted hepatitis on a holiday in Egypt with brother John. Mike returned to the family home in Toronto, while Alan went travelling before pitching up back in Canada.

As far as Mike was concerned, there was never any question that, once he'd got his feet back on home soil, there was another band to be formed. Looking back, Margo's assessment is that "Music is something that Michael will always have and will always do, he was born to it, he needs to do that. For me, I love what I'm doing or I wouldn't still be doing it, but I never felt it was my calling. I hear other singers say they were born to sing. Maybe I was born to follow Mike around!"

That need to make music was tested by the failures in New York and then London. There are a lot of talented musicians, artists of all kinds, who fall by the wayside after reverses like that, or simply because life catches up with them. It's one thing to sling a guitar over your shoulder and go make a noise when you're 19 and life seems to stretch out forever in front of you. When you get to 25 or 26, life gets a whole lot more complicated. Your choices start to narrow around you, however committed you are to your cause. Bigger decisions have to be made, career paths chosen. Neither Mike nor Al had been deflated or deflected from continuing to make music, but if their next band was going to be anything more than a hobby it needed to connect with an audience.

John Timmins was there at the birth of Cowboy Junkies, played in the band for a while too, and was perfectly placed to see it evolve in its first few months. He agrees that, in some senses, it was an act of faith, not just in the music, but in themselves. "I truly believe that in any walk of life, but in the arts especially, if you persist, you will either hit a brick wall pretty quickly or, over time, you will wear it down and get somewhere, as long as you have the talent for it. Even a nut of talent, that will grow over time. I think Mike knew that very early, when he set out for New York. He would have said to himself that what he was doing was from the heart, that he had talent and that all he had to do was have the balls to persist and not drop out. I don't believe there's been any lucky break that made it happen for them. The band made it happen. Any breaks came as a result of being earned. Ultimately, their timing was good with *Trinity Session*; that was perhaps a piece of luck. It wasn't foreseen that the time was right for that kind of sound, but they got themselves in a position to make that record first. Mike would have had a pretty good idea that the music they were making then had a good chance of succeeding because of its honesty, just because of the way he works things through, how he sees them. He's very well read, very observant, he's got a good balance of mind and soul. He's very strong that way."

Both Hunger Project and Germinal had had thought put into them before they started playing, but the new project was going to be the result of a lot more intellectualizing over what they wanted to do with music. Alan recalls that "That was one of the most important things about making this work: that we hadn't played until we had a real idea of something we wanted to do." Right from the outset, Cowboy Junkies was a highly conceptualized piece of work, yet one that has always had an emotional heart at its core, an intensity that has taken the music away from the laboratory and into the real world.

Having known one another for twenty years already and having been in bands together for the previous six, a lot of the communication between Alan and Mike didn't have to be verbalized. The idea of the two of them sitting down for hours on end making lists of what they did and did not want from the band is ridiculous – Al would probably have fallen asleep ten minutes in. Their shared record collection and shared tastes made for a shared aesthetic, a shared ideal of what this next group would represent, something they came towards intuitively. Mike remembers that "Al and I didn't really need to talk about what Cowboy Junkies was going to be. Our entire life was based round music, as kids and as adults. Even now, I don't know how many times we've been to each other's house for dinner. Hardly ever. It's all around music. That's how we connect. He has a whole other life outside the band that I'm not part of, but we connect around music and that's phenomenally strong. So, as we've gone on, we've never had to sit down and discuss what the next record is going to be like, it's never been that planned. The previous experiences guide us in a particular direction. When we were forming our sound back at the start of Cowboy Junkies, I had the ideas in my head, but it was never that formal. I liked the Joy Division sound, I liked blues, I wanted to play that way and the sound evolved very organically, not from us having any great master plan in mind. It just grows. And, because we have a shared aesthetic, when it starts going in a direction that we don't like, we both pull it back without having to talk about it.

"When we came back to Toronto, blues was the touchstone, keeping it very organic, simple. Trying to make every note you play count. Not playing a lot of them, just the ones that mattered. We married that with that post-punk aesthetic, Joy Division, The Cure, that very dark, big space to the sound, but with an American roots feel. That's what we still are, in a way. Germinal had been a completely improvisational band, no structure at all. It really freed us up to experiment with noise, what sounds we could make and how we could combine rhythms or not. So, when we moved from that to Cowboy Junkies, which is a much more structured band, we brought a lot of that with us. The idea that there was no right or wrong way to do something, we're not trying to recreate something, we're trying to make our music, and if it sounds and feels right to us that's the right way to go. Combining blues with that improvisational idea has continued through the band's life, for sure, especially live."

Alan's take on it is similar. "The original idea for this group was to bring together American roots music and some of that European, mainly British, style of the late 1970s, bands like Joy Division and The Cure, which itself was a reworking of that Velvet Underground thing which was always a big influence on us anyways. Those recent punk influences were definitely something we had in mind. It was a big shift from the music Mike and I had been doing in London, which was just wacky! That was pretty experimental, a useful period to get some things out of our system, but it ran its course. We started this band up pretty much right away once we both got back to Toronto and we started to work on that bluesy thing that was the basis for our early stuff."

A great example of that early blueprint for Cowboy Junkies came to light in 2004 with the 'Neath Your Covers Part 1 EP that was initially packaged with the One Soul Now record – and, even now, they are "records" not CDs, because every Cowboy Junkies release is a record of who and what they are at the point they made it. Doesn't apply to many other bands, but with this one the medium is not the message. It could just as easily be on shellac as aluminium. As the title suggests, it was a selection of cover versions, including 'Seventeen Seconds' by The Cure, another song that Al had singled out for special praise in his *Independent* article: "Simple, subtle and so effective, this is plaintive in the purest sense. The Cure appealed to the angry melancholic in all of us."

The Cure's original is skeletal. A repetitive guitar figure, melodic bass, drumming that is as simplistic as anything committed to tape, then Robert Smith's vocal. There's almost nothing there, but the feeling that it evokes is immense, the space playing as important a role as any of the instruments. Cowboy Junkies' reading of it is true to the emotion of the original, Alan's bass moving it along at a stately pace (it lasts a full minute longer than The Cure's version), Pete playing only what's necessary, Mike barely playing at all, injecting the song with an occasional burst of what Jeff Bird terms his "angry dog" guitar playing. It feels like a great example of Germinal's legacy within Cowboy Junkies, the genesis of Mike's highly distinctive guitar sound, his freedom to create atypical sounds within a song structure. Look at the individual parts and there's even less there than in The Cure's version, but it's instantly identifiable as Cowboy Junkies, long before Margo's voice makes its entrance. It could as easily have gone out under the name "The Velvet Underground & Margo".

"That's very true," laughs Mike. "That's how this whole thing was approached from the start, in many ways. There was the band and then Margo came into what we were doing and it developed from there. I don't think it was ever in her mind to be in a band, or be a singer – it was quite accidental in that sense. It makes you wonder just how many people there are out there who've never found their calling. That must be sad. Or maybe not: maybe it's better if you don't find out; then you don't get obsessed by it! But, now, it is strange to think that she might never have become a singer."

Nor was Margo involved in the initial formation of the band, which was, for all the thought that was going into it, a fairly loose coming together to play the blues music that Mike and Alan had become fascinated with. Mike had returned to his parents' home, as had Pete, who had been out on the West Coast, the two of them then renting a house on Crawford Street in the Little Italy district of Toronto, Alan moving in with them shortly afterwards. From there, it was inevitable that Mike and Al would start playing together. What was less obvious was that Pete would get involved too. "Al and I started the band like we always had, playing together," Mike remembers. "John was in Toronto too, so he joined in a bit, and Pete just literally walked into the garage one day with a drum kit and started tapping away on it and so that's when we started."

Having never played a beat in anger, Pete was simply following in the family tradition, doing what Mike had done back in 1979. But Mike was the older brother and had a six-year musical head start on Pete. And, though they were still a long way from being a band, still just a very loose playing arrangement, everyone knew that Mike and Al didn't appreciate people messing with their music. Takes guts just to show up like that. Not that Pete agrees: "We were living together for a while, we built a rehearsal space and Mike and Al started jamming, with John as well. They were just fooling around and they were short of a drummer, because Geoff Railton stayed in London. I just figured I'd help out. I got a set of drums from Long & McQuade in the city – still owe 'em for it! – and joined in. We just messed around; it was fun for us all to do, just to see where it was going."

23

There was plenty of time to work on the music because, as Mike points out, "We were all unemployed at the time. We were goofing around, played a lot, all day and all night and the sound started to happen, based on the ideas Al and I had, but not verbalized in any way. If we'd told John and Pete those ideas at the time, they wouldn't have known what I was talking about, so we just played and found our way into it. It started taking some kind of shape and we needed a vocalist. I always knew Margo could sing because as a kid she'd be in the school play and just floor people. People would just be open-mouthed, this voice coming out of this 6-year-old. Just like it is now – not big, just round, full. We invited her in one day to try it with what we were doing. I sat with her a few times playing different ideas, because she wouldn't audition with the rest of the band around. She sang a few songs and she never left. The rest of the band came in, we played a few more songs, we started to put things together, we got to the point where we had forty minutes, and then we went out looking for a gig."

Having failed the audition for Hunger Project, Margo wasn't brimming with confidence when she tried out for this new group. "If it weren't for Mike, I certainly wouldn't be singing, that's for sure. When I was in grade 6, I did a play, *Oliver!* I played Nancy. The whole town was there, the mayor came, it was a big production. There's a heartfelt song, 'As Long As He Needs Me'. She's going out with Bill Sykes, who's beating her up. I'm 12. I have no idea of what's going on here, I just have to sing a song. I think that Michael, aged 14 or whatever, not knowing his life was going to lead him in this direction, I think he really heard me for the first time. I wasn't a stupid little sister any more. It was, 'My God, Marg can sing!' I think that stuck in his head until the day he was ready to get this band together and he came and asked me to be in it. I think he was waiting for me to grow up or something! I knew I could hold a note, carry a melody, but it's not my personality. I have two sisters: one wanted to be an actress, the other wanted to be a model. They were ready to go out there, so when Mike asked me to sing, it was wacky. 'Sure, OK. You want *this* sister, right? What about the other two? They're better for the job!' It was a weird request, but it worked out.

"I wanted to be my mom. That was my goal, to have six kids. I'd follow her round in the morning, making the beds, doing the laundry. I loved her systematic way of handling that, I admired her for that and that's what I wanted to be. My sisters were always into makeup, *Seventeen* magazine, but that didn't interest me. I loved music, we all did, but I never felt I had the personality. I didn't want to stand up in front of people. Not that I wouldn't – if you asked me to do it, OK, I will. But I didn't have the need to be seen which my sisters had.

"Michael had a need to write even when we were kids, before he started playing guitar. He wrote poetry and I still have a lot of that – he'd give it to me because I'd tell him he was a genius. He didn't need to be seen or heard, but he needed to write, to express himself. My expression is nurturing. I took care of Pete; he was my first baby. Still is, actually! As things have gone on, I think my role in the band is that when things get rocky – and they do, we get crazy on the road, not rock'n'roll crazy, but it gets kooky with all those people trapped on a bus – I try to deal with it. I don't like things to get to a point where you can't return from them. Sometimes you'll say something and you can't take it back. You have to talk before you get to the stage where you're saying evil things to each other. So, if I see things happening, I'll go and talk. 'You're not happy. What's going on?'

"I think the reason we get a lot of people back to work with us is because we do run things as a family, we don't let things get ugly and mean. If things are getting mucked up, it's still my job to step in and unmuck them, to calm people down or whatever. I had a great teacher when I was a social worker who told me that I'd never make it in that job, but I'd always use my social work skills in life – and I really think I have. That's my expression and that's why I don't think I ever needed to be seen. My role in the family, always, was to know where everyone was, what was going on. Nowadays, I can't stand that role, but that's a whole other thing. It's too complicated now we're all adults!"

Cowboy Junkies was now a five-piece. Mike, Margo, Pete and John Timmins, and Alan Anton. Didn't he ever feel outnumbered? "I was really happy when Margo joined in as well, because she always had this incredible voice. Sure enough, pretty soon after she came in, things started to come together. We began to think, 'This is pretty good, we can sell this.' I guess it was a strange dynamic to have the four siblings in the band. You have to be used to it, for sure, but that's why it's never been an issue for me, because I grew up with them. They have a different shared history, but when we were younger it never really was much of an issue because Mike and I were so tight. If I'd just come into the band from a 'Bass player wanted' ad, it might have been different. Now, thirty years down the line, it's not even something we think about – it doesn't get any harder, that's for sure."

Slowly, the five began to piece their sound together. Just like Germinal had, they paid a lot of attention to volume, but at the other end of the scale, according to Pete, "We had problems with volume, that was a concern for sure. Initially, we tried to soundproof the basement and the next-door neighbour came around as soon as we started playing because we'd woken her baby. We moved out to the garage, thought we'd soundproofed it, but two hours into our first rehearsal there the police turned up because of complaints about the noise. So we soundproofed some more and turned down. Then, when Marg started singing, she was pretty quiet, so the playing had to reflect that. And then the blues itself dictated that kind of approach. I was playing with brushes. There was no one thing that meant we were quiet, it was all just pretty natural."

It did take time to find that sound if the hidden track on *200 More Miles* is any indicator. On an early rehearsal recording of 'Bad Boy', there are some recognizable Cowboy Junkies elements, particularly Alan's bass, but it's hard to believe that's Margo, trying to shout out the blues. No sign of the controlled delivery that was to be her hallmark later. As she says, "Everyone that you saw at that time sang loud. I was totally untrained, I had no clue what I was doing. I was just trying to find my own way into singing, so I tried to be upfront like everyone else, but it didn't suit my personality. One of the big influences that took me away from that was Emmylou Harris. I saw her playing a show in Toronto and she just seemed to open her mouth and this voice just came out. It didn't seem she was trying to do anything, and that's that gift. Leave it alone, it'll happen. That was one of the things that gave me the confidence to find my own way. From the start, our music was very simple, because Pete and I couldn't do anything else! I used to take old blues lyrics and match them to whatever the boys were offering, reinterpreting them to go with the playing, and that taught me a lot. That sparseness gave me time to listen and to think about the next line before singing it. The music became quieter and my voice sat inside that instead of on top of it."

While Margo's lack of experience offered no problem, Pete's did. Mike recalls, "We were really happy to have him in the band, but he had to dedicate himself to it more. He'd only just started playing, he had ground to make up on the rest of us and it was holding things back. So we fired him." Ian Blurton took over the drummer's gig, while Pete got down to work and hired a teacher to learn the basics. When Blurton quit a few months later, suffering from tendinitis in his wrists, Pete was ready to reclaim his place.

Most bands start out in a rehearsal room by playing cover versions of old songs that they share a love for. Cowboy Junkies did that, too. Sort of. Alan: "What we were looking for was a sound of our own and we got that going pretty quickly, that was a really important thing to focus on, to get our own style together. We were playing other people's songs, but not really the way they played them, which is sort of what we still do now when we do covers."

Coming up with original material wasn't on the agenda at that stage, though what they were doing was tantamount to a correspondence course in songwriting for Mike. The coolest kind of correspondence course, because they could work with some of the greatest writers of all time. Even if they were dead. "As it turned out, doing those covers was a good way into songwriting because we didn't do them exactly like the originals; we were interpreters of the songs. Blues had got a bad name from the mid-1970s. I guess people got burned out on it, all those musicians who came along and played it badly. There's nothing worse than blues when it's played badly. I think a lot of people picked up on it and didn't put any twist on it, it was just recreating the music. There's no point in just doing that because it's not about the form, it's about how you play it and interpret it, and a lot of people just missed that totally. They'd just play a 12-bar and say, 'Hey, I'm playing the blues.' Well, no, you're not. You're playing really bad music!

"We didn't want to play 12-bar blues, we wanted to take the aesthetic that we understood and mix it with that blues attitude and this is what we came up with. We were coming from listening to a lot of jazz and blues, which is really all interpretation – there are probably four blues songs ever written, but it's about how Lightnin' Hopkins played his guitar, not what he wrote. I guess Robert Johnson was the exception, because his writing was pretty spectacular. But we established our feel, our vibe, the Cowboy Junkies sound. Pete and Al would create a groove, I'd improvise on that, then Margo would throw in old blues lyrics and try and find new melodies for them."

27

That Cowboy Junkies sound continued to evolve. The departure and then the return of Pete affected it, as did the fact that Margo was slowly becoming more comfortable with the idea of being a singer. And then John quit, a change that had dramatic consequences according to Mike. "John left to move to Montreal with his wife. We sat down and talked about whether we should replace him or just leave it. We had a few gigs lined up and didn't have the time to replace him for those. So we played those and we liked the sound of the four of us. We left the space where he would normally play, left it blank and it worked. It gave it a weird vibe, taking it more back to the aesthetic that Al and I had talked about before we started. It enabled Margo to sing quieter, it meant we could all really hear the sound of our instruments and that slowed things down. That was how we developed the sound – part intentional, part just happenstance."

John Timmins, the Stuart Sutcliffe of Cowboy Junkies. What does he remember of that brief period as a founder member? "I think I played an important part in the very formative years, just bringing in the musical influences even before they were playing music. Mike had decided that this was what he wanted to do with his life and he had applied it, he'd had bands in Toronto, New York, London, learning his craft, but it was still relatively unformed. When he came back home, all I had to do was play with what was already beginning to take shape and bring whatever I could to that. I like to think I reinforced his vision and encouraged him. I have good memories of visiting him in London, playing some music there, then back in Toronto. I stepped out to do my own thing in Montreal, and by the time I came back to play on *Trinity Session*, in my estimation, the music had really begun to take shape. The distance between those first two records is quite considerable while still maintaining the vision, which made it easy for me to get back into it. The very fact that I could get back into it again for *Early 21st Century Blues* is testimony to the consistency of vision that the band has. It's held up through that time."

While sad to see her brother leave, Margo is very clear that in the long term it served the greater good, certainly in terms of the band's internal operation. "If John had stayed, the dynamic would have been very different because of his and Mike's ages, and their place in the family, and I doubt the band would have survived it. I don't think John could have followed Mike and I don't think Mike could have fought with John because of that older brother–younger brother thing. Mike is very respectful of that family hierarchy, so telling John what to do would have been hard for him. And Mike is the leader of this band, so it would have been really difficult to work out.

"In some ways, even in the family, Mike is sort of the older brother because of the way he is and that's OK with John, but in the long term, in a group, that would be tough. Mike and my sisters Sue and Cali, they all have that intense drive, they're really smart; then me, Pete and John, we're a little bit mushier! John is a bit different to Pete and I, I guess, because he's the firstborn and he felt he had a responsibility from that. I'm in the middle, so who cares, nobody noticed me, Pete's the youngest, so he's not worried! John has our personality but he's out front and I don't think that fits with him. For me, I had siblings to watch and you can work things out from that, and John didn't have that chance, he was on his own. When I was young, I'd watch Suzanne fight with my mom and I decided there was no way I was going through that. I'll be the good girl, I'll make my bed and then go off quietly and do what I wanted to do because everyone was happy.

"It's fascinating really, the way that large family structure operates. Pete and I don't want to be leaders, so that fits Cowboy Junkies. The dynamic between the three of us works because Mike has this drive to do what he does, he likes to be in control of that, where with Pete and with me we're both followers in that sense. There are things we'll do and things we won't do, Mike knows that, and we both need our expression, which we get in the band, so the dynamic works out. Mike is the leader, but he knows he couldn't do what he does without us, so that's OK, the balance is good, that's one of the reasons why we're still here.

"More than anybody, Mike has always trusted Al's opinions, he's like a business partner in a way. If Mike is confused about things, and as his sister I pick up on that, I always tell him to call Al to talk it through. There's great trust there because they've grown up together, they know what one another thinks. The same with Jeff Bird now – he's the only musician around here! Mike has always had a great deal of faith in Jeff's opinion, in his musical knowledge, so those two are his fallback positions, his consultants. I really believe that in this band all of us have played our roles, and played them happily, seriously, and still do."

Germinal had never made it out of the rehearsal room, but Cowboy Junkies was always going to be different. For once, Mike and Alan had got their timing right, as Alan says: "Going away was good, because by the time we got back to Toronto there was a pretty good music scene going on here. Roots-orientated music was suddenly very popular; there were pockets of it happening in the States, too." Just as Hunger Project had never had any qualms about getting in the station wagon and trying to find gigs across the States, so did Cowboy Junkies, though naturally they looked to build a reputation closer to home first of all. That didn't take long, for their live set – filled with these strange mutant interpretations of the blues that carried echoes of the Bunnymen – was unlike anything else going on in Toronto. Pete remembers that "We were out there playing within seven or eight months of the first rehearsal – the first one was at the Rivoli on Queen Street. There was a buzz around the city pretty quickly, because we had such a different sound. The scene at the time was loud, crass. We weren't making any noise at all, which got us some attention."

Back in the 1970s, Mike and Alan weren't simply students of music, they were students of the music business too. They understood that pretty well all the bands that had got a long career out of making music had done it the hard way. Learning their chops, playing the gigs, concentrating on more than their backyard and, above all, making headway into the American market. Right from the outset, Cowboy Junkies had an eye on things south of the border.

"Because of the music we played, we always felt America was our obvious market," argues Alan. "It's hard to tour Canada, it's so big, there are so few people here, so we geared up for doing business in the States. We just didn't want to live there. It was easier to tour the US, too, even though we did have to sneak across the border to start with. In Canada, it's just a straight line from city to city. They're all just north of the border, but it's eight hours or something from one city to the next, then you've got the winter to factor in as well, so it's hard to make it work. There are bands that do that. They have their whole career in Canada and make a lot of money without ever getting recognized anywhere else."

"As far as Canada is concerned, we've probably paid for concentrating on America," admits Mike. "We've only done three or four cross-Canada tours, which are always logistical nightmares. Now we try to do Canadian shows as part of an American tour, hopping over the border. Ironically, Toronto is one of our worst markets. We've had some great shows here, but we've had some disasters, too. Canadians are very strange to the homegrown acts, they're either very loyal to them or they just ignore them. Because we did so much work outside Canada, we never really seemed like a Canadian band. Even when we were starting out, it was always an issue for us that there were 300 million people in the United States and thirty million up here. Why head west when we could head south and go into that American club scene, get work, build an audience?"

Though Hunger Project had given them an indicator of just how to go about working the clubs in the States, going down there for weeks on end with no base to come back to was a real test of their desire. Anybody reading this and currently working in US immigration might want to skip to the next chapter now, as Alan reveals the truth of just what went on back in 1986. "When we first went to America, we had to pretend we were visiting friends because to get work papers just cost too much money. That's why a lot of bands don't get out of Canada because they're scared to sneak across, or, if any of them has any kind of criminal record, the most minor thing, then you can't get into America."

Margo's memory of it all is pretty sharp: "We just had to sneak into America, we'd travel separately, so we didn't look like a band. The first time, my mom drove me over, and we had the drums in the back, telling customs we were delivering them to my brother, which we were, kind of! Mike and Al were in this little brown van with the guitars, saying they were going to a party. I don't know what happened with Pete. He was probably in the trunk! But it was 1985, nobody really cared, there was no Homeland Security, it was easy to get in. I remember when Mom went back, I cried – 'Don't leave me here to do this!'"

John Timmins, safely ensconced in Montreal by this point, is full of admiration for the way Cowboy Junkies set about the job of really *becoming* Cowboy Junkies. "Determination is a big part of their story. Because if you're going to sneak across the border and tour across America not knowing where your next gig is coming from, you must believe in what you're doing. They'd play a show, then phone ahead to a club in the next city in the hope that they could get a gig there. By doing that, by sitting in that van travelling across country, you become a band."

Decades of Hollywood movies glamorizing showbusiness has created a raft of myths, among the most insidious being the idea of the "overnight success". Some talented kid will be spotted in the most unlikely of settings and then, three weeks later, they're headlining a Broadway theatre or starring in their own TV show. The advent of reality TV may actually be turning this myth into tragic truth, but if you want to be a band that endures there are no short cuts. If you don't have a work ethic, don't bother to apply.

"Getting a break really accounts for a small part of it," agrees Alan. "Most of it is getting in that van, playing 250 gigs a year and finding your audience. You need to have that talent, that sound. That's the main thing; you can't do much without that. But from there, you need to work hard. You find your sound that way, you find out how to operate as a band or you fall apart in the process. If you come through that, then you know you can work with one another.

"When we started, we did some pretty long hauls, just the four of us. Nowadays, because we're on a bus, we do eighteen-hour drives straight if the scheduling's bad. It's pretty easy, though; you go to your bunk, you get up, have breakfast, watch TV, then you're there. Back when we started, we did our own driving, we'd drive ten or twelve hours straight and we'd show up at gigs and just be zombies. Everything was still moving. It was really good for the music and it was fun, but I wouldn't want to do that again. There's a nice freedom to it; you can go out of your way to see the sights, you're a tourist almost. It was an adventure really, as we had never been to these places in America, so we saw all these places like Custer's Last Stand, national parks, it was cool. And it tests out your belief in what you're doing. If you weren't committed to it, you couldn't keep doing that. It was romantic, I guess, but it's the kind of thing you only want to do once, when you're young."

Pete agrees that the station wagon tour is a young person's game, though for different reasons. "We'd sleep on people's floors, people we'd met at the gig the night before or something. It'd be harder now, because we're older and you always have kind of a scowl on your face. 'Can I stay at your place?' is more menacing when you look like that!"

For some reason, it was usually left to Margo to ask a fan if the band could stay over at their place while they were out on the road. Ordinarily there was no problem. But just occasionally it got a little hairy. "One night we stayed with someone who had just bought a dog, and obviously he hadn't trained it yet. So we were sleeping on the floor and I woke up to find dog poo behind my pillow. I should have quit then – it was a sign from God! But I just ignored it and picked my way through the dog mess to the shower. Which is what we've been doing in the music business ever since!

"We played a small club in Philadelphia. There was nobody there to see us, which wasn't unusual and it didn't really bother us, because in the early, early days we viewed that tour as just one huge rehearsal. The only problem was that if there was nobody there we couldn't ask anyone if we could sleep on their floor. That was our biggest worry. At the end of that particular night, a very strange man walked in and he was the only choice, so we asked him. He was in a little too much of a hurry to say yes. He turned out to be a real psycho. That was the only night that, when I went to have a shower, I came out to find that Mike had been guarding the bathroom door."

Getting Margo to hit people for a floor to sleep on? Good call. Charging the taciturn Alan with the responsibility of keeping Mike awake when driving through the night? Not so clever. "No, he wasn't very good at that. Al falls asleep in a second, too. Everybody took their turn. We all had plenty of self-interest in that, so we all did it pretty good!"

THE NAME OF THIS BAND IS
COWBOY JUNKIES

"You know, [all these] years of this band, a load of records, and it's still the same," complains Mike. "We go to do an interview and the first thing that we get how asked is, 'So, how'd you guys get the name?' Is that the level of research these guys do for an interview? It drives me crazy."

Fortunately, Margo is generally in on these interviews, too, and she's a little more practised in dealing with the situation. "I think sitting through interviews is part of the same attitude that still gets me on the bus with all those boys every night. If that's what I have to do, that's what I have to do. That's my personality. Mike has it, too, in a different way. I'd rather not sleep on people's floors, but I had to do it, so I did. I always think of the greater picture. OK, this journalist hasn't done his work and has no creativity, but I need him at this moment and I'm very grateful he's giving me his time. There's a ton of other bands a lot hipper than us, but he's here, talking to me, so let's make it work. Mike gets really irritated by the image side of things, he doesn't have time for it, but we recognize the necessity of it because it's been good for us. I can deal with that, with having to have my photo taken, by doing stupid interviews. When we do one together and people ask us what it's like working with your family, where did you get the name, Michael's ready to kill them. I can just put on the face like it's the first time anybody asked me and go 'blah-blah-blah'. It's a shame, but in this industry, if you're not good at handling the press and having your picture taken, things are going to be hard for you."

So, Margo, where did that name come from? "When you're a new band, your name is really all you have to generate any kind of interest. You can't afford to take out an ad to tell people you're playing, you don't have a record out at that point – all you have is your name among all the others in the club listing in the paper. There were a lot of bands in Toronto, all trying to get gigs, competing for people's attention, so you need a good name. When we came up with 'Cowboy Junkies', we knew it was daring, that it would cause a reaction. It's worked pretty well for us."

But who came up with it? "Even we don't know where it came from," says Mike. "We had to come up with something because we had our first gig coming up, so we sat around one night and threw names at each other and the name fell together somehow. Somebody said Cowboys, somebody said Junkies, somebody said Silver Cowboy Junkies, then it became Cowboy Junkies. I guess part of the inspiration was that the scene in Toronto had an American element to it. There was this cross of country and rock happening, but it was something that we weren't any part of – you can tell that if you listen to *Whites Off Earth Now!!* That record has nothing to do with country music, so we were kind of poking fun at that scene. They were just a cool couple of words that went together without making any sense, because we didn't want to have any great meaning attached to the name. Ultimately, we just wanted something that looked interesting, to make people react, positively, negatively, but at least have a response to it. We didn't want anything to define the sound of the band, which is weird because finally it actually ends up doing that in a way, once you've listened to the music a little bit, so it was a bit backwards! You listen to the first record and they don't fit together – maybe the junkies side because of the darkness in it, but there's no cowboys, no country element there, no thought of it. We were steering clear of that and doing this bluesy psychedelic thing. But we grew into the name, which was weird."

One name it would never have had was the "Margo Timmins Band". "We agreed that from the beginning," says Mike. "We were always a band. There was no way we were just going to have Margo on her own on the cover – we weren't changing our name. Later on, when record companies became interested in us, we had so much pressure to just have Margo's name on it, but we had a pretty clear idea of where to draw the line."

Peter Moore, producer of the band's first three albums, was aware of the band right from the outset and he recalls conversations about just what direction they were going to take, conceptually as well as musically. "I remember Mike talking very early on about the name of the band. 'Cowboy Junkies' is in the vernacular now, but at the time it was pretty wacky – Ronald Reagan time, zero tolerance, all that stuff was there, so it stood out. At the time, Mike said that if a record company came along and offered them money, he'd change the name to whatever they wanted. Who cared? I think Epic were the first big players, they were very interested, but the first thing they wanted was to change the name. Mike just told them, 'No fucking way!' I thought that was so cool. Tells you a lot about them."

The name worked, and not just in Toronto. Tim Easton, a singer-songwriter who later went on the road with the Junkies as a support act – that's him getting covered in silly string on the *Open Road* DVD – caught them on the American station-wagon tour, just on the strength of that moniker. "I saw a flyer for Cowboy Junkies on the street. I thought the name was interesting, so I went along. It was a place called Apollo's in Columbus, Ohio, a Greek place that had a bar in the back. A lot of punk rock bands that came through town used to play there, and there was a sort of scene where sloppy, drunk bands, influenced by the Buzzcocks but not as good, would play around town, too. There were maybe seven of us there, a couple of people playing pool. But I was just mesmerized – that guitar playing, that voice, it was a real strong mix. They played beautiful music, very gentle, and they got a serious message across and that was pretty different then.

35

"When I read the name and went to the show, that really wasn't what I thought I was going to see. It's a strong name, great name, but at that time, and for that venue, I thought it was probably going to be a more rockabilly kind of thing, so it was a real surprise. They were just out of step with everything and I loved it so much because it was obvious they'd studied some old blues stuff, mixed it up with a little Lou Reed, it was a nice mix of things. There was nobody coming through my town that sounded anything like that at that time, that's for sure, not even close. So in a way it was no surprise that a couple of years later I was watching them in much larger venues. I went travelling actually, I was a busker basically. I was in London, going to play in the subway at Tottenham Court Road. I came out of there and saw their name on the front of this big theatre, the Dominion. That was maybe three years after I'd seen them in Columbus." While Tim was busking outside, Mike was puking inside, a rare attack of nerves before a big, foreign gig.

Cowboy Junkies certainly had a pretty good handle on marketing right from the outset. Having made waves with their name, they decided to repeat the trick with their first record, the independent release, *Whites Off Earth Now!!* Mike remembers, "Me and Al took a lot of interest in the music press, we'd read all the small print, everything. We came across this group in California and they figured that if we could just get rid of all the white people, everything would be solved. 'Whites off Earth now!' was their slogan. When we did the record, it was a bunch of white suburban kids covering the great black bluesmen, once again ripping off these greats, just like white suburban kids had been doing for the last thirty years or whatever. And we had these beautiful, ugly pictures of us on the cover. Once I saw that, it was obvious that had to be the title."

CHAPTER 4

Let me whisper in your ear

One of punk's lasting legacies, perhaps the most dramatic of the changes that it brought about, was proving that you didn't need to be signed to a major label to make a major record. In the early 1970s, it seemed inconceivable that a band could literally "do it yourself", but by the end of that decade it was no big deal to form a band, make a noise in a rehearsal room for a week, book a few hours in the cheapest studio you could find and come out the other end with a piece of vinyl in your hands. And, if your resources were really stretched, you could just come out with a master tape and then dupe your own copies onto cassette.

Having your own single or album was a step up from a cassette, though, somehow lending legitimacy to what you were doing. If you'd made a record, you were a real band, you'd moved up the scale from having a hobby to taking this thing seriously. Now you had something you could put in stores, take to radio stations, maybe sell at gigs, even advertise in the music press. You had become a physical entity. You could spread the word.

According to Pete, making an album was still something that separated Cowboy Junkies from their contemporaries. "No other Toronto bands were making records, but I guess that was an idea Mike and Al brought back from London. Bands over there would try and make a single or an album almost as soon as they formed. It didn't take us too long before we thought we were ready, from maybe September

1985 through to the following summer, eight, nine months maybe. We taped everything in rehearsal and we had twelve or thirteen songs. Time to make a record!

"Like most bands making their first record, we were pretty much recording our live set because we didn't have many more songs than that. We picked the songs off records we liked. 'No More' was actually a song we played then, but we didn't get round to putting that on a record until *Early 21st Century Blues*. We took a couple from *John Lee Hooker Live at Café au Go-Go*, a beautiful-sounding record that's got 'I'll Never Get Out of These Blues Alive' on it. Mostly just records we had been listening to for a while, things that fit in with what we were looking to do."

The biggest issue facing any independent band wanting to make its first recordings is obvious – cash. Time in the studio is costly, especially if you want to sound good. But money wasn't the only issue for Cowboy Junkies. Punk had been a reaction to the forty-eight-track studio system that had taken the means of making records away from new bands in the first place, so a normal studio environment was not something to be embraced lightly. On top of that, the foundation of their music was roots music, music that had been recorded very simply, live to tape in most cases. Conceptually, that offered a signpost for the band, as Mike explains.

"Sure, we hadn't got the money to do much, so that was a constraint. Before we made *Whites!!*, Al and I looked at studios. We'd had some experience of them, all bad. We'd never been happy with what we'd got, mainly because we didn't understand them enough. We didn't have the money to sit there and learn, because studio time is so expensive. It was a situation of, go into this foreign environment, play, get out. You never feel comfortable and you end up at the mercy of the studio and the people there, they were between the music you played and the final disc you got. We didn't know how to get it to work for us. We had that dilemma of wanting to record but knowing that, if we went to a studio and spent the $1,000 we had, it was going to sound like crap. We didn't want to do that, and we were trying to find another way when we ran into Peter Moore. He had some cool ideas."

Peter Moore was a well-established sound engineer working in Toronto, at apparently diametrically opposed ends of the spectrum – classical music and punk rock. To Moore, there was no difference between the two. His job was to capture the sound and to capture the moment. The simplest way to describe him is to say he's an enthusiast, a perfectionist and a believer in his art, every bit as committed to the concept of recording sound as Cowboy Junkies are to playing music. That passion started just as early.

"I remember buying my first set of real headphones. I was probably 12, 13, saved up my money from my paper route, and bought a pair of Sennheisers, the white ones with the yellow puffs. I was so happy! Inside the box was a 45, a demonstration disc, one of the recordings where they have the microphone inside the head and you hear different things like kids splashing around an Olympic-size swimming pool or a vocal group gathered around a mic. Hearing all these going off in my head, I felt I was totally in that space. I could escape from my world and go into that one. I've been trying to recreate that ever since, which is why surround sound is fascinating to me, because that idea only worked on headphones in the past. But the idea of being in the event as it goes on has been it for me. Right then and there, I knew what I wanted to do. It's so hard to make an emotional connection in life, but no matter what, I could do that in music. Turns out that it was a path towards working with the Junkies."

Moore is entertaining, generous with his time, always ready to talk music and willing to share his insights and opinions on the art of sound recording. For him, it's all about communication, putting as few barriers between musician and listener as you can. By 1986, though, his was a voice in the wilderness.

"As pop and rock music became bigger and more commercially successful, everything was about getting lots of equipment, about multi-tracks, ending up spending months getting a drum sound in the studio. Insanity. In the 1980s, everything was going MIDI, which was frightening the hell out of me – to me it was Big Brother. Once you have controls over everything, it can be placed in the hands of one person, a producer, whereas I always wanted to hear the combination of people. Along came MIDI, so you didn't have to be able to keep time, you get a good-looking guy or girl for the video, voice-correct them and you have a hit. But you're not presenting music, you're presenting an image. Music became slave to the visuals.

"I remember getting my first CD player, listening to Dire Straits, all this digital stuff that was designed for that. Then I got a Billie Holliday record, I threw that on one night and it just hit me. Where the fuck did we go wrong? This 1958 record was a perfect emotional transmitter. It had a quality to it that I hadn't heard in a long time, and that was a huge moment for me. From there, I was driven by the desire to recapture that emotional resonance. We were so far off the mark in the 1980s, something was going horribly wrong. It was so sterile, processed. Music coming from a factory. The focus was so wrong. By 1986, we were so far from the path of truth!

"Listen to that record and you're in a little club, sitting at your table and Billie is ten feet away, singing. That became my reference point. It just happened that I was coming to the same kind of ideas as the Junkies were at around the same time. They saw in me somebody who wanted to shift the paradigm, and I saw that in them. Musically, they were worlds away from the slick 1980s sound. That was the basis for our mutual trust. It's like the stars lining up, I was at a point on my travels, they were at a point on theirs and we intersected. You don't realize it, maybe, at the time, but looking back we were perfectly lined up.

"I'd known of them for a few years. I first saw them when they were in Hunger Project, once in Kitchener, once in Toronto. Didn't meet them, but I knew they were musicians. Greg Keelor from Blue Rodeo used to have these dinners over at the warehouse, the rehearsal joint that he lived in, a big loft place. He'd invite different types of people to get together and I went to one and they were there. We were talking about digital recording, which was brand new at that time. When they were in England, they'd done some recording using an F1 Betamax digital recorder, so I spoke to Al about the technology. I was one of the first people here to get an F1 – it was a brave new world! At that time, I'd just done some experiments recording with just one stereo mic, recording a punk band in London, Ontario. I had it in mind that you could get a great recording with just the one mic, going back to that Billie Holliday idea and that Sennheiser demo disc. They were interested in making a recording that way. My attitude was, 'We'll try it, and if you don't like it, don't pay me!' I wanted to test it out, so I wanted them to be comfortable with the experiment."

The experiment revolved around the band setting up in their garage and playing live to tape, recording to two-track. "The academy said it was madness, it couldn't be done!" laughs Moore. "It was kinda like that, actually. I was at an Audio Engineering Society meeting and we were talking about that classical recording idea and somebody said, 'Oh, you could never do that in pop.' That was it! I just took up the challenge, because to me it may be a different genre, but music is music. The industry told me I couldn't do something and that was all I needed, I was out to prove I could. There's a lot of voodoo in recording which pisses me off. All it is, is insecure people with a methodology of doing something and they don't want anybody to find out what it is, so they surround it with smoke and mirrors. And it's unnecessary, because you can replicate a methodology and it won't work, because something that you bring to it is what really makes it happen. That's the magic of the moment, of the people involved – it's a recording of a moment in time with all the variables that go with that."

"The idea of making a record in the same tradition of the blues records that were our inspiration was interesting," says Mike. "It was fate that we ran into Peter at that time, because he was ready to try something new and, if it didn't work out, all it cost us was a couple of days in the rehearsal room. We did an experiment using a couple of microphones with him and that was good. We tested a few songs in the garage and it started to work well enough for us to decide to try a full-scale session in there. He had this microphone on order from England that he wanted to use, so the plan was to record with a single mic. We scheduled it for June 26th, and the microphone arrived the day before. He came to the garage, set it up, but I don't think he really knew what to do with it. Worked great, though!"

The microphone. A Calrec Ambisonic microphone, possibly the most famous microphone in rock'n'roll outside of Sun Studios. And all because of two Cowboy Junkies records. Wouldn't it have been disastrous if anything had happened to it before they'd started work on them? "Peter had this incredibly expensive microphone, brand new out of the box," remembers Alan. "He set it up and Pete immediately knocked it over."

"I did? I don't remember that. It wasn't me! I think the drum screen fell on it – the mattresses we were using to hold the sound in pushed the screen over and that knocked the microphone over. Peter came running in having a heart attack! That Calrec still has a dent in it."

Not the perfect start to a day when Moore was already feeling pretty lousy. "The first session we did was a test run, but it was working. Then we came back to do a second one. I almost cancelled it because I was so sick. I had a wicked flu, the kind where you just don't want to get out of bed, but what was happening with the music and the recording was so cool it overcame the way I was feeling, which gives an idea of how into it we were. There was no room in the garage for the band and me, so we had to run cables out of there and into the kitchen, which became my control room!

"We were in a heatwave, there was no air, ninety degrees. Man, it was so hot in that garage. Stinky, smelly with old, rotting mattresses packed up against the wall. The room is the final performer, the final instrument. Hit a drum in a room, you create a sound and the room then shapes it, it's an active participant. That record, you're right there with them, in that space. It had that Southern, bluesy kind of feel, the heat, the sweat dripping off the face. I always say you can taste the sweat on Margo's upper lip when you listen to that recording."

Listen closely, as Mike opens 'Me and the Devil', just a couple of seconds in, you can hear Margo trying to open her mouth ready to sing, her lips sticking together as she does, then again later on 'Crossroads'. Is that a chair creaking at the start of 'State Trooper'? What's that shuffling noise at the start of 'I'll Never Get Out of These Blues Alive'? There's the sound of Pete putting his sticks down at the end of that song. Those bass strings reverberating against the neck after they've been played on 'Me and the Devil'. You can hear the band listening to one another. There are so many tiny details on offer, on top of the overall sweep of the music, that *Whites Off Earth Now!!* is one of the great headphones records – there's no better way to really get inside those songs, inside that recording, actually inside the garage. It's a remarkable achievement.

Whites Off Earth Now!! creates an extraordinary atmosphere, a shocking intimacy even now, but even more so given the layers of sound that most music was hiding behind in 1986. This was music in the raw, naked, made on the edge, as Moore explains: "First of all, it was an insane pace to make a record compared with the way things had become. To make a record in a day, that was going back to the early Beatles or something, the way Miles Davis would go in and lay down several sides of a record. But that's the beauty of limitation. That's one of the problems of modern life: we don't have limitations. It's only with them that you really become creative because you find ways around it. Our limitation was that we didn't have multi-track. We went live to two-track, like all those great records from the past, the great Ray Charles things. Everybody talks about those records sounding so great. Well, maybe there was a reason. They're being performed in the moment. There's a real psychological difference when you know that everything you're doing matters. If you screw up, you bring everybody else down. In the studio, the popularity of cocaine came about with people trying to get their energy levels up to do a take or a recording, because they were missing the natural adrenaline that comes from recording it live. When what you play is on the record and you can't correct it, you're on edge, you know there's no way of repairing it. It brings the best out of people, in a different way to a concert. When you play in front of an audience, most of the stimulation is visual. A lot of times you listen to a live recording and you hear mistakes all over the place, but in the concert hall you don't pick up on it. Recording live in the studio is much harder, because there's nowhere to hide, the concentration is strictly on the audio, on the playing. It knocks it up a number of notches, there's no forgiving mistakes there. It's a different quality of concentration that's required, everybody knows it, and that folds back into the performance. Kind of like a team sport – everyone has to bring their best game."

Moore's right. *Whites!!* sounds like a live record. Or more accurately, like a live album should, with all the nervous tension that goes with the concert stage, all the adrenaline that that implies, rather than the cleaned up versions that are foisted upon us. This was music made on the high wire. Alan recalls that session with fondness, for all the difficulties. "Because we only had one microphone, you're mixing the sound as you play instead of on separate tracks at the end of recording. The only way you can do that is by physically moving around the space so that the mix works as you're playing. That's a pretty hard thing to do and it took a lot of time to get that right."

"Making it work it together is a kind of choreography," agrees Moore. "It can be out of focus for a long time, there's a lot of changing, moving, but at the same time the band is also dynamically responding to it. So there's a symbiotic relationship, they're changing their volumes, their dynamics, and at the same time I'm moving stuff and trying to find the right space for everything to sit. That's the beauty of it. You basically futz with it for a long time then suddenly it comes into focus and you feel this energy coming off it, you've found the focus. It's a lot like writing a song, playing a song – suddenly you hit the groove. You play too fast and it won't settle in; too slow, and it's dragging; but find the right groove and suddenly the song comes alive. It's sort of like that with the recording.

"The beauty was, I didn't really know what I was doing! Nobody had done it before, so far as I know, there were no books to read. People had done single-mic recordings before, but not in a clover-leaf formation, the four lobes, the four players. A lot of it was improvised, but I loved that, the massaging, the moving, pulling distances, changing dynamics. We were sharing in that discovery. We'd try a song, listen back, say, 'That's horrible! Let's try something else!' But they were getting off on the idea of exploring. When you start getting close, when it does begin to come into focus, that's such an exciting moment. Because you always have that thought about, 'What if it doesn't happen?' That gives it an edge, it pumps the adrenaline and the elation becomes even higher."

After a searingly hot seven hours in the garage, in itself an appropriate recreation of the Delta heat, Cowboy Junkies had their first record. Mike was more than happy with the results: "I remember being satisfied with what we had when we played it back. It wasn't a whole lot different to what we'd been hearing in our own homemade recordings. Obviously, it was much clearer, much better recorded, more dynamic, but it wasn't overwhelming, the way hearing *Trinity Session* was later on. We recorded in our space, we'd heard that sound every day in our rehearsal room, so it wasn't a surprise to us. It was the record we wanted to make, it sounded like we expected, we were happy with it because it captured what we wanted to capture. There was something purist about recording direct to two-track that captured us pretty much as we were. It's so natural, so raw, you really hear the band playing together. Even though we've done records like that after *Trinity Session*, it's always been to multi-track and you get the chance to change things later, even if it's only levels. With that record, what you got was what we did. That was a very pure approach for the time. So, when people heard us, they not only heard the music, they heard the recording."

And what did they hear? *Whites Off Earth Now!!* was a piece of work that bore little relation to anything that was out there at the time. There were few, if any, contemporary reference points. Moore had achieved his goal of getting recording back on the "path of truth", but it was the music that had permitted that to happen. Recording a thrash band in that style might have got interesting sonic results, but not *these* results. This was music of subtlety, of nuance. Nothing superfluous there, not a group playing every instrument they could lay their hands on, all fighting to be heard. This was four people almost trying to avoid drawing any kind of attention to themselves, stepping back and inviting the others to take the spotlight. All were happy to play the supporting role, the overall sound of the four of them being the star of the show, four people serving the band, not the ego, like a well-drilled sports outfit with an abiding team ethic. It's the sound of an ethos, a way of doing things, a way of approaching music. As Pete says, "I think that first record captures what we are about in a lot of ways, it says a lot about us. I think we've got better and better as players, at what we do over the years, but I don't think it's a bad thing that we still have that sound that's us. It's very positive. That sound is from the heart, it's what we are. It's better than going and finding a producer to make you sound this way or that way just because that's what's happening on MTV at the moment. At least you can tell where our music is from, that we mean it."

The Junkies knew this music inside out, they worked on it, lived inside it for almost a year in some cases. At moments it could be tender, at others harrowing, at others desolate. It sounded very traditional in a sense, very much in the mould of the blues records they were absorbing. The playing had a direct connection to the heart of the blues classics, produced with a reverence for the masters like Hooker, Hopkins and Johnson, repaying that debt by picking up the music and taking it on. It was no simple recreation of the originals, as had often been the case with the blues boom of the 1960s. This was not the blues locked in a museum, but an opening up of that music to the demands of a new day, marrying that to a European take, the humidity of the Deep South of the United States butting heads with the dank, dark skies of Manchester, both put through a Canadian filter. A new kind of continental drift.

"Canadians are very good at interpreting American music for some reason – The Band are the obvious examples of that," says Mike. "We have distance from the culture itself, but still we're bombarded by it. We get to distil it through those cold winters and come up with our version of it." Perhaps as important, Canada has never really been the source of any particular movement in popular music. Rock'n'roll grew from jazz and blues in the American South. It changed again largely through the influence of the "British Invasion" in the 1960s. Psychedelia was almost a conversation between the two nations, just as New Wave was broadly a New York form and punk essentially came out of London.

For all that Joni Mitchell and Neil Young were cornerstones of Laurel Canyon, Canada has largely had a watching brief, absorbing musics from elsewhere.

Jeff Bird, the multi-instrumentalist who was to have such a big role in the future of Cowboy Junkies, believes that that's very much a facet of the national character, insofar as such a thing exists. "It's probably a Canadian trait that people don't push themselves forward. There aren't that many people in a huge country. You don't need to go far out of Toronto or Montreal to be in a place where there are hardly any people. I think the space people have lowers the whole sociological tension. People aren't fighting for space, because there's a lot of it. It's a pretty prosperous country, there's enough work, it's possible to buy a house without killing yourself with debt. Perhaps it's all just a bit too easy for us! Historically, too, there was no great cathartic beginning to Canada, no big war to win independence; it just kind of slowly drifted away from the British Empire without any fuss.

"Being on America's doorstep has a huge influence, too. That's another way that Canadians define themselves – by how much they're not American! Growing up, culturally America is everywhere. I grew up in the early days of television and we had CBC in this country but most programmes came from America, that was what you knew. Strangely, the more I travel around America, the more I find it is exactly the same as it is on TV, which begs the question: which came first?! As far as the Junkies are concerned, I think that what we do is American music at its root, or North American music at least. A lot of it comes from blues and country and that was what we grew up on, finding those obscure blues records. There's still a festival in Toronto, the Mariposa Folk Festival. It started back in the early 1960s and I'd go there and see these incredible players, a lot of them very old at that point, people who'd had careers in the 1930s and then had their careers revived by these kinds of festivals. You're looking at history and that was a huge influence on me and ultimately on the Junkies, because I know Michael's tastes and mine are very similar."

In *Have Not Been the Same*, Toronto promoter Elliott Lefko suggests, "They saw themselves not as an American band, but they never saw themselves as a Canadian band. That's why they were successful." Though Jeff Bird is right in saying that the root of Cowboy Junkies is North American music, that's not all that's in the mix. That European minimalist influence takes the music somewhere different, melding two continents together in a very unusual manner. Mike has talked of the magic of Lightnin' Hopkins' guitar playing, and 'Shining Moon', one of his songs, must have been selected at least in part because of that. But, while it is unquestionably in the blues tradition, right from the start something sets it apart. Alan's bass is grounded in the sounds coming out of England from 1976 onwards – a track like Joy Division's 'Atmosphere' is clearly an influence on his playing on a number of the songs on *Whites!!* and that tears the music away from the Southern swamp. The tangential nature of Mike's guitar playing, coming at the song from somewhere completely unexpected, makes it obvious why another of Alan's favourite punk records was PiL's 'Albatross': "The ultimate high concept rock music: Jah Wobble's bass is so low you can hardly hear it, Keith Levine's guitar so piercing it's painful."

With all that going on, it's almost surprising there's such a strong North American element to *Whites!!*, but if you're going to play from the pages of the great blues songbook, you can't escape it. And that, too, is a Canadian tradition, as Mike accepts. "There is something about the South that seems to attract Canadians. I don't know why that is, but I guess part of it is that Canadians and Americans are very close, there's many things which are similar, but for us the South is very different, it's exotic in the way the North isn't. If you go through the northeast, it's not a world away from being in Toronto. But the South is a very different place, really is another country. Its weather, the way it thinks, its culture, they're very different; it's very exotic to us, but we can understand it thoroughly because of the common language, we know its history. There's an immersion in America in general in Canada, but the South is this weird little entity and there's an added fascination because of that." Or maybe Pete has a simpler explanation: "Canadians can be as redneck as Texans, so we have our own Delta up here, so to speak!"

Cowboy Junkies' treatment of a classic form was a welcome reminder of just what the blues really were about in an age when people like Robert Cray were lauded as the new kings of the form. A highly talented technician, Cray – and Clapton, too, at that time – was under the spell of the studio, producing highly polished material that was as far away from the original reasons behind the music as you could get – blues to play in the BMW. Again, Mike credits the Junkies' distance from that movement to the principles that had been well thought out before they even got off the ground. "That came from our punk background. There were no rules, you play it as expression, how you feel. What's blues music if it's not that expression of an emotion? That was our whole approach. I never understood people who just recreate other people's music when they cover it, I don't understand the reasoning. Why you would do that? We always try to bring ourselves to a cover. That's a lost art now and the irony is that it's often used against us. What people hear as being the same thing over and over is just us. We're not going to change who we are, that's what is in the music and, to us, that's a very positive thing. It's a hard thing to do, very few bands can create their own sound which is uniquely theirs, but for some reason when you do it's viewed as a negative. I can't figure that out. People like Robert Cray were much more schooled, locked into the more traditional side of things, where we were more locked into the punk side of things, so we took that love and appreciation of the blues and married it to Joy Division. That was where we were coming from, a post-punk aesthetic and an interest in bringing forward things that had gone before it. What we didn't have was that punk disdain for everything that had come before 1976. To us that was ridiculous, but the rest of the philosophy made sense to us.

"I think it's so important to credit your sources, which rock'n'roll hasn't been great at. A lot of great blues material was pretty much stolen by some big bands and no credit was given – not at the time anyway. That's just the music fan in us coming through again. Al and I listened to a lot of jazz music, read a lot of interviews, saw movies about those guys, and we were very taken by the idea that each generation influences the next, that there is continuity. That's so vital for me, but rock music doesn't want to acknowledge that for some reason. We just wanted to show our appreciation for what other people had given us and for their impact on our lives. That was the start of it and we still cover songs by people whose music we love. It's just a tribute, a thank-you, in the hope that somebody grabs something from us and takes that forward. You borrow, you steal, you inadvertently copy, it mutates, it becomes something else. In all other art forms, that's just how it is, it's accepted as a natural thing, but not in rock music.

"For *Whites!!*, we basically culled down our live set, which was based around blues material, torn apart and put back together. It was really us going through our record collection and building a repertoire. Part of it was based on lyrics – the reason we did a lot of Robert Johnson songs was because the lyrics were so fascinating, especially taken out of that blues context and with Margo singing them. You really saw how dark and eerie they were. We made our own music and melody, because we totally changed those, so it really came down to lyrical content and how that could be reinterpreted on top of the music we were doing. That's how we chose them, so even back then it was lyric-driven, because that gave it another edge."

Those lyrics made this a particularly unsettling collection of songs. Sung by big, powerful bluesmen like John Lee Hooker, they were aggressive, nasty, violent at times, even misogynistic pieces of work. Sung by Margo Timmins, at a pitch that often didn't rise above a whisper, sung from a female perspective, their character changes completely. 'Me and the Devil' is a revelation, like hearing the lyric for the first time. The idea that this fragile young Canadian girl was going walking, side by side with the devil, that she was going to beat her man until she got satisfied, sounded incongruous, but the juxtaposition of that angelic voice and that demonic lyric was so arresting that you just knew she was going to get satisfaction before Mick Jagger ever did.

'Me and the Devil' was a tour de force, Al's nagging bassline putting you right in the middle of the story. The song's strength is in its beautiful understatement. In other hands, such a powerful story could easily have led to wailing solos, but the Junkies just let the tale unravel in its twists and turns, the vocal taking centre stage. That vocal is also a window into the future. On other songs on *Whites!!*, Margo, beguiling though she sounds, is still finding her voice. But 'Me and the Devil' sounds like she might have recorded it now, a strength of delivery that makes this the centrepiece of the album.

That's not the only hint of how Margo would sound in future, either. With a weapon as powerful as that voice, most bands would have that way up in front, swamping everything. Instead, on *Whites!!*, the vocal sat comfortably in the midst of the band, a little like Michael Stipe on the early R.E.M. records, such that some of the lyrics are hard to grasp, making them all the more intriguing, notably on 'I'll Never Get Out of These Blues Alive'.

Peter Moore believes this was a crucial decision. "That voice is another musical instrument. That's how I treated it, that's how I recorded it. She wasn't singing onto the recording mic, she's singing through a PA. The way I saw it was that, when the amplified guitar came out, that created a whole new sound, so why not do that again? What I did was get the best-quality PA speaker I could, a small Eclipse, did all my crazy technical stuff on it, and had her vocals come through that. That's what you hear on the recording, and that's why her vocal sits. It's recorded in the room as a musical instrument, not as a separate source. If it was a harmonica, played through a microphone and an amp, you'd think nothing of it, you'd record the amp. That's a tiny little thing with reeds, so I couldn't see there was anything to stop me doing it with the voice. That way, I could bring the speaker in really close to the mic and it gave me flexibility. It was just thinking outside the box, because I had the freedom to do that. That was unique, a radical spin that allowed me to make it sit in the track like they do. That's a key thing. It also set up a style. She's with the band, she's inside there. She's enveloped with the band around her. You have to listen, because the voice isn't being shoved down your throat. Actually, if you relax, the music comes to you, the voice comes through."

That was true of the record as a whole. So much of *Whites Off Earth Now!!* acts as a signpost to the future for Cowboy Junkies. 'Shining Moon' is a perfect introduction, a template of sorts, the bass rumbling in, setting the tempo, lots of space, a hypnotic quality to the music. And just where does that guitar solo come from? Within the opening two songs, you know Mike is no standard guitar player. From 'Shining Moon' to that snarling, spitting sound on 'State Trooper', that weird guitar note that flashes in on the "talk show stations" line, there's nothing you'd recognize as normal lead playing. It also recasts Springsteen's song as being from the classic lineage, its menace not suffering by sitting along the darkness of Johnson's material.

The opening three songs, ending with 'Me and the Devil', form an intense opening salvo, but there are dynamics at work on the sequencing as well as in the music, 'Decoration Day' next up and a lovely, loose recording. The subject matter is no lighter, a lamentation on loss, but the performance is in a different gear to the others, in part a product of the environment, according to Mike. "It was so hot in the garage, but it really lent an atmosphere to the record. We were in a tiny little space, completely insulated for sound, covered in carpets, mattresses. Just a little sweatbox. It was nasty, but it was also great, because we just had that spacey vibe. You couldn't concentrate, which was good in a way because it kept it loose. That again is one of the successes of that record."

That feeling set the band up for its first original, self-penned music *and* lyrics, 'Take Me'. Margo explains, "We wrote it on the day we recorded the album. Al and Pete were eating hot dogs, Mike and I weren't, so we turned on the machine. I was listening to a lot of blues, so it rhymes and repeats itself, that was all I knew about songwriting!"

Mike adds, "Margo wrote the lyrics, she sang me a melody, I played a little riff and we built it literally in about ten minutes. We recorded it straight away and we've never played it since! It was just something that happened, we didn't think much about it, we just recorded it. It wasn't like we had a game plan as to what we'd release, how many songs had to be on it; we were just recording stuff to sort out later. There wasn't a whole lot of pressure on it, we were mic-ed up, let's record. It was nice that it came about and worked, but there was no more to it than that – we didn't feel any urge that we had to have an original on there."

'Forgive Me' is a lyrical brother of 'Me and the Devil' in some senses, introducing another recurring Junkies theme of having songs that partner up on a record – 'Bea's Song' and 'Lonely Sinking Feeling', for example, on *Lay It Down* – different or complementary takes on a particular idea. This time, it's not Margo chatting with the devil, but musing on the business of forgiveness, of confession being good for the soul, of getting off the hook simply by saying sorry after blowing somebody's brains out, presaging the later existential questioning in songs like 'Someone Out There' and 'The Slide'.

Where do you go when you reach the crossroads? A typical Junkies question, asked without asking, 'Crossroads' is the only song that could end *Whites Off Earth Now!!* Slow, brooding, angel voice and devil words, Mike creating a suitably dark atmosphere almost in the background, Alan's bass up front – speed that line up, and you've nearly got 'Seven Nation Army'. You can hear his fingers moving on the strings, another stunning product of the recording method as he and Pete create the texture of the song, a late reminder of what an impressive debut this is for the drummer. Not only was Pete a musical novice when they cut the record, he's involved in something where nuance is crucial. Thrashing away like a wildman would bring the whole thing crashing down. It's not straight-ahead blues, but it would be easy to lapse into 12-bar cliché, destroying it on the way. Instead, he plays with great restraint. As Pete would admit, his limitations at that point meant that he was looking to keep it simple, but trapping simplicity is about as tough as it gets.

"*Whites!!* was pretty much what we were, and what we've been ever since, in some ways," says Mike. "For some fans, it's their favourite album, it kind of defines it in a lot of ways. That record was a real contradiction, very conceptual in many ways, but also totally freeform, it just happened. It got very good reviews, sold well for an independent. We did it all ourselves, distributed it, got some nice blurbs in pretty major magazines. We tweaked a lot of people's interest. In those days, it was a good calling card so we could get more gigs. It was an excuse to go to a radio station to hype a gig. It did well on that level, sold enough for us to be able to carry on, rent a van, go on tour, do all that stuff. It's always been about going on to do the next record, the next tour. I never thought in terms of whether we would or wouldn't last."

Not everybody got it, though, as Peter Moore learned from bitter experience. "I played the *Whites Off Earth Now!!* recordings for A&R people in Toronto and I was laughed at. One of them looked at me and said, 'What the hell is this shit? She can't sing, they can't play, this is a funeral dirge. Why is she in a band with her brother? Why are you wasting my time? Get the fuck out of my office!' I was really proud of that record, that's why I was pitching it, but I just met this total incomprehension. But we all continued to believe in it. We had no idea how big it would go, but I knew it was something special, something that would last, and that it would be the coolest underground thing going. But nothing more than that."

Fortunately, there were people listening, including Tim Easton, who'd caught that Columbus show. "The blues feeling that was there really connected with me, that slide and those dusky vocals. I was immersed in that music myself at the time. I'd gone through the early Stones stuff and thought it was time to go back to the source and started listening to my own country's music. I started playing records by Blind Lemon Jefferson, things like that, so to hear Michael playing slide really had that feel and I picked up on that. I guess that's why they had and have more of a following in America than in Canada, because they're playing American music in that sense. They started to plug into that college radio thing that was very strong. College kids have a knack of picking up unique music that's outside of the mainstream, and you have to remember the American mainstream at that time was pretty terrible, there wasn't a lot that wasn't really disgusting! But college radio set a lot of bands on their way, people like R.E.M., and the Junkies did well, too. Thank God for bands like them, people who were individual, distinctive, had their own thing going."

Deliberately doing things their own way was at the core of Cowboy Junkies, as Mike says: "At that point in our lives, our career, so-called, we were just trying to do things that were different. There was a lot of conceptual stuff going on as well as things just happening. From naming the band to naming the album and making the cover, we were just thinking that we wanted to be doing things that were completely opposite to what they should be, totally contradictory. What we wanted to do was confuse people. We didn't want to attempt to define our sound with our name, with the album title, by the cover – we just wanted to let people figure it out for themselves. That's why we had this weird mishmash of ideas, and then you've got the music. We felt that once people heard that, everything else would disappear, it was going to be about the music rather than us trying to aim it in any direction. There's no clues, you figure it out. The punk thing was coming through, the whole anti-rock idea, no glamour. I'm glad we did that."

When you line up your stock of Junkies CDs today, the cover from *Whites!!* certainly stands out. Who are those four kids? But, to Pete, it makes perfect sense. "The sleeve was just us goofing around, but in a way, with the music inside it, it captures the two sides of the band. People miss the humour that's in what we do, in the songs and in the way we are as people. That's the way it's been all the way through. At least that got us used to that criticism!"

LIGHTNIN' STRIKES

Cowboy Junkies could not have picked a more perfect song to open *Whites Off Earth Now!!* than Lightnin' Hopkins' 'Shining Moon'. Way back then, it had all the elements that would hallmark their sound. In 1986, it's a beautiful performance. Here and now, it's a convincing one. Back then, it defined their sound. Played live twenty, thirty years later, it told you who they'd become.

The song is one of obsession, the jealous protagonist keeping watch on her lover. The psychology is tender but darkly askew, a little scary even, something that would go on to be a recurring lyrical theme for the Junkies. There's the guitar between verses that's not so much a solo, but more a sound tracking a crooked stream somewhere, taking the music into uncharted territory, adding to the unease.

There's a time in life when you're just not ready to take a song like that on, not fully. On *Whites!!*, the song sounds great if you've no reference points for it, no comparisons to make. It's engaging, interesting, different. But it doesn't have the darkness, the threat, the experience in it. Margo's voice is pretty, arresting. But it doesn't nag at you, doesn't disturb you, doesn't frighten you.

Forward to the way they play it now. They're ready. There's an unhinged joy about the way they play it, a menace in the music, a knowing, predatory sexuality about the vocal. From the slightly mannered original, when the Junkies get to the "keyhole in his door" line now, they're handling one of the most sexually charged moments in modern music. Margo has gone from ingénue to femme fatale, a believable ecstatic crazy, but it's the band too, building the excitement with that gradually extending pause before they kick back in. There's a savagery in the way they play it, a dark sexuality, Jeff Bird's harmonica creaking those floorboards, Margo throwing her head back, Mike making the guitar squeal as Bird cranks up the climax. Freud would love it.

What you've got is the sexiness of maturity, something that the culture, especially pop culture, despises. These are confident people, people who know who they are, people who have a keen intelligence and a desire to share it. It doesn't get sexier than that. It's an achievement for them all, but especially for Margo, because women get a tougher time over ageing than men do.

"For women, the culture is so focused on youthfulness, and on that being related to skin, their hair, their figure, that we forget about the sexiness of confidence, of sexual maturity, all those things that come with age," she explains. "We give it to men. I find an older man way more sexy than a younger man, just because I'd rather hear his opinion on the world than some kid. If they're going to take their shirt off, OK, the younger guy looks nice. But, unfortunately, they speak! With women, it's not something we celebrate. Our audience is an older one, they're intelligent, so I think they can appreciate that."

Remember, kids, older people are having sex, too. And they've had more practice.

THE FAB FOUR

The cliché goes that a great band adds up to more than the sum of its parts, musically and personally, in terms of its sound, its aesthetic, its ethos. It's personal chemistry, like a good marriage. Have you taken a look at the divorce statistics lately?

When you head off on the road or into the recording studio to take your first faltering steps as a new band, there aren't any instruction manuals to guide you. You can look at the track record of those who've gone before, but in most cases that's pretty dispiriting, especially if longevity is your goal. Go through your record collection and see how many bands stuck together, in the same formation, for any length of time and you'll find it's not many. Ego, arguments, money, the sheer hard work, the lifestyle, they all conspire to split groups up. Keeping it together for thirty-five years, with the same line-up, is pretty rare. U2 have done an even longer stint maybe, but releasing five albums this century means they're no longer a group in the classic sense, not the primary focus of its members, but four people who get together to work every few years. In that same time frame, Cowboy Junkies have put out nine major studio releases, revisited *The Trinity Session*, added a couple of albums of bonus tracks and a slew of live albums to boot. Throw in about 1,000 gigs, and you've still got yourself a real working band.

John Timmins is in a good position to understand just why it's lasted that long, an insider on the outside: "The Junkies understand the value of a band, that it has a strength of purpose. Michael is a poet first I think, but second he's a real student of the music of his time and he's brought both parts together. Everyone has blithely referred to the great chemistry of The Beatles, but Michael knows what that actually means. There's a real internal logic to it."

A band cannot have four leaders and no foot soldiers. But nor can it have a driving wheel that doesn't recognize the value of the gearstick or the air-con switch. It's like managing an office, but more complicated – everyone on the tightrope at the same time. It is the quintessential balancing act, not least because, if you're putting your music down on record, if you value it enough to get up on a stage and play it for people, ego is a driving force. Put a bunch of big egos in a room together, and you're usually asking for trouble.

Avoiding that has kept the Junkies together, as Mike admits. "This is a real group, everybody does their thing within it and it's been that way from the very beginning. It didn't take us long to establish who's responsible for what. We not only took roles that we can do and which we enjoy, but we took roles that are right for our personalities. We all each have to do stuff that we don't want to, but we do what we can to make sure we're doing the things that suit us best. Pete does a lot of crew stuff, he enjoys that. Pete loves the road – he's in his element out there, he keeps it light, he's got a great sense of humour and that's really important. I do a lot of conceptualizing – what we're doing now and where we're going next – and Al is a good sounding board for that. Margo, although she would say it's not her natural personality, she does like to talk to people, so we try to fit what we do to who we are.

"The lack of ego is a family thing. We slap each other down pretty fast. We would feel uncomfortable in front of our brothers and sisters – Al, too, because he's pretty much family – to put on too many airs, because we know each other so well. We've always laughed at that sort of thing in other people, that side of the business. That's always turned us off and, in a way, it's made us embarrassed to be musicians, that whole pop mythology. The way bands and music are sold is very pompous. So it'd be hard for us now to put that on. We each have a lot of respect for what the others do. There's always some tension, but generally it's worked pretty good, right from the beginning."

Music was always the key, but the personalities were just as important, and Mike and Alan must have pondered that when they returned to Toronto. Family chemistry can be good or bad, but you know how it works, you've lived with it. If you go out and get someone through an ad in the music store or hear of them through the grapevine, they might fit musically, but can you get on with them? For the next however many years? It has to be a gamble. But if it's your brother and sister, the odds tumble according to Pete: "Brothers and sisters tend not to allow each other much of an ego thing, we keep a lid on that, not that there are any egos anyways. There's a pecking order established at birth I guess, which is a good thing. It's pretty clear that Mike's the leader, the elder brother. It would have been interesting how that would have worked if John had stayed in the band right at the start, but as it is it's always been easy."

Margo believes that having specific jobs to do from day one has played a big part in their longevity. "I'm the figurehead as far as the outside world is concerned. It wasn't a conscious thing, it just happened because I'm a singer, I'm a girl. We've always been a working band, we do our music. That's what really matters to us, but we've always understood there's a business side to it, too, right from the start, and we've always had control, even when we had managers, record companies and that stuff. Early on, we divided up the labour the way it made sense, so when we came into a college town, while the boys were setting up, I'd go to the college radio station because I wasn't going to unload the van. And, being a girl, it was easier for me to get on air than some big ugly drummer! Between sets, I'd go round the tables trying to sell records, I was in charge of finding somewhere to stay that night and, again, it's easier to say yes to me. Then suddenly there's three guys standing behind me! Michael handled the business and still does, Pete unloaded the van, Al did all the booking, so really nothing has changed, we still have those roles. Pete still helps unload and set up, Mike

57

knows more about the whole thing than any of us will ever know; I do press before a show a lot of times. And Al's Al. Sometimes he gets up, sometimes he doesn't! I've got a lot of the attention and a lot of people probably associate me with the band before the others, but to us we know we all need each other. I get the focus because I'm the chick singer, and they're fine with that. They're never in a hurry to come do an interview with me anytime! I always get nervous on rare occasions when Al has to do one, though he's done a few more since my son Ed's come along and I've been more busy. It's so funny, our manager will call and say, 'Can you please do this interview, I can't get hold of Al!' Or he'll say, 'Al did the interview but he didn't say anything. Can you call them back!'"

The personal chemistry might work, but what about the music? A unique band has its own sound as much as its own ethos, an identity that you can latch onto as soon as the opening notes sound. Producer Peter Moore picked up on that very early: "I knew there was a unique, cool combination of elements there, and that if you destroyed the combination, the meal wouldn't taste very good. If you mess with the unit, it would fall apart."

Irish singer-songwriter Luka Bloom toured with the Junkies in the early 1990s and came to similar conclusions. "Back then, I was trying to get myself out in front of different kinds of audiences and that meant I was working with different types of bands. No matter what the nature of the music is, there's always a tendency to ask yourself, 'Who's The Edge in this band?!' In a way, that's unjust, because with the Junkies, though you can single out a guy like Michael and say that he's obviously the musical glue that holds it together, nothing is ever quite what it seems. I subsequently learned that with regard to U2. If you took Adam Clayton or Larry Mullen away, U2 was simply no longer U2. That's the same with Cowboy Junkies. It's obvious that Michael has a gift as a writer, just as Bono and The Edge have in U2, just as it was primarily Lennon and McCartney with The Beatles. But, with real bands, they have people who bring essential ingredients to the whole mix. Writing is crucial, of course, but within the band there are other talents that perform equally important but different roles."

In terms of the sound, it's not far from the truth to say that none of the core four sound or play like anybody else. Alan and Pete are the bedrock of that sound, so what's their take on it?

Pete: "We have our own styles, none of us are technical players, which is what gives us a character. You get kids fresh out of music school and they've got the chops, but they have no feel. They play their notes, but they don't listen. We grew up with no technical training, no technique, but we listened. I'm always listening to people and I think that is a problem with a lot of musicians, that they don't listen, they just go out and do their thing: 'I'm the one who's playing here.' That's why so many bands have no dynamic, because each of them is just playing away in their own world. They don't hear when the solo ends, they don't hear when it comes down, they're interested in what they're doing, not what the band is doing."

Alan: "If any of us wasn't there, it wouldn't be Cowboy Junkies. When Mike and I and Pete sit down and start jamming, only we can sound that way, there's this sound that happens, and it's always happened ever since we started playing together, it's a mysterious thing. It's all to do with tones, with the choices you make. With this kind of music that's a little more pronounced because it's so spacious and open, different from normal rock or pop music. That's what makes it unique, the playing structure."

Pete: "We aren't the kind of band where, if somebody left, we'd just get a new bass player or drummer. The sound we have is all of us playing together, doing what we do. We fit together now. On *One Soul Now*, Mike sent a demo of the songs to Al at home in Sooke and I worked on them in Toronto. When we got together to rehearse, the kick pattern to the bass pattern were pretty much locked together already, we had pretty much the same ideas without having worked on them together. It's like being in a hockey team: you just know what the other guys are going to do without thinking about it. Making the same mistakes at exactly the same time!"

Alan: "First show on this tour, we didn't come in on a song. For some reason I just knew that Pete wasn't going to hit the drums at the right time, so I thought I'd wait, come in later. Bizarre."

There's no sense of claustrophobia, because any need to work with other musicians can be dealt with within the band, thanks to the guest musicians they've used down the years – from the ever-present Jeff Bird through Jaro Czerwinec, Karin and Linford from Over the Rhine, David Houghton and many others. But at the heart of it is the core four, doing their thing. Even the Folk Fusion Quartet of 2004 – Mike, Margo, Jeff and Jaro – wasn't Cowboy Junkies, as Mike admits. "It was a nice break in the show when we did it, simply because it is a different band. Cowboy Junkies is not the Mike and Margo show that some see it as, because when we do things that are just the two of us, or us two with Jeff and maybe Jaro too, it's a whole different thing. I think a lot of people miss that. There's a subtlety to it – to me, it's not so subtle, it's pretty obvious – but people aren't used to delving that deeply into music. It's the interaction of the four personalities, and that's what creates Cowboy Junkies."

"I don't think we could replace anybody and still be us, other than for a night or two if Al or Pete got sick or something," says Margo. "I think what people don't see is it goes beyond music. You're living on a bus under very stressful circumstances, you're tired, you're not eating right. The dynamic really counts. Ringo might have just been another drummer – I can't say anything about that, since I don't play drums – but maybe he was essential to them surviving. Maybe he brought something to it that helped get them through the days. Maybe he made them laugh, maybe he was a buffer between John and Paul's egos. Only they really know that. The dynamic behind any band is just as important if it's going to survive. People don't realize that it goes way beyond the music.

"If we ever were to quit, I don't think I'd miss the singing so much. I could keep on doing that at home. What I'd miss is the intimacy. Watching stupid movies like *Dawn of the Dead* at eight in the morning on the road to Pittsburgh. It doesn't happen in life that at 45, 55, you're on a bus with a bunch of people who are your family and friends, travelling along. I would greatly miss that relationship that I have with Mike, the intimacy of being a singer-songwriter team because we'd be relegated to what most people have with their brother – seeing each other at Christmas, talking about the kids, the new car you got – but nothing much really, because you don't share lives. I share my life with the boys. What we have on that bus, crowded and stinky as it is, is something most people don't have in their lives. That would be a huge chunk taken away from me, and that would be sad. I'd miss that.

"Most people's intimacy comes only from their wife or husband and their children. I have more than that and I like that. I like it a lot. There's a sharing of experience. They're not big things, but it's very special, especially when you maintain it for thirty-five years. And when we go in to make a new record and it's the four of us, it's like it was in the garage all those years ago. That always amazes me. Every time we start a tour, we get on the bus and settle down and it's like I just got off it yesterday. It's so weird. As sad as I am to leave my home, dreading it, as soon as I get on the bus there's this camaraderie that I really like. There are weird little moments when a door gets opened that doesn't get opened for everybody, like playing a gig at the MoMA in New York and getting a private tour of the place when it's closed. There are lots of those moments and I've shared it with these guys.

"It is like a second marriage. It's different, but marriage is intimacy and that's very rare in life. Some don't even get it in their marriage! Touring is the best and worst of being in a band, but isn't that like marriage? God, we would all love that first flush of romance when your heart is pounding: 'Will he call me?' All that. You miss that, but you have something different that's more important and lasting. I would never give up what I have with my husband. It's the same with the band. Yes, the bus is filthy and crowded and gross, but I'll gladly get on it again and again to have what I have."

CHAPTER 5

The kindness of strangers

"We toured a ton in America with that record," says Mike of the aftermath of *Whites Off Earth Now!!* "That was a huge education. It was great for us as a band, it taught us how to play live, it got us out of the Toronto scene where we'd begun to get a bit of a name. We never really liked scenes or being part of one, so we wanted to get away from that. We did a lot of touring, driving, a lot of playing to nobody, but – most important – playing. It was the experience of being solely in a band. Al and I knew what that was, we did it with Hunger Project, but Margo and Pete hadn't gone through that. We were always at them. 'Now you're in a band, this is what bands do!' It was good for them to get a taste of that, but it was great for all four of us. That whole time taught us how to be Cowboy Junkies, it focused us on the band, it made it real. If you're at home, doing your day job and playing at weekends or at night, you can't ever get that same sense of it."

Technology, the internet, message boards, fanzines, e-zines, Facebook, Twitter, blogs, have changed the whole nature of being in an independent band so dramatically that it's worth taking a minute to look at doing it yourself 1986 style. There was no website to create. You couldn't put a download or a YouTube video out there to give people a taste of your sound. There were no electronic mailing lists to get people on, no chat forums that might help you get some good word of mouth among music fans, no viral emails to send out to the world, no retweeting or liking going on. If you wanted anybody to hear about you, you got off your ass, got in the van, and you went out and found your audience, because there weren't too many ways of them finding you. You couldn't afford to put an ad in *Rolling Stone* nor in any of the smaller music magazines, either; you might not even be able to put up a poster in town. Mainstream radio didn't have your record and, if it did, it ignored it. College radio was a possible, but first off, you had to go through their town. "Two hundred more miles", indeed ...

Pete is still pretty sanguine about the business of being in a band. Nowadays, he seems the happiest of the core four when the band's on the road, not least because, for him, that's where the band really sounds like Cowboy Junkies. "I like a live sound. I love our rough mixes off the floor in the studio, but I never feel the same once it's gone through the final mix. I don't go to those, because they bother me. That's Mike's say on it. If we hate it, we'll say so, but he's the one that does it and that's fine with us. I always like it rough, before it gets EQed. Once separation starts happening, that bothers me. But when I listen to other people's records, they sound great because I never heard the rough mixes – it's all because I'm so close to the process. I think Mike is great at separating himself from what he played to what the overall sound that's going to people out there should be. I still have the emotional attachment to what went on in the room. What I heard isn't there any more to a degree, it gets cleaned up. I love those first two records because that's what we heard. On *Whites!!*, you're right there, you can hear pins dropping, you hear me put down the brushes at the end of a song, I love that. That captures the exact moment of recording, I guess that's what it is. When you go into final mixes, the whole memory of playing the song disappears for me."

From the off, Pete was perfectly happy to get out there and pay his dues in the time-honoured tradition, a tradition that was embraced by the musicians they were drawing from. What was still good enough for John Lee Hooker was sure good enough for Cowboy Junkies. "When nobody knows who you are, the only way you can sell records is by playing gigs. Al was our booking agent – he'd call the clubs to try to get us in – then, once you've played, you hope that word of mouth starts to create some interest, and fortunately it did for us. A piece of luck is great, if you get your single played on the radio, but that's the crapshoot. For new bands nowadays, that's pretty much gone, because radio is totally formatted, it's Rihanna and Taylor and rap, so you can't even get to the table to try your luck in the crapshoot now. I guess we were lucky to be from an earlier era, when getting out there was what mattered. But playing a couple of hundred shows a year doesn't just build you an audience, it builds you a band all round, as musicians, as people. You can see that in the distance we travelled between *Whites Off Earth Now!!* and *Trinity Session*. And in that period we picked up on new influences too, especially country music, which we heard a lot of as we went around America in a station wagon."

Spending literally months at a stretch trekking across the States with none of the delights of a tour bus and a hotel room at the end of the day is a pretty hard road to take, but it has its compensations, even when you're sleeping on a stranger's floor. As Mike says, "When we were touring in the States and starting to become better known, people would give us tapes of people we'd never heard of before, and that was a great way of finding out about music. They all go into your writing, and so did travel. Going through places puts them into another perspective and that feeds through, too."

One of the band's long-term strengths is the ability to be apart from everything else. They don't compartmentalize easily, you can't put them in pigeonholes. In purely commercial terms, that has its drawbacks, because if you're part of a scene or a trend or a movement you pick up sales simply by being bracketed with a bunch of other groups: "I'll get this record by that band because I've heard them mentioned by this group that I like." If you're out on your own, you're left to fight your own corner. And there really weren't too many contemporary reference points for *Whites Off Earth Now!!* other than to say that it had some similarities to the lo-fi genre that was also in its infancy around that time. *Whites!!* was, in its way, as much of a blueprint as *Horses* a decade earlier. Bands that followed that path didn't sound like the Junkies, but they shared a similar aesthetic, a similar drive for authenticity. You could argue that Nirvana were on the same road too.

The spell on the road in 1986/1987 was not unlike the time Mike and Alan had spent in London in the early 1980s. Away from their own record collections, in a foreign environment, in London, they had homed in on the blues as a way of escaping the pop music of the day.

Now, on the road in the United States, country music was the bridge that took them to the next stage in their evolution, a return to more structured songwriting.

"We seemed to play in the southern States a lot," recalls Mike. "Virginia, the Carolinas, Georgia, there was some interest in what we were doing and we could get gigs there. A lot of people we stayed with, a lot of the bars we played, the radio stations down there, there was a lot of country music being played. It wasn't forced on us, but it was part of the environment and we soaked a lot of it up. Country music was never really in our house a lot, John wasn't into it that much, we hadn't grown up with it. We heard a lot of Texan singer-songwriters like Guy Clark, some of Townes Van Zandt's stuff, but we'd never really heard hard country – Waylon Jennings, Willie Nelson, Hank Williams, any of those guys – and it wasn't until we started touring the States after *Whites!!* that we were exposed to it. Lyle Lovett's first record, Steve Earle, those guys were making a splash, then we read about their influences and it made sort of a circle. We went back to early Willie Nelson stuff, Waylon Jennings, the very early stuff like the Carter Family, and we found there was some really interesting writing in that genre, early Loretta Lynn, Johnny Cash, Kris Kristofferson. We also went to the Smithsonian in Washington and bought this huge history of country music set on cassette, going back beyond the Carter Family and then coming all the way forward, and we had that playing all the time in the van, absorbing it. And, because we were in the van, we were listening together, listening to the same things, and that glued us together as a band. Even though we had a lot of the same influences from growing up together, suddenly country music was this completely shared thing, because we were all hearing it for the first time. That was real important for us."

Discovering the United States and simultaneously discovering the delights of country music were the plus side of the never-ending tour they were in the midst of. But being an unknown band coming into a new town had its down side, too, especially for Margo. "Right in the beginning, when we were playing these weird, awful clubs, Mike, Al and Pete would be my bodyguards. They knew I wouldn't normally hang out in dives like that. I remember one night in Barrie, it was a motorcycle club, and all they did was yell for me to take off my clothes. I didn't know how to handle that it, it was terrible. Mike just said,

'Close your eyes and keep singing, just keep singing.' Coming from my brother, I knew the band were behind me, they knew how awful it was for me, so I just kept going. I had my youth, it had its rocky moments like anybody's, I saw some bands in some awful places, but I was never a hardcore rock chick.

"People ask if it's a good thing being in a band with your brothers, and my regular answer is to say I've never been in a different one, so I don't know. That's a flippant answer to get away from a question I've had a million times, but more seriously, being the kind of person I am, I think I've been lucky to have them around to support me and to take care of me. Nowadays, when people are there to see us, now that we have a bus, our touring is kinda civilized, so far as it can be. We were brought up to respect each other, we like each other as friends, we've always set a pace and a behaviour that we expect from people, and I think that's why our crew come with us time after time. They don't have to, they take a pay cut, get on an overcrowded bus instead of one that's dedicated to the crew. For them to keep coming back is great. It's fun, we enjoy each other's company, we live a normal life in an abnormal situation. It's a very gentlemanly kind of group that we travel with. We've come a long way from the station wagon!"

But, as station wagon tours always do, they gave the band a fund of stories they still remember to this day, the shared memories some additional glue to hold it all together. Mike recalls that "We'd drive all night and I did a lot of that. We were in the Midwest, we'd been moving for hours and we stopped for breakfast at a diner. We ate, drove off, and I realized I'd left my sunglasses behind, which was a big deal, because we were driving into the sun all day. It took us fifteen minutes to get to an exit to turn around, so it was half an hour before we got back to the diner. I went in and asked the waitress about them and she said, 'Yeah, I saw them. I haven't had chance to pick them up, so they're still there.'

"I went over to the table and there was a mother and son there, but the glasses were gone. I asked if they'd seen them. 'No.'

"'Are you sure?'

"'No.'

"So I went back to the waitress and she said she definitely hadn't picked them up, so they had to be there. So I went back and asked again if they'd seen them. 'No.'

"'But the waitress says she hasn't moved them. Are you sure you haven't seen them?'

"'No.'

"So I just stood there and, eventually, her son said, 'Mom, just give him the damn glasses!'"

Distance leads enchantment, and it's easy to get dewy-eyed about those long-ago days, now so far away that they've forgotten the constant dull ache of tiredness, the scratching around for a few dollars to get something to eat, the monotonous miles of asphalt and rain stretching out across the continent. Touring was a yin and yang experience – for every bad moment, there was a good one, sometimes within the same few minutes, as Mike remembered in one of his website tour diaries.

"On [an early] tour our three-day residency at a local bar/falafel joint [in Winnipeg] was abruptly ended when the owner decided that he wasn't selling enough falafels to make it worth his while. We decided to play the three days, anyways, without pay ... nothing else to do. On the third night there was one person in the audience. It so happened that he was a producer of a locally broadcast national radio show [*Night Lines* host Ralph Benmergui] and he liked what he heard. So on the way back through town, he invited us to play a nationally broadcast Halloween show ('State Trooper' from *200 More Miles* is from that show). This was a great break for us, but it also led to another typical Winnipeg moment. We were told that we would be paid $600 for the radio show (our highest paying gig yet and money that we desperately needed to get back to Toronto). We were then informed that it was a union gig and since we weren't union members we either had to join the union ($450) or pay half of the money to the union for a 'special dispensation'. Another lesson learnt."

'Lessons Learned' could have been the name of that long trek through 1986 and into 1987, when many mistakes were made, generally only the once, according to Mike. "Occasionally there'd be someone shouting, 'Louder!' or 'Rock'n'roll!'. There were always one of two of those. And often we'd be competing with the pinball machine, so we'd have to ask for that to be turned off. And we learned never to play a date in Canada during the hockey playoffs, because the TV sets were so much louder than we were. Actually, even four people talking at normal bar level could destroy it, but when we got the audience in a noisy club to be quiet and listen, it was really intense and magical."

Nights like that proved that their music was reaching people who needed to hear it, vital encouragement a long way from home. Other encouragement came from a different source, from their musical forebears, as country music became an increasingly important soundtrack to their long, long days. Listening to songs that engaged listeners, told stories, were built upon a certain truth and integrity, slowly reawakened Mike's interest in the whole form, completing a circle that had begun when he and Alan decided to form a band back in the 1970s. The simple doctrine of punk – if you've got something to say, get on with it – had inspired them to create Hunger Project and to write their own material. The music of the early 1980s then suggested that there was nothing left to say any more, and Germinal began a strange journey through experimental noisemaking in search of emotional resonance. Now, country music was bringing the relevance of songwriting as a way to communicate sharply back into focus, as Mike concedes.

"When Cowboy Junkies started, I had no real intention of writing anything. I'd written a lot starting from my teens. I wrote a ton of poetry, I've always been into words, literature, lyrics, and I think I got into music through lyrics. But at the time, though I was still writing, I was so uninterested in writing music, I just wanted to express things through the playing and Margo's voice. When we started Cowboy Junkies, we were coming from the way the whole thing had fallen apart in England and I was so disgusted with the way pop music had gone. They were trumpeting the likes of ABC, A Flock of Seagulls, and we were just left thinking, 'This is music? This is all we're listening to now? This is real?' I always liked words, but I fell out of love with lyrics, because I just got so fed up of pop music. Songs just bugged me. That's why I got into jazz, a lot of experimental stuff with no vocals just to get away from that simpering, whining thing that was going on in England! That's why we did so many blues covers, because there are so many cool blues lyrics which we could just take and use in different pieces. That was the intention, but what turned it round was becoming more familiar with country music as we travelled across America. It was very simple: the really good writers were very direct and I was hearing that for the first time. That turned me back on to writing – there is some value in songs! So I started to write lyrics again and began to enjoy it.

67

"I'd always listened to people like Leonard Cohen, Neil Young, Bob Dylan, but that had been my youth, so I guess I needed some distance from that before I could go back to those people and think I could do anything in that mould. That's why such a lot of *Trinity Session* is in that style of writing. Once I'd started again, I really enjoyed it and things began to flow. It was kinda like a dam bursting in some ways, because it had been so long since I'd done that.

"As far as songwriters go, from a very early age I was listening to Leonard Cohen. Growing up in Montreal, he was always a major figure. There were the records John brought in – the obvious people, like The Beatles, the Stones, Neil Young. But I've always drawn a lot not just from music but from a lot of fiction writers too; there are zillions of those. I've always loved Richard Ford's work, Rick Bass, lots of people. I don't have a favourite, but I take a lot from that type of writer. I used to read a ton of poetry at one point, though I hadn't done that for a while, right up until going away to write *At the End of Paths Taken*. Back in the earlier days when I was starting to work with lyrics, I'd read poetry just to get the flow, to get that style of writing. A big thing, again in the earlier days, was film. Al and I are huge film fans, we used to go to tons of movies then, during the Hunger Project days especially; a lot of the atmospheres in the films that we really liked influenced what we did musically. A lot of people say our music could be a film soundtrack. That's why: it comes from a lot of films. I get inspired by fine art in general – all kind of things just spark my imagination, and it goes away from there."

While Mike was beginning to formulate musical and lyrical ideas, Alan was beginning to look at the next move for Cowboy Junkies. "We toured *Whites!!* for a long time in our own little way, playing in front of twenty people in Edmonton or something. We'd get the record to the local radio guy – it was easier back then to get people interested in something different, so that was how we got it out there. We sold around 3,000, which was a big deal for an independent in Canada, so we'd started to develop an audience that we felt was ready for another record. That gives you confidence. Making a second record is a big thing – you feel like you've achieved something because you've made enough money to go and do it all over again. Most bands don't make it that far."

The summer of 1987 saw the band alternating between gigging and rehearsing, selecting the right material to cover and piecing together some genuine Cowboy Junkies originals. A minimalist approach was still very much in the forefront of the collective mind, but after a year of absorbing fresh influences and the further working through of older ones the band had moved on. There was a bigger, yet still more intimate, sound waiting to be made. How to capture it?

CHAPTER 6

Universal energies

Cowboy Junkies have never been a band to let their technical limitations worry them. Instead, they've put them to good use, letting them guide their sound, create something unique rather than textbook. But, in some situations, knowledge is power, you need to get hold of people who really do know their chops on a wider range of instruments, especially if you're making a far more arranged, far more structured record, introducing new sounds to the mix. And especially if you're recording it live into a single microphone.

Long-gone brother John was asked to bring his hands to the pump and, while he discussed the direction of the new material and the instrumentation it would require with the band, he made a suggestion that would have far-reaching consequences. "I know a musician in Guelph. You should talk to him."

"Our very first meeting, they called me because John knew me," recalls Jeff Bird. "He lived in Guelph, where I lived, and he'd take recordings home to them. One of them was a band I was in, so they were aware of my playing. Mike called me and said that they were getting ready to make this little recording in a church in Toronto. He sent me some tapes and we got together for a first rehearsal. I got there and literally nobody would talk to me except Mike. I found out later it was because they were afraid of me because I was a professional musician! But it changed!"

Bringing in extra musicians was unavoidable if *The Trinity Session* was going to sound as it should, but that's not to say that Mike didn't have misgivings about using schooled players, as he explains: "If you have lessons, you know what to do and what not to do, and sometimes it's doing the wrong thing that makes a song interesting. Too much schooling can make for boring music, because you're trying too hard to be perfect, which is a pointless thing to me. Occasionally I wish I had more schooling, because I know where I want to go with a song and I'll eventually get there but it takes forever, whereas if I had more formal knowledge I could go straight there. Someone like Jeff would just be able to go to it. But the good side is that, on the way to finding that spot, I might find something else that's also good, which I wouldn't have found otherwise. That's one of the reasons Jeff is so great to have around because he's got all that training but he's not afraid to discard it." For his part, Jeff admits, "There are advantages to not being a taught player and that's one thing I relearned from them, a sort of fearlessness in what you're doing."

The introduction of Jeff Bird into the band's personnel and into its sound has had implications that continue to ripple through their career to this day. An extremely talented multi-instrumentalist, a fine arranger, an inquisitive, provocative mind and a philosophical travelling minstrel, Bird is the only musician beyond the core four to have gone the distance, the mythical fifth Junkie. Yet the very fact that he was allowed to bring his talents to the band bears testimony to the way in which they follow where the music leads. Listen to *The Trinity Session* and, aside from Margo, the signature sounds are rarely bass, drums and guitar. The sounds that are given the chance to leap out of the vinyl are the mournful harmonica or the shimmering mandolin of 'Misguided Angel', the dance that's played out between pedal steel and accordion on 'To Love Is to Bury', the raging blues harp that colours so many songs – all sounds produced by players outside the band, players who take the limelight.

That's about as un-rock'n'roll as you can get. How many big bands schlepped their way across the arenas and stadia of the world with a small orchestra of uncredited musicians playing away behind a curtain, invisible to all so that the egos onstage got to eat? With Cowboy Junkies, other musicians come in if a song demands another colour or texture. And, if it's the defining feature, that's great – someone else

71

stands under the spotlight, Jaro gets the attention, Jeff takes the solo. Cowboy Junkies serve the music rather than having the music serve them, so if a session player can serve it better, get him in.

In his own career away from the Junkies, Jeff works as both musician and producer. His approach to that sits side by side with the way the band came at *The Trinity Session* and at every record since. "When I produce records and I'm picking players for them, it never really works to try to make people do something other than what they're good at. That's pretty much what Cowboy Junkies do. They don't try to change what you do. You want real strong character in the playing, you don't want to mess with that. Then it's a question of whether you like that character or not! Their interest is in making the songs sound as good as they can, whatever the setting and whoever you need to play on them."

According to John Timmins, another contributor to *The Trinity Session*, the years have not changed that aspect of the group, something underlined for him when he returned for a tour eighteen years later. "What Mike does is take all these fairly basic songs and add all these flats, minor chords, that just work so beautifully, they have such emotional twists that makes the audience sit up. Take 'Angel Mine' later on: the lyric is a beautiful little love song, the melody is so simple, but he's thrown in these little extra things that put his signature on it. Another guy would have written that as a straight song, formulaic chord changes, but Mike has an ability to stoke the emotions somehow. And it's interesting that the song can be done in different ways, because on this tour it's Margo, Mike, me and Jeff. Any musician brings their style to things if the mix will allow him in, and Mike does allow that freedom. The style I've created in my time away from the Junkies is related to their style, though of course it's changed because my experiences and the things I've listened to in the last eighteen years are different to them. There's a compatibility in what we do but, even so, they have been very generous and welcoming to me."

Jaro Czerwinec, accordion player extraordinaire, says, "They create a good environment where people can give of their best as players and as people. I stress family. It's very intimate, and when people walk in there's more family. That's the way they are, they're very welcoming and generous in that way. It's a different chemistry to most bands. I think what they have is family love, that love is energy and so you have a lot of positive energy in there. I love that energy, and I love to spread it around, too, and I know how to do that, with the accordion. If you really believe in what you're doing, the communication is even stronger and that's what we have."

Long-term guitar tech John Farnsworth says the feeling is very much the same from his side of the stage. "There's no division between band and crew, no segregation. That has happened with other artists I've worked with and then I tend not to stick around too long, but they appreciate the people who work for them. I think that comes naturally, it's not an act or something they even have to think about. I'm a professional, I would never neglect doing anything that's part of my gig, but bands like the Junkies can get that extra ten per cent out of you because you're all in it together. I'm happy to build a merchandise display for them, but other bands I might find I've got something else to do!"

In that environment, incoming musicians have the perfect environment in which to find their best work, for they are encouraged to use their own voice rather than mimic someone else's. "If you couldn't do it, you wouldn't be here" is the unspoken dictum, and many have flourished within that, not least Jeff Bird. The relationship between Bird and the Junkies has been a quietly evolving one down the years, but right from the outset he made a crucial contribution, according to Alan. "John knew Jeff and so he suggested we bring him to the session, and Jeff knew of Kim Deschamps, and Kim knew Jaro. It was a long chain, really, that brought all these people together."

Ultimately, Cowboy Junkies added five musicians to the core four: Jeff Bird on fiddle, mandolin and harmonica; Kim Deschamps, guitars and dobro; Jaro Czerwinec, accordion; Steve Shearer, harmonica; and John Timmins, guitar and background vocals. With finances stretching little further than the hire of the hall, rehearsal time together was difficult and, in some cases, impossible. "Steve lived in Toronto, so we played gigs with him," recalls Mike. "He'd come to our first gig and introduced himself as 'Honky White Trash', so we knew him a little bit. We figured John would know what the songs needed, because we'd shared so much music and played so much together in the past. We managed to get together for a rehearsal with Jeff and Kim, that was it. We never met Jaro until the day we recorded."

Jaro is the kind of guy that makes an impression, so Pete remembers their first meeting: "He turned up in the church on the day of recording.

73

We hadn't rehearsed, because he'd been touring with the Black Sea Cossacks. He turned up fresh in these shiny red boots and went straight into recording."

Jaro's own recall is characteristically colourful. "*The Trinity Session* was recorded Friday November 27, 1987. I was living in my home town of Sudbury and I got a call from out of the blue. 'Hi, I'm Michael Timmins, I'm in a band called Cowboy Junkies. I've got three tunes that I'd like you to play on for a record. Are you interested?' Nobody's ever asked me to record before, so I thought I'd give it a try. Michael told me the date and I couldn't make it, I had something else I was doing, I was already booked. A week later, he called back to tell me that the date was changed. Unbelievable. Talk about universal energies coming together to create synchronicity, because that was exactly what that was all about. Now I could play."

The band slowly assembled like a flat pack collected from the Ikea parking lot – the Junkies knew who the pieces were, but had no idea if they'd end up looking like they should until they'd put them all together. So, how to record? Finance once again dictated that recording time would be short, so methodology and location were crucial. According to Alan, the first part of the equation was easy to solve: "We could have gone into a studio at that point, there were some cheap places we could have used, but we wanted to go the same sort of route as *Whites!!* We wanted to capture the sound we had, the sound we had when we rehearsed and played."

Mike agrees, adding "We were totally locked into what Peter Moore was doing, we had no money, we loved his results. It was very much the way people used to make records, going in and cutting the whole thing in a day. We wanted to record like that again, we wanted to keep it simple, we liked the feel of hearing the band play. So we did the same thing, just a continuing experiment. We talked more about where to do it, a different space, a different environment. Peter felt that the Church of the Holy Trinity would make a great place for us to record. It had a nice reverb to it, it wasn't overwhelming and, having done some strings and jazz things there, he thought it would be worth trying a rock band in there. Nothing to lose, no money involved, we rented the church, got some musicians in on spec. No huge investment, so if it didn't work we'd go someplace else. And we were almost expecting that. But it worked."

Eventually, the results were stunning. But bringing the sound into focus in the church was a much tougher proposition than it had been back in their garage. They hadn't used the space before, because there was neither time nor money to rehearse there – they were even booked in on the day as the "Timmins Family Singers" rather than "Cowboy Junkies", to avoid upsetting the church. There were more players to cluster around the microphone, players less familiar with the material and totally unfamiliar with one another in some cases, and there was simply more room to move about in. In the garage, the options were limited. In the church, they were endless.

Peter Moore concedes, "I don't have any musical training, I just go for a sound. I'd done a ton of classical recordings in the church, and I'd just be moving the orchestra around until it sounded right. No preconceptions, not realizing I was contravening all the protocol of first chair, second chair, all that stuff! They were so offended! On the day, there were so many variables in terms of players, the room, the space, it took a while to futz around until we got it right." At one point, it looked as though things would never come into focus, according to Alan. "It took a long time to set up in there. I remember saying to Mike at about two o'clock, 'If it doesn't start happening in the next hour, let's can it.' We knew exactly what it should sound like but it just wasn't happening. We'd run through something, record it, listen back, then Peter would move the microphone or us again and then, finally, he got it and we heard him say, 'OK, that's it!' It was a huge difference."

"*Trinity Session* was a lot more about choreography," explains Moore. "There was a lot of marking out on the floor where the positions would be, like a fader move. You'd mark out where you stand in the chorus, where you stand in the verse, for your solo. Like the old movies, like *O Brother, Where Art Thou*, moving in and out according to who's playing what, when. That limitation is amazing. Visually, everyone watches the mandolin player walk up to the mic, so naturally everybody playing supports him, they sit back and let him solo. With traditional tracking now, the solo gets tacked on afterwards, there isn't that communication or interplay between the musicians."

That interplay is the heart and soul of *The Trinity Session*, the internal conversation that rendered it so unusual. "Players don't always listen to one another," agrees Mike. "I guess that's something different about us too, the same way it's different that we have an audience that listens to the music. That's part of the fun, listening to other people and playing off them. It can be frustrating if the sound's a problem, but it's what makes the live aspect of what we do the most important element. It's where we started, it's what the first recordings were about, it's what we continue to cherish in many ways. As a result, that record had everything to do with the dynamics of the moment. We were playing live and, because we'd never played together before, we had to be very intuitive, really listen to each other. It gave the music a natural grace that studio techniques have just about wiped out."

The other side of that conversation is the listener. In part, listening to *The Trinity Session* is a little like eavesdropping, but the people who really got it were also making a contribution, bringing a concentration to it that was in itself unusual in an era where music was increasingly mere wallpaper. Peter Moore is constantly amazed at how little effort people make with most music. "People have lost the art of listening. They think those first two records are the same because they're quiet and slow, but if you listen they're radically different, just because of the rooms they're made in. They're night and day to me. If I heard a *Whites Off Earth Now!!* song on the radio for ten seconds, I'd know it was from that and not *The Trinity Session*. An outsider hears Margo's voice, those cool basslines, the bluesy guitar, so they just think it's all the same, but, to me, no way. You couldn't get a smaller room to make a record than the first one, nor a bigger to record the second, so you're talking extremes."

That big room meant it took seven hours to get everything in place before the material began to sound right. It probably wasn't helped by the fact that the church stayed open to visitors all day long. "Not a ton of people came through, it's not like a huge tourist attraction or anything, but some did, we had a few takes ruined, but it was kinda funny," recalls Mike. "When we were recording 'Sweet Jane', I think the version that made it to the record, a young couple walked in at the far end of the church. We heard the door opening, but we just kept on playing because it felt like a good take. They sat down for a while and listened, then after a few songs, they left. No big deal, we were locked into what we were doing, we didn't really take much notice. About ten years later, I was having some work done on my house and one of the dry-wallers there said, 'You know, when you were recording *Trinity Session*, I was there with my girlfriend listening.' It was the weirdest thing."

While Moore and the Junkies fiddled with the sound early in the day, the rest of the players turned up in dribs and drabs, according to Jeff Bird. "I got to the church quite late in the day – that's one of the benefits of not being a full-time member, you don't have to turn up for all the fiddling around that goes on in setting something up! I just walked in – same with Jaro and Kim."

Jaro, of course, made a very idiosyncratic entrance. "I was in Montreal to play a couple of shows the two days before, then had to travel in and play in Toronto the next day. There was a lot of snow that year, and on the second day in Montreal it was a total blizzard. For some reason, I decided to hang out at the club by myself that night, I was pretty wired up, I think, thinking about the recording the next day. I didn't catch any sleep, I was gonzoed, totally dishevelled, to the point where I could feel these energies surrounding me, I was getting pictures around me. And all the time I was thinking to myself, 'If I fall asleep, I'm going to miss the train.' It was five in the morning and the train was maybe nine or something. So I stayed awake all night, got that train and eventually made my way to the Trinity church. That was the first time I ever met the folks, didn't know anybody except Kim Deschamps, the pedal steel player – it was Kim who had mentioned me to Michael; that was what got me the gig.

"I walked in, introduced myself, but by now I was very, very tired. I never drink coffee, but I was drinking cups of it, having no effect. So, as Cowboy Junkies recorded the other tunes, I went and lay down in the church. There was a cushion on the pew and I basically passed out, hearing all these tunes floating through, beautiful, Margo's voice live, incredible.

"The preparation I had was a demo of the three songs, some critiques of their album *Whites Off Earth Now!!*, and they were all raves. But the picture hit me. I couldn't believe it. All family and their best pal Alan Anton. To me they looked like punk rockers. At the time I was ten years older than any of them. Still am, except Margo, who thinks she's catching up to me! I was 37, Michael was 27 – at that age, that's a big thing in terms of experience. But when we got to the music, that glorious music, it held us together. I thought to myself, 'My rock'n'roll dream has come true. I'm going to be playing punk rock accordion for these hip dudes.'

"Then I put on the demo tape and I was listening and I cannot believe what I'm hearing. What I'm hearing is what sounds like a garage band playing, not punk rock, but some slow thing that I really liked. I loved the lyrics. 'Misguided Angel' was the first thing I heard, still number one in my book, and there's this voice, it was glorious. I kept playing it over and over and that voice haunted me, it had a magical quality. Michael sent me some ideas on what he wanted me to do, block chords, so I did an arrangement for it which came to me as I listened to it over and over, the sound of the accordion floating through the arrangement. It wasn't hard for me to put the accordion somewhere where I thought it would do justice to the song, and it happened really fast. I was looking forward to playing that one.

"The second tune I heard was even more traumatic, because my rock'n'roll gig when I was a teenager was weddings – polkas, waltzes, tangos! What kind of thing was that for a teenager to be playing when The Beatles and the Stones are happening? So, I'm listening to 'To Love Is to Bury' and I can't believe I'm hearing a waltz. I've been trying to escape waltzes for twenty-five years and this punk rock band is playing a waltz! Beautiful tune. It would have taken me a second to figure out what key it's in, but it stunned me so much that I never bothered. I just kept playing it over and over, that lovely tune. The Ukrainian people would have loved that if the lyrics had been in Ukrainian!

"Third one was 'Walking After Midnight', a Patsy Cline tune, that was going to be a blues jam session more or less, goes through the blues changes, so I jammed around a little bit with that, got the key, so I had something in mind.

"So I was lying down in the church, exhausted. You rest as much as you can in that situation, and after a couple of hours it was my turn. We don't know each other, I sit down, ready to play and I'm set for 'Misguided Angel', because that's the song I've been thinking about, first one on the demo. I'm ready to impress these dudes right here, one take, no problem, on we go. Instead, Michael says, 'We're going to do "To Love Is to Bury".'

"I turn to him and said, 'What key is this song in?'

"He looked at me with a face I will never ever forget. He can't believe the question.

"'Didn't we send you a tape? What key is it in?'

"'Yeah, I got it, but what key is the song in?'

"'G major.'

"I'll never forget that key. Etched on my mind forever. So, after hours of them recording, we're at the end of the day and I'm asking what key it's in. I'm learning it and arranging it as we go along, that's pressure. Mike's staring at me, totally bewildered. What a freaking way to start! We went through seven or eight tries, I was getting frustrated, everybody was tired, and we finally got it on the eighth – it was OK. Wow, finally!

"Michael took a break for five minutes and then came back and said, 'Let's do "Misguided Angel".' And he looks at me. I guess he's waiting for me to ask the key. But I said, 'OK.' I was ready for this. One take and it's down, man, I'm vindicated! Get that wrong, I'd have been on the bus back to Sudbury! Michael feels better now. 'Walking After Midnight' is the last one, we did three takes as a jam, don't know which take they used, but that was that. And then it's history, a phenomenal thing."

You only have to listen to the recording to realize something special was happening that day. Most of us can only hear it secondhand through the sound recordings. But, for the players, as they were working, they knew they were tapping into one of those rare musical moments when everyone is in the same mental and emotional space at the same time. You don't forget those days, according to Jeff Bird.

"It was one of those moments in a musical career that keeps you going, an incredible experience. You can't orchestrate it, they just arrive from nowhere. It's like the heavens came together, arranged themselves properly and said, 'Here you go!' Interestingly, I went back to the church in the winter of 2004–5 for the first time since we made the record, to hear another concert, a medieval chant. Jaro came to it, too, and we found out that the church is considered to be on a huge power spot. There are three leylines that converge there – two rivers converged there, too – and, long before the white people came, the natives held it as a really strong, sacred spot. Even when we went back there in 2006 to make *Trinity Revisited*, it still had something about it. It was a typical film set, lots of people milling about, lots of equipment, total chaos, very different to when we made the record. So you worry about what you'll get out of it. But as soon as we started to play, that room kicked in and it became something special. I guess we picked the right spot, we plugged into the right power source!"

The power source was one element in the mix, but so was the building, though the players have conflicting views on whether it was angels or architecture that made the contribution. Jaro admits that "I love playing in churches; it creates its own atmosphere before you start. When people go somewhere to meditate or to pray, good thoughts are happening, there are mostly positive vibes in a church, and it feels clean, the aura of it is cleaner." That struck a chord with Margo, too: "I think the stillness and the beauty of the church added to how well we played that day."

Mike is a little more agnostic about the whole thing, though he concedes the church must have offered an undercurrent to the session. "We had a Catholic background which we threw away a long time before. But, like all Catholic backgrounds, they stick with you, they're always somewhere in there. I don't think we were awestruck or intimidated by it. It wasn't, 'Oh my God we're making a record in church', but it was a familiar place to us – the atmosphere, the stained glass, the sound, the reverberation. That must have affected our psyches on the day, but how much, who knows?"

Acoustically, the church was as much a player as any of the people on the record, though that was in no small part down to the way they recorded, the nature of Margo's ethereal voice and the arrangements and instrumentation they brought to bear on the material. Jeff Bird: "It was beautiful to play in the church. The pedal steel in there was like an angel choir going into the roof, so it was a really strong experience of itself. Then, as soon as we played it back, we could see we had something special. I remember at the end of the day listening and thinking, 'There's something going on here!' We had no idea the rest of the world would think so, and it took a year for it to really catch people's attention, but they got it in the end, which is kind of encouraging, that people recognize magic when they hear it, even with all the bombardment they get. Gives you faith in the world!"

Where better to find faith than in a church?

A HOLY GHOST BUILDING

The Church of the Holy Trinity in Toronto is an unassuming, but beautiful building. A solid, brick construction, its charm is in its subtlety. It's not glaringly obvious, but there are countless beautiful details given room to breathe under its high roof.

Inside, it does what a church should do, preaching social justice as powerfully as any liturgy. The regular schedule displayed on notice boards includes a "Homeless Memorial, second Tuesday of every month". There are pamphlets detailing local projects to help the homeless and the unfortunate. Services include both a traditional and contemporary Eucharist, all held beneath banners that festoon the inside which demand "Social Justice Now".

A plaque detailing the building's history reminds pilgrims that it was created so that its seats "be free and unappropriated forever". Back in 1847, most other churches charged pew rentals – no such thing as a free Communion. It proudly proclaims that, in the twentieth century, it "developed a tradition of ministry to the needs of people in the inner city". It maintains that work to this day.

Come out of the church and you're on the patio of the Eaton Center, Toronto's biggest shopping mall, a church of the new religion – the Church of the Early 21st-Century Greenback.

The Church of the Holy Trinity should not exist amid the brutality of the modern world, an era of corporatism, of image, of lies, no ethics. But, amid that brutality, how are we to survive without solace and without hope?

CHAPTER 7

Never settle for anything less

The Italians coined the term "a cappella", meaning "from the chapel". It refers to an unaccompanied voice, such music coming about because of the restrictions on the use of musical instruments in medieval churches. For their second record, Cowboy Junkies imposed no such restrictions on themselves in terms of the number of instruments they employed. Yet they still chose to open their record a cappella.

There's not an album in the canon of popular music that whacks you over the head quite as quickly or as forcefully as *The Trinity Session*, but nor is there one that opens so quietly, intimately, sinuously, deceptively. You can scarcely hear it, the chink of metal, that whisper of air, that whisper of a voice, not forced, not demanding, but utterly compelling, totally commanding. Anyone with ears to hear and a soul to move is stopped dead in their tracks. Then there's a swoop down, a quiet count in, the harmonica wails, the guitar comes in, the accordion ghosts into the background, pedal steel, drums, bass, voice, mandolin, a second voice – suddenly there's a band there, making the loudest silence you ever heard. You're at the epicentre of a circle, surrounded and seduced by people caressing the music. How can you not love a record that starts like that?

Absorbing 'Mining for Gold' and 'Misguided Angel' is a little like watching the start of the Talking Heads movie *Stop Making Sense*, where the band slowly builds in size from one song to the next. Except, on *The Trinity Session*, it happens inside the first four minutes, and with a far greater degree of subtlety, so you don't notice it happening until there's this orchestra in your head. It couldn't be less showy, it couldn't be less contrived, it couldn't be less demanding. Nor could it be more intriguing.

Alan is typically downbeat about the extraordinary sequencing that opens the album. "The running order on a record pretty much falls together when you see what songs you have. With *Trinity Session*, 'Mining for Gold' obviously had to go first because it was so striking. It was quiet, it didn't sound like much else that was going on in 1988 when everything was so produced. It sucked you in, it made it obvious that you were going to have to listen to the album, to give something to the process rather than let it wash over you. We should do that more often."

By the time 'Misguided Angel' completed that opening couplet, you were in no doubt that this was a record of a kind that nobody else was making, though the idea of performing a cappella did owe something to another performer, as Mike concedes. "I'd seen 10,000 Maniacs in a club and Natalie would do an a cappella if somebody was tuning or had broken a string, and it was really compelling, the contrast between coming off the back of a pop song and then total silence to hear this one voice. It was very intense and it was something we started to do if I had to retune and it had the same impact. I think that song is one that Margo found, an old traditional number, and it was very powerful. We just felt, if it was so riveting live, it might be a good way of grabbing people right at the start of the record. It was a big statement, I guess, and something we did deliberately."

Easy for the guitar player to conceptualize and the bass player to shrug off, but when you're the singer, out there instrumentally naked, it's a big ask. What if they don't like your voice? They don't bother to play the rest of the record. That's a ballsy decision.

"I don't think it was guts to put that on first," Margo protests. "I think it was just ignorance is bliss. My whole life has been that way – somebody invites me to go walking up to Mount Everest, and I'm 'Sure, I'll do that,' without thinking, and you end up camping on a snow strip! I started doing a cappellas in our early shows because we didn't have guitar techs, so it took Mike forever to retune between songs. There'd be these long gaps between songs and, in those days, there was no way I was going to even look at the audience, let alone talk to them, so to fill the gap I'd sing until he'd finished. So when we were doing *Trinity Session*, I thought those were a part of what we were doing. Our albums have always reflected who we are at that time, and so I've never looked back at any of them and thought we should have done it differently, which a lot of musicians do. It's who we were at the time. That a cappella reflects that time, my place in my head as a singer. Not shyness, but awkwardness onstage. I love having that there – it's a bookmark of that time.

"It's funny, though, because that was the only song we didn't do on the day of *The Trinity Session*. For some reason we forgot, we were pressed for time at the end, and it was only when we were walking down the street after the church was locked up that somebody said, 'Did we record "Mining for Gold"? Shoot!' So a couple of days later, I had to go back and do it cold. Peter Moore was recording the Toronto Symphony Orchestra in the church, so he called me up, told me it was set up and I needed to go down and sing. I got there and the whole orchestra was on a break, top classical players who believe in everything being on time, on key. They're sitting around having coffee. I'm thinking, 'I can't do this in front of them!' When I hear it now, I just hear this one small voice among these classical players saying, 'What the hell is this?' I wouldn't have done it if I didn't have that ignorance-is-bliss personality. Don't think about it too much, just do it. Life's easier that way!"

And there was no getting out of it, because Mike wasn't going to let that record go to the pressing factory until it was done. "We knew we had to have that song, it was so important. So Margo had to go and do it and it sounded great." And anyway, Margo wasn't quite alone, because Peter Moore was there to record her. And he insists it wasn't an a cappella, either.

"It doesn't sound like an a cappella, does it? We were in an old church, built in the 1840s or whatever, and it has a really old heating system in it. We were recording in November, the heating was coming on, so we never knew if the pipes would come on during a take! For 'Mining for Gold', I actually turned off the furnace for about an hour as we were getting the sound, ready to record. Once we were ready, I turned the furnace back on, so the first thing you hear when it opens is the clinking of the radiators coming on, you hear the steam going through these ancient rads and, to me, that was the band. That's why it doesn't have that solitary 'it's just a voice' quality. Because no, it's not just a voice! You're hearing a tremendous amount of set-decorating! I timed it so that, when I turned the boiler on, the pipes would click, because it's about mining, right? It's a simple analogy in my head, it sounds like guys chipping away with chisels. It was too obvious not to use, and it solved my problem! You have to remind people it's a cappella, they don't twig it. It's cool because you really get to hear the church too, that natural reverb and decay – it has an ethereal quality to it."

It's a little playful, too, given that the Timmins family had founded a town out of mining for gold. Now a new generation of the family was mining for musical gold and, in time, a new family business would come out of the recording of that and the rest of the collection of *Trinity* songs.

Ideas being passed down the family was crucial to the second song, 'Misguided Angel', which seemed to grow organically out of the first. It was a co-composition between Mike and Margo, yet its genesis lay elsewhere in the family, according to John.

"I didn't realize until going on tour with them that Margo wrote 'Misguided Angel' with Michael – I thought it was Mike's song. But she told me on the bus that the brother in the song came from something I'd told her about pursuing your passion. I should get royalties! There's a lot I don't know about their collaboration and how they've boosted each other, and yet I know so many other things about them, of course, I'm so accustomed to them. I'd love to have that distance that an audience had when they heard Margo for the first time, because it really is a singular voice, but obviously I was used to it long before the Junkies started. I don't think there was ever any doubt that Mike would end up doing this as a career, but I'm not sure about Margo, it was never so clear. Now, I see Michael and Margo as the same entity where the Junkies are concerned and I think Mike would accept that he might not have been able to succeed so well without her."

The opening sweep of that record has become such a recognizable part of the Junkies' canon that it's hard to imagine it working any other way. Yet it wasn't pre-planned, according to Mike. "We knew 'Mining for Gold' would open it, but I don't think it was so concrete that 'Misguided Angel' would come next. It was one of those very special songs, too. When we got Jaro, Jeff and Kim together, that was the first time we'd ever played that arrangement together. The four of us had played it, obviously, but all the others had had was tapes. We'd talked about the sound, the concept of it, but what you hear on the record is the very first take of it. That was it, and that's pretty amazing. I guess that influenced us to put it up front, 'Mining for Gold', then into this magical little moment and away we go."

"Magic" is a nebulous kind of word, cheaply used. And yet that's the essence of *The Trinity Session*, that ingredient that you can't manufacture but the one that you're forever chasing. Some prefer to think of it in spiritual terms, cosmic terms, quasi-religious terms. We each have our own name for whatever it is that's out there in the ether, and we each know it when we're touched by it. Artists, musicians, they spend a lifetime trying to catch it, as Margo explains.

"Music is a very spiritual thing. When it works, it's like you had nothing to do with it, you were just there as it happened. When we've had a really great night, it hasn't been a night where we've worked really hard. It's a show where I'm not even thinking about what happens next. 'Is there a stop here? Does Jeff do a solo next?' None of that. It just flows, it comes naturally, you hear it beyond yourself. 'Oh my God, that sounded nice! Where'd that come from?' That's when it really works. The day we did *The Trinity Session*, during 'I'm So Lonesome I Could Cry', I can remember hearing my voice floating up to the top of the church and back down again and thinking, 'My God, that's so beautiful.' Totally hearing it as if somebody else was singing, for the first time. It was nothing to do with me, it wasn't 'Look at me, I can sing', it was an out-of-body experience.

"That was one of those days when it was just happening and we were so lucky to have a tape machine rolling when it did. That's what people hear on *The Trinity Session*. It's not great playing, it's just that magic that happens to you once in a while. We caught it. It doesn't get caught very often, which is what makes that record special. Live, that's what you're looking for, that's why we do this, that's why I'm sitting in Annapolis hearing about my nanny taking my baby to the farm when I don't want him to go! Because you're chasing those moments."

Everything surrounding *The Trinity Session* was kissed by fate. They turned up in the church with their own PA, only to find somebody had left a way better one in the church after a previous recording session. Waste not, want not, as the church teaches, so the band felt perfectly entitled to plug into that, getting an immediate boost in the way the songs sounded. Even rehearsals had had a touch of destiny about them. The evolution of 'Blue Moon Revisited (Song for Elvis)' is a case in point, according to Mike. "We were going to do to 'Blue Moon' as the same kind of thing that we did to the covers on *Whites Off Earth Now!!* The three of us worked on the music in the rehearsal space without Margo. We discovered that lopey groove that it ended up with, then Margo came in and started to sing those words – she didn't actually know what we were working on! But it obviously worked straight away and so we segued into 'Blue Moon' from there and it was a nice combination."

Like a lot of material on *Whites Off Earth Now!!*, trance music had plenty to learn from the Junkies, Al's hypnotic bass figure standing on the shoulders of earlier giants. "We were very much into that repetition thing, which was a very Velvet Underground kind of idea, then bands like The Fall got into that, too. That song had a great groove, so stay with it."

'Blue Moon Revisited' didn't make the final cut on the original Latent vinyl release, an omission that seems extraordinary now, not simply because the church recording is so beautiful but also because it's such a conceptual cornerstone of the record. If *Whites Off Earth Now!!* played homage to the Mississippi bluesmen, *The Trinity Session* is Cowboy Junkies' reading of the Great American Songbook, a thematic take on the subject matter that fuelled so much of the music they'd been exposed to as they slogged back and forth across the United States in their van.

"We had some new material like 'Misguided Angel' and 'To Love Is to Bury', and we just saw them as part of a tradition", says Mike. "Once we had those, we thought about the existing songs that we could add to make the record make sense and have some unity to it. 'Blue Moon' was that Tin Pan Alley side, we had to do something from Hank Williams, from Patsy Cline, and then we added 'Sweet Jane' to that, which gave it a different edge. Lou Reed is one of the great American songwriters, too, and we wanted to acknowledge that. But we also wanted to show that there was a similar darkness to a song like 'Walking After Midnight', because it's all part of a continuing story.

"The Velvet Underground were just such a cool band, everything rock'n'roll should be about. John introduced me to the Velvets when I was 11 or 12, and they've always been a very, very strong group for me. And, in every band I've been in, they've always been there. So this was our nod to them. And we picked 'Sweet Jane' because it's such a famous song. We figured it had been covered so many times and so badly by so many people that we should do it right. Of all the covers we do, it's probably the straightest, because we went back to the live version on *1969*. Not so many people know that version. Most people know the song through *Loaded* or *Rock N Roll Animal*. But we wanted to get back to maybe what Lou Reed originally heard. Even the version on *Loaded*, it was re-edited after he left the band. So it's not really the song that Lou Reed originally wrote, which is what we wanted to get back to. It really is the most beautiful song, and the rock versions just take one aspect of it and make it pretty straightforward. We felt it needed someone to do it justice after all this time."

Reed himself broke into a rare bout of public enthusiasm to claim that the Junkies' version was "the best and most authentic version I have ever heard", which is pretty much the musical equivalent of being knighted or getting the Légion d'honneur. The band met him later, and, Mike recalls, "He was real friendly. The first thing he said was, 'Fire your manager, don't trust your record company and don't talk to journalists.' When we saw him doing a show in Paris, he held on the bridge in the song which we put back in and said, 'I'd like to thank Cowboy Junkies for this.' That's pretty cool."

Another element of the Great American Songbook is the scope it gives the singer, the chanteuse. For Margo, the role of the singer, the Billie Holliday or Ella Fitzgerald figure, is an inspiration. Elsewhere, she's sometimes dismissed as "just" the singer. It rankles. "It makes me sad that in our culture the role of a singer has gone, that people constantly ask, 'Don't you want to be a songwriter as well?' As if being a singer isn't enough, as if by not writing as well, you're not really anything. That's a shame. When you think of the great singers, most of them aren't songwriters. And a lot of the great songwriters aren't great singers, either. They have a style, but you wouldn't call Dylan a singer, Neil Young a singer. Great interpreters, but not singers in that sense. In order to be a great singer, you have to have a great song. I can write songs, I've written several for us, but I don't feel they're great. When I get hold of a great song, whether it's one of Mike's, or Leonard Cohen or Neil Young, whoever, then I have material, I have something to use. That's what makes me a good singer. I have to have this material. I've always believed in knowing your limitations. I think it detracts from music that we don't appreciate the singer any more like we did in the past, because you're supposed to be everything and very few people can be good at it all.

"It's funny – some people assume I write the songs, that all the songs are about me. If they think that, then I feel like I've done a good job. When Michael writes a song, when he hands it over to me, he really does give it to me to do what I want. If people think I wrote it, we've both done a good job. That's what I strive for. As a result, some people think I've lived a very miserable life! My job is to make it believable, whether it's in the first person to make you think it is my heartache and misery or in the third person to make the characters come alive. I'm a storyteller in a way; that's what the original singers were. I have no problem with that. I love that, actually."

The problem Margo might have had on *The Trinity Session* was less one of the material and more a simple physical one – recording an album in a day puts a strain on the vocal cords. But the way the record was made, and the volume it was made at, helped overcome that, according to Peter Moore.

"Fortunately, she's not belting it out, she sings softly, quiet. And she was singing through a speaker, softly into the mic, so she didn't need to force anything. She was standing off to one side, with the speaker in the centre. I worked it so the microphone distance to the speaker was exactly the same distance she was, so she was actually mixing her own vocals by leaning in, backing off, and she heard it from the monitor. So, whatever she was hearing, that's what the mic was hearing. It was a real simple but very accurate way for her to get feedback on her performance as it was happening. It was a happy accident, I didn't so much realize it at the time as later – I tell everyone it was a master plan that I had worked out way in advance!

"There were no headphones, so it was a challenge for her not to play in the band, to be isolated from it. Live, she's in the middle, enveloped by it, but this was different. The 'vocal' speaker was on top of the bass cabinet, and Margo sang through the mic from about six feet away. She's pretty natural, too. If I say it's effortless, it sounds like it's lazy, but I don't mean that. But she is able to sing very calmly as though it's the easiest thing in the world."

Where much of the record was looking back through a catalogue of songs, one was pointedly looking outwards: '200 More Miles'. "It's more than just about being on the road, it's that sense of starting a journey, which is what I guess I hoped we were doing at the time. It uses the visual ideas of being a band on the road, but it's about heading off in a new direction, leaving things behind. You don't want to write too many road songs. Somebody once said that you know your career is over when you write your first road song. I always thought that was ridiculous, but I guess I kind of know what it means if that's all you get locked into. But the road is a really interesting place: it takes up a lot of our time, it's where a lot of our lives have been spent, so every now and then one crops up – 'Townes' Blues', things like that."

Looking backwards, looking forwards. A thematic unity. A musical approach that ran through the record. All the threads came together to bind *The Trinity Session* into a cohesive package. And, like everything, it started with a heartbeat, according to Peter Moore.

"It's always amazing listening back to the takes, comparing the ones that made it onto the record with the ones that didn't. You hear stuff we left out, those are pretty good, but you can feel they just don't have the magic. It's a lot to do with tempo. It's a group-decided thing, it's like a constantly developing conversation, there's a synergy. People don't really pay too much attention to the rhythm section, but that's where it's coming from with the band, they're incredible. Alan is a real motherfucker on that bass. He's the quiet guy, but that bass really sets it going. In some ways, he's kind of the quiet spiritual leader of the band. He knows where the groove is, and so much of their stuff comes off that, that's where its character is, taking nothing away from the rest of them. But Al is the real foundation that provided the direction and the comfort for everybody else to play. To the public, bass is the least known instrument, but to the musician, a great bass player can make a band. It's the transducer between rhythm and melody, the bridge between those two worlds. If that marriage isn't correct, you won't have good music."

Mike is absolutely in agreement with Moore's assessment of Alan's value to the Junkies. "The media view is very much the Margo and Mike show, but that really pays no attention to what actually goes on with this band. The rhythm section is fundamental to the way we sound, but it's very rare that any journalist will pick up on that unless it's for one of the musician magazines. It's not like it's Bootsy Collins or something, but it is a big element in our sound, that's what we are. We concentrate on it a lot, we think very hard about it. What Pete is playing, what Al does and what I do on rhythm gives a real sense to what we do. It's not like we take that for granted, which a lot of bands do. There's no sense of the rhythm section playing music; they're just keeping the beat. Not with us. The groove, the pulse, whatever, that is what establishes our sound. That's the blues in what we do. When we were developing the band in *Whites Off Earth Now!!* and *Trinity Session* days, we listened to a lot of that music, a lot of early John Lee Hooker stuff – not just solo, but with bands, too – and that's what they do, they get on a groove and they sit there for twenty minutes. We love that, that's fundamental to us: find a good pulse and play it. It's a heartbeat."

If you give a record a heartbeat, you give it a life, and *The Trinity Session* is one of those records that exists in its own space, its own universe, independent of its creators. A dozen years after progressive rock throttled the life out of the concept album, Cowboy Junkies brought back the conceptual record. Mike is self-deprecating about how it all happened, how there was that emotional sweep from the solitary human voice that opens it to the chatter at the end of it. "I can't remember how much of that is conscious, how much it just happened. You start with an idea, I guess, and then hope the subconscious kind of finishes it off for you!"

Peter Moore is a little more bullish about the way it was constructed: "There were elements that were luck. They played so slowly because of the room. The reverb was such that Alan especially had to play slower because he had to wait for the reverb on the previous note to die away before he could play the next one; otherwise, they would boxcar into one another. That gives it an unusual kind of tempo. It works as a cohesive record because of the way it was recorded. It is a document of a day and it has a consistency to it and it has a flow where the songs just work off one another. The sequencing of that record was amazing. It was mostly Michael's idea, but we tried a few different things. But, once we hit the right sequence, it was like hitting the right tempo – it was there, that's it.

"I worried to death about the spacing between the songs, how the fades would work, and that's not something anyone thinks about now – it's the default two-second gap. But, if you work with a guy who used to master vinyl, actually cutting the groove, waiting for the right time to come in, that's an art. I wanted to play with that. I tried to put some of the room tone there; it just goes on as long as it could, into the next song, there's no drop. That has a lot to do with the repeatability of that record, because there seems to be one energy flow through it. It, and all it is, is room tone, then Margo starts to sing, and by the end, when we end on people talking, it's this one piece. I worked very hard when we were editing on a very, very, very early digital editor which took forever to make work. That was a real tricky thing to do. But I wanted this to be a movie, to be a stage play, to open, flow and end. You couldn't break it up, change it round. It is what it is, complete. But there was no vision from God that this would change our world. All I knew was we'd made a great-sounding record that had achieved the goals we set for ourselves."

Many years have passed since most of us lost our *Trinity* virginity. But Mike still remembers the first playback. "When we listened back to it, we had no expectation it would be this huge international success, but we were stunned by it, it was a 'What have we done?' thing, we'd captured what we wanted. It was strange, we totally recognized it. The day after we recorded, I listened to it and I went straight over to Margo's house with a cassette of it and told her, 'You gotta listen to this!' We sat there and we were amazed. Then my mother walked in, just arrived without calling, which she'd never normally do, she sat down and even she got it! I hadn't spoken to Peter at that point, but that night Al was having an engagement party at his house, so I went over and played it for him as his guests were coming in. Then Peter walks in: 'Have you listened!? Have you listened!?' I guess it was kinda obnoxious for all the other people. There's nothing worse than going to a party where people are playing their own music! But we couldn't take it off! They were saying, 'Do you think we could change the tape?' after the fourth time. It was a great moment – we really felt we'd caught it."

Sure. But the world's not gonna care about a little record by a family group out of Toronto. Right?

SO YOU WANNA BE A ROCK'N'ROLL STAR?

Mike Timmins: We released *The Trinity Session* like we released *Whites Off Earth Now!!*, just as a little independent record. When it came out, I was working as a courier in Toronto. While I was driving around, I listened to this great university radio station all the time. We sent copies out to them and, as I was driving around one day, this DJ, who was my favourite, he said, 'I got this record today, and I gotta tell you, folks – if you only have money for one record this year, buy this one.' And he put our record on. That was how it started to happen for us. It was an amazing experience that repeated itself on bigger and bigger levels. That was the beauty of it, it just grew. These little wildfires would take off.

Pete Timmins: Graham Henderson saw a show we played and he called us up at the Crawford house where we were all living, and said, "I don't usually do this but I saw you play. I'm a lawyer, I'd like to work with you." And he started shopping the tape around the labels for us.

Peter Moore: We sent *Whites Off Earth Now!!* to *Spin* magazine when we released it. *Spin* was a brand-new magazine at that point and the record got reviewed really well. They were New York cool, so that counted for something. So, of course, we sent them *Trinity Session*, but we found out that the guy who'd written the first review was no longer there. That was terrible, because we'd lost our "in". We wanted to send him a record anyway as a thank-you, because we thought he'd be interested in it, but they wouldn't give us his address. So we had to send it via *Spin* and they passed it on. We had no idea he was now writing for the *New York Times*. So he got it, and suddenly I was getting calls from friends because it was album of the week in the *New York Times*. Holy fuck! All we had in New York at that time was some consignment sales at Bleecker Bob's, and that was it. But then it became album of the month. Then it was one of the best picks of the year. Then the *LA Times* are asking, "Who the fuck is this Cowboy Junkies?" They had no access to it, so they flew up to Toronto, brought a photographer and did a big interview thing to try and jump the *New York Times*. Chaos theory works.

New York Times: A special, quiet record.

Pete Timmins: A lot of people were interested at that point but they came with demands, like they wanted us to change the name of the band, so we didn't want to deal with those kind of labels. Some of them wanted all the focus to be on Margo, for Margo to shorten her skirt. There was a buzz about us, so the companies were interested because they thought they had to be; I don't think they really got it. Then we met Jim Powers, the A&R guy from BMG. He was an honest guy, which was pretty rare, because we met a lot of those guys, vice-presidents of labels, and mostly they seemed pretty slimy. But Jim was a straight guy, he didn't want us to change our sound, our name, he was happy to let us do what we wanted to do.

Jim Powers: It was my third week in the job at BMG as an A&R manager. When I joined, I was put in this windowless office with boxes and boxes of unsolicited cassettes, the ones with a covering letter saying, "Dear A&R person"! My instructions from my boss were to just take a couple of months, just get my bearings. They weren't expecting me to sign anything immediately, but to just start listening. So I was listening away and eventually I came to this "Dear Sir" letter from a guy called Graham Henderson, just a blind mailing from an attorney. It was a cassette of *The Trinity Session*, so I put it in the machine and, straight away, it was completely foreign to anything that had crossed my desk before. It was that whole era of SSL [Solid State Logic, studio equipment manufacturers], sixty-four-track recording, multilayered, the massive corporate sound, and here was this very sparse, very direct music that was just so beautiful that it gripped you right from the start. It was wholly different to anything else and I just kept coming back to it throughout the day, playing it two or three times.

And I found myself thinking, "Do I mention this to my boss or not?" It was so out there that I wasn't sure. It was the kind of thing where he'd be behind it completely or he'd sit there thinking, "Man, did I employ the wrong guy!" I was still finding my way through the nuances of the company, so I was a little nervous about it. But, at the end of the day, I took it in to [my boss Heinz], voiced my enthusiasm for it and he gave it a listen and said, "Well, go to Toronto and see them." So, with his full backing, for which I'm still grateful, I went up there and saw them playing at a small club – may have been Clinton's, but I'm not positive. It was a small place with a bar in the front as you went in and then a corner in the back where bands would play. I'm not even sure they were on a riser! No lighting, nothing, I think Margo was turned away from the front of the stage for about eighty per cent of the show, just quietly singing, and it just gave you a feeling like you were peering in on these moments in a very private world. It was fantastic, very unusual – the presence and intensity of what they were doing was rich and powerful, extremely compelling.

You have to ask yourself a couple of questions as an A&R person when you look at a band. "Am I really taken with this music to the point where I'm going to go to the wall for it?" And then, since I'm getting paid to find music that other people will enjoy, the second question is, "Will anybody possibly feel the same way I do?" I have to answer yes to both of those to be able to move forward with something. I was pretty smitten with *The Trinity Session*, but being pretty green in the job, still learning the tastes of the people who hired me, you get caught between wanting to follow your gut and not making some horrible mistake when you've just got your gig! So there were a lot of ramifications that I briefly considered, but, as I played it for people, straight down the line everybody was as taken by it as I was. You become more emboldened by that and you take it forward.

New York Times: The hippest band in the world.

Peter Moore: Jim Powers took it to Bob Buziak, the President of RCA, saying there was a buzz for them coming out of left field, and it all came together from there, they signed for BMG, the parent company, and the events meshed.

Lou Reed: The best and most authentic version [of 'Sweet Jane'] that I've ever heard.

Peter Moore: That was exactly the moment that Lou Reed became the coolest thing again with the *New York* album. *Trinity* is that kind of record: it has a world of its own, a weird kind of destiny. It felt that way even at the time. There was something special about it that I hadn't felt from other things. But what it would lead to, who knew?

CHAPTER 8

Travelled hard before

Once the deal was signed, the album was released and the hype was exploding, some things would never be the same again for Cowboy Junkies, because – like it or not – they were momentarily in the mainstream, just about the most unnatural place for them to be. Once you're there, things can't ever be the same again. We're not in Kansas any more …

Two quotes from the almanac of Canadian rock, *Have Not Been the Same*, neatly show how the perception of you changes, whether you've done anything to deserve it or not. First off: "This is one of the weirdest bands I've ever heard on easy-listening radio. How do you go from one of the wackiest bands in the underground to sliding right into the mainstream?"

So far, so good. But then: "Because the Cowboy Junkies morphed into a fairly conventional pop band, it's easy to forget how out of step and adventurous their first two albums sounded."

Doesn't sound quite so encouraging, as well as being inaccurate. When did Cowboy Junkies "morph" into the conventional? Sure, for a few moments the hills were alive with the sound of mandolins and pedal steels, but that was more a case of the mainstream coming to Mohammed. The Junkies' canon has rarely done more than scratch the surface of the mainstream in the intervening years, because the mainstream swiftly moved back to where it's comfortable, rather than worry itself sick in the midst of a music that dared to ask questions, to admit that life wasn't all cherries. But mud sticks, and once the *Trinity* hoopla died away, they'd never really have that indie chic again, because too many people only look at the surface rather than listen to the substance.

Yes, they were marketed intelligently, shrewdly. Yes, the timing was right for their music and BMG exploited that little window of opportunity. No, if they hadn't signed a deal with a major, most of us would probably never have heard of them. These things are pretty much givens in the Junkies' story. But not one of them goes anywhere near the core of that story. Success, sales, longevity – they have all come from one central place. The music. The music that hit a nerve with so many people back then … and still does now.

When they made *The Trinity Session*, there were no grandiose philosophical ideas behind it. No sense that they were making a record that would hit the mainstream like a bolt of lighting, instigating some Damascene conversion among the unbelievers. But it was a record out of time, out of step, as Jim Powers points out. "It was just so different, it ran counter to everything that was going on in popular music at the time and that was one of the things that was so exciting about it. It took us away from that overproduced sound and it truly heralded the way for grunge music that took hold just after that. It just seemed to be coming from such a pure place: the sparseness, the importance of the room ambience, the church, the space around the vocals."

In an era where technology was moving so quickly, when it was seeping into the making of music so fast that the machines had taken over from people struggling to come to terms with just what it was that studio trickery was doing to their songs, *The Trinity Session* allowed music fans to stop the treadmill, as one of its creators, Jaro Czerwinec, explains. "That music slowed people up; that was what they needed. Time to stop and think and be. The combination of sounds was the thing; that's what makes people remember. Where else do you ever hear pedal steel and accordion? Then throw in Alan's bass. When we did that record, the basslines were so slow, but he had the bass really cranked, so there was another feature – it was right out there. There are so many songs out there that they have to be special to stay with you, to be memorable. Orchestration always seems the important thing to me. That mix of harp, mandolin, pedal steel, accordion, guitar, violin, that's very organic, it's portable, it goes way back. When the mood hit them, they would play. I remember growing up, if my parents were playing cards with their pals, if they put the radio on and a hit came over, they'd be up to dance. It wasn't compartmentalized. If it moves you, you did it. *Trinity Session* took you back to that time."

It was a record of time, of moments, that ushered in something a little different. Or, perhaps, reintroduced the music industry to something we'd lost, as John Timmins underlines. "*Trinity Session* was fortunate in that it came at a time when music was so produced, so awful, so goddamned grotesque that something honest like that record was needed. The Junkies were the band doing that just at the moment that the window was open for a fleeting second. I don't think there was any way to anticipate what would happen as a result of it. I don't think we thought in those terms anyway; my mind wasn't even in that realm of possibilities. I think I was just immersed in the music, so the biggest thing for me was, were we making good music? And we did, I was excited by it, I thought it was exceptionally good. Whether anyone would ever buy it, I didn't know, and I don't think I cared that much, either. Although, I remember I wore a funny little medallion with my daughter's baby picture in it. I knew that if I did that she'd probably get her picture on the album jacket – so, to do that, I must have thought this record could go somewhere!"

The Trinity Session wasn't released on RCA until 15 November 1988, the record finding its insidious way into people's hearts and collections throughout the following year as music did begin to go through something of a sea change. For the first, probably the only time, the Junkies were riding a musical wave as musicians began to rise in Luddite ranks against the studio machinery that had enslaved them. Well, maybe in the movie. In the real world, it was just the cycle moving inexorably on, and Cowboy Junkies' section of the wheel was briefly on top. *The Trinity Session*, now with 'Blue Moon Revisited (Song for Elvis)' and 'Working on a Building' added to the running order after being omitted from the indie Latent release, was at the forefront of a more organic, earthy, human sound that had begun to grip again after years of force-fed polish. Hard on the heels of that record's success, MTV began their "Unplugged" series in November 1989, while a raft of lo-fi bands and, ultimately, grunge acts, would start to crawl to prominence, drawing on a similar aesthetic and attitude, albeit making a different kind of sound.

And it was a different kind of sound, because Cowboy Junkies made a very singular kind of music, as Luka Bloom points out. "*The Trinity Session* marked them out as being something musically very different, a band that had country elements but wasn't a country band, that had a rock'n'roll feel but clearly weren't a rock'n'roll band. They were a completely unique entity right from the start. That gave them a unity of purpose allied to their patience, that calm approach to the music world. I don't know enough about Canada to make a real judgement, but I wonder if that's a national characteristic as well as a family trait."

That music did slow you up, but it also allowed you to absorb an emotion, a lyric. There aren't too many rock songs that wouldn't be improved by being played at half-speed. Good ones, anyway. 'Help!' is one of my favourite Beatles songs, but only if I imagine Lennon playing it on an acoustic in his living room, half asleep, at half-speed. Then it goes from pop song to spiritual.

"Songs do take on a whole new perspective," agrees Mike. "The lyrics become more important because the words are so much clearer. You lose the energy of the rock'n'roll thing, which is the point of a lot of it, but sometimes you don't need that frenetic element – you want the message and the feeling behind it, too."

It was a rare record that enjoyed both commercial success and emotional resonance at the end of the 1980s, but *The Trinity Session* did. Two testimonies to its impact and its legacy come from within and without the camp. Long-term fan Bob Helm, later to have the moniker "Cookie Bob" bestowed upon him by the band, and now well beyond the 200-show mark, traces his fascination with the Junkies back to *The Trinity Session*. "That was a huge album in my personal life. It meant a lot to me for a lot of reasons and I played it pretty incessantly. That was a time that was the lowest in my life; a lot of things went wrong at once for me and I would come home from work and just play it all evening, nine times maybe, one after the other, before I went to bed. That went on for a month, maybe, and it really helped – it was a healing thing."

Peter Moore remembers that he was on the receiving end of plenty of thank-yous for his part in a record that genuinely did change people's lives. "The coolest reaction was we used to get lots of letters from people in LA, trying to get off cocaine, thanking us for *The Trinity Session*! This was the late 1980s, early 1990s, so coke was now an evil drug. They were realizing that if they needed to sell their house to pay for it, they might just have a problem! Things like, 'I've been doing coke really heavy for four or five years and, if it hadn't been for that record, I couldn't have got off it.' Those recordings obviously gave people a way to escape their trauma, to go inside it for forty-five minutes, go somewhere else. That's a pretty big thing to have been a part of. To me, the fact that that music helped says a lot. Those are my favourite letters, because they were written by people who wouldn't normally do that. That's very satisfying."

The music that brought others such serenity took Cowboy Junkies into the storm. As Alan recalls, it was all the odder, given that the recordings they made in that little church were already a year or more old before the world suddenly started pounding at their door: "We recorded it and we just carried on doing our thing for about a year after that. We carried on like we had before, there wasn't any sudden change. Then RCA put it out, and there was. The hype hit pretty fast; it was amazing. Within a couple of months, we were in *Rolling Stone*, the *New York Times*."

And Margo was winning her own little corner of weird world on top of all that, doing Gap ad shoots, and pitching up in the pages of *Esquire*'s "Women We Love to Love" in August 1989. According to that magazine, "If Marlene Dietrich wore blue jeans, this is how she'd sound." Which was odd, since we already knew what Marlene Dietrich sounded like – nothing like Margo. Blue jeans must do odd things to the voice. Stories like that can also do strange things to the mind. How did Margo survive that insanity?

"I was in *People* magazine. Gap ads. The '50 Most Beautiful People in the World' – I liked that one the best! It suddenly struck me how big this thing had got when I was on the stage ready to do *Saturday Night Live*. You think of all the people that had done the show and suddenly we're there! Even though we did all that, the record didn't really sell any more. Even that stuff, OK, it was pretty wild, but it was always outside of music, so in a way it was nothing to do with the Junkies. You just laugh at that. And, as time went on, that went away and the audience stripped back to the people who really got something from listening to us. If I were to choose, I'd rather have what we've had than being a huge pop act for five minutes. But it gave us longevity. It gave us a chance to build a crowd.

"We had a taste of being big, we could see how easily it happens, how easily it goes crazy. We had 'Misguided Angel' pulled from a radio station in British Columbia because it supposedly had satanic references! How are you supposed to take that seriously? When all the craziness was happening, we had each other. We were a band and nobody was going to break that. That was our first priority. Us. They did try to get us to change this or that, which may have sold more records, but we'd have been gone by now if we'd done that. We wouldn't have been able to deal with it. So we refused. But, at the same time, that period gave us a lot of confidence, in the listening public especially. There were people out there who recognized what we did once we put it in front of them, getting from it all the things we got. They obviously understood our music. That lets you think about carrying things forward."

"It was a weird time but we were very insulated too," continues Mike. "We were always touring for two or three years after *Trinity Session* took off. We stopped to do *Caution Horses*, but that was it. It wasn't until we finished touring that record that we really stopped and took stock. We were constantly moving and, on the road, you're in this little bubble, your world. OK, the crowds were getting bigger, more people showed up backstage, a lot of people we didn't know hung around. There was that side to it which we didn't like much, the hangers-on, but it didn't really mean much then. Looking back, I'm more amazed now than I was then. We knew we'd make another record after *Trinity* whether we got picked up or not. We wanted to continue to do our thing, so I guess that big success wasn't our dream. We weren't fulfilling a fantasy, it was just the way it was. I look at all the clippings and I can't believe we did so much press – there are folders of it from all over the world! And now I know more about the industry and how hard it is to get that coverage, it freaks me out. But, at the time, it was just, whatever, next show, next interview."

Jeff Bird's presence as the storm broke around them was hugely beneficial, and has continued to be so. Once *The Trinity Session* started to gain attention, a new Cowboy Junkies went out on the road, a much bigger unit than the core four. Suddenly they were out of bars, and into theatres and auditoriums, playing to audiences who'd come to stare through the goldfish bowl specifically at them. That's a big change – musically, too. Mike, Pete, Alan and Margo knew each other inside out, knew their musical and personal moods, knew how to make it work. Then you bring in a new bunch of players, orchestrations, and an audience full of expectation. Jeff was the perfect teacher, not only offering suggestions as Mike pieced the arrangements together, pulling out yet another instrument to make yet another sound, but giving them plenty of lessons on how to live life on the road – by pretty much floating eighteen inches above the surface of it all.

But even Jeff was taken aback by the speed with which Cowboy Junkies hit the national and international stage, and was well aware of the potential consequences, especially for Margo. "It was a rollercoaster ride after *Trinity Session* started to break. We made a little record in a church, in a day, and then suddenly we're on *Saturday Night Live*! It was quite a trip, but everyone took it in their stride. Poor Margo took the brunt of it, of course – she had this huge thing dumped on her. From hardly being onstage at all, now she was an international sex symbol. Good luck! Hope it all works out for you!

"It goes back to that strength of family; it comes from their parents. You can see them in all the siblings. Mike is very much like his father, Margo is very like her mother – there's the family right there, and on the road you can see it in action. Pete is more like his mother, too; John's probably somewhere between the two. I think if your parents have had their own business, it seems to make a big difference in how you go through the world. If your father worked in a factory, that's how you go through life: you find a job working for somebody else. But if your parents were entrepreneurs or independent businesspeople, that becomes your point of reference; you go out and do what you want."

The nature of these people was also significant, because they weren't the kind of folks who were going to be seduced by the rock'n'roll trappings, as Margo illustrates. "We were in Europe for *The Trinity Session* tour and we got a tour bus, but there were eleven of us on there and only four bunks. So the crew got the bunks and we didn't. We thought they should have them, because it was the first time we ever had a crew. We didn't know! So the boys lay down in the aisle and I had one of the seats at the front and ended up climbing over them to get to the bathroom in the night. But it seemed pretty natural – we'd only ever had a van before that!"

As that tour rumbled on, the Junkies were lumped in with another "movement" of the time, New Country, which was making waves in the UK in particular. Mike concedes, "That was useful, because at least it brought some attention our way. A lot of people had had their first records out at that point – the first Lyle Lovett record we were very aware of; we listened to the first Steve Earle record in the van all the time. Nanci Griffith was important, too. But we never really got mentioned in that context in the US or Canada – it was more a UK and European thing. We connected with them personally, they understood what we were doing, even though it was coming from different influences, growing up in Montreal instead of Texas or Tennessee. We don't have that roots element to us; it's more urban via the UK and New York. But we had a real Texas connection with Townes Van Zandt, Lyle, Jimmie Dale Gilmore, Nanci Griffith, Steve Earle. It was an interesting mix of people.

"Even then, we weren't in the middle of it. We've always been on the outside of scenes for some reason; we were never able to ride that New Country wave in North America. Which is good in a lot of ways, because it gives you freedom to do other things and you don't end up getting swept away with it when the media moves on to something else, but it has its down side, too. The whole *No Depression* thing, that magazine really paid us no attention for years. I don't care if you don't like us or you don't think that what we do is valid, but you've got to at least acknowledge that we were doing this music a long time ago! They see Uncle Tupelo as the start, but we had two records out before then, so it's kinda strange. We never seem to get picked up in these movements, but I think we're like that personality-wise too: we stick to ourselves, we live in Toronto not New York or Los Angeles or London, we don't go to parties. Being outside of that is one of the reasons for our longevity. We've sold a decent amount of records, done a lot of press, but people still feel we're their special thing, and that's important. They discovered us, a few friends know about us, they can introduce people to our sound and that keeps it tight-knit."

One of the possible disadvantages of that is that a lot of people see them solely as "the band that made *Trinity Session*", simply because they haven't kept up to speed with the releases since. There's a little irritation in Pete's view of the way the legend of that record has been retold down the ages. "The fact that *Trinity Session* sold well meant that we knew we could have a career from this for a period of time. If it hadn't been picked up and we'd sold 6,000 copies, who knows what we would have done then. But it wasn't *Trinity Session* alone that did that. We'd been touring constantly in the States and we'd built our audience that way. There was a market already out there waiting for a new album.

We'd done a lot of groundwork. Then the album came out; those people bought it. It did well off the bat and then we got the reviews and it snowballed. And it has helped all the way through, because it's become the marker. If people mention Cowboy Junkies to anyone, they'll say, 'Oh yeah – they did *The Trinity Session*.'"

Jeff Bird understands the band's slightly ambivalent attitude to that record. "I think that *Trinity Session* was certainly a magical record, and we felt it as we were making it. Some band called me from Toronto, they sent me a tape that sounded pretty darned rough except for Margo. When I heard it, I thought, 'Yikes, no!' But then you hear that voice and it was obvious there was something going on there and I wanted to be involved in that. We didn't think it would mean anything to anybody else, maybe, but we knew it was special. The fact that it sold a lot of copies was something we never expected. Then later, people's concentration on it did irritate them – more so in the past because they've gone beyond that now. I think you just have to accept that it was a defining record and be proud of it."

Mike agrees that *The Trinity Session* is something which comes up for reassessment every now and again. "I can't ever see that record as a millstone around our neck because we recognize that we wouldn't be here thirty years later – not on this level – without that one. It elevated us to a point, put the spotlight on us, and that's hard to get. We decided we wanted to build on that by making the music we wanted to make, because that's what *Trinity Session* was when we went in the church – the record we wanted to make. There were opportunities to do different marketing things, to use different producers, but we made a conscious decision to go down our road. It was a fantastic experience to go through, but, to us, it's one record in a collection. But then we recognize that for a lot of people it became something else, and that's very special, too. It gets a little tiring when people don't see beyond it. They say that it's a great record and relate everything back to it. When all they can say is, 'This new record isn't as good as *Trinity Session*.' Well, on what level isn't it as good? Tell me why! But that's music critics. Nothing to do with the music!"

And then there's Jaro's take: "The record didn't make me famous, thank God! You think I want bodyguards? Nobody really knows me and nobody needs to. I can go to the supermarket without being bothered. All I know is I was tired as hell, I went to church, got through the songs

I had to get through, I loved the music, I got paid and I went back to Sudbury. Then things started to happen. But, at the time, all I know is that from my perspective I was just recording three songs. That's part of the personal glorification machine that creates money and keeps the music business going. Thank God it happened, or I'd still be dreaming of it. But it happened and it changed everything. For everyone. When we heard it back the first time, it felt like we'd got something really good, and then we went out to a restaurant to get to know the people I'd been playing with. It was a long time coming, but when it came, the success was nearly overnight."

FEAR AND LOATHING IN THE JUNKYARD

There was a time, albeit a very brief time and a very long while ago, when the music video was seen as a promising new art form, a visual form of expression that could complement, even enhance, its musical cousin. The idea didn't last, for all the usual reasons. The companies and the corporations got hold of it, turned the big bucks on the big artists and made music commercials that sat in just fine alongside the altogether more important slots selling Coca-Cola, American Express and Nissan.

For Cowboy Junkies, the demise of the video as anything anyone could ever take seriously might have been a blessing, for videos were never destined to be their thing. On video, if you can fake sincerity, you've got it made. But what if you're the real deal working in a phony medium? The strength of this band lies in its ability to communicate directly, on record or onstage, by simply being themselves. Emoting to tape, lip-syncing to playback, playing a part in some director's vision of a song they've maybe listened to twice, is not going to give you an accurate reflection of who Cowboy Junkies are. And if you can't see and hear who they are, you really are missing the point. Even the videos that almost worked, notably the monochromatic 'Blue Moon Revisited', fell that bit short. It was just the band playing the song, but seen through somebody else's eyes, cutting at the wrong moment to the wrong shot. MTV killed the video stars and replaced them with the Real World.

As far as Pete's concerned, the death of video couldn't come soon enough. "I hate videos, but we had to do it to appease the record company. Subjecting you to somebody else's visual idea is horrible. There's never any kind of warmth to them. What we do is about making a connection with the audience, and you can't do that in a three-minute clip sandwiched between a Mariah Carey video and a Michael Jackson video. But the masses want to be stimulated by flashing lights and changing faces and morphing horses, so what can you do? Now it's the other way round. MTV screen all these reality shows instead of music. They'll play hip-hop videos, but if you want them to show anything else it has to be a hit. But, seeing as the video is your advert, how do you get a hit if they don't show your advert?"

Ironically, one of the strengths of a lot of Junkies music is its cinematic nature, both in terms of narrative and musical sweep. In the hands of Wim Wenders, perhaps, some of the material might have translated into some fascinating work. On the other hand, it's not hard to conjure up visions of some ham-fisted, ex-advertising hack cobbling together a storyboard that tries to move, literal line by literal line, through a song. Can you imagine what they'd have done with 'Townes' Blues'? Alan at a crap table, blowing theatrically on the dice. Mike the croupier, green visor over his eyes, raking in the money; Jeff playing a widow woman's washboard in the background as Margo drapes herself over a cackling millionaire, rolling diamond-spotted dice, played – naturally – by Pete. It's the great lost Junkies film …

Inevitably, making videos was rarely fun for the band, as Margo explains. "Videos are fine if you're selling something other than music. If you're a sexy pop star and you want to show off your pierced belly button, that's great. If what you do onstage is choreographed and you want to show off your dance moves, that's fine; that appeals to a certain crowd and I'm happy for them. But I don't think the world is ready to see Pete dance!

"To us, they were always just another chore, one of those little compromises that we had to make because it's a part of the business, like photo shoots or going on some stupid TV show. But, even when we were making videos, we still wanted to do it on our terms. When this is all over, I want to be able to look back and say that I never did anything I didn't really want to do. I was never embarrassed by myself. So, when we did videos, I used to say, 'Fine, I'll be in the video. But I'm not kissing anybody, I'm not wearing a weird outfit, I'm not going to dance around. I'll do the video, but I'm going to be me.' But the wardrobe people would always turn up and have these weird clothes. 'Did you not hear me? I'm not dressing up. Sorry, it's another long skirt. That's what I wear.' You should see some of this stuff, it's unbelievable. 'At what point did you think I lost my brain?' The boys would laugh their heads off, and it wouldn't happen."

One promo that didn't happen certainly would have been worth watching, as Alan remembers. "Making videos is pretty annoying, and it's a total scam on the part of everybody involved – the label, the TV companies, producers. The band ended up paying for all that free programming that everybody else made money from. The label would say they needed it as a marketing tool and then make you pay for half of it, which really sucks. We were never into being in videos anyway, so we were always looking for something different to do. Then we gave up after a while. It got to the point where we would just show up at video shoots having no idea what was going on. The director would have sent a treatment to Mike, but I didn't even care enough to ask him what it was. Just show up. Shoot it, go home. Because we reached the point where they never got shown anyway, outside of Canada – not even that much there – so they were just useless.

"There was one idea that might have turned out pretty interesting. Hunter S. Thompson had written a book called *Songs of the Doomed*, and in the first few pages he mentions sitting around and listening to something off *The Caution Horses*, then he mentions the band later on in there, too. He's always been one of our favourite wackos, so we decided to call him up and see if we could maybe work on something together. It took a while to get him on the phone, because he'd wake up at midnight, stay up all night, drinking and watching sports, then sleep through the day. But we ended up having a bunch of weird phone conversations with him.

"His idea was we'd go to his ranch out in Colorado, get a camera crew, no script and 'just go crazy, man!' That didn't really fit what we had in mind; we wanted a little more structure than that. Going crazy isn't what we do. But he wasn't into that, at all. He didn't want to write anything, he just wanted this wacked-out thing. Eventually he got really pissed off for some reason. He sent us a fax, saying, 'If you guys show up here, you're going home in body bags!' What did we do to piss him off that much?"

CHAPTER 9

When in doubt, don't

If, straight out of left field, you've released the surprise hit album of the year, there's only one thing to do next. Tour, tour and tour some more. And, while you're on the road, don't ever lose sight of the fact that the company is getting pretty hungry for that follow-up album. You wouldn't want to let down that new audience, would you? Not that the company doesn't think you're in it for the long haul. But let's just cover all the bases, shall we?

There were plenty of positives that came out of the success of *The Trinity Session*. Better pay and a little security were the obvious material gains, but maybe the most important advance came on the concert circuit. Suddenly, the venues were, for the most part, bigger and better appointed, and in towns, countries even, where the Junkies might otherwise never have set foot. And, rather than playing for a casual audience who just happened to have showed up in this town, that bar, this night, they were playing for Junkies junkies, their own audience. Weren't they?

Pete remembers things a little differently: "The buzz around *Trinity* just blew up the balloon. People come to see you because of that and then the balloon shrinks back to the people who really get it. We knew that would happen. That's fine because that part of the audience only came to sit in the back and talk. You don't want them there anyway and you're glad they're gone." In spite of that, Alan recognizes the value of that early excitement, adding, "It was good it happened early on, because it built the audience, it made people aware of us. A lot of people just came to see if they dug it or not and plenty stayed and have continued to stay. It was good to have that bubble at the beginning just to attract the real music lovers."

Would another couple of years tooling around the bar circuit on the back of *The Trinity Session* have been so appealing, having already done it after *Whites Off Earth Now!!*? The dedication and determination of the band was not in doubt, but there comes a time when repeating yourself is tiresome. Maybe there'd have been another record to follow, but without the success of *The Trinity Session* it's doubtful if Cowboy Junkies could have endured as a full-time operation. Maybe they'd still be a loose band, getting together even now to play in and around Toronto, but had they not grabbed their moment in 1988 it would surely have gone forever. Let's face it, music of integrity, intelligence and nuance hasn't been a conspicuous mainstream force in decades since then, has it?

With Mike and Alan at the helm, there was never much chance of them missing their moment. Students of the music business as much as music itself, they understood that, when you're hot, you're hot and you better make the most of it, because a band's moment is brief – fifteen minutes of fame is probably stretching it. Finally, after Hunger Project and Germinal, after touring a disinterested United States in a tiny van, without work permits and often without gigs, the world was listening. And, when it does start to listen, you can't afford to let it touch that dial because, if it does, someone else will steal your moment.

There weren't many bands with noses closer to the grindstone than Cowboy Junkies, but this was no longer the four-piece that early converts had grown used to. *The Trinity Session* was a different record to *Whites Off Earth Now!!* and, though it could be recreated by the four of them, with more money available, it made more sense to take the recording band on the road, at least in part. John Timmins did not run off to rejoin the circus, but Jaro Czerwinec, Kim Deschamps and Jeff Bird became part of the touring ensemble, Bird handling all the harmonica parts, including Steve Shearer's. It was a seismic shift and one that required careful handling. Bringing in a few players for a recording session was one thing, but introducing three idiosyncratic individuals into a touring unit was something else. Cowboy Junkies had been a very self-contained operation up to that point, so to have all these interlopers in there was a learning process all of its own.

The aesthetic was still minimalist, something they had to wrestle with, as Mike remembers. "The running joke on the tour was, 'Who stood around most each night?' We had a lot of players onstage, but we wanted to keep that less is more feel. The slogan was, 'When in doubt, don't'." That was a touchstone for the band, but it didn't always sit so well with Kim Deschamps, who later spoke of touring with the Junkies in pretty disparaging terms in *Have Not Been the Same*, saying, "It was an interesting ride, but none of us around our house really got it. It was very bizarre. I would be apologising for my gig. I'd be out there playing to people all over the world, with people like Bruce Springsteen in the audience, and I was meeting childhood heroes of mine like Bonnie Raitt. In a way I was a little embarrassed by it. There I was playing my butt off every night, trying to put a little excitement into this show that was, by definition, not very exciting."

Perhaps Deschamps' relationship with Cowboy Junkies was always destined to be a brief (if valuable) one. For a band whose trademark is restraint, subtlety and a refusal to puncture perfectly good silence with a superfluous sound, a more traditional musician whose raison d'être was to go out and play, to be onstage and perform, was always going to be out of step. Mike reflects that "Kim was never really satisfied with being in the band. He's a very good steel player, but things didn't work out between us, as people as much as musically."

Jeff and Jaro seemed to fit in with the ensemble much more comfortably, Jaro having his own special form of relaxation to get him through the long days on the road. "When we play, Al stands behind me onstage. We're often on those wooden stages, I have a wooden chair. That bass sound just goes right through the floor, through the chair and through me, so when I'm playing, I'm having a jolly good old time. Thanks, Al, for the therapeutic sound massage!"

Life wasn't always so therapeutic, not least because – even that early on – it raised plenty of questions about record companies and the industry in general, the industry in whose hands their music rested. It was quickly apparent that, a few smart individuals like Jim Powers apart, it was a business that was blundering about in the dark. "I guess *Trinity Session* was the first record of an odd nature that had sold decent numbers on a major label in a long time," says Mike. "The labels had nothing to do with it, it wasn't corporate, but music fans found it, and it had its own momentum. I guess that said that people wanted something different. Then grunge happened and the record companies had no clue what to do with that, either. I guess it signifies that record labels don't know anything!"

With one of the underground hits of the decade happening in front of them, what the company did know was that, from out of nowhere, they suddenly had a saleable commodity on their hands. But, while bean counters all over BMG might have been salivating over a multi-million-selling follow-up, Jim Powers had other concerns. "I was really excited to be working on the follow-up record right from the start of the process this time, but we all had questions, including the band, I think, of where do you go after such an unorthodox record has had such incredible success? What facet of the band will they choose to reveal and move with?"

For Cowboy Junkies, it should have been a very different kind of project, knowing that the eyes of the world were upon them, knowing they had fans, a label, critics to satisfy – all brand-new concerns. Yet none of these considerations seemed hugely significant. It was still a bunch of music fans waiting for the point at which they had enough material to make another forty-five-minute statement about who and where they were at that point in time. The difference would come, not because of the success, but because they were no longer that self-contained little four-piece, as Jaro points out.

"When we toured, there were songs that were basically the same every night because of their structure and there were others with the freedom to do pretty much what you liked, and that was very powerful. It was open, it'd start on a solo and then we'd go somewhere with a mad rush, and finally the mind gets blown and you hear things you've never heard before. I love doing tapestry work with sound when you plug into someone's energy and go with it. The audience can see when it's happening through a person.

"I used to wonder how bands could play the same song over and again, but now I could play 'Misguided Angel' forever, because it's not the same song, not energetically. Every night it moves. Jeff, Kim and myself had a special chemistry. We were a little older, our personalities suited each other, and that came out. We'd been around musically, and things just took off that were so incredible that you didn't know what you were listening to, bending all the rules. That fed into the new songs, too."

New songs were emerging all the time, some of them covers, most of them originals. The reviews and fan response to *The Trinity Session* confirmed that their own material could stand shoulder to shoulder with the Great American Songbook and not suffer in comparison, giving Mike the freedom and the confidence to write further, with the added luxury of a full band on tap to work on orchestrations and arrangements. That offered new possibilities for the songs he was sketching out. Again, he and the Junkies were not precious about the material, but were open to others taking lead roles, with Jeff Bird in particular playing a major part on a lot of the songs that eventually made up their third record. For Mike, sharing the spotlight is no big deal: "Jeff has become one of the signature sounds of the band, for sure. That comes from our love of music. We like hearing other people play. It brings a lot of ideas to us. I bore myself if I play too much, especially by the end of a tour. I want to hear somebody else. The more people playing, the better it is, because you get more ideas, more inspiration. That's what playing live is about. Who cares who's making the sound, as long as it's good? In the studio it's the same, too. Some records concentrate on just the four of us, then there's times when we want to open it up to see what other people have to say musically. It makes it more interesting.

"By the time we came to record again, we'd been touring with Jeff, Kim and Jaro for a year or so, the band was really cool, there were interesting arrangements, it was very orchestral the way those three had their parts worked out, but would still improvise too, really beautiful. I'd written songs as we toured and we'd introduce them into the repertoire and the band would develop their parts around it. We wanted to develop that orchestration for that record, that sense of intertwining, interplay."

Having a seven-piece band – soon to be eight with the addition of a percussionist – certainly did open things up, but paradoxically, that familiarity, the greater intricacy and intimacy between the instruments and the players, meant that it was harder to capture the new songs than it had been in the Church of the Holy Trinity when a group of people who barely knew one another came together to play a handful of tunes. Then, there were no preconceptions. This time, there were ideas by the score. Time, on the other hand, was a rather more scarce commodity.

At a time when you have gig offers coming out of your ears, press calls to field, TV shows to do all over the globe, the fact that you've made a habit of making a record pretty much in real time might be considered an advantage. And, initially at least, Cowboy Junkies planned to continue working in a similar vein, according to Mike: "The live band sounded good, we were very tight, so it made sense to us to record again in a live situation. We spoke to Peter Moore about it and we decided to use the Calrec again. Initially, we wanted to do it like *Trinity Session* but make recordings in a number of different spaces rather than having just the one. We thought that, wherever we found somewhere cool, we would record, and that would give a mix of environments, so that there wasn't necessarily one room sound, like on the two previous records. We'd play in different places and then choose which version was best. It also meant we didn't have to come off the road for a period of time. When we got a few days free and came through Toronto, we could just set up and record."

A tiny, sweaty garage and a spacious, cool church were very idiosyncratic environments, acting as extra players on those first two records, the church especially so. Trying to get away from that, the band set up in a room at Cherry Beach studio, but it was a disaster. "Never record when your singer has a head cold" is a sound maxim, but one that they chose to ignore. Briefly. After a few hours, losses were cut and everyone went home for some much-needed rest, recognizing that simply recording on a day off after a month on a bus or a day in a plane wasn't quite as easy at they thought. As a consequence, the second attempt at recording was much more structured, Peter Moore being set the task of finding a setting for three days of recording in April 1989.

The building that Moore found was the Sharon Temple, in the town of Sharon, just north of Toronto. Maybe there was some conceptual continuity in going from church to temple, or maybe Moore was simply captivated by an architecturally stunning building. Three wooden box structures on top of one another, something like a pyramid or the domes of a cathedral, it had some of the attributes of the church in the high roof and the sense of space – though this was space to the nth degree, covering some 2,500 square feet. The Temple had been built by the Children of Peace in the late 1820s, the three structures representing what they saw as the three pillars of society – peace, equality and social justice. Historically, the Temple had housed

Canada's first shelter for the homeless and, though the former Quakers that founded it had no musical tradition, they formed the first civilian band in the country and built Ontario's first organ. A propitious site for making music, then?

For the first two days it seemed not, according to Mike: "We had a very weird experience, almost the exact opposite of *Trinity*. First two days, the strangest vibes were happening between us all. We weren't mad at each other, but it was such a strange building. Weird things had happened there, this guy who broke away from the Quakers started his own little religious cult up there. It was a strange atmosphere." Pete reckons the problem was less something in the air, more something in themselves, much as it had been at Cherry Beach: "We sort of just blew it off at Sharon. We were really busy touring, doing press and promo things, it didn't stop. Maybe we needed to stop and really take time to record, instead of just fitting three days in the middle of everything else we were doing. We were pretty tired by then."

Things weren't helped by the fact that Peter Moore had never recorded there before, so the "futzing" that took a few hours in the church took days this time around. And the band demanded more than simply a good sound. They were looking for something a little more elusive, as David Houghton, recruited to play percussion, recalls. "I began playing that material the day I first met them at Sharon Temple, I had no rehearsal. The band had been playing the songs for some time, but they still seemed fresh. They were intent on recording them in just the right light, with just the right mood. In the end, it took quite some time for us to get to that point. I'd never recorded in that kind of situation before, but I assumed that was what the band did in search of 'the sound'. As it turned out, we never found it."

While Moore was getting his angles, his distances and his cables together, Houghton had the opportunity to get to know the new people he was working with a little better. "Jeff Bird and I had played together in a number of bands. Traditional folk, avant-jazz, ambient, we'd played pretty much every style, travelled all over North America, and had always enjoyed each other's company. After the recording of *Trinity Session*, Michael mentioned to Jeff that he was thinking of adding a percussionist to the band. Jeff suggested my name, Michael gave me a call and told me to show up at Sharon Temple. There were no rehearsals, no interviews, no auditions. I just showed up and we began recording 'Sharon'. I never asked Mike why he considered adding a percussionist, and he never mentioned it.

"I was immediately more comfortable than I typically would be sitting down with nine strangers. Michael, Margo, Alan, Peter, Jeff, Jaro, Kim, Peter Moore and his assistant were there. Margo and Mike rummaged through my boxes of percussion, and Margo fished out a triangle. She laughed – it reminded her of a music teacher they'd had in grade school. It was not the least bit apparent that they were feeling any pressure of recording a follow-up to *Trinity Session*. Over several days we spent together, they were generous, relaxed and patient."

Which can't have been easy, because for forty-eight hours nothing much was happening. And it was busy not happening in the cold, as Mike remembers: "Where it had been unseasonably hot when we did *Whites Off Earth Now!!*, this time it was unseasonably cold. It was April but it was freezing, really cold. It was a wood building, it's an historic monument, so we weren't allowed heaters there, but Peter Moore was so excited. He said the cold would make for great sound. That was fine, but we were too cold to play our instruments! You could see Margo's breath as she sang. We struggled, finding the sound was hard, we did a lot of work on placing the microphone and the band, the reverb was much bigger there than *Trinity*. It was a real struggle. We got to the third morning and had pretty much decided to write it off. But we had the use of the place, the equipment was set up anyway, so we said, 'Let's just play.' Which we did. And we got some amazing recordings out of it. Turned out to be a great bootleg!"

Those Sharon Temple sessions didn't see the light of day for many years, not until they became available as a download on the Junkies' website. Listening to different takes of very familiar material has become a more regular experience in recent years with the growth in remastered CDs with bonus tracks, in box sets or releases such as The Beatles' *Anthology* and Dylan's *Bootleg* series, giving us a look at just how songs evolved over a number of sessions. That trend has given cause to rethink the idea that any song is ever truly finished, as Peter Moore notes.

"Are there definitive versions? Most of the time you hear an alternate take, you know why it's the alternate. Some of the Miles Davis stuff that's out there now, you see why a particular take was picked, because it has a magic the other versions don't. If we'd recorded *The Trinity Session* the day before or the day after we did, it's a different record, because everyone is in a different mood, has a different attitude, so you never get something nailed down the same way twice. It's catching magic or creating an environment in which it can appear – like a seance! If the environment isn't there, the spirit won't come in – that sounds New Agey, hokey, but, call it whatever you want, there's a situation that helps create special atmospheres. On those early Junkies records, it's intrinsic to the set-up.

"And it's not the difference between working in a studio and making a live album, either. Because with *Whites!!*, with *Trinity* and with 'Sharon', though we were recording live, no overdubs, we were playing for ourselves, in the room, nobody beyond us responding to it. When guys are jamming, it naturally takes up this form of a circle, sitting round the kitchen table with a bottle of scotch. The round table lends itself to music. When you reorientate yourself for a stage and the audience is in front, you don't see each other so much, you see the people out there. Then it becomes performance, and that's something else. With them, it's a group personality, people in sync with one another. Which is why people love it. Intimacy. When you listen to them, it's like somebody sitting next to you and talking to you. That intimacy is very hard to find. You don't get too many records that are about atmospherics.

"You could see a record company wanting to do a whole Mariah Carey number on it, showing that voice off everywhere, but then it would have died a miserable death. That isn't Margo's personality, it wouldn't come across, and that's what is so special about those records. We weren't just recording songs, we were recording personality, and you don't get to do that very often. Or, if you do, too often you get to record many individual personalities, which becomes a problem because they're fighting, it becomes a cacophony, nobody is on the same page.

"I think that the circle is the key element in the one-mic recording, that's where the magic happens. Everybody has a visual of everybody else, there's so much cueing going on and everything is natural. So many times, I'm working with a band on pre-production, sitting around my table, working on a bridge or a chorus or whatever, couple of acoustics and a voice, and there's something happening and I always curse that I wasn't recording it! That moment of discovery, that magic, comes in because you're playing music, you're not projecting, musicians are playing totally for themselves and you have the back and forth of the energy – I think that's a crucial part of the puzzle. That does create the magic, some kind of focus is happening as they move in or out, I'm tweaking the sound, they're doing it, it's symbiotic and then, when it comes together, everything suddenly sounds amazing in the room. Even just not wearing headphones makes a difference – next time you make love, try wearing headphones. Even at your most intimate moment, you're pretty isolated!"

The circle – or, more accurately, a crescent – has been a Junkies motif onstage for some time, where all the players are turned inward to look at one another to some degree, while Margo, in the centre, goes out to negotiate the mood with the audience. Perhaps one of the biggest problems with recording at Sharon was that a circle was simply unworkable. Though Margo had sat on the fringe in the church, she was still very much in the midst of it. Because of the nature of the new material, as much as the environment, that wasn't going to happen this time. Having worked on so many of the new songs with the band on the road, they were much fuller in sound, in texture, in arrangement than the dozen songs of *The Trinity Session*. There, it was a slowly building band as the day went on – Jaro only played on three songs, for instance. This time, the bulk of the material featured the ensemble. Cowboy Junkies weren't exactly Megadeth, but they were a little louder than before.

"The music was lush, fuller," recalls Mike. "And Sharon Temple was acoustically more alive than the church, and harder to handle because of the size of it. With Margo sitting near the rest of us, the music tended to spill over into her mic and feed back, so that was a big problem that Peter had to solve. Eventually, we sent Margo to the opposite end of the building and we built a sound booth for her out of baffles and these smelly sound blankets. That was the 'witches hut'. Looking back, that was one of the biggest problems that we had, getting the vocals to sit properly. The room was pretty uncooperative."

For two days they laboured, trying to make sense of room, material and weather. And on the third day, there was sound …

In fact, recording *had* gone on during the first couple of days, but it wasn't until that third day when things really began to come together, when Moore found the sweet spot in the building, when Margo's vocal booth began to work, and when – having all but given up on the whole thing – the band were looser and began to nail the songs. Having done that, they all filed out of the Sharon Temple, thinking little more about the session than that at least they had some really good demos. It hadn't worked as an album, but no big deal. Then, a few days later, Peter Moore called Mike over to listen to what it was they'd recorded.

"Actually, it was kinda cool," recalls Mike. "There was an interesting vibe to it, so we decided we were done. We even presented it to the company, and the one thing they don't like is to be surprised. They didn't even know we'd been recording, so when we turned up and said, 'By the way, here's the new album', they were a little unsure."

Or, as Pete remembers it, "We handed over 'Sharon' and we made our A&R guy cry. But not in a good way!"

Had the Junkies released 'Sharon', those who loved *The Trinity Session* would have lapped it up again, because as it stands it's a fine record. For all its faults, there are some nice performances on there, some wonderful songs. But when you know *The Caution Horses*, the record it ultimately became, you can hear precisely why it was shelved. Longtime fan Jason Lent sums it up neatly: "For me, the impact of the Sharon sessions was not the songs they recorded there, but the lore of this rare bootleg and the need to hunt it down. I remember being fascinated with the whole story as a teenager. Once I found a copy of the record, it wasn't nearly as exciting."

Perhaps, on reflection, trying to chase the magic of *The Trinity Session* was always doomed to fail, for, as Mike concedes, "We were spoiled by *Trinity*. A lot of things all came together at one time on that record, and we probably didn't realize until later just how rare that was."

Where on the previous record everything seemed to fall naturally into place, 'Sharon' sounds more forced, less controlled. From the opening of 'Sun Comes Up, It's Tuesday Morning', the song seems to be running away from Margo, whose delivery is markedly different from the later version. Right away, the Junkies sound different, not so languid, rockier perhaps, a little less subtle than hitherto, more upfront. That's an impression confirmed quickly by 'Cause Cheap Is How I Feel', the echo at the start defining a cavernous musical space. Rather than sitting on a groove, the band is chasing it.

Getting away from the tempo and the stillness of *The Trinity Session* was a deliberate idea that they took into recording, as Alan explains. "Success buys you some freedom, but it also means the record company wants you to make the same album all over again. The A&R guys are under pressure too, to deliver the same sales again, so there's a lot more focus on it. Their job is not to take chances. But we didn't want to do 'Trinity Session 2'."

Yet, in trying to break away from that, 'Sharon' sounds as if they are less comfortable with some songs, trying to force them into a more upbeat setting. That's not true of all the material, for 'Powderfinger' and 'Thirty Summers' are much more in the style that would come through on *The Caution Horses*. Oddly, though, for the most part 'Sharon' sounds more like a halfway house between *The Caution Horses* and *Black Eyed Man*, even though it came first. It gives a strong sense that they're searching for another gear, a different tempo, one that they weren't ready for. On that score alone, just for the insight it gives into the way the band developed, 'Sharon' is a fascinating artefact that deserves its eventual wider release.

Initially, however, the band were pretty pleased with the results, perhaps because they were back on the road and the 'Sharon' versions were faithful to the live presentation, as Al admits: "We took the tapes with us on the bus and it sounded pretty cool. We thought we'd got it, we played it to Bob Buziak of RCA out at Peter Moore's place and told him, 'This is the record, Bob.' He didn't cry. He frowned a lot. I guess he was right, because the more we listened back to it, the more we realized it didn't have what we wanted."

The decision to shelve 'Sharon' came from the band, because, as Mike explains, "We wanted to feature the orchestration and interplay between the instruments. The more we played it back, the more we felt that the Sharon recordings didn't do that and we realized that we needed to have more control over the sound." Where *The Trinity Session* had been a record made up of songs performed by a band that had been put together for the occasion, 'Sharon' was a record made by a working band who had wormed their way inside some songs, the songs having mutated on the road and become more intricate as a result, as David Houghton notes. "The interplay between Jeff, Jaro and Kim was an astonishing thing to hear. Sometimes they would pass a musical motif between them. Sometimes they would play together, rising and descending in languid waves of sound. I was given a lot of latitude in how and what I chose to play, but I understood that their music was about subtlety and nuance." Because of those ever-changing dynamics, taming the material with a single-mic recording in a building that

120

didn't really fit the purpose was simply too much to ask. Some of the vulnerability, the colour, the character of the music was lost, though (again) if you'd never heard *The Caution Horses*, you probably wouldn't realize it.

As the band were starting to fret over whether the record caught the songs properly, Jim Powers had other concerns. "'Sharon' was pretty much in the same mould as *Trinity Session*, and I think it might have been unfairly judged had that come out, because the previous record was such a yardstick. To do anything like that again might have been looking for criticism. 'Sharon' was a good record, but it just didn't have that same kind of magic. To make a great record, it's about tapping into some truth in some way, capturing that. There were some wonderful parts to it, but had it come out, it could have been too easily dismissed as 'Son of Trinity Session'. The last thing that this band is is trendy and, to their credit, they realized the danger that they could have been seen as making a fetish of recording in unusual situations."

Eventually, the decision was made to bin 'Sharon', something they took in their stride according to Alan: "It was no big deal, because it hadn't cost anybody a lot of money to make. Peter Moore loved it, but we were listening for different things to him, just as we had with the previous records."

Of all the protagonists in the 'Sharon' recordings, it is Moore who still has some issues with shelving it, as he readily concedes. "I was really upset that didn't come out, because I thought it was a great record. Bob Buziak, the president of RCA, finally got behind it, they were ready to go, we had it mastered, and then Michael decided that he wanted to rerecord it. I thought it was a real pity that the single-mic recording wasn't going to be heard, but I could see Michael's point of view, too. It's his art, they're his songs, it's his thing, so they're his choices to make, his prerogative. And it wasn't a spur-of-the-moment thing. Michael had been away, given it a lot of thought and decided to go somewhere else with it. He'd never recorded the other way, never really done multitrack, so of course he and the band wanted to try it out.

"I guess Mike and Margo got tired of being asked questions about the bloody microphone, too! They were asked about recording, not the songs, and as an artist that would drive you insane. At that time, it was indivisible, so I'm sure that pushed them towards a different kind of recording, to get the focus more on the songs. It was odd to remake that

121

record, but it was kinda cool too, because the studio had just got a new twenty-four-track digital recorder, so that's the other side of the coin. 'Mmmm, new toy, let me at it!'

"Overdubbing allowed Mike a lot more freedom. He's a writer, his stuff is very dense and the extra layers were something he could see he could use. Saying that, I was pleased we had the other version done on one mic and actually had it approved by BMG as ready to go. That was a big thing for me. I'd won again, so that placated my ego! But there's no question they were relieved that Mike changed his mind, because they didn't really get it.

"Margo swore on one of the songs, 'Sun Comes Up', and the record company came back and said, 'We want the alternate version, without the swearing.' I told them there was no alternate version, so they came back and said, 'Can you mute the vocal track?' So I had to explain there was no vocal in that sense, this was live to two-track. That just sent so much fear through them, the fact they couldn't manipulate it, they couldn't change it, they couldn't remix it with some hotshot, they had no control. They don't like that.

"In saying that, I understand why it wasn't released. Had the record company said, 'No way are we putting it out like this,' I'd feel very differently now. And I bet that Mike would also have said, 'Fuck you! That's the record, put it out.'"

In the end, Cowboy Junkies decided it wasn't something they were happy to stand behind, so they scrapped it. That quality control is something they've tried to maintain throughout their career, according to Mike: "People would be shocked by how much stuff we scrap, from complete album mixes to recording sessions. A lot of the songs from Sharon Temple ended up on *The Caution Horses*, anyway, so there aren't so many lost songs. Looking back, 'Sharon' did work and it didn't. We didn't get what we wanted, it wasn't quite there, it didn't capture the essence of that orchestration. For sure, part of that was because we were a different band by then, there was expectation and that must have played in – as much as we wanted it just to be about us, the fact that people were listening now must have had some influence. We were learning a lot at that time, so throwing stuff out was fine; it's part of the process.

"I'm glad that we didn't release it, I'm glad we went on and did some more work and added some more songs and we ended up with a much better record. Peter Moore gave me a remastered copy a few years ago and it's a cool record, but it's not what we wanted to do. It's not as good as *Trinity*, though it was recorded in a similar kind of way, and it's not as good as *Caution Horses*, so we made the right decision. But it is still an interesting recording."

An interesting record, true enough. But it wasn't a great one. That was the challenge.

CHAPTER 10

Country and eastern

Deciding that a whole album project has gone down the can rather than being in the can should be pretty dispiriting, especially when it's the first one that you're delivering to your major label. Yet Cowboy Junkies' approach was philosophical. They knew they had the songs, or at least some of them. What they didn't quite have yet were the arrangements or the performances. Give it time and the right setting, and they would come.

The 'Sharon' song cycle was a little different to what would become *The Caution Horses*, with 'Captain Kidd' and 'Dead Flowers' both included. They would fall by the wayside in the end, to be reused on B-sides and promo releases, a decision indicative of the band's determination not to simply keep repeating themselves. Their reading of 'Dead Flowers' is riveting, sounding as if the Velvets were covering the Stones' tune, but it did cast them back into the same sort of territory as 'Sweet Jane'. Never go back, as Alan explains.

"We have a very minimalist approach – we play what needs to be played and nothing more – which was like the Velvet Underground. That was the punk idea, too: you have an idea of what the music should do and should say, and you get to the point, you don't play around it, because playing more is going to ruin it. When John was in the band at the beginning, it was a very noisy band, very psychedelic and swirly, which was great, it was a great sound, we liked it a lot. Then, as soon as he left, we liked the sound in a different way, very open, spacious, really different from what we or anybody else had and we just thought, 'Wow, this is really cool.' We recognized we wanted to pursue that sound some more.

"But it wasn't something we wanted to stay with forever, because it gets boring after a while. It's nice to have all this other instrumentation to come in and out of songs. A lot of bands would have probably made *The Trinity Session* over and over – and even that had a lot of instruments on it – and the record company were certainly saying, 'Just keep doing that for ten years and everything will be great.' But we wanted to go on and explore different sounds. That gives you problems with some people, critics or fans, who probably really liked those first couple of records and then wanted more of the same. That's the business, especially the reviewing business. Then, as we've gone on, the kids who are writing the reviews get younger and younger, a lot of the people writing them these days don't know who Jimi Hendrix is, so it's harder for them to relate to what we do; they just think it's weird because it doesn't fit in with what's going on in the mainstream."

Although the spare sound of *The Trinity Session* had been groundbreaking, it was time for the band to shuffle a step or so away from it, still taking many of the trademarks with them, but adding a few more. The new songs were fuller, and to capture that required a different approach, an approach that gave them more control of the recording process, enabling them to layer sounds, interweave them.

David Houghton best explains why it was an album that had to be put together in a more conventional recording studio format: "The sound of *The Caution Horses* is one of spectacular nuance. It's a headphones record. Many musicians seem intent on filling up silence with sound, but the Junkies restrained themselves to the point where they each played as little as possible – they got closer and closer to silence. Jeff, Jaro, Kim and I respected that, and added as little as we could at just the right moment. I've never played music that had as much space in it. It wasn't the sound of emptiness, but the sound of patience. Michelangelo said that art was the purgation of superfluities. Time and again, the Junkies have purged themselves of superfluities. What's left is sometimes so stark, it's harrowing. But, more often, it's so stark, it's beautiful."

If anything, 'Sharon' was just a little too upfront, the sound a little too big. For all that it was a live performance, the size of the building, the fact that Margo was bundled off to a corner somewhere, meant that some of the intimacy of *The Trinity Session* had been lost in these more complex songs. The only way to get it back was to go into a recording studio, yet use it in an unconventional style.

"We went into a regular twenty-four-track studio, Eastern Studios in Toronto," recalls Mike. "We still used the single mic for the rhythm section. The bass guitar, the drums, the percussion and the rhythm guitar were set up around the Calrec, as well as being miked individually. Everyone else was isolated, in the same room, but baffled. Then we played live, all together as one unit again. It gave us enough separation that we could manipulate it a little bit in the mixing, and using the Calrec on the rhythm section gave it that warmth, it uses the ambience of the room, it kept the space, the natural tones of what we do. If you isolate everything, I think it sounds very sterile. Everything sounds very compartmentalized. This way, I think we maintained that blend. That feeling of a live performance is still there."

That decision wasn't made without misgivings, particularly from Peter Moore, a born-again live-to-tape producer. "We are technology-driven – rap wouldn't exist if it weren't for a mic being plugged into a ghetto blaster and a turntable. Technology made it small, light and portable, and you could take it out to people. Technology interacts with the art. For good and bad, as we saw with multitrack. In *Ray*, the movie about Ray Charles, they go to eight-track, the point where he's having trouble with the backing singers. That's the moment it all changed, where it started going horribly wrong. Rather than dealing with the singers, he just said, 'Fuck it, I'll redo the harmonies myself.' And, from then on, you stop recording a performance, you're doing something totally different. That, to me, is the tip of the iceberg. Up to then, you had to play it live, off the floor. From there, you didn't. That's the moment it starts falling apart!"

Alan was equally unsure of the whole process, admitting: "Going into a studio was scary, because it takes your sound apart and tries to put it back together again. Our sound is what we are, so we were terrified of that. Sure enough, we struggled with it in the mix phase trying to get it back, all those separate elements. In the end, after the failed mix, we got Peter in to do it and then it made more sense."

Those nerves must have been well suppressed, or confined to conversation between the four of them, because David Houghton

126

certainly never picked up on them. "I remember the recording sessions for *The Caution Horses* being the most fun I'd had in a recording studio. Although we were being recorded multitrack, we wanted to capture performances without any overdubs. We each had to perform the song flawlessly. Nonetheless, everyone was comfortable; there was no pressure. As a drummer and percussionist, I had a wealth of experience in the studio. I'd recorded with scores of different artists and had even recorded several albums at Eastern Sound. What was foreign for me was the experience at Sharon Temple, where we huddled around one microphone and everyone had to play the song perfectly, because there were no overdubs, no second chances. If you flubbed a note, you ruined the take. It was like being put under a microscope, but I loved it.

"I tried a lot of different instruments. Every percussion instrument has a nationality, but in choosing my parts for *Caution Horses* I thought simply in sonic terms. I ended up using African percussion like shekere, Latin percussion like cabasa and caxixi, and a truckload of miscellaneous percussion including key chimes, goat hooves and emery boards. I even used the triangle that Margo had pulled out the first day I met the band."

Having seasoned musicians to work with in the studio setting was another new experience, and one that saw some pushing and pulling of ideas, some musical moments that required a little negotiation, according to Jeff Bird.

"It was interesting, because we had a big band that stayed together for a couple of years. I guess, the bigger the band, though, the less I get to play! David Houghton was a player I brought to the group, I'd worked with him as a percussionist, and that worked well – not just musically, but because he took over the sleeve design, too. We had an idiosyncratic mix – the blues influences, country, I'd bring some jazz to it, Jaro had the whole Ukrainian vibe, a European blues thing – but it all worked.

"What's interesting to watch is that they bring these additions into it, but the core is always the thing that the four of them do, a solid unwavering approach. They don't really react that much to what I'm doing – Mike a little bit, Pete a little bit sometimes, if I'm soloing or trying to take it architecturally somewhere – but generally they do what they do, so you just add or take away from it, because you know they won't change to accommodate what you're doing! Like Margo says, 'Don't try to make musicians of us!'

"I'll say, 'It would be great in this part if you'd just go down a little quieter and then build up.'

"They just look at me. 'No, not gonna happen!'

"'OK, never mind!'

"In the early days, we were doing some straight-ahead blues thing and there was a stop in it somewhere, a classic stop that everybody in the world had done, it's sitting there like a giant elephant. I tried to get them to do it and it wouldn't happen! They all came down somewhere around it at different times, and I just sat back, like watching a car crash. 'Whoa, that was a bad idea to stop. Let's just forget that!' But that fragility is one of the most appealing things about it, and that was especially the case with Margo in the early days. She's like a dynamo now compared with back then. And Pete has that, too. You feel like he could lose it at any time, but that adds a manic edge to it, which is great, because it rubs up against Al, who never changes his part, he's totally grounded."

Alan's take is that "My bass playing isn't technical, I really wouldn't call myself a musician in front of other musicians, whereas Jeff is a real musician. From his point of view, the couple of times he's had to stand in for me, he's not trying to replicate bass playing or a technique, he's trying to get a sound. That's what I go for, more of a soundscape, and that's not what Jeff would do ordinarily, so it's hard to step up and do that. He's always been mystified by that, I think. But he's a great bass player – really amazing, his jazz stuff is great, the records he has out.

"Mike definitely stays away from anything that sounds like a lick or a hook except in an arty sense. He'll either just play rhythm or those weird solos that he does. Often when he's doing that, I'll wonder what the audience thinks of it, because it's so strange. The music is definitely psychedelic, and that was where we started with John. Our idea was to play psychedelic roots music, so we've kept that as a touchstone as other influences and ideas have come in."

As time wore on, more influences did come to bear, country music taking a bigger and bigger role. But *The Caution Horses* is not a country record. It's not a blues record, a rock record or a psychedelic record. Maybe it was a new genre. Alan called it "country death", but maybe it was more a case of "country and eastern", because the East Coast sensibility was still an integral part of a record that was many things to many people all at once.

To the Junkies, too, it's a record that filled many roles. Obviously, it was album number three in pure chronological terms, but it was also that "difficult second album", the second on BMG and, to many more casual listeners, the follow-up to their "debut". It was also their sophomore record in the sense that this was the first time the world was waiting for Cowboy Junkies product, with all the attendant excitement, expectation and pressure that brings with it. It also marked the end of an era, had we but known it at the time, for *Black Eyed Man* was going to be a different kind of record, a much more marked departure than anything they'd done before. And, perhaps most crucial, it was essentially the debut of a new band that had emerged from the crucible of early experimentation, from the chrysalis of other people's songwriting. From now on, Mike's was going to be the dominant voice on a Cowboy Junkies record, in a creative rather than interpretative sense. From *The Caution Horses* onwards, fans would buy their records to hear what the band had to say for themselves, rather than saying it through the words and music of others. It was a seismic shift that opened the door to everything they would go on to become.

There was an equally important shift between 'Sharon' and *The Caution Horses*, if a more subtle one. They recaptured the sense of relaxed control that had characterized *The Trinity Session*, Pete and Alan the cornerstone of the record in spite of the fact that they played so little on it. Just as important, the different sequencing gave it a very identifiable beginning, middle and end, and the addition of three new songs gave the piece a conceptual wholeness such that it was later subtitled "A Meditation on Lost Love".

Finding an opening to the record that packed the same emotional whack as *The Trinity Session* was essential. People were bringing preconceptions to this new material and a weak start would have been disastrous. Instead, it was a triumph, with two songs that even now form the cornerstone of many a Junkies live set, 'Sun Come Up, It's Tuesday Morning' and "Cause Cheap Is How I Feel'.

'Sun Comes Up' is pretty much word-perfect, a short story that covers the range of emotions following a breakup inside four minutes, one fan admitting, "After I heard that, I wanted to break up with my girlfriend just to live through that whole song"! Approaching thirty years' worth of playing it has left Mike a little ambivalent about it, which is ironic given that that's pretty much the theme of the song, according to Margo. "It has a lot of the ambivalence that's in the record – feeling good one minute, then feeling lost the next, swinging from one to the other – which is how it is when you leave a situation, it's never straightforward."

As a piece of music, it has legions of admirers, not least among those who played on it. David Houghton: "Every musician has songs they never tire of playing. For me, one of them has been 'Sun Comes Up, It's Tuesday Morning'. I calculate I've played that song at least 200 times and every single time has been a joy. It feels like I'm playing the song for the first time, yet I know every beat of every bar."

For Mike, "'Sun Comes Up' was a very positive song, realistic too, and that was a good starting point for that record. I listen to it now and I wonder how I did it. I wrote it really fast, it just came together. I'm very proud of it, even though I don't really like playing it any more! Then, to go from that to 'Cause Cheap Is How I Feel' just shifts the mood. I was kinda surprised when we had the finished version of that, because I wasn't anticipating Margo's presentation as being quite so emotionally powerful, so dark. It's real frightening sometimes when we play it live."

""'Cause Cheap Is How I Feel' is a strange line for a woman to say," admits Margo, "so the way I sing it is my interpretation of it, which maybe isn't the way Michael originally wrote it or intended it. My way is a little more ambivalent, not as strong as maybe it was written. But Michael gives me the freedom to do that, he doesn't insist on me singing a song a certain way. That's why they become personal, because I have that freedom, and I guess that makes them more real."

Not only does it make the song feel more authentic, but it gives it a twist very distinct from any number of songs on a similar theme. Film, literature, popular music – they're all teeming with stories of men feeling reduced by guilt, of wrestling with betrayal, that whole "It's three in the morning, there's no one in the place" genre of writing. There aren't too many men who haven't at least pondered the "your body for my soul" equation one night or another. But, for a quiet young woman, onto whom the industry had already projected an image of soft, sweet vulnerability, to be singing words as harsh as these, that took the record into different territory. Long-term listeners could maybe link the song to older material such as 'Shining Moon', but to a new mainstream audience, attracted by the post-*Trinity* buzz, this was uncomfortably dark. That was to become a Junkies hallmark as the years slipped by.

It was all the more intriguing given the more traditional nature of 'Sun Comes Up, It's Tuesday Morning', traditional in the sense that a male songwriter was writing for a female singer, in the way a Tin Pan Alley songsmith might have tweaked a lyric, knowing that Ella Fitzgerald would be singing it rather than Sinatra. Having those two songs rub up against one another was highly distinctive, underlining the trust that Mike and Margo clearly have in one another. Having that female voice also offers scope for a greater sensitivity, where a male singer might tend to be either more guarded, or sentimentally clichéd. Mike certainly appreciates that opportunity, that freedom.

"A female singer does that better, for sure. But, as different as men and women are, I honestly think that if you're writing a song, if you're interpreting an experience honestly, without all the layers that society puts on male and female, the experience is the same. We experience it the same way. If a song is honest enough, cuts enough to the bone, it's the same. People might say, 'It's so sensitive, it's like a woman wrote it,' but usually that's because men don't write that way, because they won't go beyond that layer, beyond that male stereotype. Hopefully that's part of it – I try to get behind the male/female stereotypes, I like to get at the raw emotion of a scene. The pronouns get added just to tell a story, but the underlying current of the story is a human one, not gender-specific. Then Margo sings it, so people automatically put a female perspective on it, but I don't think it is. It's a human perspective.

"I don't see much point in a love song that says that everything will always be wonderful. Love is such a strange thing, beyond definition. I always feel that a song should have different facets to it, different perceptions. I don't want to say, 'This is the way it is.' I want to show something where it's in the back of your head that 'This is great now. But what about tomorrow?' That ambiguity comes from my writing from a male perspective and Margo singing from the female side. Men and women do look at relationships differently and I think that comes through in the songs."

Beyond the lyrical intrigue, "Cause Cheap Is How I Feel' is a ravishing piece of music, from the opening pulse that Pete sets, a signal that now they're sitting right in the groove rather than chasing it, is as they were at Sharon. That exultant "Yeah" from Margo after she comes

131

"up with an answer" justifies rerecording the album on its own, while that group shrug of resignation as the song closes is recognition that life never is as simple as it was supposed to be. The underlying theme to *The Caution Horses* is one of loss, but not always romantic loss. There's a feeling of dislocation, of disorientation, a reflection that, in the wake of *The Trinity Session*, the band set off to conquer the world, leaving all those they knew behind to get on with their lives.

"I guess that was partly because we were away from home so much," suggests Mike. "A lot of things changed in that time: we were away, we suddenly started getting all this attention and, without realizing it, we became distanced from a lot of people. We were very focused on what we were doing, very locked in, and we did stray from people. When I started writing, I wanted to think very much as a person, not as a 'rock star'. It just became obvious to me that, though I might be a 'rock star' for these few minutes onstage, my life the past couple of years had been pretty shitty really – from a personal perspective, anyway. I broke up with a lot of people at that point, and that's reflected in there, not always consciously, because often songs will only become clear later down the road.

"We played 'Thirty Summers' again maybe fifteen years later, and I started to get a new appreciation for it. It's very personal, there's a lot of confusion in there, but I guess that's in all my songs! I think if anybody stops and thinks about their life, what's going on, there's confusion, because there's so many contradictory elements. You're taught so many different things that don't fit together, so if you try to piece any kind of philosophy from that, any kind of direction, it is confusing. A lot of songs are about trying to get through that stuff. Then you add in the emotional side of life – the way we're driven by our emotions, that really makes no sense at all. That's always a key part of what I write about, that questioning."

Questioning, in our reductive culture, is something to be frightened of, something to repress. That's one of the main reasons why some critics rush to write the Junkies off as terminal miserablists. Mike was even moved to issue a denial in the course of an interview with *People* magazine, saying, "No, we are not depressed, or melancholy or any of those things. We don't consider the music sad, just heartfelt. To us, it's very strange when people come up to us and say, 'You must be so depressed.'" This ain't no depression, just notes falling slow.

To some, it seems impossible, incredible even, that a song can carry two contradictory ideas at once, which is pretty weird given that most of us get through the day by doing just that. For Margo, that's the strength of a lot of the Junkies' material: "I think there's a part of me that's optimistic, that there is that great love out there, so there's that in my interpretation of the songs where the words are maybe more realistic than that. We all have that thing going on – do we follow the heart or the head? There's a hope in the hardest situations, a choice where you go one way or another, even if all you're doing is moving on into the unknown. That's what I try to bring out with my vocal. I don't see our songs as sad or hopeless. To me, they're uplifting.

"'Where Are You Tonight?' is about a woman in a relationship that's not going well, but she still dreams about Prince Charming, believes in something better. It's easy to relate to that. Then, at the end of the song, I think she looks at herself and doesn't recognize what she's become and says, 'Forget it, I'm giving this up.' A lot of the songs are desperate situations, but there's a positive element to them; she's taking control and hopefully she'll go off and find a better life."

'Where Are You Tonight?', along with "Cause Cheap Is How I Feel', in particular gave an indication of the territory the Junkies would stake out for themselves in the future, music strong on a certain kind of lyrical imagery. At times hard-boiled like Raymond Chandler – "The kind of night that's so cold, when you spit it freezes before it hits the ground" – and, at others, deeply poetic – "How the cloud of dust we'll kick up will linger like a song."

Both are songs that Mike still holds dear. "'Where Are You Tonight?' is one of my favourite songs. A lot of straight imagery mixed with weirder stuff, you have to stop and think about it a bit. I don't know why that happened. I guess when I started writing again with *Trinity*, I was writing in a more formal way, thinking in terms of a country song, a tour song, a husband-kills-wife song, very much in the country tradition. 'To Love Is to Bury', '200 More Miles' – they're of a genre. With *Caution Horses*, it was more just me as a songwriter, writing about me, writing different stories. It was more looking back at how I'd written poetry and thinking about how that could be turned into lyrics, into songs. I started to appreciate songwriters again – Leonard Cohen, Dylan – started to study them more. I think it's true that *The Caution Horses* was the first record that gives you a real sense of what we went on to become, what we are now. There are a lot more of my songs on there, the writing is better, more developed. *Whites!!!* and *Trinity* are of a time, of the independent period, of learning to be a band, but *Caution Horses* is the start of the next phase."

It also began something of a tradition, maybe a subconscious one, of "partner" songs, songs that related very closely to one another, either involving the same protagonists at different times in a relationship, or different perspectives on a theme. Obvious examples came later in the two versions of 'Come Calling' and 'All That Reckoning' or 'River Song Trilogy', but other songs bear close relationships to one another. On *The Caution Horses*, 'Where Are You Tonight?' and 'Escape Is So Simple' both deal with the fragility of love, of life, of romance, as Mike agrees.

"Definitely down the line, songs will come back and the character in them will re-emerge, because essentially the character is me in a way, five years on, more experienced. I don't remember thinking they were linked at the time, but there is a very lonesome quality to that record, a loss. There was a real dislocation in our lives without knowing it. And that wasn't even necessarily a bad thing, it just was how it was. We were homeless, travelling all the time, a real sense of not belonging. It was a bus, a room, a bus, a room, and then the occasional airport, which makes it even worse! You're always in public spaces, at the mercy of circumstance – nothing is under your control. It does get to you. All the touring we'd done before, we were in our own van so we could just stop, get out, go for a walk, see stuff, eat, whatever we wanted. This was the first time when we actually had to get somewhere, there was a gig booked; we didn't have three days off between shows.

"With those two songs, 'Where Are You Tonight?' is a female song, for sure. At the time, I remember writing it and wanting to do it not necessarily from a female point of view, but a female character's perspective, because I don't think the point of view is that different, male or female. I developed the character of that waitress, the dislocation. Neither character in that song is attached to anything, but they somehow find each other, but not really. They leave together, but they're not together. That idea of separate units in the same sphere but not connecting. That, 'Cheap Is How I Feel', there are a lot of bar songs there, because that's where we spent a lot of time. I was observing a lot of that, feeling the sense of those places."

That "leaving together but not together" idea was developed again in 'Escape Is So Simple', where "You broke all the promises you knew you'd never keep", and how an insincere "forever" is still better than "goodbye". It was a telling observation on the lies people tell themselves as much as others, simply because that's the only defence mechanism that we have at times. Why do we need it? That came up in 'Witches', a song which showed just how flimsy are the things on which we base our lives, how easily they can be snatched away, often without us knowing why: "Do I answer their call or stay here with you? / But under spell of deep sleep he moans and turns away / Taking his protection and my desire to stay." Even as we sleep, a life can be shattered – how Cowboy Junkies is that? That lack of control, that sense of being adrift in a tide of circumstance, was to be another recurring theme, developed again on songs like 'Lonely Sinking Feeling' and 'Something More Besides You'.

Ironically, the inclusion of 'Witches' on the record also came about by chance. "We had 'Witches' before we started recording *Caution Horses*," recalls Margo. "It wasn't going to go on there, but it seemed to fit when we came back to it after Sharon. I'd been singing it as an a cappella, but Michael suggested we do it as a duet, so he rewrote it and that's what we recorded." David Houghton distinctly recalls hearing it for the first time: "One evening, Mike and Margo stayed at the studio while the rest of us went for dinner. When we returned, they played us their brand-new recording of 'Witches'. I'd never heard it before, and was utterly blown away."

Two more songs that weren't on the 'Sharon' running order emerged on *The Caution Horses* and were fundamental to its success – if not commercially, then certainly artistically. 'Rock and Bird' summed up one of the record's themes, Mike saying, "It was meant as an epilogue of sorts, the protagonist having had it with this strange relationship and getting ready to move on. Things are going to change."

Speaking at the time the album came out, Margo explained the song by saying it was "a look at the subject of a rejected love ('I offered you my endless skies / You countered with hoods and chains') that seemingly ends with defection ('This song I sing will be the last / To be inspired by your memory'). But I don't feel that is the end of it – she may be down, but she is definitely not out. By the end of the song she has been able, somehow, to accommodate both her concept of eternal love ('Bird with unbarred wings') and common sense ('Rock with weighted heart'). As I see it, that's how she is able to triumph over her misfortune."

A vital change between 'Sharon' and *The Caution Horses* was the decision to use Mary Margaret O'Hara's 'You Will Be Loved Again' as the closer. Mike believes "It was the perfect epilogue to the record, it was just the right note to leave it on," and it's hard to argue with that. It gave *The Caution Horses* a sense of completing a cycle, from it being cool to be alone again in 'Sun Comes Up, It's Tuesday Morning' through to the pain of enduring loneliness in songs like 'Escape Is So Simple'.

Where 'Sharon' had ended on the down beat of the Stones' typically misanthropic 'Dead Flowers', 'You Will Be Loved Again' offered hope in the midst of desolation. The sun comes up again tomorrow, Tuesday morning, Wednesday morning, Sunday morning, and we get up and we try to make some sense of it all, all over again, whatever the cost.

CHAPTER 11

A gentle offering

For a record that seems effortless, that flows from beginning through middle to its logical conclusion, *The Caution Horses* took some making. Not only had the Sharon Temple sessions been abortive, but the first pass at mixing it was a failure. "It was our first 'studio' record, so we thought we needed somebody from outside to mix it because we hadn't done that before," explains Alan. "We got it back and it was a mess, so we went in and did it ourselves." Mike adds, "I hope people hear the complexity of the arrangements, which I think are unique. As much as *Trinity* was unique in its sound, *Caution Horses* is unique in the way the instruments combine together, the lushness of it. We worked really hard on that – that was an important element in the mix."

Once made, getting the record out in the stores required some packaging and there was closer focus on the artwork than on either of the two albums that preceded it, simply because this was a big-deal release. But why get a hotshot in from outside when you could do it yourself? The design simply fell into the band's lap, in the form of percussionist David Houghton.

"I was in my final year of art college when I joined the band. When Mike set the cover photos for the record down on the kitchen table, I made a couple of suggestions. Mike turned to me and asked if I'd like to design the cover. It was as simple as that. I created the cover for *Caution Horses*, then became the de facto designer for a long period.

"In spite of *Whites Off Earth Now!!*, the band has never liked being on the cover, and never will. Everyone was drawn to the photos that Graham Henderson had taken of us walking back into Sharon Temple after getting some fresh air. The images were enigmatic, and I suppose some might read them as literally turning our backs on the hype surrounding *Trinity Sessions*.

"For me, the cover was ambiguous, and ambiguity has been a thread throughout all the band's covers since then. If you look at *Black Eyed Man* or *Pale Sun* or *Open*, you'll see the cover is related to the title, but is not a literal depiction of the title. The Venus fly trap on *Open* symbolizes a clear threat by being physically open. If a listener is going to look at a cover dozens of times, there needs to be enough depth for them to continue to find meanings in the imagery.

"Mike and Al liked the notion of *The Caution Horses* looking like an indie record, so they particularly liked the photos inside the sleeve. They were informal pictures, not staged or posed. I was getting to know the band while the *Caution Horses* cover was being created. By the time *Black Eyed Man* rolled around, I had a vision of how the packaging should look, and the band let me pursue it, and I've followed that since then, going back and forth with them on the ideas."

That indie edge which the packaging carried was important, sending out some important visual cues that Cowboy Junkies had not been consumed by the industry. Perhaps those things mattered more in 1990, when the big multinational record companies carried greater weight, before file-sharing and downloading started to chip away at them. The companies were synonymous with the Man, who was out to make money by watering down the music that you loved, packaging it so that people who bought ten albums a year in a supermarket or gas station might actually pick it up. That was maybe an oversimplification, but simply putting your record out on RCA/BMG was liable to turn off those who loved the independent nature of the first two records. Anything that reminded them that Cowboy Junkies were still the same band was important.

The record company, having shelved 'Sharon Temple', might have treated *The Caution Horses* with trepidation, but the swift success of the record calmed any fears. Jim Powers was delighted with it – artistically at first, then commercially, too. "It was a very strong record and we even got some singles success off the back of it, partly because it was still that *Trinity Session* era and they were just perfect for that moment, where people wanted something more human from music. They were such an antidote to that ultra-clean sound that still prevailed. You'd had a couple of years since the last record, where Mike had just done more and more writing. He was really getting better and better at that; there was a natural evolution within the band as musicians."

Jeff Bird underlines Powers' belief in the album, stating that "*The Caution Horses* is a great record. It has the shadow of *The Trinity Session* hanging over it, but after that band had been together a while it hit this real stride. Maybe it lost a bit of that fragility, but it's one of my favourites, because that ensemble playing had been refined." To Jaro Czerwinec, "That was the pinnacle of my Cowboy Junkies career. I love *The Caution Horses*, because I got a bigger role on it. I was here, there and everywhere on it."

The way the music meshed, the way the instruments flowed in and out of one another, in and around Margo's voice, was an extension of the life and conditions under which it had been made – in days stolen off the road as they travelled together. On the road, the band lived in and out of each other's pockets, creating a community that was also at the core of those songs, granting them that human quality. Jaro and Jeff provided some of the most enduring moments on the record: the piercing harmonica that turns 'You Will Be Loved Again' into a Delta lament, Margo sighing a vocal from a rocker on the porch; the bluesy wail that ushers in ''Cause Cheap Is How I Feel', the rise and fall of Jaro's accordion that colours it throughout, the two of them weaving in and out of Kim Deschamps' pedal steel. Perhaps the high point from Jaro was his gorgeous reading of Neil Young's classic "Powderfinger", a cover version that defined the whole genre – an artist finding something new and fresh in a song rather than giving a faithful, but pointless, retread. Mike's take was simple. "I always loved 'Powderfinger' from a lyrical perspective, but I never thought his version caught the intensity of that. He plays it as such a great rock song, the guitar solo takes it over, but there's a pretty story in there and I wanted to present it that way, just as a narrative, a country song."

For all that the personnel was similar, this was no longer the group that had made *The Trinity Session*. They'd moved on as people and as musicians, as David Houghton points out. "It was clear their fans followed the band's evolution from *The Trinity Session* to *The Caution*

Horses. 'Sharon' was in fact closer to *Trinity Session*. By the time we recorded *Caution Horses*, it was an entirely different album, so repeating ourselves wasn't an issue."

Coping with external expectations *was* another issue, particularly those of the critics, as Houghton recalls. "Stepping in after *Trinity Session*, I never saw the height of the focus, only the aftermath. *The Caution Horses* tour was called 'The Backlash Tour', obviously with tongue in cheek." Though not that far in cheek, according to Mike. A longtime consumer of the music press, he knew what was coming, but it didn't make it any more palatable. "It doesn't get a lot of notice that record, especially in the US, because it was the follow-up to *Trinity* and it got overlooked. There was a backlash before it even came out, and that was weird to watch. It was all this self-perpetuating stuff from the critics' industry because they'd all been fawning over *Trinity*, all trying to outpraise the last guy. Then they came to this new record and maybe they'd embarrassed themselves or something, but they came to it with the attitude that they were going to hate it, whatever it sounded like.

"We were doing press before it was released. I had a day with RCA in New York, and the last interview of the day was with a feature writer for *Entertainment Weekly*. He was talking to me about the backlash over the record. It hadn't been released, or even reviewed at that point! So I didn't really know what to say and then his article came out and that was it – the sophomore jinx! He'd decided that was his slant and he just went for it. RCA told us to expect that, so what can you do about it? I think it got lost a little because of that in the US.

"Those were days that opened our eyes a lot. It was very educational; we learned a lot very quickly, mostly that a lot of things that happen have nothing to do with the record at all. It showed us that the only thing we could control was our music, so we made sure we did that. We put the walls up around the music-making side of things and we've always been true to that ever since. Whatever happens when you have to go beyond the walls to do promotion, well, it's going to happen. We have to put up with that. But the music is the music, and nothing gets through the walls to have an impact on that. That's ours."

Having that refuge when you're touring the world is crucial, though at least there were one or two extra comforts, according to Houghton: "*The Caution Horses* allowed the band to travel with better buses and a better crew to better venues. I'd spent years touring North America with a variety of bands, typically four sweaty, tired guys jammed into a van with all our equipment. Those were not glory days. To be able to tour with the Junkies and have someone carry my congas into the hall was a supremely fine experience.

"One of life's cruel ironies is that, although I love to travel, I suffer from motion sickness. Particularly on a bus. I had a few instances of heaving into the toilet in the middle of a 400-kilometre stretch between shows. Thankfully, everyone was amused by it. Everyone but me. That aside, it was a fine way to see the world.

"The tour following the release of *The Caution Horses* was really enjoyable. It was immediately obvious the band had a loyal following all around the world. We began the show quietly and let it build slowly. By the time we got to 'Me and the Devil' and 'Walking After Midnight', we stretched out into long solo sections where all hell might break loose, and often did. It was like an hour of foreplay giving way to full-on sex; it was ecstatic."

The daily grind of bus, hotel, soundcheck, eat, play, hotel, bus can be pretty wearing, but that ecstatic release helped. And, so enthusiastically was the music received, it too had a reviving effect. Actually, "enthusiastic" may not be the word, given that the band's audience was as quiet as they were, certainly in Europe. It was extraordinary to watch Cowboy Junkies at work, observing the communication between them and their audience, stolen whispers between lovers trying not to bring attention to themselves, but completely lost in one another, energizing each other. I saw them first in Birmingham in May 1990, arriving at the show, for reasons long forgotten, after thirty-six hours without sleep – we were all so much younger then … You'd think their quiet, gentle music, Margo head bowed, hardly daring to look out at the crowd, the band all sat at their instruments, Alan standing but motionless, you'd figure all that would lull the weary traveller into a doze. Instead, their control of the moment, of the atmosphere, of what they were offering up to the audience, was so intimate, it was electrifying, crackling. In a typically Junkies, low-voltage kind of way, obviously.

Irish singer-songwriter Luka Bloom, the support act on many European shows then, got an insider's view and he'd certainly never seen anything like it. "The very first show I did with them, I had this big delivery, I was really into putting the song out there in an almost post-punky kind of way. I remember watching them after I'd finished and being shocked just by being in a room with eight or nine people making so little noise, projecting so little. But I was utterly beguiled by it. They lull you into a very warm place and that's an incredible thing. It takes a lot of confidence to do that, and that's an aspect of the collective thing they have. To be able to be so patient with the audience, so calm for so long with what, at that time, was a very young crowd, takes some doing. But the band was simply insistent on being exactly who and what they are, and that demands a collective courage, just to be who you are, and not, to use an awful phrase, simply 'rock out'.

"I had done a couple of tours with people like the Violent Femmes, the Pogues, the Hothouse Flowers. They were all great experiences for different reasons. The Pogues was the wildest tour you could imagine, so being with Cowboy Junkies was a little different! A couple of things really set that tour apart for me. I was struck just by how down to earth they were, but, more than that, something very unusual in the music world, was that you experience a real calm when you're with them. 'Calm' is a word you don't use much in this business, and maybe it comes as part of the deal of people working together as family. It was very obvious that they were comfortable with each other – I've been with other bands where every member had their own mode of transport to get to the gig. Family has a way of ironing out ego; they work things out together. Egos do get out of control sometimes in bands and there's no place for that in a family – they don't allow for that and, if it arises, they deal with it.

"They were very calm, very relaxed, easy-going, and there were certain aspects of the way they treated me that have stayed with me. I found a very gentle kind of generosity, in the sense that they were the only band that I ever toured with who were quite happy for me to be louder than them! The stereotype is the headliner insists that the sound engineer makes sure the support act is turned right down. At that time, my gig was very full-on, it was pretty loud for a solo performer, and they didn't mind that, they were quite happy. That said to me that they were very comfortable with themselves, their music; they accepted that diversity, they knew that their audience wouldn't be remotely affected by my kind of thunderous performance, which was very different to theirs.

"Touring with them was a singularly enjoyable experience. I loved it and I'd very happily work with them again. I just found them to be a really good bunch of people, and that counts as much for me as enjoying the music. I loved the songs, but they were a lovely group of people to be around. They had time for each other and, by extension, they had time for me. I found them to be very inclusive. So often with bands, they get into the feeling that they're off to conquer the world. They become like a Premiership football club; they'll slag off other bands. It becomes a lad thing, I suppose. Cowboy Junkies don't have any of that lad element to them! That's very consoling, that generosity of spirit. That's kind of rare, and it should be cherished."

Speaking during that tour, Margo said, "The music we're doing now fits my personality. It's low-key, it's soft, it's an offering. A gentle offering. It's *not* a demand." That was very much the ethos of those *Caution Horses* shows, very much the ethos of the band, then and now. Although their music has been dismissed carelessly as one mood, one tempo, one volume, a Junkies show encompasses remarkable dynamics, from calm to chaos and every point in between. Doesn't life? But the core of what they do is somehow the eye of the storm. All around, there is madness, mayhem, their stories are often about the struggle that goes on out there, but at once they provide a haven, a harbour where you can take a breath, where you have a few moments to reflect, to think before plunging back into the maelstrom once again. That's a valuable service.

Serving that music isn't always easy, though, as Pete admits. "By the time we'd finished touring *Caution Horses*, we were pretty much exhausted, because we hadn't had a break since we started touring *Whites!!* We moved from station wagon to a ten-passenger blue van for *Trinity Session*. That was luxury! Then we got a bus, but we were constantly on the road. It wears you down physically, but we were young, we were keen. Then, as you get more success, you play better places to audiences that want to see you, you have a nicer bus, you don't get tired of that for a while. Even now, though, thirty years down the line, I love coming out on the road. You get tired towards the end of it, but I'm always happy to do it again, there's always something good that comes with it."

And, sometimes, something bad. The more you look at the stories of the bands that have made it through, not necessarily to sell billions of records but to make a career from music, to enjoy longevity, to keep on having something to say, the more you realize there is a common denominator. Yes, a lucky break or two along the way is handy. But the ones who make it are the ones that mean it, that need it. The ones who put a shift in, play the 200 gigs a year, build an audience, treat them right and sustain their interest. You can't hide from the facts. It's a hard road.

"Sure, it has its cost," admits a rueful Margo. "In this industry, the companies rely on things taking off and then jumping on it and working it like crazy. But they don't know how to create the buzz. They don't put their energy into being creative, they grasp something that's happening and then they push you out there as much as they possibly can – every radio station, magazine, they push and push. Playing shows is one thing, that's what you do, it's part of what Cowboy Junkies is. But all that other stuff? I can do without it.

"*The Caution Horses* for me is just that period where life became so weird so quickly. I was in *People* magazine, for God's sake! I didn't know what was happening. And *The Caution Horses* is this beautiful, protective little bubble, and that's what I felt the Junkies were, floating around in this big, strange psycho-business that was pulling at us – and pulling a little harder at me than the others – but we had this beautiful bubble to hide inside.

"Overwork made me really ill at the end of the *Caution Horses* tour, but the way it worked, being sick ended up being a good thing in a way, because it taught me to say 'no'. And I realized that the record companies would run you into the ground. They don't care that you're struggling, they pile it on. After that, it was a lot easier for me. It was an eye-opener for Mike. It scared him that I got that sick, and afterwards things changed from 'Can you do this? Let's do that,' to 'Are you OK with this? Can you fit that in?' We were all smarter about what we had to do. We shifted gears a bit, which was good, because we needed to."

ONE SCORE YEARS

If the Junkies' 2005 'Blue States' trip is any guide, these things will happen on tour …

- You will get on a nice clean bus. The bus will almost immediately be full of crap, but nobody will know where it came from.
- Margo will knit, and may even offer to teach you.
- You will ensure that any beer, water or fruit left from the show rider ends up on the bus. Jeff is particularly good at ensuring this happens. It's something to do with hunter-gathering.
- Nothing – nothing – will work as it does in the real world. Including time.
- The bus air-con will break down on the hottest day of the year. The driver may or may not choose to believe this.
- Despite no obvious medical training, the same driver may have incredibly detailed opinions on oestrogen.
- At one or other venue, Pete will accidentally drink medicine, thinking it's water. It turns out to be designed to maintain regular periods. Ideal for a drummer.
- You will have little or no idea what's actually going on in the outside world.
- Whatever time of day you arrive at a hotel, you will always take them by surprise and your rooms will never be ready.
- They won't send the courtesy bus, either, leaving you unloading and reloading the gear onto your bus outside a Navy football stadium in the middle of the day. You will look like terrorists.
- At some stage, you will wake up in the middle of the night convinced that your bunk is actually a coffin.
- The bus toilet will be out of bounds for "solids". It will still smell bad. Really bad.
- Pete will raid Margo's makeup stash, use it on himself – pretty professionally – and may play a show that way. He won't use her curling tongs.
- You will learn to eat whenever you can, because the odds are that it will be at least twelve hours before you get to do it again.
- Jeff will bring DVDs onto the bus and give a director's commentary that is way better than the one already on there.
- There are never enough DVDs to watch. Not on the bus. In the world. In New York, someone will helpfully throw one through the back window of the bus, thinking you're a soccer team. Pete will tell him you're Manchester United.

- You will watch several of the DVDs many times, especially if one of them is *Team America*, which will become an instant classic. Better than *Citizen Kane*, probably. Though not as funny as *Dawn of the Dead*.
- Margo will pore over the trashy gossip magazines, passing the news onto Pete. His knowledge of the lives of Christina, Britney and Angelina is surprisingly detailed.
- You will discover that if you are travelling but in no hurry to get to the next place, a day can actually last thirty-six hours. Maybe longer. If you are behind schedule, you will find that every freeway is awash with car wrecks and construction traffic. And you'll get lost. And days only last sixteen hours.
- Somebody, somewhere, will make an incredibly long intro speech with the band onstage, ignoring the fact that Al is giving him the signal and Mike is glaring at him.
- America will remind you that there really is no such thing as America, that it is not a homogenous entity, but a huge landmass filled with good and bad and different.
- You will be confronted by strange sights, such as a car with a wrecked rear fender, the gaping hole filled with plastic roses.
- You will get somewhere, wait for ninety minutes, do something for twenty minutes, wait for ninety minutes, do something for an hour, maybe eat, wait for ninety minutes, play, wait for ninety minutes, then drive to a shower stop. Day after day.
- John will throw on a leopardskin robe and twirl a red umbrella in the confines of a jungle-themed hotel suite during a shower stop. Mike will ignore him and go on updating the website.
- You will regularly encounter the most extraordinary collection of fans that any band could have. They will bring great stuff with them, too – like the Nativity, but without the myrrh. Not so much gold, either.
- A venue sound engineer will tell you, "Hey, don't worry, it's gonna sound great when the people get here." He will often be lying.
- Everybody will lose something in their bunk only to have it miraculously turn up in exactly the same place days later.
- Whatever happens, Alan will continue to live in Alworld for the duration.
- Watch out where the huskies go and don't you eat those strange orange doughnuts they sell in truck stops.
- However tired you are, and however much you want to see your family, the last show is a downer. Though, if you've been doing this for twenty years, you're probably happier to leave the circus for a couple of months.

CHAPTER 12

Things which I dream of still

It would be pedantic to put a man with black eyes on the cover of
Black Eyed Man, so instead we used an image of a man whose eyes you
can't see. I'd seen Matthew Cooper's collages in a British magazine
and filed them away for future reference. When Mike told me about
Black Eyed Man, I knew Matthew's collages were the perfect imagery.
They were ambiguous, dark and layered. The art was so beautiful,
the band actually bought the originals and had them framed.
(David Houghton, cover designer and percussionist)

Complete estrangement from the big corporate music machine
was still some years away, but the genesis of that parting of the
ways can be traced back to the evolution, recording and release of *Black
Eyed Man*, a period when both band and industry were changing, but
going in different directions – the dream scenario for divorce attorneys
everywhere. For the business, intimacy was no longer on the agenda.
Bands like the Junkies or 10,000 Maniacs had filled a gap for a period,
a musical sorbet when both fans and industry were trying to clean
their palate of the headbands and stadium acts that had dominated
the mid- and late 1980s, but it quickly became clear to the number-
crunchers in the company towers that these new artists, who put the
emphasis on their art, were not going to be as malleable nor as saleable

to a mainstream audience as they had hoped. And, while the big record labels did employ many people for whom the music mattered, they tended to be outnumbered round the boardroom table.

As Cowboy Junkies were recuperating after the *Caution Horses* tour, and slowly turning their attention to whatever came next, the music scene changed, irrevocably, with the advent of grunge, a lo-fi movement that had records like *The Trinity Session* among its antecedents. Once *Nevermind* was out there, the future was plaid. Nirvana went global and then stadium inside a few months, Pearl Jam followed behind, along with a host of other acts, and suddenly we were at year zero again, just as we had been in 1976, when punk arrived. This time, though, the industry was smarter. This time, the movement could be turned into mega-money. Whatever the original message Kurt Cobain was trying to get across, for the bulk of listeners that was going to get swept away in the tidal wave of musical marketing and merchandising that declared it was party time again. Big, loud and obvious would follow in the wake of Seattle – introspection and thoughtfulness were no longer required at the top table, a perversion of Cobain's ideas.

Perhaps it was inevitable that Cowboy Junkies' commercial lucky streak would run out, and perhaps it was as well for their longevity that it did. There was little that was obvious about any of those first three records, certainly nothing big and loud, but they were curiously in step with more inquisitive times, particularly *The Trinity Session*, which flew in through a tiny window of opportunity on its release and gave Cowboy Junkies a place in the musical consciousness. The widespread recognition that that record earned them did much to offer a long-term, viable career in music, but this was not a band, nor a music, that could live and grow under a glaring spotlight. Cowboy Junkies were going on their own journey and, as a listener, you either bought into that, or you didn't. There wasn't going to be any sudden change in style or presentation simply to fit in with trends or the demands of the company, no matter how hard the business tried.

And it certainly did try, according to Alan. "The record companies always wanted the Margo solo album, but she wasn't interested. It would have done great, sold well; she'd have been Norah Jones or something. That's what upsets the industry with us. 'You gotta have an image, we gotta sell an image!' Sell the music. 'No, can't do that, can't just sell music.' There's no angle there.

"The idea of this band is, we put the music out there and hope that people find it, enjoy it, get something from it, separate from us as people. Margo does a little bit of a show because she has to, that's the nature of the singer, but other than that, we are as we are. That's one of the things I loved about Pink Floyd, actually: they were faceless people. They were smart, because they made the stage the focus, the thing that entertained people, and they just stood in the shadows. You have to reiterate the fact that the band deliberately doesn't have an image in order to protect and present the music. We sit down to make sure there's no distraction, that the focus is on what we're playing."

"It's natural for me now to be onstage, I love it now, but it wasn't like that then," admits Margo. "We had people telling us that if I just wore shorter skirts, if I got rid of the folky flower thing, if we made her a sex babe, if we ditched Jeff Bird, who looks like a hippie, we could cool up this band, you could look sleek and groovy and hip. Michael knew to keep people away from me. He dealt with that. That stuff is not what we're about, and he fought those battles. I knew what was going on, but I was just allowed to get on and wear my long skirts. And they'll never be short – certainly not now, anyway!

"They do try to shape you, especially in the early days when I was getting my picture taken everywhere. I always ran it past Mike – *Vogue* wants my picture, the record company are really excited, but is there any purpose to it? If Mike thought I should do it, I'd do it, because it would help the band. Then there were those where he said, 'Do it if you want, for your vanity or because it's fun to be in *Vogue*, no problem – but it won't make any difference to the band, won't sell us any more records.'

"That was really great, it helped a lot because, back then, God, they'd have me doing anything and everything, and it was hard. That contributed to me getting ill during the *Caution Horses* tour, just because there was so much. I'm not the sort of person who says 'no'. Ask me and I'll do it. It wasn't fun, I wouldn't want to go through it again. I'm as vain as any other woman, I like being pretty and all that, but I didn't need it. Even now, I still hate getting my picture taken. That period of my life was weird. I look back at magazines and go, 'Oh my God!' It helped us get off the ground, but I think that, if I'd been pushed too hard, I would have quit.

"None of that was what we were about. The name, the flowers onstage, all these things that we do, they came about pretty naturally, they weren't contrived. So the reason they've become an extension of what we do is because they always were a part of us, who we are. To be comfortable, cosy and protected is totally my personality; I'm constantly searching for comfort! It wasn't a manager or a company that came up and said, 'Margo, I've got this great idea: let's put flowers on the stage!' It was never that. And when they have come up with ideas, if they didn't suit, we didn't do them. Nothing we've ever done has been contrived or artificial."

The idea of selling Margo as "a sex babe" completely missed the point of what the Junkies were doing. They were not the hot date, they were not the quick fling, the instant gratification at night followed by the grubby feeling the following morning as you tried to slink away from the scene of the crime as quickly as possible. They required a courtship of sorts, an exploration, they demanded that you make a commitment over a period of time, gradually becoming more and more involved. It was the kind of relationship where you had to bring flowers – quite literally, as things turned out.

You also had to be willing to embrace change in the music, because Cowboy Junkies weren't simply willing to rehash former glories over and over again. Change had been subtle, incremental, over the course of those first three records, moving through the blues of *Whites Off Earth Now!!* through to the more country-tinged influence that had characterized *The Caution Horses* in particular. Though that record was a progression from *The Trinity Session*, it was the abortive Sharon Temple recordings that most suggested the next step, hinting at a more driving side to the band, one they hadn't yet captured on record. But, after another year touring, honing their craft and trying to capture the attention of concert-goers not always totally au fait with their songs, now they were ready.

A change in musical emphasis required shifts in their modus operandi. Where *The Caution Horses* had utilized the touring ensemble to good effect, now it was time to break up the band, at least in part. Although the spiralling sound of accordion and steel guitar was very much a signature, and something that could have stood further repetition, it was a stifling element for a songwriter who had new territories to cover. Changes had to be made.

Though Jeff and Jaro remained involved on *Black Eyed Man*, Kim Deschamps was long gone, a musical decision made easier by the clash

150

of personalities. The space suddenly freed up would prove critical as the music evolved, but just as important were choices made about the other side of the recording process, the actual capturing of the sound. *The Caution Horses* had seen the Junkies take a significant stride away from Peter Moore and the Calrec, a journey that was pretty much completed in recording *Black Eyed Man*, based around much more orthodox sessions. These sessions no longer required Moore, an omission that would have seemed unthinkable just three years earlier.

Yet, if you dug a little deeper, his departure from the producer's chair was a natural consequence of the change in recording, as Mike explains. "Maybe Peter's downfall is that people dismiss him because he is so blustery and they think he's bluffing, but he's not. He knows what he's doing – I guess it's just his enthusiasm. He's very passionate about what he does, he loves sound and he loves capturing it. We discovered very early on that, just as much as we love making music, he loves recording sound, right from being a kid. That was neat, because that was what we wanted. We didn't need to be influenced musically; we really just wanted somebody to capture what we're doing. He was perfect and that's why we still go to him for mastering and mixing sometimes. He loves music, but he cares ultimately about the quality of the sound and catching what it really is on tape. Even on those early records, I'd always been the producer in the sense that I handled the musical side of it and Peter was always recording. If he'd had his way, he'd have been called the recordist rather than the producer, but nobody would have understood it. If you go back to those first two records, especially, a lot of it came about because we weren't comfortable in a studio environment. Making *The Caution Horses* showed that we could handle that now, because we were more confident about ourselves."

For Moore, the parting was bittersweet, but he's realist enough to accept its inevitability. "I was sad to hand the reins over to other producers as it went on, but they're artists, so am I, and none of us wanted to repeat ourselves. But I did think there were a couple more records exploring the way we'd done the first two, to take it to another level. I enjoyed working with them, so just from that point of view I missed that. In hindsight, maybe it was the better decision to go off and do it differently. We're still talking about two or three very special records thirty years on. If we had done six or seven that way, maybe it would have watered down the impact."

After a garage, a church and a temple, there was no attempt to find an esoteric location for making music this time, the band surrendering instead to the more prosaic, but undeniably welcoming, surroundings of Grant Avenue in Hamilton, Ontario, Daniel Lanois' old studio. Before committing to it completely, the Junkies went there and recorded 'To Lay Me Down' for *Deadicated*, the Grateful Dead tribute record. Where covers had given the band their start, this time someone else's song signalled the end of an era, the final occasion when the *Caution Horses* band worked together. The elegiac nature of the performance was a perfect epitaph for that phase of Cowboy Junkies' career, clearing the decks for the next chapter.

The band's view of the studio was positive, so, as 1991 came to its close, the new record could begin to take shape, Bob Doidge and John Oliviera engineering with Mike producing, the Junkies typically working in rehearsal for the first three weeks of a month, then going to Hamilton for a week and recording a couple of songs at a time. Where previous recordings had been made in a band setting – even if it was something of a pick-up band for *Trinity Session* – by stepping off the treadmill, and leaving this an open-ended process, they were able to draft in individual players for specific songs, seeing what they might offer. It was a reflection of the increasing confidence of the core four in both their material and their playing, but, as Alan admits, it was a sometimes long-winded experience: "If you get lessons, you play all the licks that everybody knows. When we started using session guys on our records, it was really frustrating just trying to get them to play something interesting. Guitar players especially would just come in and wail away, and it took us a lot of time to get them to understand what we wanted – play less and do something interesting!"

One musician given that challenge was guitarist Ken Myhr, someone Mike had been keen to introduce to the ensemble. "Ken was a local guy that we knew in Toronto – I'd heard him play around town, he'd played with Jane Siberry on her records, I liked his style of playing, he was a nice guy – so I invited him to play on *Black Eyed Man* and he did three of the songs. When we came to tour, the *Caution Horses* band had played enough, and I wanted to hear something different, I wanted another guitar in there. I figured I was going to play a lot more rhythm, because that album is very rhythm-oriented, so I wanted to do that and have someone else to play lead."

Having lost the sound of steel guitar and accordion, to dispense with Mike's lead playing on some songs was another big step, and one which unnerved some fans, including "Cookie Bob" Helm: "When the album was released, I recall being somewhat disappointed that they had added a guitar player – a *lead guitar* player at that! I have always thought that Mike has a most original and distinctive guitar style, and I initially regarded Ken Myhr as an interloper. But I loved *Black Eyed Man* right out of the gate. I thought that the new, more upbeat sound suited them well, and proved that they were growing beyond the languid sound and reserved tempos that they were known for."

Above all else, *Black Eyed Man* is a record of maturity and of confidence. It's a record made by a band which has, to use the cliché, paid dues, as Mike agrees. "Through the late 1980s and into the 1990s, we toured nonstop and made records in between spells on the road, lived what we could of our lives in between tours. When I got married, we had a three-day honeymoon and then I headed off on tour; same with Margo when she got married. Looking back, it seems crazy. At that time, we'd been a band for a few years. We'd toured a lot as an indie band, which was something Al and I recognized even with Hunger Project: that you really became a band on the road and onstage; that's where you learn about each other, learn how to play. That road dog thing was fine, and really, whenever anybody offered us a gig, we'd take it because we were pleased anybody would want us. We hadn't learned to say 'no' at that point, because we were so hungry for gigs.

"The record company loved that, management loved it and we had two and a half years going round the world, pretty much working nonstop. We were opening ten shows for Bruce Hornsby and, halfway through, Marg got ill. I don't know when we'd have stopped, otherwise. Something good came out of it in the end – we stopped, we took a break for the first time since *Trinity* took off, and it was a chance to think about where we wanted to go next.

"I had some lyrics on scraps of paper, some musical ideas, but now I had time to look at them away from the tour bus. I realized it was time to break up the big band, the Jeff/Kim/Jaro thing, just so that we could approach the next record in a totally different way. I didn't want to make another *Caution Horses*, the same way we hadn't wanted to make another *Trinity Session*. Looking back, that break after *The Caution Horses* was a nice breathing space, even though it came about in a bad way."

Stepping off the treadmill also gave them a chance to reassess, and to work more thoroughly on the material Mike had sketched out on the road. Or scribbled out on the road, more accurately, most of his lyrical ideas jotted down on hotel stationery and the backs of menus in a few snatched moments as the tour bus rolled across the continent, then across the world. As Mike said, "We were pretty much at burnout, and Margo getting sick brought that home to us. We needed to take a break, go and rediscover our normal lives and get away from each other and the music for a little while, and figure out what we wanted to do next.

"There were a lot more rock elements to that than anything else. On *The Caution Horses*, I was very conscious of what was going to happen to the songs once I gave them to Margo. On this one I wanted to see what would happen when Margo took a song that I hadn't manipulated for her voice.

"Margo and I sat down before recording, and I decided I wanted to write in a different fashion and Margo decided she wanted to refine her singing style. I decided I wasn't going to even consider her when I was writing, because I think, in the past, I might have been writing a song and thinking in terms of subject matter and I wasn't sure if Margo could pull it off. So I decided I wasn't going to do that. I came up with some songs that ordinarily I don't think I would have written. Then I just gave them to her and she had to deal with them and work out different styles for herself, which pushed her, too. So we pushed out our own self-imposed limits. I see it as an advancement, exploring the sound of the band and a certain style of song.

"*Black Eyed Man* was a record where we wanted to break away a little bit from the sound which everyone was calling 'New Country', which was weird anyway. I've never really seen any of our records as country records, whatever people say – we never approach them as that. We just have songs. The structures of the songs on *Black Eyed Man* are pretty weird. I can't even remember the headspace I was in to write those, because they're pretty strange. When we play them now, they're really odd, they don't make any sense. Which was good, actually, to move things around. It was the most narrative record we'd done – for me, writing-wise, every song was a little story unto itself, a short story, very focused on narrative."

It's tempting to argue that, with the number of changes that had been made, the *Black Eyed Man* sessions were experimental in tone, but that suggests that the band didn't have a final destination in mind. That's some way from the truth, because Mike and Alan in particular had a clear plan, as Mike explains: "Musically, I wanted to have tons of different instrumentation, different people coming in. There's tons more we didn't use, just using different combinations. It was the first record where we worked the studio – a lot of the playing is live, but you could go and erase something now. You could put a bed down of guitar, bass and drums and then add something on top."

David Houghton underlines the importance of the studio setting on this recording: "Although it sounds isolating, I love coming into a recording studio and overdubbing. It focuses the player and the producer on a single instrument, putting it in the spotlight before it settles back into the mix. Mike gave everyone freedom musically, but when he had a suggestion, it was taken seriously. Mike knew what he wanted instinctively. Even the unorthodox suggestions he made almost always improved the songs."

Alan's view is that "We had a lot of musicians on *Black Eyed Man* because we felt more comfortable in the studio by then. It was more of a pieced-together record because there were so many players involved. The songs were pretty complex structurally, very dense, and that was a direction that carried on with *Pale Sun*, too. That was a lot of work to get those songs ready and then they go through changes as you're rehearsing them, and as you record them, even. The four of us pretty much knew what we wanted to do, we got that down as the basic sound, and then the other players came in and added their parts, they tried different things. None of them were rehearsed, like *Trinity* in that sense; they just came to the studio and did their parts, so it moved the songs around a little bit. You use other musicians, you have to accept that your original ideas will change, or what's the point using them? You want another perspective. But we knew when it was going in a good direction or a bad one."

David Houghton concurs with that, saying, "I enjoyed the *Black Eyed Man* sessions, because we were able to toy with a lot of different ideas, without the constraints of time. I tried a lot of different instruments. We even recorded a timpani part on one of the songs which, thankfully, we discarded."

While the music was going through changes, so too were Mike's lyrical preoccupations, which stretched a little further from home, ensuring *Black Eyed Man* was even more markedly different from its predecessors. The songwriting went through the roof, the material appearing apparently from nowhere. Actually, that's not quite true. It appeared from the middle of nowhere, according to Mike: "Movement was a very creative thing with this record. It was the whole rock'n'roll, on-the-road romance, coming into a town like gypsies, doing a show, then moving on. The song ideas got filed away on napkins and hotel stationery, to be worked on later when life settled down. But, on the tour, we just kept moving, and the ideas kept coming."

The grinding schedule took them out of Toronto and out of their own lives, in a sense. Perhaps that's why the songs were suddenly short stories set to music. "Cause Cheap Is How I Feel' had pointed to that direction, but now it was fully realized, a host of characters inhabiting this music, so much so that this was a record of life in the towns and hamlets of North America. Yes, relationships and their implications were still very much at the core, but these were in specific geographic settings, towns they'd passed through over the previous couple of years. Mike's recollection is that "I definitely wanted to do that, so each song had its own plotline and there is a very Southern feeling. A lot was written in Virginia, when I had met Patty, my wife, who lived in Richmond, so I spent a lot of time there. I was inspired by the surroundings, by the people down there and by meeting her. That was a part of it – the imagery comes from that place."

Jason Lent picked up on that and even used it at college later. "My first project was to produce a biography and I wanted to bring my interests in literature and music together, and the only way I could do that was to do a piece on Michael. One of the ideas for the project was to do a sketch on someone just by using existing information. There was an unofficial website back then, just a message board where you posted a message one after the other. There was no continuity, no thread, you had to skip around, just a lot of Post-it Notes on top of one another. David Houghton used to drop in and interact with us, passing on messages from the band and so on, and he helped me out, pointed me in some interesting directions with the lyrics because I was trying to find the connection between his writing and traditional literature, particularly the Southern Gothic writers like [William] Faulkner and [Flannery] O'Connor, and David confirmed some things for me. That album was a big part of my research in trying to make those connections, trying to figure out how Michael was writing in this very American style while coming from Canada. I remember the professor really picked apart 'Oregon Hill', how the first verse was very wonderfully written and the second was more clichéd, and that he felt that was because he wasn't from America and was falling back on clichés. I didn't agree with that analysis, but just the fact that we were discussing that as part of grad school was great!"

Black Eyed Man is also a document of the times, times when Western economies were in deep recession, times when, in the US, Bill Clinton was about to sweep past an incumbent president who had enjoyed historically high approval ratings at midterm, the sudden shift summed up by the Clintonian catchphrase "It's the economy, stupid!" Although the reference points were clear, that conceptual element was largely incidental, according to Mike. "I guess it does cover the decay of small-town America. That and what they call 'family values' now. But I wasn't writing from that point of view. The record is conceptual in that it's a little short-story book, they're all little stories with characters.

"The small-town thing could be because I wrote a lot down there, a lot on the road because we were touring so much, a lot of the ideas came from the road. You get a sense of America as you tour it and at that time, the industrial world as we grew up in it was disintegrating around us. I can't say it was conscious but certainly we were going through that whole rust belt area of New York, Ohio, all that, you'd travel through places and just think, 'My God, this place is gone. Where do these people go now?' In the South, into Richmond, that's like that, a once great city, the centre of the Confederacy, and now it's decayed. I wasn't consciously writing of that, but that was my environment, so it seeps in.

"'The Last Spike' definitely has that feel to it. It was something we approached in many different ways and finally we stripped it down and ripped it out. That is about the death of a dream, really, inspired by the shutting down of small-town Canada; then there's the personal element of the character losing her dreams. It's one of very few songs we've done where there is no hope. That one's done!"

The rust belt seeps into the stories, decaying towns disappearing in front of their people's eyes as collapsing industries took everybody and everything down with them. No, the songs aren't necessarily or obviously or consciously even about that – 'The Last Spike' apart – but so many of them are infused with a helplessness, a sense of being out of control that goes behind the emotional terrain of *The Caution Horses* and touches more on the external situation, the way the outside world – in this case, the economy – can devastate the personal, a realization that would later lead to the recording of *Early 21st Century Blues*, albeit in different circumstances. So many of the situations on the record involve people whose lives are out of kilter, not just in terms of relationships but because they seemingly have no future because their work, their money, their hope, is gone. There are different responses to that in the songs, but it seems to be a bubbling undercurrent, economics bringing a hardship and an edge to already struggling relationships, making personal issues harder to handle. Arguing is one thing, but arguing when you have no way to pay the rent or the mortgage is another. Maybe it's that struggle that finally pushes someone into murder in the trailer park, or simply into dreaming of that freedom of a horse in the country as opposed to the daily drudgery of the nine-to-five in a world where you can't even rely on a pint of milk any more.

At times, *Black Eyed Man* is a sombre record, one part of its brief summed up by 'The Last Spike' and the line "These foolish dreams must stop". But, again, it's one of contradiction, of paradox, where nothing is quite as straightforward as it seems, because amid all that turmoil it's also a hopeful record, one about love found, an understandable preoccupation given Mike's circumstances.

Another paradox comes out of one of the defining characteristics of *Black Eyed Man*, the musical shift away from the country elements that were upfront on *The Caution Horses*. Oddly, then, one of the founding fathers of the record was Townes Van Zandt, a legend of that scene, and an increasing influence on the band, as Jeff Bird explains. "Townes was one of those mad genius people. Difficult to deal with in the real world. I played with him onstage, which was great. He tried to be on the wagon on that tour, but there was one show in LA where he got really hammered and playing with him then – oh, oh! The tempos were about half-speed, but the show turned out fine. He was very deeply troubled, but also a very happy guy at times. He struggled with that schizophrenic, bipolar situation. I got on the bus one day and there were a lot of people there, and he was sitting in the back and he said, 'Man, I was sitting out there and I was trying so hard to think of something good.' He just found it so hard to deal with all those people. When he did get drunk, he was very nasty about it, kind of abusive. His son said that he could get really mean, he knew what buttons to push, but he was pretty good when he was on tour with us. He did the exact same set every night – the same patter, even – but it seemed like every night you'd hear the same song and a layer would drop away and become this whole other thing. It was like they were bottomless. Deceptively simple on the surface, but there was so much inside them. A line would go by and you'd suddenly think, 'Holy fuck!' While you're doing that, three more have gone past and you're trying to keep up!"

Touring with Townes was a big influence on Mike's songwriting, as he's the first to admit. "I didn't know him, really, growing up – maybe John had a couple of his records, but I didn't start to listen to him intensely until *Trinity Session* or *Caution Horses*. We toured with him on *Caution Horses*, which was huge for me. I talked to him about songwriting, watched him play every night and saw how he approached his songs. Many nights he'd sit after the show, play his songs and tell us what they were about. That made me start to think about how what a song is and what it's about can be two completely different things, so I really started to explore what songwriting was all about.

"Townes taught me about taking a subject and coming at it from a completely different angle, so that the listener doesn't necessarily know the specific scene or story that you are writing about, but understands the idea or the meaning that you're trying to get across. He was brilliant at that – you listen to his songs, and you get the feeling there's a story going on. You couldn't necessarily say what the story's about, but you certainly understand the underlying emotion.

"He was a very odd spirit in a lot of ways, and I think he only lasted as long as he did because he had some more songs to write. He wasn't here for anything other than to write songs, which is good enough reason. Townes lived on the road and loved it, and seeing him doing that, after so many years, it reinforced a lot of the things we believed in. He wrote 'Cowboy Junkies Lament' about the band. When he gave it to me, I was really flattered, then I sat and tried to work with it and in the end, I had to call him and say, 'Townes, you gotta give me a hook here, give me a clue, how's this one work, what's it about?' All he said was, 'Well, one verse is about you, another is about Margo and the other is about Pete.' When I stopped to look at it, then I got it, his observations of how we relate to each other and the world, that's really cool." It's also weirdly appropriate, and a sign of Van Zandt's insight, that Alan – the bass player so committed to standing in the shadows – doesn't get a verse.

The Van Zandt trilogy that ends the record exists almost as a separate entity from the rest of the material. In response to "Cowboy Junkies Lament", Mike penned his take on Townes and his addition to Junkie life on the road – dice. Gambling was a problem that dogged Townes all his life, and perhaps Mike's song was as much a cautionary tale aimed at his mentor as anything else – a game that was going well turns sour on him, prompting the reminder, "Never count your winnings at hour 23, of a 24 hour drive", just a warning that, every now and again, you should quit while you're ahead. It's also a three-verse biography for both Townes and the Junkies, summing up the constant rumble of the tour bus, the claustrophobia of the back lounge and the camaraderie of the road, though (as a solo artist) that was something that Van Zandt oftentimes had to do without. That lonely road was hinted at again in the Junkies' reading of 'To Live Is to Fly', with lines like "It's goodbye to all my friends it's time to go again", "It don't pay to think too much on the things you leave behind" and "We all got holes to fill and them holes are all that's real".

The trilogy offered territory that the Junkies were only now ready to cover on record, particularly 'Townes' Blues'. It's unthinkable that they could have performed that song on *The Caution Horses*, though not on a musical front, albeit that it was looser than anything they'd attempted, and that Mike would have been unlikely to come up with the solo that Ken Myhr played, very un-Junkies but just right for the mood. The real shift was in the singer, in the way Margo approached and, particularly, performed the material. Anyone who had seen her concert persona in the past could not help but be shocked by the transformation from the timid, verging on catatonic, stage performance and the way she was suddenly teasing every last nuance out of 'Townes' Blues'. You could actually visualize her moving – swinging, even. It was joyously playful, gorgeously loose, a woman "enjoying this ride" at last.

Even brother Mike was taken aback. "I was listening to some early recordings recently for the download site, archival stuff from *Caution Horses*, and the way Margo is just so quiet, not just the singing, but her whole demeanour, it's very striking. That was her whole thing. But with *Black Eyed Man*, it's the first record we kind of worked at. The first three were just done, the first two in a day, then *Caution Horses* while we were touring. This time, we sat down and thought about it, what kind of record we wanted, how we wanted to make it – we took time to think it through. Margo started taking voice lessons at that point to try to expand what she did, and I think all that was part of it. We had time off, she bought into the idea that, 'OK, we're touring a lot, I'm onstage, I might as well figure out some persona here, reach out to the audience.' Vocally, too, those songs called for her to sing out a bit more – 'Murder', 'Southern Rain', they made new demands on her. And then just confidence from doing it.

"We also wanted to approach each song individually rather than the whole album being one long song. I wanted it to have different perspectives in each song. *Black Eyed Man* is full of characters and Margo just approached it like an actress, taking on different parts in different plays. And I guess that's why that record didn't connect so directly with people so quickly as the others. You have to take the characters in and then bring yourself to it, rather than it being laid out in front of you. I think she enjoyed the challenge."

'The Last Spike' is a song that could have sat comfortably on *The Caution Horses*, the sparse arrangement and Lewis Melville's banjo notwithstanding, but it does boast a more rounded vocal performance, poignant not cloying, just as the lyric is sympathetic but unflinching, a ruthless lack of sentimentality saving it from being dismissed as bleeding heart liberalism, a lyrical capacity Mike shared with Van Zandt. It is a song of its economic times, but it could just as easily be set in the dustbowl of a depression half a century before, a tale of people trapped by a bigger world that they can't control, where you do your best but still get steamrollered.

A similarly relentless gaze falls on the scene in 'This Street, That Man, This Life'. A very dark song, Pete's drumming is especially foreboding, though it's a record where the whole rhythm section shines. Mike's writing harks back to 'Sun Comes Up, It's Tuesday Morning' and "'Cause Cheap Is How I Feel', hard-boiled, journalistic in tone, matter-of-fact but with metaphors that are chilling: "That man stalks his victim like a cancer stalks a cell", a searing line that risks a listener's revulsion, dry, unsentimental, reminiscent of Cormac McCarthy. Its realism is perhaps a result of just that, its genesis a result of real events. "The first house that my wife and I lived in together, we discovered quite early on that on the street a few years earlier, a young girl had been abducted and then found in a freezer. There's that sense that you live your life, but really you have no clue what's happening down the street, what she just did, what that guy is about to do. We all just walk around and God knows how we're going to interact."

There's a genuine air of menace to the track, a Southern, swampy heat clinging to your shoulders, a sense that, for some, there never can be any hope of redemption – "That man's soul has left him, his heart's as deadly as a rusty nail". For all Mike's protestations that this is a record about love found, there are moments on *Black Eyed Man* that are bleaker than anything else in Cowboy Junkies' canon. When you've found all that you want, the horror of losing it all suddenly becomes more real.

The sequencing is crucial, too, the downshift of 'This Street, That Man, This Life' coming after a more upbeat opening than fans were used to, laying down the groundwork for a different kind of record, the band setting off into more aggressive territory. 'Southern Rain', released as a single, is probably their best offering to that market to date, the influence of Ken Myhr coming to bear, Mike conceding that he brought a *Rubber Soul* feel to the music, "with all those weird little licks he played, very much that kind of Beatles thing from that period". This is as close as the Junkies get to West Coast, driving-with-the-top-down music, so it's appropriate that, musically, the song stands on the shoulders of 'Day Tripper', Alan offering another interpretation of McCartney's playing to complement Myhr's work.

Just as the band are putting down a marker with the music on 'Southern Rain', Mike's choppy rhythm guitar a fresh trademark, so Margo is breathing fiery confidence into every line, the apologetic tone of some previous recordings long gone. "I never thought I'd tire of a dollar" is as striking in its way as "We are miners, hard rock miners" had been two records before. This is the sound of a woman who knows her voice is worth puncturing the silence with. And then there's a central Junkies couplet, snuck in there just below the radar, but the line on which the song rises, the more you listen. "It'll never cease to amaze me, how a little rain can drive folks crazy", nails the way mankind always has to find something wrong with their lot, however good it might be, that we can find mountainous problems in the tiniest speck of irritation. It's a recurring theme through their work, a gentle admonishment that, for all that Cowboy Junkies are supposedly the experts on misery, it's we who are the architects of our own dissatisfaction.

'Oregon Hill' is next up, autobiographical in the sense that Mike was writing about a certain time and place in his own life, of the snatched moments spent with his wife to be in Richmond, the luxury of a few days of sleeping in before heading back to Toronto to record or head out onto the next leg of a tour somewhere. It's an exuberant effort, with echoes of The Band, but also of Dixieland jazz courtesy of tuba and trombone accompaniment, further placing it in the South.

A deceptively simple song on the surface, the joyousness of the performance sweeping you away initially, delving a little deeper reveals layers of imagery that would again be among Mike's lyrical preoccupations for years to come. "I guess there's some Catholic guilt there! It's a very real song, it's the place where my wife lived in Richmond, Virginia, a little redneck enclave, so all the things in there are real, except I changed the circumstances. There's Catholic guilt in all my songs! My wife always tells me I'm guilty about everything; there's definitely a residue of that upbringing in my life."

Sin and guilt, played out ahead of a backdrop of the most hedonistic music there is, the sound of New Orleans jazz horns, 'Oregon Hill' is uproarious, the most fun they'd yet committed to tape. It opens with an impressionistic evocation of the steamy landscape and its steamier people – if you can't see those girls on the porch "comparing alibis", you ain't listening – before religious imagery lies down with our baser instincts, the sacred and the profane. You've got your "Baptists celebrating with praises to the Lord", while those rednecks celebrate with gin and "me and Suzy" celebrate by not getting out of bed, which turns out to be both the pit of sin and the safe harbour amid a Sunday-morning jailbreak, different transgressors breaking free. Who it is that's doing the most celebrating is left to your imagination, but it sure seems like everyone's having a good time in their different ways. But then the guilt kicks in ...

It's a song of joyous contrasts as well as a song of thinly veiled autobiography – surely it's Mike who comes in and out of Oregon Hill in the breaks in his schedule? The prison to the north – is it too much to see that as Toronto, the place where he has to return on Monday morning, a journey that can't even be lifted by those country songs? The points of the compass are all represented, all feeding out from the centre, now transplanted to Oregon Hill and his emotional centre. So much goes on in each line – the college has to be to the east, to learn where sin begins, the college that educates us in the classics but where plenty of us got the chance to do a little life learning of a different kind, revelling in a

163

first taste of freedom. But the east also hints at the origins of biblical sin, sins that can be washed away in the huge river to the south of them, the cleansing James River, already namechecked in 'Southern Rain' as the source of stormy weather. Only a good Catholic boy, even a lapsed one, would be so preoccupied with washing his sins away.

The record is populated with sinners in all sorts of guises, and you're not always looking in the right direction for them. The title track is a perfect case in point – after all, how much more sinister can you get than a black-eyed man? – though, as Jason Lent notes, "It reads to me like a vignette on a very common Southern story: the white girl screaming 'rape' after seducing the black-'eyed' man." As the song develops, he's the victim in a song about scapegoats, another reflection of the political climate of the time. In terms of the narrative, Margo is the villain of the piece, the sultry femme fatale in a blackly comic film noir, all Lauren Bacall all of a sudden, another indication of the distance she's travelled between records. Without that delivery, the song could fall flat, but instead it bubbles along on the breath of betrayal, the man framed for poisoning the town well by his girl, grown tired of his failure to deliver the careless early promises of a lover, falling "short a star or two". One betrayal begets another in her world view, not only framing him but hanging him out to dry, testifying: "He did things to me of which I dream of still". A nightmarish vision of assault that seals his fate, but is it really more a memory of sensual fireworks, as Margo's vocal hints? Nothing is as it seems with 'Black Eyed Man'. Even Margo's apology is for her own good – "I feel better now, do you?" Like she cares. As with 'Forgive Me' on *Whites Off Earth Now!!*, this is absolution born of brutality: "I confessed, I'm off the hook."

Just as 'Forgive Me' had a relationship with 'Me and the Devil', so 'Black Eyed Man' and 'Murder, Tonight, in the Trailer Park' are uneasy bedfellows, but bedfellows nonetheless, both songs being updates of the material from their debut. Mike's assessment is, "'Murder' is a Robert Johnson view of humanity. In Virginia, there are those communities everywhere. Every night on the news there'll be a little murder happening here, another there, so I wanted to do this weird little murder mystery, who did it and why, nobody knows, nobody cares, there's no real reason, it just happens. I wrote it real fast."

That urgency is in the performance, but it's a performance born of imagination, not experience, as Mike is at pains to point out. "People often ask if I want to take these stories away from songs and actually write short stories. I'd love to have time to do it one day, but I'd need a year or so to figure out what I'm doing. I'm not going to pretend I can write a short story just because I can write a song. I'd like to experiment with it, but it means not working for two years and I can't afford to do that at this point. Maybe when I get older! But it's not autobiography. A lot of songs have nothing to do with me in that sense, they're short stories. 'Murder, Tonight, in the Trailer Park' is a short story, there are tons of songs like that. There's always an element of personal experience in most of the songs, but the great majority of it is fleshed out by imagination. You're not a journalist, you're not documenting what's going on, you're creating something out of a situation. It was the same in the studio, trying to get that mood. Tony Quarrington played on it first – he's a great jazz guitarist who has worked a lot with Jeff – and he took the song into a whole other area, and that put a more structured and fusion feel on it, which was really great, but it lost that trashiness we wanted. Ken Myhr came in and did his version, and we pieced his guitar work with some of Tony's and created the song." And then you have Alan's propulsive 'Paperback Writer' bass part. You might recall that, earlier, Peter Moore said, "Al is a motherfucker on bass." Damn right he is.

Revisiting characters, places, ideas has long been a Junkies trait, never so strongly as in 'A Horse in the Country', which sounds like a sequel to 'Misguided Angel', the passion of that youthful relationship having settled into the mundane, the spark gone and all that's left is a twentysomething girl with a whole lot of life ahead of her and nothing to look forward to. "I guess it is a kind of part two of 'Misguided Angel'," admits Mike. "I have the same relationship to both songs. We've played it a lot, I kinda became bored by it, it's very formal, but we brought it out and did it acoustically and I realized there was something to it. It's a bit complex, the metaphors are a bit odd, but it fits in with the continuum, so I like that about it." And that one-way subway ticket at the end, does it offer the salvation of escape? "Or there's no return, is the other way of looking at it!"

But there is a return of sorts, because just as the song looks back it also hints of the themes that were to come in *At the End of Paths Taken*, the frustration at the unrealistic expectations that we all have, that it should always be like the excitement that's held in that first flush of love. 'A Horse in the Country', melancholy as it is, does lay the groundwork for the reality of life, getting through every day, that there will be mouths to feed, shoes to buy, rent to pay, tears to dry. It is how it is, so best go find the joy in that.

'Winter's Song' is one of those that could have easily slotted into *The Trinity Session* or *The Caution Horses*, a delicate waltz in the style of 'To Love Is to Bury'. A last trace of that lovely interplay between mandolin and accordion, Jeff and Jaro decorate the song quite beautifully alongside Dave Allen's fiddle, Mike's lyrics poetic, a contrast to 'If You Were the Woman and I Was the Man', which, as he says, "was written in the style of that Tin Pan Alley sound of the 1930s, those Depression ballads". From the Great Depression, to the worldwide recession, it was still the economy, stupid …

'If You Were the Woman' is one of the odder songs in the repertoire. A period piece, it doesn't sit with the rest of the songs, a success in that sense given that Mike wanted songs to have a different character rather than all be of a certain style. Yet, where the other musicians add to the songs elsewhere, and where even on this tune Spencer Evans' clarinet is simply gorgeous, having another voice sharing the spotlight with Margo seems to clutter things, even though the song is blatantly a duet.

Finding the voice was a long and tortuous process, as Mike explains. "We went through all these names. My first idea was to get Tony Bennett to do it, because it was a perfect crooner song. This is way before his big comeback. I took it to the record company, because I thought they could help me get in contact and it was just met with total derision. 'Tony Bennett? Are you kidding? Come on, he's finished, washed up!' So I was never able to reach him. Two years later, he's totally back on the scene, so that tells you about record companies.

"We tried Lyle Lovett, we'd toured with him, done some songs onstage with him, but he never got back to us, and then we tried Jimmie Dale Gilmore, who we got to know through Townes. He came in, did a version, but it didn't work. His and Margo's voices didn't sit together. In the end, I think it was Graham, Margo's husband, who said, 'What about John Prine?' We called him up, we had no connection with him, but he was happy to do it, he flew in a week later, did it, it worked perfectly. We hung out that night, got along really well, and from that we did a split-bill tour in the US, which was great for us. It introduced us to his audience and it was a really nice experience."

Black Eyed Man is one of the richest records the Junkies have made, one of the strangest, opaque yet outward-looking, layered but punchy. It is a record of wilful change, of less nuance perhaps, but one where you have to dig deeper. On every level, *Black Eyed Man* is an enigma.

The final word belongs to Mike. "It wasn't a record that gripped you immediately in the same way the others had. The first three were very live records, very organic, you get a sense from them straight away. The four of us recorded this live but it was the first time we really added overdubs, brought people in to try different things, and it was our first time really working in a studio, so it all made it a different kind of recording. Now I look back on it, I think the songs are very strong. There's a unity of theme to it, it's about me falling in love with my wife, that's the period we met and those are the themes. The sense of mystery, of starting something fresh, all the things that go with it, you break with your past life, start a new one, these two unknowns coming together. I wanted every song to have an element of that; there are a lot of characters in there. When we were rehearsing for the 2005 'Blue States' tour, I had a bunch of songs from *Black Eyed Man* on the shortlist and Margo just turned to me and said, 'You know, Mike – we've played this album to death!'

"'Yeah, it's a really good record!'

"I do find it hard to get away from these songs, because I like them. I like them a lot."

ALL THESE WORDS THAT I SING

In his sleeve notes to Joni Mitchell's *Both Sides Now*, a collection made up mainly of cover versions, Larry Klein writes, "In singing these songs, I believe that Joni has achieved something quite extraordinary in that she has truly sung them as if, as Nietzsche would say, she has written them in her own blood."

In the post-Beatles culture, it's become commonplace, accepted – expected, even – that singers sing their own words and nothing but their own words, for they are the holders of the truth. They are, supposedly, the only ones who can bestow upon them the necessary passion and meaning. There are examples by the dozen of singers who've quit their band so they don't have to sing someone else's words. There's even a school of thought that implies that to sing anything but your own composition is bordering on deception. This is clearly a school that never invited Margo Timmins to sing at assembly.

If you hold to those rules and wish to be uncharitable, you might simply dismiss Margo as an actress – a very good one, but still an actress, playing a part in a song, singing someone else's life. She might even get a special dispensation, given that – for the most part – she's singing her brother's lyrics and so might have a special insight into them. But if you go back to the glory days of Tin Pan Alley, to the years when Sinatra and Fitzgerald were the greats, they were doing nothing but singing someone else's songs. And was Ella short on emotion? Whoever wrote it, once she had cast her spell, those words were Ella's, for she was a simply magnificent interpreter of the song. Yes, it's a different process to Lennon banging out 'Mother', but no less valid, exciting or affecting. In those days, Margo Timmins would have been every bit as successful as she is now, but maybe a little less misunderstood.

From the day Cowboy Junkies came into being, it was clear Margo could sing. From the second most people encountered her for the first time, singing 'Mining for Gold' at the beginning of *The Trinity Session*, they knew she had a uniquely beautiful instrument at her disposal. But singing tunefully is only a part of the interpreter's job. You have to crawl inside a song. Then you have to throw it out there again and, even as far in as *The Caution Horses*, she could struggle with those that called on her to sing out rather than look in. And then, on *Black Eyed Man*, the self-doubt has gone, and a different woman emerges, still singing like an angel, but chatting with the devil sometimes, too. From a girl to a woman is part of the journey, but it wasn't quite that simple. Life never is.

"Nowadays, I trust my voice, which is something I didn't always do. That adds a comfort zone. I know I can sing now. If you'd asked me in 1990 whether

168

I was a good singer, I don't know what I would have said. I don't think I'd have stood here and said, 'Sure, I am a good singer.' Now, I can; I feel that way. Whether people like it or not is another thing, but yes, I can control my voice, I know how to use it, I trust it. In the early days, I was waiting for it to disappear. 'Today will be the day I can't sing.' Isn't that weird? But I remember feeling like that. It felt like something that was given to me but could be taken away again. Now I realize that, unless I'm in a medical emergency, it's not going to leave me!"

For a band with such a strong body of recorded work, it's ironic that so much of the Junkies' story has been played out onstage. That is where their greatest strength lies, because they stand bare before the audience, without the distance lent by a record. While their recordings are honest, seeing them up close just reinforces how much they lack artifice, and the centrifuge of it all is Margo. The journey she has taken as live performer has fed into what she does as a singer in the studio, and then back again in a virtuous circle.

"Michael has always been amazing for me. Right from the beginning, he knew to push me, but never to push me further than I could go. He challenged me and I love that, but he never pushed it. If I wanted to turn my back on the audience when we started, I did. It's part of that honesty. If you listen to *Whites Off Earth Now!!*, we're not trying to do anything we can't do. Pete's just basically keeping time, there's no stops, nothing, because we couldn't do it. That's why it's like it is. And, if you go through our records, you watch us grow in our abilities, it's a very natural change. There was no conscious thing like, 'Margo, on this record you should push your voice this way' or 'Let's do a really hard blues number.' It's just been a case of, 'That's where we've got to, we can do that now'. Pete wasn't able to stop at the right time – took months of practice, but we got it.

"Same with being onstage. At first, I literally had my back to them, and the whole table-with-the-flowers thing started with a purpose. I put them there because I always drank tea onstage and I had to put it on the floor, which meant I had to bend down to pick it up. I didn't like that. Being modest, I didn't want everything falling out! So I got a table to put my tea on. At one point, our manager at the time said, 'I think it's time to get rid of the flowers now.' But it wasn't a gimmick, it was necessary. Where am I going to put my tea if the table goes? I still get lost and need to look at the flowers and figure out, 'What am I doing? I have no idea where I am in this song!' I still panic – it serves a purpose and it creates a certain atmosphere. I don't need the space for dancing round the stage! I've done things onstage that have embarrassed the boys, but they've never told me what to do or what not to do, they've allowed me to grow. Some nights I'm more chatty than others and, if I'm in a chatty mood, nobody tells me I'm ruining our cool. We all do what we feel is right. It's a natural extension of the records. If Mike's got a lot to say with words, it's a wordy record. If he wants to play guitar, it's a different sort of record."

169

Art, especially popular art, is a weird place, particularly as we as a culture seem to invest more and more belief in what it is that our artists tell us. I don't believe in Jesus Christ, but Coldplay, man, I've seen them, they're real. Jesus Chris, show us the path … Yet, for any musician, however much playing in a band might be a calling, it's still a job. Paradoxically, for all that some of them are giving themselves away through their songs, we're only getting to see a specific side of their personality, the bits they've chosen to show us, the elements that the industry then promotes. The rest of us, going to our daily job that we don't much care about, we tend to be more "real" simply because who cares about putting on a front during the nine-to-five, seven-days-a-week, fifty-two-weeks-a-year grind? Who can be bothered? For all that we beatify Bono or Bob, we actually know nothing about them and we know that, up there on that stage, they're going through their schtick, however heartfelt. With Cowboy Junkies, perhaps because the venues are more intimate, there is a feeling that this actually is who they are, up there or in the bar, and that is perhaps their greatest strength, the one that inspires such devotion among fans looking for a moment of integrity in a world of artifice. Al barely moves, Pete laughs a lot, Mike holds it together and Margo goes out and talks to you, that's how it is, on- and offstage. As David Houghton notes, "Margo is a shy person who has been thrust into the limelight. She has adjusted to the role and has become more and more comfortable." But it wasn't always that way, because she wasn't ready. Go back to tapes of them playing *The Trinity Session* or *The Caution Horses* tours, and Margo is verging on the catatonic up there. And then, someplace around 1991, it changed. How?

"We had some success – which helps, I guess – but I wasn't really comfortable. But that success meant we could choose who we wanted to open for us and we asked Townes Van Zandt to do *The Caution Horses* tour because we all loved him. Having Townes open for us seemed kinda wrong, we should have been opening for him! The fact he'd heard about us was amazing, and he was really excited about it. We never let anybody travel on our bus, but this was Townes, so we asked him and he agreed, which was incredible. Touring with Townes was a pivotal moment, because he realized that I was hesitant about my singing and about being onstage. If I was sitting on my own in the front lounge of the bus and Townes would come through and sit with me, I'd be freaking out inside: 'Oh my God, Townes Van Zandt is having a conversation with me!' Usually, he'd only come through to really tell me something. That was always a challenge, because he always talked in 'Townes words', which is different: 'What exactly did you say, what did you mean? I'm not sure. Can you say it again?!'"

"Townes was an interesting guy to travel with. He had his ups and downs, but he'd respect people's space, he'd go sit in a corner at the back if he was in a bad mood, but other nights, he'd come and sit up with us and play, explaining what the songs meant in that oblique way. 'Oh yeah, I get it! No, I don't – what did he say?' One night, he addressed every song straight to the bus driver, who

170

was this heavy, KKK type of guy, just breaking him down with one song after another, disarming him. Townes was an amazing man, just amazing.

"One time, he just sat down and said he was a singer and a songwriter, that's what he was born to be, and that if the world didn't recognize it, it didn't matter. And he was telling me that that was the same for me. He said that I had a gift and that I had to believe in it and enjoy it and realize it really is a gift. That's not just some phrase. It means you were actually given something. I really believe Townes could never have been anything but a singer-songwriter. That's just what he had to be, whether it was gonna kill him, which it did, or whatever. I don't have that, but I think what he was saying to me was that I was given this beautiful voice, so don't be afraid of it. Go and use it. Let it be. That was huge, because here was an icon in my life, telling me that I had a gift. And Townes didn't bullshit! He didn't use false words, ever. Hearing that was huge for me. Huge. Not that I was going to quit, but it made me realize that I was more than just a little sister tagging along. This was what I was supposed to do. I think that helped me look out at the audience more and have some contact with them instead of shying away from them.

"From there, I felt more comfortable, but it was still something that I looked on as work, I guess, something I had to really concentrate on and do well, and I'd put a pressure on myself. Then when we made *Black Eyed Man*, John Prine toured with us and that was another big moment for me. He gave me this idea that this job could be fun. Townes didn't say, 'Have fun.' That wasn't his thing! It was more serious for him. He just said I was gifted, this was my life, there was no other choice for me, good or bad. John's message was 'Enjoy it, don't be afraid, you own the stage, this is the moment you command.' That was a huge change for me. I always liked to sing, but being onstage was a little weird. But once he gave me that permission to enjoy it, it all started to make sense. I don't have to be tall, be thin, be anything, I just have to sing well and enjoy that. John would get up onstage every night and just do his thing, and that was great to see.

"I hung out a lot with John, not so much with Townes – we were on the bus, but I didn't go drinking alone with Townes – but John was that kind of guy, I enjoyed his company, so I did. I liked his spirit and that was another turning point. I didn't realize it could be fun, because I guess we were trying so hard. I'd join John every night and do 'Angel from Montgomery' and his stage felt different. The feel of his band and what was going on was so much lighter and easier and more fun than when I stepped on my stage. And, over the years, we've become much more that way, we have way more fun than we did.

"So those two helped me get to the point where I started to feel comfortable. If you let go of what you think people expect of you, you can be just who you are and that's where the fun comes in. Nowadays, after the show, people say, 'On the records you're so dark, mysterious, cool, you're so this or that, then you're standing here smiling and laughing,' and I can see they're confused! That used to upset me; now it doesn't. In the beginning, it hurt. Records, and videos especially, are just images – now, you're seeing something live, this is who I am. If you came into my house, it would be exactly the same, except I wouldn't have makeup on and my hair wouldn't be done. That's how I want it to be."

Having seen Cowboy Junkies perform over many years, having heard the records, having grown with them, it's easy to take for granted what it is that they've become. But, as Margo's eldest brother, John, says, every now and again you just catch a memory of a shy girl doing anything to hide away from the glare of the spotlight. "I never would have guessed that Margo would be such a presence in front of a live audience, it's almost two shows for the price of one: the music and Margo. That was never apparent to me in our younger days, that she had that in her. I'm still very impressed by that, by the way she talks to the audience. It's such a great raconteur approach to things, sitting there, telling her stories. That in itself is a talent, a skill.

"She's so at home there, you are in her living room. She believes that there is a space in which everyone is comfortable and the stage is hers. That was very revealing to me. It's not the privacy of her country house, it's the stage, she really feels at home there. I can't even begin to recognize that, I don't have that feeling, that experience of it. But I guess she would have to find that sort of comfort to still be doing it, to still get on a bus with twelve guys, to leave her son at home for a couple of weeks. There's got to be a powerful attraction in that stage, a revivifying thing for her; otherwise, how could she take on a tour? The thing that is striking is that the person standing and talking on that stage is the same person that I know away from the stage. She doesn't have to change hats to be comfortable, she doesn't put on a persona. Again, that is the egolessness of it. I think that that egolessness is at the heart of the success of this whole thing. I think their story is a primer on Zen rock'n'roll, because that lack of ego is everything that the music business is *not* about."

"It's interesting John would say that I'm most at ease onstage of anywhere," reflects Margo. "I think he's right. When I turned 40, which is never a good thing for anybody, especially a woman, I told Mike that for my birthday I want to be onstage. 'Find me a gig, don't care what it is, get me up there.' I didn't want a big party, I didn't want a surprise, I didn't want a Mercedes or anything special! I just wanted to be onstage. We did a literacy benefit for adults, it was in Buffalo, it was easy to get to, and it was good. That says it all. To me that was what made me happy. If I have to turn 40, put me on a stage, put me where I'm happiest. That is where I'm most comfortable, and that's such a nice thing, because in the past, believe me, it wasn't like that.

"I think a lot of it is age, experience. When you're younger, you feel you're supposed to be hip, whether you're onstage or not. You're supposed to be cool, you're supposed to be thin, you're supposed to be tall, be a redhead, you're always supposed to be something you're not, and you're always searching for it. I think that's a part of the journey in your youth; you're a little bit confused, but then you reach a point where you settle into what you are. Or you don't sometimes, but hopefully you can. Specific people along the journey have had a huge impact, but at some point, I realized, 'I like being up here! This is fun!' I didn't feel that I had to prove anything. I had to do a good show, I always feel that, but I didn't have to be thin or tall or pretty or old or young or sexy or cool or whatever. I just had to sing well. That's the only responsibility I have. When that came to me, it made life a lot easier. And it also made music more fun, too, because in rehearsal I'll experiment a lot, but, get onstage, it was all about doing well, doing the right thing. When you experiment, you make mistakes, but then I realized mistakes weren't so terrible onstage any more than in the rehearsal room, I felt I could play around more with it and that's great. We're looser and we're more fun because of that."

Somewhere along the way, the voice became Margo, and Margo became the voice. She's reached a point where all her life is in that sound, in the delivery, in the inflections, in the way she talks to the audience, the way she sniggers over a dropped lyric. She is not simply defined by her voice, but to have a life without singing is surely unthinkable, because it is such a huge part of who she is at this point, professionally and, more important, personally.

One story is specially revealing.

"Years ago, I went to Tibet with my husband. We went in November, it was very cold and, rather than being in our tents at the base camp, we went to a nearby monastery and asked the monks if we could sleep in their sheep shed, just to get out of the wind. They said we could; they invited us in. We sat around and tried to talk. We had a bunch of pictures of family and where we came from to share with people, because it was the only way we had of communicating. I think somebody brought a picture of me singing the national anthem at a baseball game – me, alone, with all these people watching, and they explained I was a singer. So the monks started to sing for me. At this point, I'm delirious, I have altitude sickness, a cold, I'd banged my head on the sheep-shed door, bleeding from my forehead! Everything, just out of it! I was in bad shape! Graham was trying to build a fire with yak dung, which is pretty hard to light – you have to be Tibetan to work that one out – so it was really cold. Jeff Long, a mountain climber who was with us, he was stuffing Hershey bars into me for the sugar, and I was saying, 'I don't eat chocolate, it's fattening!'

"The monks finished singing, and then Jeff said, 'They want you to sing for them.' 'What?' The weird thing is that, when I'm uncomfortable or sad or nervous, I will often sing under my breath, to myself. I'd been trying to get warm, figure out where I was, looking at these dead animals hanging from the ceiling, and I was singing to myself. Jeff said, 'They want you to sing for them.' I don't like singing that way. I don't go to a party or a wedding and sing for people. You gotta pay me! That's not my personality, but I wanted to sing because I was so out of body and I needed to get comfortable. So I started singing and I found myself singing this Elvis Presley song that I'd never sung in my life, and it always shocked me that I sang it. 'Are You Lonesome Tonight?'

I sang that to them and they all started to throw rice at me, which I think is a good thing. I'm not sure. I hope so! And then somebody put another Hershey bar in my mouth. Graham says he left me going into a coma, went away to stoke the yak-dung fire, came back into the room to check I wasn't dead, and, 'There I find you singing Elvis Presley!' That was a pretty wild experience."

Spaced out or not, the Margo Timmins that she's become is more assured and more confident about her role onstage and in the band, and there's nothing stronger, more charged, than that. Cowboy Junkies know who they are, and onstage Margo is the embodiment of that.

Jeff Bird: "I think we are happy with silence, musically and just in our everyday lives, too. I think that's a maturity thing, being comfortable with silence. My wife says that about Margo, that her singing commands the silence really well. I've done some recordings with her with other players and she can just leave her voice hanging after she's finished a line. It isn't like nothing's going on. That silence has a huge presence and that's what she's doing – she's commanding it. When you're a kid, you're mad! You've got to make a lot of noise! You're finding your way. It takes maturity to understand silence."

Luka Bloom, who toured with the Junkies in Margo's more introspective period just after *The Caution Horses*, points to the fact that, back then, she was graduating from making a pretty sound to having a voice. "They capture who they are on record. There are certain artists who, if you hear thirty seconds of one of their songs, you know who it is. That is the mark of something unique and that is true of Cowboy Junkies. I would give Margo a lot of credit for that, because she has an incredibly distinctive style of delivery, it's completely unique. It's so patient, so languid and sometimes you're there wanting her to hurry up! But she doesn't – she hangs back and she delivers the lyric in exactly the way she wants to, and you end up being completely seduced by that."

And, when she's really on, she owns not only the stage, but the crowd, whether it's in the Palace Theatre, Manchester, New Hampshire or the Irving Plaza, New York City, two deeply contrasting shows on consecutive nights, the second and third dates on the June 2005 tour. The first was in a sedate theatre setting, a benefit for a local Children's Aid Society. A rapt, attentive crowd, hanging on every note. 'Cause Cheap Is How I Feel' is the second song in, the sound swells and Margo completely misses her cue. The band just simply come round again as Margo shakes her head, smiling ruefully. Nobody's worried – those are the kind of mistakes that give a live show a special charm – but there's a professionalism at work here, too. When she sings "The sound of clinking bottles", jaws drop around the theatre because she has wrung everything out of that line. At the end of the song, the end of the set, everybody's going to remember the way she sang that line, not the mistake that preceded it.

Twenty-four hours later, in the capital of the world, a heaving, sweaty rock club, people out for a raucous Saturday night, a world away from Manchester. The band battles through the first song, beset by onstage sound problems. As the last note dies away, they're already scratching away, trying to find solutions. A pregnant pause. Margo starts to chatter to the crowd, but it's quickly becoming clear that this is going to take some time. So, with 1,000 rowdy New Yorkers out front, "We are miners, hard rock miners", just a single voice in this huge room. And you can hear a pin drop.

Mike's songs, Neil's songs, Bob's songs, Townes' songs. Margo takes them, but she does not diminish them, does not overpower them. She enhances them, breathes life into them. Her greatest gift is that she does not sing them as if she's written them in her own blood. They're still Mike's songs. But they're her skin.

CHAPTER 13

Words misunderstood …

"I don't remember making that record."
"You were having a baby then – you don't remember anything!"
"OK. Do you remember it?"
"No, I think I went crazy when we were doing it, but I don't remember."
"I could make some stories up, if ya like!"

Al, Margo and Pete discussing *Pale Sun, Crescent Moon* in an Italian restaurant in New York City, fourteen years after the record came out. Somehow, that exchange captures what is a "nearly" record. There are some strong songs on there, songs that have endured better than some of their best-known material. There's some great playing, some of their best to that date. But there's something weird about that record, something a little scary even. This was a new incarnation of Cowboy Junkies, but one they don't have a handle on, now or then.

It doesn't invite you in, doesn't welcome you, not the way *The Caution Horses* or *Black Eyed Man* did. As the years have passed, it's become one of those records in the collection, there on the shelf, that I take out, hold it for a moment or two. I know that if I put it on, I'm getting to enjoy it, but I stand there and look at it some more. And then I wonder if there's not something else I'd rather put on. Having lived with it all these years since it was released, and having spent weeks on end listening to it day in, day out, in preparation for this book, it still feels that way. It's oddly, indefinably foreboding and, no question on this one, as a listener you have to give it plenty of work.

"That's true, you do have to work at it, but I'm not sure why," says Mike. "It contains some of my favourite songs like 'Crescent Moon', 'Ring on the Sill', 'Anniversary Song', too, though we've played it to death and I don't particularly like the version on the album. 'First Recollection' I like a lot as a song, 'Hunted' has been a staple in our repertoire.

"But it is a dark record, a nasty record in a lot of ways. On *Black Eyed Man* there was a lot of storytelling for people to get into, where there's very little on that one. It's a bit oblique, it takes a lot to get into the lyrics, you have to work at it. Even though *Black Eyed Man* came after we'd toured with Townes, a lot of the songs on it had been written already. So a lot of those songs on *Pale Sun* are the real reflection of hanging out with him, listening to him every night, talking to him about songwriting, that's in there, too. I was trying to use his approach a little bit where you're writing about one subject but talking about another. It is hard to get into on that level. As a body of work, I like it, I like the intensity of it, the darkness – I don't regret it, for sure, but it got away from us a little."

In its way, it's a halfway house, leaving one home but not yet getting to the next place, a record made on the train tracks in the middle of somewhere out of focus. Like the recordings in Sharon Temple, it was a portent of things to come, but not yet fully formed or realized. Again, the songs were there, the frameworks, but the realization of them was at times off-centre, a criticism that might also be levelled at *One Soul Now*, another in-between record of sorts.

Small wonder that Mike says, "Of all our records, I'd like to rerecord *Pale Sun*. That's not to say I don't like it – we approached it the way we wanted to and did it as we wanted, I'm happy about that. But I like those songs a lot and I'd like to revisit them, redo them, because some of them we didn't capture it when I listen back to them. 'Anniversary Song' is too slick; I like the way we do it now acoustically. We've found the groove for 'Hunted' better than we did in the studio and it was great that we finally got it down when we rerecorded it on *Sing in My Meadow* in *The Nomad Series*. I love the lyric to 'First Recollection', but we never captured it musically and there are a lot of songs like that. But then 'Ring on the Sill' is good; 'Crescent Moon' sits fine, I like it a lot; 'Cold Tea Blues', the same.

177

"But even the artwork, it's dark, it's murky and, again, that wasn't successful. We had this idea that we never captured. It was just one of those records. We had the image, but we couldn't catch it, in every sense. We went through various versions, it got darker and darker and there were even two versions of it. We did ours and, when they finally went to re-press it, the company wanted to change it because it was hard to read. Even the booklet isn't a booklet, it's a pull-out thing and I hate those. Why did we do it? I think David Houghton suggested it, I got talked into it, but looking back there are lots of elements I would redo, given the chance."

As designer, David Houghton should have the right of reply. Not that he's arguing much. "The cover bears the strongest influence of Alan. He knew Juan Sánchez Cotán's work and suggested it for the cover. Al knows more about fine art than I will in my lifetime, but plays a background role with the CD covers. Mike and I will work closely together, then run the artwork past Alan, generally toward the end of the process. It took long negotiations with the Art Institute of Chicago to get the rights and I was ultimately dissatisfied with the result. I tried a poster format instead of the typical booklet and set myself the difficult task of making the cover type by knocking out process colours. The CD actually has two covers with different colours of type; I thought that would be something the retailers could play with when they racked the CD. I also struggled with the songs; *Pale Sun* is the record I've least connected to. I loved reading most of the lyrics when Mike first sent them to me, but never got comfortable with their connection to the music."

Margo has a similar attitude to the album: "I don't even remember making *Pale Sun*, writing it, rehearsing it, but we got an album at the end of it. I agree with Mike, I would love to rerecord it too. Hopefully I'll remember it then! We were in the studio, 306, but it was very quick. I have no feeling for the making of it, where I do with all the others – I can place myself in time, which dogs I had, what knitting I was doing or whatever! *Pale Sun*, there's none of that. I think I dusted all the leaves on the suffering plants in the studio – a little bit of madness there.

"There are some beautiful songs on it, but it's one that gets a little bit lost, just because of where it is. *Black Eyed Man* was such a pivotal album for us and, because *Pale Sun* was in the wake of that, it got lost in the shuffle a little bit. Then there was the end of our time with BMG, so that overshadowed it a bit, too. We didn't tour so much, so for us it was over pretty quickly, where something like *The Caution Horses* had taken up two years of our lives. I think there's some very strong writing on it, but I'm not sure the recording is as good. It was the first thing we did as a studio record in the sense of being isolated a little bit. When we did *Black Eyed Man*, we all went up to Hamilton every day, even if I was just sitting around doing needlepoint while Pete was doing his thing or whatever. On *Pale Sun*, after we'd done the initial stuff, that was different – we'd go in more individually. Now we're used to that, but I think, then, it maybe fed into the record because we were still finding our way in the studio."

Where *Black Eyed Man* had seen the relationship between the band and their record company begin to fracture, perhaps some of the shortcomings on *Pale Sun* were down to the fact that it was now apparent that they were in this for the long haul, that Cowboy Junkies was becoming a career. And in dreams begin responsibilities, as Mike concedes: "By then, there was a Junkies machine – the stakes were higher, I guess. We had a crew, sidemen, managers and accountants, our lives were structured around Cowboy Junkies, so if it fell apart it meant big changes to a lot of people. And you have to keep feeding that machine."

Among those relying upon the Junkies for work was guitar tech John Farnsworth, who had joined the travelling minstrel band on the *Black Eyed Man* tour. "Back in 1992, I got a call to offer me a position with the band, but I was committed to the tour I was with, with a bunch of friends basically, so I hadn't really accepted at that point. I was sitting in the hotel room with the lighting guy from the Lee Aaron band, talking about the Junkies, but when I told him I wasn't going anywhere, he said, 'What do you mean, man!?' I told him that I had decided not to go, and then the tour manager who was in there with us, he said, 'Farns, let's step outside!' So I followed him out and he said, 'Look, we love having you work with us, but this is the next step. You have to take it, you have to go, you've got our blessing.' They were right and so I came out and joined the Junkies. Twelve years later, I was still with them, but they had the same attitude, too – they gave me their blessing when I couldn't go out with them, when I was working with someone else. First tour I did was for *Black Eyed Man* and we rolled into the Iron Horse in Northampton, Massachusetts, with real production, a semi-tractor trailer, basically emptying it out onto the sidewalk, pulling out the bits and pieces that we needed, leaning a monitor console up on the front window because we couldn't set it up straight! That's a tight place to play if you bring anything with you – the stage is the size of a matchbook!"

The Iron Horse was the venue that sold the band on another long-term member of the crew, according to Margo: "Chas was our lighting guy for a long time. He was English, but he'd lived in the south of America for years. The first show he came to was at the Iron Horse in Northampton, but it's a tiny place, no lights there! So his first night with us, he just sat in the dressing room without saying a word. And that's why we decided to keep him! We're quite loser-y when it comes to people we have with us, like the crew. We can employ people just because we like having them around. But, if we like them, they usually work out pretty well, because they're like us and they get the job done."

A reciprocal loyalty is a pretty rare commodity in the music industry but it is a cornerstone of the Junkies' story. The normal story is that fans are loyal and the band, once they've reached a certain point of success, are free to abuse that loyalty whenever and wherever possible. Similarly, crew are just employees to be hired and fired at whim. That's not the case with Cowboy Junkies. Most people they work with either last a few days and don't fit into their very understated road life, or they stay pretty much for the duration. And, when you go to a Junkies gig, there is a genuine warmth between band and fans. That doesn't make them unique, but it is pretty unusual. But loyalty, however freely given, carries a burden. Perhaps that fed into the making of *Pale Sun*, and certainly the speed with which it was made.

Once again, when they came off the road following the relatively short *Black Eyed Man* stretch, Mike had a batch of material sketched out and ready to be finished and, before long, "We got the itch to quickly get back into the studio to start working on a new album." Speed was very much at the centre of things, quite deliberately so, the band wanting to catch something of the pace at which they had lived their lives, a conscious step away from the languid style of the past which had caused one critic to liken their shows to "watching bread rise".

"It's a bit quicker than watching grass grow, I guess!" laughs Mike. "When we have a repertoire together and we've been on the road a while, shows change from one night to the next depending on the kind of place it is, the crowd. We have to figure out how to put across all the elements of what we do, the subtlety and the quietness as well as the louder stuff, so we do try to build it. I guess if you slam the door too tight, the bread falls, so I'll take that as a compliment!

"But we did want to show another side of us. If you look back through the records, I think one of the breaks happens after *Black Eyed Man*. After that, the whole country side of the band begins to recede a bit. There is a very country influence through *Trinity*, *Caution Horses* and *Black Eyed Man*, that was what was feeding into my writing. By the time we'd done that, I was getting tired of that format. Those influences had begun to wane and I wanted to go in another direction, writing-wise. There was a lot of instrumentation on those records – fiddles, violins, accordions – where *Pale Sun* was basically a five-piece band, us and Ken Myhr, very traditional. We wanted to get away from that instrumentation and make something more straight-ahead. I wrote it and we recorded it really fast. It was intentionally a break from what we'd done; we'd run the gamut with that."

Where detailed, intricate pacing remains part of the leavening live experience – and anyone who has watched Mike piece together a set list before a show knows just how much thought goes into that – going in to make *Pale Sun* was about catching a messier aspect of the group, songs that were a little frayed at the edges, detailing characters' lives that were starting to come apart at the seams. "We wanted that kinetic sound, you know, just get it down. Looking back, I think we might have rushed it a bit, so that there may be some weak spots on the album, but it gave it a different quality. There was some great playing in a way that we hadn't played on records before – some blowouts, I guess. It was a real release and it was the first time we'd really done that. *Black Eyed Man* we did as a four-piece, I did a lot of rhythm, then we left it and the other guys played on top and I sat there as producer.

"With *Pale Sun*, we did it live off the floor, a lot of experimenting, turned things up, tried using feedback. It was a lot of fun to do that. We worked with Ken as part of the band, because I'd liked his playing on the previous record and on tour, so he was part of the unit. He came to rehearsals before we went in the studio, contributed to the way we arranged things. It was just another way to push the band somewhere else."

The record turned out to be their most extreme exploration of opposites, Mike characterizing it as "sun–moon, yin–yang, dark–light, hot–cold, male–female". Some of the situations had a savagery that put 'Murder, Tonight, in the Trailer Park' in the shade, but while a physical violence bubbled just beneath the surface, more troublesome yet was the emotional intensity, a rare ferocity that pushed all kinds of buttons. Vicious? You hit me with a hammer.

"It's the most direct record about female–male relationships. That's the core of it: this weird, constant circle; that's the sun and moon side of it," says Mike now. "How couldn't it be complicated? It is complicated, but there are some really cool songs on it. The general theme is that there is love and there is all that conspires to steal love away. That was how we described it at the time, and that holds up.

"There's a sense that mundane, everyday life crushes the feelings you have when you first fall in love, it's a part of the record, it is a theme on *Pale Sun*. *Black Eyed Man* is about falling in love, that first flush, going forward, breaking away from your past. *Pale Sun* is being in the middle of it and realizing that that first flush goes and never really comes back in the same way. That's how it is. There are all sorts of other angles that are just as good, as meaningful, but it's very different, the reality of a long-term relationship. At that stage, my relationship with my wife wasn't even that long-term, but I was just beginning to realize, 'My God, this is serious. This is a lot of work, it's complicated.'

"The emotions being experienced by the characters could be explored more powerfully using an internal dialogue rather than the external type used for most of *Black Eyed Man*. These songs are more about how someone deals with themselves when they decide to trust their heart and soul to another person.

"There are very large concepts there, 'Crescent Moon' is a very big metaphorical song, then 'Ring on the Sill' or 'Anniversary Song' are very mundane, the beautiful little things in life, the hard little things in life and how you have to balance them. Those two fit together. 'Ring on the Sill' is one of my favourite songs that I've ever written: it's a Raymond Carver story or a Hopper painting, her washing dishes, him over there, then the last scene is the two sitting together. It does sum up a lot of what that record is about, that sense of 'What the fuck's going on? We gotta make this work somehow.' Then it's sort of sweetened by 'Anniversary Song', because where else can you go after that?

"It's interesting: a lot of the records don't necessarily start off with a specific theme. There are vague ideas and then, as it goes along, a theme suggests itself. I tend to write a lot of songs at once and so I'm writing about a particular period in time, in life, and the theme comes out of that. It's rare that I'll sit down and decide to write a ton of songs on a particular theme – *At the End of Paths Taken* was one where I did, but that's been fairly unusual.

"About halfway through the cycle, the songs are going in a certain direction and then I might start to gear songs towards that. Some songs drop off because they don't work in the context of where it's going, and then I'll start to fine-tune from there. Every record has a theme to it on some level, whether it's highly conceptual or pretty obvious. Even the way we arrange and sequence the records, what we do as far as adding musicians, how we produce it, they're all conceptualized on some level – they're not just thrown together, it's not haphazard; all those aspects are thought out. They're not obvious to some people, but they're there. That's the way we make it cohesive."

That said, being cohesive is not the same as being easily comprehensible. This is the record whose themes lie most deeply beneath the dust, in need of excavation before they shine. Ironically, in so doing, they pretty much give the game away, making an admission that they're not going to make this easy for you in future.

"There's a line in the song 'Pale Sun' which is my mother-in-law's favourite line," Mike reveals. "It says, 'Is it better to have words left unsaid than to have words misunderstood.' I think that's a good conundrum; we're all fighting that. How do we present ourselves? I think we're more comfortable leaving those things unsaid! We're quite happy to have people misinterpret us now rather than fight the stereotypes they have of us. The same with the music. A lot of people try to put themselves across in a certain way. I'd rather have people come see us and figure out their own way into it. I like to think we give a lot of respect to the audience – we think they have a lot of intelligence, we don't have to spell everything out, we can leave it to them to fill in the blanks, or not, as they choose. There's a lot of leeway and openness as to how we want them to listen to our music. The danger there is that you leave yourself open to a lot of misinterpretation, but again there are more important things to care about."

As a lyricist, little wonder that Mike has plenty of respect for the damage that words can do, a preoccupation that dates back to an early song that he wrote along with his sister, 'To Love Is to Bury' from *The*

Trinity Session: "Then one night, a terrible fight, words spoken better left unsaid." OK, maybe words better left unsaid don't always lead to murder, but you never can tell. Maybe it's not a risk worth taking.

Where 'To Love Is to Bury' dealt with one American archetype, the settlers disappearing off into the west with only each other to cling to, the song 'Pale Sun' appears to deal with American history on a more monolithic level, not least the way the Native Americans were dealt with: "White Cadillac, white man at the wheel, white faces on the mountain, wounds that will never heal." The mountain clearly references Mount Rushmore, the memorial to the great and the good of the American body politic, but where is the memory of those that came before, that were wiped out in the drive to take charge of the land? It's a song that captures the dark genius of American iconography and its forward march as well as the nation's ability to sweep less savoury passages of history under the carpet. It might be the New World, but they took a trick or two with them from ye olde one.

"A lot of the images in that song come from a drive my wife and I took through South Dakota, all through the Great Plains, the area where all the Indian wars happened. There's that sense of destroying something all around you. The song does have that sense of American iconography of how they deal with what they don't understand. We're talking here in Annapolis, in what was the centre of the slave trade. You go down to the water, they've got those cutesy statues at the bay of Alex Haley and the kids listening to the storyteller, and it's become kind of a theme park attraction. It is very strange the way they do appropriate things here and sanitize them." Words left unsaid, indeed …

Running from the truth, maybe running from the cares of responsibility, or the threat of responsibility, is a theme that rears its head time and again on the record. 'Crescent Moon' is a version of the siren's song, luring the unwary mariner – or musician – to his doom on the rocks. "I know I'm not part of the life you had planned" seems to speak directly to the guy whose game plan was to keep clocking up those '200 More Miles', following the music, gig to gig, escaping domesticity.

It's a terrific performance. As Jason Lent says, "The best songs on that record remain some of the best stuff they've done. The opening chord of 'Crescent Moon' jolts me still," and it really sets the bar extraordinarily high, signalling from the opening seconds that this is yet another kind of Cowboy Junkies record. Sonically, 'Crescent Moon' is a real quantum leap in using the studio, Margo's voice having that West Coast rush and that East Coast grit – some balancing act. But the change is not just musical; it's lyrical, too. The sleeve notes point out that the opener owes a debt to Townes Van Zandt, and there is certainly a more elliptical element to the lyric than in the past. Jason Lent again: "Revisiting the album, more and more of the mystery reveals itself with time. I think this album works on the same levels as the writers he references in the lyrics [Márquez and Faulkner]. There is more going on beneath the surface than the writer allows us to see, and it takes multiple visits to grasp it all."

That very style suggests the weird mysteries of love, of relationships themselves, the seductive pull of finding yourself plunging headlong into something you don't understand, which you know will change all the rules and all the certainties, but which you can't escape. And nor would you want to, because that rush is a life force itself, that desperate need to find out more, to unwrap the layers, to get to the heart and damn the consequences. And who among us could turn away from the promise that "Your heart will lose its pain"?

The run of four songs that opens the record – 'Crescent Moon', 'First Recollection', 'Ring on the Sill' and 'Anniversary Song' – are all of a piece, rubbing up against one another, fighting like feral cats in a sack, tearing at each other, so that just as you think you've got an emotion nailed, just as you think you know what this love is doing to you, you catch another swipe and all the pieces are back on the floor again. It's mystery, it's doubt – of the self and of the other – it's mundane, it's little glimpses of pure joy, it's the everyday in its dirt and its gold. And at the end, there still aren't any answers, any rules, any roadmap. You just are left with this swirl of things that fly round your head and your heart, little flashes of insight that buzz past, so you're trying to catch fog in a butterfly net. That's how it is. No wonder we're all so fucked up.

It's so fleeting, like the waxing and waning of the crescent moon, but it leaves so indelible a mark, it demands so much, that there is that impulse to run from it when put to the test. The romance of 'Crescent Moon' swiftly dissolves into the grind, the mundane, the needs, the little sacrifices that take you away from who and what you are, or were. And then there are the compensations – that life doesn't just get in the way, it enhances, it takes you somewhere else, creates a new world and, somehow, maybe if you hang on to that, to the memories, you can find "the balance between this fear that they feel and the love that has graced their lives". No, you can never go home again, you can never go back to how it was, but maybe you can get somewhere better, to "a face in a crowd of people that lights up just for you".

It's a long journey, one that the band covers well initially, although 'Anniversary Song' is so unlike anything they've done before or since that it can't help but jar as the fourth and final song in that sequence. And, inevitably, it's since become the most requested song in the catalogue. But the key song is 'Ring on the Sill'. It's easy to see why Mike is so proud of it, because each line sits beautifully on top of the last, layers of a painting that can only exist because the previous one is there. Layer after layer of the workaday, and then, the flash of colour, redemption of the mundane by a memory of a time past and a hope that it can get better, that it can become the life it was once again – the same, only different.

The way the two sides of the coin are addressed in 'Ring on the Sill' is phenomenal. There's the abject terror with which you confront yourself in love, when you become naked, despite the self-doubt that, "Once inside, you were afraid they'd find nothing to hold on to". The fear that you'll be found empty echoes the concerns in 'First Recollection' and then later on Ray Agee's 'Hard to Explain', that you won't be up to the job, that in the end you will have to run. But where 'Hard to Explain' is about exasperation, about wishing love had never come knocking, 'Ring on the Sill' ends on determination, that in the end you will stand and fight instead. Musically, that's caught beautifully by the outro, which is reminiscent of 'Let It Be', a statement of acceptance. As Mike explains, "The outro to the song is supposed to give that sense of hope. The last line lifts up the song and the outro takes that on; it's beauty and hope and going forward. Lots can come out of this – there's not just washing dishes, there's more out there, you've just gotta find it somehow."

The sequencing of *Pale Sun, Crescent Moon* is another of its difficulties. Actually, maybe not the sequencing. Maybe it's the fact that most of us were now buying it on CD rather than vinyl. "The transition from vinyl to CD was a hard one in terms of sequencing," says Mike. "As a fan, I always thought of them as records – side one, side two, a minute break between them while you got up and turned the thing over. That's more important than it sounds, because if it's a record you need to really listen to, that little break halfway through is great just to give yourself a moment before you go and listen to the rest. I found it really hard, and it wasn't until *Pale Sun* that I started to get a sense of it being one continuous thing."

That's maybe where 'Anniversary Song' and, to a lesser extent, 'Cold Tea Blues' and 'White Sail', slot in. With the intensity of the material around them, they act as that little break on the CD, although that's maybe harsh on 'White Sail', which is a beautifully romantic tale, perhaps a better take on the same kind of subject matter as 'Anniversary Song'. That interlude is just as well, because if you thought the opening set of songs were challenging you ain't heard nothing yet. Even then, 'Seven Years', 'Hunted' and 'Floorboard Blues' are broken up as if having the three together would simply be too much to take, certainly as a closing suite of songs.

It's these songs, especially the last two, that make *Pale Sun, Crescent Moon* feel like such an anomaly in the catalogue, a record that has a chill edge to it as opposed to the warmth of the others. The subject matter is very dark and, as a finale, maybe that colours thoughts of the record as a whole, giving it its air of menace.

It could not have been otherwise, as Mike explains. "Another element of that record is about a friend and she was very viciously raped. 'Seven Years', 'Floorboard Blues', 'Hunted' – she's a big part of those songs, and that's that very nasty, dark, brutal side of the male–female thing. In what you think is a common, everyday marriage, there can be that 'Hunted' side. It's about all those weird relationships, things of how we do and don't deal with each other. She becomes the aggressor in a kind of way in 'Floorboard Blues' just to flip it for a song, but that violence that there is in the record comes from that whole incident."

With that backstory, songs that have long been daunting suddenly become harrowing. The ferocity of 'Seven Years', hammered along by Pete's drumming, is a musical *Cape Fear*, all blues language and biblical thundering – it could be Bogart or Mitchum at their most merciless, offering no escape. The quote from Marquez, "Memories are just dead men making trouble", is inspired, but Mike's own words are as effortlessly chilling, especially those eyes, "As cold as a stonemason's chisel".

Going straight to 'Hunted' from there would surely be too much, and the delicacy of 'Cold Tea Blues' is a welcome interlude, though the take on Dinosaur Jr.'s 'The Post' is less successful, musically at least, a stab at a more psychedelic sound that pales in comparison with 'Hunted', which features some terrific playing from the band as a whole. The guitar playing is startling, incendiary, yet it's Alan's insistent bass figure that is the most unsettling element. Then there's the singer. The nervous Margo Timmins that sang with her back to the audience had continued to come a long, long way.

"When you do a song like 'Floorboard Blues', which comes from a place I've never been to, thank God, you're a storyteller. It's acting. When he handed me *Black Eyed Man*, that was the first song that was really totally beyond anything. The girl in the song is deceitful: she's tricking the guy, he's a scapegoat and she's using him. There's not one part of my body that would ever treat anyone like that. But I liked playing that role, it was exciting. Had I had it two years before, I'd have shied away from it. It must be the same with writing – you know there are things you just aren't ready to do, then a few years later you can.

"*Whites!!* is a very intimate record, even more than *Trinity Session*. But you can't be that thing forever. When we do a record, we do it for ourselves. We don't think about what people expect or want. We please us. What do we need? To continue doing the same thing, in any part of your life, is idiotic. Life's about growing, changing, so we've done that. Those first two records are so intimate, because that's who we were. You wouldn't catch me dead singing big. If we were to do the exact same songs now, it would be a totally different record. I'm thirty years older. I look back and that's who I was – it's a time capsule.

"Michael's writing changed after *Caution Horses* and I still have no idea how I managed to get all those words into the songs! I get the lyrics, and I'm thinking, 'Oh no! This doesn't rhyme, it doesn't fit with the melody, what am I going to do?' Each song is different. Some he hands to me and I know that he doesn't truly understand the meaning of the song himself, even though he wrote it. Because it resonates so strongly with me, it might be totally different to what he intended, but it speaks directly to me. I've never asked him if he wrote a specific thing about something that happened to me, and I don't care. When you hear the song and it speaks to you of a bad time or a broken heart you once had, that's what it means. Nobody can tell you it doesn't.

"Some songs I just know how to sing them and, if the band isn't playing it the way I hear it, I will push them: 'We've gotta do it like this.' Others, I have no clue. I don't know what he's writing about, it could be Italian! I sit there bewildered and often I'll wait for the band to figure out what they're doing. I won't sing with them, I'll wait and then attack it like it is Italian, go for melody, for phrasing, the beauty of how the words flow. Forget putting the meaning across, because I don't have one. I let the listener interpret it for me. If I'm really stuck, I'll ask for a hint or ask if I'm going in the right direction. Most of them fall between that; certain songs I feel strongly about the chorus; there are even songs that I don't get until years later. I'll suddenly get it onstage, I'll realize what it needs. I don't look back and think I screwed up the record, because I did the best job I could at the time. Songs are organic, they have their own life, their time – they come and they go. I try not to worry about it too much."

Her performance on 'Floorboard Blues' was a record maker, all femme fatale, sashaying towards the hunter and facing him down, an important twist off the back of 'Hunted', which took the record away from being lazily labelled misogynistic, ending on a fiercely defiant note. Margo is totally in control, while the band sit back and leave the final bow to Jeff Bird, his harmonica like police sirens going off, the sound of rescue coming after seeing off the danger, the bleaker side of relationships put in the hands of others.

Pale Sun, Crescent Moon is a weird one, simultaneously perhaps the most and least successful record in the canon. In the finish, it does what it sets out to do in the most peculiar way. It's there to show that love, relationships, they're messy, they're complicated, incomprehensible, that it's not straight lines and hearts and flowers, that it's also concrete, barbed wire and broken bottles. The record sounds like a seething, steaming swamp, with no way out. Sometimes, so does life.

CHAPTER 14

Lonesome words scrawled

"The term 'music business' is an oxymoron, because it has nothing to
do with music and, as a business, it's so poorly run. They just throw
the spaghetti against the wall really fast, really hard and see what
sticks. There's not much long-term thinking. Bob Buziak was smart at
RCA, he signed Lucinda Williams, Cowboy Junkies, Michael Penn,
thinking long-term. Singers and songwriters, that's what develops
the catalogue. He was right, but BMG wanted hits fast and they took
the company elsewhere. Building a stable was not on the agenda, but
if they'd listened to Bob they'd have been in a lot better position."
Peter Moore

If it's signed to a big label, a band is a little like an automobile, heading
out onto the open road. You start off in the low gears, building up
a head of steam and that's OK, nobody minds that. You need to get
going, but too much too soon can wreck the engine. But there comes a
point when the voice in the back starts to demand: "Go faster. This isn't
the way to the city – don't you have a better map? Do you really think
you should be driving this car? Do you know what you're doing? What
kind of idiot are you not to do exactly what I tell you to do?"

That backseat driver is the record company. When things are going
well, the band is driving and the company is paying for the gas, maybe

helping navigate. But you can bet your life that, one day, that company will tell you that you should get a bigger car, the car that everybody looks at as you drive past, paying less attention to the little details that used to make you so idiosyncratic, so intriguing, and more to the blinding, gleaming chrome and leopardskin seats. The car that everybody can admire but that fewer people really love any more. It's nice, but it's not, just not, not quite, that thing – the thing that made you want to pore over every inch of it time and again. You know, that thing it had that made it special …

Bigger isn't always better – it's not always worse, either – but success in commercial terms, in mass culture terms, comes with a price ticket. Just round off those jagged little edges. Try not to use difficult words of more than two syllables. Drop the questions, offer some answers. Wear a nice hat. Be obvious. No, really. Really obvious.

Above all, don't make a record like *Pale Sun, Crescent Moon* just at the point where you about to cross over into the mainstream. Make a record like *Out of Time* or *The Joshua Tree*, a sonically expansive record with some big choruses and radio-friendly hooks. Before the R.E.M. and U2 fans come out of the hills baying for blood, that doesn't mean that those bands necessarily made a calculated decision as to the record they were going to make and what it was they had to do to suddenly shift mega-units. They both benefited from right time, right place, right record, and both had already earned hefty audiences via their previous work, primed for just one last push over the edge. But it can't be denied that both of those albums contained a number of songs that were perfect for a mass, radio-fed audience. Where they were records of the wide-open spaces – *The Joshua Tree*, in particular – *Pale Sun* was claustrophobic, introverted, complex, structurally sophisticated. Above all, it was taxing. It demanded things of the listener. That's most of the casual mainstream audience gone right there.

"*Pale Sun* was a very dense album," admits Mike. "And it's the one where our relationship with RCA dissolved, because they were totally clueless as to what to do with it. I had lots of meetings, getting together with our manager, I even went to New York at one point and sat with the vice-president of BMG International, because the record gave them heart attacks. When you make a record, you're not thinking in terms of 'This is complicated or difficult', whatever. You're just making a record. This is our record – you figure out how to sell it. They were complaining there was no single, but I couldn't see what that had to do with it. So a lot of talking went on, and it finally came out and they didn't work it – they didn't understand it, so they let it slide. From that, we just felt it was time to go. If we deliver a record and they decide they don't want to work it, where's the point?"

A changing of the guard within the record company proved crucial, too, as Pete points out. "Jim Powers was pretty much the only guy we liked at BMG, and he left there and then a little later started working for Geffen. Actually, a few of the people we worked with at BMG went – Bob Buziak, Heinz – so we were out on our own a little bit."

Alan's take on it is similar: that the new faces at the company, all desperate to make their mark, were more interested in banknotes than musical notes. "When BMG signed us, they had just bought the RCA operation and they were all together and rah-rah-rah for the company. Really positive about the future. They assured us that they would be together forever, and within two years everyone was getting fired or leaving! To us, the company didn't exist without Jim and, when he went, we didn't feel the same.

"That was the start of the move to where the business is now. The marketing end ruined the music end of the industry. Because they're not into handling more than a handful of products at a time, they can't deal with it. They made radio into what it is today, playing the same forty songs over and over again, shutting it down as far as artist-orientated music goes. OK, that happened a long time ago, but college radio tried to combat that when it got big in the 1980s and it helped sell a lot of records – it became a market in itself, and that helped us. But the industry shut those college stations down in terms of having any influence and now playlists for the whole country come from a head office, so in any individual city the FM station there doesn't make any decisions that reflect their community, the artists around there, so that kills music right there. If you've got a great up-and-coming artist in Chicago, the stations there aren't allowed to play him – it all comes from above.

"And they still refuse to accept that that has a bad effect on music. The marketing guys love it, because it's one-stop shopping for them – here's the new Taylor record, here's $500,000 to sell it, and it's so easy for them. The ownership of media in the US is so closed up. A company will own TV, radio, record company and it all gets tied in – they release a record and they make sure it gets played on their TV and radio shows; the media blitz goes on. So A&R became redundant at the lower levels.

Jim Powers signed us to RCA and he got so frustrated with it that he left to start his own independent label."

Alan's analysis rings true – truer by the day – and it's apparent why, in the long term, Cowboy Junkies had little alternative but to return to the idea of *Whites Off Earth Now!!* and become an independent band again. But that was for the future. Back in 1995, in the days before the internet revolutionized the movement of music, that wasn't a viable option.

But nor was working for a company that had no interest in the music you were making, as Mike explains. "*Pale Sun* got lost, because it was the end of the relationship with BMG. They were never happy with it, they didn't work it very hard and it was the first time on a record where we stopped touring halfway through. So we didn't get to Europe, and that was a terrible mistake because, with changing labels, doing *Lay It Down* and getting ready to go again, it was five years between tours. The same thing happened in Canada, so we lost a lot of that audience. It was funny; BMG were just non-committal towards it. We couldn't understand it. 'You guys have sold a lot of our records, you made a lot of money on us, I don't care if you don't like it, go sell it. That's your job. If you're not promoting it, we're not going on tour.' In the end, we just said we wanted to leave and it was very amicable – they were nice about it. I think we'd just gotten bored with each other.

"Personalities do matter when you're working with a big company. The turnover of people at record companies is huge, and a lot of people who were at RCA when we signed, people who championed us, they left. In our time there, they had three presidents in the US, two in Canada; Jim Powers, who signed us, left, and we got to a point where it was stale. They lost their direction. From looking at building a stable of core artists over time, within a year they decided that wasn't doing the bottom line a lot of good and the focus changed.

"We'd deliver the record and it became like dealing with music critics. 'Great record. guys, but what's the angle, how are we going to sell it?' We kind of thought that was their job! So after *Pale Sun*, we went to them and said we felt they'd run out of ideas with us, they weren't working the records while we were killing ourselves on tour. We just didn't feel they knew who we were any more, they weren't marketing us and we asked them to let us off the label. You hear horror stories about that, but they went away, thought about it, and we managed to make a deal. We offered them *200 More Miles*, which was fine, because we wanted to put out a live record and we had to agree to *Studio*, which we weren't wild about, but at least they let us put it together and it was a good record, so we had a very amicable split. RCA put out a second 'greatest hits' later – but don't get me started …"

The ins and outs of record company politics are issues that we fans are blithely ignorant of – after all, we just want to be able to go and buy the next record, and we want it to be a good one. Ironically, the fallout from the band's departure was another album, and a good one at that. *200 More Miles* was no straightforward, nostalgic live record, culled from a single performance or from a couple of shows on the most recent tour. Instead, it acted as an aural history of Cowboy Junkies onstage, as the subtitle, "Live Performances 1985–1994", made clear. From their first performance at the Beverley Tavern in Toronto in November 1985 with John Timmins still on second guitar, through the line-up changes, the musical changes, the shifting continents, it sums up the essential Junkies dichotomy: they sound totally different from one end to the other, yet still they sound exactly the same. Who they are remains bigger than what they are, and that seeps into every performance.

Alan is pretty ambivalent about live records in general and, had it been left to him, the album might never have seen the light of day. "*200 More Miles* was kind of a contractual obligation at the end of our time with BMG, but we had control over it and it worked out great, I really like that one. But, really, Pete's the only one who listens to this stuff. All the live albums are his choices. When we're getting a live record together, I only hear it when it's finished – I'm not going to sit and listen to fifteen live versions of a song to pick the best one. That's just crazy! Why would you do that to yourself?"

"I just like to listen to the introductions!" explains Pete, but that belies another side of the band's rigorous attention to detail that is masked by the personable nature of players and performance. "We've always taped gigs right the way through our career for the archive and because we like to know what we're doing and how it's sounding. Over the years I've been able to judge myself from the records and by listening to [tapes of] the live gigs." It's a process that Pete continues to this day, often listening to DAT tapes of the show on the bus that night or the following morning. The joker in the group is as conscientious as they come.

194

Margo Timmins waits for her cue. *The Trinity Session*, Toronto, November 27 1987. *(Cowboy Junkies Archive)*

Making *The Trinity Session*.

(Top) Another take, another decision.
Mike Timmins, *The Trinity Session*.
(Cowboy Junkies Archive)

(Right) The Church of the Holy
Trinity, Toronto. "Seats be free and
unappropriated forever". *(Dave Bowler)*

(Opposite top left) Jaro Czerwinec finds
the key... *(Cowboy Junkies Archive)*

(Opposite top right) "This record could
go somewhere!" John Timmins and
medallion. *(Cowboy Junkies Archive)*

(Opposite bottom) Working in a holy
ghost building: Kim Deschamps, Pete
Timmins, Alan Anton, John Timmins.
(Cowboy Junkies Archive)

You sell a million records, you get to have your picture taken… Alan, Margo, Pete and Mike, February 1989. *(Paul Natkin/Getty)*

Recording at Sharon Temple, April 1989.

(Top left) Mike leads the band through another rehearsal. *(Cowboy Junkies Archive)*

(Below) Not your typical recording studio. *(Cowboy Junkies Archive)*

(Bottom) Gathered around the Calrec: Peter Moore, Jeff Bird, Mike Timmins, Alan Anton, Jaro Czerwinec, Pete Timmins, Kim Deschamps. *(Cowboy Junkies Archive)*

(Top) "Live, from New York, it's Saturday Night!" Cowboy Junkies take to the *SNL* stage, February 18 1989. *(NBCU Photo Bank/NBC Universal/Getty)*

(Left) "So that's how they got the name!" Margo checks if the press got the story right. *(Cowboy Junkies Archive)*

You sell two million records, you get
to do interviews... Margo and Mike,
London, February 1992. *(David Tonge/
Getty)*

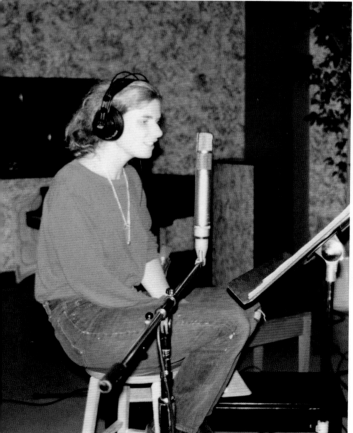

(Top) Breakfast in (North) America. Pete, Mike and Alan chew the fat, 1991. *(Cowboy Junkies Archive)*

(Left) "All these words that I sing". Margo in the studio during the *Black Eyed Man* sessions, 1991. *(Cowboy Junkies Archive)*

Whether a contractual obligation or not, it was an album whose time had come, as Mike agrees. "I'm really proud of *200 More Miles*; it does capture another dimension of what we do. It was time to do it, so people could hear what we were like away from the studio – a lot of people didn't know or understand there was a whole different aspect to what we do.

"We had tons to choose from. It was a pretty big project just to find the tapes, though. At the time I wasn't really collecting the stuff, so we ended up going to radio stations to find stuff in their vaults – that was fun. We left some of Margo's introductions in because we wanted people to get a flavour of what we're about and they're a big part of the live show. Looking at it, too, we've played at some pretty historic venues: the Albert Hall, CBGBs, the Fillmore West, wherever. You do feel the history of the places being fans. Even somewhere really small like the Iron Horse in Northampton is pretty historic; playing there is neat." Or, as Pete says, "If you're in the dressing room in the Royal Albert Hall in London, you have to feel something from it – Bob Dylan paced up and down here!"

200 More Miles is, of course, not your average live record because Cowboy Junkies don't do your average live show. There's a trajectory to their concerts, just as there is to their career. They are constantly changing, and they're always the same. The oddity of 'Bad Boy' aside, the hidden track that dates back to their first ever gig with Margo searching desperately for a voice and a persona, there's a consistent thread that shines through a series of different band line-ups, through different kinds of venue, through different levels of success. And even 'Bad Boy' has an intro that's not dissimilar to 'State Trooper'. Theirs is a truth put on plastic, but it's never a plastic truth. The songs remain heartfelt, and are played and sung that way, time and again. When you're rolling into the first few bars of 'Sun Comes Up, It's Tuesday Morning' for the five hundredth time, that's some achievement. It's a huge compliment to the quality of the songs and the arrangements, which are often revisited, that they can stand such heavy exposure. But, more than that, it's testimony to the nature of the players and their commitment to their instrument, their music and their way of life.

And to their professionalism, as Margo explains. "I remember asking Emmylou Harris, 'How do you keep singing the same old song again and again when you feel you can't face it.' She said, 'You just look

195

at the audience and you find that face. You know you're making them so happy, and you go with that.' It's true. To make somebody happy by singing a song – how great is that? I just believe that people have such hard lives that, if you can give them a moment like that, give it to them. I would never not sing a song just because I've sung it too much. If somebody asks for 'Sweet Jane', OK. It's four minutes of my life."

Possibly the hardest thing for any band is to retain its sense of vulnerability onstage after playing two hundred gigs a year for years on end. Early on, they were fumbling around in the darkness, looking for a sound, trying to figure out what they're doing. There's an edge there, and there's a sense of exploration, a search for something that's out there. There's the joy of working with new material and the surprises that brings every night. There's the thrill of playing in Poughkeepsie for the first time ever, of getting in the van, of taking music to audiences that like it.

And then they become professional. They've played a lot of shows, they know how it works. Instead of a voyage of discovery, they now know the tricks of the trade, the buttons to push. And, somehow, on that third visit, Poughkeepsie just doesn't hold the same charm any longer. They've played the hit more times than they care to think about. It's very easy for things to harden, for shows to be done by rote rather than by inspiration. Suddenly, the creative spark of live playing is going, the show atrophies and before you know it they're phoning the gig in – how many of those shows have we all been to? When it really is a show, a performance, where the music takes a step outside and has a smoke rather than demands its place as central to the evening?

Again, the fact that the Junkies are music fans first and musicians second is a huge component of their ability to sidestep that trap. There is plenty of stagecraft going on, they know their jobs, there's nothing amateurish about what they do. They're pros, through and through. But they're not going through the motions. They take playing live – and its attendant huge responsibility to give of their very best every night – very seriously. That's evident onstage. It's apparent when you watch them going about their work in what are often exhaustive soundchecks and it was obvious in Mike's online tour diary, which talks about their travels, largely across the States, and which, in the timeless words of *Spinal Tap*'s Marty DiBergi, "capture the sights, the sounds, the smells of a hard-working rock band, on the road". But there was more, a lot more. Like a dissection of the previous night's show which often reads like a reminder to Mike and the rest of the band to stay on their toes, not to let the standards drop. He certainly mourns the passing of those diaries in the new social media world: "It's funny, even with a band, the website is now pretty irrelevant; it's all moved to social media. When the website started in the late 1990s, we had discussion forums, blog posts, tour diaries – you could write, you could say something, you had space, and people would read and respond. You can't do that any more; nobody pays any attention, you're just whistling in the wind. It's all on Facebook now, these tiny posts, and if you dare put anything longer than a paragraph, no way will people look at all of it. And if you put something up without a photo, forget it. That's the way the culture is, not just for serious things but everything – you can't communicate, it's pure selling. That's a real drag; you'd have thought that would have been the thing that would have continued on, but it's been totally wiped out. For all the communication tools there are, there's less and less actual communication. Everything is progressively being dumbed down – it's amazing."

In spite of their serious approach to their craft, they somehow maintain a sense of fun onstage that escapes many other outfits, as a band that, over the years, has unquestionably loosened up, as Jeff explains. "A lot has to do with Mike's attitude onstage. If he's not happy, usually either with Pete or himself, he gets mad and that sets a tone. You can fall into the trap of being too hard on yourself and of worrying about your mistakes. When you've been in a band this long, with this strong a following, you know the crowd really wants to be there. A show that we might think falls short is still great to them, because they see you once a year. You almost want to say to them, 'Can't you see we're playing terribly?!' But you have to remember that they're probably loving it."

Equally, mistakes are, by definition, a risk you take with a Junkies show, simply because these are inquisitive musicians who are always digging further into the songs, particularly on those that really open themselves up for improvisation, like 'Lay It Down', 'Dragging Hooks' or 'Blue Guitar', for example. They don't sit the same way every night, they're prey to the vicissitudes of mood and of inspiration and, as such, they're a different thrill each time they are played, be it intellectual or visceral.

A shared experience is at the core of their shows, as is a very real and often touching sense of humour. Like so much of what the Junkies do, it's subtle, it's understated and, often, as a result, it's missed. But it's there. The decision to leave in some of Margo's song introductions on *200 More Miles* was a masterstroke, giving the record a real character all its own, from the self-deprecating opening of "Before I do some rock'n'roll, I always like to sit down", through to the bus-head story that prefaces "Cause Cheap Is How I Feel'.

One of the strengths of *200 More Miles* is the opportunity to hear the material handled by different ensembles, and the ways in which they've been reworked. The addition of Spencer Evans' piano to 'Misguided Angel' is particularly affecting, while 'Oregon Hill' gives up a new reading shorn of the brass section of the studio recording, no longer so rooted in the Mississippi, the lyric notwithstanding – ironic given that the lyric is given more emphasis in this version.

Even the choice of the opening cut, the gentle, hypnotic 'Blue Moon Revisited', confounds expectations, because rule one in the rock'n'roll book is that your first song, especially in a live show, should be designed to pin the audience to the wall with 1,000 decibels. But volume isn't the only way of getting an audience to pay attention. Give them something interesting, give them some layers of sound to explore and it's amazing just how carefully they'll start to listen. And that's why Cowboy Junkies are what they are – by being who they are, by having total confidence in themselves, their music and, above all, their audience. Have a little faith in your fans. They're the ones that like you, after all.

Confounding expectations is a Junkies stock-in-trade, for all that they're dismissed by some as still being "that band that did *The Trinity Session*". Cookie Bob Helm recalls his first encounter with the band and, even for a man who has taken as detailed an interest in their catalogue as any, it was still something of a surprise. "I got into them *Trinity Session* time and that was pre-internet, so you were just scratching around for information – that was the time when you just hoped you'd hear about it if they came near your town! I wasn't hearing about it until 1992, when they were playing Buffalo, New York, about seventy miles from my house, so the precedent for travelling to shows was set right at show number one. Actually, I was sick that day and I was thinking about staying home, but a friend who was going with me, he just dragged me up there! We got there insanely early for reasons I don't remember any longer, but we got there as they were soundchecking. They were playing Led Zeppelin's 'Kashmir', which seemed a little odd, because I didn't really associate the two bands. At first, I didn't think it was them playing, but the house PA. It wasn't what I expected Cowboy Junkies to play, that's for sure!

"We got into the show, we were on the front table, resting on the stage directly in front of Margo, I'd brought my *Trinity Session* CD booklet to get signed, and as soon as they'd done the encore, before they got offstage, I handed it up to her and she signed it there and then – I couldn't believe it! I was immediately hooked for life and remember wanting to see them again real soon.

"I absolutely loved *Black Eyed Man*, which was the record they were touring at that time, thinking it was a step in a positive direction for the band. I was so excited to finally get to see the band play live, and there were so many things to consider, that that first show was just sensory overload. There was much to consider musically. Did I like the band as well with Ken and Spencer? How does this band compare to the earlier version with Kim? Will Mike play *any* solos, now than Ken has been hired? How does Bird play so many instruments so damn well? How does the live version of the band compare to the only other version that I've heard – the one on their recordings? This was a lot to consider at one time, especially while trying to enjoy the show in the moment."

The oddity is that, despite being a band that many – even a former member like Kim Deschamps – dismissed as being on the point of coma onstage, as Helm intimates, there is an extraordinary amount going on if you know where to look for it. As another uberfan, Jason Lent, says, "The little nuances from show to show are what brings me back, not just changes in the set list, but changes in how the songs are played, watching the band interact onstage, watching Mike direct Margo and keep her focused on where it's going, Al just standing there but controlling the sound with Pete. From the back of the stage, Al expands and contracts the rhythm section during each song as Pete follows his lead. I don't recall ever thinking Pete led Al during an extended instrumental. Throughout their journey, it sounds/appears like Al leads the rhythm section while Michael guides Margo. If you watched Michael hold Margo's hand with just his eyes during a rough first night of 'Lonely Sinking Feeling' in San Francisco one night like I was lucky enough to do, that might make more sense. It was one of those brilliant little moments you notice after so intently watching show after show."

From an onstage perspective, Alan adds, "It's an anti-show, it's music. When we started, we used to turn our backs on the audience most of the time. And that was cool for a little bit in the late 1980s, but not really. In the 1990s, it was all about a big show, people paid a lot of money and they wanted to at least see your face. So we had to turn around. Because the focus is totally on music and because our audience is definitely a music audience, to see it happen live and to watch us working it out onstage must be kind of exciting, even though nothing much seems to be going on."

As Mike concedes, part of that is a question of scale. "When you get in a stadium and it's the Rolling Stones, it has to become a spectacle, because there's no way to translate it. Gestures have to be large, you need the distractions. We've played the sort of places we do for a long time now, and the way we survive onstage in a lot of ways is to go inward. Margo deals with the audience and the rest of us deal with ourselves – we have our little thing happening. A lot of the people who come to lots of our shows enjoy that side of it, the small interactions. Once you've seen Margo a few times, you start to focus less on her and see what the rest of us are doing. That's fun. I like to do that when I go to see bands, too, to see them communicating. There's a lot of fun onstage."

There's also a great back-and-forth relationship between band and audience. The crowd is generally the missing ingredient on live records, but the Junkies were keen to give a nod in the direction of their supporters, not least in the packaging put together by David Houghton.

"*200 More Miles* and *Studio* were, as Al says, 'contractual obligation' discs, one a live and one a greatest hits collection. Nonetheless, I wanted to make the packaging as interesting as possible. The images on *200 More Miles* celebrated some of the souvenirs the fans had given the band over the years; the images for *Studio* were a look behind the scenes at the making of Junkies records.

"The cover for *200 More Miles* came together quickly. Once I discovered that Margo had kept every letter, every stuffed toy, every trinket that fans had ever given to the band, I simply FedExed boxes of them to Hans Neleman in New York and let him play. He had such a wealth of souvenirs, he could have taken a hundred photographs. He loved the project, and it shows in his luminous images. At the same time, I knew my father was dying. I had him write out the lyrics to the title song at his kitchen table. I'd grown up seeing his scrawly handwriting and I wanted, in some way, to memorialize him. He loved Hank Williams and had instilled in me a love of country music that served me well on *The Caution Horses* and *Black Eyed Man*.

"I spread the lyrics, in my father's handwriting, throughout the CD booklet, alongside pictures of Mike, Margo, Pete and Alan. I'm very happy with the result, and it has a lot of resonance for me. It captures some of the emotion of the time I spent touring with the band. Except, of course, the motion sickness. It made me realize how much I missed travelling with them. I was pleased to have had the experience, and it was unforgettable. It's a chapter in my life I'll always be very fond of."

The record captures that sense of transience in its permanence, weirdly enough, fleeting minutes when a hall full of strangers suddenly comes together and shares something and then goes its separate ways, back to the everyday, yet subtly changed. In the *Rolling Thunder Logbook*, Sam Shepard writes of a Dylan show that "He's infused the room with a high feeling of life-giving excitement. It's not the kind of energy that drives people off the deep end but the kind that brings courage and hope and above all brings life pounding into the foreground."

And that's what the Junkies do, night after night. Supposedly the most melancholic band around, their strength is that they are life-affirming. *200 More Miles* gives you a sense of that. It tells you that they are a live band, not just a band that happens to play live. There's a world of difference.

THE GREAT FLOWER CONSPIRACY

"I don't really remember when I first began to put flowers on the stage, but I know it was early on when I was still very nervous about my position out there. I was very unsure about that part of my job. The singing was OK, but interacting with a bunch of strangers? Are you crazy?! So I found it very difficult to look at the audience. In the early, early days, I didn't even turn around very much, I spent more time looking at Pete, but that made it very difficult for the onstage sound. And if we were going to carry on playing live, communicating with the audience was going to be a big part of that, so I realized that I had to face them. To be honest, even when I did, I still didn't really want to look at them, so I needed to find a way of coping with that.

"I always got great comfort from flowers from a very young age. My mom always used to put a crocus next to my bed in spring and, since then, I've loved being surrounded by flowers. I used to bring flowers into our rehearsal space, which back in those early days was just a garage with mattresses on the wall. It was pretty grungey and gross. We found the mattresses on the streets, so I'm sure they were crawling with bugs and vermin and who knows what else, so I brought flowers in to make things a little nicer in there. I had that in my mind, that was already becoming a little part of what I did when I sang, a little part of what made me comfortable. Because I was so scared and because I knew I had to turn around, I just thought, 'Why not take the flowers onstage too and see if it made things easier?'

"I still wasn't talking to anyone, didn't want to make eye contact, but the flowers were there to help me at least look forwards. If I got lost in a song, or when I realized what I was doing and wondering what the hell I was doing there, I'd focus on the flowers instead of the person in the front row. It was something to comfort me. It still is, to a degree, though I don't need them so much now. But if you find me staring at flowers a lot, it's because I'm panicking and trying to get a hold of things again.

"I always drank tea onstage, just to protect my voice. I'd find it hard to bend down and get my tea off the ground, it wasn't very graceful. So I got a little table to put my tea on and the flowers went with that. It was partly just being practical, but in those days, too, I liked the feeling of protection. I had the microphone in front of me, the table, it was like a little environment that was all mine and I felt a little more at home.

"After a little while, they came to be a part of the show, I guess, a little focal point – people associated us with that, and it seemed to fit with what we were doing. As we got to a point where we could ask for things from venues, I always asked to have flowers there for us at a show. Naturally, the promoter didn't always get it right, and sometimes, when I was introducing a song, I'd complain about the lousy bouquet – a bouquet is more than two roses, OK!

"But you soon learn in this band to be careful what you say, because our fans really do listen! If Mike writes in the tour diary that he can't get a good bottle of beer somewhere, by the next show we'll have cases of the stuff waiting outside the bus afterwards. So, when I started talking about flowers at the shows, people stated to bring bouquets for me and that was really great, because it's nice to have them on the bus when I'm on the road with all these stinky men. I put them in the cup holders and the boys have to hold on to their beers, but they've got used to it.

"So I'm a little spoiled now. Which is great, I love that! Wherever we go, there are flowers waiting for me and I'm always really touched by that, that people would spend the money and make that effort to send them – that's very special. Some people send them once in a while when we go through their town or if there's a special occasion or something – I got a huge bouquet out in Saratoga one time from a guy called David. It was his birthday, but I don't think he got the concept! On your birthday, you get, you don't give!

"It's always amazing when I get flowers from people who we don't really know. But then there are some people who always seem to show up with flowers, wherever we go. People like Crazy Ed."

"I really like the fact that the audience, especially the fans who go to a lot of shows, have an impact on them. In the beginning, they would play almost the same set list night after night after night. But once it started to happen that two or five or fifteen people would be going along for the next six shows, they stopped that, they started to change the songs around. I've seen them respond to our presence, both as a group and individually, and a lot of the fans respond to that, again, and want to do something to make their lives easier, because we know it must be tough being away from home so much of the time. So when Bob brings them cookies or Po brings brownies or I bring flowers, it makes a difference. Some days they're busy, they're having a tough time and you go see them, say here's my offering, and you back off. Other times, there's a chance to talk and you can see that you've made a difference.

"When Margo rearranges the flowers you brought to the show, you know you've helped her feel a little more comfortable onstage, you've had a part in what the band is doing. People who buy the CD, go to the show, go home, they don't get that, nor do they need it – that's not what they're after. But some of us have been drawn into the whole thing more by their acceptance of us; it's a two-way process that's always developing.

"Back in the fall of 2000, Bob and I were following them on a tour in the Midwest, a bunch of shows in Ohio, Illinois, we'd been there a week or so. On the message board on the website, there'd been a lot of talk about a show in Elgin, just outside Chicago. A lot of people made arrangements to go – we were going to get together, meet up and have dinner, so I knew there'd be a lot of people there who really knew the band. Bob and I drove around town and found a florist, got a bouquet and took it to Margo before the show, knowing there'd be plenty more that night because of all the fans coming to the show. I gave them to her and said, 'I know you won't need them tonight.' But she said, 'No, Ed. The more flowers, the better.' Then she told me a story about the early touring days, when they'd been in Nashville and they'd gone to see Nanci Griffith."

"We were driving around the United States, just the four of us in a van, and we arrived in Nashville. Nanci Griffith was playing a show so we got all our money together and managed to buy tickets, the cheapest seats in the place, way up high at the back of the theatre. So we were looking down on Nanci and she had all kinds of flowers all over the stage. It just looked so beautiful from where we were, especially as we were playing a lot of grungey little bars. I can remember sitting up there, thinking to myself, 'God, wouldn't it be nice to play in a beautiful hall, and have flowers all around?'"

"That story got planted in my head! The next time they were coming to my area was in Northampton the following June. They weren't playing the Iron Horse that time, it was the Calvin. The sound's not great, but it's a beautifully restored theatre, the place looks great. I had a few email addresses of fans that I had corresponded privately with. I sent out maybe twenty-five mails explaining that if people wanted to donate whatever they thought they could afford, I would buy as many flowers as I could, get them to the theatre, get them on the stage – they could send a card that I'd take, too, and give it to Margo so she'd know who it was from. I said I'd try to get a few pictures from the show; make a recording of it, too. Obviously, I couldn't just put a message out on the board, in case Margo or any of the band checked in and saw it.

"Some people didn't respond, others sent questions and decided against it, but then maybe twelve people or so said, 'Sure', and sent some money. I got hold of a wholesaler and I bought 200 yellow roses, about fourteen vases full of flowers. I knew that Margo had an appointment before the soundcheck, so while she was away I showed up at the venue with these flowers, vases and buckets of water. There's an unused bathroom next to the stage, so I got all this stuff in there. While I was in there, they started the soundcheck. So I'm cutting the stems off, peeling off the leaves, arranging them, stuck in this bathroom until they finish soundchecking. Finally, it went quiet, I peeked out, nobody around, so I got out and left.

"Now, I always bring Margo flowers, especially in Northampton, but obviously, that day, I hadn't sent any. She actually sent John Farnsworth backstage to try and find some, because she didn't have any and she knew I must have sent some. But John said there was nothing there and, apparently, she couldn't work it out. Anyway, the opening act finished and then, the stagehands, John and I just went into the bathroom, took out all the vases and arranged them around where she sits. I'd also got a basket with all the cards in it and put a big card on top that listed everyone's name alphabetically, but in arranging everything else somebody had put the basket to the side. She came out for the start of the show, saw all these flowers and didn't say anything. She wouldn't even look at them; she was looking out at the crowd."

"That was really freaky! It was really odd that Ed hadn't sent any flowers in the day, and I missed them. 'Doesn't anybody love me any more?!' So, anyway, we went out to play and, as I walked onstage, wherever I look, there are vases and vases of roses, and it scared me to death. It made sense why Ed hadn't sent a bouquet before the show, because he'd obviously gone crazy! Oh. My. God! From flowers making me feel calm, I really felt uncomfortable, because in my mind suddenly Ed has gone from being the friendly flower guy to a serial killer, the guy in 'Floorboard Blues'! The only explanation was that Ed had crossed the line and we were going to have to do something about him."

"I could see that she was trying to ignore it and, because the basket with the cards in it had got hidden, I could tell that she thought that I had personally bought all these flowers, that I'd gone a little bit beyond being a friendly fan and now I was a stalker! A couple of songs in, she said, 'OK, I can't keep it in any longer. What is this?!' Then she said, 'Ed, I hope you're not responsible for this, because if you are, you're a real, certified …' And then, as she was talking, Mike pointed to the basket with the cards. She said, 'Oh, I've got mail!' She opened the card and started to cry; she dedicated 'Misguided Angel' to all the people who had contributed. It was very heartfelt; she went on the message board afterwards and sent a big, long thank-you to everyone, saying that she didn't have to dream about sitting on that big stage surrounded by flowers any longer. That had happened for her now.

"To see the way she felt and how touched she was that people had taken an interest in her, I think that was a transition point in our relationship with the band as fans, though she said afterwards that, at the time, she felt really bad because, when she thought it was just me, she thought we couldn't be friends any longer. The people who were involved, some of them knew they wouldn't be at the show to see it, but they still sent their money because they wanted to take part, they wanted to give something back to the band. That's pretty unique."

YOU CAN ALWAYS SEE IT COMING, BUT YOU CAN NEVER STOP IT

Lay It Down is an insidious record, a misunderstood record, one that some see as among the Junkies' most commercial work, yet a record which is, without doubt, among their most emotionally draining.

The death of love, the loss of emotion, the desolation of hopelessness, are all there. Maybe all you need to know about the record comes in three songs – 'Lonely Sinking Feeling', 'Bea's Song' and 'Now I Know' – an unconnected interdependent trilogy that flows through the second half of the record.

They are songs of betrayal, because it wasn't true that, "Tomorrow may be the day that our love betrays us." It happened today, or yesterday. Not deliberate betrayal, not human betrayal, but a betrayal wrought upon us by malevolent gods watching down and deciding to crucify someone for the sport of it. One day you're there, the next day you've been hit by a truck. One that nobody was driving because, really, it's nobody's fault. We love to apportion blame, but sometimes it's just how it is and that's even worse. You try to hold on to it, but it has run through your fingers and out the door, and nobody did anything wrong. It just left, the same way it just arrived. From out of fucking nowhere.

"Just when I thought I'd discovered the joy of loving one so completely, that lonely sinking feeling creeps up on me."

"The slightest move and this river mud pulls me further down, John's at my side but he's not noticing that I'm drowning."

A relationship in tatters because love has moved on; is quixotic, mischievous, savage. And you keep fighting, and you grow emptier. You try to hold on for those around you, the innocent victims, because you don't want to put them through it, because they've done nothing. And you try to hold on in case there's a change inside you, the other innocent victim who is guilty and condemned and collapsing. And days pass, and weeks, months, maybe years, and all that happens "seems as clear as spit". And you no longer have any idea who you are, because you're being somebody who has closed down just to try to get through every day. But, really, everybody is lost and there is no way of getting it back. And there is no comfort of those "extra few feet in my bed" this time. This time, it's walking "away, like Judas from the table".

"Now I know what it means to be broken. Now I know what it means to be bared."

CHAPTER 15

Wink once and flash me that old grin

If you've just broken up a long-lasting relationship, it makes sense to sit back and reflect a little before leaping headlong into another. What went wrong? Where do you go from here? What do you really want from a partnership, and will getting into bed with somebody else ever really work out for you?

If it's a business relationship, though, time may not always be a commodity that you have much of. Back in 1994, 1995, if you were a rock band operating in the commercial league – and Cowboy Junkies were, a point emphasized by Oliver Stone's use of 'Sweet Jane' as part of the soundtrack to *Natural Born Killers* – you needed to maintain a profile, and to do that you had to work with a major label. The internet was still a long way from being a tool that allowed bands to communicate directly with their fans, much less sell things to them. Back then, you needed a presence in the market place, you needed a promotional budget and you needed people getting out there, putting your albums in the racks, your posters in the stores, your name in front of the DJs and in the magazines. Without that, how would people know about your new record? Basically, you still needed to work for the Man, the company.

It's a concept that never really sat well with the band, as Pete points out. "Musical control has always been what we've been after, not world domination, not those huge numbers. We just want to do what we want to do. Back before we signed to BMG, we thought about some smaller labels, too, and we almost went with Cooking Vinyl, just because we were scared of what a big label would do to us. Even if they promised us our freedom, we thought they might take that away. Michelle Shocked was big with them, so they were a real possibility, but then we stumbled on Jim Powers and that eased our minds about BMG."

Fears of the corporate machine had been both eased and intensified by the BMG years. The more they dealt with the big company, the tougher it got. The more they dealt with an A&R person they could trust, the better things went. Sometimes, fate smiles.

"Jim Powers left around the time of *Caution Horses*," recalls Mike. "He was a young guy, we got on well, and once he wasn't our A&R guy we became even better friends! He was very honest, straightforward, and it happened that, as we left BMG, he'd just joined Geffen, so it was a pretty simple thing. They gave us a really good deal – there was no more to it than that."

Powers agrees that the stars were neatly aligned for a few moments. "After I left BMG, I moved back to Chicago to start a label, Minty Fresh. BMG being a record company, the turntable keeps moving and people change jobs every two years, so that was frustrating for the band, to not have a constant person to deal with at the label. I did some A&R work with Geffen while continuing to run Minty Fresh, and one of the first things I wanted to do when I got there was work with Cowboy Junkies. I knew they were ready to move on from BMG and so the timing was pretty much right."

Had Powers not been so involved at Geffen, it's hard to say just where the Junkies would have ended up, or if the decision would have taken a lot more agonizing over. Time and again, the band has drawn its conclusions based on "who" rather than "how much", so once Powers was available the die was cast, according to Alan. "Early on with RCA, when things were going big with *Trinity Session*, we always had Jim Powers as an ally and if we ever had a problem, he'd deal with it. With them it was, 'Who do these guys think they are, just making a record and delivering it to us without us guiding it?' They got pissed off with that, because we were the only band who did it.

"When we went to Geffen with Jim, he told Geffen that they couldn't touch us, that we'd hand over the record and they released it, and if that was a problem don't sign us. So we've been very lucky that way we've been shielded from that crap, and the only things that bothered us were the promotional things where we had to give in and do stupid things that they thought sold records, just because that bought us the freedom to go our own way musically. It seemed a good move. Geffen was bigger – they had a cool history, they'd done well off the Nirvana catalogue. They offered us basically the same deal we had with BMG and, with Jim there, we knew it would be safe, we could do what we want, deliver an album, no questions asked."

Of course, nothing is ever quite that simple, not in the real commercial world, as Mike concedes. "There was more pressure on us as we went in to do what became *Lay It Down*. Jim was happy to sign us, but he said, 'I don't want to tell you what to do with the record, but I want to feel free to talk about it, to listen to it and offer my opinion.' That had never happened in the past. I'd always blocked out the company because I thought they had enough influence anyway, without letting them in to say anything. Jim felt a bit wounded at that, maybe, but by then we'd known each other long enough that I was happy to let him offer his opinions. Definitely the dollar figures were bigger, so there was an element of pressure there, for sure. You are aware that the stakes are higher."

Artistically the stakes were high, too. *Pale Sun, Crescent Moon* had attracted mixed reviews and was something of a staging post for the band, featuring some strong material, some good playing, but so lyrically and sonically dense that it hadn't always been easy to find the songs within. Everyone involved, in and around the band, recognized that, just as *The Caution Horses* had ended a chapter, so *Pale Sun* had ended an era, *200 More Miles* closing that book. As Jim Powers said, in 1995, ten years into their career, "It was time for them to shake the tree a little bit, to reinvigorate it. I think Mike felt that it was time for them to strip the sound down again after working with a lot of outside players, to say, 'Where are they now when it's just the four of them again? What are Cowboy Junkies about today?'

"Mike was also challenging himself as a guitar player, cranking it up a bit, playing more lead guitar, and I found that very exciting. Personally, I wondered what Margo's voice would sound like in a more multilayered situation simply because, as an instrument, it is phenomenal and I thought it could be exploited in a number of other situations, using reverb, whatever."

Yet again, it's the central Junkies paradox. Go as far out as *All That Reckoning* and they don't sound anything like they did twenty-five years before, and yet they sound exactly the same. Musically, it comes from the fact that there is always progression, but there are always touchstones. Beyond that, maybe it's what Frank Zappa used to call "conceptual continuity", the fact that everything Cowboy Junkies does comes from who Cowboy Junkies are.

There is also a strange internal cycle of events going on that has twice worked itself out. *Pale Sun* could almost have been labelled a "Michael Timmins solo project", the rest of the band seemingly less involved in the building of the finished arrangements and songs, more there as players – certainly compared with a record like *The Caution Horses*. A similar point was reached on *One Soul Now*, another insular, claustrophobic record. Leaving aside *Early 21st Century Blues* – largely a record of covers, a palate-cleanser in the way that *200 More Miles* had been – after *One Soul Now* came *At the End of Paths Taken*, a piece that involved new instrumentation and orchestration, the use of an outside studio wizard and a far greater involvement from Margo, Alan and Pete from the bottom up. It's as if, for the band's leader and guiding light, the tunnel vision that goes with the territory occasionally needs to be thrown back into widescreen. Or maybe Mike's not so sure: "I do see the parallels. Also, *Lay It Down* had a primarily white cover, as does *At the End of Paths Taken*. Freaky, man ..."

Cover art was still a long way off as the band started planning their first Geffen record. What was on the agenda was the idea this was going to be a much more band-orientated, band-focused offering, centred on the core four. Sure, other players and sounds might make a contribution as recording went on, but this was going to be the essential version of the Junkies, according to Mike: "*Lay It Down* was very stripped down, which is what we wanted. We'd done a couple of records with other musicians and it was time to get back to the four of us.

"The way we put it together was really important – it was a way of working that we hadn't used in a few years. We found this place called Rock Island, not so far out of Toronto, but far enough that we didn't go home at night. We were all married by then, so it was the first time since *Trinity Session* where we'd gotten away from our lives and got together as a band for a few days, just to play music together, live together. We weren't on the road, so there weren't those pressures, no other people – just us and making the music again."

While isolation plays its part, Alan reckons the big influence on the record might have been more primeval: "*Lay It Down* was the meat record. We went away to work on it in this out-of-the-way place, so we took a lot of food with us. We bought so much meat, we were eating it for weeks. Maybe meat is the secret.

"Actually, for those sessions, getting away from it all was really helpful. It was a little like being on the road: you get all day to think about the show, whereas if you're at home and you've got a gig that night, by the time you get there, your focus is scattered because you've been busy doing your normal life stuff all day and you never get that same intensity. On Rock Island, there was nothing to do but rehearse the material, and that was fun."

Being so heavily involved from the get-go also brings with it a greater sense of ownership of the material for all the band, and a heavier emotional investment in the end product. Even today, Margo talks glowingly onstage of *Lay It Down* being one of her favourite records and that must – at least in part – be down to the fact that the music breathes more easily than on *Pale Sun*, that the arrangements are looser, the feel more relaxed. Above all, it feels and sounds like a record made as a group, start to finish.

The Rock Island location also provided some source material, not simply as a result of the environment, but because of the people they were exposed to. There are two versions of 'Come Calling' on the record, a "his and hers" coupling that is based upon the life of the caretaker at the house they used. Mike explains, "It's a very sad idea about the end of a very long relationship, a true thing based on the caretaker there. He was this East German pilot from the Korean War. He'd escaped to the West and emigrated to Canada, brought his wife with him and, in the last few years, she had Alzheimer's and was slowly dying while he was slowly drinking himself to death. You had these two lives that had been together, this really loving relationship, her brain was failing, his liver was going, and they were dying together in horrible circumstances. More generally, it's about these two entities falling apart and that's why I wanted to have his song and her song. His is, as usual, 'I gotta do something'; her version is a bit freaked out, just waiting."

'(Her Song)' captures a desolation that's missing from the other, its languid sound more typical of the Junkies. It's rootless, helpless, alone, stuck in the midst of an unfolding tragedy, the narrator enveloped by the inevitability of the ongoing, impending, worsening loss. As Margo says, "Men and women will approach the same emotion differently. That's why things are so complicated. I took a lot of direction on the '(His Song)' version. This one came much more naturally to me."

Where '(Her Song)' has a melancholic acceptance of what will be, hinting at the slide into dementia, the male version is more aggressive, catching that sense of raging against the dying of the light, however futile. As Mike says, "We were experimenting with different rhythms to see if we could turn the song around a bit. It devolved into this version and we really liked it. It brought a whole new attitude to the song – you really get the devastation of what's going on. It's a song about two people, and the perspective shifts in and out. So we made it two perspectives on a relationship."

It's not necessary to know the backstory to get anything from those songs, for it could be any collapsing relationship, at any stage in life, the male voice thrashing away at the decay to try to beat it into shape or otherwise just escape it; the female voice waiting to see where the pieces lie when the storm has blown out, to see if they can be rescued. Although that pairing of songs has not endured in the concert repertoire, they are integral elements on a record that is about making choices, about uncertainty, about being at a crossroads, about being forced into corners. The material was a logical progression from that of *Black Eyed Man* and *Pale Sun, Crescent Moon*, moving from the first flush of love and the excitement of a new relationship and on into the realization that turning that into something lasting demands a lot of work. Then come the next batch of questions. Does it really have to be this hard? Isn't there something more fun out there? When did I become this two-headed monster? Why can't I find myself any more? What happened to him/her? Why has she/he turned off? When did I turn off? Who hid the switch? What the hell do I do now? Is this worth it any longer? What if this is as good as it gets? All the big questions, all the time. Life with Cowboy Junkies ...

Where *Pale Sun, Crescent Moon* asked equally huge questions, there was a lack of clarity there, hiding the subtleties and the nuances of the songs, certainly in the initial plays. While nobody has ever accused

Cowboy Junkies of being obvious, for *Lay It Down* it was important that the songs be presented a little more accessibly. The writing and arranging process of the core four had seen the songs take form and shape and, for the most part, it was a shape that needed but minimal augmentation.

They were also songs that saw Mike take a step into the foreground again and pick up lead guitar, or at least his version of lead guitar. "Even when I play lead, I work inside the rhythm of the song more than the melody. For me it's the feel that's most important – how I attack the notes, as opposed to which notes I play. I've always appreciated blues players. I can't really play that way, but I admire the soul and effort they put into every note." In another nod to conceptual continuity, it's when Mike has the most personal statements to make that the guitar really comes into its own. The rage on the guitar solo in 'Basquiat' on *At the End of Paths Taken* has echoes of some of the material on *Lay It Down* – the title song, in particular – where there's a similar impotent frustration, albeit from a different root. In those circumstances, it makes sense to have another set of ears either helping with or running the production.

"The *Pale Sun* experience had been exhausting for me," admits Mike. "We did it in a very short period, it was a ton of work, so I didn't want to produce the next one. It was a whole new thing with Geffen, because we had to force our way to getting it made. We had songs, we were ready. We knew there was a record in there somewhere and the only way to find it was to make it. Jim put us in touch with John Keane, which was perfect. John pushed for us, too; he thought the time had come. It was the first time we'd had to do that, because in the past we just recorded when we wanted. This time we had to negotiate just to go and make it!

"Working with John was great. He had a nice, cosy little studio in Athens, Georgia; we went there to hide away, that was cool. His studio was very comfortable – it was a big old house, it got us out of our environment in Toronto, and it worked. We'd developed our ideas on Rock Island, then when we went to Athens it was the same kind of working pattern. After we'd finished recording, we didn't go back to our houses every day, we went back to the place we'd rented, [to] watch the thunderstorms and the fireflies. That was good for us, to get that feeling back again. That was a big part of the record.

"We ended up with a very relaxed-sounding record. That's a big credit to John: he was very laid-back, Georgia is a relaxed place, hot as hell, no pressure on us. John had a schedule where his wife had just had twins, so at five o'clock or something the session would stop, so he could help out at home. We'd have a couple of hours off, we'd go eat, come back do a couple more hours – it was a nice way to work. I was more relaxed personally, too. I had decided I was not going to deal with the studio side of it. I was just going to play, and that was great.

"John Keane was very different for us. He's from the South, which is very different to being a northerner. He's a very quiet guy – we thought *we* were quiet until we met him! He was very unexpressive in some ways which was because he was so thoughtful, he takes his time. We hadn't worked with a lot of producers outside of our own circle at that point, so we didn't always know how to interpret what he was saying, his personality. It was an interesting album to make, because he had great insight into the music; he kept it simple, which was great for us. We needed that at the time."

Georgia itself certainly played a big part in the making of the record, according to Alan: "It was so hot when we went to Georgia to make *Lay It Down*, 100 degrees, really humid, normal weather down there. It was insane. Everybody was really low-key, struggling through the heat, and you can see that in the record – it's kinda loose. Environment is really important to the process; it shapes what you get. Even if you go in with all the songs written and ready, which we did then, the environment still dictates a certain part of the performance." Small wonder, then, as David Houghton points out, we might not have been talking about *"Lay It Down"*, after all. "*Lay It Down* might have been called '*Athens*'. It's an instinctive process. Mike and I generally talk about album titles, because there's typically more than one alternative."

Pete was very enthusiastic about working in Athens, adding, "John had a great studio, he'd done Vic Chesnutt's record, he'd worked with 10,000 Maniacs and R.E.M., so that was interesting, just to get his view on our sound." In spite of the big-name credits, Jim Powers was initially attracted to Keane as a producer for rather more low-key reasons: "He'd worked on Grant McLennan's *Horsebreaker Star*, which I thought was a really ingenious record with a lot of breadth. They met John and hit it off, and away they went."

To suggest that either *Black Eyed Man* or *Pale Sun, Crescent Moon* had been strident records would be too much, but in Junkies terms they were certainly rockier than their predecessors. *Lay It Down* went back to using silence as a starting point, that Zen-like approach to the music where nothing – the state of nothing – had a real value and should only be punctured if there was something of value to say.

That attitude was helped by the fact that this was very much music made only by Mike, Margo, Al and Pete, as Margo agrees. "We have always been happy with silence. That's something we always had. When we get new players with us, that's hard for them to learn. 'Just don't play. That's OK!' If you stop, it doesn't mean the song falls apart, because there are other players. Even silence is a sound; it'll add to it. I love that space as a singer. It gives me a place to work, because I don't have a voice that can go over the top of these big electric guitars! Don't not play on purpose, but if it doesn't make sense to you, don't do it.

"Even people close to us find it hard. When we started rehearsing for the 2005 tour, when John rejoined us, he was playing all the time, and he slowly learned to rein back. It's the same with my singing style. I can put everything into a perfect note, but not everything has to be that way. Some nights I will sing it perfect if that's how I feel; some nights it sounds different, more emotional, maybe. For 'Now I Know', on the end of *Lay It Down*, I wanted to do it really from my heart, because I love those words. I've felt that, I think everybody's that's been alive has felt it – just that crushed feeling. I wanted that to come across. I told Mike that I'd know when I was ready to sing it, because I didn't just want to go in the studio one happy afternoon and try it. So, one night, I said to Mike, 'I'm ready to do it.' And I knew I just wanted to do it, not retouch it, so I sang it, and when I'd finished I said, 'OK, that's it.' John Keane was great with us, but he said, 'Really? It sounds like crap!' But that was it, how I wanted it to be. That goes back to honesty. It might not sound great in technical terms, might not be 'perfect", I'll leave a mistake in because, if I fix it, it's going to ruin the whole thing. I don't know when records started having to be perfect. Those old blues records with the guys just jamming away, tons of mistakes, but they were so real. Some music should be perfect – that's its style, but it's not ours."

'Now I Know', following on from 'Come Calling (Her Song)', sees the album end on a sombre note, and very deliberately so, bringing it to a close, very much like an anthology of short stories, as Mike explains. "'Now I Know' was the very last song that I wrote for the record. I did it in Athens and, to me, that and 'Something More Besides You' are bookends – that was the conceptual element to the sequencing. I knew I needed a final song; the themes in that record had to have a summation and that's what that song is. It's an understanding of grief in a way, of loss, coming to terms with it. This is what relationships are about, what life's about – constant evolving, the losing of what you think you have – and that's the overall feeling from that record."

As far as what can loosely be described as their "relationship" records are concerned, *Lay It Down* is perhaps the most tortured of all, because it's gone past realization, gone past questioning. Now you're at the point where you turn back to the heart of it or you turn away for good. Where you inflict loss, or suffer loss, or where you encounter mortality and the greater loss that brings with it. Or where you try to rediscover that spark that was there to start with, the thing that kicked off the mad notion of trying to hold on to someone in the midst of a world that does everything in its power to make that impossible.

Mike would later write of "The rare good will of the random world", but on *Lay It Down* that randomness tends to the malign rather than the benevolent, right from the outset in 'Something More Besides You'. A gentle musical opening that barely scratches the silence, in the verses at least, this is the sound of the Velvet Underground almost thirty years on. Lyrically, it's deeply ambiguous, yet with open-wound rawness to it – not surprising, given its source.

"'Something More Besides You' is another of my favourite songs. It's really personal. A lot of weird things were happening in my life at that point and it focuses on those. It has a real sad side to it, but the chorus has this odd question about it. 'Is there something more besides you': is that a positive thing or a negative!? Ultimately it's very hopeful – there's nothing out there as great as you; there can't be anything better – but I guess you could interpret it as 'You mean there isn't anything better? Shit!' That summed up the situation I had, in a strange way. It's a perfect opening to the record; it sets up this sort of idea where you're never quite sure where you're going with this thing."

It suggests you're never quite sure where you're going with your life, either, an echo from the opening stretch of *Pale Sun, Crescent Moon*. From wider questions of faith ("I still wonder is there a point to what we do?") to the deeply personal, the song stretches across thirtysomething questioning. Weren't we supposed to be settled when we got to this age? Wasn't it supposed to start making sense by now? Then there's the railing at our own lack of patience, victims of the instant, consumer, jump-cut world that we inhabit, that has smashed the concentration span so totally that we are becoming ever more immune to moments when "Small mysteries slowly unfold". Who can be in anything for the long haul now when the long haul doesn't exist, when we're being reprogrammed to want new experiences all the time? Then there's that final glimpse of … is it fear of the unknown or a shaft of hope? "Do I dare believe that there is something more besides you?"

It's a song of impatience, at our own failings, at the way life squeezes you into mundane patterns, taking the little joys with it – and at our own stupidity and inability to recognize those small blessings that still surround us because we're too busy looking for something bigger and better. Maybe it's actually sitting right in front of us. And maybe the ongoing struggle with dissatisfaction is what makes us human.

The random world, dumb luck – call it what you will – its impact crashes in again and again, be it the worry that destiny can pass you by, simply because you looked in the wrong direction at the wrong moment on 'Something More Besides You', or the caving in of the ceiling from out of nowhere on 'Lonely Sinking Feeling'. That moment where everything that was going fine just calcifies in front of you as the other person switches off. And you did nothing. And neither did they.

"I thought of it as a Roy Orbison-type of ballad, a little formulaic almost, but with a twist," says Mike. "It's about that feeling of a lack of control in relationships; that's something that's hard for everybody. How it can be fine, you can be doing OK, then suddenly you turn round one day and it's just gone. 'Bea's Song' is paired with that, too – it's the same kind of idea. I love 'Bea's Song', it has a lot in it, it sums up ageing, sums up life. 'You can always see it coming but you can never stop it' – it just keeps on coming at you; there's no place to hide!"

If forced to pick a single line that summed up Cowboy Junkies, that would be as good a place as any to start. A universal emotion rendered deeply personal, a sense that you are adrift in the world, that you can't get away from it, but with that nagging thought in the background that it's pretty much your own fault and yet, at the same time, that you really do have no control over your emotions, much less those of someone else. It's almost giving permission to go through that much-maligned process, the midlife crisis, not in the sense of buying a Porsche or a Harley, but in opening the book and allowing the questions to flood in, even when you know that the answers – if you can find any – are going to be ones that you don't want to hear. Of 'Bea's Song', Margo says, "I can see where this woman is sitting. I know that feeling of 'I'm not OK, I'm not in a good place.' There's nothing specifically wrong; she just knows that she's not happy. It goes, 'John says I look at the moon and the stars these days more often than I look into his eyes.' She can't disagree, so she doesn't say anything." Is it better to have words left unsaid than words misunderstood?

Even for Cowboy Junkies, 'Lonely Sinking Feeling' and 'Bea's Song' are pretty heart-rending, and a casual listen would only reinforce the impression that this band are minimalist miserablists. Thing is, Junkies records don't cater for casual listening, as long-term fan Jason Gonulsen says: "It's serious music, but that doesn't mean it's depressing, which is how a lot of people write them off. I've read a lot of quotes from songwriters who say they turn on sad songs to cheer them up, and I can understand that. Life isn't all champagne and strawberries – there's a lot of harder things that go on – but the fact that other people have gone through that and have written about it is hopeful and I think they pull that off really well. I don't play their music to depress me and I never leave it depressed, so there are obviously hopeful messages in there."

From on board the boat, Jeff Bird has this view: "There is something about embracing the pain of the world, people take comfort from that, that you're not alone. On the road over the years, there are many people who've come and told us stories of how this music has helped them through. People dismiss it as depressing, but it's very hopeful, kinda like the blues. That came out of pain, oppression, the worst situations you could be in. And a lot of religious music does likewise – perhaps misguided in some senses – the sentiment that it's not always that great here. I guess the idea of heaven came from that; it's got to be better than this somewhere!"

Neither 'Lonely Sinking Feeling' and 'Bea's Song' offer much in the way of resolution, but most of the time neither does life. Where's the guarantee of a happy ending anywhere in life? If you've got the paperwork for that, can you send the rest of us a copy? You offer that happy-clappy idea up and it might sell you more records, but who are you fooling? 'Most of the people, most of the time', is probably the answer if you look at what sells, but there are plenty of us who don't want to live in a delusion. Tell it to us straight. We can take it. Along with our Prozac …

Both songs are about the death of a dream, in the heritage of 'The Last Spike', but now in an emotional rather than an economic sense, a subject matter that Mike returns to later on songs like 'Ikea Parking Lot' and 'Morning Cried', both of which were collected on *Notes Falling Slow*. Sometimes, just the knowledge that you're not the only one that got mown down is enough solace, knowledge that plenty of us are going where life takes us rather than where we want to go. This music makes you feel better about your own imperfections, gives you a sense of shared experience. If these people are troubled, then it's OK to be troubled yourself. It's no fun, but it's a part of life, of all our lives. Maybe that makes it easier to carry the load.

You have to be pretty lucky, or pretty insensitive, to get from the crib to the casket without being broken at some time – by ourselves, by others, by chance, by the simple passing of time – but there's something in the human race that sees most of us find a reason to go on, even in the face of crushing defeat. There isn't anything more uplifting than that triumph of the spirit. That's what so much of this music is about.

Margo is right on the mark when she says, "Music is something to get you to the next day. Life can be really hard and, if you can put on your favourite record, and cry along to it, that's what it's for. If I hear our music has done that, then I know it's been worthwhile. You can get so wrapped up in the business, but if you hear a story like that, who cares? If I never sing another song, we've touched someone and made things a little better for them. That's a good job. I love that."

Life is light and shade, and so are Junkies records, the light on *Lay It Down* coming in no small measure from 'Angel Mine', a song that splits opinions inside the camp. "I never really liked 'Angel Mine' all that much," says Mike. "I was never sure it should go on the record. Then it was slated as the second single, it was that or 'Speaking Confidentially', which would have been a much smarter choice, it was a different kind of song – it had that string thing in it, but there was no chorus, so they left it. 'Angel Mine' is too floaty and sappy and it was a lousy song to follow up 'Common Disaster' with; I think they really screwed up. I enjoy doing that song live sometimes as an acoustic thing, but to play over and again it's another one that's too straight, doesn't go anywhere."

For Margo, it's a song that came of age later, a fresh emotion coming through a decade on from its recording. "When we first did it, it was a poppy little song. But we took it out in rehearsals for the 2005 tour and I started looking at it again and it just hit me as a whole different thing, the 'I can't promise' line. I'd been married seventeen years at that point. I can't still be the girl my husband married, because I'm not her any more. I'd love to be, God knows! It was so much easier then! But it was two decades ago. But I can try, and I can always promise that, no matter what happens, I will never, ever betray him. To me now, that's what that song is about. I'm not cute any more but I will not hurt you, I will always be there, that's what I can promise. That's what 'Angel Mine' says now. It didn't when we made the record, believe me! It was a la-la-la pop song. Rediscovering a song like that is so exciting.

"We hadn't played it in a million years, but it was so funny when we brought it out again. I hated it then because it was too poppy and stupid, but years later I love it, it's saying something I feel as a 45-year-old woman who's been married a long time. I'm not the girl, I'm better, just different! And for me, there's a sadness in it, too. With women, in their mid-forties, there's a loss. We have a more serious mourning of our youth than men do, because men just go on being stupid!"

Musicians can be a little stupid, too, according to the singer. "For years, they would do songs in a key I couldn't sing in and they wouldn't change! I didn't realize they should change for me, that I'm the singer and I can't retune! I only have this range. Now, though, we'll change it and that helps a lot. 'Angel Mine' isn't a key I should be singing in, so I can't hit that last note in the chorus, but I didn't know we could change it. Jeff was always shocked, I think – 'She can't sing that; why are we playing it like this?'

"Saying that, it's emotion that matters more than technical perfection. Some people are born with a good voice – your aunt Mary sings at weddings, she can hold a tune or whatever. But I don't think it makes her a singer, just because she has a pretty voice. It's all the other stuff: the phrasing, the interpretation, the control, the being able to hear something in your head and making it happen, using it as an instrument. I think *Lay It Down* was the first time that I really felt I had that kind of control and ability. Yes, before that my voice was pretty and hopefully I'd been a good interpreter because I always approached it from my heart, always from a feeling. Around *Lay It Down*, I started to take lessons. It's not that I didn't need them before, but back then I was afraid that I'd lose something, that my voice would disappear. Because I didn't know how I was doing it or what I was doing, I thought that, if

I had lessons, the teacher might take away whatever it was people were responding to. I wanted to stay away from anybody tampering with it.

"By *Lay It Down*, I realized I knew what I was doing and I could go away and learn technique without ruining the stuff that was making people happy, what made my voice unique. I had no technique up to then. There's a lot to be said for not knowing what you're doing. Lennon and McCartney weren't trained, Mike's not, but they find things because they don't have that technique, they come across different ways of doing something that a trained player might not. As a band, we've grown together, we've never asked anything of one another that's beyond what we could do. Which isn't to say that Michael hasn't challenged me, but he knew I could do it and he pushed me to be better.

"Same with Pete. Listen to *Whites Off Earth Now!!* and it's very basic. But, as you go through the records, you hear him, and the rest of us, becoming more skilful. If we couldn't do it, we didn't. 'Sweet Jane' was meant for *Whites!!*, but we didn't have it at that point, we couldn't do it well enough. So we waited until we could. That's fine, no problem. First time we tried 'Thunder Road', one of my favourite Springsteen songs, I just couldn't handle that material. I could sing it, but it didn't mean anything. We came back to it years later, and I found a way in, and there's a lot of songs like that. We've always known that things change, that things have their time, that we will improve."

Musically, the band had never sounded better, in particular the rhythm section, Alan and Pete reaching a new peak, as Jason Lent suggests. "Pete's development from *Whites Off Earth Now!!* to *Black Eyed Man* was rapid as he grew into Al's style. Then he moves outward and reaches a level of perfection on *Lay It Down*. To me, that album is flawless on drums and the best example of everything Pete does well. Since then, Al and Pete's playing on the studio recordings has felt more 'equal' – that's the best word I can find – though onstage they had reached that level on earlier tours."

Jason Gonulsen is of a similar mind, and adds, "The hardcore audience appreciate what Al and Pete – and Jeff, too – bring to things, but you can't get away from the fact that Mike and Margo are going to be in the spotlight. Without Al and Pete, though, the package wouldn't be complete. Al just stands there, he doesn't have any tricks he does, but he's an integral part to it, he grounds what they do. Pete's a very underrated drummer, but I guess he gets overlooked a little because he's the kid brother and because the focus is so much on the singer and the song. But that relationship is a very important part of who Cowboy Junkies are. These are people working together as a real band, a real team, and if you don't understand that I don't think you really understand their music."

The interplay between Alan and Pete is crucial to the overall feel of the Junkies, and they perform the not inconsiderable task of giving the band an energy – when called for – while still being hugely understated. Which is pretty much the way they are as people, too. Ask Pete when it was that they really started to feel comfortable as a rhythm section and the reply you get is, "Oh, we're still waiting for that to happen! Mike and Al were friends before I was born, so we spent a lot of time together growing up, we'd play tag and I was always 'it'! We knew each other pretty well, but it still took a while to lock in. It used to be a lot of work when we were putting together a new song, where now we can piece it together in an hour or something. Back in the early days, a song would take us a week if we were lucky. And a lot of that hanging on a note or hanging on a beat came from that – it was tricky getting into the chorus! It's still growing."

According to Alan, "Our underlying sound has always been the same, it's who the four of us are and what we like from music. I guess we're a real band in that sense and in that Cowboy Junkies as a unit is more than the sum of the parts when we come together. That's pure luck, really; you just need the right chemistry among the people. When we started, Pete was very raw, he wasn't quite good enough and we got a couple of other drummers to play with us at different times, but it was never the same. We wanted them to play songs the way Pete had and they tried it, but there was just something about it that was missing. It's the personality thing that comes through when the four of us play together.

"People say it's the family connection, and I guess that helps, but a lot is luck. Look at Led Zeppelin: there's a studio veteran who somehow finds a 19-year-old singer who says he'll only be in his band if the drummer can come as well; there's a session bassist; and then they just have the greatest chemistry you could wish for – it was explosive. You need that luck.

"As a rhythm section, we don't work the traditional way, where the drums and the bass are just locked together – we have some songs like that, but it's not something we do all the time. The way Mike brings the song to us is just him strumming on an acoustic guitar with the lyric and he wants me and Pete to do something with it and take it on, because he doesn't want to do that, he wants to go and make noises or whatever, he leaves that structure there for us to work around. It's an interesting way of working a song, because it starts with nothing, really; there is no music there yet, just a sketch of what the chords are. Musically, they are group-written songs in a lot of ways. Usually we get an idea of what kind of groove it needs right at the beginning, but sometimes we won't and it goes through all kinds of changes and mutations – faster, slower, different groove, whatever – as we're trying to find it.

"The funny thing is, we all know when it's not working and, when it is, there's no argument about it, we all just feel it at the same time. There are one or two songs that we've dragged with us for as much as seven years before we've finally found a place for it to sit, but that's pretty rare. Usually, it's not so much of a search. I was reading the Dylan *Chronicles* book and he was talking about the way he operates, specifically about *Time out of Mind*, which he did with Daniel Lanois. He went to New Orleans, and Lanois got the musicians together, and Dylan played the songs and tried to get the band to play along and it just went off in all these directions. Lanois' input was huge: they worked on one song for two weeks and argued about it every day – Lanois is going one way, Dylan's going another. It was just such a struggle. It's amazing; that must be so frustrating to do it that way, because that's totally alien to us. They came out with a brilliant record, but the process seemed all over the place. But a lot of people work like that: they go in with the producer, the musicians, they record, scrap it, get another producer, on and on and on. For us, that would be terrible."

Pete, in particular, is very much a player who likes to get to work, get his part down and get on with something else. That spontaneity acts as a nice contrast to the more "worked-out" elements in the music, giving it a fragility that is often its greatest strength. Just as Margo admits she's not a technically perfect singer, Pete isn't really a schooled drummer, as he freely concedes: "I always feel weird at festivals when you have other drummers and it feels like a talent contest in a way. I'm not a technical drummer at all, but sometimes you get up there and follow the guy who just did 1,000 paradiddles and I'm going up there to do my pitter-patters. But it's the pitter-patters with the bass, with the guitar, that makes us. It's not about the drummer or the guitarist or the bass player, it's about Cowboy Junkies. I hate rock drum solos. I like the Max Roach solos or some of the jazz drummers where you can feel the fury coming off them, but then you get into the quarter-note kick drum solo and it's embarrassing, especially if they go on record. How do you listen to that over and over?"

Pete's drumming brings another very human element to the mix, a vulnerability, a feeling that it's all in the moment, that it could all come tumbling down, that the band could suddenly get a lonely, sinking feeling all their own. And yet it doesn't. What you have is a guy up there showing you who he is, who he really is, and God love him for that. That idea went out with those great old Blue Note sleeves, didn't it?

They always say that a drummer is like the goalkeeper in a group, and there are times when Pete really fulfils that function. "A lot of the time, we're not really playing the way a rhythm section usually does, because Al is more melodic in his basslines, so it's not the traditional kick drum/bass guitar punch that's happening. The guitar plays a big part in that, Mike kinda weaves in and out between us. I have in the past – and still do, if things are going wrong, like if Mike has a bad solo – tried to cover up by doing something different. That happens. But when the band isn't right on the money, maybe the start of a tour or something, it's about playing what you know, keeping it solid and helping everybody along by giving it that base. Al is usually pretty solid, too, so we try to lock in, and that gives us a base to work from. Then the band goes from there."

The chicken or the egg – which came first? Did Mike's guitar come from out of nowhere because Alan so often plays such melodic basslines, or did Al develop that style to keep out of the way of what Mike was doing? In making *Lay It Down*, Alan's influence was as a prime mover according to Mike, as it was with *At the End of Paths Taken* – spooky, man …

"We really wanted to keep it spare. If we weren't sure whether to add something, we didn't. The melodies are also more economical. Everything is more precise, so you hear the individual instruments better. Alan's bass was very melodic; he managed to create even more space in the songs. And John Keane pushed Pete to hit the drums harder. When Pete heard how it sounded, he was encouraged to go even further in that direction."

225

An obvious example of that sound was the first single to be taken off the record, 'A Common Disaster', a song that remains a staple of the live repertoire to this day, based around that infectious groove. Sequentially, though, it strikes an odd chord because, conceptually, it feels like the final part of a trilogy that includes 'Something More Besides You' and 'Hold on to Me', with the latter really the jumping-off point for 'A Common Disaster', going from what appears to be a simple love song that is more twisted if you delve into it. "Would I see it for the precious thing?" Probably not. Because we never do. We don't value what we have, because there's always a new horizon to head off into, something new to explore, some greener grass somewhere. From there, 'A Common Disaster' details the stupidities we inflict on ourselves to escape from something that wasn't so bad in the first place: "Run away with me from a life so cramped and dull / Not worry too much about the happily ever after". So why aren't those songs in that order?

"I didn't even think about that!" says Mike. "With that record, a lot of sequencing decisions such as putting 'Common Disaster' upfront were strictly the label saying they needed the single on early and I guess we had to give them something, so we worked round it. Those are the type of things that happened with Geffen: we compromised a bit on things like that because it wasn't such an issue – it was a good song, it hooked people into the record, we're not going to fight that one. That conceptual side of it, maybe we let it slide a little bit. There are a lot of songs on that record that are love songs with a twist, asking that question: 'Is that a good thing?'"

'A Common Disaster' pushed the band back into the kind of limelight they'd last enjoyed/endured with *The Trinity Session*, a genuine hit single that certainly got Geffen's juices flowing. "'Common Disaster' came out of left field for them," recalls Mike. "It took off and, once that happened, they put their weight behind it. Then, as soon as the single was done, they pulled back. It was very odd – the first time we really felt the nastiness of the industry. We'd always been sheltered from it with RCA, because we just did what we did and they didn't know how to deal with that. These guys were top of the heap and they felt they knew what they wanted to do, so it was tough.

"In the end, with a big company, you realize that it doesn't matter how good your record is, because if it comes out when they're trying to promote one of those mega-artists, you won't get a look in, you get lost in the shuffle. There are all these demands, these pressures, the hoops we're supposed to jump through just to please some people at the company – it's such a waste of energy. Geffen was really positive in the beginning and really negative at the end, and we just got to a point where it was zapping our strength and we couldn't do it any more. And it all comes down to luck. With *Lay It Down*, Jim Powers especially was adamant that we didn't record until we had the songs ready, and that was fine. I wrote a zillion songs, we found John Keane, but I don't think Jim could hear a single. I thought that was too early, we hadn't started working on them, how do you know how it'll turn out? Even 'Common Disaster', which ended up a pretty big single, the company couldn't see that – at the demo stage they didn't even want it on the album. They don't know any more about singles than we do, and we know nothing!"

You don't sign to Geffen without having to make some compromises, and the same was true in terms of the sleeve design, as David Houghton points out. "There was pressure to put the band on the cover. We chose to shoot with the Guzmans, a New York husband-and-wife team who shoot simultaneously to keep their subjects off-guard. The band felt it was a harrowing experience but I like the results. The whole package is absolutely stark, stripped down. It's the kind of thing you'd least expect from Cowboy Junkies, and that's part of its power. The sequence of images was intentional: you see the band on the cover, then you see them much closer inside the booklet, then you're left with an empty chair. There was something ephemeral there that appealed to me."

Margo remains less sanguine about the whole experience, however: "We had this big photo shoot, the first record with Geffen, and they brought a hairdresser in. I've always done my own hair, but I got talked into it, and she did my hair and the boys were just in pieces. I'm almost in tears, she's put so much crap in my hair that I don't look like me. I went to the bathroom and started wrecking her hairdo. If you look at the cover of that record, I always point it out to people: 'I'm really pissed off here!' I was so mad.

"That's a little thing, but, if you take that and exponentially add on to it, you can see where it leads. If I'm Margo Timmins, alone, like so many people are, and you're constantly being pushed, you lose your direction, you lose that ability to see it as it is. Somebody always says, 'Do this and you'll sell more records.' Wouldn't that be nice? It's a big push, especially if you're young. But you only sell records once, and

227

then people see through the fact that you're manufactured and they lose faith in you. The real fans you had before think that you've sold out, they don't come back, and the new ones only buy what's cool that week, anyway. But nobody tells you that side of the story, and a lot of them are very young.

"I remember when Edie Brickell was just first happening. They were the New Bohemians first. Then it was Edie Brickell and the New Bohemians, then Edie Brickell. I knew exactly what was going on with her, on a way bigger level, because she was selling ten times more records than us. She was way younger than us – I was 28, it wasn't like I hadn't done anything or been anywhere; I had a life and I could easily go back to it. She didn't have her brothers to just say, 'Edie, forget it.' They convinced her that her band wasn't good enough in the studio, they got her a new band, and it's hard to stand up to that as an individual. We've been lucky – that's where we've been able to fight them off. Of course, now nobody pressures us at all. I'd like a little more, damn it!"

Let's not be offering our sympathies to big record corporations, but playing devil's advocate for a moment, you can see why they have had such a problem getting a handle on what Cowboy Junkies do. Take a song like 'Just Want to See', another example of Mike as a short-story writer. That song has all the Junkies stuff in it inside four minutes and twenty-three seconds – loss, hope, fear of the unknown, all bleakly, blackly comic. It's no wonder that so many people miss what's going on. They can't keep up.

"You could be right!" laughs Mike. "It's pretty odd, pretty complicated, I could've written three songs there instead of one. Maybe they even started that way and I just put them together. The genesis of it was sitting on the bus and us coming to a screeching halt because we nearly hit something, and thinking, 'God, what a horrible way to go, not seeing what kills you.' Then thinking through all the ways you could go. I guess AIDS was becoming a big issue then; all those things came together. It's pretty odd. The song itself is a couple going to a friend's funeral but, in the end, they're reevaluating everything about their relationship."

At its heart, that is what *Lay It Down* is about, hitting a crossroads, reworking, rethinking, deciding or deciding not to decide. It's about how life can be going serenely by and then, suddenly, it changes because tomorrow may be the day our love betrays us. Life hangs by a thread, not just physically but emotionally. Out of our control, it can all be going great, then your life is a train wreck for no apparent reason.

"The record is about turmoil inside a person's mind. An individual being forced into a corner and trying to make choices – that's really what the whole record's about. It's about people coming up to a crossroads and having to take one road or the other. And 'Lay It Down' is the ultimate song of that theme. It's the darkest song, musically as well as lyrically. The character is faced with a decision. The chorus is suggesting that he lay it down, whatever is forcing him to decide. It's fairly open as far as the specifics are concerned; you can find your own corner in it."

Find your own corner, but you don't find any hiding place. All the big questions, all the time. Yep, that's life with Cowboy Junkies.

A STONEMASON'S CHISEL

They're an odd band, Cowboy Junkies. Their greatest strength, the attribute that has given them such a devoted audience, is their integrity and, yet, what you get with the Junkies isn't always what you see. On the surface – and, in concert, it's mainly Margo who offers up that surface – they're light, sunny, in sharp contrast to the more thoughtful, sometimes sombre music. And in contrast to the deep, and occasionally awkward, relationships within the group. How could it be any way else inside a family?

What is undeniable about the core four is the deep sense of love and loyalty that exists between them. It's a family – including Alan – in the best sense, but it's also a family with entrenched roles, perceptions, joys and irritations. No family, especially one placed in the unnatural environment of making and touring music, can be all sweetness and light. Tensions, differences of opinion and simply weariness of one another's company are occupational hazards that cannot be avoided. But they can be coped with, got past, survived, and few bands have survived as healthily as Cowboy Junkies. For that, a large slice of the credit must go to Pete.

In a lot of ways, Pete has the toughest job in the band, and in the family. You can't ever get away from the pecking order dished out by birth and, as the younger brother, it's perennially tough to be taken as seriously as your older siblings, especially when your older brother calls most of the shots in the band you are in, reinforcing that hierarchy on a daily basis. And if your older sister refers to you, however affectionately, as her little brother from the stage and, away from it, points out that you were her first baby – there are tales of ballet dresses and toilet training that we won't rehash here – it is a constant reminder. Then you are in the rhythm section with a guy whose musical intellect is up there with the very best of them.

And in this band, the drummer rarely comes out front, for it's a group where songwriting is at the core and where the extraordinary singer takes the bulk of the public plaudits. Yet so much of the Junkies' music is about nuance, and, especially live, so much of that nuance is provided by the drummer. The trouble with subtlety is that it often goes unnoticed.

Although the band has not changed its line-up since John left, Pete is always the new boy. Mike and Alan had paid their dues and were seasoned musicians before the Junkies ever got off the ground; everyone knew that Margo could sing; but Pete simply turned up with a rented kit and, an untrained player with little or no experience, demanded his chance. Even getting kicked out for a few weeks didn't dampen his enthusiasm and his determination and, eventually, Pete was back and the music and the band have been the better for it ever since.

Yes, Cowboy Junkies could have existed without Pete in a way they never could have without Margo, but in the hands of a different drummer this would be a different band. Given the clarity of Mike's vision, there is no other conclusion to draw, except that Pete is the drummer they needed, for all that Mike (by his own admission) doesn't always give Pete the credit he deserves. It's a man thing. And a brother thing.

"Pete is very interesting – he can be our absolute strength live, which he is most of the time, but occasionally he can just lose concentration and then we're screwed! That's true of any band, but especially us, because if we're going to improvise and feel out songs, the drummer has to be there. When he's there, it's fantastic; he's so much fun to play with, he keeps it locked.

"Having Al as his partner in the rhythm section is very different, because Al isn't a traditional bass player, he doesn't hold down the groove, he's doing a whole other thing. He's almost playing free. Sometimes he'll play with me because I play a lot of rhythm, so we become the rhythm section, which is unusual. Pete doesn't have that solid bass to latch on to and that's hard for a drummer; he doesn't get much help. That frustrates Pete sometimes, I guess, but he also knows that's what makes it special. He's developed a style and I don't know if you could even define it. He's unique and, again, that's a big element of our sound.

"We have played a few shows without Pete when he's been sick and we've just had to get a drummer in to sub for him, and it is completely different to play in that band. I think that goes back to how we play our instruments – we all play our own style, they're unique to us and they're all personality-driven in some way instead of technique-driven. If we lose one of the four, it's a very different band, because atmosphere or aesthetics is central to what we do. We all have similar taste, not just in a song, but in how it sounds, how a recording sounds, how to approach a vocal or a guitar part. We like the same things in music, which can have a negative side, but it also means that we have a very focused vision. We know when it's not there, when it doesn't feel right and we all know that without saying anything. We can have disagreements over small discrepancies in a song – but the general feel, we all know if we've got it or we haven't.

"When Pete injured his back and we did some shows without him in 2006, it made a difference, and it happened right before we began to think about recording *At the End of Paths Taken*, which was interesting. There were certain songs which just didn't feel nearly as good, classic Junkie grooves, I guess. We did them, but not to my satisfaction; they never had that open-ended, loose feel. Other songs, more straight-ahead, tempo-dominated songs, worked better. That's not Pete's strength – he's a looser drummer, so it was a challenge, it was refreshing in a way. I guess Pete didn't feel like that! There was no way round it:

the shows were booked and we had to play. There was nothing easy – we all had to focus on every song, we couldn't fall back on anything.

"It was interesting to be out there without Pete. I've always known what he brings to us. I appreciate his strengths, probably not enough, and his weaknesses piss me off, probably too much! That's a big brother thing, I guess. We all have strengths and weaknesses in our playing, we're not classically trained players, we all fumbled our way into this, and I guess our weaknesses are intensified between ourselves because we know each other so well, and yet that also brings something to our sound. He's not the normal rock drummer. A lot of it is subconscious, too: he's learned to play drums by being the drummer in this band, so his whole style has evolved around what we do and it's a push–pull thing. What we do influences him and what he does influences us, it goes back and forth."

Earlier on in the band's story, there were certainly greater tensions as Pete tried to find his way into his new career, into the music and into playing the same material night after night. Back then, the pressure was on in a different way to how it is now, because, for Mike and Al, Cowboy Junkies pretty much represented the last big hope of getting a working, recording band off the ground. Then, once success came, the treadmill in those first few years moved swiftly, the band played a lot of shows tired, they lived on small buses and in each other's pockets and the two brothers let off steam in each other's direction until it reached a point where both agreed it was being counterproductive. Time changes things, too, as Alan points out: "There's the family dynamic where Mike is the leader because he's older than the other two – that's my younger sister, that's my really younger brother – but that's changed a lot now. When we started, Mike and I had been in bands, this was our band and we asked them if they wanted to be in it. 'We know what to do, you guys don't, so we'll tell you what to do.' That's how it started."

It's important not to overstate the differences because, as bands go, Cowboy Junkies is – and always was – one of the more harmonious. If you've ever watched Mike and Pete watching the Stanley Cup together, hollering at the TV, you pretty quickly realize that any differences of opinion they might have are purely professional and have no impact on their personal relationship. And the Junkies know how to enjoy the experience even in tougher times, as David Houghton will testify. "Pete seemed very comfortable having me on board alongside him as a percussion player. He started out as a very instinctive player, so I think my influence helped steady him. He's grown with each passing year, and is now a very strong player. Onstage, my percussion rig was set up between Peter and Michael, and the most entertaining role I had was to ferry messages from Mike to Peter during the show. In the middle of a song, Mike would call me over and say, 'Ask Pete what the fuck he's doing over there!' or 'Ask Pete why his fucking tempo is dragging!' I'd relay the message to Pete, he'd howl with laughter, then so would Mike."

Only experience really shows you the way of making things work, no more so than within personal relationships, and Mike accepts that things have changed over time, to the benefit of them all, on and off the road. "We keep family and business separate. It's hard – you can't completely separate them, but we try not to let it leak over. When we get back home after a tour, the last person Pete or Marg want to see is me, and vice versa, so we give each other space then. To say we ignore each other is too strong a word, but we kind of do! Then, at family things, we know that that's a bigger thing than the band, so we very rarely ever let it cross over, we hardly ever even mention business in a family context. And we want that break, too. We don't want to be the Cowboy Junkies every minute of every day, so we just make a conscious effort. That's one of the big reasons why this 'family business' does work, because we know there is family at stake. If there was a nasty breakup of the band, that would definitely affect the family, so we're all very conscious of smoothing things, making them right in the band context very quickly if anything goes wrong, so that it doesn't spill over."

The internal relationships in Cowboy Junkies are fascinating. Those between Mike and Al, Margo and Mike, Pete and Al are all obvious from a musical standpoint, but the personal relationship between Pete and his sister is every bit as crucial. On the surface, it's very playful, the two laughing at and with each other constantly, swapping opinions on gossip and celebrities: "I like Kim Cattrall." "You didn't really mean to say that out loud, did you, Pete?"

When Margo turns her back on the audience to lean on Pete's drum shield, it seems to take both of them out of the pressure of performing for a few seconds, maybe even back to the Timmins household of all those years ago when they were kids, Margo tapping away at Pete's cymbals, Pete trying to clip her hand with his brushes. That's a very Junkies moment, warm, one that maybe few of the audience sees, but which actually feeds back into the show in more obvious moments later. As Pete says, "I see making this fun as being one of my big roles, even in photo shoots. That's the most horrible thing you can do, and generally, if we're smiling in one of them, it's because I've cracked a joke. In some ways it's expected of me. I'm not a clown, but I like to make people smile, I see things in a weird way, maybe. I don't want us to put on a serious show, make it all dreary, and Margo's the same: she's open and talks a lot to the audience, tries to lighten it. Al's just Al, you know! Mike's busy working – when he plays, he's very focused on what he's doing and you can't blame him for that, because he's got a lot of chords to play! So I try to keep it fun, because, if it wasn't, why would you do it?

"Me and Marg hang out a lot together even when we're not on the road. I talk to her on the phone a lot and it would be hard if she wasn't there, just because Mike is the leader of the band. So, if he's coming down on us, we talk it out between us, we have each other to vent, and that's really what you need, that's an important dynamic. After a show, I use her room a lot and we talk about stuff, go through the show. She's good friends with my wife, which is a great connection, so it is a big partnership, it does play a big role for both of us.

233

"Musically it's changed over the years. Nowadays, with Al living in Vancouver, he comes in a week before when we're doing real recording, and we rehearse. I still jam a lot, but not with Mike, I just get together with friends. We didn't really ever have Tuesday-night jams or rehearsals, so it doesn't make any difference Al not being there. I wouldn't see him, anyway. He'd be sleeping! When you're on tour, you get so thrown together that when you get to the end of it you're happy to get away from each other. But that passes real quick and, before you know it, you're back on that bus."

A huge part of the Cowboy Junkies story has been played out on the road, where they learned their chops, learned to be a band and earned their audience over time. While others might be ambivalent about certain parts of the process, Pete laps it up. "I love touring, I love the road. I love getting away from home, not in a bad way, but just to get distance, to look back on it, reflect on it. So many relationships you see, you just think, 'If they'd only go on separate vacations then come back, they'll see each other again.' But you get so stuck on the same path, butting heads. I go back home and it's full appreciation again, because I realize, 'Holy smokes, she's great.' Where if you're together every day, working out who's taking the kids to baseball, whose turn it is to cook the goddamn dinner tonight, it gets to be such a grind. And I like getting out to meet people, there's that gypsy feeling, the circus feeling. I like to work, I don't like sitting still, so I love to pack the trailer, I like working with the locals, the stage crew and stuff. It's like joining the circus or going to camp.

"We're driven to go out and play music because we love it so much. It'd be real hard to be the drummer for Julio Iglesias. You might make a million bucks a month, but not liking the music must be a really difficult gig. This is a release. You can be in a bad mood, but you go out, you play, and that fixes it, you come off stage feeling great. It's therapy in a way. I love going out there. Making people happy, what more do you want?"

Making people happy extends to the hours that surround the gig, too. There are few people whose company is more enjoyable than Pete's, as Jeff Bird explains. "People take on different roles on the road. Pete loves being on the road and he has such a good sense of humour that he rides the problems pretty well. He doesn't have the same set of responsibilities that Mike has, but he does his bit to keep it light. The touring business is such that you could spend your whole time being mad about something if you wanted to, because there always is something that isn't quite working out the way it was supposed to! It could get very tiring, but Pete is so funny that he keeps himself amused and the rest of us, too."

The paradox is that, while Pete seems to take things the least seriously of all, there is nobody more professional. He is very much the glue that holds the mood of a tour together and, while he may be the joker, like all good comedians, he works at it. Musically, too, he is always looking to ensure that he's doing the right job. Back on that 'Blue States' tour in 2005, after a drive through the night,

Pete was up at eleven in the morning, listening to a DAT of the previous night's show, trying to work out what worked and what hadn't while, outside the doors of the bus, New York City was waiting. That's dedication.

"I'm not that Keith Moon wild-man drummer, or the Bruford round-the-kit drummer. I play the song, so you have to be true to that. It's important to listen and to be able to take criticism, from Mike especially, because he is the reference point. Go on the road and play a song night after night, it will evolve into something completely different, and it can be something horrible! It doesn't always get better, so you have to watch that. And Mike is the director – he is the one who knows what it's supposed to be – so he'll sometimes point stuff out, give advice on it. Some people would get mad at that, but my attitude is it's like being in a soccer team or something. It's a drill, and if you don't do it right, it won't work. We all want it to work and, for that to happen, somebody needs to have the final say. That's what breaks up bands – egos, not being able to work stuff through.

"Ego gets beaten down in most family groups – it's not allowed. If you're all sitting round the kitchen table as kids, if one acts up, the others jump on you, it's picked on! We respect each other's moods, that's for sure, but if it gets out of hand, somebody will stop it. That's one of the big things with being on the road: you're close together and you have to respect it if someone wants to be on their own one day or isn't in the greatest mood. After a twenty-four-hour drive, or after you've been on the bus for four weeks, it gets really tight, but we know it. When we're playing we read each other's minds, and when we're on the bus we do the same, I guess. Maybe for other bands that's harder.

"If we had a bust-up on the road, I could quit, but Margo is still my sister, Mike's still my brother, I can't just leave that behind the way you could if you just walked out on another band. We're still going to get together at Christmas. That takes some of the pressure out of it, because there's something bigger than the band, it goes beyond Cowboy Junkies. With a lot of groups, it is a matter of wanting the recognition for it, the Lennon/McCartney thing – who actually wrote it? In this band, it's defined. Mike is the architect.

"I look at it as being Mike's church, I carve the gargoyles, do my stonemason's work, but it's from his idea of what it's supposed to look like. I put my bits and pieces in to help get to that final idea, but there's no gargoyles without the church! And when we play through something in rehearsal, things get added. I might stop by accident when we're playing and Mike'll say, 'That was good, that stop.' 'I did? OK.' And that goes in and becomes part of the song. Mike opens it up for interpretation to a degree; we put our things on it."

Recording is the side of any band that remains shrouded in mystery to the fans, and the Junkies on record and in the studio are a different proposition to the live band, showing different facets of the whole. For Pete, recording is an area where he has become more and more important, even if his brother Mike isn't so sure if the finished recordings that they make are quite his thing.

"For Pete, it doesn't matter how much we do stuff, he doesn't really like the process of recording, the adding and taking away. He has this thing where, for him, what is in front of his face is real and the rest of it isn't there. His animal paintings are kinda like that, too, the prints we sold online in our Junk Store. They keep going, right the way through the skin, it's all right there in front of you. Pete would be happy to make *Whites Off Earth Now!!* every time we go in, and that's fine. He loves playing, likes to get it right, but doesn't want to mess with it beyond that. But, to me, rough mixes are great, but only for you because you're the player sitting there.

"Pete gets off on us playing, and that's it. He has an attachment to the moment more than to the idea of a record. As a musician, you hear everything you play, you were there – you're not actually hearing it, you're extrapolating, understanding it, even what isn't there. The idea of mixing it is to offer something to a listener who wasn't part of that and has no interest in the making of it, maybe. Whether you're trying to recreate that session or bring something new to it, you're trying to put it in a form everybody else outside that circle can understand. Even *Trinity* and *Whites!!*, which are performances, they're high-tech recordings, not just rough mixes – they're not just tossed off.

"We did it a little differently on *At the End of Paths Taken*. 'Basquiat', 'Mountain', 'Doesn't Really Matter Anyway', those are based around the recordings that we did when it was me, Pete and Al just trying to work the songs out. Those are those rehearsals basically, and then things are built around it. But that's when Pete is at his best, when he's finding his way in, when he's playing, and I made a point of recording him doing it, because we've realized that over the years, that when Pete goes into record mode, he sometimes overthinks it. This stuff is fresher and you get a spark. And it's part of keeping it earthy and rootsy, it's us rehearsing, but recording it properly in the hope we'd capture something, which we really did. Pete played great on that.

"Using Pete's early takes is a good way of working, because he doesn't like to repeat himself. He has a good ear, he finds stuff quickly and then he goes off as a session goes on. It's best to capture him when he's not paying attention! I mean that in the best sense, because everything about Pete's drumming when it's really working is about feel and about his instincts rather than having an intellectual approach to his instrument. That's how Pete's brain works, just as Al's works another way, mine another, Margo's another, and over the years we've worked out how best to put that together, how to get the best from each other."

Listen to Pete's work on 'Handouts in the Rain' from *Early 21st Century Blues* and you will see that he does shine on record, but Pete will happily admit that he is no great fan of repeating himself: "I'd rather play drums with no audience, in some ways. Making records, jamming in the Clubhouse, it's fun. Take it on the road and it becomes a recital a bit, the record becomes the focus and you stop doing something new. When we were rehearsing for the *Trinity Revisited* DVD and we were rehearsing for the cross-Canada train at the same time, because people sent in all their requests for songs they wanted us to play, the set list was different every night, and I really liked that. Whereas when you're on tour and you're pushing a record, you're connected to that; you have to play seven or eight of those songs, and I prefer a bit more variety."

His enthusiasm for changing the set list or performing new music is the clinching evidence of a highly inquiring mind. His eldest brother, John, makes a very perceptive point. "Pete has his role as the comedian because he's always been the little brother, but there's a lot more going on with him than that. The sharper the humour, the sharper the intellect, and Pete really is very funny.

"I am always amazed by him, especially when they play live, because he has become an exceptional drummer and that just came out of nowhere when we started the band. He didn't even have the benefit of growing up with a highly musical peer group – when we started playing, he suddenly found himself in a professional rock band virtually from the day he started playing. And it's not a band where it's easy to be a drummer; you can't disguise a lack of technique by just thrashing away. Right away it was very restrained, using brushes. Talk about balls – he's really shown that through the band's history."

Over the Rhine's Linford Detweiler, who joined the band on keyboards for the 'Waltz Across America' tour and then on *Open*, is another big fan of his work. "Pete is a great antidote to the intensity of what they do. He's very much a jester, keeps it light, but don't let that detract from him as a musician. His playing is very interesting, he's pretty much got his own thing, which is really hard to do. You listen to a record and you can say, 'That's Pete Timmins!' and that's not easy. There are scary moments with Pete where you wonder if it's just going to fall apart around you, but there's a real subtlety to it – he has a lot of power in terms of what he's doing, he has his own sound." And, while we're talking to the Pete Timmins Fan Club, Jaro Czerwinec insists he was a founding member, too: "He's one of the most interesting and intelligent drummers you could find. He never does what is obvious. He's a great guy, nothing fancy, he loads the gear in even now, so you don't want to mess with the bronco! Pete was the person I was closest to early on. We had a kind of big brother/little brother thing going on; we'd horse around and knock the shit out of each other!"

Talk to Pete himself and he's pretty reticent about his own playing. The most you'll get from him is "I try to go for textures, colour, dynamics, it's not about people seeing me, it's about people hearing the songs. Partly that comes from the drummers I like: Levon Helm, I love. Kenny Buttrey, Dylan's drummer on a couple of records. Kenney Jones from the Faces. Jim Keltner is a great studio guy: pretty dynamic, great cymbal work. There's a long list. I love the drummers on a lot of those old blues records. A lot of the time, it was just the producer came out and played the kick and the snare, and it sounds so cool – it wasn't even a drummer, but it sounds fantastic, it's all feel, just playing right along. Then you've got Fred Below.

"I like the old guys who weren't even drummers, it seems! I think that's so important to us, that we don't know what we're doing in a sense – we're none of us technical performers, we're not trained that way, so we don't get caught up in rules. My big concentration is to know where the one is and, once you know that, you can find it again, so you can stray from it and come back. If we're jamming on a piece, I can hear a roll coming in my head – I'm not technically thinking about it, I'm thinking about how the sound is going to be. As long as you know the return point, you can do pretty much anything. Al's bass licks, it's not standard, it's an eight-beat pattern most of his stuff, and that influences my drumming. It becomes a two-bar pattern, so that makes us different right away. That's how Al has always played. We pretty much read one another now. When we demoed *One Soul Now*, I was in Toronto, he was in Vancouver – we didn't hear what each other was doing – but when we got our tapes back and put them together, it was pretty much dead on, which was pretty funny. Al tends to hang back, work around what I'm doing and, if he doesn't like it, we'll talk about it and switch it round, try different things for hours. Again, it doesn't become a fight; we're just willing to keep trying things until we settle on what we want to do. We don't get mad, we just want to work out the best plan for the band as a unit."

Mike is right that so much about Pete at his best is instinctive, but equally you can't go with your gut unless you really know what you're doing – not unless you have worked out who and what you are as a player. Everything about Pete, especially on those looser, loping songs, is unmistakably him, to the point where, after Margo, he probably commands the most attention from the live audience. Even the fact that he drums with his entire body, moving like he's taking a course of mild ECT as he plays, is an absorbing spectacle.

Always thinking, always trying to improve, he says, "I'm learning a bit of guitar to learn chord structures and the relationships between them and that kind of thing, but as far as going to school to learn music, no. Just trying to get into a music school would be interesting! You see the people that come out of there, the jazz players, and they can't swing. You ask them and they say, 'Swing?' Like you've insulted their mother! I'd rather be able to swing and not know my chords, thanks!

"And, away from the band, I have a lot of things going on, because I think if you load it all into one area, I think you'd go mad. Different passions, I guess it is, and they all feed each other. The music is still the biggest focus, but it's not as all-consuming as it was thirty years ago when we were trying to get it off the ground. We tour less because we all have kids, we all have other things that we do. I love painting, and that's something I've pursued more. I've got into graphic design, I love carpentry, I work construction, too, because that's a great escape, being with the guys I work with, coming across problems and solving them. It's just living and having passions. The construction work is something I'm careful with because of my back, but I've learned to do things differently.

I've always had a bad back, but I've just functioned with it. I used to do the work myself; now I have guys helping me, so it works out. Actually, travelling is the worst thing for my back: bad flights, bad food, different routine, sitting on those buses, foam on plywood, sitting sideways. Then you go to your bunk and you wake up the next day and feel like you've been through a tumbler. But that's part of the job."

The biggest part of the job is being the drummer that nobody else could be for Cowboy Junkies. Pete is the heartbeat of the band, if not its pulse. Timekeeping in the strict classic rock sense is maybe not his forte, but his individuality is something that gives that band its sound. Perhaps that's what prevents them becoming a "normal" rock band at times, because he's not the kind of drummer that drives a song. Pete is about colours, tones, decoration. His drumming is nothing if it isn't about feel. Live, especially, that can mean they sometimes sound on the edge of a nervous breakdown because it isn't rock-solid, but they sound far more human for it. And just how often does it break down? Pretty rarely. That's a mark of his ability and his professionalism.

You know what, without Pete, Cowboy Junkies could not exist, after all.

CHAPTER 16

What will I tell you …

"They'll be round to turn the lights out soon."

Loss. The currency of so much popular music, so much of the Junkies' work, too – much of their best work. But so much of it is about romantic loss. My baby done left me. Anyone who's nursed a broken heart knows the keening pain of that, the desolation, the dark nights of the soul. The need to play *Blue* for the seventeenth time in a week. But generally, we get through it. We survive, we move on. As cliché has it, there really are plenty more fish in the sea. Life might be less fun for a while, it might be more complex, it might create misery, but hearts broken by love do – for the most part – mend.

Other loss is more final, irrevocable and there is no mending it. I lost my dad following a catalogue of abysmal medical care, and I still wonder where I went when he went. There are bits of me I've never come close to finding again. It happened so slowly, months of being bedridden with misdiagnosed back pain. It happened so fast, a few weeks after cancer had been found – a final weekend of screaming agony, misinformation and horror. Images etched deeper inside my memory than pretty well anything, obscuring too much that was good. A failure by the medics and the ancillary care services to answer calls for hour upon hour because a public holiday means a skeleton staff. Rage at a nation that was happy enough to send him off to maybe get killed in the war sixty years earlier but now wouldn't lift a fucking finger to ease his pain. I still cannot look at this country's flag without feeling physically sick.

My dad being carried out of his home of near fifty years – for the last time, as it turned out – screaming and delirious with agony. Being told that afternoon at the hospital that the problem was minor and would be treated that day, only to turn up that evening to be told that any operation would be an effective execution, and that the problem had occurred because he'd been left on steroids too long by a medical industry so incompetent it had cancelled an appointment at which he'd have been taken off them. Then, to be told the following day that a successful operation was possible, but it might be better not to do it, because of the future horrors that lie in wait (spinal disintegration, anyone?); to have to make the decision; to be told that there was a fifty-fifty chance that drugs would see him through anyway; to be sent home that evening because there was nothing immediate to worry about; to be woken in the middle of the night to be told he was gone; to have to call my mom; to have to go to the hospital at three in the morning for a final farewell in a ward full of sleeping patients and trying not to make a noise. To carry the blame for taking my mom home and for letting my dad die on his own. That does not mend.

Loss, devastation, anger, impotence. Howling at five every morning, because what else can you do? Writing this chapter was avoided for month after month, always hidden behind something more pressing, because I didn't want to confront it. It's still raw. The quote at the top was from a letter Dad wrote in hospital which I stumbled on as I was ready to start writing this, and it brought it all back, yet again, like it comes back time and again. But now, it's kind of controllable, however much it still disfigures everything. Back then, it coloured everything. Back then, there were just too many feelings, too many emotions. For weeks, months maybe, I couldn't pick up a book, watch a film, couldn't do the things that I normally do. I couldn't go back to a normal life because, if I did, that would be the final defeat, the final admission, the final throwing in of the towel. And because I didn't want anything else to make me feel anything. All my feelings stemmed from the situation, not from some external stimulus. But, even in that loss, life ultimately does have to go on.

Eventually, it was time to approach the outside world. And when I did, it was Cowboy Junkies, and only Cowboy Junkies, for quite some time. I didn't analyse it at the time, didn't think about it, but a year later I found myself on a bus in America with them, just talking to John Timmins about life, and trying to explain why it was the Junkies. And, actually, it was very, very simple. They were the only band I could go to and know that they wouldn't fuck with me.

There are other artists I love, but when you're that scarred can you trust them? Would they manipulate you, would they press buttons for effect, would they offer cheap sentimentality, let you down? Or would they talk to you? The Junkies don't fuck with you. They are an anti-personality in the obvious sense, and yet everything about them is about catching personality and putting it on tape or onstage.

I realized then – or instinctively responded to something I already knew – that you can trust them with your life. There's a warmth in there, a truth. More than that, there's solace, shared experience, empathy, music and emotion that is heartfelt. I was in a fragile state, but that music did not take advantage of it. It opened up to me, opened me up, and slowly I started feeling other things again. It wasn't the only reason I did, and without it, in the end I would have moved through the grieving phases some other way. But the Junkies helped, that music healed, soothed. If music is at the centre of your life, that's what it can do, that's why it matters; why, as Frank Zappa said, "Music is the best." The more you listen and the harder you listen, the more you hear and the more their music repays you. It's an ongoing story, a two-way street, not a static monologue.

To John, that assessment of the Junkies was no surprise, because he's seen the band evolve from close up. "As you get older, if you pay attention, you don't find any more answers but you should at least find better questions. There has to be some growth as you grow older, and I think Mike has continually shown that in his writing.

"This band has had incredible results in supporting itself. It's a very independent band in many more ways than just the 'indie band' sense, even when they were on a major label. They're independently minded, there's something that's driven them to create over these years that is very true, very much part of the human soul. The thing that is their engine is the humanity that appeals to those of us who listen to their music so assiduously.

"There is no pretence or artifice. They've accepted that they're getting older. Mick Jagger is 75 or whatever and still pretends to be 25, which makes his records redundant now. He's not telling me what being 75 is like, so I'm not interested, and the kids who are 25 must think he's a joke. There's no point to that. What the Junkies are about is total selflessness. 'I'm 40-something, here's what goes with that. We're going through this together, I'm doing what I can to serve you.' Ultimately, that's what we should all be doing for each other.

"They are a very egoless group because they really do serve the music above all else and, if that requires other people to come in and add something, if that's what Mike is hearing when he writes a song, he's happy for that to happen and for them to take centre stage, as happens sometimes with Jaro or with Jeff. Of course, there's ego because otherwise you would just make music at home and not put it in front of other people, but that's not a dominant characteristic of the individuals or the band itself and I think that's pretty special at this time, in that genre of music. I think you actually hear that absence of ego, you sense that when you talk to the band, or when you hear Margo doing those wonderful monologues between songs. I think that's why she's so well liked, because it's so true. She's not innocent in the sense of being naive or simple, neither is she some sort of diva, but she has this incredible egoless sensibility that is very refreshing for people to come in contact with. And for that to survive these years intact is remarkable. But I think that egolessness is a very important characteristic of the band and the music, and it's evident in their own personal lives, too."

That was the other reason to turn to that music for comfort in my time of need. Hope. The hope that gets you up in the morning when there seems no reason. Nothing concrete, not a promise of an outcome, but hope. Nothing any more nor less nebulous than that. But the most important thing, the only thing.

My theory is that those who are dismissed as miserablists, as the Junkies all too often are, are actually the most life-affirming people. They see the reality of life, confront it, and conclude that it's the best thing we've got and go on. Those who are happy-clappy, constantly looking for fun and a "good time all of the time" are running away from something they can't face – the reality of life. In the end, that masks an absence of hope, and that is the most crushing thing of all.

243

Hope is a much-abused, devalued currency these days, not one the world deals in any longer, preferring fear to keep the people down. It's not an emotion we're encouraged to feel any longer. Dumb ambition, sure. Naked greed, check. The weird dream that you will be the next American Idol, OK. But hope? We don't do that any longer round here, not for real, only for television. Because, for all that it gives us the chance to soar, hope is the most grounded of emotions, the one in touch with our reality, because it's the one that grows out of our fears, our experience. It's the one that gives us ideas, that can see us change things, change who we are, what we are, where we are. Martin Luther King didn't have a dream, he had hope. Kennedy offered hope, Lennon wrote of the hope we would give peace a chance. Look what happened to them. Hope no longer springs eternal, but burns infernal.

Hope is the thing that makes you think, that lifts you out of the mundane, that brings people together. Hope is about change, real change that we can believe in. Did Obama really put hope back on the agenda? It seems not – not in any lasting way. But the corporations, the establishment, the governments, they're not big on hope, because they're not big on change, not big on losing the control they exert over us all. Change is the most threatening weapon we have in our personal lives and in our political lives. That makes it our most dangerous tool and the one that popular culture looks to numb, to reduce, to extinguish. Look at the floor, never at the horizon. Hope is crushed and most films offer that emotional outlook – also, a lot of television, the bulk of music. Cowboy Junkies are an endangered species, because they are fragile, they're sometimes bloodied, but they keep getting up. They remain hopeful.

Their central theme is the ongoing struggle with life, wrestling with it, sometimes coming out on top, sometimes not. And that is anything but depressing. They're among the most optimistic of bands, because the hope they offer is realistic, attainable, logical, not sentimentalised, romanticised. Mike Timmins: "The songs are about life, so of course they have a lot of different emotions in them. There's a lot of loss in life of various kinds and that's what a lot of it is about. But we all have the same thing – we get through it and go on and do other things, that's the hope. When I read a really great book, I hear a great song or see a great piece of art on a more conceptual level, I think what you really get out of it is that sense of bonding, that togetherness, that hope. I have the same aspirations and hopes, desires, confusions as this guy does. That's where the hope is, once you connect with somebody.

"That's the great thing about art: it does offer that hope. We believe that what we put across in the songs is hope, but so many people miss that. We don't get upset about that, because what can we do about it anyway? It's a very unsubtle world. Most people don't have time for that, that's why so much stuff passes them by, not just us. They don't even have time for hope, nobody sells that to them. It's the nature of the times, odd times. But there are people who dig deeper, who get what we do; otherwise, we wouldn't be here."

My dad made that final trip to the hospital on Good Friday and he was out of his pain on Easter Sunday. You don't need to be the Pope or the Archbishop of Canterbury to see something in that. I've wondered since, was it because of 'Good Friday' that I picked up *Miles from Our Home* first, and pretty much lived inside that record for forty days and forty nights? Or was it because that was the record where Mike and the band first really confronted loss on that level? The setup for what to follow was there in the booklet that accompanied it: "Last year we spent a lot of time in a 125-year-old mill, overlooking a four-acre, creek-fed pond. At the beginning of the year we said goodbye to a man whose passing made the world seem a little less significant, and in the summer, the passing of another man brought that significance back. We did a lot of sitting and walking and watching things changing. And a lot of waiting. These are the songs that we stumbled upon."

For all that *Miles from Our Home* is perhaps the most "produced" Junkies record, that it also features co-writes with other musicians, it's a ferociously intimate, personal piece of work, an internal dialogue perhaps disguised by the studio sheen that was added to it as the band went in search of a big-budget pop record from the old school. These songs could easily have been showcased "*Trinity* style" and, had they been, fans might have looking back at the record as harrowing, akin to *Nebraska*. As it is, *Miles* is perhaps the overlooked gem in the catalogue, partly because of Geffen's collective nervous breakdown ahead of its release, but also because it's outgoing nature jarred with the expectations of many long-term fans.

There is an odd juxtaposition with the material and the way it was written, Mike having ended 1996 by gathering together scraps of ideas, musical and lyrical, prior to heading off to put together the songs in similar style to the Rock Island period ahead of *Lay It Down*. This time, the location was Maiden's Mill, in Warkworth, Ontario. "That whole record was written in isolation," recalls Mike. "I lived a good part of the year out in the country and my wife would come out now and then, the band would come and work on the songs I had from time to time. We rented this house and I just had a lot of time, much more than in the past, to just sit and think, really go through stuff. It says on the sleeve notes that we stumbled on the songs and that's from just walking around, being inspired by what was around me. I'd write all day, sit and work, think, go for long walks in the country. I was doing a lot of questioning, I guess."

Questioning is very much the essence of *Miles from Our Home*, for, amid the rural quiet, it was a period of real turmoil for Mike and his family. "A lot of songs on *Miles* are about death, which was Townes Van Zandt, who died as I went out to Maiden's Mill, and then about my granddad, who died that summer, but there's a lot of hope in that record, too. At the time, my wife and I were adopting a child from China, so there was a sense of expectation, of anxiety, of waiting, of things happening a long way away and out of our control, it was a huge two-year waiting period. It's not directly about that, but there is this feeling in those songs of something else coming and not knowing what it is. There's a finality with the death of Townes and of my grandfather, then there's a sense of future but not knowing what it is, when it's going to happen. That's what life is, right? You lose things, new things come, it's a constant circle. That whole album was full of songs about that – 'New Dawn Coming', 'Miles from Our Home', 'Darkling Days', 'Good Friday', 'Someone Out There' – and then it was bookended by 'Blue Guitar' and 'Those Final Feet'. Obviously, it wasn't planned that way, but the idea of death and rebirth just dominated my life at that point."

These were themes touched upon on *Lay It Down*, songs like 'Just Want to See' and 'Something More Besides You' perhaps hinting at the subject matter Mike would move towards on *Miles from Our Home*. Thinking more deeply about those issues is a function of growing older or, perhaps more accurately, a function of life experience. Approaching the age of 40, one of life's milestones, pushes those questions further forward in the brain as you begin to receive hints of your own mortality, and that, plus Mike's isolation as he wrote the songs, along with the circumstances of two death blows around him and the band, meant that would inevitably surface in the new material.

These were songs about blasphemy, death, anger and love. They make up perhaps the heaviest Junkies record, certainly to that point, even if it didn't sound like it, not at first glance. It was a record that's about anything but first glances, yet they were songs that went back to first principles in many ways, back to the first lessons most of us are taught as children. Surrounded by life's biggest events and by nature's great wonders, it's no surprise that Mike found himself asking the fundamental questions about spirituality, religion and why does it all seem so screwed up?

His brother John finds himself similarly intrigued by the teachings they absorbed in their formative years. "We had a very strong Catholic upbringing. Not in the strict orthodox sense of the word, it was just at a time when Catholicism was dominant in Catholic lives. We were all old enough to be influenced by what was going on when the Catholic Church started to be questioned. I remember going to church with my parents every week, it was always a big deal, being bored out of my mind. I'm sure Michael remembers that, too, though the age difference between us was more significant then, so he seemed much younger when my father started to question out loud, for our benefit, what was going on in the Church. I remember him commenting – just a couple of times and memorably, impactfully, because it was such a rare thing – that he didn't quite agree with what the priest had said during his sermon. Then the next thing I remember was we weren't going to church any more.

"But in those early years there was the presence of the Church in our lives. I've learned in later years that my parents grew up in an even stricter and more dominating period of Catholicism and that was a very influential force on them. My father's younger brother is a priest and he was big in our lives – we all have fond memories of Uncle Peter when we were kids, he was just a really great uncle, but he was always a priest, too. So there were strong influences there, then there were the Catholic schools we went to; they were very formative years in which we had experience of the Church. So I'm not surprised when I see Michael using references to religion in his lyrics, in very interesting ways. He's having a conversation with God almost. There are elements of doubt in there, too, as if this is a questioning Catholic mind trying to figure out where the hell he's coming from on this topic, what his own beliefs are. I see that questioning still and I've done a lot of that myself.

"I've done a lot of reading over the years about Catholicism, I became the editor for a Catholic diocesan newspaper for a while, not because I was enamoured by the Church but because I wanted to get back into it and see who I was dealing with. That was very interesting – I got out pretty fast! But it was a very strong early influence on us all. I can go in any church today and still feel something happening. Whether it's a knee-jerk fear reaction or something more profound, I can't say, but there is an environmental influence." Evidence of that came at a gig played by the Mike/Margo/Jeff trio at Islington's Union Chapel in March 2007, a London church that regularly plays host to concerts. While setting up for the show, Mike stood by the pulpit and started to raise both arms. Halfway to the cross, he laughed and said, "No! I can't do it, I'm a Catholic!" Maybe he just didn't fancy messing any further with "that fucker up there".

"That whole Catholic upbringing, the iconography of it is always there," he admits. "So when I talk about God, I'm not necessarily talking about the guy with the beard, I'm talking about the essence of something great out there. With the death of my grandfather and of Townes, waiting for this child to be born, we didn't know what was going to happen. There was a lot of confusion, a lot of injustice; I just felt everything was so fucked up. Because of those ideas that were driven into me at a very young age, a lot of that came up and I used it to voice that sense of outrage and frustration. It's an internal record in many ways, but it's also inspired by all the world around me."

Central to that feeling was 'Someone Out There', very much Mike's song, yet it fell to Margo to give it voice, one of the harder tasks of her Junkies career. "There are times when Mike will give me a lyric and it's not something I want to sing. Not very often. There's a song on *Miles*, the one about 'that fucker up there'. That was really hard! I didn't mind the sentiment, I understood where it was coming from, I know why Mike wrote it. But it was such a personal song for him, that feeling that he was having, it was so deep in him – it wasn't mine. I did struggle with it and I told him, and his thing was, 'Sing it or don't sing it, it's up to you. Either you can find a place where you can get into the song or it won't work, anyway.'

"There are some songs I will pull away from because they're hard. They're hard for me to sing and it's hard for me to figure out. And Mike will say, 'Just do it. Get in there and sing it.' He'll just push me into doing it and, usually, once I'm in there singing, it's fine. But there are some, like that one, where he knows not to push it. If he'd said, 'Just do it,' I'd have said 'Screw you!' and not done it. He knows the approach to use on me; he knows when I'm just being wimpy. My personality is to just say, 'Skip it, I'm not doing it. Let's go have some tea!' But he knows when to back off, he knows when it's not me wimping out, he knows when I'm genuinely not sure about the song, if I'm not sure I want to put my voice to these words. I have a right to do that, he respects that, so when it's a song like that, he'll let me find my way through it. Or not.

"I played with it, I tried to find how to go about it and I hope that I did. I'm proud of it because, again, those songs, whether they're challenging in the sentiment or in the music, to come through and record them is very satisfying. Sometimes they'll hand me a piece of music and I don't know what the hell to do with it. 'There's no music here. Where's the melody? What do you want me to do with this thing?' I am proud of that song, I got into it as a sister, my love for Mike. I knew the pain he was in – I knew why, I knew why he was angry – so I felt 'I'm your voice, I'm going to sing it for you.' That's how I did it. It has nothing to do with me, it's about Mike. Not all the songs are that way. Some he gives me and they become my songs. That's his egolessness as a songwriter. Once he's written it, he lets it go.

"It's different to sing about falling in love, or breaking up, or a murder. It touches on something very deep. A lot of people don't read credits I've found out, and they think I'm writing this. When 'Someone Out There' came out, people would ask me, 'Why did you say that, what did you write that for?' Really angry, some of them. I'm the one who goes out and talks to people, like a sucker, so I'm there defending myself. 'I didn't write it, it's him! Go tell him!' There is a lot more religious imagery in our music now because, as you get older, it doesn't become more clear, it gets more confusing, there are more and more questions. In our culture, when you ask questions, we do go back to the roots that were instilled in us as children, this God thing, and I think that just confuses people more. It's there, I think that it hurts a lot of people because I think people get all sorts of strange takes on it. It's in us – we all grew up Catholic, I went to convent school, it's very much a part of us.

"I think that when I'm singing words like 'God' or 'Jesus', we're doing it because that's our reference point. It's asking a higher power, if there is one, 'What the hell are you doing?' It gets more and more complicated and, as that happens, you look everywhere you possibly can for answers and you get more and more frustrated. And that's what our music is about right now! It's weird: we were out with Over the Rhine on tour and they're a Christian band and they'd do their show and then we'd do ours, and I think our songs had way more mentions of God and Jesus and the Cross than any band ever, and that was really funny!"

'Someone Out There' sits slap in the middle of the record, asking the big question: "With so much suffering, so much going wrong, so many people drowning, couldn't He just, you know, fix it?" "To me, it's the central song on the record," says Mike, "because it summed up, without pulling any punches, the outrage. It just said, 'What the fuck? This is bullshit.' I didn't want it to be hidden in metaphor, I wanted it bold and in your face but unfortunately it was up to Margo to put that across! I think she felt uncomfortable with it, but she went through with it anyways, and then, when we delivered it to the record company, they were appalled! 'We can't put this out, blah blah blah!' They even came back and said, 'If we release this, Wal-Mart is not going to stock it, they sell thirty per cent of the records in America.'

"'Fine. How many of our records do they sell?'

"'We don't know.'

"'OK, go find out.'

"Apparently they sell about one per cent of our total sales in the US, so it wasn't really an issue! There was a lot of fighting with it. Even my parents, for the first time, my mother actually said, 'Do you really think you want to put this out?' My reply was always, 'Of all the records we've ever put out, this is the only one we've ever had a conversation about, we're talking about it, discussing it, questioning it.' To me, that was a really positive thing. It got on the record, nothing was made of it anywhere else; all the doom and gloom was just a waste of time!

"It's pretty simple. If God is up there, why the hell isn't He paying attention to the mess down here?! It's something we all say in one way or another, so all I'm doing is putting it maybe more crudely, to make the point."

Yet, at the same time, *Miles from Our Home* refuses to wallow in self-pity and reflects the potential there is for good in the world, turning on us as much as the Big Guy, railing against our wilful destruction of it all and our unwillingness to get up and fix things for ourselves – don't we have free will, after all? 'New Dawn Coming', the clarion call that opens the record, is a withering salvo against a generation that feels it can change precisely nothing and shouldn't even try.

"'New Dawn Coming' is about faith and about apathy, which is the thing that grips the times. It set up the sense of things dying but new things coming. You don't know what it is, but you've got to believe it will. You're gonna be apathetic and believe it's all dead? You can't – you have to have faith there'll be something else. I guess that's why there's a lot of religious imagery in that song, because that, to me, is what religion was about and it's what we've forgotten. That's why I don't really hold with any formal religion, because that idea of faith, to me, is the key to any philosophy, and it seems to have been lost, left out, it's not convenient any more – that's the key to that song." It would be easy to misinterpret the song as an evangelical, born-again anthem, not least because of the "Are you born yet" refrain, but it's anything but.

Pete's incessant, hypnotic drum pattern sets the tone from the start. A bubbling, burbling rage, like water crashing against rocks but still carrying its onward tide, pervades the album once you begin to dig into it, and it never goes away – certainly there's no trace of resignation, of giving up the fight, of surrender to the inevitable. Rage against the dying of the light, against those that take flight. That is the cornerstone of the album, the call sign coming in 'New Dawn Coming' in the verse that runs "Ain't got no answers here. What I see is not clear. Time to shake it around. Turn my world upside down and watch as the stars come unhinged". From there, the hope – "Soon there'll be a reason to see it through one more day."

How could Mike not have hope given his surroundings – a hugely influential factor, as he acknowledges. "The natural world was very important to the record. It was written in the country; the colours and the photographs in the CD booklet all reflect that. The band would come out and we'd record, work on the music, go cross-country skiing, go hiking, it was a fun time. It's a beautiful place – every night the sky would be different; it was the year when the huge comet [Hale–Bopp] came over, and we'd sit and watch it, fireflies every night. The scene changed as the seasons went on; it was really inspiring."

251

'Good Friday' was a song that spilled over with those environmental influences, rubbing up against the religious imagery with which Mike was preoccupied. "'Good Friday' is a song I love; it's so much fun to play live. It was written very quickly, actually on Good Friday. I was out in the country and it was one of those spring days where the ice was breaking, the water was flowing, all the things in that lyric were happening; one of those days where you're uplifted, completely inspired by the world, really attached to what was around me. And then it's the day when Jesus, whether you believe he's the Son of God or not – I believe there was certainly a man called Jesus and he was persecuted along with a lot of other people – it's the day when he was tortured to death, and so there was that weird juxtaposition. So I went through the themes in the record, that sense of loss, hope (which is again in the whole Christian mythology of the death and the resurrection, what was happening with us with the death of people close to us, then my sense of hope with the arrival of this child); it all built up in there. The whole cycle is there – people leave us, new ones come – and that's what the spring is about, too, so it all locked together."

Musically, it's a piece where everyone is totally locked in: an emotional vocal, understated drums like a rumble of thunder in the distance, an atmospheric harmonica from Jeff Bird that tails off at the end like a train whistle in the distance, rambling yet focused guitar part that contains the same kind of frustration that Mike was to recapture on 'My Little Basquiat', and gorgeous bass from Alan. He above all seemed to benefit from working with producer John Leckie, who captured a richness of sound that conjured up images of another bassist he'd worked with in the past, and one whom Alan was finding increasingly influential. "I didn't really realize until later on that Paul McCartney was such a great bass player. It didn't stand out like Burnel's did, because that was the dominant thing, it was always tied to the music. A lot of it is quite simplistic, but his phrasing, the space, it's really interesting. Once I started listening to bass players more, I guess I stole a lot of ideas from him through the years! I think there's a lot of his style in my playing, probably from *Lay It Down* onwards."

The playing on *Miles from Our Home* was especially cohesive, following on from the way in which *Lay It Down* had been recorded, an approach Pete is especially fond of. "We were just hanging out, the four of us. You go in the studio and work, then you come home, listen to what you did that day together. If we're in Toronto, we work, then we go home, pick up the kids, do the dishes. It's good to listen together; you keep that sense of purpose going and I think we got a really great record out of it. We did that on *Lay It Down*, too, and I think that brings a lot of the music together."

For all that the four of them were very much in sync, outside influences also added plenty to the mix, including a number of musical co-writes on 'Darkling Days', 'Someone Out There', 'Miles from Our Home' and 'The Summer of Our Discontent'. "I did those with a couple of friends from The Corndogs. I put some records out with them in the early 1990s. They have a really interesting harmonic structure, their chord vocabulary is extensive and odd, and that was an early attempt to break free of what I know. We got together, worked on songs, they'd give me those interesting chord progressions and I'd build round them, and that was a nice change. I always intended to try to do that kind of thing again, but lost touch with them a little bit. It took until *At the End of Paths Taken* to really get involved in that kind of collaboration again, I suppose. There's always a danger that other people will take the song somewhere you don't want it to go, and then it becomes not us, and I don't want that. I want to add to what we have, and it's really the way I learn at this point, working with someone who has a different way of operating."

The most unusual collaboration on the record came on 'Blue Guitar', credited to Mike and Townes Van Zandt, whose death as Mike headed off to write the album had had such a profound impact on its shape. "It was odd to co-write a song with a dead Townes. That was so weird. When I heard he'd died, my part of the song was written, but I knew it wasn't finished, it needed another part; I didn't know what to do with it. Margo and I were invited to the Bottom Line in New York to do a memorial show for him while I was writing. His wife was there, and she made these books for everyone of unreleased lyrics from Townes. I was reading through it and I came to one that had these passages in it, 'Screams from the kitchen', and it was just so clear. This was it: 'The song needs Townes' voice.' So I added that in, and in a weird way we co-wrote it after he was dead, which was kinda perfect in an odd way. I love the recording we did of that."

It's a recording that benefited from the work of producer John Leckie, a song seemingly overloaded with different parts, yet each one distinct – "a transparent denseness", according to Mike. Old colleague David

Houghton was one of the musicians involved in the recording, adding another element to it all: "I doubled Mike's guitar part on kalimba. The combination of the two instruments sounds like he's playing a guitar filled with water."

Englishman Leckie, a veteran of working with McCartney, PiL, Pink Floyd, Radiohead and the Stone Roses, certainly enjoyed the process, on that song especially. "'Blue Guitar' was a great track to work on. If you record something and play it back, you hear it a certain way and there's a precious balance to it. And, though you can fiddle away with the components on your twenty-four tracks, there's still something about the blend you have and the pleasure you get from it when you decide that you've got what you were after, and that's the best recording of it, that first playback. Very often, you recognize there's something precious in the way it resonates, the rhythm, harmonics. Nowadays, with computers being such a big part of recording, you can tamper with it too much and you lose something. Maybe I'm old-fashioned in that, because music now is pushed forwards, everything has got that radio sound, loud and compressed, all the things that used to be in the background are now pushed forwards, and I think you lose atmospherics as a result."

David Houghton certainly noted a shift under Leckie's watch. "*Miles from Our Home* had a very different sound than anything the band had ever done. John Leckie created a complex wall of sound, but still kept the groove unstoppably strong. Even though it sounded very different from the recordings that preceded it, the album exuded confidence. Right from 'New Dawn Coming', there were layers of sound but each was distinct and clear. Pete sounded solid as an iron girder and Alan's bass never sounded so rich. Around that time, we recorded 'Ooh Las Vegas' for the CD *Return of the Grievous Angel: A Tribute to Gram Parsons* and we captured one of the strongest grooves the band will ever record, as well as one of the best guitar solos Mike will ever play. It's like a fully laden freight train at full speed, and it's certainly one of my favourite Junkies recordings. The band were really in strong form, really in the groove."

"There is a certain Canadian thing going on, there's a very different feel for rhythm compared with most bands. Neil Young has that, too," Leckie adds. "Pete had problems at times with dynamics, whether to thrash it out or hold back at times, and this was all done on tape, unlike in a big studio now. It was very much a playing, performance feel, so there was a very definite idea about when they'd captured the feel they wanted. They knew what they were heading towards and they knew when they'd captured it. Mike was very into getting the parts right on his things – he would write a part before he came to play it, it wasn't an improvisational thing in that sense; he had it very much down before we started recording."

The irony of that is, of course, that 'Blue Guitar' became one of the great improvisational set pieces in the Junkies concerts, the interplay between Mike and Jeff Bird's electric mandolin a real feature of many shows, veering in different directions from night to night. It's a fitting tribute to Townes and the enduring nature of his work that a song that is tinged with Mike's confrontation with his own mortality via Townes' demise should go on to live a life of its own, morphing daily.

The record's other bookend is 'Those Final Feet' – addressed more generally to loss, more personally about Mike, Margo and Pete's grandfather, but in a positive sense, coming out the other side of grief – a bittersweet closer to the formal album. "I don't think our brains are capable of understanding death," says Mike. "I don't think we could function if we did, because it does make no rational sense that people are there one day and the next they're not. There's this wall there and you try to go through it or round it, you try to figure it out, but you keep hitting this thing that non-existence makes no sense. I guess that's why we have religion, the idea of heaven, spirits, because non-existence makes no sense. That song is pretty personal, because my grandfather always used to say to me, 'Never grow old, Mike.' 'Thanks, Grandad! How do I do that?'"

It was a widescreen musical ending to the album, as David Houghton explains. "As soon as I heard a demo of 'Those Final Feet', I knew what I wanted to add – the sound of a battalion of drummers on a distant ridge. I think we achieved that, and it's ominous and stirring. I remember the sessions as tremendously powerful. I stood alone on the studio floor when we recorded my overdubs, but I could feel the power of what we were creating all through my body."

Additional musicians like Houghton made a significant contribution to the record as a whole, not least keyboard player Vince Jones, whose valedictory organ part on 'Those Final Feet' brings the record to a fitting conclusion. Jones was introduced to the band by producer John Leckie.

"I got Vince Jones in, who I'd worked with in Grapes of Wrath. I'd done their previous record, been out to Vancouver a couple of times.

When I got to Toronto, Mike said he really needed a piano player, so I immediately thought of Vince. He came and played all the piano, the Hammond, the overdubs, and he sounds fantastic, like a part of the band, although his parts were put on afterward, and it was great to make that introduction, because he did add a real zest to some of the tracks."

Leckie was very much a part of the whole recording process, from a fairly early stage, as he recalls. "I was very busy, doing a lot of records one after the other at the time, but I got a letter from Jim Powers at Geffen in June 1997, telling me the band were interested in working with me and would I get in touch and think about going and doing some demos. From there, I had a phone conversation with Michael and I was on board. I knew of them, I'd heard them from *Trinity Session* onwards without actually having the records. They sent me a copy of *Lay It Down*, and I was blown away by it, actually; I was delighted to be able to work with them. Then I was into the business of proposing a budget, because, with American companies, once they hire a producer, it's in your hands to work out how much it's going to cost, how long it's going to take and then bring it in. Just from that conversation and from the demos, I had to gauge it from there, so that's a real discipline, but I guess you can say that from there the record was tightly planned."

From its inception, the band had seen *Miles* as a significant departure from the lower-key productions of the past. It was a widescreen collection of songs and that required a similarly cineramic recording. After the success of *Lay It Down*, and now at a label like Geffen, a big budget was finally available to them – something Mike relished.

"The whole point was, 'We got a big budget, so let's use it, let's use the studio, get a great producer like John Leckie and learn what we can do in there and find out what we sound like when you pay attention to those details.' I love listening to that record, because there's so much in there. A song like 'Darkling Days', there are so many cool elements, it's one of the best recordings of the guitar we've ever done, and there's lots of just great little things all over the record. John Leckie was so great, so open with the attitude to it, to try anything. 'Run it backwards? Sure! Whatever!' That was our rock-star record, a huge budget and we knew we might not get it again, we didn't know why we had it then, so we thought we'd blow it, just use it as an experience. It was great fun. That's why I love that record, because it was the first time we could really experiment, try studio things, put in those extra touches. On 'Darkling Days', it's a very complex little arrangement, it takes a lot of time to do that and, when you're recording, that means money. So we used it!

"I knew people who like us were going to have a tough time with it, because they'd never heard us with that sheen before. I knew it would be an issue, but I really wanted to do it. I think for the audience, hearing the songs live, it made more sense to them and they went back and listened to it a lot. It's got a real sparkle to it; it's one of those records I still enjoy hearing. John Leckie was amazing with us, a lot of fun, interesting guy, taught me a ton about the studio and about attitude, just about how to approach a recording – it was really refreshing. It's our only big-budget record and it's not what you want to do every time, but it was fun to get a chance at it. I don't think it's dated, either. A lot of big productions do, but John isn't of a moment, he's very song-oriented, and he's been working in the business so long that he's not tied to the current big thing."

Leckie adds: "We did some work together up at Maiden's Mill where they'd been for about six months, but the PA hummed – we only had one speaker, I think – so we were a little underprepared by the time we really started work. The brief was very much that they were after a bigger-sounding record than the ones they'd done before and that was why we went into the big studio, McClear, in Toronto. I'd never worked there before, but it was the biggest in the city, it was used to handling film recording, orchestras, that kind of place, so it was well kitted out. We booked in there for the first seventeen days of September and then we went to a little place called Chemical, a little back-street-garage type of place, but the guy had really great equipment. It was a real musician's kind of place, instruments lying around, you could experiment more and, once we got in there, the atmosphere changed a lot. I think McClear made everyone, not uncomfortable necessarily, but it wasn't quite right – it never really captured what I was hoping to in that big place.

"Even then, I remember it being a lot of fun, very loose, intense when it needed to be, but an enjoyable project to work on. They always seem comfortable with what they're doing once they've got it moving. They seem to have to get themselves onto the level, ready to do it. There are often distractions – people go away and play hockey or have a building job to do, knock down a wall or build a garage or something – so there's an element of trying to put off the moment of actually recording, which

257

was all part of the fun, but once they've committed to it they're very confident. I drank a lot of beer and went to hockey with Pete; he kept things very light, he's a good foil for the rest of them. It was a good place to be, a great environment.

"They're a pretty unusual group in the way they operate. Mike obviously orchestrates things for them. This was a departure for them, a denser record, a lot more guitar overdubs and specific guitar sounds, which Mike was very keen on. He'd worked that out in the demo process and wanted to follow through; he was very definite on the arrangements. He controlled the situation musically, he was demoing everything, playing all the parts, and we built from there. We laid the tracks down as a band together, everyone playing, but there was a lot of reference back to those demos, because Mike had a very strong sense of where he wanted those tracks to go."

That included seven guitar overdubs on the title track. Alan's verdict was, "It seemed like he'd lost his mind when he was doing it, but it worked out very cool. John Leckie was really good at finding a place for everything in a song, and that was important, because we'd never gone so crazy on overdubs before." In its final incarnation, 'Miles from Our Home' is a great pop song, but it comes with such a rush that the lyric can get lost. Very much in the tradition of the Junkies, "Out here searching, out here fumbling" tells the age-old tale – "What am I doing here, I don't know anything!" Along with 'Darkling Days', it was very much a song of frustration, the waiting for their adopted child, the chosen who becomes beautiful. That frustration boiled over in 'The Summer of Discontent', a paper sea of bureaucracy, a song of savagery yet beauty, too; their trademark duality carrying the album towards its climax, the desolation of 'No Birds Today' and the redemptive nature of 'Those Final Feet', itself an echo of 'Hollow As a Bone' – a glorious rush of sound, a powerful summation of the strength of love and the fragility of life, wrapped up in a beautiful piece of production, Margo's breathless double vocal a delightful effect, justification enough on its own for all the money spent on producer and studio.

Of course, after the basic tracks were put together in Toronto, there was a further phase of work to be done – adding strings and mixing the whole thing. And, if this is your rock-star fantasy record, and you have John Leckie in tow, where else are you going to do it except Abbey Road?

"As far as making it, it was a pretty indulgent year," accepts Mike. "I got a year out in the country just writing it, we got to spend a lot of money on a pretty decent studio in Toronto, nice big room where we'd set up – like all the photos you see from the 1960s where bands set up in huge rooms, dividers everywhere, amps everywhere. Then we went to Abbey Road because, hey, what the heck! There's a pub in the basement, tea ladies who come round with tea and scones – it's hilarious."

Alan recalls, "Only Mike and I went over to Abbey Road to work on *Miles*, though Margo and Pete showed up for the last week, too. It was amazing, walking through the hallowed halls. And everybody working there has been there forever, there's still a buzz about it, and they'll point to places – 'Over there, that's where John sat for the "All You Need Is Love" satellite broadcast.' Such a cool place to be. While we were there, Plant and Page were recording, as well. They'd never been in the building before, either, so they were walking around in awe just like us, getting somebody to point out all those Beatles moments.

"We were having something to eat in the cafeteria, the four of us and John Leckie and those two and Steve Lillywhite, and those guys knew each other, so they were talking back and forth and Steve asked John who he was working with. 'Oh, Cowboy Junkies.' Plant's eating his dinner and he looked up, said, 'Oh yeah, they're good,' and goes back to eating, not even realizing that we're sitting in the corner! Really weird. I would guess they'd enjoy it on the level that it's roots music. I'm sure Jimmy Page would always be interested in hearing a version of a Robert Johnson song or whatever – that's what he takes inspiration from all the time!"

Things were a little more fraught than they might have been, though, as John Leckie points out. "For the strings, I'd already worked with Craig Leon in the past and had him in mind, but while I went over to Canada to record, I gave him the demos and told him we wanted some arrangements on certain tracks. We knew where they were going to play, but not what they were going to play, as we recorded our material in Toronto, but by the time we got back to Abbey Road, Craig hadn't done anything, because he'd been so busy. There was a studio in Wheeler End near where I live in High Wycombe, run by Stuart Epps and Gus Dudgeon, who do Elton John's records. It used to belong to Alvin Lee but, since then, Oasis rented it for years. Every morning, before we went in to Abbey Road, Craig would come and work with me, Mike and Alan on the string parts. We had one for 'The Summer of Discontent' I remember very well. There's a record by David McWilliams called 'Days of Pearly Spencer' and the strings on that were very much what we had, and they were meant to be all over the start of that song, but as it is there's just a little taste of it left there now over the solo. That was meant to be the main theme of the piece, but it was taken out in the mix, which I never understood because that was the big hook, the single!"

The matter of the mix is still something of a moot point for Leckie, because – the simpler 'No Birds Today', 'At the End of the Rainbow' and 'Good Friday' aside – the rest of the record was taken away for remixing. "My disappointment with it was that, when it was mixed, it wasn't the same record that I'd been working on. They came over to Abbey Road to do the strings and to mix it and there was some talk after the first group of mixes were submitted about getting an outside mixer to do it in LA. They did, and I'm not a fan of it! It was a shock, startling, to hear the change, and that soured my feelings towards it a little bit. It was no longer my record, I suppose. It wasn't the one that I'd worked on, having been right through it from the demos, knowing the direction and the intentions, and it wasn't that record any longer. But that's just part of the job, I guess. I felt like there was a pressure to be more radio-friendly from the company; certainly they wanted a commercial production but, given the material, that was always going to be difficult. They do what they do, they're who they are, they're not a singles band – let's put it like that!

"We did want that big 1960s pop-record sound; the harmonies are a big part of that, with Margo double-tracked, singing harmony in a lot of places, and maybe that was why I was asked, given my involvement at Abbey Road. I'm sure they also knew me from the Stone Roses and Radiohead, and probably the Dukes of Stratosphear records, as well. There are a lot of little references to that in there, backwards things, but in the mix, to me they're not balanced right. There's some backwards reverb on the vocal to give this ghostly feel to things that makes it sound misty, but if you have too much, you can tell how it's done, because it doesn't join up, there's a little bump and there's a couple of places where it's too loud and it just sounds wrong to me. Probably nobody else would notice because they hadn't heard the earlier versions, but it jarred with me."

According to Mike, having the album mixed elsewhere had always been on the agenda. "When we got John to produce it, we looked at his credits and we hired him as producer, not a mixer, because we noticed he hadn't done a lot of that. The idea was he'd get a shot at mixing it but, if it didn't work, somebody else would get a go. That's normal. As a producer, he brought so many elements to it and I thought he lost it a little bit in the mix. If I listened to it now, I'm sure it'd be fine, but I was going for a certain sound and I wanted it all to be out there, sparkly, so you could hear every element, and his mix was more blurry, certainly compared with Chris Lord-Alge's mix. Chris was in LA, he does his thing, he is very good at separating things if you want that, and it really worked. It's always good to have somebody outside it all to give you a different perspective. We've always used a mixer: Joby Baker and Jeff Wolpert worked on *Paths*, Jeff Wolpert did *One Soul Now*, Peter Moore did *Open*. I find that helpful, to have a fresh set of ears to push it somewhere else."

As listeners, all we get to hear is the final versions of the material and we make our judgements from there. Certainly *Miles* stirred controversy amongst fans, many of whom found it hard to warm to the big sound that the band had captured in the studio. Yet the years have been kind to it, and it's a record you can approach in different ways. Lyrically, it certainly has all the depth of previous efforts, although it does signal a change in subject matter, pointing the way towards *Open, One Soul Now* and beyond, a more personal, introspective take on things with the short stories of 'Murder, Tonight, in the Trailer Park' becoming a rarer species.

Equally, it is a shining, glittering pop jewel of a record, a big, fat-sounding thing that's great fun to listen to, giving up new layers every time you approach it, little musical moments of detail that you hadn't heard until now. In the vein of The Byrds, The Beatles, that intelligent, literate late 1960s pop, it has its place in the musical lineage. "That music is in our blood," says Mike. "That stuff John brought into the house, it's always there on some level, even if we're deliberately ignoring it! It's a presence. On that record, I wanted to use more guitars, I wanted to use different textures, more guitar licks. I definitely called on a lot of those ideas, that sort of late 1960s thing. Then we had John Leckie as producer – it's his thing, too. We went to Abbey Road; that helped emphasize it even more when we were recording. It was definitely in our thinking and it was the first time The Beatles idea popped its head up so clearly, though there were bits of it on *Pale Sun*, too, because of Ken's playing.

"More than that, I think that record did mark the end of a phase of the band that really started with *Caution Horses* – completely breaking away from the country side of things, not having so many narratives in the songs, a little more towards psychedelic-y stuff, more guitar-driven."

That shift was no better illustrated than in the hidden track at the end of the record, 'At the End of the Rainbow', atmospheric, dark, sullen, Leckie explaining its lack of credit by saying, "It obviously didn't fit in with the rest of the material. It was a bit extreme, so I think it was probably done to show that it was something separate to the rest of the record."

Elsewhere, the recording encapsulates the bucolic idyll in which it was made, a musical sunlight shimmering on water. Those colours were carried on into David Houghton's artwork for the album. "I was able to work with two very good friends, Douglas Walker and Russell Monk. Russell took the photos of the band and Douglas took photos of Maiden's Mill. The mill was the focus of the entire package and we were able to capture some beautiful scenes: the brilliance of the waterfall, the dark tunnel of trees that line the road nearby. Everything we needed was right there: the skies, the trees, the barn boards, the sunflowers. It was a special place; I'd grown to love it myself, because I'd spent a few weekends there with my wife, sipping coffee as the sun rose over the pond.

"Actually, I prefer designing CDs to LPs. Although it's a much smaller format, being able to create a little book is perversely thrilling to me. I love telling a story with a beginning and an end, and the CD booklet allows that. The LP was a big canvas to work on, but rarely had a booklet inside. And cassette packaging just sucks, no matter how you look at it. It's way too small to be legible and folds out into idiotically long scrolls. It's like designing for a roll of toilet paper."

There are some who say that major record labels don't know the difference between selling records and selling toilet paper. Geffen quickly proved the truth of that suspicion. Armed with perhaps the most commercial record Cowboy Junkies have ever made – a question of degree, we're not talking Madonna – they dropped the ball. Actually, they never picked it up. The band found they were with a record company that, having given them a fortune to make the album, was disintegrating.

"Geffen was a disaster," admits Alan. "We joined them just as they were fracturing, everybody was fearing for their job, and rightly so, because they all ended up getting fired. It had an impact on the business for us, but musically it didn't change anything because we made our records like we always do – we go away, write what we want, record what we want, deliver what we've done. We've never let the labels interfere, though they'd love to. 'We don't hear a single!' 'Really. Why did you sign us, again?' That was always a fun conversation."

"That was always a fight we had with major labels," agrees Mike. "We tend to shy away from the obvious. When we do come up with stuff that's a little bit too straightforward, without any textures to it, we tend to throw it out. What's the point? That's the way all our minds work and, as a band, that's our aesthetic. It's not even as conscious a thing as that sounds. I think subconsciously we just naturally gravitate towards the other side of the obvious, because if it's obvious, who's interested in that? A lot of people miss that in our music, but I think the reason why we've lasted so long and why we haven't 'succeeded', in a larger commercial sense, is because we've always been more interested in it being artistically satisfying to us. We know what does and doesn't sell in the mainstream – I'm not saying that we could go write a hit single tomorrow because that's impossible, there are so many variables involved – but we know that there are elements in what we do that don't fit the marketplace and that, if we took those away, we could maybe sell more records. But that doesn't matter to us.

"Yet *Miles from Our Home* was a record where we made a very conscious decision to really 'produce' it. Right from the start we decided to spend money on it, spend time on it, mix it until we were happy with it, but we also decided upfront that we were going to make a real great pop record in the sense that there were going to be lots of layers on there, lots of sounds, a pop record in the way they used to be. *Lay It Down* had been pretty successful – it sold more than anyone expected, we saw them work hard on it, there was a sense of excitement that next time we'd be able to spread the word a bit further. Geffen was excited about the next one, so we thought if we could give them a record with some sparkle to it, let's see what they can do with it. We did all that, made the record, looked up and the record company had gone!

"The Geffen empire was crumbling – we heard they fired all their field staff, which was one of their strengths. Jim Powers got let go halfway through the record and, with Geffen, the A&R guy was product manager too, so we had no representation in the company any more. Literally as we released it, within a week, the company was officially dissolved. We couldn't get anybody on the phone. We were so mad, so disappointed. Then we had to cancel gigs in Europe, because we lost our tour support. The international release of it was a mess, it was just ridiculous. And the worst thing was we'd spent this huge amount of money when we could have given them a piece of crap and taken the money for ourselves! But I love that record: there are so many cool little things happening on it, so many textures – it's fun to hear it again."

Pete's view is philosophical. "That record got lost a little bit because of what went on at Geffen – that's frustrating – but you can't get too down about it, because it's out of your control. And it's still out there in the racks in the stores; it's a document of that time. People will always come around to finding it if they want it."

Mike agrees with that assessment, though clearly the circumstances still rankle. "When you have distance from it, what matters is we've got a record we're proud of. We worked really hard on the record, we did a ton of stuff on it. Looking back, I wish we hadn't released it, held onto it and bought it back and released it ourselves, which is what Aimee Mann did. But we wanted it out there after we'd done so much work on it. We parted ways with our manager, too. He should have seen that coming and said, 'We're not going to release this, it'll get dumped on, nobody'll see it – just buy it back and release it in six months with somebody else.' But the positive side is it made us realize we needed to get back to controlling that side of the operation. We'd let fate determine too many things, like when to record and release stuff; we'd given too much control to the company. It was a wake-up call."

CHAPTER 17

The high plains of expectation

"I can't do this any more."

If there is a single sentence in the English language guaranteed to spread a swifter sensation of dread in its recipient in a wider range of circumstances than that one, I'm not sure what it is. Delivered at several thousand feet up with nothing but faith and air between you and the ground, it can take on a more sinister tone yet. So, for Margo Timmins to utter that fateful phrase to her brother Mike in such circumstances gives you some sense of her state of mind in 1998 in the aftermath of the Geffening silence that came from their record company's promotions department.

"*Miles from Our Home* is our lost record," concedes Margo ruefully. "When we were on tour with it, people came to our shows and had no idea it was out. That taught us that people would come to see us whether they thought there was a record out or not, which was a positive sign for the future, but these were real fans of ours and they had no idea we had a new album out. Isn't that awful? And we were on this major label! If I were running the label, I would be embarrassed.

"I don't ever understand that attitude. If you've got a job, you do it as best you can, whether it's making coffee or running a business. You're there, you're getting paid, you might as well do a good job. I never understand not doing that. But you run a record company, you have tons of money and people at your disposal, and you can't even let the fans of a band know? Never mind new people – the fans! I don't know how you can do that and go home and look your wife in the eye. You're just a big loser!" she laughs.

"It was shocking. So that was a weird time. It was a great tour, as far as playing goes, I love that album, but it was terrible as far as the politics and business of being in a band goes; it was falling apart so badly. I remember at the end of the tour I was on a plane with Mike and saying, 'Mike, I can't do this any more. I can't work this hard on a record only to have it lost. I can't be constantly fighting with our record company. We both want to sell records, so why do we have to fight with them to do it?'

"I'd thought a lot about it, because I didn't want to give Mike an ultimatum – we either leave the record company or I quit. I didn't really know where he was at, so on this flight I was telling him about how I felt, that I didn't want to quit but that I didn't know if I could continue. I found it so demoralizing. I didn't so much care that they didn't sell any records, but they've gotta try. That's all I was asking. We were working as hard as we could, but they couldn't put the CD in the store, put a poster in the town we were playing. That would have been good, you know? Just something.

"And Mike said, 'I've been feeling exactly the same way and I've got some ideas.' Mike always has a lot of ideas, they're always good ones, so it was 'OK, great, I'm there!' That was when we decided that we had to go independent, which was the best thing we ever did for ourselves. It was a total renewal of hope. Not hope we're going to sell huge numbers of records and be rich. Just hope that we could keep doing this thing. All we want to do is just keep going. Sure, we'd all love a hit and make millions of dollars, God knows, but that's the lottery, the fantasy, I don't know how you do that or if you can do that. But really, we just want to stay together, enjoy it. And Geffen had taken the enjoyment out of it."

And, if the enjoyment has gone, the chores of being in a band – the lousy hotel rooms, the interminable days on the bus, the promo grip-and-grins, hours stuck in hotel rooms – begin to pall. They begin to become more important than the fun of being out there, playing for your fans, writing and recording. So why carry on doing it? Though

Jaro Czerwinec wasn't party to the decision, he sums up the logic in his own special way. "As a musician, you get glimpses of another world – I know when that's happening, when I'm hooked up. When I'm sitting there and I'm hearing the accordion as if it's being played by someone else, I'm just listening, I'm not aware that I'm doing anything, that's it. I like that: you just let it happen, you don't want it to end. It's inspiration, there's no mind blockage there, it's just happening through you, the creative energy is going through you and you're just floating along with it. Music is everything, because everything is sound. Everything is vibrating, giving off its sound: the people, the plants, the animals, it's the music of the spheres, and you tune into this physical universe, the primordial sound of creation, this big 'aum' sound – all sound comes from that. I've plugged into it a few times and it's phenomenal."

On a slightly more grounded level, Mike has this to say. "If you're going into music, it has to be your calling, something you're driven to do. If not, forget it. It can't just be this thing where you hang out with cool people. It's not like there's another career option. I guess it works for some, but for the great majority it doesn't happen. It's a lot of work, a lot of dedication, there's no logic to it, it doesn't make much sense. People get into it for all the wrong reasons and they quickly get disillusioned. A lot of people involved in music don't seem that interested in music itself.

"First and foremost, we're music fans; that's how we approach everything we do. We look at it from a fan's point of view – what would we like to see, what intrigues us. We always fall back on that position, that's in us still. It's still inspiring to hear a great record and that drives us; we want to make records like that. I don't want this band to become something that just goes out in the summer to make a few dollars and play a few songs. I want it to be something vital, I want it to be moving forwards, moving towards the next record, having something to say. I don't want us to just rehearse and go play 'Sweet Jane' at a few festivals every July, that would be horrible. Read this back to me in ten years when we're doing it because it's the only way to make a living, and I'll tell you something else! I really hope we wouldn't do that. Plenty of bands are, but it becomes a cabaret act.

"I don't blame anyone for doing it, I'm not going to say they're artistically impure. They're musicians, they've built something up, more power to them, but at this point that's not something I want to do. I guess the other side is you do that for a couple of months and I have the rest of the year to work on something else and then pay the bills in two months by going out with Cowboy Junkies. Who knows? I have no intention of that, but reality takes you to weird places. But I can't see it. I think we'd disgust ourselves and stop! Integrity is a big part of what we do and I hope the audience picks up on it. I think that's why they stick with us, and I wouldn't want to be gross enough to prey on that."

The deeper truth behind the Junkies' decision to keep on going was, and still is, a simple one. Naked ambition. Not ambition to be the biggest, not to play twenty-five nights at Madison Square Garden or Wembley Stadium, not to be ubiquitous, not to be celebrities. It's a more dignified ambition that that. The ambition to make a better record next time. The ambition to live up to the legacy of those who have gone before and who are still bringing the music on home. The ambition to keep learning their craft, to keep sharing their ideas, to keep on doing the wholly worthy job of the professional musician or writer. It's a notion that's come under increasing fire in the wake of music made by TV "talent" shows and, had the Junkies had to make their choice five years later, who knows if they could have carried on in the new climate.

Not that it was straightforward in 1999, but in their favour was the memory of a tour when the band had really been on top form. It came off the back of a run of albums that had done nothing but add to the reputation established a decade earlier by *The Trinity Session*, in spite of criticism from some quarters that argued they were becoming a more "conventional" band than in those early days. It's a thin argument, and one that Mike doesn't really accept.

"I guess we are more conventional than we were when we made *Whites Off Earth Now!!* or *The Trinity Session*, just because there was an element of doing it ourselves then, of not really knowing where we were going, of trying to find our way a little bit. But *Black Eyed Man* is not conventional, the albums since then haven't been, but people hear it as being a lot straighter than it is because, on a few songs, the structure is familiar. But there's a lot more to it than just that.

"Over the years, we've gone in record stores all over the place and you find our records in the rock section, the alternative section, blues, folk, country – every section, really. And when we were with major labels, they always used that as a negative, saying they never knew how to market us, not just in retail but radio, too. It's funny; we get people who say it's too straight and then we have people who think it's too outside – that's radio people, marketers, audience, everyone. Depending on how you approach it, what you come to the music with, it can take on either aspect. It's been an issue from that point of view but certainly not as far as the health of the music is concerned. People want to pigeonhole us: are we country-rock, alt-country, psychedelic, blues, 'Just what are those people doing?!' So, to say we're a just a conventional band, I don't think that holds true."

They were about to become anything but conventional, walking away from a big record company and their management, part of a top-to-bottom review of how Cowboy Junkies were going to operate into the twenty-first century, as Mike recalls. "When we decided that we were through with Geffen, we had to do a lot of thinking about what was next. There was no way to make that relationship work, because the amount of energy we were spending on dealing with the company, and the fallout from that, was getting to be way too much. It was so much effort to manoeuvre things so that we could get done what we wanted to get done that it was no fun any more. It was beginning to impinge on touring, on recording, it was leaking through the walls, and we had to figure out where to go next.

"The big thing was we'd looked after ourselves and put out our own records in the past, so we weren't frightened by that. We had to strip back down and reassess how we were gonna do stuff. We were totally certain that we wanted to go and continue to play music together, so then we had to look at the economics of it because, at the age we were, we all had responsibilities to deal with. We wanted to make a living out of it, not just busk it while we carried on with our day jobs. We wanted to be independent – we wanted a situation where we didn't have to answer to anybody, to play that game, to keep the company in touch. We just wanted to do our thing.

"We decided to part with Peter Leak, our manager. I was the one who dealt with him most and he did a pretty good job for us, all told, over ten years. He handled the labels, and right up to maybe the last year he was good at that: he kept them away from us, he let us do our thing in our bubble and he dealt with the crap. But when we decided there wasn't going to be a company any more, his job kinda disappeared. And that meant the managerial cut was going to take a lot of money out of our pockets for something we didn't need any more, so really it became inevitable that we would part."

Crucially, Alan and Pete were also on board, recognizing change had to come. "Geffen was falling apart – there was no way it was going to fix itself," says Alan. "We entertained the idea of going with another major afterwards, but things were changing. We'd built up this substantial fanbase, and with the growth of the internet we suddenly had new ways of communicating with them. We could do a lot of what the record company did ourselves and then hire in the other elements as and when we needed it, and probably sell just as many records. A major will pay attention to your record for the first week and then they move on. We could focus on a record for a whole year and hire people to do that with us in different markets. So, if we sold fewer than we did through the first week with the big machine, we'd still make more money, because we could extend its life and we get a bigger cut of the sales.

"If you have a label, you probably do more touring, and much more pointless touring in markets where nobody is interested, because they force you onto the road as part of their plan. The guy in Virginia who is responsible for three states down there will say, 'I have to have them for a promo tour, then a radio tour and then a concert tour.' But you still don't sell records there. We used to do a lot of touring in markets where we were weak, nobody would show up, but they'd keep sending us there! Now we can make our own decisions on what we focus on, which is a lot better for us."

When *Whites Off Earth Now!!* had been released, over a decade earlier, the DIY idea was vibrant among bands, just as it is again now – back then it was gigs and vinyl that did the trick, where today's newcomers use Facebook, YouTube and downloads. In the late 1990s, that independent ethos had slipped into the background. Everything was dominated by the big companies, in the stores and on the air, while independent releases got pretty short shrift – and tended to be more expensive, thanks to the move to CDs. As Alan notes, the expanding reach of the internet was to come to the band's aid and was to offer up a new business plan and a modus operandi.

Their decision to fire up Latent Recordings came at the point where running your own label was once again a viable option, as Mike explains. "We talked to people we trusted on how to approach things after leaving Geffen, what the possibilities were. We talked to a few labels, big and small, just to get opinions, but we never really felt as if we were going to sign to a label again. We tested the water with the *Rarities* record: we put it together ourselves, licensed the various tracks from the different labels that owned them, then we put it out on the internet through Amazon. We had a direct deal with them, which pissed off a whole bunch of retailers but which made that record work very quickly for us.

"We were on the cusp of labels starting to drop or lose decent-selling bands – the Geffen shakedown was the first – but I guess, now, a lot of people have done it in various ways. Once you get to a certain point, depending on what you want to accomplish, you don't need them. You want to sell ten million records? You need a label. If you want to make music, play some shows, you don't. They help you reach your audience at the start – they definitely do that, you can't match their marketing muscle – but if you're not concerned about being a huge superstar, once you've connected with the audience, you can do it yourself."

Ironically, the *Miles from Our Home* tour gave them an indication of just how they might go about things, according to Linford Detweiler from the support act Over the Rhine. "It was interesting. Over a couple of years, we saw them both with a major label and then when they left Geffen and looked more into the independent approach. We were definitely independent when we started touring with them and I think they might have taken a few small cues from us in that department. They were surprised to see how many CDs we would sell at a show, that kind of thing. We had a fairly independent ethic, which has been part of their philosophy, too, I think – even though they were signed to majors, they have a very strong idea of who they are and have been true to their vision. I think it's been a good transition for them and they've been helped by their amazing work ethic, which is maybe the biggest variable in making it happen as an independent – that willingness to go out and work at it.

"They work hard and they're very focused. I think the idea that each would have specific roles was evolving somewhat as they contemplated taking an independent approach. They were figuring it out. Michael's a pretty strong leader, he's very organized, good at delegating, doesn't waste a lot of energy on undefined areas; he's good at dividing things up, spelling things out. When we were getting ready to go out with them, we got a pretty long letter from Mike which pretty much laid everything out – 'No rock stars, we run a pretty tight ship, we show up on time for soundcheck, these are our expectations' – and that was great. It just makes it all an easier process; everyone knows what they're supposed to do and when they have to do it. That mentality makes it so much easier if you're running the thing yourselves."

Another former support act, Luka Bloom, is of a similar opinion. "For myself, a lot of the time, not only am I not particularly interested in wild success within the music industry, but I find that a lot of the time I'm working in spite of the industry, which is a whole other issue! But Cowboy Junkies understand that and have managed to overcome it because of that singular sense of purpose, which is to express themselves through music. They have constantly looked for the most effective way of getting that across to people."

Jim Powers, who had gone indie himself with the creation of the Minty Fresh label, saw the departure from Geffen as wholly logical. "They know exactly where they're going, they're utterly impervious to market forces! Mike has been a man of his convictions right from the day I met him and I think that he's well respected for that. *Trinity Session* earned them that respect. If you create a record inside fourteen hours for $250 that goes on to sell two million copies, you've earned a certain amount of leeway! This guy's gotten pretty far by following his own instincts – who are the labels to tell him to follow a more 'traditional' pop music path?! That's not what they're about, and I think Mike, in particular, is a visionary in that sense.

"I think they've consistently looked inward at what drives them as people and as musicians, and I think they find what goes on around them in the industry largely irrelevant. The fact that they are this small, intense, creative cell means they're pretty adept at making things work, at adapting when they need to. There are no grand pretensions – they're very straightforward, simple, direct – and, with those attributes, and by being as realistic about their ambitions as they've always been, they can continue to develop the very strong following they have, and that in turn affords them even more freedom."

The recording industry has rarely allowed artists much leeway to follow their vision, and as the 1990s ebbed away, and grunge – perhaps the last time bands called at least some of the tune – receded into memory, music was becoming ever more corporate. A parting of the ways between the Junkies and the old ways was inevitable, as Pete admits: "If you want to move a whole load of records these days, you have to play ball with the accountants. If you want the big, generic audience that fills stadiums, they don't really want to be asked questions, they pretty much want to be told what to do, because we've moved away from thinking for ourselves, certainly in the mass culture. 'Hey, these guys are superstars, they should have all the answers!' It's easier to listen to, you don't need to engage with it, you don't have to work at it, think about it."

"You have to simplify," adds Alan. "There aren't too many intelligent records out there that move a lot of copies – most of it is bubblegum, manufactured. That's what record companies do these days: they manufacture music the same way they manufacture cars."

Fans of the band, such as Jason Gonulsen, see the decision to leave that corporate world behind as a wholly positive one: "Operating independently has given them so much freedom, so much control: they can release a CD when they want to, release a DVD, not have to worry about fitting into a company schedule or into their marketing strategy. It's really a case of, 'This is what we were feeling at the time, what do you think?' If you've seen the stuff that Wilco went through when they moved labels, the stuff that was in that documentary *I Am Trying to Break Your Heart*, I'd guess it was similar for them with Geffen. You need to feel that you are able to make your statement exactly how you want to make it. But a lot of bands don't really care about that, not the majority; they sign up to the deal and that's it. So, the way Cowboy Junkies go about their work, that's really refreshing. I just couldn't see them fitting in with a big label at this point – it'd be like putting the wrong kind of battery in your remote control!"

The Junkies don't fit into the mass-produced format. If anything, they're an idiosyncratic, hand-built, vintage model, the kind that appeals to a smaller market, but a devoted one. In that climate, the decision to escape was so simple.

"It's hard to say whether we could have survived had we stayed on Geffen," admits Mike. "We love playing music together, so we could certainly put up with a lot, but it wouldn't have been so much fun, for sure. We survive financially now by doing lots of different little things, like making records like *Early 21st Century Blues*, *Acoustic Junk*, downloads, tribute records, doing shows. Money trickles in, and all of it is relevant to the end-of-year figures! In the past, a label would give you a big chunk of money and you'd get on with things. We wouldn't have got that with Geffen any more, but we'd still have been controlled by them, we couldn't have done those side projects so, financially, I think it would have been hard. Mentally, it would have got harder, because they were in such disarray; we'd have had a few years of real struggle.

"Looking back, thank God we decided to go our own way because record companies have continued to be in chaos ever since. And it was also the spur to get us touring more again, because we needed to go out and connect with the audience, especially in America, which is where our biggest audience is, but that also meant we neglected Europe for a number of years, which was disappointing for us and the fans over there. We've tried to redress that a little bit, but it's not always easy." As Pete says, it seems to be working. "We figured it would make it hard to keep working in different markets outside the US, but our fanbase in Europe actually seems to be increasing. When we get there, we're getting good crowds. Better than we do in Toronto!"

In part, that's because the audience has become all the more fervent since the band went independent, according to Pete. "I guess we're not a huge band, we're everyone's private little secret and people care about that like they care about the local park or something. They want to spread the word, they want us to succeed, and they really want to help, I do get that feeling. I think they feel like we're friends, in a way. We're pretty approachable after shows, we'll talk to anyone, where most groups just disappear. Al works the merch, I do the trailer, Marg goes and talks to the crowd, we're there, we're visible and that plays a big part – people like that. But that's who we are. It's not like 'We're musicians, and you're down there'. We're just working. We could be a construction company! There's no stars here; we're not better than the people who come to see us."

Back at the ranch, along with Mike, Alan is something of an industry-head, taking a close interest in the minutiae of the way the music business operates. From that perspective, going back to the DIY model is almost ideal. "Being our own label isn't that hard for us, because it's always been our way of working. It was harder to try to fit into the industry. We spent a lot of time and effort just trying to do that, hoping they were doing their jobs properly, which normally they weren't. They didn't know what to do with a band like us that didn't fit into their marketing strategy.

"The industry end of it is so screwed up and has been for twenty years or more. It's conglomerated, people get fired all the time, they missed the boat completely on the internet, so badly that Apple managed to step in and launch iTunes, did a beautiful job, and left the labels scratching their heads. They're so out of touch – they continue to lose money because they put out crap and can't sell it, however much advertising money they use.

"It's all about pleasing the crowd now. We did a show in Washington a few years back, finished our set at maybe 10 p.m., then a whole other gig followed us, a rap thing; we stayed to watch a bit of it. Their mission was to tell the people to have fun, dance, do it. That's what they're there for – they're not there for music. It's not music in the sense that you listen to it; it's the music of a machine that wants you to react to it. You don't put it on, sit down and listen. Fewer and fewer people are listening to music any more.

"We could have chosen worse times to go independent, for sure, because the record companies were a wreck. There's more work to do, but it's no big deal. Like on a tour, I'll sort out the merchandise, check what we have, what we sold, but there's not a lot to do during the day anyways, so it's nothing."

Margo is equally happy to be hands-on: "When we got rid of the company, the management, everything, and started doing it ourselves, it was great. That year was crazy. We put the website together, we were putting an album out, organizing a tour, I was trying to figure out T-shirts – it was crazy. I hate paperwork and I was trying to figure out how you get T-shirts across the border! 'Can't we just smuggle them?' We had to pick up everything. I'd call venues, because we wanted them to link to our website if we were playing there – if you bought a ticket online, you could click through and go straight through to our site. It was my first foray into the web, it was all new, so I'd call, talk to the promoter and, at the end, they'd say, 'Sorry, are you Margo? Margo, the singer Margo? Why are you calling me?'

"'Well, who else is going to do it? I could get Pete, but he can't speak, Mike's busy and Al's asleep, so it's me!' It was so funny the way people reacted. I didn't know what I was talking about, but it worked out great. We did it all ourselves; we had nobody else at that point except our booking agent. We did a tour and it was the best tour we'd ever done. Everything ran perfect. Posters were in the town, CDs were in the store, links were on the websites, it was a beautiful thing. Even when something did go wrong, it was your own screw-up, so it wasn't as frustrating and at least you could do something about it. We learned things, things we didn't know to do, but we picked it up for next time. It wasn't like you turned up in a town and nobody had a clue you were there in spite of the multi-million-dollar company, who didn't know you were there, either!"

Easy, maybe, but I'm having a hard time imagining Beyoncé doing all of that. That lack of ego again, that belief that you simply do your job, that you don't put on airs, that you serve the music in whatever way you need to. And that included putting your back into running the kind of website your fans want to visit, week after week. It's all migrated to social media, now that everything that needs to be said can't go beyond 280 characters – but, while it lasted, the content was great.

"It needed to be an extension of who we are and what we do," according to Mike. "Margo had always gone out and talked to people, we knew a few people came to shows pretty often, but the website became a focal point for them. It was very important to us, too; we knew people were taking a real close interest in what we were doing, voicing their opinions, sitting there and talking. Certainly, the first few years, I was very active on the message board, to make it obvious that it was our board, we were involved, we were there. Slowly it became self-sustaining, which is great – thank God, because it took up a lot of time! Later, we had people to help out with the technology, so that eased it a lot. It had its own momentum, but in the first place, to get it up and moving, it was non-stop, trying to work out what did and didn't work, the pitfalls of it. You need to give people a reason to keep coming back."

As a working band, you need to give the people something to buy other than tickets. They concluded that the best way to put a tentative toe in the water was by gathering together material that was already around in various forms. "We decided to give the fans a bonus, by using the website to sell a record featuring unreleased songs," says Margo. "We had a lot of tapes, several recorded songs we never used, other songs we used in a different version. We started working on it and, little by little, we started realizing that it was becoming more like a real album rather than a mere collection of loose songs. Then it made sense to sell it through the more normal channels instead of just from our website."

Those normal channels included this newfangled internet shopping gizmo, Amazon. A nice piece of synchronicity, as Mike admits. "When

we put *Rarities* out, it was through Amazon first and it did really well –
that was when we had the site running but before we had a store, so we
needed a storefront and Amazon were great for that. They bought a lot
from us and our timing was good, because they were trying to get into
that market at that time, trying to compete with the big guys, so they
were keen to get any splash they could. They gave us a great price per
CD, bought them outright, no returns, we made good money from it
and got a lot of attention, too, so that was great. I think we did 30,000
or 40,000 that way, which was great, then after that initial period ended
– they had a six-month exclusive – we went into proper retail after that.

"It's a nice record, it hangs together well, for what it is. It was a good
point to look back, and a good time to do something smaller again.
We'd gone through *Lay It Down* and *Miles from Our Home* with Geffen,
and that was a much glossier kind of record, where *Rarities* was a look
at the other way we'd made records, which people liked, too. It was
important to collect some songs together from the live show that hadn't
maybe gone out before – we'd been playing 'Five Room Love Story'
nearly ten years by the time it came out on that album. It was nice to
find homes for those songs that never really fit anywhere else, plus a few
other songs that had appeared in different places over the years."

For a record that was born out of a need to confront the new, the
modern, the internet, *Rarities, B-Sides and Slow, Sad Waltzes* was an
endearingly backwards-looking record, gathering up scraps from their
back pages. Yet, despite the fact that the material covered a lot of ground
and a few different styles, it was surprisingly cohesive. Summarizing the
record on the website, Mike wrote, "In an odd way *Rarities* has become
a rather special CD to us. Probably because we did it all ourselves for
the first time in a long time, but there is also something special and
revealing about collecting lost moments scattered throughout one's
career and making those moments … found." Which is a pretty decent
description of what Cowboy Junkies do. Flakes of paint, slivers of wood
from "everylife", dropped, discarded, covered up maybe by a fresh coat
or a new frame, maybe forgotten or half-remembered, but moments
that make up the whole, that illuminate it.

'To Lay Me Down' and 'Five Room Love Story' are archetypal
examples of that, in a personal sense and a musical one. That Grateful
Dead cover brings an era to a close, as it was the final recording made by
the band that toured the *The Caution Horses*, and beautiful it is, too. But

more important perhaps are Margo's recollections: "'To Lay Me Down' means a lot to me because it was the first thing I recorded after I'd been in hospital with pneumonia. I was really scared that my lungs were damaged, that my voice would be gone." This recording was conclusive proof that that scare was over.

Musically dating back to the crossover period between *The Caution Horses* and *Black Eyed Man*, 'Five Room Love Story' fell through the cracks, the interplay between Jeff and Jaro rooting it in that earlier record just as the band were looking to expand their range on the following collection. Based on a newspaper clipping that told of a couple who had lived their whole lives and brought up their family in five rooms, it was at once heartbreaking and celebratory, the husband, now widower, filling his time after losing his wife, sticking things to the walls of their home in her memory, "because he had a lot of time on his hands".

That bittersweet weariness to the record, its wry, reflective mood, is caught perfectly by David Houghton's sleeve art. "I wanted *Rarities* to look just like a worn, old, vinyl album. I wanted to give the experience of finding something old, valuable and forgotten. Margo dug out the photo of the band from her archives and I had a retoucher give it a sepia treatment. I studied blues albums of the late 1950s for the typography, and put a wear mark around the cover as if the vinyl platter had worn away the thick cardboard.

"From my perspective, not much changed after the band left Geffen. Michael has always tried to ensure my freedom as a designer, and profit has never been a motivation for me. When the band was with BMG and Geffen, the record company often took it upon themselves to design CD singles, and the results were, to my eye, absolute shit. It was clear the designer had no understanding of the band and no regard for their music. It incensed me to see these discs mixed in with work that I'd done in the racks at the music store. The major labels also had the irritating habit of putting a sticker on the front of the package: 'New Cowboy Junkies CD'! Like it was a bottle of aspirin. It destroyed the cover and I wanted to tear the cellophane off every copy of the CD in the stores."

'If You Gotta Go, Go Now' initially came to light in the same way as the Junkies' material, as Dylan mined his own archive for rarities. A contemporary of 'Five Room Love Story', the treatment is radically different, anything but a slow, sad waltz. This has last song of the night written all over it, the *Black Eyed Man* touring band really letting its hair down on a high-velocity rock'n'roll number. Then, to further make the point that, if you think you've got Cowboy Junkies pegged, you really haven't, there's 'Leaving Normal', written in that same period, but from another genre entirely. Knocked off in a couple of hours, apparently, this is a great pop song, from the era when that was not a pejorative description. Fun, feisty, concise, a master of the art such as Paul Simon would have been happy with this one, and you can only wonder if the movie business is even more stupid than the music industry given that the song was rejected for the film of the same name. It's a great tune, redolent of the sentiments on 'A Horse in the Country' from the same era – was this Cathy's song after she'd bought her one-way subway ticket?

Even on a compilation, the tradition of partner songs continued, 'A Few Simple Words' and 'Love's Still There' looking at domestic bliss, or otherwise, from different viewpoints, the words we cling to in the wreckage of real life that enable us to face the day and to hold it together. With a few simple words, a heart really is sent soaring, small blessings amid arguments, moments when you really have to hold onto those feelings that you know are true. The similarity of subject matter is perhaps because Margo was largely responsible for the lyric to 'Love's Still There', as well as the chorus to 'A Few Simple Words'. They're classics of a kind that she has contributed every now and then down the years, kitchen-table dramas such as 'Misguided Angel' that have a different feel to the way Mike would treat the same subject matter.

'The Water Is Wide' was another song that got the bum's rush from Hollywood, this version rejected by the producers of *The River Wild* for being too sad. The version used in the film is more uplifting, but the band prefers this take and they're right – it's another gorgeous waltz that has increasingly found its way into the live repertoire as the years have passed. Its wistful tone is shared by 'Sad to See the Seasons Go', an item from the *Miles from Our Home* period, this a demo of a song that didn't survive the transition to the studio. It shares the shimmering quality of so many of the songs from that Maiden's Mill period, whereas the two songs from the *Lay It Down* sessions, 'River Waltz' and 'I Saw Your Shoes', are of a very different character.

'River Waltz' was the first part of the 'River Song Trilogy', initially slated to feature on *Lay It Down* until late in the day, when it was decided that the record as a whole didn't work with the three pieces on it. Only 'Bea's Song' survived the cut, 'Dragging Hooks' eventually pitching up on *Open Road*. It's a shame the three songs weren't released in that complete fashion, because it's a fascinating story arc, but perhaps it's a blessing, too, making it easier to appreciate each on its own merits.

The other *Lay It Down*-era song forms part of the first of fun bookends to an otherwise pretty serious collection. "When we recorded 'I Saw Your Shoes', it was hilarious," recalls David Houghton. "I ended up banging on a steel beam in the studio during Mike's guitar solo and embellishing the song with vibraslap, an odd, comical instrument I hadn't found a use for in ten years. When we listened to the playback, we burst out laughing." The album ends with laughter, too, 'My Father's House' the hidden track, a piece of tape they'd rediscovered from way back when they were recording in the Sharon Temple. Mike wrote on the website that "Margo was singing to help Peter Moore find his mic placement. The rest of us had obviously been sitting around too long and were getting bored so we spontaneously joined in. Just one of those weird, beautiful moments … and the tape was running." Always run tape, a truism they were to adopt more and more as time went on.

Disparate songs from disparate times, somehow fusing together to make something coherent. Cookie Bob Helm puts his finger on one of the reasons why it worked so well when talking about another song that would surely have made it to *Rarities* had it not been required for the *Studio* compilation.

"'Lost My Driving Wheel' shows just how much the band can do with a cover song, a masterpiece of subtlety. It starts off so gently that you almost feel the need to lean in closer to the speakers. As the song progresses, it also builds in intensity, although since you are so well distracted by Margo's vocals you hardly notice it. By the time it reaches the end, the song is an unleashed geyser, leaving you wondering how it got to that intensity without you noticing. Try putting this song on repeat and note the contrast between the beginning and the end."

It's a great example of "the pulse", the element which Mike sees as their real inheritance from the Velvet Underground. "What Alan and I got out of the Velvet Underground when we were starting bands was that constant pulse and that groove they had set up. Their influence isn't so much the songwriting or the instrumentation; it's that feeling of getting the band chugging along and moving in one direction. When the Velvet Underground get going, they don't stop, they churn, and that's what we try and do with a lot of songs, get it moving along and let the instruments come in and out of that."

Ultimately, it's the quality threshold that gives the record its place as a worthwhile addition to the canon. Consistency is undervalued, as Jason Gonulsen points out. "In all the years I've been going to their concerts, I've never seen them do a bad show or release anything that seemed like they were going through the motions. It seems that there's always strong artistic motivation there. It's a shame that Michael's songwriting doesn't get the wider coverage it should, because he's a great writer – I really believe he's up there among the very best. He's a great storyteller, people can relate to what he's saying, he uses the essential elements in life that we see every day. I find it kind of weird that they don't get the credit, and it really irks me.

"I've always thought that, for that kind of music, the media will only offer a certain amount of room. It always seems like there's only one band that can represent that area, and for a long time it was Wilco. They're the one, there's no room for anybody else. It makes no sense. You say to Cowboy Junkies, 'Sorry, your slot got taken by Wilco. We can only cope with them.' It's frustrating because they're making great music, there are still a lot of possibilities out there for them, they should have a wider audience, but people didn't get the chance to hear them because of the way the media is. I love Wilco, I was happy to see them get a lot of attention, but why can't Cowboy Junkies get just as much?"

It's a question that has exercised Mike, too. "It drives me nuts. Why is that, because there are dozens of Britney Spears or rappers or whatever? It's crazy but we can't control that, one way or the other. I'm sure Wilco has the same attitude we have – they do their thing and they're happy they're getting the attention they're getting. I'm sure when Jeff Tweedy was in Uncle Tupelo and we were getting all the press for *Trinity Session,* he was saying the same thing then!

"It goes in circles, but it is odd that this kind of music does get ignored. I guess the consolation is that if you're never part of the fashion, of the trend, then you don't get swept away when the trend disappears. That again is part of the reason for our longevity. But from a major label point of view, that was one of the difficulties, because they didn't know how to market us. That Wilco documentary was interesting, because so much of it was recognizable, the whole label thing of 'this next record taking it to the next level'. Maybe this kind of music won't ever go to the next level. A lot of people don't want to stop and listen, stop and think. You have to spend time on us and most people won't. That's fine. Enough do."

The next job was to go out and find those people without the aid – or hindrance – of a record company. Time to call in the fans, people like Jason Lent. "They started to use the fans on the website to do some grassroots marketing for the *Rarities* record. They hired a promotions company and then put the fans to work in specific markets. I signed up for Denver and, basically, we just set up merchandise displays, took the record to college stations. That was fun and it was rewarding because, at the end, Denver was really successful, so it was nice to feel I'd done a little to help them out."

There was no skimping on the live show, because Cowboy Junkies needed to prove they were still functioning at the top of their game, whether they had record company backing or not. They set off on the *Waltz Across America* tour, replete with backing from Linford and Karin from Over the Rhine once again. "That was a very important tour," concedes Mike. "Since we released *Trinity Session*, we'd only toured on records, following up the release of something, part of the record/tour cycle. You get the backing of the company, the promotion machine, people would meet us in cities, we'd go to see radio people. This was the first time since the independent days at the start where we just went out and did it. We had the *Rarities* record, but there was no machinery. We hired a publicist and then made it up; we had no idea how it would go. It was our first time exploring the summer side of things, going into outdoor venues that are bigger than we should be playing but you get more people because it's a summer show. Our agents pushed to get us into those and it went great, and it was very uplifting for us. It showed us we had an audience out there, and that was very important at that time."

It was a fun tour and Linford was delighted to be along for the ride. "We'd enjoyed doing the *Miles from Our Home* tour and it was great to be invited again. Originally, we came to be involved through Peter Leak, so it was ironic that he stopped working with them after that tour. Peter had signed us to a publishing deal, he was managing Cowboy Junkies and, after they had made *Miles from Our Home*, which was one of their most fleshed-out studio projects, I guess they were thinking about maybe adding musicians to the touring ensemble. I think Peter suggested Karin and I as possibles and Michael flew down to Cincinnati to see an Over the Rhine concert, then we went to Toronto to do an audition. It was funny – they stressed the 'getting to know you' part of it more than the playing, which was interesting. Michael's words were, 'We know you can play, but this is about chemistry and whether it will work personality-wise.' We really liked them, we're fairly laidback people so we fitted in, but we were really excited to work with them. Like a lot of people, *Trinity Session* had ended up in our permanent record collection, we kept our eyes and ears open to them, we were interested in what they continued to do, so it was a nice idea."

For Margo, it was a rare luxury to have another woman on the bus, and a more pleasurable experience than the brief Lilith Fair festival junket had been in 1998. "I thought Lilith would be great, to see some women on the road for a change, but actually, it was very hard. I have one girlfriend who I grew up with, she lives in Montreal, we see each other twice a year. That's perfect for me – not too much responsibility! I like being with women; especially if my sisters-in-law come on the road or something, I cling to them: 'You don't want to see your husband, do you? Come with me! Let's go out!'

"I love having women around but, with Lilith, it was weird. Maybe there were too many women. I'm more a one-on-one person. I don't do those girls'-night-out things. My sister Suzanne has tons of girlfriends and they're all around her, but that's not me. So Lilith was overwhelming for me. And because I was the girl in the band, which allowed us to do the tour, I felt responsible for holding up the female end of the band and I didn't know how! It was strange. Fun, I'm glad we did it, but it was too much.

"When we had Karin with us as backup singer, she was great, she got me. She loved to shop, and first – whenever we got somewhere – she'd say, 'Come on, let's go shopping.' I hate shopping, you won't catch me dead shopping. But she was good for me; she'd drag me out once in a while and make me buy something, make me paint my nails a different colour. What I liked was when I do get ready for the show, like any woman who's going out, you just want to hear you look good! I don't get that from my brothers. Jeff might say it sometimes, John has a couple of times on this tour and I can't tell you what that means. Even if it's a lie! I gotta step out in front of people, so it's nice to hear. Karin was great at that – she always made me feel pretty, and that was a nice thing. But it's rare. Most of the time, it's a male zone. It's hard when I get really tired. When I'm tired, I find they get bigger and louder and smellier! What I do to protect my brain is rearrange the bus. I'll get up and clean and make the bus my home and then I can handle it – there's a place for everything. It's about comfort, not because I feel that's my role as a woman. I do it because I need a space tidy for me to be comfortable. It's a survival technique."

On the *Waltz* tour, Margo and the band survived and prospered, calling it the best they'd ever done on the sleeve notes to the accompanying live album. Being in charge of their own destiny again energized both them and the music. "The songs evolved as we went on the road, but it's hard to predict what is going to happen out there," says Detweiler. "You might have a song you think will be pivotal to the set and then, a week in, you're not even playing it any more – some songs just won't translate to the road. We've always been the kind of band where we've seen the songs change when we play them live, so it was natural for us to be part of that. It was fun to hear what they had, and then go away and think, 'What can I contribute here?' It was a very nice, unforced, process.

"I tried not to mess it up! There's something very special about the four of them and I was always pretty happy during the songs when I could just walk offstage and listen. My approach was I didn't want to get in the way of that, I wanted to supplement what they do best, but I didn't feel like I needed to be out front, it was a supporting role. They, on the other hand – and this is one of the things that is very special about their approach – they feel, when someone else comes in, they really want to pass the hat around musically. They want everybody to step forward and have a conversation onstage. That's very traditional, very old-school, part of their love and fascination with American roots music, because that's the way that was made – different people stepping up and doing their thing.

"I didn't think of myself as a lead player or anything, I was playing piano and Hammond organ, but they very much wanted me to do something and that was a really good challenge; it was a vote of confidence, too, and I really appreciated that. I think they had an influence on me, that trust. I loved the feeling of taking it, then passing it back to Jeff halfway through 'Cheap Is How I Feel' – I would play the first half of the break and then pass it to Jeff, and there was this feeling emotionally of dropping an expensive vase and him catching it right before it hit the floor. A very pregnant moment and, when that's firing on all cylinders, that's one of the things that draws people into their performances. On the one hand, there's a strong vision, Mike is at the helm steering the whole thing. Then, within that, there's looseness and a generosity to let people be who they really are."

That's something Luka Bloom picked up on back in 1990 when he supported them on *The Caution Horses* tour. "They are generous musically, they will let other people come and join the music and add to it, and again that goes back to the family, because Clannad were similar in that sense. It's so difficult for a group to stay together; that's probably the single most difficult aspect of being in a band. When they can overcome the endless needs of the individual ego, then they can achieve an awful lot, because there's suddenly a huge unity of purpose – I guess that's what enabled bands like U2 and R.E.M. to stay together for so long. But I think that must come easier to family, and that was very apparent to me with the Junkies."

Of course, passing the hat to invited guests does occasionally end in it getting dropped, as it did in Bearsville in 2007, when Garth Hudson was set to appear as a special guest. According to Jeff, "He was supposed to be there to play on a couple of songs in each set. Through the first acoustic set, we kept looking to the side of the stage. 'Garth here yet? Nope. OK, carry on!' He turned up midway through the main set and I could hear him behind the curtain, working on 'Blue Guitar' as we were playing it. We should have had him with us for that!" Al's memory of the night is of Garth shuffling past him to take up his position onstage, muttering to himself, "Now would not be a good time to fall over. Now would not be a good time to fall over."

With one eye on the bottom line and the need to generate money, now there was no record company money coming through, and with the other eye on posterity, a great tour needed a great live recording, and that's what *Waltz Across America* was, a real old-school live album. It wasn't one show – it was pieced together from several – but the way it was sequenced, using Margo's between-song stories again, made it feel as if you were sitting down in front of a single gig. Another Junkies paradox: every night is different, but every night is the same.

Let Alan explain. "Our music isn't just about playing the notes in the right order. A lot of our music is about atmosphere, and a bad show for us is when we don't capture that. It doesn't happen for a whole show, but if there are three or four songs where it's missing, that ruins it for us. I don't think the audience gets that, they don't go away thinking it was terrible, because we're professional enough to play through it, but it upsets us because we know something is missing.

"Not many bands trade in musical atmosphere now. There used to be a lot more – that was one of the strengths of the punk thing; it took away that kind of spectacle of the 1970s and replaced it with a musical idea. One of the acts I am always buoyed up by is Nick Cave; he plays fantastic shows every time and he still understands that element of it all, but there are very few bands that do that. Springsteen is another, especially with the acoustic show – just him and his guitar, that's a very powerful experience."

Translating that to a recording can be tricky, but Linford explains how it was done so well. "*Waltz Across America* truly was a live record. It wasn't messed with in a studio, they had Mike Sponarski, the front-of-house engineer, mix the record, so it was very much a mix pretty close to what he would try to do while we were playing. That's another part of the ethos of Cowboy Junkies and their love of roots music: they have been able to just put people in a room, play together, roll the tape and get what you get. That's a brave approach today. I was glad to have that document."

Each night, the Junkies picked from a repertoire of around sixty songs; each night the set list shifted; each night, an atmosphere was created, different from the previous one but always from the same roots. More than anything, the warmth in their records came across onstage more strongly than ever. In going independent, the band and their fans were somehow more united, the connection more direct, not least because the fans now realized that the future of Cowboy Junkies was in their hands, as Cookie Bob points out.

"Since they went independent again, I think the fans got more devoted to them, to help them keep going. The explosion in the internet kind of coincided with that and certainly their website brought a lot of hard-core fans together. There's definitely a feeling that we want to support his band, that we should buy direct from them if we can, support the shows, buy the merchandise. The support network is strong and it's fun. New album comes out, I get two copies: one for at home, and then another for the music store where I work part-time, to play in there constantly and see if I can get some people to buy their discs. Regular customers come in and I talk to them about what they like, and I target them – if you see someone come in who you think should like Cowboy Junkies, I'll put the CD on while they're in there and often they'll come and ask you about it. That's great; it feels like you're helping. I think fans do feel pretty protective of them. We just get so much out of the experience, from the records and the concerts, that I think we want to give them something back."

It's a relationship the band appreciates, and one that Mike does not take for granted. "The fans are very devoted and protective of us. I think that's because our contact with them has become that much closer. We've always been grateful that people buy the records and come to the shows, but even more so now because that's what makes us able to keep doing this thing. I don't feel that it's been intrusive or too demanding. I think our fans treat us with respect and we do the same with them. I have no problem with somebody taking issue with a lyric or something I said, or whatever the set list was. I'm quite happy to defend anything like that, as long as the whole thing doesn't become nasty or abusive."

The release of *Waltz Across America* also saw the band becoming more defiantly independent of mind as well as of the industry. The material has none of that overproduced sheen of many a "live" album, nor is there the obvious selection of crowd-pleasers – the likes of 'Sun Comes Up', 'Black Eyed Man', 'Common Disaster', 'Angel Mine' are conspicuous by their absence. This was very clearly a band guided by its inner compass. This was a showcase of all its facets: the sass of 'Townes' Blues', the raw fun of 'I Saw Your Shoes', the delicacy of a new version of 'Hollow as a Bone', the swing of a reworked 'Sweet Jane', the fury of 'Hunted', the exploratory psychedelia of 'Blue Guitar' and the intrigue of 'Dark Hole Again', a pointer towards the next studio record. The opening of another era.

WHO ARE COWBOY JUNKIES, AND WHY DO THEY KEEP FOLLOWING ME AROUND?

Arcane. A lovely word, conveying the hidden, the secret, the abstruse, suggesting a connection with the past and all its dust-layered mysteries. A word that's perhaps fallen into disrepute and misuse in recent times, used dismissively, pejoratively, to suggest something that is out of step with the modern world. Yet, in its proper setting, it expresses much about what is special about Cowboy Junkies: music, ethos, principles from a different musical era, when it was about depth of feeling and the communication of emotions and ideas rather than the distribution of bland 0s and 1s.

Ironic, then, that a band whose roots clearly lie in an older era should find its future in the most forward-looking of technologies, the internet. Without the internet, could a band a decade and more into its existence have continued without major label support? Could they have maintained contact with their audience? Could they have rallied the troops when a new release was on the way, or when the touring show was rolling through their town? Doubtful. Very doubtful. The further irony, of course, is that the internet and file-sharing are now making it increasingly hard to make a living from recorded music, but at least, in the case of bands such as the Junkies, the close connection with the audience that they've assiduously fostered over the years means they have an unusually high percentage of fans willing to spend a buck and put it in the band's pocket rather than simply grab a free file.

Mike's view is that "We all feel we're in league with our fans; there's this weird communication that goes on through concerts but on a larger scale through the records, and it's nice on a record to put out there that we appreciate them. The idea with any kind of art is just to connect with another person, to realize that you're not alone, that sense that it is OK out there, after all."

Increasingly, though, it's the communication that goes on when they play live that is the lifeblood of the band, and of the fanbase. Without the Junkies hitting the road so regularly and so extensively, would their support have such an intense and loyal edge to it?

Jason Lent admits "I love meeting the fans. There's a certain shared feeling about life, the way the world is. The lyrics resonate because you see beyond the happy endings; you see where the lyrics are going and what they say about life. And I think there are some fans who have had something really major happen in their lives, relationships that have scarred them very deeply and they're attracted to the lyrics because they feel that they're in there; they're reaching out for a kind of community with the other fans and with the band."

Keith Bergendorff has a similar take. "I've only known about Cowboy Junkies since 2001, but this band and its music attracts a truly amazing bunch of people. The joy of communing with other llamas, to see and hear Cowboy Junkies create their magic onstage, has brought me from New York to Texas, Wisconsin, Illinois, New Hampshire, Massachusetts, Pennsylvania, Maine and Ontario. When I'm really lucky, friends from Scotland show up or I get to see a basement full of rare tropical frogs. I actually met some of my best friends on their message board.

"By the time you've been to half a dozen post-show meet'n'greets, Margo really feels like an old friend. She's always genuinely interested to find out what you think about the band's performance or their new songs. The second time I saw the band, at the One World Theater in Austin, she actually did some shopping for the fans between the first and second night's shows – after the last show, she walked out to [fan] John Olson's now-legendary truck and gave us all matchboxes with llamas on them that she had discovered in town. When I introduced my 19-year-old son to her on the sidewalk outside the Iron Horse Tavern after a show in Northampton eight months later, the two of them spent ten minutes consoling each other over the demise of their favourite TV show, *Buffy the Vampire Slayer* (I have to admit I was a little jealous). They literally had to drag her away from us fans and put her on the bus that night."

Bob Helm, "Cookie Bob", may not be exactly typical of the Junkies' fans given he's seen well over two hundred shows, but his story and his rationale for seeing them so often is not that far removed from that of those who see slightly fewer concerts. He sees himself and the band following in historic lineage. "The idea of being part of a community is in the line of what the Grateful Dead did. It's smaller and maybe better in a lot of ways, and I say that as a fan of the Dead. I go to shows mostly in the Northeast, but I've been to Canada, to the West Coast, I like driving, I like seeing the country that way. Normally I'd be up for work at five in the morning anyway, so instead I just get on the road and, as long as I bring the right CDs, it's great. Roads are empty, the sun's coming up, it's peaceful. And, wherever I go, I see someone I know and that's nice. It's a great community, it's a good way of meeting people – we communicate over the internet, we meet up, too. It becomes an extended family almost, when they go on the road.

"And why not come to this many shows? They're different all the time, I love the music, they mix up the set list a lot of the time, and in part that's because people do come to lots of shows – they've said on the website that, because people go to more than one concert, they don't want to bore us! I'm always going to see somebody, I love music, I saw the Dead a whole bunch of times, Phish too, and it got to the point where it was easy to see Cowboy Junkies all the time. Their music is what I like the best, but when they're not on the road I go see other bands. It's just what I do, what I love.

"I guess we're season ticket holders from a sports perspective! Nobody sees that as strange if you were following the Yankees or the Red Sox, yet you don't know if they'll play well, if you're going to get rained on. But you go see Cowboy Junkies and, even if they're having a bad night, you know you'll still love it.

"It's interesting to watch the ups and downs as they play different nights, different venues. On one run in the Northeast, the Northampton Iron Horse shows weren't quite as good as you'd hope, but the Annapolis Rams Head shows I loved. I could have just gone to the Iron Horse and ended up going home thinking that I'd had an OK night, but by hanging on and going to the Rams Head too, I got to see one of those great nights. And, even if the songs don't change, the way they play them does and so does the way they are onstage. One night will be pretty serious; another night, Margo and Pete will be sharing a joke – that's fun to watch, too. When you go to a lot of shows, there's a continuity to it where it's not just this show in isolation, but a chance to think about how it relates to the body of work they've done in the past. It's an ongoing story and I want to see how it works out."

Crazy Ed Casey, another long-term fan, has a similar view – Cowboy Junkies shows offer him a chance to catch some great music and to see some more of his vast country. "I remember the early message board; one guy said he was off to see a bunch of shows and somebody responded, 'Get a life!' I got a little miffed and asked him what he did on vacation. 'Don't you go places? I happen to go see the bands I love on vacation instead of sitting on a beach somewhere.' That doesn't make me crazy! I look at the tour dates, I look at my schedule, my money, and I make my arrangements to see the most shows in the time I have, and then I ask my boss for time off. I don't just drop everything for the band. I'm a sane human being that happens to love seeing their shows.

"If I've never been to California on my motorcycle and I have two weeks off and I want to do that and Cowboy Junkies are playing some shows I can catch while I'm there, then I'm gonna schedule my vacation to make that fit. What do you do on vacation? You go different places and meet different people. So do I! I've been in Boston before, to see Cowboy Junkies and other bands. But I haven't been here and sat talking with you! It's a method of choosing how to spend my time. I have criteria, and one of those is I want to see Cowboy Junkies and the things that go with that, interacting with people, eating dinner some place new. Sure, sometimes it's drive, get there, see the show, drink a lot of coffee, drive on and on until you burn out. But I love that, too!

"Beyond that, there's grown to be a more personal connection. They treat me better than I feel I have any right to ask, it's beyond what I would ever imagine. I want to go to the shows, but to be included in the sense that I am sometimes, to be given little glimpses into what goes on, that's incredible. I love to watch soundchecks, I love to watch the crew putting the gear out and taking it down. I love the process of rock'n'roll. Not the business of it, but the work of it, so to get the access I have is just really exciting for me.

"There have been times when I've got there very early. It happened at Cape Cod one time, and I walked through a fence and down some stairs looking for the back door and there were the band sitting at picnic tables under a canopy with a buffet laid out and they just called me over. 'Hey, Ed, grab a seat. What do you think about the new record? What do you think about Bush? What do you think about this or that?' It was like a friend had stopped by. So, you tell me why I wouldn't go see them? I like 'em!"

Musically, the band take a particular interest in not repeating themselves, and in making each show different, and part of that comes from an obligation to those who go the extra mile – or 1,000 miles – to catch a few shows on a run. On any given tour, there's rarely more than fifty per cent of the material that is core to the show, the rest changing from night to night. On top of that, during the afternoon when he's putting a set list together, Mike will regularly consult online sources to figure out "What did we play last time we were in this town?" The set will then be altered accordingly to avoid repetition – just another piece of attention to another little detail that strengthens the bond. And then there are the requests …

"Some nights we get five hundred requests and I can't dedicate a song to everybody – we're not a wedding band!" laughs Margo. "But I do feel obligated to do it sometimes. But you can become a jukebox, and that's where Mike and I are a good balance. If it were up to Mike, he wouldn't do any of them and I'll push him to make somebody's day. So we get a fine balance between the two – of being polite, nice, and of having our own show. If I were boss, I guess we would become a jukebox. Push whatever button you like and we'll play it. I'll even dance! When I go see a show and John Cale's up there being mean and rude to me after I just paid $50 to see him, I don't like that. You have to react to the people that are there."

"I get tired of being a jukebox. Margo doesn't!" admits Mike. "She's right in a way: people are paying their money and she wants to sing songs that are meaningful to them, and I understand that side of it. The other side is that I keep an eye on the overall picture, I look at what we played the last time we went through that town, what we've played in recent years, what we're trying to put across as a band this time, what I want the whole audience to walk away with, not just what three or four individuals want. If it fits into that concept, fine, we can do it. But if it's something we played last time around, I don't really like to do it, because the chances are this audience have heard it, we're tired of it, we have to drop something we'd rather play or that they haven't heard. It's important that we keep adding new songs to the live show and going back and picking out things from the repertoire that we haven't done before or not in a while – otherwise, it gets very stale. That's the difference between our jobs, because hers is very much to get that individual contact, so we compromise on that."

That personal connection is the single most potent weapon the band has in bringing people back time and again, as another veteran, Jason Lent, says. "I

291

was in Florida when *Lay It Down* came out and that was when you could start getting information on the internet, you could find where they were playing, so that was my first tour. I drove around Florida to see back-to-back shows, about sixteen hours' driving, and I thought I was the coolest fan ever, I didn't think anyone else would ever do that. They were spectacular shows, they had the guy on cello with them, which gave it a great sound, and that just took my appreciation of them up a notch. My first show, I'd been much too shy to stay behind for the meet-and-greet, but I met Margo after those ones. I got up the courage to ask her about the *Whites Off Earth Now!!* title and she talked about how the Black Panthers had that as their slogan, and I was just amazed at how casual and open she was with the fans, and that just further cemented my attraction for them."

Next witness, Jason Gonulsen: "Margo comes out and talks to the audience and I can't think of too many other bands where that kind of thing would happen. And where it does, you feel there's an ego thing going on: 'I'm going to see these people who love me.' I don't get that from Margo. I really think that she's genuinely thankful that people are still buying the CDs and coming to the shows and she's appreciative of that. It's very weird, because she's probably the most down-to-earth musician I've ever met and I find that talking to her is like talking to somebody you've known all your life. I haven't had that experience with any other band and often I'll think that a lot of people whose music I love, I really wouldn't want to meet them, because you think you're going to be disappointed! But, with Cowboy Junkies, they are just the most down-to-earth band I could name."

At the centre of it all, it can look a little different, as Margo admits. "I used to feel nervous when I first did the meet-and-greet thing, when I wasn't as comfortable with the whole thing. That was one of the reasons I did it, because of the discomfort. I never liked the separation between me and an audience. Record companies and management try to widen that gap, to create an image. If you're a star, you have to be untouchable. I hated that. It wasn't me; really bothered me. So I'd go out and talk to lessen the gap. I'd show up in the lobby and ruin our whole image! It helped me onstage, too. I figured if I knew who was out there, if I sang to people instead of a big, black void, then it might be easier. Early on, I felt vulnerable because it was odd and there was a lot of gawking at me, and I had one of the crew standing right next to me. Now people are so used to it, it's no big deal.

"I know our audience – they're thinking people, they love the band but they don't necessarily love me like they do a lot of female singers. I don't get weird sex mail or all that crap. They yell out, 'I love you Margo,' but I don't think they want to marry me! It's not sexual. I don't feel threatened by it. I think I'm their friend as opposed to anything else. I hope they find me sexy, because we all want that, but it's not a sexual thing – it's about being female, about the lights, about the way we present the music; it's in the context of what we do. It's not that I have a nice belly button or big boobs or my outfit is revealing. When you do that, you're inviting that kind of adoration and that's frightening. You're turning people on and you get a lot of kooks! I don't think I do that.

"But it's important there's a sexy side, a sensual side to what I do, because that's part of the music. I'm the visual part of it, the front person, there's not much else to look at with the guys just sitting there and Al not moving! The least I can do is brush my hair and put on a nice dress – I wish I had more of them, but I don't. My sister Cali lives in LA, she's an actress, she has a closet the size of my bedroom, and I remember her opening Trixie, our wardrobe case, and freaking out. 'That's all you have? My God!' I have three dresses in there. I do my best. One pair of shoes.

"Even in meeting people on the street, I get stared at a lot – especially in Toronto, of course – but it's always nice. Our audience aren't silly little kids, they're grown-ups. They come over and say something nice, like, 'Your music helped me through a bad time', 'I love the new record', 'I've been following you forever'. It's never crazy. But we've never appealed to that kind of audience. We have a thinking audience, which is why we could last a long time yet, because it's not about turning them on sexually, it's about turning them on to music. There's not a sell-by date on that. Our music is our personality, it's who we are, what we are. I like our fans. Some bands have really yucky people who follow them!"

And, for the yucky few, there's the Junkies police, as Crazy Ed explains. "People like Bob and I took it upon ourselves that, as new fans popped up, we'd take them under our wing and try and show them that this wasn't a normal rock'n'roll situation, you didn't go barging in on the band; you sort of sat back and absorbed the music, you thanked them for it and you left them to get on with their lives. We're very protective of their privacy and, if somebody violates that, they pretty much get ostracized. Somebody stayed in the same hotel as them when they played in Manchester and she went and knocked on Margo's door and freaked her out, but we haven't seen hide or hair of her since – she got a pretty cold reception from everyone. Maybe she didn't even realize she'd overstepped the mark. But, hello! You don't interrupt their privacy. You need to have a sense of what's right and wrong."

That kind of situation is pretty rare, as Margo says, with a mixture of relief and gratitude. "I think with fans there's always a part of them that feels they own you a little bit, but ours have been pretty amazing. A few have come into the dressing room and sat there and we've had to get them out because we're preparing for a show. But they don't try to get on the bus, they don't feel we owe them more than a good show, they don't try to tag along when we go to dinner – we've never had that problem. Generally, they give us a lot of space and that's great. For me, more than the others I guess, it's a real balancing act, because I want everybody to feel welcome. I'm happy they're there.

"I guess the fact that I tell stories about our day when I'm onstage makes everybody feel a part of who we are and what we do, and it's great if they do, because they are a part of it – if they weren't buying the tickets, we couldn't come to their town. And, in doing that, maybe you do invite people to think it's more than it is, that they are my friend, that they know me.

"I'm not threatened by the llamas or anything. I like the fact that they're there. But I'm not a llama! This is my job, it's what I do and I'm doing it for all the people who are there, not just the llamas. I'm doing it for them; for the person who's just spent his money and come out of curiosity, never heard us before; for the people who turn up when we go through their town but don't follow us – for all of them. I don't want it to get too close, too intimate, because that's a little awkward, a little intimidating. I want them to have a good time, I'm happy to chat after a show, but there needs to be a little distance, or it gets weird."

Llamas. A collective noun for a breed of Junkies junkies who pay particularly close attention to the music, frequent the message boards and who always, when the opportunity is there, go to the show. But why "llamas"?

"One of the regulars on the old message board, Skippy Peanut, posted a message saying how much he loved the Junkies," recalls Mike. "He'd seen us many times, but as he was walking out after a show he heard a couple of guys saying that I was playing to tapes, I wasn't doing it all live. So people started speculating and, in the end, I wrote back saying that I wasn't doing that, but I had a bunch of pedals in front of me and I could basically make the guitar sound like a spitting llama if I had to! So then everyone got dubbed spitting llamas on the board, and that got shortened in the end to 'llamas'. And that ended up being a galvanizing thing for fans, too, one of those weird things that come up on the internet."

The thing that most galvanizes and most unites a pretty disparate crew of people is simple. The music. As Crazy Ed says, "I keep coming to the shows because, every night, without fail, I get a burst of electricity up and down my spine and the top of my head starts to scratch! At some point, I always find myself standing there with a big, dumb grin on my face, or my mouth wide open. Why wouldn't you want more of that?"

That's why you can go to a Junkies show night after night after night, because it's never the same way twice. Not that it's sloppy, because they work very hard at their craft. But the show is loose. Tight, but loose. You know they're going to play a good show, there's that bedrock of professionalism that pretty much guarantees that, but you don't really know how "Dragging Hooks" or "Blue Guitar" is going to get from point A to point B from one night to the next. There are no fancy lights, no pyrotechnics, no explosions, lasers, film shows, dry ice or any other cliché. Marshall McLuhan wasn't quite right. The music is the message.

"It's all about the music," concurs Alan. "It's not a spectacle, a show, it's about playing, and being on the road is when we get chance to play. That's why we always do an hour-long soundcheck, every show. It's not to just get the sound onstage right. It's to hear each other properly, to feel it, to get to a point where we're comfortable on that stage, that hall, which you can't do in just a couple of songs."

Mistakes are made, but they're human ones, they're covered or excused by the warmth and personality of it. "We're not perfect, we're just like you." It's part of the show, it's live, we're in this room together, let's enjoy it. That warmth gives the players the freedom to make mistakes, to carry on. The band is constantly reaching out and embracing the audience and constantly in touch with each other. Lot of stagecraft in what they do, but technique never swamps the human side, doesn't become a technical exercise, instead they use experience to overcome any issues they have onstage, be it lack of rehearsal, equipment problems, etc. And they can always turn it round by laughing at themselves, with a joke between them onstage, from a throwaway comment from the back from Pete, or especially by Margo cutting loose – ad-libbing through "Sweet Jane", snake-dancing through "Dragging Hooks". On a two-show night at the Rams Head in Annapolis, the first set was halted as Pete dashed off the stage to go to the toilet; then, in the second set, the band stopped, there was an awkward silence, which was eventually punctured by Pete calling, "We're waiting for you, Marg!" And then they can just hit their straps and put in a big song that turns a place upside down.

There's a constant chain of reaction and interaction going on through the shows, as Pete points out. "As years have gone by, now there's a real connection between Margo and the audience, here we all are together tonight, instead of a big gap between us and them. We thrive on what the audience gives back to us – especially in America, where they are pretty boisterous; they let you know what they think about you. Canada is sometimes pretty bad for that, because it's very low-key. In Europe, if you're not playing well they don't respond. If the Norwegians clap in unison, you know you've done well. If they don't, it's been lousy, so you wait for the end of a song and hope!"

Alan feels they keep things fresh because the music has room to breathe. "A lot of the songs we play have room for extending, so that keeps you sharp onstage. You don't just go through the exact same part every night, because we don't have many pop songs! The few we do have, we get bored of them real fast and end up not playing them after a week or two of touring. That was pretty funny, because it would drive the record company crazy when we wouldn't play the single because we were bored with it. Luckily, 'Sweet Jane', there's something about those three chords, there's so much pleasure in them, so many things you can do with the song."

Returning to the band for the 2005 tour, John Timmins was left astounded by the people coming to the shows. "There's a quality of listening, of concentration, that people bring to the Junkies' music that doesn't come to too many bands. I was swept away by the dedication of their fans. I've never had the opportunity of experiencing that first-hand and I find it thrilling, especially those stories that people give you of how important the music has been to them.

"The sensibility of the 1960s is very much part of the Junkies and I found the music we played on tour, some of the instrumental sections, are just so reminiscent of that period. I really loved doing those. You need guts to stand up and play that free-form stuff that could fall on its face just as easily as it can soar. A lot of younger musicians are tied into technology – into formalized music, too. They feel they have to play the notes in front of them, play the guitar the way they were taught. I guess that if you're not too schooled in an instrument, it's easier to try that free-form style. If we'd all taken formal music lessons as kids, chances are there would be none of that improvisation, because we would never dare do some of the things we do now, because you're taught not to do it. That's true of many great bands: they're not taught players, so they find their own way to make sounds.

"Musically, there was a pattern of progression on that tour for me. It started out with no idea of how well it would go. Then, after a couple of shows, naturally I felt more confident. I had a base to build on, and then – and I knew I'd reach that point – I lost confidence again! But that was good, because if I'd been sure of myself I wouldn't have been progressing. I reached a point where I need to reassess what's right and wrong, which is a little bit nervy. It's fascinating just how much of a mental process it was and I'm very lucky that the band was patient enough to let me go through that.

"There's some freedom in songs like 'Dragging Hooks', 'Bread and Wine'. When they work, they work beautifully, but when they fail, it's horrible. That's the nature of free-form music and that's why it's so great to watch, because you know the band's taking a horrible risk out there. One night it just didn't work and I felt like every cell in my body was screaming at me to run. I just didn't know what to do – the riff I was doing wasn't working, because we were too slow, and you don't want to go for a walk when you're not really sure where you're going! Being with this band is a great way to learn that stuff because of their high quality of work and because of the forgiveness afforded to me. Everyone is of the same nature, where you forgive the mistakes of the others but demand more of yourself. If a show hasn't gone well, everyone thinks it's down to them. There's no finger-pointing. There's a very distinct sense of responsibility among the group."

While it might not be such a thrill to the people up there, even those songs that don't go where they were supposed to can be fascinating for the seasoned viewer. In a world where too much music is straitjacketed, seeing it go where it will is a spectacle in itself. "If they have a train wreck up there and a song goes really wrong, it's interesting to see how they get out of it," says Cookie Bob. "I remember Margo blew the lyrics of 'Dragging Hooks' and Pete was ready to just carry on with what had happened, and Mike was trying to step over that and make a smooth transition out of it, and it was fascinating to watch them working at it to salvage something. Maybe they're not so happy with it, because I get the sense that they're always shooting for perfection, but it's great to see them experiment and try to reach for something, even if it fails. That's what live shows are about."

Each fan will have their tales of a particular show, a particular night, just as Jason Lent does. "When I got to college, *Pale Sun, Crescent Moon* came out in my junior year and they played on campus. It was $7; greatest deal ever! I'd been dating this girl for three years – we were serious, I'd started putting money aside for an engagement ring – but there was always something that felt a little off, somehow. The concert was on the night of her birthday and I decided to go to the concert instead of going out with her. I'll never forget in 'A Horse in the Country", Margo singing the line 'When your guts just burn.' That just connected with me; it was one of those moments when life just makes sense for a few seconds, and it ended up that we broke up a few months later. Cowboy Junkies are still my favourite band many years later, so I stand by my decision!"

Keith Bergendorff hasn't had his life changed so dramatically, but, as a regular at the shows, it's the nuances that capture his attention. "Margo's stories. Sometimes they're hilarious – I mean, like Margaret Cho hilarious – and sometimes they're not, but they're always warm and entertaining and utterly unpretentious, and they always seem to say, 'Let me share a little of my life with you, I'll bet you can relate.' I always look forward to hearing what she has to say, even when she's good-naturedly complaining about Americans' ignorance of geography or the pathetic size of a venue-supplied flower bouquet.

"The band has so much presence and is so much fun to watch onstage, despite their low-key style and shunning of theatrics. Margo with her head hanging below the mic, the often-intense visual interplay between Mike and Jeff, Pete with his eyes closed in concentration and bouncing like a hyperactive 6-year-old, Alan … well, maybe not Alan. I especially enjoy seeing Michael smile after a particularly good jam, or roll his eyes when his sister flubs his painstakingly composed lyrics yet again."

For Crazy Ed, finding the Junkies was a happy accident. "A lot of people will say a record grabbed them, that they were breaking up with their girlfriend and a record was a soundtrack to it. For me, a young woman I knew had a similar interest to me in alternative music and we agreed that one day we'd go see a band. One day, she came up to me and said, 'Cowboy Junkies are at the Iron Horse in Northampton, shall we go?' I knew they'd been on the radio but I hadn't paid much attention at that point, but I agreed. We walked up to the door, got what were probably the last tickets. We sat way in the back with a pole in front of us, but half an hour in I was spellbound. It was the tour just before *Caution Horses* came out, Margo was dressed just like on the promo poster for that – the grey V-neck sweater and ripped out jeans – just sat on her stool, staring at the microphone, and she was just so quiet, just like the band. There was such musical tension. You knew this band could really let loose if they wanted to, but they didn't – they kept the tension. I walked out of there reeling, wondering what I'd witnessed."

Jason Gonulsen enjoyed a similarly revelatory evening in their company. "I saw them the first time in St Louis, and after the show I couldn't believe how much effect the live show had on me. I immediately got online to find out when they were playing round here again! So, the next time, I drove a couple hundred miles to Kansas City and saw them in a tiny club; I got right in the front row and that was great. Margo has a real ability to make eye contact with the audience, which is really important; it makes the performances so much more powerful. Afterwards, I had a really good conversation with her and, ever since then, there have been times where they've let me into soundchecks, which is a thrill and then afterwards we've chatted, which makes you feel like she really cares about the fans. The best thing was waiting in line for a show in St Louis, reading my book, and out of the blue Margo came past to go into the club, saw me, stopped and said, 'Hi Jason, what are you waiting here for? Do you want to come in for the soundcheck?' What other band does that?! It makes you feel such a part of it."

Like every good relationship, there has to be give and take. When it comes to on-the-road comfort eating, the band are only too willing to take from Cookie Bob, hence the name. "When I really started touring, around 1998, Margo said at a show that they were tired, they'd been on the road for months, they missed their families. I'd been staying behind at shows to get stuff signed, so we knew each other a bit and I just wanted to do something for them because they were so nice and they'd done so much for the fans. I just figured one of the things you miss is home cooking and my mom has been baking cookies forever for church functions, for friends – my sister's boss would call her up sometimes to ask for them in the office – so I knew everybody loved her cookies. So I asked her to make a couple of dozen for the band. I felt pretty weird about it the first time, but it was the best thing I could come up with. Just dumb luck, it was Margo's favourite that I brought with me, the band loved them and so I've been bringing them ever since. Even if they quit touring, I could see myself getting an address and sending cookies to Toronto periodically, just because I know they like them!"

Yet, where the fans are protective and supportive of the band, it's a two-way street, as Margo points out. "It would have been difficult to do things the way we do now if we hadn't tried to concentrate on our fans over the years. They're very loyal, which we're very grateful for, and I think they've always known that. When we did *Whites!!* and then *The Trinity Session*, we never expected to get a record company, ever. Not because we weren't good enough, but we weren't playing the popular kind of music, so why would they be interested? Then, when we did, the record company figured if we sold 30,000 of *Trinity*, that would be great. So, when it started to sell, everybody was surprised. Our whole career is a surprise. That we're here thirty years later and people are paying $50 to sit and be entertained is still incredible. There are a lot of choices out there, we're not on the radio or in the paper all the time, but somehow people hear about us and it's great that they come. We never took it for granted. That's why we want to put on the best show we can within our budget – it's sometimes frustrating that we can't always put on a bigger show, but people seem happy with what we're doing.

"I find our audience really interesting. You'll get a young kid, then you'll get an older couple, then a factory worker, then an artist, another who drives a forklift truck for a living, but he follows us whenever he can. What brought them here? You get a retired couple who haven't listened to anything new since Bob Dylan put out his first record. I love the way, even now, even in the world we have, music can still find people, even though it's so easy to miss it. I don't read the paper every day, I don't feel I need to know everything, I don't want to know the tragedies, how many people died today, because it's too much, and anything major is going to be forced in my face, so as far as music goes I don't get to hear about a lot of stuff, I even miss the big guys like Springsteen when they're touring. 'What, he was here last night? Oh no!' And yet people find our music, find out about us.

"What I've always been curious about is the attraction for the fans. To me, this is what we do. Yes, I think it's good, but it fascinates me why, thirty-five years into it, we have this loyal following that doesn't seem to be going away. People love it, and they love it as much as they ever did. We put a new album out, we get people saying, 'This is the best thing you've ever done!' That's great. But what are people hearing? Why have we been able to do with this and not had that great hit? We just go quietly along. You look at our audience and it's such a range, from congresswomen to the guy in the factory, and they're both getting something from it. A lot of bands, their audience is the same – same age group, all working class, all university kids, whatever it is. Not us.

"There's a trust between us and the audience, certainly on my side. I trust them. Through these years, the one thing I've always trusted is them, I've always believed they got it, the people who love our music. I think we share something and that's important to us. It's nice to have that, because I can't say I felt like that about record companies, journalists, the industry. The only thing I've trusted apart from the boys is the fans. They stick with us, they give us a chance. I don't love every record Springsteen or Dylan or Neil Young have done – I have my favourite – but if there's one I don't like, I'll still show up for the next one and give it a try. I think our fans do that."

With such a passionate following, there are inherent dangers. In a show where there are maybe 1,500 people in a theatre, maybe twenty per cent are the real committed fans who know every song inside out and travel wherever and whenever; maybe another few hundred mostly follow the releases and see the show every year or two when the Junkies are near enough to their town. And the rest are those who've picked up a couple of albums down the years and think, "Cowboy Junkies? Didn't they do 'Sweet Jane'? I'll go check them out." Pleasing all of that audience is a tall order, but, as onetime support act Tim Easton notes,

299

that's part of the challenge. "What they show is that there aren't any short cuts if you're a band making serious music. You have to get out on the road and find your audience, build it up, because they're not going to come to you, because there aren't too many places you're going to hear that music any longer. You have to stick to your guns. They were influential on me in that way. Do your thing. Just write a good song with a good melody, that's your job."

Good songs and good melodies still attract people, even now. And those people sometimes go to extreme lengths to find them. To end, here's the North Bay story, which is pretty typical. Your host this evening is Cookie Bob.

"North Bay was just about in the centre of what was probably my favourite tour ever. It was in March 2003 and I had some concern about driving through Canada then – we frequently get real bad storms here in New York about that time, and I expected that Canada could offer much of the same. I expressed my concern in an email to another fan on the message board, John Olson, and jokingly dubbed the tour the 'Blowing & Drifting' tour. He used that phrase on the board, and the tour had an unofficial name.

"Many folks travelled a fair distance for this run, a bunch of shows that were mostly within an hour or so of Toronto, as they were testing out material for *One Soul Now*. The Trinity St Paul show was the final 'homecoming' show. The band had been experiencing weak ticket sales in Toronto prior to this show, but not this time. I think the 'Trinity' in the church's title deceived some people into thinking that this was the venue that *Trinity Session* was recorded at, and they bought tickets accordingly. The show was way sold out, and scalpers were getting high prices on the street. Once again, there were many llamas in attendance, as this was the same Toronto-based tour as North Bay. The prior night in St Catherine's, Margo did not receive any flowers from fans, and had only one very poor specimen on her table that was provided by the venue. She good-naturedly heckled the flower and the person who was responsible for it.

"Everyone seemed to take her flower tirade to heart, and for the Trinity show, Margo was literally swamped with flowers. Her table was far too small to contain them all, and many bouquets were just draped across the front of the stage at her feet. Most people seemed to purchase the flowers from a florist directly across the street from the church, and the woman who owned it was so impressed that she came over to meet the woman who inspired such devotion (and probably provided her best business day outside of Valentine's!).

"The way the tour worked meant a lot of people made the trip and our friend Judy really stepped up. She made a deal with the Toronto downtown Days Inn for a group rate, and most folks stayed there as home base and then travelled daily to each show. North Bay was the exception. It followed a show in Barrie, about ninety minutes north of Toronto. North Bay was another three and a half hours north of Barrie, and all but the most hardy decided to skip this show and lounge about Toronto for a day and then reconnect for the following show. To the best of my faulty recollection, there were eight of us who attended: me,

Crazy Ed, Scott Tromblee, Greg (he was known as Rare Good Will on the message board), John and Nic Olson, Mike McCorkle (aka MJM), and Chris Sansenbach from California.

"John Olson found a deal on a fully furnished fishing cottage resort on Lake Nipissing that cost big bucks in season, but we were able to get it for a song in the midwinter. All of us stayed there, and the post-show activities there probably remain best unsaid. I do remember Scott grilling some food for us at 1 a.m. – without the benefit of a coat – in completely frigid weather.

"The show was in a monolithic theatre called the Capitol Centre. The place was a little big for the Junkies, especially without the tourist traffic that obviously sustains the town in warmer months. There was ornamental metal artwork set into the side walls of the theatre, just to each side of the stage. I found it to be somewhat intimidating, and it struck me as a perfect venue for a Wagner opera, but the small crowd was attentive and appreciative. The band was opening with 'Mining for Gold'/'Misguided Angel' and you could hear a pin drop. Margo's voice sounded great in the theatre, and my recording came out really well. You can hear the echo of her voice decay as it travels through the theatre. 'Cold Evening Wind' was played during the first set, dedicated to all of us who made the trip, and it couldn't have been more appropriate!

"The day after the show, myself, Ed and MJM were travelling together back toward Toronto. We left North Bay after a night of very little sleep, and all of our collective faculties were not fully functioning in the early morning hours. We opted to get coffee on the road in an effort to expedite our departure. After all, there's a Tim Horton's on every corner in Canada, right? We ended up driving almost an hour before encountering an establishment that offered coffee for sale. We were severely in need by this time, and gratefully pulled into the general store/truckstop. We got in line and slowly notice some familiar individuals in front of us – the band! Who are Cowboy Junkies and why do they keep following me around?"

301

THEY ALSO SERVE

Any tour involves more than the musicians. A collection of crew make the trek, too, without getting any of the adulation that the band get, though Margo always makes a point of namechecking everyone who has worked on the show at the end of the night.

The Junkies' road crew contains many warriors who have made it through year after gruelling year, for reasons guitar tech John Farnsworth explains: "The road can be frustrating, because there are so many little screw-ups going on all day because, a lot of times, you're at the mercy of things outside your control. You have to let a lot of that go, not get mad at it. It's easy to do that with them, because I don't get called on stuff that others do: 'How come I'm set up nine inches in the wrong place?' That doesn't happen; I don't have to pull a measuring tape out.

"If something goes down onstage and I've had to change something around for some technical reason, they trust me that I've done what's best and they deal with it. There's no fuss, no tantrums. So I can walk into a venue, look around and, instead of getting upset about all the things that look wrong, having that spill onto the local crew, having bad vibes all day, I can just go to work and do what needs to be done and we have a good environment to work in from there. And that's because I know the band won't come back and complain, because they know that a lot of the places won't be perfect, so they deal with it."

Of course, not everybody passes the test, as erstwhile tour manager Blair Woods points out. "We had this monitor guy and he was terrible. He didn't watch the band, there was no eye contact, he was always looking at the computer. The stage sound was terrible. We got to an outdoor show in Seattle. Mike and Margo were doing 'Bea's Song' and Marg couldn't hear the guitar – she was frantically trying to get this guy's attention all the way through it, but he's not watching. Margo had no idea what Mike was playing, so eventually she stormed offstage to yell at him. But, because it was outdoors, it's not like going into the wings in a theatre – the people can still see you. So she was yelling at him and discovered the whole crowd was watching her freak out. He got fired."

And then are other misadventures, ones Pete would like to forget, but can't. "We were in Vancouver, last night of the tour, and everyone was sitting in the back of the bus. While we were there waiting to get going, somebody got on the bus and stole the tour manager's bag with all the money in it. In Italy one time, the tour manager came back to the hotel and said, 'Guys, I've been robbed by gypsies!' Italy is weird. We got lost in Florence for four hours one time. The road manager ended up crying."

Being stuck on a bus for hours can unhinge even this most sedate of touring parties from time to time – can't it, Farns?

"We have a lot of jokes on tour and I've been on both ends of that, more often on the giving end, maybe! They all have a great sense of humour, especially Pete, and that's important to break up the day. We dropped a dummy out of a lighting truss in Vancouver one time, it was supposed to be me, and after it fell I crawled out from behind the drum riser like I'd fallen out of the sky, and a couple of guys carried me off the stage. Margo was speechless, the whole crowd went silent – they couldn't believe what had happened – then it dawned on Margo that the guitar guy wouldn't be on a lighting truss; she realized she'd been had and she called me out to take a bow and explained it to the audience. That was maybe too real for the crowd!

"We dish it out pretty good. We have a lot of fun with opening acts, like gaffer taping people to chairs and leaving them to sit out onstage. Over the Rhine were with us one time and we got a dancing girl get up there with them, so when Melanie Melons was up there in her little outfit I don't think Karin knew what to do! Nothing pornographic, but it was sure fun to watch. But, later on, Karin climbed a lighting truss that was side-stage and, from fifteen feet up, she cut open a feather pillow and dumped it on the band. We were still finding feathers in the gear seven years later! We had to shut a song down because Margo got one stuck in her throat, so we had to wait for them to settle – it was a real showstopper!"

CHAPTER 18

Which way you looking?

You can't escape the allusion to life as a journey, be it in art, literature or in advertising, those lovely, cuddly banks and insurance companies now promising that they're with you for the duration, having worked so assiduously over the last thirty years or so to fuck up the world's economy and destroy countless millions of lives in the process.

For all that Oscar Wilde said that, after 25, everyone is the same age, in the modern world where people are encouraged to remain children – or at least childish – for as long as possible, it's maybe not until the mid- or late thirties that you fully realize that you really are on a journey. Maybe it's the realization that you've started going to funerals more often that does it. Suddenly, you realize you're heading somewhere and you've come from someplace else, a process the Junkies began to confront in ever greater depth on *Miles from Our Home*.

Like any journey, you reach a point where there really is no turning back. The effort expended in getting you to where you are seems to have taken all the reserves you had, yet there's still such a long way to go. In marathon running, they call it the wall. In life, it's often the midlife crisis, existential ennui which takes on many forms, particularly in the male of the species as the earlier zeal of the hunter-gatherer gets replaced by something approaching exhaustion and a realization that you're no longer the youngest, the strongest, the fittest.

The symptoms take many and various forms, the popular culture caricature being the sudden urge to buy a huge motorcycle or an ultra-expensive sports car and take on a coterie of young female companions. But it can also be a whole lot more subtle, and a whole lot crazier, than that. Sometimes, men and women can just shut down completely. The energy of curiosity can be replaced by simply settling for what you have; by complacency and by sheer exhaustion due to the routine, from the effort. There's a tendency to look over your shoulder, back towards a golden time, rather than confront the black hole in front of you, one of ever-narrowing options. That is the space that *Open* occupies, as angry a record in the Junkies canon as you'll find, a barely suppressed fury informing great chunks of it, raging against the dying of the light and the onset of intellectual and emotional conservatism. Cowboy Junkies were open, not closed. But it's not easy.

It's a record of just how complex life gets as you get older, no matter what you do, and just how exhausting that realization can be, the awareness that those cherished dreams of youth, that one day it would all fall into place and just make sense, are just that. Dreams.

"We were reflecting that in the record," explains Mike. "But then the other element to it was the album title, 'Open'. Despite all the problems, the only way to continue to grow is to be open. It's so contradictory, so confusing, so much comes at you that you want to shut down. But if you shut down, you're going nowhere, you're dead, there's no more growth – what's the point? You see so many people who get to a certain age and that's it. They never listen to anything new, they never go to see a movie that's challenging, they don't read any more books, they feed on what they know. It's a really natural thing for people to do in this day and age where so much comes at you so quick but there's so much access to the familiar, too, so that record is also about fighting that, realizing that things are totally unprocessable in a way, but that you still have to be open to them, you have to accept all that change and try to process it because, otherwise, there is no point."

Margo adds, "I think the records we make are like time capsules of our life. When I listen to *Open*, it was such a passage. Turning 40, all that that brings in your life. It's about growing older, realizing that life does come to an end. One day you wake up and think, 'My God, I'm ageing!' You have to continue to be open to life, to change, not be afraid of it, or try to run from it."

For John Timmins, that's the key to his siblings' success. "There is no filter on what the band does. The songs are written and performed with an attitude of, 'This is who we are, what we do; this music is about our lives, probably yours too.' That's the thing about art: it can have that universal message or appeal that we can all tap into, there's a current in it. Therein is the story of the Junkies – staying tapped into that universal consciousness, if you like – which is primarily Michael's doing through the songs. Tapping into it is one thing, but staying true to that given all the pressures to go down different roads is tough, and that's where the others come in and help keep that focus. I think a lot is to do with family intimacy: they understand where he's coming from, they can play off that understanding or play around it, and Michael knows that his writing will find a supportive and understanding group. It's quite phenomenal.

"They've accepted that they're getting older. Just as their records at the start were about being in your late twenties, now they're about being in your late forties, and that's why there's such truth in them. There has to be some growth as you grow older and I think Mike has continually shown that in his writing."

Or, as William Burroughs put it, "The function of art and all creative thought is to make us aware of what we know and don't know we know. You can't tell anybody anything he doesn't know already."

And so, if you're willing to enlist, remaining open becomes a conscious battle, day upon day, a fight against stagnating, a refusal to surrender to ageing and to the age, and, above all, it becomes a struggle with time, with the everyday. Anyone under the age of 30 reading this, you have no idea of the simple weariness that's coming towards you, physically and emotionally. You want to do anything that requires physical exuberance and emotional independence? Now's the time to get it done, kids. Your times, they will be a-changin'.

But, on the plus side of the ledger, experience is a teacher that no money can buy, as Pete points out. "Whether you're an electrician, a plumber, I don't think you're anything until you're 55 or 60. That's when you really are at your peak, that's when you know all the tricks, the skills, the secrets. Same with us. We're still learning and that's our attitude. I don't think we're as good as we can be yet and hopefully we'll keep on getting better and better. I respect the older guy that knows his stuff. Maybe that's because we had such an interest in the blues when we started and a lot of the guys we listened to were making great records at 60 or whatever. I wish Mick Jagger would just sit down and play his harmonica, I wish they'd all sit down and just play. I still love the Rolling Stones, but it makes me queasy when he's jumping round the stage and stuff. Why not just be 70 and tell us what you found out getting there?

"It's like a woman who is beautiful at 50, but when she tries to be 40, then she's not. She's a beautiful 50 not a beautiful 40. It's a matter of accepting what you are. I think that we have always tried to be what we are at that time and I think the audience has come along with it because we're all around that same point. People get something from the idea that we're all in it together, we're all getting older, we're all still learning, we don't know all the answers. As you get older, you realize you don't know any of the answers. And having that strong base of what we've done in the past, the fact that people know we do what we do, we're not going to bend to appease this person or that company – people trust that."

"We're not very complicated people," adds Margo. "It's subtle: we live the same life that our audience lives, we all go home to our mortgages, our children, our bills, the leaky pipes in the basement, the same problems. We've never had any pretence about us."

We move on, we age, we change, we look different, we like different things, we act different, we have different preoccupations, but if you strip away the layers of the years, underneath there's the kernel of what we are and what we've always been, always will be. The artifice, the star machine, the need for reinvention means that, in so much music, that character is hard to find. In Cowboy Junkies, here is a band whose main motivation each time around is to get who they are onto the record.

"I think that's it," agrees Margo. "Maybe we've been lucky not to have had a huge mega-hit. We've had success, I've made a living out of music, that's great, but not having that huge hit has maybe allowed us to keep doing what we want without too much fighting. We've always fought for the fact that our music is our music, that's what we do, so when record companies have tried to change it, we never understood it. If the music changes in a way we don't want it to go, if it's not expressing who and what we are, where we are, that's how bands break up. It stops being fun, the music becomes work. Touring is the work, getting on the bus, leaving home is work. But playing isn't work and, if it was, that's wrong, so we've always closed ranks and guarded the music really hard and always done records the way we wanted to do them.

"*The Trinity Session* was a whirlwind, it gave us a glimpse of the next level up. Sure, I'd love to be there as far as the financial things go, the security you have as a band. Being on the next level up makes that easier. But it also costs. You have to do more, you have to be out more, get your picture taken more, get the crazies hanging round. The people that follow us are great, I like them all, they're musicians or tapers, they're really into music, they're normal. The crazies we had early on when we were the next big thing are gone. We saw a part of that world where it's not about playing any more. I used to think of R.E.M at that time – they got to a place where it was just screaming kids, they could have done anything onstage and people would have liked it, they became something beyond what they were about.

"With some bands, they become so successful that they just repeat what got them there; they stop trying new things, asking questions. Our records have changed because they're what we are, they're about having kids, being middle-aged, losing people, living in a world that's falling apart knowing your children are growing up into it. That's who we are right now, so that's what we do. It makes me sad when you see people still doing the same thing they did thirty years ago. But I see older women onstage, like Emmylou Harris or someone, and that's great – I can do that, too."

Long-term fan Jason Gonulsen adds, "The Junkies still have it together, the songs always seem to come and are just as strong as ever, the albums are complete projects and the music is what matters to them. I read an article before *Open* came out and Margo had had her hair cut shorter and the interviewer kept talking about that instead of the music, and she said something to the effect of, 'You're talking to the wrong person!'"

But the wisdom of the ages doesn't come free, and one of the costs is a simple fatigue and, in part, *Open* expresses that, but not with resignation, and that's crucial. Fatigue can lead to apathy and, of all attitudes, that is not on the agenda here. Making a record that acknowledges weariness, particularly in this most kinetic of centuries, is fraught with danger, with the possibility of alienating listeners ever more programmed for instant gratification, for a caffeine jolt from their music.

That's something that irritates Pete in particular. "More and more so, anything 'artistic' or 'difficult' just goes over people's heads. People don't have the time to sit down and listen to a song these days. The old saying in A&R is 'Don't bore us, get to the chorus!' People give songs three seconds now, then click. The whole idea of a record as a statement, actually as a record of a point in time, that's becoming history. The fact you don't have two sides like you did with vinyl is a part of that. It makes it harder, I think. It started with iPods, where people just bastardized albums, chop them up, create greatest hits playlists, everything is greatest hits; or you have the iTunes thing where you just buy one song off an album; then Spotify, where you just stream songs and can move to anything that's ever been released with a click. It's like chopping up a painting and taking the smile off the *Mona Lisa*: 'That's the good part, the rest of it is crap. It's a lot of black canvas and she's not so great-looking, anyway!' That's where everything is going – it's so crass."

It hardly needs saying that that was not the Junkies' philosophy. The end of the millennium ennui, the frustrations, the little joys, they're all in *Open*, and if the band were pretty much preaching to the church by this stage, the congregation was ready and willing to take on the reading. After all, this is where we all were – we're all feeling it, we're all dealing with it; hopefully, we'll all get through it.

For those who came to the record fresh, without any working knowledge of the band, the first impression was of a band that really could kick it out when the mood grabbed them. There's a vitality, an energy, an urgency about *Open* that continued to take them into new territory, albeit that records like *Trinity Session* and *Whites Off Earth Now!!* remained touchstones. The more things change, the more they stay the same.

Songs suffused with a bubbling rage were reason enough for the record to encompass some playing where the group really cut loose, but the method in which they made the album also had a big part to play, leaning on the touring ensemble that had cut the *Waltz Across America* record. With Jeff Bird and Over the Rhine's Linford Detweiler and Karin Bergquist in tow, *Open* wasn't quite guerrilla recording, but it was brisk, focused, pieced together in downtime between concert dates, and that gave it a different energy to previous recordings.

"We took the live band into the studio every time we got a break to just go in and play and then see if we had a record at the end of it. We'd be on the road two weeks, go in the studio for a couple of days, play live, then go back on the road. It's a very dynamic-sounding record because of the process," according to Mike. "I guess it was a very live record, so there was a lot of aggression as a result. We'd written it and then played it a lot onstage, so by the time we went in the studio we were really recording our live show. We went in as a seven-piece band and recorded live off the floor. It was material that we really had a handle on, so that gave it a certain sound. And some of the songs that were on it, like 'I Did It All for You', 'Dragging Hooks', the way that record develops from those two, we wanted to take a certain sonic statement that we'd made live, and we wanted to translate it to a record.

"The songs were getting a little longer. They go through distinctly different sections sometimes, and that was partly from playing more live, thinking about how the music will translate. You open them up in live shows and we wanted to get more of that element into the recorded side of what we do, to play more in the studio. We deliberately freed ourselves up from budget restrictions by using cheap studios or eventually going into our own studio so we could experiment, have fun, see what happened. It was a few hundred bucks a day, so if we didn't get anything, no big deal, do it again tomorrow. That was a big part of making that record, as was having Jeff on there again, and Karin and Linford. I like to hear other people play, it's inspiring. That's how the songs take on a life, other people stepping up and giving their interpretation."

For Margo, the different process played into her hands, perfectly suiting her favoured approach to recording. "I much prefer to be familiar with songs, go in, close my eyes and sing with the band. I don't like going in a booth. If I don't think anybody's listening or paying attention, I can experiment a lot more and try a lot more things with my voice. *Open* was a different way of making a record, because it was made from the road. A band connects in a different way on the road, because you work and travel together, it's so close all the time. We all have walls up on the road just to survive, and some of us have thinner and thicker walls than the others. That's always been the same. I find *Open* fascinating for that reason."

It is an intriguing record, a step away from their past, not just because it was their first album proper as an indie outfit again, but if sonically the songs got different treatments, as a whole the record had a greater thematic unity than probably anything they'd done before, the summation of what they'd become as people, where they'd got to. In the early conversations we had about putting this book together, Mike was initially keen for it to be a non-linear affair, but when you sit and listen to the records, end to end, it becomes crystal clear that each one stands on the shoulders of its predecessors, that building blocks are being laid down and that no record exists in isolation from the others. You keep coming back to the fact that this musical catalogue is part of a wider journey through life, and you have to keep coming back for the next one to find out how it's turning out.

Open pointed the way towards an increasingly conceptual approach to their albums, not in the sense of something like *Tommy* or *The Wall*, where there was a storyline, but in terms of an overarching theme, further reflection of Mike's increasing ambition as a songwriter. John Timmins is particularly proud of his brother's willingness to take on the big themes. "Life is hard, terrible things happen sometimes, but in the end we carry on, and that's what their music is about, that sense of hope. I find that there is hope in great art, period. If we as human beings can create these things, there's hope in spite of every other stupid thing we've done. It's like a really good story: the lyric is the same thing as the music, you're getting the feeling two ways. If you haven't quite figured it out through the words, then the music will talk to you."

For Mike, "*Open* is a dark record at times, it picks up on some of the themes from *Miles from Our Home*, but I guess it does start a new phase, too. Lyrically, and *One Soul Now* was the same, I think it's more mature, maybe old – 'weary', I guess, is the word! That's the first time that's in there, that was off the back of the years leading up to it with the Geffen situation and all, figuring it out. I'd done a ton of thinking just trying to make it work, so just that weariness probably seeped in there."

Perhaps that thinking and the need to find a new way of operating beyond the confines of the record company machine forced the band to find fresh energy simply to survive, to keep going. Sitting back and leaving it to somebody else was not an option, and it was a case of all hands to the wheel. Fortunately, the band's work ethic was never in question, perhaps a reflection of their upbringing.

Certainly that ethic is harder to find these days, according to Margo. "Out there right now, there are young people with something to say, writing their songs, playing in clubs, they're the next generation

311

to speak about their time. I want to hear them, but I'm not going to be in a club at one in the morning when they go onstage. The problem is, I don't know how easy it is for them to come to people like us now. The record companies aren't spending any money on young bands because they spend so much on Beyoncé or whoever, and the extra cash they have goes on lunch instead of a new band! That scares me. It was always hard to find new music, but it's getting harder.

"I had a nanny for my son when he was very young and she's a great singer, but she didn't know whether to sing or go to teacher's college. I'm like, 'You're 20, you can go there any time. Try singing!' The sad thing is, if she does sing, her road will be way harder than mine – and mine was hard enough. That any label heard *Trinity Session* and thought there was something there, that's a miracle. A lot of it is luck, but I don't know if there's a lot of luck out there to go round any more.

"Attitudes have changed, too, because we got there by a lot of hard work and not too many people want to do 250 shows a year for five years before anybody's heard of them. We worked all day, rehearsed all night; we'd drive five hours to Montreal, play, come back, go to work. You can only do that if you're young. But I find it fascinating when we've had kids, 20, 22, come out and sell our T-shirts, and they're tired. How are they tired? Go out all night. Believe me, you can do it, but not for much longer! You have to work hard and we did. That was down to Mike because, otherwise, Pete and I would have been having a drink somewhere! But work did everything for us. It made us into a band, taught us how to play, got us an audience. There are a lot of clubs in Toronto, and a willing audience, so you can generate your own audience and think you've made it. But go an hour's drive to Hamilton and nobody is coming to the show. That teaches you humility and it teaches you your chops. You get used to the clubs in Toronto, then suddenly you're on a different stage, different PA, there's a bunch of drunks out front who don't know who you are – it makes you realize you're not a hotshot. We always did that. We could have stayed and been the kings of Toronto, but who cares?

"And then there's the time where you have to quit the day job, there is no money coming in, you just play and pray to God you make enough money to pay the phone bill. Which you don't. So there is an element of courage to jump in the deep end and believe that it's gonna work. There's a small window, two or three years, when you can do it before life moves on. I know a lot of great bands in Toronto who just stayed, and that was that. I don't know where they are now. I've always felt, to have success, yes you need talent, but you need to work hard and be aware of the business. Don't hand it over, know it. Understand advances, royalties, contracts. You have to do it all to make it work – that's what people don't tell you at the start.

"I love Mary Margaret O'Hara, she's so talented, but Mary could never handle interviews, that side of it, and you need to. She just couldn't, and so there's a piece of the puzzle missing, which means it's harder to find your audience and to keep going. Townes Van Zandt was like that, so talented, but he couldn't go beyond the stage and his guitar. And that's the advantage of being a band, not a solo artist, because there's always somebody to help, you all do different parts of the puzzle. If this had been 'Margo Timmins', it would have ended years ago. I wouldn't have had the strength to fight the companies, I needed Mike for that. And I wouldn't have had the attitude to take the criticism. I'd have just said, 'Screw this, I don't need this, I can travel the world without this!' I don't need to stand onstage, however much I enjoy it now. I would have quit years ago, because it would have been too yucky. But, with the boys around me, I live in this little pod and it's nice."

Finding the pieces of the puzzle is the ultimate conclusion of *Open*, the record passing through a very definite arc, from initial anger and a desperation to escape a situation, through characters trapped by self-loathing and self-destructive behaviour, a refusal to accept the passing of time, all of which gradually give way to people finding a way to handle those issues, to hold on to their idealism. The record ends on a note of acceptance, a willingness to simply close your eyes and walk into the future, placing your faith in the ride. It's a compelling document that goes to the heart of the central idea of remaining open – a very hopeful concept, but one which can't do anything but leave you vulnerable, leave you beset by questions. Do you want to face them? Which way you looking? Do you close down, or do you keep questioning, taking the good, the bad and the ugly which that inevitably brings?

The irony of *Open* is that the trajectory of it could all have been very different, as Mike concedes. "That record is very dark but there's an aspect to it which is very up and that's in the second half of it. I initially sequenced that record pretty much up in reverse, going from light to

313

dark, and I gave it to our A&R guy at Rounder, Troy Hansbrough. When we signed the licence and distribution deal with them, he said, 'Use me how you want to use me. If you want feedback, ask; if you want to play me demos, fine; if you don't want me to hear it until it's finished, that's OK, too.' I hadn't really used them, we wanted to do the record how we used to, just making it ourselves, no input, just us as a unit. So we did it – gave him the final mixes and said, 'Here's the record.'

"So he went and listened to it and said, 'I'm giving you my opinion, take it for what you want. I think the record is fantastic, but what about sequencing it the other way, from dark to light.' And that was strange, a record company offering some useful opinion! So I took it away, played it to Al, and he said, 'God, that's it – that's the way to go.' So we are willing to get perspective from outside if it's from somebody who understands what we're doing. It's not as easy a record to get into by doing it that way, and that was what we had in mind when I sequenced it, but it's more powerful the way it ended up; he was right. It's also the first record where the CD was a real advantage to us, because it has one flow to the album, it's the first time where I haven't felt there's a side one and side two.

"It has some extremes of mood and of playing, and that was what I was maybe fighting with in the sequencing. The songs were coming as we played live. I didn't write them all at one time, the way *Miles from Our Home* had been done pretty much – they came along over a period; a lot were developed over a long time. A song like 'Dragging Hooks' had been around a long time lyrically but musically, it was totally developed live, then something straighter like 'Small Swift Birds' kind of balanced it out. We didn't want to make a specific kind of record – we wanted a jumbly kind of thing with some psychedelia, some straight love songs, some pop, something complex. It is a hard record to get into, a lot of people have difficulty with it, but I think it's the kind of record where you can listen to it a lot and you gradually get into it. I like those types of records. And it's endured, because things like 'Dragging Hooks', 'Bread and Wine' and 'Thousand Year Prayer' have been staples of the live show."

Starting the record with a song of absolute finality coming at you from a migraine of feedback made it pretty clear that *Open* was enmeshed in darkness, that its core subjects were not going to be easy to handle. There's no starker expression of the desire to escape from a situation than committing murder, with 'I Did It All for You' covering similar terrain to 'To Love Is to Bury', still more threatening, an orchestrated killing, the dead and the living engulfed in flames. "She took his dentures from his mouth, placed them in her own" is a pretty unsettling way to open things, but it was actually one of the older songs, according to Mike. "That song was originally recorded during the *Miles from Our Home* sessions, that's a demo that I made. I'd got the first recording unit of any quality that we had, I did a lot of experimentation. That song was a sound experiment, really, as much as a song to start with, and I loved it but it didn't fit on *Miles*. We tried to rerecord it so the sound fitted the other songs, but we just didn't get it, so it ended up on *Open*, and it's a good way to start the record."

Ominous in sound and context, built round Pete's hypnotic contribution like a bell tolling for the dead, the first reference to the river – "River, like magnesium, burns" – sets it off on a recurrent theme. A more guitar-driven record than most, the guitar becomes that river, snaking through the songs, sometimes serene, sometimes choppy, meandering, then churning, going through the mixed emotions of the record and its cast of characters.

That's nowhere more true than in 'Dragging Hooks', the third part of the 'River Song Trilogy' and a musical tour de force on the record. "The river is the ultimate image for life," agrees Mike. "The first part of the trilogy is about the river's beauty and it goes downhill from there to part three, where they're dragging the river for bodies." Possessing some of that Southern Gothic feel that so informed *Black Eyed Man* and *Pale Sun, Crescent Moon*, the musical take on it is a departure from that era, considerably heavier, Mike's "angry dog" guitar harking back further to some of the atmosphere of *Whites Off Earth Now!!* The swampy, swirling sound gives it an atmosphere akin to 'Somewhere Down the Crazy River' by Robbie Robertson and PJ Harvey's 'Down by the Water', a perfectly logical place to be dragging hooks.

For all that 'Dragging Hooks' had been written some time before it was recorded for *Open*, it still contains a key definition of that first half of the record, "They say even the weariest river in the end will find the sea, but here among the cat tails all we discuss is breaking free." Tethered to earlier decisions, to the life it brought in its wake, the frustration is palpable, "the taste of this river mud" the taste of life sucking you under.

If death and destruction inform those opening two songs, 'Bread and Wine' taps into the sacred and the profane and that favourite of Western pop psychology, the midlife crisis. Whether it's consummated or just a fantasy is never clear, but such a blatant story of infidelity isn't one that every writer would want to put out there, knowing his wife was listening.

"We don't talk about lyrics too much!" laughs Mike. "She tends to not take things personally! Occasionally she'll pick up on something and say, 'Let's sit down and talk about this one!' But she doesn't listen that closely now. She used to a lot more, but, just because she's there, the nature of our lives, she knows what I'm writing about anyway. Maybe down the line she'll come back to a song and talk about them, but she doesn't listen to them as much now – probably self-preservation!"

It's maybe a function of an ever more prurient society that, while nobody would ever imagine that the Junkies' songs about murder, for instance, are drawn from their lives, once a song has a more traditional relationship at its heart, then that surely must be just real life played out loud. Margo finds that level of stupidity pretty exasperating. "It's weird – in music, it's expected that everything you write or sing about is autobiographical, nothing can be from your imagination. Our culture is so silly. If you can write, you use your imagination, you're open to people's lives and emotions, so you draw on that when you're writing a character. A good actor does that all the time. For Michael, it's his writing, so obviously it's closer to him than anyone, but it isn't necessarily about him. Some of them are things he's going through, others are things he's seen people around him dealing with, some are just imagination.

"When you get a song like 'Bread and Wine', he's fortunate that Patty, his wife, is a very intelligent woman! She understands how much he's influenced by what he's reading, who he's talked to. When they're songs about relationships, she lives it too, as do I, as do you. God knows I love my husband, but is it bliss every day? Of course not. Relationships are hard work, raising children isn't easy, living is tough. We all understand that, that things break down, too, even if it's not happening to us. We all see it around us, so it's something that goes into the songwriting process. But it's not a diary."

Where 'Bread and Wine' is particularly intimate is in its religious imagery, something that has increasingly found its way into Mike's lyrics over recent years. "I look to it more for hope than anything," he says. "I discarded religion many years ago when I was younger, because there was no place for it in my life, I had no need for that aspect of things. I've sort of come back to it a little bit because of my wife – I wouldn't call her religious, but she's in an organized church in Toronto, the United Church, which is very left-wing, socially conscious, and I like that side of it. To me, that should be the point of organized religion: creating a community that can then better your neighbourhood and take care of people. I sometimes go with her.

"I'll go in, it's still Christian, the symbols are there, they use the term 'God' now and again, and my back kinda goes up! She tells me to substitute the word 'love' for 'God', so I try that, so I guess I've returned to it a bit more, physically at least, because I spend time in church, I know the ministers, they're interesting people. It does make me rethink the whole Catholic side of my life, makes me more angry about that whole way in which its doctrine tries to dominate.

"If somebody asked me am I a Christian, I'd say 'no' because I don't believe in Christ rising from the dead, being the son of God, but I do believe in Jesus. I believe in his teachings – they're about as valid and as pointed as it can get; I believe in that. But the imagery and all that stuff, it's just very powerful symbolism that connects with a lot of people."

And "Your cross ain't nearly as heavy as mine"?

"That Catholic upbringing stays with you! I can't even write about this kind of stuff without feeling like I've sinned! That guilt and doubt runs through all my songs."

Maybe the definitive recording of this song is on the *Open Road* package rather than *Open* itself, because the power and the glory – there goes that imagery again – is more inherent in that live reading that really thrashes away, abandoned, sinister, summing up the fact that the narrator of the song is forced into a corner, wrestling with so much pent-up doubt and with nowhere to go. It's a spiteful, claustrophobic, tortured song, dripping in "soul full of holes" self-loathing that simply has to be followed by 'Upon Still Waters', its natural sequel.

Given it's safe to assume that the "curly blonde disaster lying out there" is not Harpo Marx, she must be the fantasy from 'Bread and Wine', the subject of an internal monologue while the married couple simultaneously have a broken conversation, talking at, rather than to, one another. The ferocious music which ebbs away at the end is anything but calming, but that lull which follows the storm offers the record's first glimpse of light, the suggestion that, rather than railing against your situation, maybe you should embrace it, find the good in it.

Reconciliation is the last thing on anyone's mind in 'Dark Hole Again', however, an exhausted spit of self-pity. Musically, it's a superb set-piece, Mike's guitars cutting across Detweiler's contribution on keyboards, the loping rhythm the kind that might, in other hands, have been the backbone to a nice little pop song. But Mike's were not those hands, not this time, for this song was built to be "menacingly beautiful", as he said later. Oddly, given the subject matter, it's a joyous performance, Mike remembering that "We got it on the first take, the seven-piece really locked into that one." Not that the expanded band was to everyone's tastes, as Jaro Czerwinec says. "You have male energy in that band and then you have Margo. They had a combination when they had two musicians from Over the Rhine playing with them, a keyboard player and a woman singing with them. I came up to see them play and, to me, it was a different thing. Instead of the whole focus being on Margo, and therefore on the lyrics, now I'm seeing two. It was distracting – the energy wasn't right for me and it took away the sharpness of the focus."

Going under for the third time in 'Dark Hole Again', the character has touched bottom figuratively and is willing to do it literally. But there's always that kernel of hope, that, no matter how terrible, somehow we go on, providing "Someone gives me a reason to stay clear of those rip tides again". From there, instead of the water being destructive, as it was throughout the opening salvo of the record, it starts to bring hope as 'Thousand Year Prayer' opens with the sound of waves, a studied calm against this seemingly insoluble maelstrom.

Never mind its central position on *Open*, 'Thousand Year Prayer' stands as one of the most simply beautiful performances the band have ever produced, from the nuanced playing through to an open-hearted lyric that bids farewell to one century and ushers in a new millennium on a note of hope, noting mankind's destructive impulses and contrasting that with the possibilities that lie before us.

Mike sees it as "the turning point song – that's where the light starts coming in, that's why we had the waves on there, the sound of the ocean, the tide turning! Even when we started it, before we recorded it, when we were rehearsing, we talked about it in those terms, having waves;

there was something about the chords that said we should have gentle waves on it and, when we finished it, we thought, 'What the heck, put them in!' It's about reflecting on doubt, guilt, remorse, realizing that there is so much on offer and to be reckoned with. It's a very positive song, I think. I really like that song, especially as a kind of defining statement for a lot of my views on things."

The dialogue between writer and God continues, contrasting our destruction of His planet with the fact that He took Jimi Hendrix too early, which leaves us quits. Maybe we should have played cards for him … The most intriguing phrase, however, is "I am cursed by too little or is it too much belief in the strength of another man's words." Is that a religious reference – the fact that the first draft substituted "I was" and "was it" suggests that it might be. Whatever, it's a fascinating, beguiling paradox that keeps nagging away long after the song is over, given Mike's position on religion. Are these the words of an atheist who wants a reason to believe? Is it the guilt of someone raised Catholic who doesn't have the faith but can't shake the indoctrination? Or, like so many of us, despite professing a specific stance on religion, does the writer find the sands shifting beneath his feet sometimes, particularly in extremis, the emotional resting place for the characters in the first half of *Open*.

If 'Thousand Year Prayer' does usher in some light, nothing in the real world – and therefore in Cowboy Junkies records – is ever quite that simple. 'I'm So Open', a musical co-write between Mike, Pete and Al which thunders along on an archetypal Junkies groove, a song of deceptive complexity, is the keynote address in some ways. "It sums up the album," says Mike. "The persona of the song is reflecting on the ideas of hitting the age in your life where you're halfway between childhood and death. You can either try and hold on to what has passed, your youth, or you can open yourself up to your present and future with all of those exciting and terrifying mysteries still to unfold."

Yet, for all that 'I'm So Open' echoes Beckett's famous ending to *The Unnameable* – "I can't go on, I'll go on" – it doesn't seem entirely comfortable with the conclusion, that the only option is to carry on the fight, there's no alternative. Rather than any kind of Zen acceptance, instead there's a resentment that you've got this far in life, you're halfway there and what's that you say? There are still no answers? Fuck! What kind of deal is this? That paradox is picked up in David Houghton's work on the record's packaging, too.

"Mike and I were standing in his kitchen when he told me the title of the record. *Open*. I said, 'Which is both accepting and vulnerable.' I went home to create the package. I found the Venus fly trap in a stock photography book and photographed my nephew's eye for the cover of the booklet. It's interesting how the arc is so similar in both images. The outside cover is black and the booklet is white – again, another expression of the duality of being open. I tried to match the photographs to the imagery the lyrics evoked. None of the images are specific or articulate; they're suggestive, and that's where the interest lies.

"I've always found in Mike's lyrics certain lines that really resonate and have that ambiguity I seek. We often feature those lines inside the package. On *Open*, it was simply, 'Which way you looking?' On *One Soul Now*, it was, 'Abandon all those precious things.' They're like koans, provocations."

The further into the Junkies journey you go, the more obvious it becomes that they're less and less willing to puncture the silence if it's speaking eloquently enough on its own. "It's very Zen-like, isn't it?" says John. "The music, and Mike, is very contemplative. I think we all are that way in the family. It wasn't as if my parents were practising Zen Buddhists or anything! I can remember growing up and being told by their generation of parents that I shouldn't be afraid to speak up, but that I should only speak up if I had something to say. I think we've taken that lesson and translated that into something that my generation lives by, a quiet, contemplative way of being.

"Again, that indicates a lack of ego, too, even comes from that, because you don't rush to make a statement or judgement, and that's something the Zen Buddhists would agree with. When something is said, it's heard, it's understood, because it's meant. Given that way of communicating, you can get right to the heart of issues without offending, because you know it's not ego-driven; things are said because they have to be said, because it's heartfelt, it's been thought through and it's a nice way to communicate. That's very much there in Mike's music, too: 'I'm saying this because I really believe it, I'm writing these lyrics, playing these notes because I mean them.' I think the audience picks up on that honesty, that truth."

The audience quickly picked up on 'Small Swift Birds', a perennial favourite in the live act and perhaps even more central to the record than 'I'm So Open', coming out of the other side of that song's irritation and finally taking that moment to stop and smell the flowers. Appreciate what you have while it's there. Maybe tomorrow it'll be gone. To react to that with "It's just the way life goes" is pretty much the antithesis of what's gone before it, but then again where's the option? This time, we're focusing on the light at the end of the tunnel. Careful, we're getting kinda jaunty here. Blame Al – he wrote the music, another big contribution to a record where, as per usual, Anton is the understated but crucial presence, holding it together both sonically and conceptually.

'Close My Eyes' is the final summary of it all, the opening section of rejection harking back to the earlier songs, Mike noting, "It's about getting to the point where you feel that the only solution to the turmoil in your life is to turn your back and walk away and then coming to the realization that there are reasons to stay all around you. It's those sorts of moments that make you want to bow your head and close your eyes." Whether that reaction is a refusal to look at the truth around you, or simply the chance to take a breath and be grateful for what you have, that's left open too, the return of the feedback that ushered in 'I Did It All for You' closing the record on a dissonant, disquieting note that hints that this one is to be continued …

And it is to be continued, not least because 'Beneath the Gate', the song Mike described at the time as "the most personal one on the record", was in many ways its catalyst. After all, it's about the daughter he and his wife adopted from China, the child that was on her way to them during the writing of *Miles from Our Home*. As he says now, "A lot of *Open* is about moving in to that phase of my life – parenthood. The fear and uncertainty and the need to open oneself up to possibilities and fate and deal with what comes down the line." When there are others relying on you, you can't run, and there's nowhere to hide. You simply have to get up, get on and cope with it.

Which is not the same thing as saying it's easy, for, as all four of the Junkies would concede, age, the coming of children and, to a degree, the loss of big label tour support, only made life on the road that bit tougher. Crew member John Farnsworth was amazed at the energy they showed in getting the *Open* show on the road, but is clear that, because of their attitude to those around them, plenty of others were willing to go the extra mile to make their new-found independence work.

"To take on the whole package as they have done – the record label, management, everything, Al doing the merchandise, Margo responding to all the emails onstage, Pete loading and unloading the gear, Mike managing the band – that takes a lot of hard work. But they never forget the people that work with them. Every night I've been with them, I get thanked onstage by name and the same with every member of the crew, and that's not just lip service or something Margo says. It's because they genuinely feel the crew is a part of the family.

"They just do it because they enjoy it, they believe in the band, it's their livelihood and they want to keep on doing it for a long time yet. They took on little pieces at a time, because they've realized they need to be in control, and, the more efficient you are, the easier it is to be successful. We'd customize things, we tweak things, everybody is really just so pleased to do anything for the cause. And it is a cause – it's something that people believe in, that we all, fans too, want to do our part to help them carry on making this music. And they're out there working side by side with you. If you're in that situation, you want to do more, you'll miss the occasional dinner for the good of the cause if something needs to be worked on. And they allow you to do more – it's not even so much a team effort as a family effort, it's something just a little different. I know a lot of bands, but none let me come inside the way they have, and there's nobody where I would feel comfortable about talking about things the way we do. I can't tell you how many times I've cried on Margo's shoulder over the years about being away from my wife, my family now – we have common ground there, because we both adopted children from Russia. When I'm away from my own family, it's hard, but at least, if it's with the Junkies, I feel like I'm still with family, and that's a nice experience.

"Long bus rides are something I don't even think about with them. Other bands, it's, 'Twenty-four hours on the bus? Man!' You just crawl into the bunk. But with these guys, you get up in the morning together, you make coffee, you start off on your day together, we're not hiding from each other, we watch movies together. Even on days off, we're always together. I always get a call in my room because we're all getting together for lunch or dinner or something, and nine times out of ten everybody is there, just to be together. I don't do that with any other band. But, with them, we check in and, next thing you know, we're all in the lobby bar, hanging out. It makes an abnormal kind of life pretty normal from day to day. It doesn't seem like the road, because there are such consistencies in the days. We're real close, we know each other inside out, we know each other's families. If I'm down, they'll pick up on it and I've had many home-style chats with Pete through the years. Touring is hard. We had one time where we took twenty-eight flights in twenty-five days across Europe and we ended up just holding one another up. If you can't count on one another, that sort of deal can just drive you crazy.

"I'm a classic rock guy, one of the last of the long-hairs, and every once in a while I have to step it up a notch on the tour bus and enjoy blowing off some steam with a little AC/DC going on, but a lot of bands wouldn't let you anywhere near the remote control – that's theirs! I've been with bands where the back lounge on the bus is set aside for the singer or whatever, but Margo gets a bunk just like everybody else. There's no difference between any of us out there."

Inevitably, being away from home is a problem that's harder for Margo to handle than the others, though her son, Ed, has accompanied the Junkies on their travels at various times. This is something that got harder to arrange as he grew up and school interfered, stopping him from running away to join the circus as often as he'd have maybe liked – as this conversation from back in 2005 illustrates.

"I find going away and leaving my son the hardest because, with the others, their wives are running the home pretty much, so things stay pretty much the same for their kids," admits Margo. "It's hard on my husband, because his life suddenly really changes – there's no milk in the fridge! But, again, it's what we've been doing my whole life and even my marriage is part of that. For Graham, it got harder because we had Ed and I have to be a little more cautious that I'm not gone too long. It's easy to fill up the summer and, all of a sudden, I'm not home. I have to weigh it up, to say no to things. Mike got it, he's never tried to sway me away from it. He's always said any time that I want to take Ed on the bus, it's my decision and he can get on there and rip the place apart and nobody can have their laptops open! He's always said, 'You decide what to do and I'll make it work.'

"Balancing everything is harder the older you get, trying to make things work out between work and family. My husband has a very powerful job, it's very stressful, lots of travel – like, tomorrow, he has to be out of the house by 6.30 and neither of the nannies want to get up that early because they're young and can't seem to manage! But I have to fix that, remind them it's their job, and, that way, Graham doesn't need to worry about Ed. I feel bad because we're sitting talking in Annapolis, it's 100 degrees or something, I've just come off the phone to the nanny, who's taking him to the farm, when I'd rather he went to the pool to stay cool! But I can't control it, and I don't want to, because it makes it harder for everybody – it's tough. It's tough on Graham, too, because life gets harder as you get older.

"He wouldn't say it, but I'm sure there's a part of him that would like me to stay home now, and there's a part of me that's sad because I can't say 'yes' to that – and I know I can't. Not because of the band, or Michael, or anybody else, but for me. I need this now. Before, I might not have, but now it's a huge part of my personality, my expression of myself. It's my moment to express myself, away from being Mom, from being a wife. It breaks up the routine, it gives me something new to take back every time, so it's hard but it's important. It's such a gift, because I have a lot of friends who don't have anything but raising their kids and, great though that is, don't you just want to get away? It's hard to get away when there's nothing to go to – 'I just gotta take a week to get away from you people!' For me, it's easy, it's 'I'm working – gotta go!' I'm lucky, I have a nice balance. It's not every day, I don't do the nine-to-five and have to leave him while I go to the office. When I'm home, I'm home. But, even though the balance is good, it's not easy.

"Logistically it's hard, even for my brothers, even though their wives look after the kids and their lives don't change so much when the boys are away – it's probably easier not having to look after Pete, too! But it is harder for all of us now that our kids are getting older. They don't like it when Daddy goes away, and that's tough for them to deal with. But it's totally different when I leave, because Ed's life really changes a lot. But it's important that I have balance and I believe that will give him a happier life, too. The story of Cowboy Junkies is the intimacy we share, not just the music, not just the four of us, but it extends to whoever gets on that bus with us. That is important to me, it's fulfilling, and I bring that back to life at home, which makes that better.

"And, if I were to give it up for the sake of Ed, that's a huge burden for a kid to carry, that they took that from you. You might give it willingly, but when it dawns on them when they're teenagers, that's a lot for them to carry. The only reason I'd quit because of Ed is if, God forbid, he were ill. In those circumstances, you do what you have to do and nothing else matters.

"I think I'm a better mom because I have Cowboy Junkies. We were talking about it at home, and I said to Graham, 'I have a job where, at the end of the working day, people form a queue to tell me how much they love me! They're happy, they bring flowers, they're excited to see me. In what other job does that happen?' It's a constant feeding, and it's positive for me and for everyone around me. Why wouldn't you want more of that? Our audience has got older with us, and when you go home to your teenage daughter screaming at you, or you work later and later to find the college fees, it's harder to find things that make you feel good. If we can provide a nice evening for those people, that's way more good than I could ever have done as a social worker.

"I think people get confused when they give up huge parts of themselves to look after their children. The culture now says that to be a good mom you have to be with them twenty-four hours a day, constant, constant, constant, you have to look after this Golden Child, they're supposed to be so breakable. I'm not sure that's a good thing, I think it's too much. It's hard not to do that. You want to do the best, you want to protect them, but the more you do that, what happens when the day comes that they have to go out there? When somebody is mean to them, or hits them over the head? They don't know what to do. You want life to be perfect for them, but you know it's not going to be because life isn't, so it's important that they're exposed to that while you're around so you can help them through it, so they'll be ready for things when you're not around.

"And it isn't always a breeze when we're out there. It is harder because we don't have the big record company, we have less money because things are so expensive. The gigs, the venues are getting better, which is huge for me. If we go in smelly, awful clubs, it flattens me. That's when I start to think that I can't do it any more, when I go into rooms that are disgusting. I don't need five-star hotels, just a little cleanliness instead of the smell of vomit and beer! I'm too old for that. I don't have a false idea that we'll be catapulted into luxury – this is it, we're where we are – but it has to be at some level of civility, or it brings me down. It always did. I remember having a conversation with Mike some years ago when we were in some terrible hotels. For the boys, I don't think it's such a big deal, but I go into these places and I smell the mildew and go into depression! And now, most of the time, our hotels are decent."

Much as those couple of hours up onstage can be so fulfilling, it can't be underestimated just what a grind touring can be, particularly in the way the Junkies did it in days of yore when they conducted those mammoth tours such as the one in support of *Open* – 100 cities, 15 countries, 108 gigs, 410 miles by sea, 31,977 miles by air, 34,744 miles by land. Just 200 more miles, all day, every day. Having spent a couple of brief runs on the road with them, doing a gig, heading for a hotel to shower, piling back on the bus and heading for your bunk as you drive through the night and arrive around midday ready to load in, wait a couple of hours, soundcheck, wait some more, try to find something to eat, do some waiting, play, then do it all over again – that must lose its glamour pretty quickly. There's never time enough to do anything but wait; like being trapped in an airport. OK, that's overstating it, but even road veterans like these can be a little jaded at times.

"That famous Charlie Watts quote about twenty-five years of the Rolling Stones being five years of playing and twenty years of waiting around – that really is it, it's deadly," says Mike. "There are aspects of touring that are great. Just having time where you don't have to do anything is great, because I don't get that at home any longer with the kids, responsibilities for all that business stuff. There's something nice about walking aimlessly through a street and getting a coffee. But it gets a little tiring after a while! It's not so bad if you get a good night's sleep, but you rarely do because we sleep on the bus a lot, and that means you're tired a lot of the time. It tests your strength of purpose, I guess.

"At 25, it's a big adventure, you can stay up all night, it's fine. At 35, 45, 55, you like to be more comfortable! But playing live is still so much fun that you put up with it. We know what we're getting into when we do it, you steel yourself, but it's always open to question as to just how we're going to do it, especially as things get more complicated back home. We do shorter bursts now, pretty much since the summer of 2005, after Ed's arrival changed things for Margo, but we've learned that it's best not to set things in stone, because things are always changing around you. Logistically, it's tougher because of keeping crew, because they only get paid when they work, getting buses for a few days rather than the whole summer. But we figure it out – we've always been good at that."

You couldn't hope to find a more equable, totally adjusted tourist than Jeff Bird, but even he finds life on the road a strain at times.

"Touring is really hard work for those two hours onstage. The travel is brutal, it's relentless. Laptops are great. I do my income tax, my billing, some other work, all on the road. I save it up so that I can fill the time! But the thing of adulation, if you could sell 'canned adulation', the world would be so much happier! Standing up in front of 1,000 people who all love you, that's a pretty powerful thing, and that keeps you going through those long drives or days with nothing to do. And you know that you're making audiences happy for those couple of hours and you're sending a bunch of happy people back out to their homes. The way things are these days, that has to be a good thing.

"Touring can be disorientating and tiring, you lose touch with what day it is and where you are. You don't see a lot. I find that the best thing is to not try and see anything, don't plan, but just walk around and let a place come to you. You only get a couple of hours, so you just are better served by letting it happen naturally. I think I've spent around three weeks in New York City now. I've just been there twenty times to do it!

"It's weird – a couple of days off in one place can actually take away the rhythm of playing, it actually makes you feel more exhausted, too, which is crazy because you should sleep better in a hotel room than on a moving bus! But you're looking to fill your days when normally they're filled for you. And you probably do more tiring things, you go walk round a city or visit a museum, you go out for dinner together and stay out later, so it does knock you off centre because, after a show, you just get on the bus, maybe have a drink, then crawl into your bunk."

For Al, the bunk is home, albeit temporarily. "We all leave the bus less now than we used to. I guess we've already seen a lot of places, but it's about being older, too. It's a survival thing – you save your energy, you stay in your environment."

Pete admits that the passing of the years takes its toll. "It gets to be harder to travel and keep your focus and not drink a lot! You like your comfort more, you want to get into bed, not a bunk on the bus; after a while your body can't take it, playing at eleven one night then doing two shows the next. Everyone thinks you're going out and having a big party, but the actual work – not even the playing – but just the work of getting from one gig to the next is hard. Not just physically, but mentally, draining is what it is. And there's no time to do anything. You get to a town or a city and you have an hour before you have to do something, then you load in, maybe, then you get an hour and you soundcheck, then you get an hour before you eat, then you get an hour and you play, so you don't get time to do anything. We were in Pittsburgh the other day, but there wasn't time to go find the Warhol Museum.

"Then, if you get a day off, you just want to be in your room, lie in your bath, don't want to see anybody or anything, just get some sleep! But days off can drag if you've nothing to do, because the day has no structure. Normal days, we have to be in places at times. Days off, sometimes the hotel room feels like a prison. A nice one, with a plasma screen.

"In Europe, we pretty much live on the bus, so we go out after a show and we just walk around and check out the cities – it's too scary to do that in the States! In the States, we travel at night a lot, but I've seen a lot of the country from the days when we would travel in the van. We got time off then, so I know a lot of cities from then. You can't find time now – you can't plan anything, you can't plan to go see the Warhol Museum, but then you might step off the bus, go round the corner and fall upon something really great. That happens a lot and that's really cool. I guess it's the thing Jeff always says: 'Don't expect anything on the road, let it come to you.' You can't expect to have the best BLT, but you might just find it – it is out there. Or you might get mini-burgers the size of your thumb in the green room at MoMA!

"I like painting and sketching, it's another release for me; it's good for those long road journeys, too. On the long tours we've done, when I get chance, I'll go to my room and sketch what's through my window, so I have a series of impressions of where we've been. And if I really like the room and the hotel, I'll write down the room number and the hotel on there, so if I go back with my family some day I know what room to ask for! I like detail, too, so I've developed this thing where I draw cut-outs, cutaways of buses, so you can see what's going on inside them. They look so big from the outside; you get inside, you just wonder where the space went. The European buses are double-deckers – they used to be horrible, but they've got a lot better. You get a little bit of headroom, you get an upstairs and a downstairs lounge and the bunks up to the front, driver below. They work pretty nice."

"When we visit a new place for the first time, I still go and check it out," adds the intrepid Bird. "I try to go for a walk every day and you usually find the most interesting stuff when you're not looking for it. I guess experience teaches you how to handle it – you have a better idea of what you need and what you want while you're travelling, we're probably more tolerant, we're in nicer hotels often. The soap smells nicer nowadays. It used to smell of smoke in all those motel rooms we used to go to in the early days. If it's a place we play regularly, you start to know a bit about where it's good to walk or to eat or whatever. Some places you look forward to, some you don't! And it takes you places you'd never choose to go to, which is great a lot of times. It's a nice surprise. And, if you don't like it, you'll be moving on soon enough!"

"It's hard to keep yourself amused on the road," says Margo. "On the bus, we have a quiet lounge where I sit. It's the needlepoint lounge, actually. Then there's the back lounge where the boys play video games and kill things! Sometimes we get stuck in a van and there are no games, no TV, nothing. The boys have had this game for years where they attach the word 'anal' to car names. So if an Explorer goes by, it's an Anal Explorer. Even now, after so many years, they'll sit there saying, 'I can't wait for a Probe to go by'! When the Intrigue came out, that was just too much for them.

"Next time we do a DVD like *Open Road*, instead of how many bottles of wine and beer we've drunk, we should have something that says how many miles we've aimlessly walked while we're on tour, how many hours of bad TV we've watched."

That *Open Road* DVD is a perfect example of why Cowboy Junkies don't fit in the mainstream, but why they have such a powerful following. Not the glossy, glamorized, airbrushed documentary for them. Instead, the film that captured the tour really does just that – captures what the experience was like. There's some great music, of course, but the nitty-gritty comes in sections on the venues, the crew, the audience, the bus itself. Their website calls it an attempt at "capturing the spirit of being on the road. The excitement, the hard work and, most of all, the insanity. It is our salute to all of the varied and sundry elements that cause the fevers that rule our lives."

Any music documentary must inevitably tread the path worn well by *Spinal Tap*. Some pretend it isn't there, others embrace it and attack their film with one eye on the absurdity of it all, such as an inflatable doing the snake dance behind the stage in Quebec. Or the way in which support acts like Tim Easton get treated …

"They have a great sense of humour, band and crew, and they played some of the most fantastic practical jokes that have ever been played on me. One night they switched the key plates on my harmonicas, so

I thought I was playing one key and I was actually playing another – this was in front of a very serious audience, at an art museum, the Mass MoCA in Massachusetts, a very quiet audience, and I just totally baffled them with this noise I was making! I looked over in the wings and they were all standing there, giggling. Then there was the night they covered me in Silly String onstage.

"One night, they taped me to a chair while they played 'Sweet Jane' onstage for the first time on the tour. I was stuck down to this chair, a complete S&M kind of scene, right out of a Lou Reed song, with Margo gently tagging me with a rose as she was singing! It was really funny for us, but I think the audience was probably a little freaked out by it – I don't think they got it, it was a carnival scene!

"That was my first real tour of America with the whole thing – tour manager, hotel rooms, per diems and all that. I was very excited about it, but it was tough to keep to the schedule because I was doing my own driving. I think they saw something in me that was a little more rootsy and different from other singer-songwriters – I would hope they did, anyways! They knew that I was from the old school when it comes to writing, that I had studied Doc Watson, Mississippi John Hurt, that I wasn't shy about wearing those influences and trying to take them to a new place. They were very patient and cool with me and basically taught me a lesson that the road itself isn't a big party. You've got a job to do and you're not going to be able to do it if you're out of your mind or hungover, so they taught me some things about that – about professionalism, I guess. Theirs was a very subdued stage act, which was where my head was at the time, too. After playing in so many rock'n'roll bands, I really enjoyed that tour. They didn't assault you with loud instruments, it was very relaxing and a lot of the places we played were theatres with seating, so that was great, too. It was a nice contrast."

In the early days of going indie, there was the inescapable need to put "product" out there, as Mike concedes. "Being an independent means you have to be more creative in finding ways to fill the gaps between records. You need to put things out there for financial reasons and also to keep your profile, to keep people interested. *Open Road* was part of that and it was a nice package with the CD and DVD, we're really proud of that. It's a pretty accurate look at being on the road and that was what we were after – a documentary that says, 'This is how it is.' Every aspect, including the performances, is in that DVD. It took a lot of work, more than we thought, but it was a lot of fun and it was worth it in the end. The documentary was the heart of it. We didn't know what we were gonna do, we had all this stuff, the documentary was what we were after and the concert footage would just be extra, but we didn't know how to approach it. First, I started writing something that I thought Margo would do a voice-over for, then I just thought that would be too tortuous, so we went through a lot of ideas. We just stumbled on the idea of dividing it into the chunks of what touring is all about and went from there.

"We like doing added-value things like *Open Road* or the 'anatomy of an album' thing we've done on *One Soul Now* and *At the End of Paths Taken*. Partly it's market-driven, because you want to give more value for money, but it's fun to do, too. When we were on major labels, they'd never let you do that so when we finally got off them, and when we kicked off the website too, then we realized we could do what we wanted because you don't have to sell zillions of those things to make them pay – if you already have the material, the only cost is to physically make them. Sell a few thousand off the site and you've made your money back. As a fan, it's the sort of thing I'd like; it gives a different perspective, it gives you more information, so it's nice to put that out there. A lot of our decisions come down to that, by flipping it around – as a music fan, what would I want to see, what would be interesting or useful to me?"

Margo is equally keen on retaining that perspective. "Before anything else, we're music fans. What would I want to see Neil Young do? Even to the artwork – poring over the picture, 'Look, I think that's his dog back there!' That kind of detail matters if you really love the music; I want to get in behind it. So we approach things that way. What would the fans like to see? Not necessarily what's the picture that might sell more. It sells or it doesn't sell. Whatever. We still maintain the love of music, so it's not hard to put things out with that in mind.

"I know other bands don't, but I think they get caught up in selling. They're listening to too many people. They want to put out a blue shirt, but people tell them, 'Pink's in.' So they put it out in pink, but it doesn't look right because blue was what they should have done – that was in their heart. It's easy to do that. But we've always been a four-piece. It's never been just Mike trying to make decisions or dealing with the company. When they pushed him, he'd come back to us and say, 'They want us to do this,' and I'd say, 'No way, I'm not doing that,' or Pete would turn it down, Al might refuse to wake up! Maybe we'd say, 'OK, let's try it and see what happens.' There was never pressure on one person – it was on the four of us and it's easier to fight off the problems if there's somebody with you.

"It even comes down to doing certain TV or radio shows. In twenty years there's just one radio show we shouldn't have done. We were on the road, we were tired and we got talked into it because we didn't have the energy to resist! It was some weird sex show where people would call in, and I was just shrinking into a corner because it was just awful. Like a Howard Stern thing, and I just shut down – 'I'm not talking.' It was icky. I didn't know how to handle it. 'I'm Canadian, I don't even know how to talk about kissing, let alone what you're talking about!' Michael tried to ride the storm out to protect me. We didn't walk out, because we'd said we'd do it, but it was just terrible. One time out of millions of things they pushed on us. The show had a huge syndication, it was part of another record company, they promised to play our record, blah, blah. So all these things they try and push on you is to help sell the record, that's great, but you have your soul, your integrity. At the end of the day, you don't want to have to take a shower to get rid of all that!"

As a proud brother, John particularly admires that attitude. "The spirit of the music of our ages says to you, 'Just stand up and play it'. It has a sort of subtle, polite, Canadian punk to it, it really does. It doesn't wear its punk roots on its sleeve or a pin through its nose. You don't have to do that. Often the pin through the nose is a compensation for not really having that power within you or your music. But their music is the real thing, it's honest, sincere, giving. It's very childlike in many ways, there's great excitement there. The music isn't driven by the need to score big and be famous and impress a lot of people – it's driven by the virtue of the music. And that's been the struggle for this band for the longest time. There have been opportunities for them to change the way they do things for commercial advantage, and many bands would have done that without a second thought, but they exist for the music. It's a very pure thing."

While they may exist for the music, you cannot live in a bubble, and during the *Open* tour, events overtook them. Waking up on the morning of 11 September 2001, it was clear the world would never be the same again.

"When the attack on the World Trade Center happened, we were in Tampa with a show to do that night, and we woke up to all that stuff happening on TV," recalls Mike. "Just being away from home was the hardest thing, because who knew what was going to happen next? This chaos, this uncertainty. We forget now, but at the time there was this feeling of the future being totally destroyed. It was really odd, and then, if you have kids, you just think, 'What's their world going to look like, what are they growing up into?' That's still out there, but at the time it was just so overpowering.

"So then we had all these decisions to make about the shows. We had a European tour planned for October, everything was so unsure. We only lost one show, in fact – the night it happened, that was cancelled – then the next day was a day off anyways, so by the Thursday we were playing again. The first couple of shows were horrible nights to play; nobody came, everyone was down, but by the weekend people were coming out because they were sick of it, they didn't want to watch CNN any more, they didn't want to see the buildings fall for the hundredth time, and I'll never forget those shows because they were just incredible. There was a release, we were getting it out of our system, playing it out through the music, and people just wanted to make contact with one another, with the band. All the venues had extra security, but they were having fun side-stage! It was an amazing feeling, a communal thing. Houston has never been a great town for us, but we played there, a horrible little club, and we were backstage afterwards and the merch guy came back and said, 'You wouldn't believe it out there. I've had the most amazing night of my life – people are just coming and talking all night long, they won't stop.' It was really like that: everybody wanted to be a part of something. That happened for a few shows, then slowly it started to die away, but for a while it was really special.

"That's why I get really angry about that time and the way it was lost, that spirit, because that was a microcosm of what could have happened, taking that nastiness and turning it into something really phenomenally positive, something that could galvanize the world, taking it to heart – the idea that what happened to the US, to the West, was horribly wrong – but we're obviously doing something wrong out there in the world, too. There's something not right in this world; let's try to fix it. America has the strength and the power to do that. It had the goodwill of the world at that point but, instead, Bush decided to beat people up instead and the moment went. It was a lost moment in our history."

Margo recalls, "Waking up and clicking the TV on just as the second one hit, literally. I sat there thinking, 'This is a weird show!' I thought it was a movie or something; it looked fake. Then the announcer came on and started talking about it. I had a serious headache, too, so I couldn't make sense of it – all too much for my little brain.

"After I understood what was happening, I just wanted us to get out and to play, but we had to cancel, that was the situation, I understood that. Then, when we played again, the first night, very few came. It was a stand-up bar, they were all spaced out, separate from each other, like zombies who'd come out of their houses for the first time. There were cops there, because security was crazy everywhere. We played, and by the end of the show the thirty people were close together and it was a cathartic night, for them and for us. Even the cops were talking to us later, saying, 'That was great!' Everybody in that room had needed something to happen that was normal again. By day three or four after it happened, people were saying, 'OK, I can't take this any more. I can't see the towers falling on TV again. I can't take this sadness, I have to scream or sing or dance or something.' That night, we played 'Sweet Jane' three times, it was a crazy crowd, we just played and played and it was real fun, because people were ready to be up and have fun again, to laugh again. It was interesting to see those two shows, and the difference was just a day. It was like a mourning process. It's over – now I have to go and laugh. I'll never forget that

"That time in the States was very hard. It was almost like the rules were forgotten and people were voicing everything they wanted to voice, and it wasn't all great, I have to say. We saw a lot of local news being on tour and there were lots of stories of mosques being attacked and American Muslims keeping their children out of school. That part of it was heartbreaking. The thought of that still makes me so sad. I just kept thinking what it would be like to look like an Arab in this country. People were mean and I don't like meanness.

"I was so sad and I just needed to play, because that's my therapy – it makes me feel better. Even if nobody comes, let's just play, play for ourselves, and for the maybe five people who turn up because they do want to hear music because they're so heartbroken. If there's any band you should see in a time of sadness or confusion, it's us. I really felt we could make some people feel a little better. Even if nobody came, I wanted to play for me."

As Pete says about the band, "People talk about the depressing thing with us, but the blues makes you happy. It's uplifting, it's a release in its way." Seeking the life force in the presence of death is the most human reaction there is. And there's nothing more life-affirming than talking about life's travails, accepting that they happen, but refusing to be beaten by them.

JUST WANT TO SEE

Like me, John Timmins was pretty much a tour virgin going into the 'Blue States' trip – I vividly recall him sitting in the dressing room at the Northampton Iron Horse not long before the first show, just the two of us. I got up to leave him to his preparations, only to hear him wail plaintively, "You're not going to leave me here alone with my demons, are you?"

Whether it was an innate curiosity to see those electorally sensible states passing before him or just a simple willingness to be closer to the impact if the worst happened, I don't know, but he spent time aplenty on the bus riding shotgun alongside driver Kevin.

Driving a tour bus is a pretty specialist occupation, chasing up and down the freeways, living like a bat, sleeping in the daylight, driving through the night, with not much by way of company. Though I guess Kevin was pleased to have such sedate inmates as these sleep-seeking Canadians, after the rigours of driving the Kings of Leon and Slipknot all across the land – "Those guys didn't go to bed till midday. Plenty of times I got a pizza down the back of my neck at seven in the morning while they were fooling around."

Intrepid reporter John regularly brought back slices of "Kevinlife", life that we in the back, asleep in our bunks, or drinking and learning new sexual techniques from repeat screenings of *Team America* in the back lounge, were too timid to find out at first-hand.

If we've got the energy, we all talk too much at two in the morning. Maybe it's the intimacy of darkness, maybe it's sleep deprivation. Or beer. But, if you're a bus driver, having anybody to talk to at that time of night has to be a blessing, so I guess it's inevitable that you're going to chew the ear off your new friend. Do you court weirdness if you're a bus driver? Is it an occupational hazard when you're on the road, eleven months out of twelve? Or do you drive a bus to escape the weirdness back home?

You're going to end up a little strange if one of the things that worries you, when driving through upstate New York, is the chance of running into a moose and totalling animal, bus and passengers in one huge collision. John gave us the story after we'd finished watching a Viking classic on DVD, an example of the Bird collection that came with many subtitle options but not, sadly, the original Norse. Once Tony Curtis and Kirk Douglas had slugged it out for the hand of a pneumatically chested Janet Leigh, the moose tales began, of cars thundering into bewildered beasts, like Terry Gilliam filming a Woody Allen routine.

Like a lot of Kevin's tales, there was a dark side. The story got gorier and gorier, but as John recounted it we shifted uneasily from humorous interruptions about the Berkowitzes going to a fancy dress party, to a cloying, stunned silence. His brother was out driving one night and was killed in an accident with a moose, slamming into one in the dead of night, the deadweight animal crashing over the hood, through the windshield, taking his head clean off in the impact – not the kind of injury you're coming back from.

Later, it was left to Pete, as so often, to say the unthinkable: "Most of the guys who drive the bus are OK, but it's an odd way to live. And you get the guys who are driving because that's all they've got left – they're on the run from life, I guess. And they're always tired, because, however much you sleep in the day, driving at night's a hard road.

"Everything in life is fleeting. The kids kiss me when I go out the door to go out to a restaurant – maybe they don't think I'm coming home for six weeks again! But I kiss them, too. Never leave the house mad, because you go out there, anything can happen. That's part of the anxiety of being on the bus. Is the driver OK? Is he on top of his job? Living on that highway food, driving every night. A lot of them used to be Vietnam vets; that made me a bit nervous. It'll be Iraq vets next – the guys who signed up as truck drivers and who ended up driving convoys and being shot at. Jesus, what does that do to your mind?

"When you've been on buses like we have, you always have the thought in the back of your mind that, one day, you'll get the guy who decides at four in the morning that life's not worth it. And, if that happens, he's not going to think about the people asleep in the back, he's just going to take the bus over the cliff."

EXIT STAGE LEFT

We're in the Palace Theater, Manchester, New Hampshire. The band are into the second set of the second show of the tour, June 2005. After the rust was sheared off at the Iron Horse, things are cooking, in spite of the break. I'm in the wings, taking a few pictures. 'Dragging Hooks' starts up, Margo strolls off the stage, coming my way.

"How ya doin'?"

This is kind of like Paul putting his bass down on the Apple rooftop and strolling over for a chat while the rest of the band hammer out 'Don't Bring Me Down'.

"Pretty good."

This is the point where you try to retain your cool as all that journalistic objectivity leaps out of the window. It gets tougher because, as the band played on, suddenly Margo is in the middle of a story, the kind she leads into a song with, but this time there's no audience.

"Back when we started, the boys would just play these really long jams and I never really had anything to do, so it got kind of embarrassing to be up there. What am I gonna do up there – dance!? So I started coming offstage and watching from the side. I didn't have to do anything which was great! Then we had one show in a theater like this, and while I was standing here I saw the stage door and I figured, 'Wouldn't it be cool to go and watch from out front?'

"So I slipped through the door, and stood in the aisle and that was nice, seeing them like the audience does. It's time for me to get back up there and start singing again and, of course, the door has locked behind me! I go chasing after the security to let me back in. They don't believe I'm me, they think I'm some crazy person, and I can see the boys up there, looking around wondering where I am, carrying on playing. Finally, they opened the door for me and I got back up there, so I guess it's safer to just stay here and watch. OK. Gotta go."

With that, she's back off to stage centre. Anybody else, and it's a moment that would seem wholly incomprehensible, the shifting between on-, off- and back onstage again, but with Margo – and Cowboy Junkies – it seems the most natural thing in the world. If you take a look at the stage, going to their show is pretty much like being in their living room. It's all carpets and chairs up there, everybody sitting pretty close together as a unit, like they're all together for Sunday afternoon tea. You suspect that Margo would be out offering us all tea and cookies if she could. It's a far cry from the 1980s, when she would barely acknowledge the audience's existence, never mind keep them in the palm of her hand. Experience is a great teacher, as is learning from others.

"I still watch singers, but more so in those early days when I was trying to figure out how to be a front person. When I saw Emmylou when I was a young singer, I noticed that onstage she was always really gracious. She always made you feel like she was happy you were there and you felt that, if you went to her home, she'd treat you exactly the same way. That's how I am as a person. I would never be rude to anybody, so I just thought, 'Why don't I do that – why don't I get up there and make people feel welcome?' It's my natural way of being. I figured if she was cool doing that, I could be cool, too! My approach onstage is to be who I am, to make people feel comfortable and invited. It would be the same if you came to my house. I'd want you to be comfy and feel you're welcome, and that's my personality. Sometimes people who come to a show for the first time say that they feel as if I'm their friend and that's nice, that's the greatest compliment. I want them to feel relaxed.

"My era was the punk era and that attitude of 'screw you', dark, angry. When we first did our shows, not that I was going to get onstage and tell everybody to 'Fuck off!', but I just didn't feel I could get up there and babble on like I do now. That was not cool. I was babbling then, but just not onstage! So I liked what Emmylou was doing and that gave me somewhere to go, I guess.

"Who am I onstage is close to who I am the rest of the time, but it isn't exactly me. I wouldn't want it to be, because then it's too revealing. It's pretty exposing up there, anyway. It's not an act, it's just a different side of my personality that I don't necessarily go around showing. In real life I'm much more reserved, not that I'm that demonstrative onstage compared with some. Some nights I feel more inhibited, some less. In the old days, if I was feeling sad or lonely or uncertain, I would bring that more to the stage than I do now, basically because I couldn't do anything but that. I wasn't a skilled performer. Nowadays, I can rise above my own mood and do the best I can possibly do. Some people might see that as fake, but I think it's a good thing. When people are paying a lot of money for a ticket, you have a responsibility. They want you to be real in the song, but they also want the song. On those nights in the past when I wasn't feeling confident, it wasn't a very good show. I wasn't singing well, interacting and I don't think that's fair. When I hit the stage, I might be acting initially, but the show pulls me out of that mood and it becomes real as the night goes on. I can go on with a splitting headache and twenty-five minutes later it's gone, because I'm happy by then, this is great!

"A lot of our audience is older and, if you've chosen tonight to get a babysitter, spend your money on your ticket and it's a big night, that matters. I know what a big night is, the babysitter thing just kills me: 'I have to pay to go out now?!' But that's what I want you to walk away with. I want you to walk away with good music, but also a feeling that it was well worth it, that it was a nice evening, you weren't berated, somebody wasn't rude to you again. You get that all day long; you don't need to go out and pay to have that! Nowadays, I think people need a little bit of gentleness as balance, and that's something that matters to me.

"I think we've always been honest, I don't think we've ever hidden. I've never gone onstage and tried to be mysterious or cool, because I can't pull it off – my personality isn't that way even if the music is. I meet a lot of people who ask me who the real me is: the person singing the song or this goof girl who meets people after the show. It's both. I'll be really cool for the first set, then I'll forget and lose it for the second!"

There was a moment, fleeting, but nonetheless there, when the mainstream found Cowboy Junkies in general, and Margo Timmins in particular, to be very cool indeed, its very epitome. In 1990, she was on Maclean's Honor Roll as one of "12 Canadians Who Make a Difference", she was in *Esquire*, she was getting her picture in *People* magazine as one of the "50 Most Beautiful People in the World".

"I hate that picture! It was a horrible, horrible situation. I was going to a ball, my first New York ball, and I arranged for the photo session to be over at a certain time. This guy came in and he wanted me to do my photo nude, just holding flowers up. There are certain things I don't want to do, but I'm not good at saying 'no'. I know he's a photographer and he's come with a vision and I want him to get the picture he's come to get. But, on the other hand, there's only so much I can do. I'm not a model and I'm uncomfortable in that situation. There were big arguments and the whole thing was very embarrassing, I felt like the little prima donna in the corner – all because I wouldn't take my shirt off.

"Our audience has never come to our shows because of the sexy chick singer, because I never pranced around or wore those kind of clothes. Well, maybe they did around *Trinity Session* when there were a lot of photos, the Gap ad. That was a terrible period where we would do shows that were jam-packed, but only because we were the band of the moment, it was the groovy place to be that night. In Toronto, it got to the point where we'd do shows off the beaten path because we didn't want that audience, we wanted people who really wanted to come and see us. It was necessary because, within that audience of people just hanging out, there were people who really loved it. Usually, by the end of the night, the people who were hanging out were at the bar and those who liked us were at the front, so it was a time of generating our audience. If we hadn't had so much press, they wouldn't have known to come. It was necessary, but it was painful and, yes, they did come to see the pretty chick singer. But I was so busy trying to figure what the hell I was doing, I really didn't notice! It wasn't until later, when I was cleaning out my basement and sorting through those magazines that I realized, 'My God, I got so much press.' When it was going on, I didn't really take much notice, which is just as well, because I would have gone mad!

"I guess it was because there was tons of press, but really slowly, over a long time, and so our growth was slow. When *Trinity Session* came out, we had a van. Then it got taken up by RCA, the audience grew a little larger and we started to make a little bit of money, the company started to put money in, so we got a bus. Then we got proper crew, but it wasn't like we went from a club to a huge arena like someone like Tracy Chapman did. She was set for life from that and I'm glad she's got security in her old age, but what does it do to you? She releases a beautiful record that launches her onto a level she probably wasn't ready for – you have to grow to know how to be yourself in front of big crowds, it's hard. We had the luxury of time to do that. She didn't. She was suddenly a star, expensive tickets, expectations. The first album sold ten million, the second sells five million and people think it's a failure. How do you survive that as a songwriter and write something real again?

"I was the focus of it to start with, I guess. I did the press and there were a lot of dumb questions, over and over again. Even at my most angry, I've always been polite, I hope. The occasions I haven't, I can still remember them and I get angry with myself that I lost it. So, if I'm doing an interview, being asked stupid questions that I've been answering all day long, and inside I'm thinking, 'Why are you asking this? Don't you do any research?', I still just sit there and answer as well as I can. They're doing their job, and I do mine by taking the monotony! When I do interviews with Mike, I think it's my job to answer so he doesn't have to, because he's not as polite as I am! That's our teamwork. If Michael was alone in this, he'd be like Neil Young or Bob Dylan and would have just refused to do interviews years ago, but you can't do that at our level, because you need to be out in the press. On the business side, that's what I can bring, that buffer, just as he's been for me with the companies.

"Because we've never been rude to journalists, they've always treated us well, they've always given us something in the press, and we're thankful for it because we need it. We make a good team, even in the early days when we got reviews that weren't positive – sometimes they were mean, especially the English! The boys would laugh so I never got brought down by it. I was never allowed to become a star, a diva, I've always just been somebody's sister. Sometimes that's a drag, because I'd love to be a star sometimes! I've met a lot of singers, especially women, who do get brought down by the press. It's hard to take – people attacking what you look like, what you wear, whether you've gained weight, this whole stupid thing – but it does affect you.

"It's a rare thing being in a band where everyone can rely on one another right the way through. That whole band attitude seems to be something from the past. I guess it went out with records, LPs, the A-side and B-side, that concept of a team, everybody having one goal. Nowadays, music is so much oriented on ego, image, individuality, and that's the record company influence. They tried to do it with us. They were constantly wanting to pluck me away from the band, bring some sidemen in for me to stand next to. If not that, then constantly trying to pluck me away in a publicity way. I did all the publicity, I did the photos, but again it wasn't because the record company wanted it, it was because it was what we had decided to do as a band. The boys didn't want to do press – neither did I! – but somebody had to do it.

"We've always, always, protected the band, musically, and each other's spots in it. Now there's not the pressure, but in those days it would always amaze me what we would get asked to do. Peter Leak, our manager, would try to do these things to push me and he wasn't some evil man trying to break things up, he was just doing what the industry did. But I'd keep saying that he was trying to drive a wedge between us. Businesswise, it probably made sense and that was why he was doing it, it was his job, but I always thought that this band, they'll be around me a lot longer than you'll ever be. They're my brothers, they're forever, even if we break up tomorrow. Because, long after it's over and I'm an old woman and I've got my Cowboy Junkies collection on the shelf, that'll be mine. That's what I put on the earth. But it's not what I did. It's what *we* did, me and the boys. I won't be thinking of RCA or Geffen when I'm playing the records in the nursing home when I'm 99.9 years old. That means nothing. The records mean Pete, Mike, Al, Jeff, Jaro, whoever was playing on them. That's what I'll remember. I remember really seriously thinking that. You guys are just a little part of what we do – you come, you go, we're grateful for the help you give us – but the music and the band is permanent, forever and ever and ever. We all felt that way; we knew we had to protect it."

Protecting the band has made for a pretty hard road over the years, but it's one that is clearly more satisfying artistically and one where the audience gets far more from records and shows than they do from their more processed musical brethren. Even if it isn't always a perfect night.

"Our audience is very forgiving on every front, I guess. They don't mind if I sometimes forget the words or Pete gets the wrong intro, because that's part of it being a live thing, something that happens there and then. I've never understood why that should be perfect. Shania Twain came to Toronto one time and there was a big thing about her lip-syncing and there were huge discussions about whether it was OK or not. I don't get it. If you pay for a ticket, you're paying to hear someone play, not to listen to a record. OK, her show wasn't so much about her songs as her belly button, her hair, her dancing – and God knows I'd hate to have to dance around and sing! But, for me, a live show is that, live. When I go see Springsteen, when it's live, it's intense. He's broken my heart. Leonard Cohen did a show in Toronto, and I was in the audience, so close to boo-hoo-hooing! It was so amazing. With that intensity comes mistakes, but that is what touches your heart: a real person telling you how they feel, sharing something with you in that moment. Patti Smith never remembers words, she's way worse than me, but her shows are so great. She is amazing. I know images are just images, we've seen some of that, but even now when you meet somebody you expect that image and then you find there's someone underneath! I met her once and she's not crabby or mean, she's really nice! She is so natural – that's something so important. She blazed the trail for women to do what I do."

What Margo does has certainly evolved over the years, her confidence growing and her influence increasing all the time, not least onstage. In a sense there are two sides to Cowboy Junkies. In the studio, it's very much Mike's band. But onstage, as she guides the audience through the evening, there's a very real sense that the Junkies have become hers.

"That's a good observation, I think. It's always Mike's band in that he drives it, but it's always our band, too; that's part of that weird glue. Mike's always in control, but he's not so tightly in control that it strangles it. It goes back to that egoless thing. He doesn't feel it has to be his way or no way. Our input is important, and he realizes that and respects that. Even though he's guiding it, we let him, our personalities are such that it's OK. I don't want to be boss, nor does Pete, and Al certainly doesn't because he'd have to get up earlier. Mike's lucky in that, but he also appreciates our input.

"Onstage, you can't have everybody leading. During the show, I will make suggestions like, 'Let's not do this song now' or 'Let's play that one' – not too often, because Mike writes the set list and that's fine. But I have more of the pulse of the audience and if I feel 'I'm losing them, we gotta do a big song right now' or 'I can't sing another big one, let's do a quiet song', he'll go with it. Mike knows I'm watching them; my job is to keep an eye on the audience and know what's happening. It's his job to know what's going on behind me. I have no idea. Pete could fall off his drum kit and I wouldn't know, that's not my job. I'd laugh, because it would be funny, but that's Mike's problem. It's just become a natural division in our responsibilities. Nobody's said it or laid it down, it's become that way because we trust each other to do our jobs.

"As a front person, I have a good sense of audiences now – Mike will trust that. Sometimes before an encore, I'll suggest something and he'll say 'no', and there'll be a reason for it. Pete's not playing that type of song right that night or Mike's not playing well or Al's fallen asleep, so there's that, too. If the band can't play it, we don't play it. But, over the years, Michael and I have developed a really good relationship on so many levels – doing interviews, splitting our responsibilities in the band. I hope he knows I'll be there. I know he will; there's no danger that Mike will ever let me down and I certainly wouldn't let him down. That's really nice to have in this kind of job. I think it must be really hard for people who are by themselves and have different bands every time they go out. To do all this by yourself and not have that fallback, somebody to turn to, to pass the ball to – I'm playing shitty tonight, sing great for me! There are nights I fall apart, I don't know what I'm doing and I know the others will pick it up for me. Even now, there are nights when I look around at them and pull the 'I don't know where we are!' face! 'What are the words? Somebody help!'"

Oh yes, "all these words that I sing". There are a lot of them and very few are conventionally easy pop songs. The sheer volume of them, combined with the fact that none of us are getting any younger, has required an onstage addition – the lyric book. Fan Ken Hoehlin vividly remembers one of the catalysts for its arrival.

343

"In St Louis in 1997, or 1998 maybe, Margo wasn't using a lyric stand at this point. There are a lot of examples over the years of her forgetting the words, but this time, they were doing 'Anniversary Song', and in the second verse she just forgot the lyrics. It wasn't like she stumbled on them, she just went blank. Nobody in the band knew them, so by this point they'd stopped, and she asked the audience if they knew them. We were all dumbfounded and, of course, when somebody asks you something like that, you can't think of them, either. So, instead of going on to the next song, finally somebody went backstage and got the big book with all the lyrics in before they could carry on – it was pretty funny! I saw them a couple of weeks later and she had the music stand up there and she was using that to help out!"

"Man, at this point there are a lot of songs we can do and I don't know how I'm supposed to remember them," laughs Margo. "I can't do without that book now! I've always had difficulty remembering words, that's nothing new, and I don't like it when it happens, but I figure it's a live show, I don't have a great memory; you get what happens on the night. It's not going to get any better now, so I've always struggled with it. Then I thought, 'I'm 40 years old. I'm going to bring up on that stage whatever the hell I please! If having the lyrics bothers people, too bad for them.'

"The reason I didn't do it before was Mike and the boys felt that, when people see you with lyrics, they feel you're not into the song, you're not singing it, you're reading it. But I'm not reading them, it's just to help me when I blank out so I can find my spot again. There's the blank when you forget a word, but then there's the blank when I don't know what the next line is, and then I'm lost. That's a terrible place to be. But, at 40, I was old enough and cranky enough just to bring it up. And I saw Springsteen and he had a teleprompter and I figured, 'He's The Boss, he leads me!'

"It also means we can change the set around a lot more, because we don't play the same set day after day. I have my black book which goes onstage with me; then there's the blue one, which is all the other stuff. The black book is the stuff in our repertoire, the songs we rehearsed, then every other song is in the blue book. Last night we were talking about requests, we were going to do 'Powderfinger' for the first time in a while, and I knew I had that in the blue book, so I took it out of there. At a show the other day, they asked for 'Common Disaster', which wasn't in the repertoire, but we did it and now it's something we've added to the show. That's why requests often aren't a burden, because sometimes you pull out a song that somebody's asked for and it works, so you keep it in. On a long tour, we'll keep adding songs to keep ourselves interested. And we know that people come again and again and we don't want them to see the same show all the time, so it's nice for them to hear different stuff."

One of the things they often want to hear, no matter how many times they've seen the band, is 'Misguided Angel', one of Margo's handful of co-writes with her brother. Is she never tempted to pen a few more songs, given the success of that one?

"Michael has always written from his heart, what's going on in his life, but I think he's had great freedom as a writer because, although it's very personal, he's not singing it, he hands it over and it's not as exposing as it would be if he were singing. Because we're close in age, we're family, we have a lot of the same beliefs and values, we're going through the same age conflicts together and always have. When I'm singing it, a lot of it resonates, but it's not my diary. I think that's allowed him to stay honest, and me too. There are times onstage when I sing something and it really affects me, but it's one step removed. That's one reason I've never become a writer – that, and talent! When I have sung songs I've written, it's exposing. Maybe that's what's allowed us to keep it honest.

"Songs grow with you. When 'Misguided Angel' was first written, it was obviously a romantic love song, loving the bad boy. At that age, that's what you did. You didn't want the boring guy who was getting a good job – you wanted the drug dealer, God forbid! Now, I have nieces, there are the children of friends who are teenagers, and the misguided angel just isn't good enough! I'm now the mother in that song! Sometimes, I'm trying to sing it from that perspective, as a sad thing, that this girl is in love with this person that she can't help loving, but he might not be the right person, sort of, 'God help me, let's hope it goes OK.'

"When I first sang it, it was, 'I'm in love with him, he's great, it's going to be so great, you guys are stupid, you don't know what you're talking about.' From the perspective of being that age. Now, it isn't always part of our repertoire, we just put it in once in a while because somebody wants it. If somebody wants it, I'm just singing it as a gift. They've come to hear that song, they're usually young. I start singing it and all the girls in the front row get this glow on their face: 'I have a misguided angel'! I want to go give them therapy afterwards, some counselling. 'You stay away from him.' So that's how I sing it."

One of the big paradoxes of the Junkies, one that knocks you off balance at times, is that the words often read as though some growling Tom-Waits-like character is going to sing them. Then, when you hear the music, the voice is from somewhere completely different. According to Mike, "Without a doubt, it's our biggest strength. Margo's voice is what has allowed us to reach as many people as we have. We wouldn't have sold as many records without that because, if you hear that, you don't have to get into the lyrics. I like to think that the music and the lyrics are what has kept us where we are, but Margo's voice is the hook; that's what made people stop and listen in the first place. Then they get deeper into what we do and they stick around if they're that kind of person, that kind of music fan.

"The other side is that it's kind of the element we fight against, too. If you're not willing to sit and listen, then you're not going to get so much out of it, and you can just take it as, 'There's that voice again!' It's very defining and distinctive, and so whatever we do, in some ways, you just can't escape it. It's a double-edged sword, but I wouldn't want it any other way, because without Margo's voice we wouldn't be where we are. And, as a songwriter, it's great to know she'll be singing what I write. It is an amazing voice – there are often times when I'm writing and I lose perspective or just plain forget just how great it is. Then I give it to Margo and, those first few times of playing it, your jaw drops because it's amazing to watch a song bloom when she takes it.

"The funny thing is, at the start of the band, that double-edged sword thing, we discussed it a lot, especially Al and I. We were very aware of it – that, with Margo's voice out front, we could get away with doing all sorts of stuff underneath it that we wouldn't get away with otherwise, because people wouldn't understand it. But, with that voice, that would distract them from it at first and we could have that dichotomy happening, and that was exciting."

That dichotomy is something Margo also relishes. "Punk was a huge influence on the three of us – Pete was a little young for it. But that era of music was our twenties, you're becoming an adult, being seriously influenced by things beyond your parents, your home, taking on the world's influences. It was a great time in music, a great message, because prior to that music was so big, rock-star-ish, diva. That was part of our teenage years, but punk, we were the perfect age for it. I remember going to New York overnight just to see a band, driving ten hours there, ten hours back, and at that age you could do it and go to work. What happened to those days? Now we go on at ten o'clock at night and I'm worried it's too late!

"Alan, Mike and I went to a lot of those shows together. Mike and I shared our entire lives – the fact that we're the two in the middle put us together. John was older, I was a baby when he was home, then Pete was my baby, but Mike was my peer, my age – we went to the same proms together. But punk, it still affects us, Al's playing. I hear it in our music.

"Sometimes I'm singing and I'll turn round thinking, 'What are you guys playing?' I'm singing la, la, la, 'rock and bird', and there's this noise going on! Al's playing a jazz lick, Pete's playing a waltz and who knows what Jeff's doing, and I do wonder how it works and it shouldn't work, it should all fall apart, but it doesn't and it's always been that way. That's why our sound is distinct. I can't tell you what kind of band we are, but that is our sound. It works. I don't know what Michael does with his guitar. He doesn't play it. He bites it, somehow. I think it comes from that time. And Pete has turned into a mesmerizing drummer. When I get to turn round and watch him, it's great. He has a really hard job, too, and he's found his own place, we all had to do that, it's always been that way, even way back to *Trinity*, which is quite a simple record. As I was listening, I thought, 'This shouldn't be working!' It's the only music I've ever had to sing to, so somehow it makes sense to me! I listen to the groove; that's how I was taught to sing. When we started, those first two records, it wasn't really about the lyrics, it was the groove, and that's all we worked on as a young band. On *Whites!!*, we'd find a groove and it would be, 'OK, those lyrics work, we'll use them.'

"Pete and I have similar personalities. If he was running the band, we'd never rehearse – 'Let's get a coffee' – where Mike will say, 'No, it's not good enough, we need to rehearse again!' Thank God for Mike, because we'd sound really terrible without him! Michael's always pushed Pete in the right way, even when he was fired and told to 'Go out and learn if you want to come back, because you can't just laze around.' To his credit, he got a teacher, he learned his job and, over the years, has become a great player with his own style. He's someone we really need in the band, not just as a player but as a personality on that bus."

Like all the real groups, they all need to be there for Cowboy Junkies to function. Ask Jeff Bird why it took Mike such a while to be successful, despite moving to New York and London with Alan, and he has a simple answer. "He didn't have Margo singing then! It's a very formidable combination those two, and it's pretty unique, such that I've not even heard many covers of their material.

"Michael's songs aren't the easiest in the world for anybody to learn, and then lyrically they're very, very dense, there's a lot of literature in his writing. That's a whole other thing about them and their songs – that they operate on two levels. Early on, especially, playing in places where the sound wasn't great and she was singing so quietly, it was completely incomprehensible what Margo was singing, but it didn't seem to matter because it was so strong musically. Then you'd sit down and look at the lyrics; you have a whole new experience with the song. The llamas were always quoting them on the message board, and often, when they did, it came as something new to me!"

Jeff is always looking to bring new experiences to the others, not least in attempting to get them to play with other people.

Margo is the one who has been most receptive to the concept. "I've done a lot of it. Things like backup vocals on albums, a few shows, the album that was on the download site. It's just our personalities are better suited to being with the band. I've done it to challenge myself, because it's amazing how much you learn, good and bad. You realize things that we do, better or worse – even just setting up stages and getting through soundchecks. But none of us are big social people. I don't have many friends, I don't hang out with the gang, I'm not the sort of person who's going to break into song and jam along. If I'm thrown into a situation where I have to, I can. I've created situations where it's forced on me and it's always been helpful. It's funny – I know I'm a good singer but I still have reservations about it, as if I'm not. It's an odd feeling. Michael's probably the same. There's a shyness, an embarrassment. I'm not sure if I can keep up with other guys, so I keep away from it."

That's one of the endearing things about the band: it's a very humble, modest thing.

"I guess that is an extension of us – the audience does realize it's not pretence, we don't put it on. But, as a result, we're very closed ranks. I've had opportunities to sing with people that I left. I never sang with Townes and that makes me sad.

Why did I never do that? That was stupid. Stupid! But he changed the songs every night, he's worse than I am about changing lyrics, so it would have been hard! I think Michael is an amazing guitar player, a brilliant songwriter, but I don't know if he knows how good he really is, so he's not comfortable to sit around with other people and play. Away from that, he's got his family. They're his friends. I have my sisters, my mother, that's enough.

"We're all just a big bunch of losers together! Social life is too much work – I have to call all these people!"

CHAPTER 19

Where the winds of confusion swirl

Mike Timmins, 2005: "The more I think about *One Soul Now* as I get more distance on it, I kick myself a bit. With that album, I wanted to bring forward some songs I'd written and liked but hadn't made it on other records. A lot of the songs I wrote for it didn't get on there. It was a weird process I went through as a producer to bring it forward. Of all the records, it's the least formed thematically. Saying that, there are a lot of songs on there that I love: 'The Slide', 'He Will Call You Baby', 'One Soul Now', 'Why This One'. But I think they're individual songs. Where our other records are very strongly of a period, that one, because of the way I grabbed ideas from the past and wrote new ones, it doesn't have that same feel. There's not so much integrity in the structure of the album, because it's not written that way. I think it suffered because of that and it makes me mad now! Maybe over time I'll get another perspective on it, but it was that kind of record. That's why it's so dense, because there's no thread. I could make one up, there are strands in there, but it doesn't really work. When all's said and done, I'll probably look back on that record as the one we shouldn't have done."

Mike Timmins, 2010: "*One Soul Now* is an album that I would take a 'do-over' on if I had the chance. There are a few songs on it and recordings that I really like but I think we should have sat back a bit and thought about how we were going to approach the album as a whole. It was the first album that we recorded in our studio space, so the actual process took over and I never really did a good job at shaping the album – I'd have to give myself a 'D' as a producer on that one, although I love the production on songs like 'One Soul Now', 'Why This One' and 'Notes Falling Slow'. 'He Will Call You Baby' is one of my favourite songs that I've written and I really like the performance on the album, and I still love to play it live; I love the production on 'Simon Keeper' – but it's from the *Open* sessions – and I am also very proud of the writing on that song. 'From Hunting Ground to City' and 'Stars of Our Stars' should never have been on the album and should have been relegated to the archives; and I think we lost 'My Wild Child', 'The Slide' and 'Long Journey Home' in bad production decisions. It could have been a much better album."

If there is such a thing as a runt in the Cowboy Junkies album litter, it's *One Soul Now*. Its moving force would like another crack at making it, his band colleagues barely remember putting it together, and a number of long-term followers have relegated it to the "play once in a while" section. It has the same sense of foreboding around it that *Pale Sun, Crescent Moon* had, yet more opaque, impenetrable. It's as though the band had come full circle, where they needed to purge themselves of a more difficult collection of songs after a cycle of more, if not mainstream, then at least llama-friendly tunes – *Pale Sun* came after the classic American songbook trilogy of *The Trinity Session*, *The Caution Horses* and *Black Eyed Man*, and *One Soul Now*, after the clutch of *Lay It Down*, *Miles from Our Home* and *Open*, records where the band had moved away from those early roots and forged what would become an identifiably Junkies sound, still touching on those foundations, but meandering into new areas, down the jagged river often forged by Mike's guitar playing.

But does *One Soul Now* deserve that kind of dismissal? The answer, like the record itself, is less than clear, more complicated than a simple "yes" or "no". Perhaps the best comparison isn't *Pale Sun*, for all that it bears the same hallmarks, but the *Rarities, B-Sides and Slow, Sad Waltzes* album, in that it's a more random collection of odds and ends, not from over a career, but from the recent past, songs that couldn't quite fit on other projects but which needed a wider audience. In earlier days, possibly they might have found their way onto B-sides and 12-inch singles as little extras to entice the buyer, but those days were pretty much gone, certainly for the indie Junkies.

The problem lay with the songs themselves, not so much in terms of their quality, but their sheer awkward cussedness. They were angular, singular pieces that stood alone and, by now, Cowboy Junkies albums had started to become very much of a piece, conceptual, thematic, coherent. That coherence was lacking in *One Soul Now*. In current terms, and it's a generalization again, these were mostly independent observations that a novelist might throw into a short story or onto a blog because, by their very nature, they wouldn't be so happily moulded into a wider theme.

Perhaps it was always going to be that way. These were chaotic, crazy times. We were all still picking our way from the debris of 9/11 and the aftermath that Bush and Blair created in Iraq and Afghanistan, with America's shift from the nation that had the world's sympathy to one whose belligerence, right or wrong, was beyond the comprehension of many. Serious people were trying to formulate a coherent response to it all and, as this was the Junkies' first record since the Towers had fallen from the sky, it's perhaps inevitable that they were thrashing around trying to find some sense in it all, the same as the rest of us. We were all in pieces one way or another, so little wonder the record was equally fractured.

For Mike, the title track was about that sense of the dislocation between the personal and the political that very much defined the times. "The song 'One Soul Now' does define a lot of things for me at the point I wrote it. Current events, politics, where I was in my own life, it's a statement, almost like a rallying cry – that term is so important, more important than ever – that people find that connection that binds us all. The song deals with that connection through nature, but conceptually it's just we're at such a horrible time in history. Part of that was, because of my age and my kids' age, I was that much more in tune to it, I think. Obviously there have been periods a lot more horrible than this, but it seemed a very dysfunctional time to me – and that hasn't changed."

When the album came out, writing on cowboyjunkies.com, Mike noted that the phrase "one soul now" had been inspired by a line in Steinbeck's *The Grapes of Wrath*, adding, "The idea behind *One Soul Now* is that we are all interconnected. I suppose that it could be a political statement for these times, but more importantly it is a statement of personal politics. I think that, to certain degrees, we all go through the same life cycles and have to deal with the same bouts of loss and confusion as we struggle through. It seems that there should be a way for us all to pool our energies, our souls if you will, and conquer these interminable cycles. I suppose that is why the notion of a God was invented: a focal point for all of our inner energies. I suppose that is why music was invented, too."

Written initially at Maiden's Mill in the period that led to *Miles from Our Home*, it was a song that needed to wait for its time to come. With the world splitting into factions and tribes, each blaming another, a call to link arms was timely, albeit destined to fall on deaf ears – or ears that chose to be deaf, as peace marches, anti-war demonstrations and the rest were studiously ignored by the hawkish forces of the establishment on either side of the Atlantic.

'One Soul Now' was about those rare moments when the world seems to make sense, when for a brief second you feel yourself tapping into the "universal force", for want of a better explanation, a sensation that Mike knew well from those long hours of writing. "When I look back at something I've written, if it's something I'm especially happy with, I look at it and think, 'I don't know where that came from! That's pretty good!' I talked to Townes a lot about this, because his stuff was so amazing and he'd say that, when he was doing his best work, it was as if he wasn't doing it himself. He described himself as a conduit. His job was to make a space where he was receptive to it. And that's hard. That's the writer's job – to get to a place where you're open enough to take that in. Once you do that, it's there, it comes out. I believe that, too.

"There's nothing arty about it. It's your life, you have all those experiences, it's what happens on the news, what happens when you go down the street; all the stuff is coming at you and, if you do put yourself in a position to absorb that, that's what you do as a writer. The more open you are to letting the reality come out, the more honest it is.

"When I'm writing, I read the material back and every now and again, I'll stop and say to myself, 'Do I believe that? Is it true?' If the answer's 'no', then I throw it out. It doesn't matter how clever it is – if it doesn't have that belief, if it doesn't mean something, it goes. That's hard, a lot of writers don't do it, and there's value in that, too, on a different level, but the stuff that really affects me is the thing that, when I read it, I go, 'Wow, that's me! How does he know that about me?' That's the real stuff and that's the editing process I use. You fool yourself many times and you let stuff go by, but when I'm being really honest, that's the way it works."

As you look back at the Junkies' body of work, there's a pronounced sense that their music is like the sea, constantly changing yet without you noticing it. Like the sea, too, they're also relentless, always there, not going away: "You can ignore us if you want and then we'll make another record and maybe you'll like that one, you won't get rid of us." A sense of defiance amid the ephemeral nature of modern music, celebrity, art.

"You get the sense that Mike is not depleting the pot from which he works, but that he's drawing from an endless fountain and that's very exciting," points out John Timmins. "There are few artists like that and those that aren't, you can anticipate the demise of their career just by the weakness of their writing, their changing styles in an effort to disguise it. One contemporary that comes to mind is Bruce Springsteen, who just keeps going as strongly now as he ever has; Bob Dylan, too, I suppose. They've all made records that are better than others, but there's that sense of integrity – 'I've got more to say.' It's so pronounced."

"Writing that record was no easier or harder than it'd ever been," admits Mike. "I've never been short of things to write about – if you've lived another year, there's stuff to write about. But, strictly in practical terms, it does get harder. I think back to *The Caution Horses*: I was writing all the time because the band was all there was. I'd get up and write, go for a walk, come back and do some more. But now, I have to gather ideas in snippets, themes, maybe a line, directions for the next song or record, and I write them down as I go along, and then I start to get an itch – I feel that it's time to sit down and start really putting it together. I have to go away because it's impossible to do it at home with all the normal things you have to do with your day-to-day life: kids, the business and everything.

"I need to totally immerse myself in it, so I go away for a couple of weeks, get totally isolated and that will usually start the process. I get a ton done; it just comes out. I will have been building them prior to that, but getting time to sit and work at them, that's when it begins coming together. I do that a few times over the course of a few months and, once I've got the bulk done, then I can start to do some writing at home because things are clearer. That's how I've done the records, pretty much since *Lay It Down*, because you need some space away from kids, wife, business, just to solely concentrate on the writing. As we go on, there's just more stuff to do in terms of business, admin, that kind of thing, and you have to get away from it to write, to free your mind up."

Writing is a very personal thing, as each has his or her own different style or approach, and some are more open about it than others, according to Linford Detweiler. "Mike was fairly reticent about the creative process. He's a very solitary writer. I was somewhat stunned at his willingness to bring out six or eight new songs when we toured with them. I never got the sense that he was agonizing over the writing. Maybe I'm wrong, but it seemed an effortless process and that, when the song was done, he didn't try to second-guess it too much. Mike and I are both pretty strong introverts at the end of the day – there's a part of me that needs to get away by myself to write – but Karin and I tend to collaborate too, which is a different thing.

"We had conversations about music and influences and all that stuff from time to time, but I never really delved into Mike's creative process, never really got under the hood and worked out what made him tick. I guess we both play our cards pretty close to our chest and we don't want to go into it too much. When they go onstage, there's an intensity to what they're doing. It seems like you can put that serious part of yourself into your performance, your writing, get the music across; then, by the time you've done that, you really need to be silly for a period of time to bring yourself back into balance, so we didn't really get that opportunity.

"We even did a little Q&A workshop together at a university where kids were asking us questions and suddenly we were talking about it, but I guess I had the feeling in mind when we went on the road that I'd find out a bit more about his writing. Probably my fault for just not pouring the drink and saying, 'So …!'

"I have a lot of respect for his writing, but I just don't know that much about how he gets there. I picked up on the fact that he's a bit of a collector, like any good writer. When he's reading, a line will jump out at him – he was reading *Cold Mountain* and 'The rare goodwill of the random world' just stood out, like 'Hey! There it is!' I think all good writers are going around with their butterfly net, something will jump off the page and stick with them."

If *One Soul Now* had started with a thought from *The Grapes of Wrath*, its bookend, 'The Slide', was bittersweet, too. Where the

(Top) "Never count your winnings at hour twenty-three". On the road with Townes Van Zandt. *(Cowboy Junkies Archive)*

(Above) Extended family. Long serving crew member John Farnsworth with Margo, 1996. *(Cowboy Junkies Archive)*

(Bottom left) Musical chairs, piecing together the *Lay It Down* cover, 1995. *(Cowboy Junkies Archive)*

(Top) Recording *Lay It Down* at John Keane's studio in Athens, Georgia. John, Margo, Mike, Alan, Pete. *(Cowboy Junkies Archive)*

(Left) Alan and Mike haul the gear onto Rock Island, where the band readied the songs for *Lay It Down*, 1995. *(Cowboy Junkies Archive)*

(Right) Pete gets ready to play at the Colonial Theatre, Phoenixville, 2007. The Blob didn't show. *(Dave Bowler)*

(Bottom) Playing with the Boston Pops Orchestra, Symphony Hall, Boston, June 24 2007. *(Justine Hunt/The Boston Globe/Getty)*

Trinity Revisited, Royal Albert Hall, London, October 2007.

(Top) Lights, music, soundcheck. Mike, Jeff and Margo working through the acoustic material with singer Thea Gilmore. *(Dave Bowler)*

(Left) On mandolin, harmonica and all kind of shaky things, Jeff Bird. *(Dave Bowler)*

(Opposite top) Walking after midnight. Pete, Alan, Jeff, guests Thea Gilmore and Ryan Adams, and Margo. *(Dave Bowler)*

(Right) Alan Anton, the Sage, Gateshead, 2007. Al! *(Dave Bowler)*

(Top) Working on Margo's Farm. Pete and Alan during early recording for *At the End of Paths Taken*, June 2006. *(Cowboy Junkies Archive)*

(Left) Mike Timmins, getting in tune at the Union Chapel, Islington, 2007. *(Dave Bowler)*

(Right) Margo Timmins in full cry, Manchester Academy 2, 2007. *(Dave Bowler)*

(Left) "Let's just keep it simple and make four albums in eighteen months…" Cowboy Junkies prepare to defy the laws of physics, 2010. *(Cowboy Junkies Archive)*

(Bottom) "Sing me a song of love". Massey Hall, Toronto, 24 May 2018. *(Heather Pollock/Cowboy Junkies Archive)*

opener was about the excitement of those small epiphanies when everything crystallizes and the world falls into place for a brief moment, 'The Slide' was all about accepting that those moments are few and far between, that all we can do is give ourselves up to the winds of confusion, an echo of the sentiments found on the later songs on *Open*. That way might lie pain, loss and the rest, but also those great little moments in life, the moments we treat in too cavalier a fashion, according to Margo.

"You know in *Annie Hall*, the bit where he tells a joke about two women who complain about how terrible the food is in a restaurant and then say, 'And such small portions!' I like that – that's the way life is. And that's kind of what the music is about. Life is hard, it's a fight and it's all over so quickly. The highlights in life aren't going to the big party at the end of the week, it's just having a nice dinner with your family or having a good day. Big moments like going to the ball are the perks, but it's the everyday that matters.

"I think, in our culture, unfortunately we've turned it in on itself. Big things are supposed to happen every day and, if they don't, you should be unhappy. Even with our love lives, there's this expectation because of what gets put across in these short movies that show a life compressed into ninety minutes. But, in between all this adventure, there's the laundry! A lot of people are made sadder than they need to be because they're expecting more than what life is, what is real. Our culture is so weird, I find it frightening."

'The Slide' also revisits some of the themes of *Miles from Our Home*, not least in another of Mike's conversations with God, albeit through a third party this time. "I love 'The Slide', the lyric, the idea of having a blunt and true conversation with God, whatever that is, but that you have to get to him through his son. I like that idea. Not believing in anything, but wanting to and trying to figure out the channels to get to that belief. Ultimately it gets very personal, about sitting and realizing what you have, that special little flame of your family and those around you who you love, and the bigger picture, the God issue, you can choose to put on top of it if you want, but it's not the core."

Musically, 'The Slide' is at the lighter end of the spectrum, and it needs to be, for it follows hard on the heels of 'Simon Keeper', one of the most challenging songs, not just on the record but in the band's career. Stripped of all the redemptive qualities of the album's end-pieces, it is a storytelling song that bared its teeth, harsher in its disgust with the everyman protagonist than something like "Cause Cheap Is How I Feel' had been, a sign of a decade's worth of developing maturity as songwriter and performers.

As Detweiler notes, "Mike is not afraid to ask big questions in his songs; there's a spirituality to some of the music that is fairly exceptional. There's Catholic roots stuff in there – it's an interesting mix. Most enduring songwriters aren't afraid to go and ask the big questions, but it is the exception in rock music today, for sure. But they are more interested in the tradition they're drawing on and contributing to, where that approach isn't particularly rare. I want writers who are willing to put themselves on the line – the ironic thing can be fun and clever, but at the end of the day I want someone to tell me how they really feel in their gut. This is what I'm thinking about."

The irony of a song that deals in ironies is that 'Simon Keeper' was written for *Open*, didn't fit that album's template and so was resurrected for *One Soul Now*, by which point the times suited the piece far better than they would have three years earlier. "We put it on there because, after September 11, it made sense, it had a context, but that's not what the song is about," explains Mike. "I wrote it for *Open*, but it didn't make sense on that record; it was a song that was very removed from the others. That's what's cool about songs, about any art: it can suddenly take on a new life in a new setting and that song did. It makes so much more sense now than it did when I wrote it for *Open*."

At its core, it was a parable of corporate greed, the way in which that can distort the morality of the individual and the way in which that innate dishonesty can be used to create similar results from different environments, from big-company bookkeeping to street preacher, always looking to throw a line to hook the money fish. As Mike noted, "The song is about selfishness and greed – all done, ironically, in the name of selflessness and generosity," the kind of corporate spin we see all around us. But do they ever come through on those promises? Hardly. And was this the kind of greed that brought the world to its knees in the banking crash? Exactly. Is it still going on, unpunished? You betcha.

By the time 'Simon Keeper' did appear, the Enron scandal had been exposed and, as noted, the spectre of 9/11 also hung over it, largely because of the opening verse describing "a job in the towers cooking the books". These were not necessarily the World Trade Center towers, though – just any giant office block that looks down on the pawns below, lives turned inside out by the decisions made high above them by people with little thought, or interest, in the consequences, as long as the skids are greased, the money flows in, the bonuses stay high and the taxes low.

That idea of the population going about their daily lives while those lives are manipulated in the towers and the government offices also plays into one of the big themes of Mike's writing: the way in which chance's juggernaut can suddenly mow you down without you having done anything to encourage it. "It constantly freaks me out, that chance element. I can't get over it; it's just the thing that makes it exciting and terrifying. You never ever know what's round the corner and I can't get away from that!"

'Why This One' is the most obvious manifestation of that on the record, yet its genesis went back almost a decade to the sessions for *Lay It Down*, where songs like 'Something More Besides You', 'Lonely Sinking Feeling' and 'Just Want to See' hinted at the same kind of "Why now, why me, why this?" questioning in its various forms.

"I've always had that song in my head," says Mike. "We completely reworked it from then, because it never worked musically, but I always liked the idea, so it was a matter of finally getting things to fall into place. That's a regular thing, it's always happened on all our records. I never throw stuff out – I put it to one side, often never to be worked on again, but at the start of every writing period I look at what I have that wasn't finished, because I know that something in there will pop its head up."

The release of the *Anatomy of an Album* CD-ROM that went with *One Soul Now* was especially illuminating for those fans who really wanted to get inside, not only the songs, but the process of committing that final definitive version to vinyl. Or tape. Or aluminium. Or digital. Or whatever it gets committed to these days.

The CD-ROM included a sixteen-track demo version of 'Why This One' dating back to 1996, a very different version of the tune and, listening to it once you know how it finished up, it's a slightly unsatisfactory version. It's apparent why the band threw it out at that point, but there is clearly something in the lyric that might work. That said, had they released it on *Lay It Down*, and that was the only version we had of it, maybe we'd see it as a classic now. Who knows? But, as Mary Gauthier put it in the press interviews following the release of the Mike-Timmins-produced *The Foundling*, "Good enough isn't good enough. The world doesn't need any more good, there's plenty of that out there already." The band's quality-control-driven willingness to consign that version to the work-in-progress pile rather than release it before it was properly finished was totally vindicated by the version we got on *One Soul Now*.

For each track on *One Soul Now*, the *Anatomy* CD-ROM provided "liner notes" on the song, copies of rough draft lyrics, some accompanying photos, and two or three musical versions, tracing it from demo to almost-finished version. Given that some of the versions were little but the most rudimentary sketches of Mike singing lines alongside an acoustic guitar, it was a pretty bold move to put it out there, although it's probably better than letting people hunt through your garbage.

"*Anatomy of an Album* was pretty exciting, opening up the songwriting process the way Michael did," says Jason Lent. "I don't ever remember anybody else doing that in that kind of depth. 'Here's everything behind the songs, see what you make of it.' It goes against all the ideas of mystique, ego, everything that rock is based on. Because, when you just have Mike singing or humming to an acoustic guitar, it sounds pretty much like anybody else, but to follow that journey through the rehearsal room to the finished version is so cool."

"It was daunting to put my demos on the CD-ROM," admits Mike, "but it was a safe way to do it because it was very left field, very small scale, we only made 2,000 of them. It was a nice way to sneak it out and I knew only people into that side of things would get it and listen to it. It's something you really have to go to, it's a very active process to go through, to navigate, so again I hedged my bets a little! It was fun, I knew it would interest people who really want to get in behind the songs, but I didn't expect or didn't want it to be any bigger than that. Rounder wanted to package it with the record when it came out, but I didn't really want to do that – it's not for everybody. It did open a window on what we do, going from two-track to Clubhouse, and you can see the moment where it takes on a life of its own. People always ask about the process so I wanted to show it to them – that's pretty much all of it in front of you."

And maybe *One Soul Now* was the perfect time to showcase that, because, if ever a record was defined by process, it was that one, perhaps the single biggest reason why its overall focus slipped. This time, Cowboy Junkies were really going it alone in every sense, recording in their own time, in their own studio.

Margo explains, "When we were touring *Open*, we sent out word on the internet that we wanted to upgrade our recording equipment and as we went round the world, we bumped into people who had great microphones and, because the crew were with us, they helped check things out. We gathered up equipment and the Clubhouse became more of a studio. We were ready. We'd done nine studio albums and, by now, we were ready to do it ourselves, though when we saw Mike reach for the manuals we lost confidence every now and again! It was great – there was no pressure to get something recorded, which you have when you're on the studio clock. If it was working, we worked. If it wasn't, we came back later."

Mike agrees that "Recording at the Clubhouse with our own equipment was great. There's time to fool around, to try things out, experiment, not care about cost and time and schedules and that's been a big benefit to us." That looseness also helped enhance some of the Junkies trademarks. "There's a fragility to what we do, which is an important part of it. I don't know where it comes from; there are so many different elements to it. Some goes back to Pete and Al, because there's not that solid grounding, it's floating somewhere."

For all the advantages that having their own recording space would afford, especially long-term, initially it didn't make for the easiest of recording processes, according to Alan. "*One Soul Now* was a record where Mike had a lot of other things to think about because it was the first one where he was actually recording it, working the studio equipment, so I guess he was less immersed in the actual playing of it when we put it together."

Margo adds, "Albums have their own character, because they're always been a reflection of who we are and what we are. Depending on what's going on in our lives, you're either really focused on the record or your mind might be on other things. And I don't necessarily think that's a bad thing. *One Soul Now* was very much a Mike record. I've been meaning to listen to it again recently, because it's a real lost record, even to me. Personally, it was a really difficult time when we were making it, so my head was not there. And that happens to us all at different times. Making *Pale Sun*, I look back at my journal and it's all, 'And Al had a baby!' Day after day, it's that, so Al had other things going on then, he was in his own world even more than usual! So, at different times, we're in different spaces, and that can be a good thing sometimes, it's not always a negative.

"But *One Soul Now* was very much a Mike project and we all felt it that way. We did our thing, we were involved, but it's not something we were one on, and that was because Mike was figuring out how the equipment worked and how we recorded things properly. I don't mean we disagreed or we didn't like it, because if we're not happy it doesn't come out. But it was more a case of 'Whatever you want to do, Mike.' From my perspective, I didn't offer much inspiration. Mike was in the studio all the time doing his thing, and then every now and then he'd call me up and I'd turn up dutifully, do my part and get out. Get out fast, because it was really weird!"

There's no better example of the jigsaw approach to it all than 'No Long Journey Home', as captured on the *Anatomy* CD-ROM. The germ of the idea came in 1999, when Mike was home alone, looking after his daughter while his wife was in Virginia as her father's life neared its end. "It suddenly hit me how surreal or hyperreal this whole thing was. My wife was about to lose her father. I found it hard to get my head round that. I began to think about life and all the clichés that we try to use to describe it and how futile they are in the face of something as enormous as the death of a parent. So I started to list off all those clichés: 'a long journey', 'a trip across the tracks', 'a dead-end' and put them to melody. And that's as far as I got. Three years later, I decided to readdress this skeleton of an idea."

Lyrically, 'No Long Journey Home' sits up with some of the Junkies' best work, though perhaps it's one of those songs that only works when you know how it feels when a death knocks on your door. Death is the weirdest, most smack-between-the-eyes, most abstract, most absurd thing we have to deal with. You think you understand it in some kind of rational way before it happens around you, but once it does there's no way it can make any sense. Surely, it can't just be that simple, that one minute your heart is beating and the next it isn't? That's it? And you just go away? What you have to do in the aftermath is find your own soul again and try not to let the sheer trauma of it close you down, something captured perfectly in the final verse, which is echoed later in 'The Slide':

A cautionary tale for all who come this way,
A warning writ in water.
Act one you'll see it all so clear.
Act two you'll watch it disappear.
In three open your eyes and stare down your fears.

In spite of the anger that sparked the initial song, there's a sense of humour in 'No Long Journey Home' that captures the human survival instinct perfectly. If you've ever been to a funeral, you'll recognize that moment after the trial is over, when everybody convenes to eat. From the sombre, the atmosphere slows, shifts to the reflective, to the bemused and, often, to the almost hysterically funny. Maybe it's a collective release of steam, a relief that the horror of the final goodbye is over or, perhaps, simple relief that you weren't the one going in the box. Bleak, black comedy, perhaps, but historically the way in which people have coped with realities so monumental and so awful. Humour is the only escape, the only road back towards hope.

"People do miss the sense of humour in what we do," says Mike ruefully. "I can understand why they miss out on that, because it's not too obvious, but there are so many things that people miss because they're only looking at the surface of it. The artwork doesn't get any mention either, and that again is an important element in what we do. From loving music as fans, we always used to pore over the covers, specifically the days when we'd get Factory and Rough Trade stuff from England – how many records did I buy just because of the sleeve! It was yet another issue with the major labels: they wanted to take it over, but we were always, 'We'll give it you when it's ready. If you don't like it, tough!' It's part of the whole – it reflected the music."

The relationship between the band and their artwork is just as conceptual as the way they think of their music, as David Hougton explains. "The genesis of nearly every cover has been the same. Mike will send me lyrics first, then tapes of rough mixes and the name of the album. There's usually one line of lyrics that will crystallize the entire album for me. That will be enough to get me searching for the right images. On *Miles from Our Home*, it was, 'No one in sight for fifty miles.' On *One Soul*

Now, it was, "I don't understand how these things feel the way they do.' With the guidance of those words, I can find the perfect images.

"*One Soul Now* was the most difficult cover to create. I couldn't figure out how to relate the music to imagery. I had tried to find the right thing for two or three months and was having no luck. I tried trees. They were overdone. I tried water. It was overdone. I tried symbolic imagery. It was overdone. One evening, I was digging deep into the Communication Arts website, which lists the work of literally thousands of photographers and illustrators. I'd looked through about 789 people's work when I came upon James Reeder's photo illustrations. As soon as I saw them, I knew we had our cover. The hardest part was choosing which images to feature, because he had such a catalogue of great stuff.

"I typically assemble a virtual team: a photographer or illustrator, a typographer or calligrapher. I've never met most of the people who have helped me create the covers. Matthew Cooper, who designed the collages for *Black Eyed Man*, lives in England. Karen Cheeseman, the calligrapher on that CD, raises dogs in northern Ontario. Hans Neleman, who shot the cover for *200 More Miles*, lives in New York. I've never met any of them. Ten years ago, we used to work by fax and phone; now we work online. It's like laying down overdubs in the recording studio. I know what their skills are, and each of them plays their part individually.

"I feel every cover should be different from the one before, so when you walk into a music store there's no question you're looking at a new Cowboy Junkies CD. When creating a new cover, I keep the previous cover in mind, and try to create its opposite."

In those days when CD singles still just about survived, at least in the promo sphere, the illustrations carried on into a cover for 'The Stars of Our Stars', one of the more upbeat pieces on a pretty introspective collection. Mike had begun this song with a morning's fun at home with his daughter, who decided it would be pretty cool for them to write a song together, the innocence and simplicity of the idea providing a nice counterpoint to the heavier elements elsewhere.

"'Stars of Our Stars' is an undefined expression of things that are larger than us – that childhood perspective," says Mike. "It's not just stars, which are intriguing and fantastical enough, but 'stars of our stars', something way out there, that we can't even define. The way it was written, the idea behind it, it fits, because this was the first record that was heavily influenced by having children. *Open* was to a certain degree, but *One Soul Now* is much more focused in that direction – not specifically children, but family in general. If you look at *Open*, it's kind of the beginning of that love affair with your kids, that sense of a whole new adventure. As you go on, reality creeps in and you start to realize, 'My God, this isn't an adventure, it's a slow slog through the muck!' So much of it is great, but so much is just hard work. It's almost like the earlier albums, like *Black Eyed Man* was the first bloom of a relationship, and you move into *Pale Sun*, where it gets darker, then *Lay It Down*, where it's really dark; it's kind of a similar cycle with kids over *Open*, *One Soul Now* and then when we went on and made *At the End of Paths Taken*."

The song is deceptively simple, because it actually took a lot of effort to make it work in the studio. "We tried recording it off the floor a couple of times, but we couldn't get it to move properly. So we decided to track it individually … The final touch was finding the appropriate instrumentation to fill out the instrumental sections that pop up throughout the song. I tried a couple of things, but none of us were happy any of with it. Richard Bell did a pass on organ, which worked pretty well. And then Jeff took a couple of runs at it and nailed down a repeating electric mandolin riff that gave the song the lift it needed."

Jeff's electric mandolin has become very much a live feature of the band in recent times, and it's had its impact on Mike's guitar playing, too. "I got bored with playing lead and really got into playing rhythm, which I enjoy just as much. And, as a songwriter and arranger, I kind of enjoyed using other instruments and other people to do the solos. But just over that period of *Open* and *One Soul Now*, I began to enjoy playing lead a lot more. And that definitely influences the way I write a song, and the way I conceptualize it in terms of the arranging – I'm leaving more space for myself to play. On any record, I tend to work with one or two guitars. I don't change between them a whole lot, I tend to gravitate towards one. The sound you get out of it is very personal, subjective, it's how you approach it, what you put it through, the amp has a big part, though that's a constant with me, I always use the same amp. It's the tone I'm looking for: if I want it soft, brittle, hard, if I'm going to play a lot of lead, if I'm using a pick or my fingers. I know how the guitars I have will react to what I'm trying to do. But, though I'll record a song a certain way, on tour sometimes, especially later on, I'll reapproach it with different guitars because I want a change. Realistically, I could use one guitar and play every song, it's not like a huge difference, but it's enough for my enjoyment."

For all that it was recorded piece by piece, 'The Stars of Our Stars' is a fine example of just how much a band Cowboy Junkies is, as Pete points out. "Mike will generally record the song with him singing and his acoustic guitar on a two-track demo and from there it goes off in different directions. We all bring our parts, and then, if it's something Jeff's working on too, he's great for ideas and he can take it somewhere else. That's what makes for a real collaboration. Mike works pretty much in a short-story format a lot of the time and that gives you a lot of scope to bring our imagination to bear on it. I love his writing; it's great to work on that material."

"The songs very quickly take on their own life when all four of us are working on them," agrees Mike. "It soon becomes a Junkies song, not mine, and that's great. I usually send Margo my demo and we sit and work on it and then we send Pete and Al the demo with the two of us on, but sometimes they get my demo with me singing on it and that's kinda weird, because that's very personal. I like having Margo as a blanket there, a wall. That's happened more and more recently because of circumstances, but once we get by that and we get in the studio to work, the first day, that song has gone and it's ours not mine."

With its very pared-down lyric, 'The Stars of Our Stars' would surely have appealed to Lou Reed, who once said that good lyric-writing should be compact, concise, not a single word too many. "That's very Lou Reed!" laughs Mike. "I don't think there are any rules. Leonard Cohen, some of his songs are extremely wordy and are just as interesting in their way as the more concise ones. Same with Tom Waits. In a pop sense Lou was right – he had a great facility for that."

'My Wild Child' is rooted in the parental experience, albeit a rather more complex take on it. "Along with all of the love and all of the small and large blessings that children bring into one's life, they also create a distraction and confusion and do a number on relationships that existed before they came along. The irony is that, through all of this chaos, we, the parents, are supposed to be the stabilizing forces in our children's lives when more often than not it's the children that become the stabilizing force in the parents' lives. 'My wild child, she's my stone.' The verses deal with the notion of love as being a tricky, fickle force. It caresses us with one hand and smacks us with the other. The chorus is a simple, unabashed declaration of personal truth: my wild child, love, brings me home."

As Margo says, "I think that, as life goes on, as we get older, it's only going to get more complicated, more confused. I don't think you get smarter as you grow older, I think you get more confused. So there's a lot still for us to write and sing about."

Mike adds, "The records are about the struggles we go through in life. They're not autobiographical necessarily, but they are sparked at some level by experiences. People ask, 'Don't I ever run out of ideas?', but how can you run out of ideas? Just live a day and things are always changing. If they're not changing, you're not thinking, I guess. That's what the songs are about – about living."

'From Hunting Ground to City' drifts back towards some of the ideas on *Black Eyed Man*, the urban decay of a song like 'The Last Spike', and it's part of a trio of songs, including 'He Will Call You Baby' and 'Notes Falling Slow', that illustrate well the way in which Cowboy Junkies are viewed by supporters and detractors alike, both taking the same elements and revelling in or reviling them. It's best summed up by Mike's pithy dismissal of some of that criticism: "They're not depressing, they're just slow! We've fought that forever. If a song is quiet or slow, then it's sad. It doesn't have to be – try listening to it!"

Margo elaborates on a theme that clearly gets under the band's skin. "We get a lot of criticism that our music is gloomy, but I hear a lot of hope in what we do. I think that response stems from those who are often afraid of their feelings. In our culture we suppress them, we're bombarded by TV, fake emotions, so when they get confronted by something real – a book, a painting, music, anything that does stir them – they tend to shut the door. 'This is depressing, this is sad. It's making me think! Go away!' They label it, they dismiss it, they don't allow it to affect them. Yeah, maybe sometimes the words are sad, the melodies are sad, but the reaction it brings out in you isn't sadness, it's hopefulness, a feeling of community, understanding. When you're happy, everything's going fine, then great, I don't need anybody! But when they're not, that's when you need. I don't know what it is, but you need, you reach out for something.

"That's one of the reasons why we haven't sold tons and tons of records, because people are afraid; it's too much sometimes. Those who do get it, they really get it, it makes them feel OK. The culture has changed so fast over the years since this band started. People don't want to think now, they don't want to be asked questions – our culture gets more and more bland. We're sitting talking here in New York, but go out of this Starbucks and you'll see exactly the same stores that you'll see in Rome, the same clothes; you can't find anything unique to take home for people, because they can get it wherever they are. We're so homogenized, we're happy to be told what to think, where to stand, and people are afraid. We were in Moscow one time and I was sitting in a cab listening to the radio and it was the same crap they play here, with a few local songs thrown in which sound just as bad!"

In that vein, 'He Will Call You Baby' specializes in that dry morality and language – "leave you twisting in the wind" – that is so often at the heart of the great westerns of yore. "I know what you mean. It's about trying to make things simpler, to cut it to some bare bones to a degree, which is what westerns do – good guys and bad guys.

"It's a song about all the weird games we play with the ones we love. The conscious and subconscious games that play out in any long-term relationship. It's also about the loneliness and the sadness inherent in any great love. A happy little ditty." But no less true for that. This is life, warts and all, and the more we face up to that rather than hiding in the make-believe, the better equipped we all are to make it through the days and years. That's where the hope is, the real hope. You might have to go looking for it, but that's what makes it precious when you find it.

"I do believe him though I know he lies" is a similarly telling line from 'Notes Falling Slow', which also has a gentle prod at those detractors – "This ain't no depression, just notes falling slow". "When I played 'He Will Call You Baby' to Jeff Wolpert, our mixer, he said, 'Nobody plays that slow!' We do, and we're proud of it.'

Perhaps that comes from being Canadian?

"I don't think you can write to your geography, but I do think that the vastness of the country, that space, is in our music. It may be coincidental, but I do believe that environment influences how you write, how you think, how you interpret things, how you express yourself."

If you're not in a hurry to get anywhere, you get to the end of a song when you reach it. Is that the impact of driving 1,500 miles across country to the next gig?

"Could be. You sure learn patience!"

Taking a breath in songs, allowing reflection even as they're progressing, is a rare quality these days, but when there's such lyrical depth it's critically important, because these are words for ruminating over. "That song is a meditation on relationships, age and children, the basic themes of the album," says Mike. "People are great at deceiving themselves. It's our defence mechanism – we all do that, you have to. That's what's very healthy for me about writing songs. I can try to get down to the truth of things, but then I can get away from it and go back to living normally! Every year or so I get to sit down, try to get past the bullshit, the lies, the deceptions, try and figure it out, but I don't live my life like that all the time. I don't think anybody does; it's too hard. To a certain extent we all think we're savvy, we know what's going on, but I don't think we really do, and I don't think we wanna know!

"If it's a lyric that I finish, then I pretty much know what they're really about. But there are times when I've started songs and I've left them because I don't know what it's about, then years later I might come back to it and it might make sense to me then. When I'm about to start writing, often I'll go through a lot of old manuscripts just to get going and I'll come across something and I'll pick that up again. Maybe it's because I've got distance from it, because of things that have happened to me since then – then it starts to work again.

"Usually I know what they're about, I have a sense of it, but there may be other readings of it, and that often happens, too, where a few years later, I think, 'So that song was really about that. How did I miss that?' My perspective on it will often change and that's neat, too. The band don't really want to know what they're about – Pete loves the musical side of it, Margo is pretty involved. Al won't ask, but I think he listens hard to them and appreciates them, which is important. Margo does ask if she's having trouble finding a way to approach a lyric. I won't tell her, but if she's having real problems I might help her out a little. It's a weird thing to sit down and say, 'This is about ...'"

There's no getting away from the fact that *One Soul Now* is a difficult record to take in, both musically and lyrically, something Mike readily accepts. "*One Soul Now* was like *Open*, only more so. It's not an easy one to get first time around, but the more you listen, hopefully the more you get from it. We made a lot of changes on that record – we did a lot of work on the songs in the studio, because we were recording in our own space by then. A lot of the records went through many versions, different feels, grooves; we didn't put a deadline on when it was going to be finished, we just wanted to do it to the point we were ready. I guess it is like a little like *Pale Sun* – it is a dense record. It's a scattered record; there's no focus, because the songs were taken from lots of different writing periods. Even the making of it was unfocused: we did some songs off the floor, we did some individually, it was my first record completely engineering, so that was something I concentrated on. It was a weird record to make. I don't really have a sense of it. Sometimes records go off on their own. They sort of happen – you don't really force them in any direction, they happen. That's not necessarily a bad thing, but you step back afterwards and think, 'That was weird! That wasn't supposed to end up there!'

"I guess the timing of it, that made it look a little out of step, too. It didn't have those kind of recurring characters and situations we've had in other records. I've always written about me and those around me, or where I am. *Black Eyed Man*, a lot is about meeting my wife and dealing with that relationship. All those characters are intertwined. *Pale Sun* isn't so romantic, because reality creeps in – it's not as storybook, it's more Carver-esque, I guess. It keeps on going. *Miles* sees the idea of family and children start coming in. *Open* is a very dark album about middle age, really, and those sorts of questions. *One Soul Now* is a confusing record to me. It doesn't hang together thematically or lyrically; there are elements there of what you get in *At the End of Paths Taken*, which is the other side of middle age, of realizing where you are. In the sense that those characters keep turning up, it's because they're always there, always evolving, lives are changing and new things happen. It wasn't so much that way on *One Soul Now*.

"The other intention of that record was to learn how to make records in our studio, so I was more focused on that almost, and that was fine, that was one of the reasons for gathering these songs together, playing them and trying different ways of catching them. So it was never a body of songs in that way, it was a little bit of an experiment and the songs were fodder for that. Maybe it seems a strange record, because that's not really the way we do things these days. Records do tend to have a theme to them with us, where that one doesn't. As songs, I really like a lot of them and a lot will be in the repertoire, but it is a collection of individual songs from different periods – they don't have that focus which people maybe expect from us."

It was, nevertheless, a repetition of an enduring Junkies pattern, where they appear to have put together a trilogy of albums and then broken them up with something looser before embarking on another one. *Pale Sun, Crescent Moon* was of that mould, and so, too, was *One Soul Now*. "That's true. There tend to be bridging albums, and *One Soul Now* was definitely that way. And a lot of songs I wrote for that one didn't actually get on it, things like 'Cold Evening Wind', 'Ikea Parking Lot', 'Morning Cried', a couple more which were specifically done for the record but which we didn't use. Instead, it was mainly songs we brought back, things maybe that weren't finished or hadn't worked out, things we changed around. I did know that I somehow wanted to get all these songs out there and that just seemed the point at which to do it. Maybe we did that job better when we put out the extra disc in the *Notes Falling Slow* box rather than as the 'new album'.

"Saying that, looking back, *One Soul Now* was kind of an introduction to *At the End of Paths Taken*. Really, I should have continued writing, but I couldn't have written *Paths* at that point. *One Soul Now* was something we had to do to get to that one in every sense, as songs, performances, in the studio. It's almost like those songs should have been tagged onto something else. I try not to feel regrets for stuff we've done, because you do it with the best intentions, and at the time I thought it was a valid record. But now, I don't know! The songs are valid, but as a piece, I don't know.

"It's probably the perfect download album, a project of individual songs, some reworked, some new. That would have worked. To me, *Paths* is a real album, which *One Soul Now* isn't in the same way.

"Even *Pale Sun* doesn't have the feel that *One Soul Now* does. That's a pretty focused record, written very quickly, and again, a lot of the songs are in the repertoire still, because they've lasted. I do like *One Soul Now* a lot, but I would like to rerecord it maybe, approach the actual recording of it from a different angle. Maybe we'll do that one day: go back and revisit some things. That would be kind of cool ..."

369

CHAPTER 20

Things wrought by prayer

Most of the time, life comes at you from nowhere. However tightly you plan, however hard you strive to keep control, the unexpected always gets you. For good, for bad, for mundane, mostly, it throws its grenades at you from out of a clear-blue sky.

When those two planes came out of just such a clear blue sky to bring the World Trade Center buildings crumbling to the ground on 11 September 2001, the world, and our responses to it, changed inside half a day, half an hour. We still live in those changed times, and we still struggle to make sense of what we have found in the rubble.

It's the job of the artist, the songwriter, to help us do that, or, if that proves beyond reach, to show we are not alone in our confusion, our terror, our incomprehension, because they're just as lost as the rest of us. But, in picking through the debris and the aftermath, maybe some sense will emerge.

The aftermath of 9/11 gave us the "war on terror", the 2001 attacks on Afghanistan, the invasion of Iraq in March 2003, the seemingly never-ending wars waged in all our names, even when apparently half the population and more of most nations were against them, or at best undecided. Marches against the wars, peace groups and movements began to spring up across the globe. Words, books, songs began to be written. Some of them in Canada.

"When we were working on *One Soul Now*, we had 'December Skies', which was a statement and we left it off the record because it kinda clouded the personal issue," recalls Mike. "It was too broad, too galvanizing a song, but I wanted to use it somehow, because I thought it was relevant and important to get it out there. More and more we wanted to make some kind of statement about the way things were. With the small platform I have, I felt a responsibility to use it. I think, as we've got older, we're more interested in either making statements through the records, in playing benefits for the homeless and that kind of thing. It all comes back to us having kids – feeling a greater sense of responsibility for the world, being less focused on yourself.

"Being a musician or an artist of any kind is a very self-centred thing – you're constantly thinking about projecting your ideas – so with kids, you suddenly realize you can use that sense of self to give things back, so it has become more a part of what we do; I've become more conscious of it in our writing. I don't want it to turn into blatant propaganda, or for us to be a band that only does political stuff, because that's not what we are, we have a wider focus than that. And when we do cover that area, I like to be more subtle about it and I think we achieved that with *Early 21st Century Blues*. It's a pretty subtle record, because we come at it from many angles, whether it be veterans, loss, and you can take those songs as just songs, too.

"Ahead of recording, we were talking about how we could do that, what we'd put it with. We had 'This World Dreams Of', which was a song we never got a good version of on the previous record; we'd got 'Isn't It a Pity' already – and, from somewhere, we had this idea of using those as a jumping-off point for making an album on that kind of theme. Make it small, use mostly other people's words, which makes an interesting angle and, initially, just release it through the website, though subsequently we put it out wider than that.

"We really downplayed the album. There was no big promo tour, we didn't do press or radio very much – Margo and I would normally spend two months doing that, flying everywhere before we even get on the road. It was the kind of record I'd like to see bubble, for people just to find it, without it being pushed at them. Sometimes people are more willing to spend time on a record if they've found it for themselves, if they discovered it, rather than reading all about it and then buying it. If they hear about it, they come to it with expectations and, if those aren't immediately met, they leave it quickly because it doesn't match what they thought. It became a subtle record, very much about hope. All the songs are about violence, war, loss, but ultimately they're about people writing about it, trying to do something about it, discussing these things, bringing them into the open to talk about them. That's the positive element. All you can do is get people thinking about the issues."

As Mike notes, writing is at once both a selfless and a selfish act, putting thoughts out there for others to receive and process while simultaneously exorcizing, purging, releasing. The Junkies' online diary offered another outlet, and close observers of it would not have been surprised at the direction taken on *Early 21st Century Blues*. Take this extract from 8 October 2003:

"So do we now start referring to this as the 'Post-Schwarzenegger World'? You know what I mean, we start saying things like, 'in the wake of Schwarzenegger, rule number one for all public discourse will be Inanity'. I'm at a loss. I know that the democratic process is fucked up and that money is usually the order of the day when it comes to getting elected in the US of A, but you Californians just elected a man because you like the characters he plays in the movies, and don't try and pretend that you didn't. All of the polls indicate that most people felt that he didn't address the issues in his campaign, but they thought that he showed tremendous leadership skills and that is why they voted for him. How exactly does one show leadership skills in a two-month campaign where nothing of substance is talked about? It leads me to conclude that Arnold showed great leadership skills in his movies and that seems to be good enough for the populace. Tell me that he would have got ten votes if he wasn't a movie star: the same looks, the same life story, the same money spent, the same campaign, but he owned a highly successful restaurant chain instead of being one of the biggest movie stars in the world. Do you honestly think he would have been elected? I know that the people of California are pissed off at their government, and they wanted to send a message, but good God people, the message you just sent to the rest of the world has us all shaking our heads in disbelief and a little bit scared. You just put a man in charge of an economy that is larger than most countries' economies, because he's good at destroying killer androids sent from the future. My question for discussion today, class, is: can the rest of the world's democratic institutions survive if the United States continues its headstrong march towards a system best described as a 'mock-ocracy'?"

Then again, getting an action movie star elected is now looking like the good old days.

Then there's this from 7 November 2004, just after the world awoke to find that John Kerry wasn't going to be president after all.

"I can't finish off this round of the tour diary without touching on last Tuesday's USA election results. Politics has swirled around us throughout this entire tour. I was pretty dismayed at the outcome, like most out-of-touch-big-city-elites and like most of the democratic world outside of the US (except, apparently, for Russia and Israel). Analysis of the election results will, no doubt, continue for months and the long-term effects (positive and/or negative) that it will have on the internal life of the US and on the rest of us outside of the US borders will be felt for years. But I have come to the realization that fretting about it will only give me sleepless nights and a bad stomach. So I have decided to be optimistic about the future and to search for the silver lining. I have come to the conclusion that the world that my children will come of age in will be a better and brighter place: 1) if God does indeed exist; 2) if this God's temperament is more like the loving, just God of the New Testament rather than the vengeful, blood-thirsty God of the Old Testament or the psychopathic, hate-filled God of Osama and his pals and; 3) if George W. is indeed getting his marching orders directly from this loving, just God. If these three things are true, then we should all be OK. I'm not quite sure what to think if any one of the three is false. In the meantime, if I were you, I would hedge my bets: take care of yourself and your family and look after your neighbour (no matter who they voted for). We will be back in touch in 2005, with a new tour and some new music. Until then, peace, peace, peace."

The response that they would make in 2005 seemed a deliberate move to counter the apathy that was swirling around us all, to avoid being swallowed up by it and to make it clear that there was another path. More than thirty years before, John and Yoko had set up billboards saying "War is over (if you want it)". If the same were still true in 2005, if we really lived in true democracies where governments have to respond to us, did we want it and, if we did, could anyone be bothered to make the effort to ask for it?

"Apathy is everywhere and that's one of the things that makes me feel more responsible, that there is a need to make a statement, because you do feel people aren't paying attention," agrees Mike. "There's so much going on, there's so much you should be looking at and paying attention to, come on! But we were in the States through the 2004 election and I guess people aren't that bothered. I'm not that cynical, but I guess people feel the forces at play are so huge, it's so hard to move them, they just can't see how they can do anything. It's harder and harder to effect change because the engines are so enormous, the momentum is so powerful, so much power is concentrated in so few hands, more and more and more.

"I'm not sure what happened exactly, why musically nobody has really taken on a political attitude really since Live Aid and the support there was for organizations like Greenpeace in the late 1980s. On those very large levels like that, people have become more cynical, though I guess Live 8 was a step away from that, though again what has there been since then? I think music still makes a difference on a personal level and I think that any change that any art brings comes from a one-on-one basis, and then you get a groundswell from that. Maybe that huge social level, those times have changed, have gone, but I still think it's influential on a personal scale underneath.

"I think that is so lost now, that feeling of the 1960s. I think people just feel they can't do anything now. At the end of 2002, when we were getting ready for the war, there were a lot of protests and that was amazing. Millions of people were on the streets, it was so huge, they were enormous demonstrations. And they had no effect. It was almost part of the process – we protest, you do what you want. That was the feeling, that it had been absorbed into the equation, and I guess that disheartened a lot of people. The frightening thing is they're right – you probably can't do anything. But, to me, you don't stop talking about it.

"And people are running scared, too. Back when the Dixie Chicks said their piece about how ashamed they were of Bush, the reaction was pretty scary – the idea that you're not allowed to say things like that in a country that talks about freedom of speech all the time?! That you get taken off radio? That was weird. I guess people with careers see that and get scared. Unless you're known as somebody who speaks out, like Neil Young, and then it's OK."

Jeff Bird adds, "*Early 21st Century Blues* was a very political statement, far more than anything else the band had done. It's interesting going through America; you see how things change. We were here on 9/11, we've watched how it's changed to the point where life is very different – our tour manager had the FBI at his house in 2005 because he deposited $9,000 in cash, and they wanted to know where it had come from! There's nothing like that happening in Canada, so when you do see it up close, it knocks you over. We were down there when they went to war in Iraq the first time, too, in 1990, so to see them repeat it, you just think, 'What the hell are they doing?'

"You see an apathy among people down there, you want more of them to pay some attention to what's going on. That's very frightening and I think that's what we saw in 2004, when the election was going on while we were there, and which inspired *Early 21st Century Blues*. Really, the country was divided on Bush, but there's a huge population that was completely disenfranchised: 'Which rich, white bastard do we vote for this time?' Why bother? But that's not unique to America, it's similar in Canada: voter turnout is low. Just in my little town, we had a mayor who was progressive, trying to make things better for everybody, so consequently she wasn't as sympathetic to developers as the mayor who beat her in the last election. But only thirty-three per cent of the voters turned out! In Canada, too, things are pretty nice, so people don't get that riled up about anything, because their needs are met. They're pretty well looked after and, when they do get riled, it's usually about something stupid!"

Musically, there was something of the guerrilla approach to the record that had characterized an earlier school of record making that was just as political in its outlook. John Timmins, back in the fold for both record and tour, certainly saw some similarities.

"The record had that sense of *Sometime in New York City* [John Lennon and Yoko Ono], about having something to say about the world, that you can't sit around and wait to say them, that you need to get it out there. It is a powerful statement, a powerful reaction, delivered in the only way that we know how – with music. We all really felt the temper of the times, very frustrating, very stressful, so it's not surprising that, at that time, that record should come out. People don't make protest records any longer, nor sustained protests of any kind in the numbers we saw against Vietnam, for example.

"One of the biggest concerns I have – and this may be a trait of our family temperament – is the anaesthetized behaviour of people around us. Personally, that's always really bothered me just in day-to-day life, the sleepwalking way that people go through every day. But, if there was ever a moment where we were all asleep at the wheel, it's these last few years. There is so much that is evidently going on, somehow, for some reason, and you have to conclude that we're not doing anything about it because we're asleep. That really gets Mike's goat and he's fascinated by it. There are so few political choices that you can make. It's a systemic global problem: that there are so few differences between the political parties now and we've allowed it to happen. We've allowed ourselves to end up with a system that has been co-opted by a certain world view. If there was ever a time to take back control of the wheel, it's now.

"I compare it to my knowledge of the 1960s, and I'd say we're in a worse situation now than we were then. Democracy has to get up and fight back, because it's been knocked down too often by this neo-conservative agenda that is rampant throughout the world. Regardless of whatever government stripe they wear, everyone in power these days seems to have that same view.

"But the Junkies are not saying, 'Do this, do that', as some artists might. The music is saying 'Wake up.' It's trusting the audience, it's saying that you can figure it out for yourself if you'll make the effort. 'I don't need to tell you what to do. I don't need to figure it out for you.' It's calling on people to do their thing, because they believe in it. If you do what you believe in, you'll probably do the right thing. It's music that's addressed to the human soul. There's nothing party political about the way the music is being presented, about the choice of songs, and yet it goes right to the heart of what drives politics, to the heart of the issue. That's their gift, that's what the Junkies do well: they go right to the heart, in their music, their personal lives. It takes a lot of soul-searching to achieve that honesty. We can all become so honest that you're almost immoral, too honest for your own good, too self-appointed as the holder of truth, but I don't believe that struggle exists in an overt way for them, at least. They hold that lightly."

'This World Dreams Of', one of the two songs that kicked off the project, has tended to be overshadowed by the other, 'December Skies', but it sits in an interesting place in the canon, merging the sparseness of the earliest recordings with the altogether more mature, confident delivery of later-period Junkies. Lyrically, too, it cuts to the heart of the mutual mistrust that has grown up between the Middle

East and the West in recent decades, something built on centuries of misunderstandings of one another's cultures, misunderstandings oft seized upon by those in power for their own ends: "Vengeance has been tasted, hatred cultivated, it's an old game."

It's a sentiment that Pete picks up on. "The people in the Middle East, they've lived on top of the world's most important resource of the last 100 years, the main supply of it, and still most of them have nothing. Then we go and invade their country and try to kill them on their own soil. It's no wonder they're raising the next generation to use guns. What else would they do? Revenge becomes one of the reasons to live, it's your release. The sad thing is, they've run out of options.

"On top of that, you can understand them being pissed at us in the West, especially in North America. We have our Macy's Thanksgiving Day parades and our consumerism, and all for what? The excess is just disgusting – we deserve to drown in our own sewage, because we're producing it, man. Do you really need 1,000 choices of soup or bagel? You go to a deli and you just want a sandwich. But what kind of bread? Do you want this on it, or that? Extra cheese? What kind of cheese? Do you want to get something to go with that? Dressing? Stop, please! I just want a toastie! It's hard not to buy into it when it's surrounding you. You're out on the street with the kids: 'Can I have this?' 'Can I have that?' No, no, no ...!"

It was 'December Skies' that courted the most controversy, though, not least in the USA during the pointedly titled 'United States of Canada Blue States' tour in June 2005. Playing in Annapolis, that bastion of the US Navy, the line "Time to kill our children and sing about it", caused a restlessness in the audience, just as the decision to play 'No More', a song about slavery that they'd played at their very first show in 1985, made a few waves. "I like that!" enthuses Mike. "It's a very good thing. I have arguments very often about stuff like that, and my attitude is 'Look, we're discussing it now. If nothing else, that's positive. We're talking about how something made you feel; how can that be anything but positive?' If they're uncomfortable with it, they're being forced to think, and people don't do that enough. We let things go too easily. Even if you don't agree with the sentiment, don't understand it, to be moved enough to talk about it is what we're about. That's right down to the basics of making music.

"It's really about our attitude to war, the way we glorify it, make it seem a noble calling in some way. We celebrate the fighting, the glorious dead, and we make it seem that death on the battlefield is something to aspire to. If we concentrated on the human cost of those deaths, the lives that are broken by it, maybe we wouldn't rush to war so easily."

True to so much of the most thought-provoking music, it's a song that means different things to different people, albeit that its roots obviously lie in bodies falling through 11 September's skies, as well as Timothy Findley's book *The Wars*. According to Alan Anton, "It's a bold statement – people aren't used to that any more. A lot of people don't get the idea, 'What do you mean, kill your children and sing about it?' Mike gets tagged with trying to explain it and he's pretty diplomatic about it, but my version is from the way I remember things after 9/11, the day after, when the senators and congressmen and women gathered on the steps of the Capitol Building and sang 'God Bless America'. That's my image of it – that was the first song that led to the killing of everybody that followed. That's what they do: they sing about it. When you are about to go to war, there's a lot of patriotic songs about that are supposed to make it OK."

'December Skies' is a song that takes its responsibilities seriously and which offers solace to those most in need – including, ironically, US soldiers fighting in Iraq, who have written to the band in numbers to thank them for the music they listen to at the toughest of times. Those soldiers have become the forgotten people in the political elite's determination to desensitize us to their machinations, a project that seems to be working. It's as if we think all the battles were won after the Civil Rights struggle, Vietnam, Rock Against Racism and the like. We've fallen asleep in our post-Cold War material comforts. But racism? Still there. Civil rights issues? Still there. Vietnam? Moved to Iraq, but it's still there. The need for dissent? Still there, more than ever. It's not a song about killing our children, but about saving them and thousands like them. It's a reminder that war really is over – if *you* want it.

That's why, though Margo found it a hard lyric to sing, she knew she had to work it through. "As a mom, whatever the context, it's still a very shocking line. I struggled with it for a time before I found a way into it, but that's OK, that's my job. It was important that I did sing it because I'm very supportive of what Michael is writing about.

He's expressing the way that we all feel in the band: that there have to be alternatives to war and that we should all do more to make our voices heard."

Mike understands that reticence, given he has the luxury of greater anonymity than his sister. "Margo was a little unsure – she doesn't like overt political statements, probably because she is more the face of it, she has to take it out there – but I think she became more comfortable as we did it. Al was very excited by it and, once it was done and we took it out on the road, I think we were all pleased with the album and felt it was something worth doing."

At a time when iTunes was starting to take over the musical world, putting out an album that carried a coherent statement was very much out of step, as Alan admits. "The album concept is pretty much over for the mainstream, the mentality of an album having an arc from start to finish, because people are editing in iTunes now. I even do that myself – I put my Pearl Jam records in, and I love their quiet stuff but not the hard-rocking things so much, so I got all the quiet stuff together in a playlist and it's great.

"Bands used to think in terms of side A and side B, so they were almost making two different albums at one time, and there's a whole artistry to that, I loved that. That's all gone. The fact that CDs are so long isn't always good, either, because suddenly people were putting out sixty- or seventy-minute records because they think they have to fill it up, where it used to be forty minutes. It's not more value for money, because you just get a lot of filler now. *Early 21st Century Blues* is sixty minutes and, by the time I got to the end of it, listening to the master, I'd forgotten what was on there! 'How did that go again?' Because you don't have a break to get up and turn it over, it's a lot to take in in one listen.

"Because of the length of the record, we had a big discussion about whether or not we should put 'Handouts in the Rain' on there – because it's so long, for one thing – but I thought it would be a shame to lose that lyric from the concept of the album. Such a great lyric, the most relevant one, really."

Including it was the right choice because, ignoring its sentiment for a second, it's also a beautiful performance: rolling drums and guitar cascading forwards, creating a simple, irresistible momentum, topped off by a genuinely gorgeous vocal from Margo, the moment the voice comes in for the first time just heart-stopping, the beauty of the music a vivid counterpoint to the righteous anger of Richie Havens' song. The lyric asks questions of us, of who and what we are, of what we teach the next generation, of whether we can ever call ourselves civilized in a world where we own ninety-eight pairs of shoes and three cars, yet a billion people go hungry every day, some of them within our own supposedly advanced nations.

If the human race lives long enough to write history books 500 years hence, if our descendants have approached something like genuinely enlightened humanity, they will look back on us with no greater respect than we accord our forefathers from the dark ages, or those more recent who thought that owning slaves was reasonable behaviour. Perhaps they'll judge us more harshly yet, for we are the generations who have created extraordinary technological miracles and yet use that knowledge to kill people more efficiently rather than to feed the starving. 'Handouts in the Rain', like much of the rest of the record, comes from a place of confusion, of wearied anger, from bewilderment at the choices we make, that we allow to be made in our name. But, while the record bubbles with anger, while it's a contemplation of loss, of war, greed, at its core it is a hugely humane album, something signified by the peal of laughter with which it opens. It's a warm, spontaneous moment, captured without any artifice, as Mike recalls.

"We were in the studio, a late session, we were pretty tired, Al was supposed to start us up on 'No More', and I asked him to play it as slow as he possibly could, which is pretty dangerous, because Al can play real slow! So he was getting into a kind of slow trance and Margo said that watching him get ready was like watching him melt! That was what cracked her up. And then it just seemed a nice way to open the record – it set the tone, a very human sound, human contact. This is a record about people."

Opening with Dylan's 'License to Kill' after that laughter is something of a mission statement, musing on the world we created and mismanaged, a song suggested by another longtime Junkies friend who features on the record, Jaro Czerwinec. "*Early 21st Century Blues* is fantastic and I'd like to do more with them in that style, back to their roots, that spacey, slow, bluesy style. Nice that they found 'License to Kill' in the end, I played it for them in 2004, but couldn't remember the title of it, but at least they got it in the end. That's a beauty – who the hell can beat Bob Dylan lyrically? I would love to hear the combination of sounds that we had on *Trinity Session* again, that's for sure, because I think it stirs up people's inner feelings, it touches earth, touches base. Technology has advanced to a point where it overwhelms everything – we're being eaten alive by our own technology. Your brain gets overloaded by so much information."

The possible list of songs was pretty overloaded, too, and plenty of options fell by the wayside, according to Alan. "We recorded a version of 'Us and Them' by Pink Floyd, that was my choice, and I guess there's a similar kind of floaty quality in what we do. The original of that song is really weird – the long sax solo which I hate, it's so cheesy, then it just stops dead at the end. I listened to *Dark Side of the Moon* again recently and it's an interesting piece, and I guess it has a life of its own now, which it never had when it came out because of how successful it became. I prefer *Wish You Were Here*. We left 'Us and Them' off it, because the record was so long. 'Isn't It a Pity' is sort of that song: we sort of Pink Floyd-ed that song, that was our idea when we played it. We left off 'Cortez the Killer', too, another one I suggested." If Pete had had his way, the record would have been more radical still. "I said we should put out a songbook for kids instead. Coulda made millions! I wanted 'Sweet Emotion' by Aerosmith, but I've been saying that for years!"

For all those thwarted ambitions, making *Early 21st Century Blues* was a real pleasure for the Junkies' drummer. "That is one of my most favourite recordings, because we were all in the Clubhouse, elbow to elbow, mucking about. Making records and especially the mixing is a very tricky thing. I still prefer rough mixes off the floor; I never feel the 'proper' mix has the same feel to it as a rough mix. The fact that we're now working such a lot in the Clubhouse and now The Hangar is going back towards those early days and I like that. And that's also part of the new way of being a rock band that a lot of people are getting into. Building your own studio, saving money, getting away from the companies, not blowing your recording budget on whisky and women. Studios are the biggest ripoff in the world – just for a room they'll charge hundreds of dollars an hour. That's a bad situation to be in, because the best music comes when you're relaxed and comfortable, so if you're watching the clock and it has dollar signs on it, that's not great. You lose the first hour just showing up!"

I watched Mike, Alan and Pete working on the album for a few hours in the Clubhouse and it was genuinely eye-opening, even though they were just going through playbacks. There was a genuine democracy going on there – to the point where I got asked for my opinion – and the quality of listening they brought to it was really interesting to watch, if that makes sense. Pete was sat at the back, behind the drums, and insisted on using headphones with his eyes shut and his hands over his face to block everything out, listening ferociously.

"I find, if you close your eyes, you hear it better. Even if we're playing a show, if things are going wrong, I'll close my eyes and try to figure it out and find a way back from there. But how can you make music if you don't listen? The quality control just isn't there. With a painting, I'll work on it, work on it, work on it, until I fool my own eye and, once I can do that, then I figure I can fool somebody else's, too – not in a bad way but the perspective is right or whatever. Music is the same. If it's good, it's good, but if it's shit, it's shit. You can't get away from that. But people just let it go."

As well as having something to say about the world in 2005, the album was in part motivated by that indie band ethic that propels the Junkies in the post-Geffen world, as Pete points out. "I never dealt with the industry at all, so in that sense leaving Geffen didn't make so much difference. For Mike it did, because he had to deal with that, he likes control, and now he's the manager, the record company, so I guess he's happy with that freedom even though it means there's more work. I'm not gonna question his decisions, because this is Mike's church. We talk about stuff, sure – I do wonder if maybe we should get a manager to go out there and do that schmoozing. Mike does not schmooze. That's fine, I hate schmoozing. But in this business, you need it, I think, even in this day and age, just to get your foot in the door. It's all word of mouth. With lawyers and agents it's not about music, it's about who you had a drink with last night; there's a lot of that. It's gross, but it's the game you have to play and Mike doesn't do that. I like that he doesn't. But maybe there's a role to be filled that would help us. But then you gotta put up with a schmoozer coming in and talking to you! Maybe we could rent one once in a while! You do need somebody at the party repeating your name; otherwise, they don't think about you. The media, the radio, is so closed these days that it is very difficult to get your music out there in front of people.

"We appreciate that, nowadays, we have to have a consistent trickle of things going on to keep the keep fans coming back to it. And that's our source of income – the records, the website and the touring – so we know we need to keep ourselves in people's minds. But we love to play, so that's not hard. We have more freedom now: you can do what you want when you're ready to do it. It's nice to have that voice, especially when you have something to say like with that record. I love the way it was recorded, that it was done real fast to make a point. It's like some of the old Elvis Costello records. *My Aim Is True*, they learned all the songs that day, then went and recorded them, a flying-by-the-seat-of-your-pants type of thing and that's where you get that edge."

Mike concedes the business imperative did have an influence on getting *Early 21st Century Blues* out there so quickly. "A record like that does buy time. We have to maintain some presence in the marketplace and to have new things for our fans to check out. It's hard to come off the road and then go straight into writing, because I'm burned out, I don't have the energy or the headspace to do it. So we're always looking to try to bridge the gap between our records with something. Between *Open* and *One Soul Now* we put out the DVD – that keeps the interest levels up, gets us a little money, gives us an excuse to go and do a little more touring to get a mention in the press and maintain the profile. You have to keep yourself current. But those sorts of records are fun, because there's no pressure, no expectation, but they're still artistically valid things to do.

"I was very happy with how the whole *Early 21st Century Blues* thing worked out. It turned out to be something a whole lot bigger than we imagined, initially. It was a nice project. The record was quick and easy: we recorded it within two weeks; from first note going to tape to being on sale on our website was ten weeks, which was phenomenal. It was initially just a website thing, but Rounder liked it, Cooking Vinyl wanted to put it out, so we slowly put it out there after a few months. We didn't intend to tour it much, but we had that summer tour back in 2005 and it grew and grew and it was nice, it wasn't strenuous, but thirty-five, thirty-six shows over two or three months, we did some weird places, we went to Alaska, it was fun. It sold decently considering we never did any concentrated touring or promotion, didn't play Canada, didn't get to Europe, where it sold well, so it ended up a nice, self-contained project, a buffer between *One Soul Now* and *At the End of Paths Taken*."

Even the artwork gave the album a different slant, another positive created out of a potential problem, according to Mike. "Because we did it so quickly, we didn't even have the artwork until after we finished recording. David Houghton was away, and my wife just suggested we use the painting my daughter had done a few years before – she'd done it at school right after the invasion of Iraq, and I'd kept it. It was perfect; it made it a complete statement."

For the first time since *Whites Off Earth Now!!*, that statement was made, for the most part, through the words of others.

Though cover versions remain an important element of the Junkies' work, especially onstage, Mike's writing has come to dominate the recorded version of the band, a responsibility he's well aware of, especially as those records have changed in character, rounded statements that offer no room for covers, as he admits. "They have become very conceptual lyrically, so it is harder to find a cover that fits in. Because we're a band, it's taken to be our statement, so I try to be sensitive enough to everybody's viewpoints that I'm not saying things that someone in the band would violently disagree with. I'm not saying I speak for everybody, but I'm representative of their basic philosophies. We know each other so well, we've lived together so long, I think I know enough to know that's true. If I was going to do something that stepped outside that, then we'd definitely sit and talk about it. I run the stuff by them and see if they're happy. Everybody gets to look at stuff like press releases, liner notes, just to see if everything sits OK – I don't just throw stuff out there without checking. But, if I'm making a statement like *Open, One Soul Now* or *At the End of Paths Taken*, I try to make sure that it is reflective of the whole band, because those records are very lyric-driven.

"There is a pressure to it and there are times when I look at bands who have a couple of writers, and I think, 'God, that would be so great! I'd only have to write five or six songs!' But I love songwriting – I like the responsibility, I love getting away to write, just sitting by myself and working away, though it's great that Al has started getting more involved in it, too, over the last few records. I like that the band will allow me to have an album of ten songs because that becomes a complete statement. Obviously, the music has its impact and Margo plays a huge part in delivering the words, but the lyrics are one complete statement and I like being able to put that out. This is me, I wrote this, this is what

I'm thinking. I'm really proud of that; it feels like an accomplishment when the record is finally ready."

But, as great interpreters of other people's work, Cowboy Junkies ensured *Early 21st Century Blues* was just as cohesive. It was also, perhaps, a sign of Mike's gathering self-belief. After all, putting two of your own brand-new songs up against cherry-picked material from the best songwriters of all time, measuring your work against that which you've selected from one million songs and 1,000 songwriters, might be seen as a little daunting.

"I don't know if I see that as a challenge," said Mike. "We don't think in those terms – competing with somebody, trying to compare ourselves. It's a continuum. I've always viewed music as this person feeding the next person, then the next, and it just goes on down the years. In rock music, that doesn't happen so much, unfortunately. It's very much our generation and their generation. But in jazz, blues, country, there's a real sense of feeding everybody. You borrow and you cover, you take examples and experiences from other people and you blend it into your own work. We've always felt that's what we're doing. Maybe we'll cover something or do a Neil Young-type of song of our own – it's not really a sense of competition. I like to think we fit in somewhere, but *where* isn't really important; it's just becoming part of the continuum is what it's about. If anything, if we've got a Neil Young song on a record, I always feel the others never will match up, so why worry!? There are people who have inspired me so greatly that, from my own perspective, I'd never compare myself with them because I don't feel I could match up to Springsteen or Coltrane, whoever, because they've touched me so deeply. I just want to use the input they've given me to give that to somebody else.

"That's part of the spirit of that record in a wider sense – that on a wider scale we are part of a continuum of life – and that sense only increases when you have kids. The feeling we had when we made that record was that, all of us, we need to come together as people, we need to work for change together. That was why we had 'One' as the last song on the album and why we ended our live show with it on that tour. I'm not a huge U2 fan, but the line 'We've got to carry each other, One' pretty much summed up the record."

The irony is that, in asking people to come together, in questioning the war in Afghanistan and Iraq and especially America's role in it, the band created fractures in what is, after all, its core audience, according to Jason Lent. "It's interesting that they should make such a statement with *Early 21st Century Blues*, given that America is their biggest market, because I guess they could alienate some fans with that. I know their message board had a lot of talk about that, and there are people on there who were pro-George Bush, very conservative, though a lot of them disappeared around the time of the 2004 election. As Michael and the band have become more open about politics, some of the regulars have disappeared."

You can't help but wonder if that's just a microcosm of the rest of the world, that we're all so entrenched in our positions that we can't hear what the other side is saying – if we could care less, anyway. How many other artists made a big play of releasing anti-war records in the wake of the war on terror? Probably the most blatant was Neil Young and 'Living with War'. Was that a reawakening, or was it just the same old suspects saying the same old thing? All these years later, looks like the latter.

NUNC SCIS TE IN TERRA
INCOGNITO ESSE

I never met William Burroughs, and it's too late to rectify that now, but that's an omission somewhat mitigated by having spent two hours in a hotel room with Jaro Czerwinec. That pretty much equates to meeting the famed novelist – if he'd been on speed at the time.

Jaro's conversation seems to come from the cut-up method, full of jumps, right angles, dislocated thoughts that tumble and pile one on top of the other to make some kind of fractured psychedelic sense. He is the kind of man who quite probably eats his lunch naked. He certainly inhabits his own universe, one that crackles along at a pace often at odds with the nature of the music he makes and the sounds and moods he conjures from that accordion. It's a yin and yang balance that is probably essential to saving him from keeling over and collapsing under the self-imposed strain that comes from simply being Jaro.

"I like songs that come from the heart. I'm an accordion player, I play heart music. People can relate to that. I've come across songwriters who can create fantastic images, but so what? Tell me something I don't know. If I want to go for a cinematic ride in my mind, it can be useful, it's a kind of craftsmanship, that's another thing, so I don't want to flush it down the toilet. But I call that mental music.

"I'm not versed in jazz because I like melodious, harmonic things – it calms me down, it energizes me, though I can see what an hour or two of discordant jazz can do for you. It's like therapy, it's purifying. But I'd rather experience something, then write about it and transfer it to other people so they can relate to it. We're all the same, just in different bodies. We all think we're running the show, but we're only visiting; we don't know when the axe is going to fall and how it's going to fall. That's what keeps it real. Otherwise, it would be Disneyland!"

It's testimony to the scale of Jaro's ability and the force of his personality that someone who has played comparatively sparingly on the Junkies' catalogue is still so closely associated with them, seen as producing one of their signature sounds.

Naturally, he has his own view on just how inevitable it was that he should play on their breakthrough recording *The Trinity Session*. Bear with him. "Live recording is the way to go – it's a great way to do it, because you get a special feeling that you don't get if you play all the elements alone. It's energy, love and conviction coming together, and that can move mountains. Then, if you put an accordion with that, watch out!

"I got a cartoon once and it was in two pieces. All the people going up to heaven were getting harps, but all the people going down there, they were handing them accordions! That's what I'm having to deal with! My father was right that if I stayed with the accordion I would be OK. If it hadn't been for him, I would have killed that thing so many times! Who wants to watch Lawrence Welk when you're 17 and The Beatles are happening? But it's all OK now.

"When I was 13, I was singing in the Ukrainian choir in Sudbury – in the alto section, because my voice hadn't changed yet – and the first big road trip that I took with them was to Timmins, Ontario. I was hooked by that. Party on the bus, party, sing and dance in Timmins, party all the way back. What kind of life is that? Pretty good!"

I took advantage of Jaro pausing for breath to tell him that, when I first came across to meet the band in Toronto, the map that you get on the back of the plane seat suddenly flashed up Timmins, a town I didn't even know about at that stage.

"That's the things that happen – there are so many incidents of synchronicity which are totally phenomenal. This happens a lot; it's a recurring thing. These things happen all the time, but we don't notice. The grace of God is showering upon us all the time but we aren't aware of it. Our minds are in the physical world, and we don't see that everything is connected to everything. Then we're meeting to play music in church. The fact that the church is still there is amazing, because they were going to demolish it at one point but there was an outcry. In the middle of all that concrete, there's this little church which is pretty incredible. So I guess this trip with the Timmins family started a long way back for me, when I was 13!

"Music is communication and that's what's happening between the four of them. Which is why you're grateful to be invited onto that trip with them. It's like a dream to do that – it's something that would have been so far-fetched to me when I was playing waltzes, polkas and tangos at 17. Yet it manifested itself twenty years later. I played at the Fillmore, that was amazing. Immediately we played there, I got transported back to being 17 in Sudbury, reading the magazines about Haight-Ashbury, and then I play there. Be careful what you think, because you might get it. That's the way the mind is; the thought is a seed and then it goes out to make it reality."

Go back to those early records – *The Trinity Session* and especially *The Caution Horses* – and they are awash with Jaro's accordion, mingling and intertwining with the pedal steel of Kim Deschamps, indicative of the way in which the Junkies were always willing to put their ego to one side in service of the music.

Not that Jaro necessarily buys that interpretation. "This business is wholly about personal glorification! Ego! It's all to degrees and what you do with it. I love to hear that people like the way I play accordion, that I touched somebody, of course I do. I don't have to flaunt it, I don't have to make it obvious, but the whole thing is ego-driven. It has to be. Look at what I can do, I'm good at this. I have a real strong ego, so I know all about that.

"But they're a family, so that's different. And, at this age, to still be travelling around together, wow! They have beautiful personalities, it's a wonderful thing that they can still communicate so easily together, because even in families there are big squabbles and problems. But this is a very well-tempered family. What you gonna do: jump up and down because you're on TV or you sold a lot of records? It must give you a bit of a buzz, but you've seen it, done it and, if you like doing it, all you want to do is continue to do it in one form or another – that becomes the main thing."

Jaro – or, more specifically, the sound that his presence requires the Junkies to make – has become something of a problem child within the family. Unlike Jeff Bird, who brings a whole range of sounds and possibilities to the band through his virtuosity on a variety of instruments, that accordion imposes its own very particular boundaries on the music. To fans, it's a much-beloved part of what they do, something they seemingly can't get enough of, yet if the Junkies had continued to employ it extensively, their music would have calcified around that *Caution Horses* sound.

No bad thing in itself, but, as Jaro accepts, Mike's ambitions always had broader horizons than that. "The nature of the mind is to look for something new, and I think it's true that Mike's attitude is to immediately go away from what he did last time around, just so that he can make something new. But, to me, I ask the question, 'What got ya there in the first place? If it ain't broke, don't fix it!' It was that slow, quiet music and that's coming back again. It all goes in circles, cycles. The accordion sound is very distinctive – you can't get away from it, it's pretty obvious, and there aren't many accordion sounds in rock'n'roll, either. So I can understand that Michael might not want to use it all the time, because it automatically makes people think about the music in a certain way.

"The way Margo and the accordion sit perfectly together was one of the features of Cowboy Junkies music at that time, *Trinity Session* and *The Caution Horses*. What happens is that the accordion has more of a human quality than a lot of instruments. It sits on the heart area and it breathes. That's what we are. That's why the dynamics are so immediate – and I have been playing it over sixty freaking years now! The mind always wants to play lots of notes because that's its nature, but energetically speaking, after sixty years, in one note I will convey what I want to convey from heart to heart, energy to energy, and when you hook it up with a voice, well, you can't get any more personal than that, no more personal than a beautiful human voice like Margo Timmins has. So, when that's hooked up, people who know how to make that a living thing instead of just a sound, then you have something special. That's what Margo and I have, and when people hear it they love it.

"I love the style we have when we're together. I don't have to leap about the stage doing punk rock accordion – I couldn't do it now. This music just sits. At the time we did *Trinity Session*, the music had specific traits. First, Margo's voice, smooth, silky, sultry, from the heart; that's what people feel. Then you've got Michael, who writes. He's got so many songs, he has to carry around books with him to keep them all in. I was flabbergasted by it. Before we started out on the road in 2004, I had a nervous breakdown because he's got like fifty-eight tunes that he wants us to learn to take out there, to play from memory. I'm getting senile or something – I can't do it! Too many tunes, man. I was overwhelmed, but in the end it worked out really good, and people start asking where I've been these years, that I fit right in.

"The past has gone, the future is just something in the mind, all there is is the now. But try staying there any length of time! Music helps. When we play together, there is a certain magic. I understand Mike uses other players to experiment, to get other sounds that he has in mind, but you can't easily find magic like we have. That's not for sale, can't be bought – it just happens among people. It makes me melancholy in a way when I'm not playing with them, but I never give up hope. I think perhaps the next one we can do it again."

In spite of that hope, Jaro is pretty down-to-earth when it comes to the heavy demands that touring makes on the body. He's not a fan of that aspect of it all, forcing him into finding a series of practices to help him cope, as David Houghton remembers.

"Jaro was a mystery. He always roomed alone and, at one point, I suggested I might room with him. People shook their heads silently and pursed their lips. It was not encouraged. I never understood why, but it was clear that Jaro was a riddle. He spent his days alone and lived for those precious hours onstage. He had rituals that had to be fulfilled, like a single red rose on his microphone stand every night. Some crew member would have to drive all over every town we performed in, looking for a red rose."

Jaro admits, "Touring is very physically demanding: you have to have a strong nervous system, you have to be fit before you go out there. It's not a normal schedule, not a natural schedule, eating differently all the time, different places, different kinds of weather. Some places actually made me ill, like the Beacon Theater in New York City. It might be an icon, but the thing is rotting – you can smell it when you walk in. We started a tour there and I got sick the first day, so there was no place to go but up from there! Until we hit Toad's Place in New Haven. My God. The floors are sticky, the whole place is gungy, it's horrible. On top of that, I had this wicked migraine. I wasn't there; I had to drop a couple of Advil and I had to sit there. One of my worst gigs – I didn't want to be there. I faked playing it, there was no joy in it, but I was too sick to do anything else. It was so horrible. You go downstairs to the dressing rooms, there's mould, and you want me to eat there? Are you kidding?

"I have a really sensitive system, so eating different foods is a problem. I'm an aquaholic, thirty-five or forty years now on clean water out of glass bottles. On tour I have to drink plastic water; it screws me up. Water was clean – they put it in plastic and poison you with it. How stupid! So I have a very hard time of that. Three or four weeks of that, I'm dying to get back to the fridge to my gallon-glass jugs of pure water from an artesian well. It's crucial.

"The whole road thing is debilitating, because it's buses and hotel rooms, TV, travelling, trying to sleep, odd hours and waiting. As you get older, the body just can't handle it as much, although some musicians – B.B. King, for instance – that's what they did, forever. When you have a family on top of the tiredness, I can't even imagine how hard that is, because I'm a single guy.

"But you play for two hours and you forget all the troubles. If it wasn't enjoyable, who the hell would want to drive themselves through that? It's the music that drives you. And you have to keep doing it while you still have the vitality, because there's going to come a day when you can't do it any longer and all there is are memories."

Where Jaro is not a natural road warrior, in Jeff Bird Cowboy Junkies found themselves the perfect tourist, both in terms of what he offers musically and, just as crucially, what he brings with his personality and attitude – as Margo explains.

"Even people close to you, they think you go on tour, it's your little holiday, because you only have to work two hours a day onstage. It's not like that! That's the holiday part, those two hours. The rest of it is the work, the day, getting on that bus after the show, going to a hotel to get a shower, then getting back on the bus, sleeping in your bunk, waking up in another town in the morning and having to wait hours before you go and soundcheck. You get on there and, no matter how you feel, you have no space, it's noisy and crowded and your body hurts. That's where Jeff is great for us. Apart from being a great musician, he's been amazing for us, as far as giving us some sort of Zen balance or something. He's great to have on that bus."

Jeff's explanation of it is typically phlegmatic. Where, for Jaro, eating on the road is a daily crisis, for Jeff, it's just another opportunity to come across something different. "However hard you try, it is hard to eat healthily when you tour. But it has an attraction to it – you never know what's going to turn up. Here we two are, we found Dmitri's diner in Ridgefield, we've eaten well, we've talked. It's been good. That wouldn't have happened if we weren't on the road.

"It is a strange existence, especially travelling and sleeping. The first time Jaro slept in the bus, he got up and said, 'Somewhere last night, I lost my body!' I've had times where I've woken up only to find that, somehow in the night, I've gone 180 degrees and my head is at the wrong end of the bed, which is pretty weird!

"Having the right mindset is the key. Some people are just frustrated all the time, because they want it to be a certain way – and it never is. No expectations, and you'll be a far happier person! Walk in, say, 'What have we got here?' and deal with it. The world is how you want it to be – if you want it to be miserable and upsetting, it will be. You're always discovering something. The weird thing is, wherever I go, people ask me for directions, so I guess I look like I'm at home wherever I am!"

Jeff would have been the perfect person to have in mind when Defoe was working out *Robinson Crusoe*, although Bird's matter-of-fact approach to being shipwrecked would have sucked some of the drama out of the situation. But on a tour bus, where everybody is packed in whether they like it or not, or during a soundcheck when there are musical or technical problems to solve, having Jeff around has to be a godsend. He keeps a lid on the tension, doesn't make a drama out of things, just deals with what is presented to him, a lesson he brings to the Junkies experience from a former career.

"Although you're travelling and going to new places all the time, you're also living in this very closed, insular little world as well. You don't have much chance to get away from it or from the people, so you need to learn how to handle that. I used to work as a guide taking people canoeing, and a lot of people came as a single adult – often they grew up camping or canoeing and, after they married, their partner wasn't interested in that, so they came alone – and that was fascinating, throwing these strangers into the woods for a week. That's kinda like what we do now!

"Being with this band in particular was a learning thing: you realize there are times when you have to make yourself scarce. 'Whoa, family stuff! Gotta go!' It's a question of being sensitive to it and, as you get to know them, the dynamic and the hierarchy becomes very clear. I seem to be able to get along with everybody. It's never been a problem."

Jeff also knows how to keep himself busy. Once he's taken his constitutional, clad in straw Panama if the weather is amenable, strolling around like a Southern gentleman, it's back to the bus and the laptop and some editing work. Filmmaking has become a passion, and the results have ranged from bizarre to beautiful and all stops in between. *Rink* is particularly gorgeous.

"There's a skating rink that's across from my house, so we're in a perfect position to see it be born and die each year – it melts away. The guy who built it escaped from East Germany in the 1960s. We've watched it for years, it has a life of its own, and I kept thinking somebody should make a film about it. Well, I guess I'm in the best place, because it would be very different if you didn't live there, because you'd have to turn up, set up, whatever, where I just shot a lot of it from out of my living-room window. I'd look over and something was going on, so I'd just grab it.

"I had about fifteen hours of footage and whittled it down to twenty minutes, edited it on my computer – it's shot on video. That was the investment I made, to buy the camera. Then the music is from the first meeting we had in my house for what became the *Deep Breathing* album. I recorded that. It's got a different energy to it: it's denser, faster. When we made the actual record in the church in Guelph, you want to hear the room, so you play it and listen to it, whereas in my living room you play more, so it has a similar vibe but more energetic – in parts, anyway. We were feeling out ideas for what we might do at that show, and what I had worked out great for the film, and then the CD has more extended versions because you maybe only use a minute or so in the film.

"Getting it out there to people is the tough thing. I worked really hard on the film. I approached festivals and TV companies and stuff – nothing. But what kept me going was that the man on the street loved it. It went all over the world via various friends and family, it got out to Germany, to Brazil, Indonesia. People tell me it makes them cry! It resonates with Canadians, of course, and when we premiered it in a little theatre in my home town of Guelph, everybody came out. Udo, the guy who makes the rink, he was there, and my other neighbour is from Germany, too, and he was there. He said, 'Back home, when you honour someone, children come up with a flower each and, in the end, he has a bouquet'. So we honoured him that way, and when the credits rolled and his acknowledgment came up the place exploded! It was quite something.

"My take on why the commercial people don't go for it is that it isn't a true documentary in the reality sense. I worked with a guy and rewrote these folktales. I found one about the North Wind, and it wanted to get married, so he marries the East Wind and he says, 'What kind of a dowry do you have?' So she freezes the lake and makes everywhere beautiful, and he laughs at her and blows and melts it all, and that was perfect. That's what the rink is, what the film is: about the weather as much as anything. I tried to find more like that and couldn't, so I worked with a writer on the rough cut and wrote these quasi-folktales. So it's not a documentary, it's not a drama, there are no talking heads in there – a documentary's gotta have talking heads!

"I really started doing films when I got a digital camera years ago with an MPEG function that would shoot fifteen seconds, so I started doing films with that. I kind of liked the limitation. I filmed something with Jaro and I thought, 'Someone should make a film about him!' So I started right then with that little camera. I brought out my video camera for that year he was out with us in 2004, so I have a lot of footage, but it takes time to go through. The great thing is he never pretended the camera wasn't there, so when you got the camera out, he'd talk straight to it: 'Today, I'm going to tell you about this!' He's mad as a hatter but, musically, he's a huge talent. The first time we played in the Trinity church – the focus on his playing, that intensity – if everybody could conjure that up, you'd have some amazing work. His command of the accordion is terrific. He's a virtuoso.

"I have a lot of film of him, and he has this background in Ukrainian show bands, which he's kind of sworn away from, but I got him to play some of those tunes. It's heavy, heavy playing, blistering tempos, left-hand stuff – people say they play the accordion, but can't do anything with their left hand – but he's like a machine, incredible. Stop, it's too much! I have a lot of footage of that. Josh Finlayson, who comes out with Cowboy Junkies sometimes, he lives near Jaro, and we've both had it in the back of our minds that he should make a record of him, but he's very resistant to it. It would be great, just him, but he always sees it as a band and he doesn't want that. To get Kevin Breit to play with him on that stuff would be something, because Kevin has that same kind of facility and speed on guitar, and he doesn't know that music, but he'd learn it really quickly, so it would be interesting."

From his inquiring mind to his equable personality, Jeff acts as a kind of glue that holds things together when the band are at the midway point of a lengthy trek and still miles away from home.

John Farnsworth has spent many years as a part of that travelling circus and had plenty of opportunity to assess Jeff's contribution to keeping the show on the road. "Nothing gets to him. They appreciate him not just for his musicianship but his worldliness, the way he picks up on stuff in the world, the way he fits into the world. No matter what's going down, Jeff's the kind of guy that will always make things happen. We all know how to get by, but Jeff just seems to be so much more a part of it. He's a lot of fun to be out with. He's taught me so much musically, too, with all the instruments he's brought out over the years, listening to him every night, his willingness to try something new just to keep people on their toes! That's become a part of them, the way they change the set list every night. That's just an awesome thing to do. To have such a huge repertoire, to be able to tailor it for the venue or to do two completely different sets in the same place in one night, that's amazing. Jeff has a big role in that."

Pete goes further yet, according Jeff the accolade of being "the fifth Junkie – he pretty much is part of the band. I certainly wouldn't want to go on tour without him; he's a great musician, a utility player, too, which is really important on the road."

Mike says, "Jeff is a perfect complement to us. First he's a very skilled and practised musician – he's studied music, which none of us have. So when we need somebody to figure something out musically, he does that for us. He's egoless, too. He's the consummate sideman for us because, whoever he's working with, he wants to make it the best it can possibly be. If you don't like what he's doing, he's quite happy to throw that out and do something else. He's totally open to ideas, he loves music, he can't live without playing it. He's a real musician that way. And the multi-instrumentalist side of what he does has been so valuable: whatever we want him to play, he'll play it. Then just his interest in music in general introduces us to a lot of things. He fits in with us so well."

There's no debate over the way in which Jeff's ability, his willingness to experiment, to throw in new instrumentation, has stretched the band over the years. What he offers up in concert often subtly edges the band into a new direction when they go back in the studio – though, characteristically, he tries to downplay his influence.

"In the live shows, certainly my part has tended to get bigger over the years. I'm flexible, I guess I'm the utility chair, and that's what they need. I said that to Mike when I first started playing. The four of them are sort of fixed, because of who they are, the relationship, their musical training; it's difficult for them

394

to change. I've approached it like that: they're one thing and I'm another. They have their groove, Mike has his songs, they do that and I add things to it. They keep asking me back, so it must be working OK!

"I think the fact that I had been involved in music for some time before I got together with them meant I did help them with things early on, but they have pretty strong ideas on what they want to do. I make suggestions when I have something to say. When we were working with Over the Rhine a few years ago, they'd been in rehearsals with the band for a few days before I arrived and Karin picked up on that: 'Oh, Mike listens to you!' That's not entirely true, by the way!

"When you work with somebody else's band rather than your own, things are more defined around you. I'm very much a decorator with Cowboy Junkies: I add to it rather than change it. Sometimes, not playing is the best thing you can do. One of my talents is in orchestration, I think – being able to see the bigger picture musically of what's going on, knowing when just to add a little, when to come in strong – and that's always come easily to me, because I have a very broad interest in music. But Mike has a very strong sense of where he's going. I don't always agree; musically I might have a different opinion. That's not to say either way is right or wrong, it's just personal taste."

Jeff's ability to play a host of instruments is a key reason for his longevity in the band, but he is a great resource for the band in every sense, a low-maintenance traveller in complete contrast to someone like Jaro, who finds the road a much more difficult place to be. In that sense, the two are poles apart, yet musically they have been perfectly in sync from the outset, as Jaro recalls.

"First time I met Jeff in that Trinity church, I took a look at him and it was one of those connections where I felt I'd known him forever, even though we just met. He was like a long-lost brother. Maybe we've done the trip not just in this lifetime. On the 2004 tour, there was a lot of air with the accordion and the harmonica happening – that creates a whole other dimension of sound and people love that, because it sounds like one huge harmonica in the sky!"

Jeff doesn't argue with that, adding, "We were in a big circle around the microphone, and after the take I remember Jaro coming over to me and saying, 'Who are you, man? You're like my long-lost brother!' We instantly fell into the same orchestral ideas for the music, it really was instantaneous, and the same with Kim Deschamps, the pedal steel player – the three of us just did this beautiful dance together. Somebody would initiate a line, then another would join, it would get passed on. That was very organic: we never worked at it at all, we never talked about it. Jaro and I have made recordings away from Cowboy Junkies, and there's a beautiful one that we made in a church with a piano player called Witold Grabowiecki, and it's sort of meditative, improvised stuff and we just fit together beautifully. There's some intense, minimalist playing from Jaro – he can wring such heart and soul out of one note of that accordion, and I've never heard anybody play like that.

395

"It can be a mystical experience when it really comes together; you suddenly get shown how the universe works for a few seconds. But you never can remember how it works when you come offstage, so you're constantly trying to find it again! I have the feeling that that happened to Jaro, that he saw the universe laid out in front of him once at a very young age, and he's never been the same! That's true of a lot of genius, I think – it's too much, the universe is coming right through them, so they have real trouble dealing with life on a mundane, day-to-day level.

"I do love playing music, not just with Cowboy Junkies but anybody. Actually, I feel a little sorry for them that they don't play with other players, because I have a whole other musical experience away from this that they don't. I try to introduce them to people, like David Houghton. I've had Margo sing with some of my favourite players, but I guess it's harder for them, because their whole focus really has to be on Cowboy Junkies. And maybe if they played with other musicians it would destroy the tightness of the unit, though I can't seriously imagine that would happen.

"But they are all very idiosyncratic players and I don't think anybody knows just how it all sits together and works. I don't think you can analyse it, take it apart and say it works because of this or that – it just does. There have been a few occasions where Al has been snowed in or sick and I've had to play bass, and it becomes a completely different thing and it just doesn't work as well, though it has got better. I think, the first time it happened, they were frightened when they looked over at me: 'That's not Al! What's going on!' It's always a last-minute thing, figuring out what to do twenty minutes before the show. I always say that I'm not going to play like Al, I don't have time to learn that, my job is to just get through as best I can. With bass, there's no hiding. You have to lay it down, you have to know what the changes are. Normally in the band, I can just wade around, or not play at all – it doesn't really matter. But, with bass, you can't do that: if you're not coming in big and strong, then it flounders. It's just not the same band at all. He never changes his part once he's got it down, whereas I've played bass in jazz bands where you hardly ever play the same thing twice, and I play bass without a drummer a lot, too, and that's a whole other approach.

"It is very interesting to play with them and then go back and do jazz things or something else. I've worked with classical players on recordings and you have to tell them what to do, which is kinda neat, because they do exactly what you ask them! But you have to be very clear, write up parts, number every bar, so you can talk to them: 'Bar thirty-seven, that quarter note on the fourth beat ...' That's not going to work with Pete! He has the absolute control; there's nothing you can do! I've played bass with him, I've tried to get him to change if the tempo's wrong, but it won't happen! When Pete hurt his back in 2006, we had to go out for a few shows with Randall Coryell, who I've worked with for years. It was a shock – Mike would count songs in and they'd come in at that tempo!

"Margo always jokes about me trying to make musicians out of them! They have improved dramatically just in things like being able to recover from errors onstage, and that's just a question of experience. A lot has to do with Mike's attitude onstage. If he's not happy, he gets mad, and that sets a tone. Everybody else I play with, when we fuck up, we laugh, it's a joke. Because it's really no big deal, it's usually less than a second, so to dwell on that is harsh. That was how music was taught – that conservatory approach where you're defined by what you can't do, it's all grading, I remember that as a kid and I hated it. That has coloured my approach to mistakes, I guess, and I think the audience actually enjoys them, too; it's a human moment. And 99.9 per cent of the audience don't realize unless you make a big deal of it, because it's a split second in time. It's scary to think of how much stuff you have to remember! I think they've got better at accepting that over the years – you have to with the number of shows we play. Mike has started to let a lot of that stuff go over the years. A lot of it is to do with age: it doesn't affect him the way it used to, unless we get a night where there are lots of technical problems, and then it can get hairy, because that can turn a show into a struggle.

"The sound when we did the private MOMA show in 2005 was really bad. The people weren't there to see us, so all you can do is play really loud and hope that gets you through. It's one of those situations where you play well – it's not that you don't care, but it's not the pressure or intimacy that you have if it's your own show in a theatre. There's more abandonment, I guess, abandoning yourself to the songs instead of being careful to play the songs 'right' for your audience. Unleash the hounds!

"Actually, the shows can work better if you're distanced from it some way, if you're not feeling so good, if you're struggling with equipment or sound problems. It can distract you from worrying about playing technically well, and that often frees you up and allows you to play better.

"But, musically, they remain what they are, so that in a way they're almost one musician, which is why it works so well when Jaro is with us. I love the space I have when we work as a five-piece, but I do sometimes miss having that other 'decorator', a player who has a similar role as me. It brings a little more dimension to it. Jaro is especially good at that and of course he has a breathing instrument in the accordion, like the harmonica is – it's not a percussive thing like a guitar. Bring in another guitar player and it's trickier, because there's more chance of that clashing with what Mike's doing.

"The electric mandolin is a kind of signature now; it's come into its own. I think it's because, like the harmonica, it has its own place in the register. The guitar and bass and vocals are kind of lower down and I can get above that. I play a lot with Margo, I follow her lines sometimes, but most of the time it expands the sound, makes it wider, where another guitar player makes it harder. I stay out of the middle, because that's where most people are!

"The electric mandolin thing I learned with them. I was playing the acoustic one and then I found this electric one in a store in Boulder, Colorado, but didn't know what to do with it. It didn't work as a mandolin, it didn't sound good as an amplified mandolin, so I sat with it. And then, one day, I turned it up, got some pedals and took off the second string in each of the four pairs, because there was just too much information otherwise, once I added distortion pedals. I really got into that instrument with the Junkies – that whole sound came from them. Mike and I have both influenced each other in that kind of psychedelic, psychotic, 1960s kind of yahoo stuff! Sonically we explore whatever the pedals will do. I introduced him to the wah-wah pedal, because I had a spare one and he's just taken that off someplace else. And I've learned a fearlessness from him, the idea that 'I'm just gonna make some noise now! But I'm gonna mean it!' I missed being a metal guitar player in the 1970s, but I'm making up for it now!

"The things I play are mostly high, so that sits up with Margo or above her, so you don't get in the way, and that's true of Jaro, too. Dave Henry came with us to play cello one time and that was nice, too – it brought a texture to it. Those are the easiest kinds of things to bring into the band, because they don't get in the way of the four of them; it really is an addition, a complement.

"Away from Cowboy Junkies, my favourite playing has always been trios, especially if you have really good players. It seems to be just the right size, so you can think on your feet, nobody gets lost, you can arrange on the stage, on the spot. You can make a lot of noise with it, but you don't have to be playing all the time, too, so that's my favourite. I think of Cowboy Junkies as that, anyway, because the four of them are this immovable unit, so you add a couple of people and you've got a trio – there's the other players, and the band which is the third member.

"I'm happy enough with the way it's worked out. I came in as a sideman and it just happens they've come back to me more often than anybody else. I enjoy that freedom. It's good for me financially, too, and it does mean I don't have to do the things I wouldn't want to do, like the promotion, the interviews, the photo shoots. That's their problem!"

CHAPTER 21

Working in a building

The Trinity Session remains one of those great foundation stone records, one on which a whole vein of taste was built, one that opened up vistas of new music for the young who discovered it on its release, one which exists in its own space, as its own reference point. It's one of those records that truly matter. It was also the record that gave Cowboy Junkies a career.

Two decades on from its making, there was a sense that the Junkies were at a fresh staging point, one where the challenges of the future would require different answers, different ways of operating, different musical challenges. There was also a sense that those opening twenty years needed to be acknowledged, celebrated and rounded up, putting an end to an era, tying up some loose ends and clearing the way for a fresh start.

Early 21st Century Blues certainly had echoes of those early one microphone records, for even if the recording techniques had become more complex it was something of a return to the sound and style of earlier days. The musicianship and the songwriting were more sophisticated, but there was a very definite sonic link to the roots of the band, redolent of a period of reflection in the wake of passing time and the uneasy relationship they had with the making of *One Soul Now*.

Making peace with the past, even subconsciously, can be an important step in providing impetus to drive on again, Mike summing up the dichotomy that confronted them at the time: "You think, 'I'm 45 and in a rock band! It's amazing! I've been living off of this for twenty years!' Then you think, 'I'm 45 and I'm in a rock band! I gotta do this for another twenty years – otherwise, what am I going to do?!'

"The anniversary was really just a number; it didn't mean that much, other than giving an excuse to stop for a second and sum things up to that point. Normally, I don't really like the idea of looking back, I don't want to be anybody's nostalgia trip – it's enough work to make people look forward all the time anyhow, without giving them more of an excuse to keep looking backwards! But twenty years was a time to stop, collect things together and then get on with what we do.

"I hope that, corny as it sounds, we are very sincere about what we do. We always feel that it's our name on the jacket, we're the people who have to look back twenty years down the line, and I don't want to be embarrassed by it. There's stuff we've done in terms of promotion where we've had to hold our nose a couple of times, sure, but you accept you have to go on a stupid TV show sometimes. But, as far as records and concerts go, we've never, ever compromised on that, we've never allowed somebody to push us in a direction we didn't want to go. Of course, we've taken suggestions, but we never put out a record that we can't get behind, one that we wouldn't want to own up to in twenty years. People ask if there's anything we'd do different – well, sure, there is, you change. But I have no regrets. If I listen back to our stuff, I know why we did things that way: it was honest; that was what we wanted to do at that time.

"We are really proud of the body of work we've put together. It gets overlooked in a weird way. It's like, 'Oh, another good Junkies record, what's new?' Isn't that a good thing? There's a flippancy towards longevity, not just hanging on but doing it with some quality, which is why we wanted to stop for a moment for the anniversary and acknowledge what we've done. A little recognition, even if you're not into what we do, would be nice. I think there should be some awareness that we do our thing and we do it well. It's unusual in this day and age.

"So we started to think about the twentieth anniversary, what we were going to do to mark it. One was the book, *XX: Lyrics and Photographs of the Cowboy Junkies*, that kind of fell into our laps with Enrique Martinez Celaya. He was an up-and-coming painter from Los Angeles, he was getting well-known on the international art scene, and he put this book together, which we're really proud of. I think it's really beautiful and it was nice for us, because it was his concept, he did the whole thing and it's beautiful. It's very different, an art book really, and then, obviously later on, he was involved in the whole 'Nomad' idea.

"Initially at that time, we wanted to rerelease the catalogue, too. We were looking at a box set, but that involved getting in touch with the companies – it was moving too slow, it wasn't a priority for them. So, instead, we started looking at what we could control and what we could do relatively quickly. It made sense to go back to *Whites Off Earth Now!!* because, after the success of *The Trinity Session*, we licensed it to RCA and they put a CD out that was a straight copy of what we had. There was no remastering at that point, so as far as CD went it was a sort of an afterthought.

"We got the chance to do a high-density, high-fidelity vinyl version, which was perfect, really. It was important that there was a straight remaster of it, and that sounds so much better now, because the version we put out was so early on in the digital days. The company that did it did a great job, the sound is amazing.

"What we did is go right back to the original tapes with Peter Moore, the things we did in the kitchen that day. They're old tapes, very early digital, so Peter corrected them, got rid of the pops, remastered it and it sounds incredible. All the information is there, but, because it was so early in digital recording, you couldn't get rid of that high-end stuff, where now there's so much more you can do.

"Peter transferred the whole two hours across, everything that went onto tape that day. I've heard bits and pieces. There are other songs on there that didn't make the cut – there's a version of 'Sweet Jane' that we did for that. When they came to redo it, there was the temptation to put everything on there, the alternate takes, everything, but I really wanted to do it as the album, and just put it out as it was. When they're putting a record out again as a remaster, I don't like having extras on there, because it spoils the original, it takes away from what the album was. I don't mind adding a separate disc, but with *Whites!!*, because it's an audiophile release, it was expensive anyways, and we didn't want to add to that.

"And the other things got left off for a reason: they weren't good enough! There's some cool stuff on them, but they didn't really work out. We might make them available as downloads at some time. We'll see.

"On top of the remaster, Peter also did a 5.1 mix of it. You usually need multi-channels for that, but this is a two-channel recording. Peter and a friend have developed some software that creates a surround-sound effect, which is really cool. I heard it in Peter's studio and it is amazing." As an aside, the surround-sound system that Peter has developed is truly extraordinary, scraping dirt off old masters. He played me a version of Buddy Holly's 'Peggy Sue' that his software had created, and it was just a revelation. It's a technology that deserves – *demands* – widespread adoption.

Having returned to *Whites Off Earth Now!!*, it was still clear that any anniversary or celebration would have to hinge on *The Trinity Session*, the record that really got things moving. Any relationship that has gone on for twenty years has stood the test of time but, equally, you have to be wary of taking it for granted, familiarity being that most insidious of dangers. To ward that off, plenty seek to renew their vows and commitment after such a lengthy period. If you're going to do that, where better to do it but in church? And so the Junkies headed back to the Church of the Holy Trinity to take a fresh look at their own icon.

"When we got talking about the twentieth anniversary, marking the recording of *The Trinity Session* gradually became the thing that made most sense. That was a more focused event, it was the thing that pushed us to wherever the hell we are now, so we decided we should try to go back there. Even then, the whole concept was weird. I was of two minds about it. Going back seemed desperate in a way: 'Why are we doing it?'

"It was stupid to just recreate it, because the point was it was one day, one recording; it was very special so you couldn't recapture it. We decided to revisit it, and when we had that concept I liked that. It made sense, I was comfortable with it, it was a celebration of an important record, fine. We invited some new guests – we had Natalie Merchant, Ryan Adams and Vic Chesnutt – and we got together for a one-day rehearsal, one-day recording, go back to the church, film it and see what comes up. It felt good, it was exciting, it was fun, intense, which was what we wanted. We wanted to put musicians together that would give it a new spark."

It's an odd record, is *Trinity Revisited*. Let's rephrase that. It's an odd record to approach. You have to be in the right frame of mind, the right sort of headspace when you sit down to listen to it, because, if you come to it with the original album in mind, you can pretty quickly get disorientated. Margo's view on the project is tellingly accurate.

"That album is very special to a lot of people and, as a fan, I know it's important not to tamper with those things, so we really had to find the right feel. People were saying, 'So you redid *The Trinity Session*, then?' No, we didn't. We covered it, really, like we do a Neil Young song! It's twenty years later – we're all different people and players, we brought in different guests, so it's a different thing, not a re-creation.

"Going back to the church was nerve-racking. It was something people have always tried to get us to do. We've resisted it, because you can't go back and recapture it. But, when we did it, the music was fantastic, the place was just inspiring again, and then, working with Natalie, Ryan and Vic, they were amazing. The original recording was a wonderful day in our lives and we didn't want to ruin it, but we didn't; it was like a continuation, another day at the Trinity Church. When we were trying to pick the takes to use, there wasn't one we couldn't use because so and so screwed up – they all were great. Different, but great. That's the sound of the church, it's so good, it gets you playing."

"It was freaky going back to the church and thinking back to the fact that that was where it all started," adds Mike. "I don't think I'd been back there since the original recording, actually. And back then, it wasn't as surrounded: you could see it from Bay Street; there was space around it. Now it's just hemmed in by buildings. But we got to the church and, literally, from plugging in, right away, it sounded so great. It brought back tons of memories: 'Now I remember, it sounds so nice in here!' It wasn't just a lucky day back then – part of it was the environment was so conducive, it feels great to play in there. It was bigger than I remembered, more beautiful. Back then, we knew it sounded good, but with twenty years of experience under our belt, playing places that don't sound so great, we appreciate it even more. We should make a record there!"

The second record they made there was done in very different circumstances to the time when The Timmins Family Singers showed up all those years before. Back then, there were no preconceptions, they were nobodies, there wasn't a career hanging on it. This time, despite Jeff Bird's wise entreaties that "no expectations" is always the way to go, *Trinity Revisited* was a real production number. The guests were high profile, the music was well-known and well-loved and, just to ratchet it up a notch further, there was a camera crew filming the whole thing. No pressure, then.

"I was nervous about the cameras, because I don't like them," admits Margo, "but the crew were great, very friendly, they totally understood who we are and what we're about. I never felt there was a camera in my face, so I was totally relaxed."

Jeff adds, "I think we all wondered about the production, because they had a ton of stuff. It was a huge thing – cameras, lights – but they were totally conscious of not being in the way, they were great. They said they had a hard time, because they're used to actual live shows with an audience where you don't stop. Obviously, we were stopping and they found that disturbing, because they're like a giant machine and, once you stop, it's hard to get it rolling again, double-checking the cameras, the sound."

"There was a lot of stopping and starting, lots of takes, but that was kind of like the original recording, anyway, though that took way less time," agrees Alan. "It was grinding that way. We had this giant camera crew working things out and telling us to stop all the time; we'd be playing and they'd yell 'Cut!' which was frustrating. But it sounds pretty good, Ryan sounds great, Vic and Natalie too. In a way, it's a rougher version of *Trinity* than the original in terms of playing – we weren't as precious as with the original, when we were trying to nail it all. This was more a fun kind of thing. The visuals are pretty sweet – really nice lighting, they had great gear – so everything was there to make it a good show."

Perhaps watching it on DVD is the best approach to *Trinity Revisited* because, from the outset, the film makes it very clear that this is a fresh take, on top of which, it looks just gorgeous. The church is beautifully lit, it captures an atmosphere all its own, existing on its own terms, where on CD alone it's hard to escape your own internal dialogue with the original. Seeing it as well as hearing it offers an easier route into what is "the Cowboy Junkies revue", Rolling Thunder without actually rolling across the country.

A recurring theme of this whole tale has been the willingness of the Junkies to stand aside and let guest musicians take the spotlight, but *Trinity Revisited* took that to a new level. Inevitably, perhaps, given the lack of rehearsal time – and the stature of the guests – a lot of the performances saw the Junkies taking a backseat, playing around their guests. It couldn't be any other way, given their intimate knowledge of every aspect of each song's DNA compared with guests feeling their way into material they'd never performed before. At times, Cowboy Junkies are almost the backing band on their own record, which is both its strength, in the way it casts new light on old material and, for the diehards, its weakness, because who doesn't want to hear more of Margo singing or the band at centre stage?

At times, having new people working on the music is quite revelatory. Vic Chesnutt's vocal on 'Postcard Blues' is mesmerizing, the more so as you watch him deliver it, like Kaa in *The Jungle Book*, hypnotic. Then, on 'Dreaming My Dreams', that singular, late-lamented voice carries an ache from somewhere deep within that suits the song, creating a haunting duet with Margo.

Natalie Merchant's contribution is, as you'd perhaps expect, more confident, more forthright. Where Chesnutt slips beneath the songs, almost hiding inside them, Merchant sits on top of them, a more forceful presence. On 'To Love Is to Bury', her contribution is dazzling, a luscious vocal allied to a beautiful piano accompaniment which meshes perfectly with Jeff's violin work, while on 'Misguided Angel', when she takes the last line, perhaps simply because the song is just so well-known, such a central part of the Junkies' canon that you're just waiting on Margo's final, wistful delivery, it jars a little when you hear it sung with the confidence that is otherwise such a strong calling card for Merchant.

Slotting Ryan Adams into the mix is trickier still, particularly as a singer, for his phrasing and approach to vocals is so idiosyncratic – allied to his compulsion for never doing anything the same way twice – that the whole focus tends to fall on him. At times, that's simply breathtaking, as when he sings "Did you ever hear a robin weep" on 'I'm So Lonesome I Could Cry', whereas on '200 More Miles', after twenty years of hearing Margo sing it, his delivery feels awkward. His part as one of the slinky, 1960s backing vocalists on 'I Don't Get It' is terrific, though.

As a guitarist, he adds some delightful touches, on 'Misguided Angel', '200 More Miles' and 'Working on a Building' in particular. The DVD shows him keen to be a team player as they work the songs up, but he can't help himself from bringing his strong personality to whatever he does, including the donning of Lou Reed dark glasses for 'Sweet Jane'.

The trio of interlopers have a hard road to follow, however welcoming the band, for (as shown so often on the record) the five of them have an almost telepathic communication, something that clearly thrills Jeff. "The church, it's an amazing sounding room, so beautiful. Having the guests, that changes it up, too, but really it was another gig, it's playing – that's what I do! Playing live makes you be present, in that moment, where you should be. It's where you do your best work, I think."

Jeff is in particularly fine form and *Trinity Revisited* gives him particular scope to stretch out on electric mandolin, the sound that has come to be such a live signature for the band, but which wasn't there on the original album. Playing with minimalist restraint on 'I'm So Lonesome I Could Cry' gives an indication of one side of that instrument's potential; there's a contemplative edge to it on 'Dreaming My Dreams'; then there's the real psychedelic tint to the intro to 'Sweet Jane', illustrating the range of possibilities the instrument offers.

Watching the DVD also gives the opportunity to really appreciate just how unusual, and how good, the rhythm section is. Where twenty years earlier Pete was still feeling his way into things as a drummer as the least experienced musician, listening to – and watching – him on *Trinity Revisited* is to see someone completely at home with his role, his ability, his place in the scheme of things. He's still a very idiosyncratic player, but he and Alan are perfect foils to one another. Listening to that loping groove Al puts down on 'Blue Moon Revisited (Song for Elvis)' never gets old, but throughout the performance, rock solid and assured as his performance is, there are all kinds of subtle touches and nuances that decorate and enhance.

Working with an additional guitar player always increases the opportunity for clashes, but Mike's role as MD includes consciously taking up a backing role. His signature style of playing is all over everything, of course – the lovely meandering solo on "Working on a Building" particularly outstanding – but there's a sense of straining at the leash at times, reining himself in to play a captain's role of bringing the ship safely home to port.

The elephant in the room is the fact that Margo isn't singing on everything. Great as some of the performances from their guests are, that voice is so much at the heart of the band that, when it isn't there, it's startling. Like the others in their roles, Margo steps away from the limelight with good grace, but when the chance does come for her to sing, she's not shy of really reminding us just how good she is, however stellar the company around her.

Ultimately, *Trinity Revisited* about hits the mark. It works on its own terms as a recording and especially a DVD, and puts that full stop on the twenty years that led them towards rerecording it. It also served as that re-dedication to their craft and their band. The idea behind "two hundred more miles" was embraced anew, the commitment made. And how better to prove it than, as soon as the recording was done in November 2006, jumping on a cross-Canada "Roots on the Rails" train to play pretty much the entire canon to a bunch of Junkies junkies on board? It's not the kind of thing Lady Gaga would do, is it?

"The train trip across Canada was something we talked about for a long time," admits Mike. "At one point, after a long discussion, we decided it was crazy and turned it down. We told the promoter 'no', because it seemed too intense, we didn't know what we were getting into. Then we stepped back again and thought about it. We've never stepped away from an unknown experience before. One thing about the band we've always enjoyed is the chance it gives you to go to weird places – we do a gig in Slovenia not knowing if we're going to make or lose money, because how the hell else are we going to get there?! Losing control is kinda fun in a way.

"So we decided, it's only three days, if it was a nightmare, it lasted three days and it's done. How bad can it get? We can hide in our berths and only come out for the show! The promoter was a very straightforward guy; it was on the up and up. We're pretty open with our fans, anyway – if you want to talk to us, show up and we'll talk – so we knew the personality of our audience. The wildcard was a couple of crazies might show up, but we hoped if you were that insane, you couldn't afford it, anyway!"

Musically, the trip hinged on a complete live performance of *The Trinity Session*, the first one ever in front of a live audience, but there were workshops, request shows and other musicians in tow, just to keep everyone busy, as Mike notes.

"Playing *The Trinity Session* inside a railcar instead of a church was weird, but it gave the whole thing a focus. We'd never done it before, we'd just done the *Trinity Revisited* thing, so it seemed obvious. The mood was strange, it was the third night, we were all exhausted. We'd never done it front to back before like that. It works as an album, but I don't know if it works as a concert, though we have done it that way since and it's worked better. And just the five of us meant we had limited instrumentation, too, so that was awkward because we couldn't get the

407

textures that are so important. Then, the real quiet stuff – there's that constant rumble from the train, which made it hard!"

Although the music was the point of the whole trip, as Alan points out, the restrictions imposed by being in that confined space, and operating within its confines, did make life uncomfortable at times. It must have been easier for Boxcar Willie to play than it was for the Cowboy Junkies.

"Playing while the train was moving was difficult. Then, while we were playing, we'd pull in to a station or just stop for whatever reason, and then it was really nice. Then we'd start up again and things would start falling over. I don't think the sound was great for the audience, either, so that needs figuring out, but you are so confined – it's a railcar. I don't know how much you can do with it."

Although there were deprivations, Pete found plenty to enjoy during a trip which he likened to one of those marathon bus drives from the early tours. "You lose track of time, you go along for the ride and you get antsy at the end, whether it's six hours or four days, and you're happy to get off. Fortunately, there were enough cars on there so that you could escape the drunk if you had to! You just keep moving! But it was something different, and that's nice. You just have to have the right approach to it.

"The workshops were fun, too. Playing with Jeff on bass is always a fun change; playing with Andy Maize from Skydiggers was good, he's great onstage, outspoken; Josh Finlayson is a good buddy, too. We got to know some other guys, too, so it was worth doing. Playing on the moving train wasn't too bad. I had half a kit because of the space we had, so that was a great challenge for me. I'd be hitting stuff that wasn't there, so that means you're reappraising all the time.

"And the whole train idea was that it was kinda absurd anyway, very loose, whatever happens, happens, and you get good performances out of that. If it's a concert hall full of 1,000 Italians and an opera played there the night before, you're looking for perfection and that gets you a different kind of show. When Jeff is there, he's played so much, it doesn't matter. Even if you're in New York and all the record companies are there, Jeff is always saying it's just another gig, which is a great way of conquering those inner demons.

"When you think back, we have played some incredible places. The Royal Albert Hall. Holy Christ almighty! It's hard to separate yourself from that and from the voices in your head that scare the crap out of you. You start staring at your foot, then the other foot: 'Don't stop now!' I've had to talk individual limbs through concerts. 'Oh God, no, not tonight!' Nerves are a good thing to a point, because you should be aware of what you're doing. They make you sharp; otherwise, don't do it. And then you go the other way: that you've played so many gigs that you're not even thinking, you're just riding the music and that's a great feeling. Something takes over – it's like painting, it becomes Zen, meditation almost.

"Everybody gets distracted when you're on the road; that's why we try to juggle the set lists, because it's always making you think about what you're doing. 'How does this one go?' The train was like a very intense tour and, having those request shows, it gave us something to work on in that same way. We played songs we hadn't played in years."

"Pete's right: we rediscovered a few songs because of the requests," agrees Mike. "And a few, it reminded us why we never play them live! It was a hardcore audience, so people deliberately requested songs they hadn't heard, from tribute albums; weird little songs we did in the studio, gave away and walked away from. Songs like 'Darkness, Darkness' was a studio thing, we never played it as a band, it was pieced together, so it was odd playing that and we won't go back to it. We did 'Ooh Las Vegas' again, which was fun. We did a lot of studio vocals for the Gram Parsons record, but it's basically just a blues song and we enjoyed it. 'Seven Years', we did a different version. 'Dead Flowers' is real fun and that went back in the repertoire. We did 'Handouts in the Rain', which we never could get a feel for live – it's a long song, there's a weird tension to it and we never felt comfortable enough to get up onstage with it. We did it during one of the workshops when we had a few other players up there with us, so we hammered away at it!

"The music was great; it was nice to be with the other musicians; it was cool – a lot of music, five or six hours a day; it was good. We hung out with people, we met some pretty intense fans, it was interesting to hear their stories. We had people from England, a woman from Norway who had never seen us live before but was into the music, a couple from Australia, a lot of Americans from all over, so it was neat. It was very invigorating to hear how the music had touched people. At the end, it was great to hear from so many people that they'd really loved it, that it was even better than they were expecting, so it was really worthwhile, but pretty exhausting."

"It was hard work, but when it's done you look back and think it was an interesting experience," agrees Margo. "The music was a lot of fun, the people were great, really nice to us. But it was like a three-day cocktail party. You arrive and everybody is a bit stiff, not knowing what to do and, as it goes on, and they get more into it, it opens up. The second day was great, because people were loose, but not losing it. By the third day, the drinkers were starting to drink first thing in the morning and getting drunk by mid-afternoon, which was their way of coping with being cooped up. We did *Trinity Session* straight through that night, which was the first time we'd done that, and there were a bunch of drunks being pirates in the bar car, so I asked them not to bring that into the performance car, because a lot of people paid a lot of money to see that show, and they were fine."

"It was fun to do once. I'm not in a hurry to do it again," says a wary Alan. "My son was with me and he said it was OK, but it was a day too long, and I agree with that – two days would have been good, three days not so great. The food was really weird: everything was buffalo this or buffalo that. The disappointment was the scenery. It wasn't spectacular enough, because we went through the Rockies at night, which was crazy, because that was what everyone was looking forward to after days of flatness. So the scheduling on that has to be sorted out, but overall it was OK. Just making it happen must be a really tough job.

"It was very intense, to be in such a confined space with fans for so long. They were good, we know our fans. But, because you're in that space, because there's a party vibe, there's a tendency to drink, because there's not a lot else to do. We had the odd guy who talked way too much that you had to creep away from, but otherwise it was pretty good. It could have been a lot tougher in that way, let's say that."

Bearing the brunt of the fan attention was, inevitably, Margo. The public face of the band over twenty years, the point of contact between band and fans onstage, the one who goes and does the meet-and-greet after the show, she is the focal point of the Cowboy Junkies in the public mind … even if, as Mike explains, they've tried to share things out a little more over the years.

"From our perspective of listening to bands, we always liked it when there was a focal person, even if there were lots of players, lots of writers. Then, when we got signed to management and got a record company, the rest of us didn't really want to do interviews anyways, so that was fine! Margo was the spokesperson: she's great at it, she's a hell of a lot better-looking than us and, strictly from a commercial point of view, it helped. Having a good-looking girl always does. But we are a band, we know who we are. There's never been any problem in that way inside the band, but, as we went along, there was Margo fatigue. Journalists who were coming back for the second or third time wanted to talk to someone else – they noticed that I wrote the songs, so I ended up doing some, too. And it's gone on like that, and now people want to talk to Al more – we've been pushing him out there more, just because it gives us another voice to talk to the same channels, and that's been a natural progression.

"As far as people listening to us goes, the more records we put out, the more people appreciate that we are a band, that we all have an input. But we never had any big meeting to say to Margo, 'You're doing too many interviews!' She got as tired of it as anybody, which is why I started doing some, and, now I'm tired of it, Al is doing more. That's never been an issue and that is another reason why we're still going, because we never fight about that kind of crap! We all have the same sensibilities musically and anything else is unimportant. However we can best serve the music, that's what matters. And then the rest is marketing, totally the business, and we do what we have to do in that sense. We know that the bigger the picture we get in the paper, the bigger the interview, the better the TV show, it helps us sell records, so, whoever they want to talk to, we'll talk! It doesn't affect the music – we all know what the questions are going to be, so it's not an issue, it's easy. In fact, what we've done sometimes is, if they want to talk to me, Alan will do my phone interviews as me, and nobody knows! We can all do them – the questions are never really that left-field that one of us would be unable to answer, so that's kinda fun! The whole marketing thing is pretty ridiculous at heart, so we don't worry about it."

Even so, Margo has been the band's ambassador for the most part, and as such has moved from being the painfully shy girl who wouldn't look at the audience at their early gigs to someone comfortable dealing with the Junkies' fanbase, from the more casual punter to the most hardened llama. But her ability to do that has its limits, something she discovered for herself over the course of the train trip.

"The train trip was very weird, we'll leave it there! It was a new experience. I had no idea what the train would look like, who'd be on it, what would we see, how would it sound, nothing. When we got to the train station, at seven in the morning, I realized what I was doing. That was my first 'Oh my God' moment. 'This is going be weird!' There were people milling around, they'd wave at me because they know who I am, but I had no idea about them apart from a few llamas I'd met before. I immediately went and sat next to them, because it was somebody I knew. But it was really early, some of the people were tired because they'd travelled a long way just to get to Toronto. Some were hungover, too! It was strange, very quiet, no real communication, because everybody was finding their way into this whole idea.

"The cabins were 1950s things. Tiny. The lighting was something that reminded me of what I imagine my prison days would have been like – a bad-coloured light bulb. My husband had to back out because our son was sick, which was just as well, because if we'd both been trapped in there we'd have had a nervous breakdown, it was so tiny!

"So I went to explore the rest of the train and everybody's having the same 'What have I done?' feeling! We played pretty much immediately, we did a workshop, and that was fun; playing gets me normal. I think it helped get everybody focused – this is why we're here, they've come to hear us – and from there people started to mingle and feel more comfortable. We did a show that night. I really enjoyed it. I don't know it was the best playing, but it was fun, really loose, because the sound was terrible, as you'd expect. You make do with what you've got, and it was fine.

"The next morning, I got up for breakfast. Our car was the furthest away from the restaurant car, which had the performance car beyond that. So, if I wanted to eat, or if we were playing, I had to walk through all the sleeper cars, and of course everyone's saying 'hello'. It's like being the Queen on a foreign tour or something! It was really funny, but it gets kind of wearing! There was no specific seating in the dining car, so I sat down and I haven't even had a coffee yet. And, of course, it's with people who love the band, so it's 'Hey, Margo, come and sit with us.' Very nice people, but I need my coffee first! I'm not mentally ready. I don't wake up as Margo Timmins of Cowboy Junkies!

"That was very weird to me, because onstage, or when I talk to people afterwards, I think I'm still me, I think I'm pretty natural, but there's

412

obviously part of myself that I don't show, and that was interesting to me. I don't know what it is, but I obviously don't show the breakfast part of me! I'm sitting at this table with three very nice people, chatting away and I was answering the kind of questions I get asked a lot, about the music and the band or whatever, and after a show I'd chat away like that, no problem. But I'm sitting there thinking, 'I'm not ready for this, I can't handle it.' I felt invaded. It takes a lot for me to be rude and I hope I wasn't, because they were really nice to me, but I had to say, 'Look, this has nothing to do with you, but I'm really not ready yet. I haven't had my coffee and I don't want to be in public yet.' So I went back to my cabin, 'Hello, hello', all the way back to people I met in the corridor, and back to my cell, which was looking great now! The purser obviously saw me and came to see if I was OK and she brought me a coffee and a croissant, which she then did every morning, and that helped. Then I was able to come out when I felt I was ready to face the day. But it was a strange sensation, a moment I always remember, when I really discovered there is a line between Cowboy Junkies Marg and just Marg!

"By the third day, I was ready to get off the train, but I think everyone was getting antsy by then. We got off the train in Jasper and I really wanted to get away on my own for a while, but of course the town was full of train people. I went as far as I could, but suddenly this guy came running out. 'Margo, can you talk to my daughter, she's on the cell phone?' And I snapped a little bit: 'I haven't even talked to my own son. I don't want to talk to anybody!' And I could see how upset he was, and he started apologizing, and I started apologizing, and in the end I spoke to his daughter. I would never be that rude ordinarily, so it was time to get off that train – it was too claustrophobic, overwhelming!"

However far they'd had to travel, anniversaries had been celebrated, milestones marked, punctuation marks applied. Now it was time to look forward and take out the new body of music they'd written and recorded. As an artistic statement, it would be every bit the equal of anything from the two previous decades of work.

413

IN THE ZONE

There are all kinds of time zones. There's GMT, PST, EST, CET. Then you've got AAT. Alan Anton Time. Or, put Jeff Bird's way, "Al is either the coolest man in the world, or he's full of shit!"

It's the percussionist who is supposed to march to the beat of a different drum – that's their occupation, after all. In Cowboy Junkies, it's Alan. The man who deliberately steps just outside the spotlight that's trying to find him; the one who never cracks a smile onstage; the only one who spends all the show on his feet; the one who isn't a Timmins; the one who, from time to time, Mike defers to.

Alan Anton is an alchemist, an illusionist. Talk to the rest of the band and, only half joking, they'll tell you Alan spends his life asleep, that nobody ever quite knows where he is, that he's not so much clued up as switched off. But, on the road, it's Alan who makes the merch work, who's the stock-taker and the accountant. Around the bus, he's the one that, in some insidious way, gives the day its rhythm, its mood, while floating above it all. And there's nobody sharper than Alan.

David Houghton admits, "Alan is a tough guy to know. He doesn't reveal much of himself. In my time with the band, I learned he has very refined tastes and is a tremendously underrated bass player. He's a stabilizing force in a band that is already well-anchored. And I can assure you he makes the best cappuccino available on any tour bus."

Before a gig at New York's Irving Plaza, pretty late in the day, I paid a visit to the Strand Bookstore with Pete and Alan. We were there a while and, in the rabbit warren of it all, Alan drifted off from us. It got pretty close to showtime and, after a cursory look for him, Pete concluded we needed to dash back to the gig. We didn't waste any time and got back a little breathless, wondering where Alan was. Of course, he drifted into the dressing room with time to spare, no rush, no hurry, no sense of panic, no problem at all. That's AAT in action.

To describe Alan as an enigma is to trifle with understatement, but to underestimate him is foolish, as Linford Detweiler notes. "I always felt Al was a huge part of the puzzle, but I couldn't put my finger on it. What you can't do is imagine them without him. Starting with his playing, if you pulled Al out of the mix, it's not the kind of thing where you just get a good bass player to step in. Obviously, when people play together a long time, there are just connections that happen on a lot of levels that are hard to quantify. Musically, he's a dark horse, he doesn't draw a lot of attention to himself. I always felt he was a really significant part of the whole picture,

414

but I couldn't quite decide why or articulate it. I feel like Al is very proud of his role in the band and he was the guy that would sit around and talk about music. Mike obviously wants to talk, too, but Al was almost more of a fan in some ways."

That last observation is especially pertinent, reflecting as it does the way in which the development of Cowboy Junkies has altered the way Mike and Alan are able to look at music. There's no doubting that Mike is every bit as much a music fan as ever he was, but such is his central role in Cowboy Junkies that so much of his time has to be given over to the mechanics of making that music happen – the simple business of getting the show on the road – that maybe the fan side of it all has to take a back seat.

Alan, meanwhile, admits music still does it for him, something you quickly pick up on if you share a drink or two with him in a bar, when he can be at his most animated in discussing an old record or something he just heard. "We don't really get the fans' thrill from a Junkies record, because we're hearing it as we go along, so there's never a kind of unveiling of it for the first time, though we had that kind of moment with *Trinity Session*. We did it so fast, then listened to it the next day and got knocked out by it! 'This is really cool!' But I still get those moments when I buy a new Nick Cave record. I still get the same excitement as a fan that I had before we started doing all of this."

The circumstances that led to Alan sidestepping the leadership role to a large degree gave him an enviable position in the greater scheme of things – utterly crucial to the band, hugely influential on its thinking and direction, yet with a greater degree of freedom than his musical partner. It's a dichotomy that might frustrate Mike at times, but one he knows is right for the band.

"Alan is a very unassuming guy. He's very passive and that helps our relationship because I'm very aggressive – I'm the one who pushes things and he's quite happy to ride that. But he won't let something go in a direction that he doesn't like. He'll say something, he'll question it and so he allows me to drive stuff, but he's always there saying, 'We should probably turn left here!' Then I moan a bit and say, 'Yeah, you're right!' Our personalities just work well that way."

The relationship between Mike and Alan is at the heart of Cowboy Junkies, or, perhaps more accurately, it's the brain of the band. Where Margo and Pete are more instinctive in their approach, it's Alan who is willing to intellectualize what it is the band should be striving for next; he's the man who will talk in conceptual terms about what Cowboy Junkies are, what they represent, where they are going. He's also the one that Mike takes account of, as he admits.

"Al plays a huge part in this band. He's my sounding board. When we're talking about music, because of our shared experience, when Al says something, I know what he means. Even if he says something like, 'This is black', I'll know that what he really means is that 'That's white'! We read each other's moods pretty well after all this time and I know that if we ask each other the same question the following day, we'll get an answer that relates to what's happening around us.

"That's why Cowboy Junkies is very much a band, whatever spin gets put on it from the outside. I couldn't operate without Al; he's hugely important. Everything gets bounced off everybody, but because of the way Al and I go back, and because I have huge respect for the way he hears things, then he's the one I really listen to. With Pete and with Margo, I listen to what they have to say, too, but in a totally different way. As far as the overall feel of the thing, the big picture, Al's the one I look to the most."

"The big picture" is another key phrase, because Alan is extremely interested in the art world, and the conceptual nature of modern art, in particular, strikes a certain chord with him. His appreciation of great art feeds into his desire to be involved in making some, because – on both an intellectual and a gut level – he understands that art can reveal things that would otherwise stay hidden.

The way in which he responds to art is evident in the music, that innate understanding that the abstract can only work if it has an internal logic and a structure that binds it together. Listen to 'State Trooper' on *200 More Miles* and, off in the distance, Mike's apparently channelling Jackson Pollock, spitting out notes in a seemingly disparate, abstract pattern, while Alan is locked in, holding it together, making sense of disorder. It's very indicative of his unusual style, according to Jeff Bird.

"Al's approach is interesting: he never changes his part once he's got it down. Ever. He and Pete lock in, in a weird way – it's not a tight kick-and-bass thing. Margo said to me, when Randall Coryell was playing with us when Pete had his back problem, "Al sounds really good!" That was because he had a kick drum, a drummer who was following his bass pattern, so suddenly they had a point on them that defined them. Randall loved it because Al was so consistent, he could play round it, knowing it was always going to be the same. But Al and Pete do have this weird style that's all their own and it's very effective. When we did *Trinity Revisited*, one of the things that struck me was how good they sounded together. They've got their own thing going and it works for the band.

"As a bass player, Al very much plays within a two-fret box. There's a specific method; things that he does all the time, and harmonically everything is right there, lying under your fingers. He almost never plays the root, except on the lowest string, he'll go up the neck rather than across, so there's always the same kind of harmonic pattern from song to song. That's very much Al's style – no other bass players that I'm aware of do that – and it also means his sound has a very specific tonal quality and that gives a terrific warmth and roundness to the sound."

That playing is very much an extension of who Alan Anton is. For all that he has his own way of being, his own timeline, there's a genuine warmth to him and, when the spirit moves him, he can be pretty animated. Ferociously intelligent – it's unlikely he'd have been Mike Timmins' musical partner for this long if he wasn't – he also appreciates the life that music has given him, and he's pretty sharp on the way in which the industry is trying to deny similar good fortune to the next generation.

"I love Led Zeppelin, but they were just one great band among dozens of them in the 1970s. That's what's missing now. You're lucky if you have two great bands now, and I try to explain that change to my son, and he's amazed that you could choose from so many amazing bands then. It was such a rich scene then: Pink Floyd, Genesis, Zappa, Steely Dan, Bowie, all doing amazing work at the same time, stretching things, constantly reinventing themselves. Nirvana was the last great band in America and it's thirty years since they first emerged. Look at the catalogues the record companies had in the 1970s, putting out one amazing record after another, week after week. What do they put out now? Crap, and they only have a big release once a month, and then they'll pick out six singles from it and make that record last for a couple of years, just so they don't need to find anything new.

"The way things are, it's important that you maintain a close relationship with your fans. Even huge bands like Metallica understand the value of that – my son is big into them, so that's how I know. They put out a lot of things for the fans. When they released the DVD of the *Some Kind of Monster* documentary, it came with eight hours of extra stuff, which is amazing. They obviously force that on the company, because the company wouldn't want the hassle or expense of that, but that's what ties you to your audience. I've a lot of respect for those guys.

"I think the nature of what we do has a big bearing on the fact that we have such a strong fanbase. They're pretty loyal. We don't have hit singles, so we don't pick anyone up on that basis, but people find the music somehow and, once they like it, we seem to be able to keep them with us. There's a depth to what we do and it's the difference between real music and the manufactured stuff; that's why people stay with you.

"We know the kind of music that we make means that we're not going to have those huge-selling records that put you on the cover of every magazine in the world. We know the music is pretty selective, so there's no point thinking, 'Wouldn't it be great to be number one?' or anything like that. And no, it wouldn't be great, because then we wouldn't be doing this music – we'd have to be U2!

"We don't look back at what we've done so much. It's nice to hear from fans that our music has meant something, has moved them, affected them, because that was always our goal and still is – that's really gratifying. It is unbelievable that this is my job! I was in Australia one time, having dinner with Jean-Jacques Burnel, sitting on a beautiful deck in this restaurant, looking over the water and I just said to him, 'Isn't it amazing that we can play bass guitar, be sitting here halfway around the world and not have a job!' That's pretty special. And the other side is, if you stop doing that, what do you do then? You're going to go

417

and have a regular job? Sure, this gets more complicated as you get older, but the music is strong enough to plough through that."

As with all the members of Cowboy Junkies, Alan has a very strong sense of who he is, what he will and won't do, and what works. Like the others, his is an ego that stays in check, recognizing that he finds himself in a particularly singular group.

"I think we know we have something special as a group, and we don't really need to go beyond it. I'm not interested in playing with other musicians, because it's the sound we have together that draws me. I'm not a bass player who needs to be out there playing bass every day with anyone and everyone. I like playing with these people. I can't remember the last time I had a jam with anyone else. I don't think I ever did, matter of fact, unless I was forced into it! I don't consider myself a musician in that sense. I don't know other people's songs; it just wouldn't be fun to me."

Cowboy Junkies know what they are. Alan doesn't feel the need to make an Alan Anton record, and there's not going to be a day when all four members unleash solo albums on an unsuspecting public the way the likes of Yes did back in the day. Alan is great at being the Cowboy Junkies' bass player, a part of its sound, a key part of its think tank. That's enough. And that's an attitude that stops the group tearing itself to bits the way so many others did. Family is a big part of that, but the non-Timmins in the quartet plays a pretty huge role, too.

There were bands before Cowboy Junkies – Hunger Project and Germinal – and those two early incarnations were necessary steps on the road to forming the Junkies and that band being what it became, but the common denominator has always been Mike and Alan. While Mike has done the lion's share of the writing, being a founder member of a band gives you a special sense of ownership of the project, whether you get the limelight subsequently or not. Because you were there getting it off the ground, physically, musically, intellectually you are always going to be at the centre, nudging it, pushing it in various directions, towards certain concepts – not always explicitly, but simply by being around and having the clout that history brings with it.

Not that it's quite as easy as it was, given that Alan and his family now live on the other side of Canada, in Vancouver. Everyone seems to have a different take on just what that has meant to the band. Alan first.

"I don't think it's made that much difference that I don't live in Toronto any longer. By the time we had enough money to buy houses, get married or whatever, we didn't really hang out, because we were together so much of the time with the band, anyway. The three of them did obviously because of family stuff, but we'd go long periods in Toronto when we didn't see each other if we weren't working, because you just want to get away from that. So it doesn't seem that much has changed."

Mike sees things a little differently. "The fact that Al isn't around has changed the dynamic. Not initially, because the way we were working was very

418

cyclical: work on a record, tour, take a long break. We had very distinct projects, so Al would be there for that. But now we're working on a ton of little things, we're doing stuff all the time, it is a drag that he's not there, because there are times when I'd like to just get him over to work on something and we can't do that. We have to wait for a few things to come together, so it makes sense for him to fly across country. We used to get together a lot more just to play, but now we need a project to do it. But a lot of other things have changed, too – family, kids – so it's just something else we work around and figure out how to do. Being able to use the internet to mail each other things has helped, and that's been something we've done more and more of, but it's not the same as being in a room together."

As someone looking in on the partnership, Margo's view on Al's presence is a particularly incisive one, not least because, while the outside world views Cowboy Junkies as largely a collaboration between her and Mike, she sees a very different dynamic.

"Al is the silent partner. He's been there from the beginning, so their relationship on a personal level is like brothers. They've been together through everything, literally, since nursery school. They're no longer friends socially, they don't go out together – Mike doesn't go out with anybody, he has his family and that's that, where I still hang out with Pete – but they have such history that they don't really have to talk about anything any more.

"As far as the band goes, Al is very much a force behind the scenes. He's a big part of creating the music at its initial stages. Michael totally respects his opinion, so when we're writing and recording he does depend on Al. And when Al isn't there for him – and Al's personality is such that he drifts off, goes to sleep – that's hard for Mike.

"I sometimes think that Al doesn't realize just how much Mike does need him. There are times when I've had to push Al to help, because that's the way he is. Michael gets most of his stability from Al, he trusts him. I'd love to be able to help Mike more musically; I just don't have it in me. I have an opinion, but I don't have the same sense of music that Al does.

"Al has a completely different work ethic than Mike. Actually, we all do. The whole world does! Certainly Al does, and I think that frustrates Mike, because he wants more from Al and can't necessarily get it, or get it as quick as he wants. There's a tug-of-war between them. And Al lives on the other side of Canada, of course, so now we communicate by phone, email, whatever – it's frustrating. But I guess, in a way, it's no change really, because it's always been frustrating. Even when we were all living together, paying rent, Al would be asleep for three weeks. 'Did he pay his rent?' 'I don't know. I think he slept through it.'

"It's weird, because Mike will put up with a lot from Al that he wouldn't from Pete or I or anybody else. They just have this relationship that is like a strange, old married couple – they know how to do it. I think Mike's right: if he were to push Al, it would make no difference, where if he gets cross with me, he'll get some kind of reaction, good or bad. They have this dance they do around each other, but it's totally necessary. If Al were to disappear, it would be very interesting, because he's Mike's anchor, his sounding board."

Jason Lent makes an intriguing point on the finely balanced relationship that exists between Alan and Mike. "Does Michael 'need' Al's approval? Absolutely. To a certain extent, I think Al is the most interested in Cowboy Junkies. I felt a level of involvement and commitment from him that seems to eclipse Margo and Pete. 'Alter ego' seems to be the right description. When expanded to the dictionary terms, it can be 'trusted friend' and the 'opposite side of a personality', which could be interpreted as 'opposite side of the music'. The Cowboy Junkies sound has the ego (the lyrics and lead guitar) as the conscious mediator between the band and reality (the listener), and an alter ego working behind this transaction to complete the process. That's Al: essential to the music of Cowboy Junkies, while adding legitimacy to Michael's leadership. I'm not sure Michael would be the force he is without Al being there. I am sure the band's sound would never have developed to such great heights without Al."

As ever with this band, the subject of family isn't far from the surface. Having Alan around unquestionably gives Mike's leadership of the thing a greater legitimacy. He can't pull the big brother act on Alan the way he might be able to with Pete and Margo at times, so if Alan is on board with an idea – be it in the studio, on the road, wherever – you can be sure that he's thought about it, challenged it, even if only in his own mind, and concluded it's for the good of the band. That has to give strength to any idea that makes it through.

Understandably, Mike argues that in some ways, Alan really is family, pointing out, "I've known him longer than I've known Pete, because we were friends before Pete was born!" Even so, blood is thicker than calendars and by definition there has to be a different dynamic because of it. They are part of something bigger than Cowboy Junkies and that fracturing would be something in a quite different realm to simply having to get another drummer or singer. There's a level beyond which arguments with family members can't – or shouldn't – go.

Because of that, in some ways, the relationship with Alan is almost closer than a family one, because it's one that has endured out of volition rather than tradition. For the Junkies, that is an incredibly healthy thing, because it means that at the heart of the band there is a key partnership where the two genuinely can say anything to one another without any danger of destroying a bigger unit. Of course, it wouldn't be Cowboy Junkies – and it certainly wouldn't be Alan – if it was that straightforward, as Mike concedes.

"He's such a strange entity, because he's not very vocal, he's not an obvious balance in that way, he's not aggressive. It's easy for him to get washed over sometimes, but he never allows himself to drown. Somehow he always gets his point across and, I must admit, sometimes I wish he'd make it more forcefully, because it would make it a lot easier for the rest of us. But then there would be more arguments, more tension; it probably wouldn't work. It wouldn't be Al. The way he does it is fine – he's a really important person to have in the mix."

Or, as David Houghton explains, "Michael is the head. Margo is the heart. Peter is the spine. And Alan is the opposable thumb: one simple thing you take for granted, but wouldn't want to do without."

CHAPTER 22

In their caves of wonder

Rock'n'roll is not a commodity that deals much in age, maturity, growth. If you want evidence, look at the Rolling Stones, still straddling the globe, Mick Jagger up there onstage canoodling with the female pop star du jour, young enough to be his granddaughter. Nice work if you can get it, you might say, but what is it telling us?

If it's telling us anything, it's that we have moved back to the dark ages in popular culture, away from that brief flowering in the 1960s – of which Mick'n'Keef were such a vibrant part – when it was all about "us" to a stage where, once again, it's about "them", where we the people cease to be a part of it all other than in our role of handing over money and adulation, where the communality that existed all too briefly in those moments when we were going to change the world has been replaced by an attitude where we mere plebs are simply spectators at the feast once more, where we observe, where we genuflect at the feet of the great ones who are full of grandiose, but ultimately empty, gestures.

The world can do you bucket-loads of ersatz emotions like sympathy, but if you are looking for empathy, for understanding, for somebody to take the time to truly care, you're going to find yourself looking for a long, long time. That is one of the most jarring things about *At the End of Paths Taken*: the fact that somebody is actually sharing your load, talking your language, rather than offering up the simple platitudes that pass for emotional engagement, but which are really full of the same cheap sentiment as the worst greetings card in the tackiest rack.

Oscar Wilde noted that a sentimentalist is somebody who wants to have the luxury of an emotion without having to pay for it – a perfect description of the culture of surface in or, more accurately, on which we live. Cheap sentiment has, of course, long been the staple of popular music such that, along with the dumbing down of the rest of our popular culture, it is what we have become conditioned to respond to. It is the music of the mainstream, swamping those artists who look to reach deeper, convey more, offer genuine feeling. The tsunami of schmaltz has swamped simple truth and washed real emotion away with it.

It's pretty much incontrovertible that the last great Stones record came about a decade before Cowboy Junkies started making albums of their own, that McCartney has had only a slightly better hit rate in that time. Those intervening years have seen the Junkies release one classic after another while Macca and the Stones have atrophied, but still effortlessly fill stadium after stadium for a public anaesthetized by having wealth and fame rammed down our throats with the subliminal, stupid message that attaches itself to every episode of *American Idol* and its ilk – one day, all of this could be yours. If there's anything left to have.

Meanwhile, the Junkies work every hour God sends to keep the show on the road. Why? Because they are talking about reality now. The real-world consciousness has been so manipulated that, now, it shrinks away from us rather than celebrates, and we close our eyes to it because it's all too real. Why the change? Because "us" leads to empathy, to love, and love is too dangerous a concept for those in power, those who rule and ruin the world, to let it fall into the hands of the people. Look what love did in the 1960s and 1970s – it played a huge role in finishing a war. We can't have that happening again, can we?

At the End of Paths Taken does not fit the modern model, not least because the life it talks about is probably yours, or something very like it. It is also a record that is exclusively about love. Not the first flush, hearts and flowers, la-la-la, happy, chocolate-box kind of love, but the kind that's put on a pound or two, wears its bruises and its scars openly but is still standing on its own two feet, even if it is up against the ropes at times, still going after a fifteen-round slugfest. The real kind of love they don't package up for mass consumption any longer.

It is also the kind of album that they don't offer up much these days, one that is a continuous whole, from beginning to end, one you couldn't cut up into little pieces for your iPod, not if you were really going to understand it and get full value from it. Building on the bricks laid down over the previous records, it was never going to be anything but a recording with a strong lyrical theme to it. *One Soul Now* had been fragmented, a collection of songs to be finished from here and there, while, if *Early 21st Century Blues* had consistent subject matter, it was largely drawn from other people's words and music. It was time for a cohesive statement again, something Mike had at the forefront of his mind as he set off to write a new clutch of songs.

"I always write from a very inwards perspective, what's going on in my world, personal politics, the micro that can also be affected by the macro. The writing was very personal on *Paths*, about what's going on, my reflections on my family unit, but that had to be affected by outside forces, because I'm thinking about that all the time.

"To get the songs together, I rented a great place north of Toronto, straight up the highway, an hour door-to-door. It was the old post office of the town; tiny, backing onto a forest and a little river. In the fall, we went up with the kids. There was a weird little stream with these huge salmon coming up, it was beautiful. Patty went up to paint, so we split the weeks: I'd go up for three or four days, then she'd go up the next week. I just wanted to write – that was all I did, and I completed sixteen songs, we recorded thirteen of them – so it was a really good time.

"Musically, I approached it very differently. I didn't use one standard tuning anywhere – I wanted to relearn the guitar, so I found these random, weird open tunings. I had a book of them, and I'd just pick one. If I liked the sound of it, I'd just feel my way round it, figure out how it worked.

"We've been doing this a long time and it is hard to find new ways of coming at the writing. This time I really felt I had to do that. I didn't want to sit down with my guitar and write fifteen songs, then bring them in and build them up. I wanted to come at it differently. I wanted everybody to rethink how they approached the songs. By taking away my instrument and thinking about how to play it again, that was a start. For me, it was great, because I rethought melodies, how chords go together. Lyrics sometimes came from that, and so we had some songs that were very weirdly structured, odd tempo changes, strange little bridge sections, and that's fun.

"Also, I'd sit and write lyrics without the guitar, it was a very nice way of working. I brought up a lot of E. E. Cummings with me to read, I like the sparseness of what he does; I wanted the lyrics to have that feel, and I think it worked."

Working in a post office would seem to be the perfect place if your job is sending out messages to the world and, in this case, it proved to be the ideal setting for Mike to compile a cohesive body of mail. The sheer pace with which it came together was partly a reaction to a year or more spent working on other people's songs.

"I tend to write in chunks anyway. If we hadn't released *Early 21st Century Blues*, *Paths* would still have come out at the same time, maybe three or four months earlier, because touring delayed it a little bit. It didn't impact on my writing schedule, because I just wasn't ready to write until the fall of 2005, but it did have an impact on what I wrote. When I come off tour, I'm too tired, full of being on the road, don't want to pick up the guitar, which is how I felt after *One Soul Now*.

"*Early 21st Century Blues* was a good way to get round it. I didn't have to write, we got to play, I got to produce and engineer, which I like doing, so it kept me busy and playing without having to write something new. But it definitely led to a weird touring set, because it was so top-heavy with covers. We do a lot anyway, but we were promoting an album of them, as well. Normally, I don't think in terms of the mix because, once we do a cover, it's our song, it's in our repertoire. But so many people began to mention it to me that I realized they were right! It didn't mean anything, but it made me anxious to get some new material together, and to do something different.

"Usually when a band reinvents itself, they've got a new hat, or they've gone in some terrible direction that a producer has suggested. The twenty years thing that went on around *Early 21st Century Blues* did maybe make me think it was time to change things, and to add to what we've done, so how are we going to do that? That record was very traditional-sounding Junkies, it was approached in a back-to-our-roots way, just sitting and playing, not much overdubbing. That was nice. We love to do that, we love to sit and play, it's the rock of what we do, so it was a nice little treat. From there, I felt a need to do it all differently. Going into *Paths*, it demanded some changes."

Creation is all about change. You want to keep creating, you gotta keep changing – that was Miles's philosophy and, pretty well every time you got a new Davis disc, you got a charge of electricity that raced up the spine and knocked your wig off, for good or bad. Not many of those guys about. You find another one, you better relish that, better cherish it, because those are the artists that are worth having around your house, in your ears, taking space in your head. They're the ones that are going to wake you up, challenge you, maybe open you up to something instead of reinforcing what you already think you know – better yet, make you ask yourself some questions, or help you strip away some dirt from the answers that were there all the time. That is why Cowboy Junkies remain relevant, while others wither on the vine.

Agreeing with Mike, Alan was also very clear that, going into a new decade of Junkiedom, change had to be on the agenda. "I guess the twentieth anniversary stuff, and *Early 21st Century Blues*, put a top on something. We did that record really fast: 'This is what the Junkies do, let's put it together in a week and see what we have.' When the time came to make a new record, we definitely didn't want to do it like that – we wanted to rethink it – so that period of looking back was a catalyst, for sure."

That Mike and Alan were thinking on such similar lines was no surprise, but it underlines just how much Mike welcomes reinforcement from his longtime collaborator. "The relationship with Al is still the most important, as far as behind the scenes go, making things happen. Getting him on board is the big thing for me. If I can get the concept across to him, then everything else will fall into place.

"Musically, Al is so important and he had a lot more input on *Paths*. I always try to get him involved, but it's never been easy and, now he's on the West Coast, it's harder still, that's a real drag. It's important he's there for his family, but for us we never get together just to work on music or fool around with songs the way we used to. It is frustrating – we'd get things done quicker – but that's reality. There's tons of stuff in life that make things harder; you just deal with it.

"Getting him to come up with basslines to work from was a way of substituting for that. I've tried to do it in the past, but getting stuff out of Al isn't easy! I think 'Dragging Hooks' was developed like that, 'Upon Still Waters' too, so I've done it before, but I wanted to do it again, and more of it. Finally, I got him to start sending me stuff. He really began doing that on *One Soul Now*, but it was too late and that record was already down the path, but I kept that stuff with the intention of building stuff around it.

"Al played a big part on *Paths*, because he had some music demos, too. He gave me a tape with some bass parts, some drum patterns – some piano patterns, too – that we ended up using, so we took what I had and reworked three of the songs to work with what he had. I stripped my guitars off and rethought the melody, the structure, and it went from the bass rather than guitar, which was a nice switch. I put melodies and lyrics to what Al had done and that was cool, too, a different way of approaching it. It worked out with 'Basquiat', 'Mountain' and 'It Doesn't Really Matter Anyway', which are all based around his grooves. I love his bass playing, so it's great to feature it. People miss it, they don't understand it – that it's a big element of our sound.

"A lot of the piano parts and the little weird melodies are his, too. He's got a great sense of that. And, even when he's not obvious as an influence in terms of what he's playing, he's still a huge sounding board and helps push the music in certain directions. We understand each other on that level. I know when he doesn't like something. I don't necessarily have to agree, but I know what he means and why he doesn't like it."

Although change was already very much on the agenda, a stroke of bad luck in February 2006 reinforced the thought that the new music needed to be recorded differently, as Mike explains.

"We had a few shows in February 2006 when Pete was sick – he had a back problem – and we had to get Randall Coryell in to sit in for him on that little run. Randall did a great job with us, but Pete not being there maybe brought it home again what we do best. We missed what he gives us, and that was a useful reminder, I guess.

"I always wanted a lot of songs to be open-ended on this record, not drums-dominated, and there's some of that on *Early 21st Century Blues* – the drums are buried in there. And, to Pete's credit, he likes that, too: sitting back and simmering underneath. That's when he sounds best, when he's sitting back there rather than trying to drive a song. He's great at giving it a texture. Where we get in trouble sometimes is if we have the drums drive a song. That's not what we do, it's not our feel. It works for us when the three rhythms – the guitar, bass and drums – are all together. And I really wanted to make sure that the songs went in that direction, to be a part of the texture, not upfront."

For Pete, staying home was a bittersweet experience. "It was so weird when I missed those shows and Randall went out instead. They were rehearsing at the Clubhouse and I was like a block away, flat on my back at home. Al was staying with us, so he'd go rehearse, come back, tell me stories. He was nice about it, he likes Randall, but it was, 'He's not you, man!'

"Then they went off for the tour. Al was getting the merch together, everything was behind schedule by a couple of minutes, so Mike was getting uptight about it, which is good, because if he didn't we'd never get anywhere! So they got in the cab and it was a funny feeling, like, 'Cool, I don't have to do this bombing mission!' Much as I like it, at that moment, it was nice to think I didn't have to get on the plane, go through the waiting, I can go back to my bed. And, of course, I was still high on painkillers, these Oxys, which is the new ecstasy, so I was in a very happy mood. I just wanted to melt into the carpet! But, to then look on the website, see the tour diary and read the message boards, that was hard. Then they called from the bar one night and that made me sad, because I wanted to be there. But there was no way I could have gone – you just have to accept what your body is telling you, especially as you get older."

Fortunately, by the time it came to working on the new material, Pete's spirit was willing and the flesh was no longer weak, enabling the band to hunker down and start to work … but work with some very definite parameters in mind, according to Mike.

"I wanted to write songs that would open up, so people could come in, and bring something. Even if I split myself into songwriter and guitar player, the guitar player wanted to open up too, not go back to the familiar things I do. That's why I had those unfamiliar tunings: I messed around until I found cool combinations of notes and chords, not knowing what they even were, and then I let the songwriter come in and explore – it was very open. It took me a long time to bring the songs to the band this time, because I didn't want to fall back on the pattern of saying, 'Here's the song, figure out your parts, let's go,' because that's how we've made a lot of records in the past.

"For Pete, there are a few songs where there's not a lot of drumming. There are cymbals, patterns and things; he played congas on some, lot of tambourine; some real simple stuff where I just wanted the kick pattern to get a nice groove, not using his hands, trying to get us all to rethink what works, rather than falling back on what we all normally do.

"It took a while, and we did a session where me, Al and Pete got together and played, and a lot of the drums we used are from what I'd call that demo period. I miked Pete up pretty well, taped everything, and a lot of the feels we got were Pete just searching around for something that worked. I got some really nice grooves from that. Al brought in some bass parts and I put lyrics and melodies on top of those.

"Pete is really good at listening after the fact, where Al is good at interpreting what's going on now. We're very compatible in how we view the music and where it's going, so we have a good understanding of what we want, what's cool, what's not working. Pete is good afterwards, to play songs back to, because then he'll come back with an idea of something else we can do with it.

"I wanted to get away from what we did on *One Soul Now*, because I didn't feel it was healthy, I wanted to try and find something new, and it is a different sound on some levels; that was why we involved other people like Henry Kucharzyk with the strings, Joby Baker later on, too. I think it's very different, but it gets thought of as 'another Cowboy Junkies record'. You can't fight that – you just do what you think is best for your music and go from there."

Alan agrees on the importance of that trio phase as setting the tone for what the record was to become. "We kept a really open mind for the songs, so, as we started doing the record, as we were beginning to play from Mike's demos, we all kept it in mind that this might not be how it ends up, this may just be an acoustic guitar number, it might end up being bigger. We were all prepared not to play on songs, maybe – there's no guitar on one song. It didn't matter. We just wanted to find the right vibe for the song and we consciously went to the extreme of stripping away potentially everything and having a guitar and a voice or a drum and a voice – whatever. Piano, even. It was just a question of seeing where it could go, to get away from the idea we all had to be playing on a song, which gets tedious. I find it an interesting record to listen back to because of all that other input. Jeff Bird contributed a lot of sounds, probably a lot that didn't get used, but that helped us get somewhere else. It's all a big blur now. I don't know who did what, but it worked out great, a bigger collaborative project. It sounds really cool. I'm really happy with it."

"I think Mike got a little bit tired of the sound of the band after the *Early 21st Century Blues* record and two years touring it, and he was ready to do something different," says Jeff. "He asked me to send him copies of all the various things I was working on, because he wanted different kinds of input. He sent me early versions of the material and I sent back a lot of things to go with it, most of which ended up not getting used. Of course, I was disappointed, but it's only what I do to other players on my records: I make the choices. And, anyway, by the time the songs had been around a while, they'd gone through a lot of changes, so some of the things I'd done for the earlier versions were maybe not right for the directions they'd gone in. That's just the way it is when you're a contributor. It's not my record!"

"Jeff ended up only playing on one song, on 'Cutting Board Blues' – these atmospheric things in the back," notes Mike. "But he sent stuff for four other tracks – one of the songs didn't make it to the record, 'Shrike' – some stand-up bass on 'My Only Guarantee' which I wanted to try, but I ended up liking it pretty spare. On 'Basquiat', he did percussion, but we decided we didn't want anything extra on that one, either! It's part of the process and finding out what you don't need is as important as finding out what you do.

"Live, Jeff makes all sorts of things possible, but recording, we haven't used him a ton, considering what a big part he is of things. He was involved on *Open*, because it was the live band, that was the idea. But, in the studio, we can cover things because you're piecing it together. And where his electric mandolin is so important live, to add to the four of us, in the studio, it's not such a necessity – we get there in different ways. Jeff is a very distinctive player – the harp and the mando especially. He's on *Trinity* and *Caution Horses* a lot with that and they were signatures of that time. If we use him, it tends to make people think of those records immediately. Same with Jaro, too – the accordion is too reflective of an earlier period. It has that effect on me, too: it takes me back and makes me write in a certain way, and we've already done that.

"I felt it was important that we approached *Paths* very differently; that was a conscious thing," Mike reiterates. "I set that out for all of us right at the very start, but at the same time, I said I didn't know how, where to begin, even. That's why it took a long time even for us to start. I had the songs written by December 2005 and we didn't really start recording until the following June. So we had six months trying to figure how to start. What we normally do is get everybody together, say, 'Here are the songs,' and start to work out our parts from that. I didn't want to fall into that set pattern this time. Even with Margo, I didn't give her the songs, I just gave her the lyrics, no demos. I just wanted her to read the words and get to know them as poems, just to understand them, and then figure out how to approach them later. I didn't know if I wanted to start with her, with the band or what. Even the actual recording, I knew I wanted to do that myself, but we didn't have the proper equipment. I wanted to upgrade what we had, but I didn't know where to go, so we were waiting for that, too.

"All these elements were floating around and then they started to fall together. I had an idea about isolating the four of us up at Margo's farm for two weeks in June 2006, just to play around with the songs, experiment. The Clubhouse was a big asset for us, but it can make things feel a bit like going to the day job, too. If we use it, we go in at eleven, come home, deal with the kids, dinner and stuff, then go back and do a few hours – you're in and out of that world. At Margo's, the four of us stayed there, focused on music, did whatever we wanted to do, whatever hours we wanted to keep – a really intense period to kick-start it."

For Pete, recording *Paths* was a big shift from the way he prefers to work, but this time he found the more "academic" approach appealing.

"We looked at shaking things up for this record. Mike put a lot of parts down to clicktrack and then, when we went to work on it at the farm, he became the producer/engineer. We all had input on it – we'd move the microphone a few inches and see how the kick drum sounded, we all had a consensus of opinion on the boom, the chick and the boing – but he was the guy on the knobs, he hardly played.

"Usually I don't like that, because when I'm playing I do it through the feel and I don't know if it's good unless we all get off on one another while we played. So, a lot of stuff we've done as one-offs in the past for soundtracks or tribute albums, it's often Mike's idea, clicktrack, my drums on top of that, and I hate that process. But this time, I found that there was something to it. Maybe I'm more used to it, but I enjoyed it. Then there were songs you couldn't play that way, there were a couple we tried live off the floor. But, having Mike as engineer, you could do it on a take, where before, on *One Soul Now*, it was hard because you're waiting for him to press the buttons and you lose that feel. You look at it a different way; it was more dependent on the playback rather than if it felt good as we played it, distancing yourself a little bit. It was a new way of looking at it, to gauge it. It was an interesting challenge.

"For all that Mike gets frustrated sometimes with engineering and with producing, he likes it, too. There's something about writing on those sheets from the recording studio, the tracks, the tracklisting – something there gets to him! When he'd make compilation tapes when we were younger, he loved to list everything down. He used to take that Letraset lettering and do the whole thing with that. That's his interest: he loves the idea of making music and getting it recorded. And he gets better and better at the producing as he goes on – working with bands outside the Junkies is valuable for him and having the new studio space the last few years has helped him, too, because the Clubhouse was getting kinda small. I think it's good practice, but it also brings new ideas, too – all part of the learning curve."

"Once we had the ideas together," says Mike, "then it was easier to go back to the Clubhouse. I could get different people in at different times. And we had a few sessions, too, [when] Al would fly in for a week every now and then and we'd throw ideas around if something wasn't developing properly, but that period at the farm really did get things moving. We hadn't had a period for a long time where we're together twenty-four hours a day while we're recording, and just focused on the record. I don't know how much of that we kept on the finished thing, but a lot of ideas came from there – we developed a lot of stuff, evolved things and threw things out. A few times, we took songs so far and just realized that wasn't where it should go and we started again. It was very liberating; we got to a point where everybody felt they were part of the process, which was good for the band. Al played a lot of keyboards up at the farm, too, which I've always wanted him to do but Al, you've gotta place him in front of something to get him to do it! He's really talented, but it's getting him to do something.

"After that, we had the ideas, and things beyond that started to fall together – like getting Joby Baker involved on the mixing, he added a lot of keyboard parts with Al. The approach to instrumentation, the whole sonic ideas came together, but at the same time, right from the beginning, even before I'd started to write, I knew I wanted to use strings on this.

"I'd already met Henry, who arranged them, at that stage. We'd talked about it and I was determined to use him, but the problem was that I didn't know how to start a dialogue because he's in a whole other world, the modern classical composition world, I'm in this world, and we didn't have a common language. I talked to Henry before I started writing songs. I was almost hoping to write around his parts, but we were never really able to get that dialogue. I was trying to bring the two worlds together and I couldn't, so I decided to go on writing and put in sections where he could score. I wrote in the spaces. It was pretty open. It wasn't written in stone. As I got songs together, I sent them to him and he'd feed me ideas back and that started moving, too. So, we had all these elements making progress on their own until, finally, late in the summer of 2006, we were beginning to really put it together, take this idea, that idea, throw that one out, take a piece of that part. That's why it has a different sound – it's focused, but it isn't. The band stuff is, but the added instrumentation comes from areas we wouldn't normally work with."

At the End of Paths Taken was to be a record that followed the blueprint of *Trinity Session* and *The Caution Horses* albums in terms of the number of people closely involved with it, albeit that it sounded radically different. What it did have, though, was the cohesive quality of their best work – something they laboured long to achieve, according to Alan.

"We had a solid base of ideas going, the songs were together, but the idea was to get to that point and then let it fall apart, let other people have a crack at it. We had four outside people taking a major crack at the songs – Henry, Joby, Jeff Bird and Jeff Wolpert in Toronto, who has mixed a few of our recent records. He doesn't play anything on it, but he adds radical enough sounds to it so that it sounds as if he has. He really loves to change things, he's a major creative guy for us. Everyone was really enthusiastic about the record. We were lucky that we've found the right people over the years to help add to things without taking it away from the direction that we want. This time, with Joby and Henry, we'd never worked with them before, so it was a real crapshoot if they would get what we were doing and could contribute to it properly, but they were both amazing.

"Joby is a guy I met out in Victoria near where I live. He runs a studio, he's a producer and engineer, great musician – plays everything.

We hired him to mix a couple of things, but he kept hearing things in there and kept recording them and adding them on and sending stuff. He was really enthusiastic, so he did a lot of things and we picked what we liked. He plays piano on 'My Only Guarantee', beautiful piano part. Mike just gave him the acoustic guitar track and said, 'Can you make this piano?' so he just sat down and did this Keith Jarrett thing, really nice. The whole song is based round that, so it was great to have someone able to contribute. It makes the whole song. We've never really had that before. The way Henry changed songs with his input was amazing too, so going fifty-fifty with these guys on arrangements, that was very exciting."

"Joby was the wild card," agrees Mike. "Al was doing some work with someone else and he found this studio, run by an English guy, Joby Baker. He's a phenomenal musician, plays everything, he's got a very interesting ear, and he's a studio engineer, too, so he knows all the toys in there. We got him involved on a couple of songs. We had the piano parts that Al was working on, but we don't have a piano here, so, when Al went back home, he took the files and went to do that with Joby, who suggested some ideas. Al left it with him; he put a Wurlitzer on, put bass on a song that we had left without bass, some cool ideas, treated things – not straight playing, but playing the studio at the same time. So we gave him a couple of other tracks that I felt could use some of those elements, and some we used, some we didn't. A couple of songs went in a different direction, which was refreshing. He was ideal for the project, because we wanted to have a whole other angle on it anyway.

"We talked on the phone, we emailed each other. He's a good musician; he throws stuff on there, sends mixes back, not directed by me at all. That's great for me. People think I'm a control freak but I'm not. I'm just the one who has to move things forward or they sit and nothing gets done. But, if somebody walks in with an idea, that's fantastic. Not all the ideas we go with, but I love having the chance to look at them and then decide if they work or not. That makes it fun. All our lives as Junkies, we've had tons of musicians come in and do different parts, so in a way it's nothing new – just a little more of it on that one, maybe."

The most obvious "outside" element came through the string arrangements, something that Alan especially enjoyed after supervising their addition with Mike and Pete in the Metal Works Studio just outside Toronto.

"We let the arranger do what he wanted and bring it in. The original idea was, 'Let him go crazy and we'll cut it down, take it out if we don't like it.' That was the idea I had going in: 'It'll be used sparingly.' But after we recorded it, everything sounded so great. At first, I thought some of it was dangerously over the top, but the more I listened, the more I liked it, and I don't think we ended up editing any of it. He got his full gig in there, which was nice. Makes a real imprint on the record, for sure.

"The obvious reference points for our generation is The Beatles and Led Zeppelin. And ELO. I guess the whole classic rock era. Younger kids probably think of The Verve or Spiritualized or something, that kind of stuff – Oasis, even. There's not a lot of bands using strings these days, real strings, written stuff, played stuff, so it always sounds really old school when you hear actual orchestral players on a pop record. It gives it a different feel.

"I think it's a bit dangerous – it can turn a lot of people off automatically, they think it's pompous or whatever – but if you listen to it, you can hear that it works. That's the only thing that matters. It's not so conventional to be bland. Some is pretty straight, but there are really weird chords on top. I like it. Pete's not so big on adding strings, Mike likes it, Margo's just, 'Whatever, who cares, I just sing', so it's interesting."

Pete remembers, "When we did the strings, Henry was our go-between, between us and the string players. He was the conductor in there with them, where we were in the control room. They had their own ideas, which was interesting, because normally for those kind of sessions, you better not have any ideas, you just play what's written! Mike and Henry had a nice rapport, but I guess it could get pretty ugly if you get a producer who can't relay it to the conductor, who can't then relay it to the strings. That must be pretty tense. They talk a completely different language. We talk about music in terms of fuzzy or dark or whatever, where they're talking minors and majors. For them, it's a bit of an autopsy. They've got this music on the table, but it's not what they're used to seeing. It's not 'in time' or whatever. But that's rock'n'roll, man! You push a chorus or a solo. You don't really have backbeats in a symphony!"

A sense of looseness was something that Mike was determined to retain throughout the whole process. Again, in using outside musicians, particularly classically schooled ones, there was a danger that their influence might have swamped it, made the music more conventionally regimented, but the Junkies were on the lookout for any telltale signs that things might be drifting the wrong way. They also had an interesting new way of countering it.

"I didn't want to lose the casualness of the demos. I didn't want it to get too formal, which is a danger of the studio: you correct things and you look for 'perfection', whatever that is, and by the end we make a judgement on whether we like the song or we don't. It doesn't have that emotional aspect to it any more – it's like something we've built in the lab, it's not even the same song any more, it doesn't have the same vibe as the demo.

"Because I don't have any formality in my singing, because I don't know how to sing, I don't have enough technique to guide it in any direction – that's what you get on my demos. It just comes out. So I thought that, if I put my vocals on some of these songs, and make them more prominent, that'll force the song to stay casual. 'Still Lost' was one of those, and 'Someday Soon', too. It was just not going to work if we'd developed it, it would have totally lost the idea of the song, so I wanted to keep my vocal there to keep a sense of groundedness, to keep it there.

"Over the years, I've thought about singing one or two songs, then I've given it Margo to have a shot at. She'd just do it, you hear that voice, and you think, 'Fuck! Why do I want to sing? That's so stupid! She sounds so amazing!' That was why it had to be a conscious decision to sing, don't let go of that idea this time. It was something I had decided on even before we started the project, just to give it a sense of being thrown out there. She had to adapt to singing with me, she had to sing around me or with me, as opposed to bringing what she normally does. And that was part of the intention, too – I wanted her to sing differently, less how she would do normally."

"It was a challenge this time," Margo concedes. "A lot of time, my voice is on the top of the songs, like icing. This time, it was the anchor, with all the weirdness going on around it. It was hard. The idea from the start was that my voice would be the only melody. Usually there's a guitar riff or something fooling me. This time, just me. When Mike suggested it, I immediately thought, 'Oh God, oh God! Too much work!' I was very familiar with the words before the music turned up, which was new, so when we started to work on it, ideas began to flow from the music they were giving me: sounds, sometimes; it wasn't always music!"

"Margo approached the actual physical recording in the same way," says Mike. "She takes a while, she'll take a pass at a song, take it away and listen to it, then do it again, and that will happen a couple of times, maybe, before she nails it through listening and talking it through. All the vocal performances came out great and they went through stages – there were songs that hung in the balance because the vocal wasn't right but, in the end, she nailed them all.

"Even 'Basquiat', which is my favourite song on the record, that vocal initially did not work at all. So we went at it a different way and, rather than trying to get the vocal to fit the music, we kept the vocal and changed the instrumentation around that, stripped a few things away, added that weird minor keyboard part in the choruses, and all of a sudden the vocal worked. Normally we finish the instrumentation and Margo has to sing to that, so that was an interesting thing – a backwards approach for us, in a way.

"We did a lot of new things with the record, so you had to keep on top of it. The problem with any studio production is you can lose perspective as you get inside the job of using the studio. For me, using the acoustic was important to that, because it's very basic. A lot of the rhythm on this is acoustic, not electric. A lot of it was played without a whole lot of attention to detail, just strumming away and we'd build on that, which gives it a natural feel, an immediacy that you can't escape, it's not perfect, and then everybody has to play round that. And there are a lot of 'human noises' in there: the bar noise, the count-ins on songs, Margo sighing at the start of 'Spiral Down'. We wanted there to be a human atmosphere around the record."

For all that there is a real kitchen-sink element to the production, with everything you can imagine thrown at some of the songs, it's still a very intimate-sounding record. It's also one that pointed intriguingly towards the future, as Alan explains.

"Playing live is fun, the gigs are good, but it's the records that stand. Anything you do in between just gets lost really. The people who are at the shows have a good time that night, hopefully, but that's pretty fleeting. You make a reputation and a history from the records – that's what people know. That was one of the great things about The Beatles, especially later on: they didn't have to tour, and so they put out so much music instead. Fifty, nearly sixty, years on, that's still what we're talking about and listening to. They were smart!"

And they had the songs to back it up. Just like Cowboy Junkies.

CHAPTER 23

What wears most is the constancy

As Alan says, in the end, it's the records that tell your story – they're what people hold on to, your songs. Some groups can sell out enormodomes, yet leave not a trace on the bigger picture, while others enjoy a few moments in the sun but generally embrace the dignity of labour, taking their work around the theatres, releasing records that leave an indelible stamp on the hearts of those willing to make the commitment to listening.

At the End of Paths Taken is an album of unflinching realism, one that their peers in their forties and fifties could relate to – a far cry from the teenage preening of all too many rock'n'rollers, busy having their skin stretched beyond the realms of elasticity while dipping their head in a bucket of dye. Instead of pretending that life in middle age can be as energetic, lively, exciting and open to possibilities as it was in your early twenties, you reached the end of that path and found a record that was weary. Life-affirming, but weary.

"I think that's where we are, the age we are," agrees Mike. "Everybody I know of my age is just exhausted. Was it supposed to be this fucking hard?! You have kids, a job, you're trying to go forward, deal with the hits that come from outside. Then you start thinking about your kids' lives and you really get freaked out. But, at the same time, we're all in the same boat – there's something very positive about it, and most people are doing things they enjoy, maybe not their job, but the kids, or other interests. Families are difficult as hell, but there's something really great about it; you can be proud about that. That's what *Paths* is about.

"We wanted to get some of the record's theme across with the cover, too. The young hand is my daughter, the old hand is my mother. It worked really nicely. Initially we found a very cool photo of a young boy sitting in a field – you only see the back of him – then there's the wheatfield and this huge sky, which can either be beautiful or nasty depending how you interpret it. It was a nice summation of the thing, but the photographer had already sold it, so then we went on a three-month journey to find what we eventually had. It was frustrating, because it was the first image that came, and we said, 'Yeah, that's it! Perfect! We don't have to go through this whole stupid thing of looking at a million photos!' But I'm really pleased with what we got in the end: conceptually it's nice; it translates into lots of formats, like the booklet, posters, T-shirts and things, which is great, because with *One Soul Now* that never happened. They were nice images, but they didn't live beyond the CD. But this really tied the whole theme of the record together, being in the middle of young kids and ageing parents, and not having any place to turn!

"I guess every generation is the same, but all my friends, we look at one another and say, 'I'm raising kids? How the hell did I do that?' There's a sense of getting the job done – of achievement, I guess. But, at the same time, it's so exhausting. You don't have time for anything, trying to put everything in there: job, family, passion. It's hard, so the record is trying to sum that up. And then you think, 'I got it easy. It isn't World War II!' Imagine doing this then?

"It's so strange – there's nobody on your side except your little circle. The big thing is, up to your thirties or whatever, you always feel there's somebody looking after you, you can go to your parents. Then, suddenly, you're looking after everyone: your kids are too young, your parents are too old. All the responsibility falls on you, you're the one in line. There's no recourse, the buck stops at your desk, whether you want it or not.

"*Paths* is about the family as a whole, how the people in it affect one another, generation upon generation, how you get into ruts over the way of doing things, relating to people, each other, that you don't really realize unless you step back and start to think about it. How your relationship with your father affects your son, his relationship with his son, it goes on and on. You perpetuate these things that are sometimes good, and sometimes aren't healthy, and you'd be the last one to recognize it, for some reason. There's some weird evolutionary thing going on there that masks it from you.

"That's part of what the record is about, *At the End of Paths Taken*: you go down these paths, you get to the end, and you think, 'My God, how did that happen? How did I get here?' You're always having paths open up, choices to make, but you look back and think, 'I didn't make a choice at all, it just happened.' And you get to a point where you are at the end of a path, when the choices are really narrow, if there are any; the reality is that you are at this point in your life and there's no turning back. It's a terrifying point to come to. All your life, you're told you have these thousands of choices, and then suddenly someone's taken them away, it's the weirdest thing. When you're young, everything is open to you, you just walk here or there, that path, whatever. You can always back up or jump to the other, but all of a sudden it's, 'I can't move, I'm here.' You've taken a path and you don't realize you've done it.

"Part of it is influenced by where you've come from, your past relationships, not just yours, but your parents' past relationships and what happened to them. It's hard-wired – it's very difficult to break away from, even if you are conscious of it. But I think at least it's healthier to be conscious of things even if you can't avoid them. That's the basis, but then there's also the way the world comes in on that, which extends from *Early 21st Century Blues*. The outside pressures, what's going on, where we find ourselves, how you relate to your kids' future, that's another element.

"But I think mostly it was where we were in our lives. You get to a certain age and you realize that the decisions being made politically now are going to affect our kids. A few years down the road, what their lives will be like is being influenced right now by decisions being made. Their safety; will they be able to travel so freely; the environment; the whole situation in the Middle East and how we're dealing with 'terror' – that's a path taken, that can't be just erased; the whole fuck-up in Iraq and Afghanistan – that's going to affect us for decades to come. There are solutions to that problem, but there was a path chosen in the aftermath of September 11th that was the wrong one. So many people knew it, so many people said it, but it was totally ignored. Now we're here and now we have Trump, now we have populism everywhere. What are we supposed to do? I don't know. I have no idea how you get out from under this. It's just fucked. And that will be part of our kids' lives forever. So that's in there, an underlying current, those are the times the songs were written in – it has to be there.

"'Brand New World' set the tone for me. This was my subject matter, and I wrote it almost as an introduction: this is what the record is about, the day-to-day slogging, the idea that I don't fit into this world, that I don't get it any more, that I long for the time when I can just lie back and watch the shadows move across the walls. That weariness. But also that sense that 'Only love will stop the withering', that answer to it. The big outro was a very cathartic idea, the way to start the record. That sums it up. Then, at the other end, 'My Only Guarantee' was pretty much the last song I wrote. I always knew I was going to write it, that was the final destination. I didn't know how it was going to come out, but I always knew that sentiment would be there."

Margo feels that "'Brand New World', it's about all that stuff you have to do, and you're willing to do it, you do it your best, but all parents, and all children of aging parents, have that moment at 4 a.m., when it's dark and you just realize, 'God, this is too much.' There's not a person that hasn't had that 4 a.m. moment, because that's life. And people don't admit to it, which I think is the big problem. We share a lot in songs, books, art, but we don't really talk. Girlfriends don't say to each other, 'This mothering thing is too hard' or 'Sometimes I just want to kill him.' If you do find somebody who does share that, you don't feel so much like a bad mother or a bad husband when you say, 'I wish I could run away for a week. Or a year. Or forever!' We all go through it. But we're so inundated with what we're supposed to be, with bad pop culture, TV, magazines, and it's really screwed us around. Our normal feelings are portrayed as abnormal, so you're lesser. Our radars are really off, and that's the worst thing pop culture has given us, this whacked-out sense of reality."

Pete echoes his siblings' view on both life and the record. "As you get older, time gets shorter, somebody steals it. Kids, too, they eat up the time, picking up, taking, playing. You just don't know what it is when that happens to you. I think it's the same with getting old. I look at my dad and I see things change, things he does or doesn't do, and

I say to myself, 'Why is he like that? How did he get to be like that?' But it's because there's no fighting it – age does things to you, it tires you out, your body wears out, and you might be able to appreciate it mentally, but I don't think you really understand it until you get there. People don't talk about these things, they don't talk about death, even when they're 90 and they have to be thinking about it. People don't say anything, so we're all left there not knowing."

Margo is on the same page as her little brother. "I've always believed with records that they go out and they can fit other people's experiences. Michael writes the song, brings his own life to it, hands it us, we bring our things to it and it ends up as an album. But then it goes out into your world and you bring your life and your interpretation to it. I love that part. To me, there's no greater compliment than somebody telling me what a song means to them, or what they hear in a song, and their connection with it. That communication is what we're about.

"Part of the strange culture we have is this lack of talk about death. It's beyond me. We're all going to experience it, we'll all have people die on us. I was out walking with Ed and our two dogs one day in spring – he was 4, I think – and there was a little groundhog family we'd been watching. I said to Ed, 'Hey, maybe we'll see the baby groundhogs again.' Just as I said it, my dogs pounced, grabbed one of them and threw it in the air. Oops. Ed's face was just so stunned, I reached for the parenting books to see what you say when you've watched a groundhog being savaged! So I explained, 'The dogs are hunters, it's their instinct', and then, of course, he wanted to see the body. He really looked at it for a long time, and I had to explain, everything dies eventually.

"Next day, he wanted to see it again, but of course it had gone. I had to explain that something had eaten it, thinking, 'Oh God, I've messed up my kid again!' But I called my mom afterwards and told her about it, and she said something really wise to me. It's better that these experiences happen with you around so that you are there to explain it, rather than him going through it without you. I think that's one of the really strong things about that record, that it talks about coming to the end of your life and we all have to handle it."

Warming to the familial theme, it's back to Pete: "These books about having kids and raising them, there seems to be something missing from all of them. There's a lot they don't talk about, like, 'One day, you're going to want to throw the kid out of the window.' Being a single parent must be the hardest job in the world. I don't know why there's not a suicide rate going through the roof on that. To be locked in a one-room apartment all day with a child, however much you love them, can drive you crazy. They should get a lot more support instead of being blamed for everything. All this pressure to be the perfect parent, bring up the perfect child, and nobody knows what that looks like, anyway.

"Mike's songs address that – a little extreme sometimes, but in a good way – to get the point across. He's right: the only guarantee is I will fuck you up because what else do you do? Then your kid becomes a teenager and you find you're fighting with yourself, you've programmed them! A lot of those conflicts explode because of that. You're mad at yourself, because you see all the bad things about yourself in this person and you don't want them to go there, but how do you stop it? You have to let them go through it. They have to make their own mistakes, because we're just not very good as people at learning from anybody else's."

The way 'Brand New World' starts, it sounds like it could have been on *Early 21st Century Blues*. It's a very traditional Junkiesque song and then it goes through so many changes and sums up a lot of the music to come, the big string parts, the cathartic outro. There is a real urgency in that closing section, the whole primal thing – let's just get it out, let it go.

"I love that primal scream at the end," laughs Margo. "I feel so good when I do it onstage, because you can't do it in real life. But you do want to, because you do feel so overwhelmed. And then you wake up the next day and do whatever it is you have to do. How you do it, you don't know. But you do."

"The line 'My heart is missing' is one a lot of people have picked up on," notes Mike. "The way I view it now is that it's referring specifically to that sense of waking up at four in the morning and everything is flooding in on top of you and not having the strength to deal with it, the sense of being overwhelmed. It's just those moments when you think, 'Fuck this, I can't deal with it.' And then you carry on."

Mike's point about the way people coped with all this stuff in the past while war was raging around them does make you wonder if the touchy-feely way of life that came through the 1960s was all for the good. We have surely lost the stoicism that characterized previous generations. We blow up everything that happens into a big deal, when there's no need. Are we the thinnest-skinned generation there's ever been? And, if we are, how much worse are we teaching our kids to be?

"You might be right. We take everything to heart, everything is urgent. I often think that about raising kids. My parents didn't deal with it like this. They didn't sit and talk at dinner every night about how the 7-year-old was acting and, 'Is it because we're doing something bad? Should we do this?' They just let it go – it happens, it evolves. We tend to agonize over everything. We don't just hunker down and say, 'It's life, let's just get through it!'

"I guess it's part of the whole 1960s thing that the world will change and we will change it. Even though we were at the end of that, I think it carried over into our generation. Bringing up kids now, it's like bringing up a glass vase. When we were kids, if you fell out of a tree, you fell out of a tree! We were expendable – they had six of us! I'm not saying we should go back to that. My dad was great, but he wasn't involved in a lot of aspects of my life, because dads weren't, and I don't want to be like that. But I don't think it's totally healthy that we're involved in everything, either, but you can't seem to get around it now. I don't know where that's come from, but it's weird. The modern media tells you that you have to be perfect at everything – child-rearing is such a huge industry with so much to sell you. Even then, for all the books and the DVDs and the programmes and the magazines, there's nothing that ever prepares you for a baby."

Small world and big planet converge upon one another on this path, a connection made more explicit on 'Still Lost', the song evolving throughout its writing, according to Mike. "It wasn't so much about the individual path when I started it, though it turned more into that, it was about the world's path, I was thinking a lot about that. The whole, 'Guiding light, inspiration' idea was about the thing that 'We are the West and you should follow us!' That song in many ways is the example of the micro and the macro coming together.

"I guess exasperation is just the human condition. You choose a path, you follow it and you're still not satisfied. I wish it wasn't like that and maybe you do get to a point where you're OK with things. And then you die! It's probably right at that point. Damn! But at the same time, that dissatisfaction is a big motivator, it's what gets things done. Without that, if you're satisfied, there's no need to continue to explore, to continue striving. But it's frustrating, because I'd love to get to a point where I was really happy and I could enjoy it! And then, if you're thinking about work, even if you get to a point where you're satisfied, then you have to worry if it's bringing in enough money for the family and all that side of it. The dynamic is always changing with kids: every day is literally a new day, there's very little stability, it's always shifting."

> Here we stand at the end of paths taken
> Guiding light, inspiration, the slow decline
> Crumbling foundation, the station and now the cross
> We're still lost, we're still lost.

The central refrain of the song takes in pretty well the story of the West, its dismantling of any founding morality coupled with its belief in its philosophical supremacy over the rest of the world, while simultaneously focusing on the trials and tribulations of ordinary, workaday lives that exist beneath it, neither world nor individual seemingly coming to any kind of satisfactory resting place. If anything, from its opening salvo of a gaggle of voices gathered together but saying nothing (recorded in a bar by Cookie Bob Helm), to the exasperated defiance of its end, 'Still Lost' is a gospel song, a twenty-first-century spiritual for we latter-day cotton pickers huddled around the water cooler, crooning in harmony about standing at "the edge of salvation".

"The new slaves – that's funny!" says Mike. "It's kind of what it's meant for. It's a record about now, about real lives."

"I love 'Still Lost'," adds Margo. "If there's an anthem on the record, that's it, and that's why I dedicate it to the llamas, because to me they get what we do. The last song I had for them was 'Cold Evening Wind', because I always think of them travelling and how far they all come! But 'Still Lost', that's about all of us and I think they get it. It's such a simple song, but so meaningful in its simplicity, too. It's not so complicated, our situation here in life, but we're so fucked up. The whole album, if you listen to it from beginning to end, it really has the power to suck you in, it pulls you in. Gospel songs are like that: they drag you in and make you part of something bigger. That record has so many layers, you go in and I think you can get such a strong sense of sharing something from it."

The way in which the album was put together was, as already noted, more complex and piecemeal than in the past, but there is a blast of live electric Junkies up next – 'Cutting Board Blues' – which opens with a steam-hammer riff that offers a real jolt after the gentler 'Still Lost'.

Mike says, "It's the one that is live off the floor and it doesn't really fit so easily as the others with the theme. But it was just such a cool song we had to keep it in there! It's more abstract – lyrically, I don't even know what it's about – more than the idea of not knowing what's beyond the next door, spiritually or physically. It makes some sense in those terms, but musically it throws the balance out which is good, you don't want it too perfect, that's why it's there. We liked the vibe of it, it's earthy, it's what it is.

"It's about the same kind of restlessness that 'Still Lost' has but it's also about the stupidity of that restlessness. It was written really quickly. The actual line 'Leave my cutting board behind' was something my wife said to me – she's an artist and she uses a cutting board. We both used the house I wrote the album in, she'd go and work there too at times, and we were wrapping it up towards the end of the time we had it for. I was packing some things up and she just said, 'If you're leaving tomorrow, leave my cutting board behind.' As soon as she said it, I thought, 'I don't know what it means, but that's such a cool line!' It just went from there, the sense of leaving, and the groove was great right away. It's great to play live, either as an acoustic song, which again goes back to the demo, or with the full band.

"We did a few shows in Europe as an acoustic trio – me, Margo and Jeff – and played 'Cutting Board Blues' then. That was a weird tour, a lot of fun to do, fairly simple, because you don't need a whole lot of equipment, but we're playing our songs and yet, really, we're not Cowboy Junkies. I guess it's like when John did a record with George and Ringo: it still wasn't The Beatles! There's something about the four-piece that defines what we are. When people ask me to define our sound, I always say, 'It's the four of us playing together.' That's the chemistry, it is what it is, we don't try to fight it. It's nice to have that organic feel to it all, and that's pretty much what the performance on the record brings – it emphasizes that."

From savagery to a sigh, 'Spiral Down' is a delicate contemplation of the most delicate subject matter – mortality and its irresistible march towards you and yours. The dawning, sometimes sudden, realization that your parents are getting not just older, but old, perhaps are on borrowed time, is a blow that debilitates. It might be the natural order, but when the time comes it is genuinely bewildering, coming with a crash to the pit of the stomach. There's a rising tide of panic, a sense of something approaching betrayal and a coruscating wave of loneliness that only intensifies with time.

It's also something that we don't like to mention in polite conversation, except in the most abstracted way, such as the sorting of affairs, bequests, etc., "laid out on paper". Rarely do we sit face to face and talk it out, talk out what's happening, how we feel, simply because it is far too painful, too real. It's one of the great taboos that remain, the abstraction of art the only way in which we approach it. Even then, it's a brave thing to take on the subject when its main characters are still around.

"I guess that song will take on different resonances in the years ahead," admits Mike, "because that's what the song is about – it is about loss, it's about the slow decline of whoever it is, particularly parents, and there will probably come a point where we don't want to play that in the future. It's just a recognition that this is where we're going. The idea of 'now it all begins, or continues to' is that you suddenly notice it, but yet it's always been going on, that getting older, that process. When you write those things, you can't second-guess yourself and say that this is going to be painful in however many years. Any of those things outside the moment of writing, when you're alone in the room, you can't let that affect it. 'Can my parents listen to this song, should I be saying this in front of them?' You really destroy what you're trying to do if you think that way. I don't worry about it until it's too late!

"But sure, impending loss is there; that's the straightforward realization that your parents are getting old. That came up a little bit on *One Soul Now*, but it's very strong on this one. Death is one element, but also losing who you thought they were. As you get older, and as they get older and begin to decline, you realize that the impression you had of who they are isn't necessarily right – you start to reinterpret that. Most people think they were brought up pretty well if they were fortunate, they did their best. And you look around and think, 'Yeah, they did their best, but it was kinda fucked up!' We had a great upbringing, but it was fucked up. You can't escape that. There's not a right way to do this, to bring up kids; there's not a manual. You flounder around, try to be as supportive and kind as you possibly can, but ultimately it's fucked up, because you bring all your stuff to it, it's what you know, you can't help it. I'm not saying it in a bad way, that parents are evil, it's just reality. The whole idea of losing them is hard to even imagine, but you see glimpses of it and that's in there, too. It's a very happy record!"

As the singer of these songs, Margo has to carry the emotion out to the public while all the while feeling the closeness of the subject matter, one of the more difficult balancing acts of her career. "There are nights when I sing 'Spiral Down' and I think of my dad. To me it's about him, especially the line 'I laid it down on paper', because he has everything organized. It's ridiculous, but that's my dad, that's the beauty of him. If I think that way then, yes, I'm sad. But I've never been afraid of that emotion onstage. I've shed tears up there, but that's OK as long as I can keep singing. There's only been the once or twice when I couldn't, and even that doesn't embarrass me, I'm not afraid of those emotions. I'm singing a very sad song and tonight it's even sadder because that's how I feel, or I'm allowing myself to feel the song more. Some nights, I'm just singing the song, I'm not going any deeper than that, I'm doing my job. It might get to a point when I won't be able to do it, but then, in time, you get to the other side and you can do it again and it's about my dad, and it will be a different kind of connection. It will always make me sad, but it will make me happy too, because we're still tied together that way."

The inability to confront mortality, and this generation's general contempt for the concept of growing up, is something that clearly frustrates Pete. "What's going to happen when we all get old? Western civilization is going to be clogged up with all us old people in twenty of thirty years. There'll be too many old people. How do we stay afloat? How do we sustain that? We don't die of natural causes any more – we stay alive until something really goddamned awful gets us! We should talk about that, but we're all so afraid of it. We're in such a cushy life that we don't want to lose it."

The elegiac nature of the sentiment in 'Spiral Down' could have fallen prey to that enemy of emotion, sentimentality, not least because of the musical accompaniment that comes with it. Mike was well aware of the dangers as they pieced it together. "The string arrangement could easily have been too soppy on a song like that, but it isn't. There's a lot of cool little harmonic weirdness happening, which I like a lot. Henry

449

did a great job. His whole sense of harmonic structure and dissonance and what works and what doesn't is totally different from mine, so it was really fun to work with him. I think, for him, it constrained him, put a few boxes around him and that was an interesting challenge on his part; whereas, for me, my brief to him was, 'Go outside of what I've given you, but not so outside that you lose the song.' I think he found a nice balance: there are some beautiful melodies and then those weird moments. As opposed to the strings being a sweetener, they're an integral part of the song and that was important. Ultimately, it's a rock record and I was clear with Henry that it needed to retain that sense, but I still wanted him to do something that made people think differently."

From children to parents to parents to children, *At the End of Paths Taken* is a revolving door of relationships, passing by in the same kind of blur that a life does, impressions forming as you chase your tail just to stay ahead of the other rats in the race. Just as you fear the future taking your parents away, so you worry what that future is going to do to your children once you let them go and can't protect them any longer. Where will their drives, needs, ambitions, talents, luck take them? And what kind of a world will they be doing it in?

"The opening image in 'Basquiat' is very real," says Mike. "My son, back then he drew all the time, just at this insane speed; that's how he gets his energy out. I had tons of his drawings with me on the road – I use them for writing set lists. I'm a big Basquiat fan anyways. I love that primitiveness, that fury in his stuff, and I remember watching my son draw, thinking, 'My God, it's just like Basquiat!' And it went from there.

"So my wife says, 'So you're labelling your son as a junkie who dies at twenty-four! That's great, Mike!' But that feeds that anxiety, I guess. I don't know what he's going to be. Who knows if your child ends up as a junkie? I don't know what's inside of him, what will drive him, and where to. You have no fucking idea where these kids are gonna go, however much you try. You can pretend you're in control, but you have none.

"That's where the solo comes from. I love that guitar solo, I'm so proud of it! I wish I'd written down how I got that sound, because I don't remember! It really breathes, which is great – it was a combination of things. It's the only one on the record, really. It's short, it's intense and I really like that. It's all the anxiety and fury of parenthood, and I'm really happy with it. And, in the song, it's so sparse and then this thing explodes.

"That song actually developed from the demo ideas that Al sent me with some basslines, drum machine, keyboards, and one of those was perfect for 'Basquiat', so I moved the song around his part. It's really liberating, it gets me out of my habits. Then Joby got very involved in and a lot of his ideas are on there. It's all based on Al's bass groove and then we put tons of percussion on it and it never really worked and, when we mixed it, there was something missing, it wasn't happening. Finally, I just said to Joby, 'Thanks, you've done all you can on this one, but I'm going to get somebody else to take a shot because it's not working.' He was fine with that, that's the gig, but he called me the next day and said he had an idea that he wanted to try and then send to me. 'If you don't use it, fine. I'm not going to charge you for the time, even, but take a listen.' So he sent it, and it was just there. He found the song that was in there. He stripped it all away, went back to the groove and just had these little textures and it was perfect. He did a great job on that, hearing what was missing – or what wasn't missing, actually, because there was too much on it. It's very spare: bass and drums and sprinkles here and there.

"And then I had to spend all our time in interviews explaining who Basquiat was! I kept pushing for that to be the radio single and somebody eventually said, 'The problem is, the DJs won't know how to pronounce it, so it'll never get played!' OK, good point. You win the argument!"

Musically, Basquiat's closest bedfellow is 'It Doesn't Really Matter Anyway', no coincidence given that it too is built around a bass groove from Alan. If anybody wants to dismiss *Paths* as "just another Cowboy Junkies record", play them this.

"We haven't done anything like that before, that's true," agrees Mike. "My vocal in the background is weird and it's funny how that happened. Al had his bassline and we were working out the drum parts with Pete, and I was recording as we did it. There's the main part and then a section that goes through these changes, so, to try and get the spacing right, as they were playing, I was giving them the lyric. I had a microphone really close, because I didn't want my vocal to get in Pete's mics. I didn't want to use the vocal: we were just working things out, giving him timing. But, of course, it was there on tape, too, and it kind of worked, it was so odd, but we kept it. I didn't want to go back and

451

redo them because I knew, if I did, it would lose that atmosphere. We call them the 'Creepy Man vocals'!"

They are perfectly in keeping with a piece that is musical film noir. Mike says, "That was from Al's bass again, building from there, and it took a while. Joby had a big part – he brought those little string samples, which really added. Al did the main keyboard part and Joby added a cool Wurlitzer to it. So there are lots of nice little elements to that song which really made it.

"It is a really dark, dark, dark song, there's not a lot of hope in that one. And, whatever people say, we haven't done too many songs like that. In most of our songs, even in the darkest moments, there's a little light somewhere. But that is dark from every angle – the music just intensifies it. It's a real downer! One of the things that it's about is miscommunication. There are times when it doesn't matter what you say, it makes no difference, the other person is going to hear it a different way, interpret it a certain way. It's got a very dark tinge to it, that song, but that's how life is. There are moments in life, in relationships, when you just think, 'I have no idea what's going on here!' That sense of frustration.

"It's a direct result of a fight with my wife, words just crossing, and thinking, 'What are you hearing? I'm not saying that!' And the same on her side, too. We're talking and the communication is completely missing, it's flying over our heads, and it's chaos. How did that happen? You have no idea. And then you don't know where to go from there, because you can't understand how you got there. It's like two different languages; it's so weird when that happens. 'I don't even know how to fix this – I don't know what to apologize for!' It's in that moment that this song exists. And then you apologize anyway. 'What are you apologizing for?' 'I don't know, what do you want me to apologize for! The death of Christ?' Those moments are so weird! I hate those situations, but I think the song catches it, the weird voice in the background mimicking everything but with a different attitude. Musically that was a happy accident, I guess."

Is it better to have words left unsaid than to have words misunderstood, as Mike had once mused, as far back as *Pale Sun*? Resurrecting a domestic argument is always fraught with danger, especially doing it for the masses, so it's at times like these when it's handy to have somebody else singing your words. Is it easier to be completely honest if you're not the singer?

"It's true. I do have another wall," agrees Mike. "I can write certain lyrics and there's a filter between me and the listener, for sure. If I'm feeling vulnerable about something, I'm never totally out in the open, because Margo's there singing it. That is a big part of what we do, being vulnerable, and Margo's voice is a big part of putting that across, she's very able to communicate that side of what we do. People hook into that and that's what keeps people there – we're saying something they want to say or that they're feeling. We're attempting to get to the heart of the matter and people recognize that.

"It's hard to know if Margo offers greater security than just writing anonymously for other people who I don't know. I guess that part of it is that she's my sister, but it's also that we've worked together so many years now, so I know so much of what she knows, she knows so much about what I do, we have that unspoken relationship on that level. If I was to work with someone else, who knows? I've been offered that opportunity, but it doesn't interest me. I like writing my own songs and playing them with our band. Songwriting as a craft doesn't interest me. I don't want to write the perfect pop song, I like to write songs that we can play and record. I don't want to write the songs they want you to write in the Brill Building. I want to write my own!"

Having Margo as the front does mean that she is regarded by many casual listeners as singer, songwriter, leader and head Junkie. The fact that those of us in the congregation know that isn't the case meant that the opening to 'It Doesn't Really Matter Anyway' courted some controversy – "Singer brought her to tears, but they were my words, not hers", all delivered with laced contempt – is a pretty potent concoction. If you happen to have a tame psychologist in the house with you, now's the time to go and get him or her.

Mike: "It's funny, it sounds stupid now, but I had no intention when I was writing that song of talking about me and Margo. That isn't what those lines are about. I never noticed it, it didn't cross my mind. Isn't that weird? The whole scene is a couple watching somebody perform after they've had a fight or something, and one of them is crying, but it's nothing to do with the performance – it's being provoked by what happened earlier, the other side of the triangle. I never thought about Margo. Not that anybody will ever believe that!"

Margo: "No way! Come on! Isn't that fascinating? I thought it was the greatest song ever, all about us! That's something – a psychiatrist would love that! We have a circle of people who hear our music first, and some people's reaction to that was kinda negative: 'How can he say that about you?' To me, it just totally expresses a very strange singer/songwriter relationship that we have. It works great, but it's very strange.

"I get a lot of credit for a lot of stuff that he doesn't get noticed for and, I don't care how egoless you are, there has to be a part of you that says, 'Fuck that!' There's no problem between us. I'm happy to tell everyone they're his words and I think he's brilliant, I'm honoured to sing them. But some people got really out of joint about that song. But one of the strongest things this band has is that we're very realistic. There's no pretence. We are what we are, who we are. The media can think what it thinks, that it's all me or whatever, but we know how it is. Al and Pete hardly get any attention at all, but, God knows, we're not a band without them. Al is probably the most musical of all of us, but people outside don't get it."

It's odd that anybody could have imagined there was tension between singer and songwriter on the basis of 'It Doesn't Really Matter Anyway', given that the two of them had already offered up 'Someday Soon', what they refer to as their "Donny and Marie moment". Mike's vocals had already played a part on this record and others in the past, but this was a full-blown lead vocal, one that had to work or take down the song. If you want the best opinion on it, go to Alan Anton.

"I like Mike's singing on this record, especially 'Someday Soon'. We're used to it anyway because, a lot of times, that's how me and Pete hear songs first, from his demos, before Margo has even heard them. I really liked him singing 'My Only Guarantee', actually. His voice worked perfectly on it, but he didn't want to do it, he wanted Margo. I think he's got a good voice, really different sounding, but it works in its way and it's added something to this record, a different character."

"Singing together made sense for the song," adds Mike. "When I wrote it, it wasn't meant as a duet, but it was one of the last songs we worked on and, as we got towards it, I started to think it had to be either really elaborate or incredibly simple. There's almost too much melody in it. It was going to become too formal and I wanted it looser. My vocal was initially just a guide, but she started work on it and it started to work with her singing around me; we all liked it, so we kept it. I won't be singing it live, though!"

"The 'Someday Soon' vocal took forever," recalls Margo. "We worked so hard on that to make it sound like we were just sitting around singing in the house one afternoon! Live, it's hard, because there's so much work going in to make it sound nonchalant on record; live, I struggled to find the right space where it's supposed to go, because I can't give it that same feel, because it's not a duet any longer.

"I love it when Mike sings. As long as he doesn't take my job! It makes a lot of sense that he's singing on that record. The theme of the record is that we are sharing things, our responsibilities towards our parents, our kids. 'Someday Soon' is about a hope that there is something that will come along that will make sense. We've always had that hope. People dismiss us as depressing and melancholy, but if you really get what we're doing you realize there is a strong sense of hope in there, too. You hear that; that's why people who like us really love the music. I think that hope comes from our being brought up the same, having a similar outlook on life, even though we express it differently: Mike certainly isn't a talker, like me. But we take our responsibilities seriously, we're the middle kids, the responsible ones, and I guess we both sometimes feel overwhelmed and like we could use a saviour ourselves.

"The other day, I was with Ed in Washington, and I just felt like, 'I wish somebody would take care of me. Just for one day! Somebody go get me something to drink!' The song looks at a more global picture, but if you are in midlife, with kids and older parents, there is always this sense of 'What about me? Somebody take the load off my shoulders for five minutes! Please!'"

For Mike, the song expresses the idea that "the answer" is round the corner. Except, when you get there, somebody says, "No, not this corner, the next one."

"It is like that, but it's a bit tongue-in-cheek: I'm going to find a saviour, a prophet, a leader who'll make it OK. And it does go back to that weariness, the hope that you can look up and get rid of that responsibility because the leader will show us the way. Going back to the macro, there are elements of that song that talk about the attraction of Bush as it was then. 'This guy is going to lead us, yeah, great!' The line 'With only a wink, he'll tell me all I need know', that's him, that wink, the good old boy, great guy, and he knows everything, too! Somebody's going to kick some ass for me, great! It doesn't really happen that way, but more and more it's what people seem to want. That's Islamic fundamentalism or the Christian Right, absolutely. I don't want to have to think, I don't want to have to make decisions, I don't want to process the data any more, I don't want to have to decide what movies I like, just feed them to me. Whatever level, nobody wants to think any more. Maybe they never did. But maybe marketing's become so smart that we've all lost interest or been beaten down.

"Or maybe we're just exhausted. When you talk about the responsibilities, it sometimes sounds like you're saying, 'If it hadn't been for those pesky kids'! How simple it would be without them, time, finances, stress, all of it. Then I think, 'If I didn't have kids, I'd be miserable, I'd be dead, mentally anyway.' My life wouldn't have moved anywhere. It would have been easy, I'd have had so much time on my hands, but what would I think about?! I guess I could see more movies and read more books, but there wouldn't be the advancement as a person that family and responsibility brings. Just the confusion, too, which is a big part of growing and creating, the sense of being thrown off balance. When I see friends, we always say how hard it is, but at the same time it's pretty great. It's all we talk about!

"The final sentiment in the song is just 'Gather those around you, do the best you can, help where you can, move on down the road, because that's all you can do. Nobody's going to show up to save us or guide us, as a civilization or an individual, so it's up to you to do the best job you can for you and those around you. Sorry!'"

Junkies albums have long featured songs that partner up, and *At the End of Paths Taken* was no exception. 'My Little Basquiat' and 'It Doesn't Really Matter Anyway' sat neatly together musically, while 'Someday Soon' and 'Blue Eyed Saviour' shared a particular viewpoint, as Mike explains.

"The saviour part reflects back to 'Someday Soon', that idea that somebody will come and help make sense of it and it will suddenly all be OK after all. The first verse is the macro thing and one of the things built into it comes from the Iraq War: 'She won't let him through the door.' When they talk to widows or parents of the kids who've been killed, they always talk about the Marines coming to the door and they know what that means. Almost to a person, they refuse to let them in the house, they close the door on them. It's like they're trying to stop time, they know what they're there for, but they don't want to be told.

That starts the sense of loss on that song, that finality that comes with it. The next verse, to me, is about losing a parent, then the last verse is again a parent reflecting back on a child: 'Where the hell is this life going to go?' It's that anxiety and fear of losing what is close and tight to you, through various ways – like old age, war, that constant nagging fear about our kids. It's the promise of a future and, once you lose that, what do you have?

"'Hope, the belief that loved ones will never die' is a quote from Joan Didion's book *The Year of Magical Thinking*. I took it with me when I was writing this record and it's a beautiful book, a reflection on loss. It's really intense, beautiful writing, very circular in the way it refers back on itself. It's so well done, some beautiful lines in there, and that was one of them. I agree with that sentiment actually, but in the song, I'm dismissing it – 'never heard such lies' – because you don't want to face that; it takes on the character of the people in the song. I guess, when you're writing, you're more hyperaware of things that you read or you hear or see, and that feeds into the process. I love that. It's the way it's supposed to work: art is supposed to feed art. That's how you gain inspiration, in spite of what the copyright lawyers say!

"It's another that went through changes. I wrote the song and we started playing it live and, as we did that, I felt it needed an extra section – it hadn't felt like that as I wrote it, but with the whole band playing something was missing. Just before we recorded it, we put in the extra section, and I was never really happy with it lyrically, it was just superfluous. We recorded it with that section, we didn't like the recording, and Al just said, 'I really like the demo you guys did.' So I went back to that and, for the finished version, I used my guitar from that demo, and that didn't have that middle part on it, so we just kept it, because I just liked the feel of the guitar. I didn't lose any sleep over not having that middle section on the record, though live it still feels good to have that.

"We played that song and a few others before *Paths* was available. Some people say now that you shouldn't play new material before the record is out, because there are so many trading sites and it dilutes the new record. For me, there's no point fighting the technology. I don't get it – if you're out on the road, you have new material, but you're not playing it because you don't want people to hear it yet? I don't get that. What are you hiding? The people who are into the music enough to listen to a bootleg of new material are going to buy your record. They're your hard-core fans. They really care about what you're doing, they've heard this stuff for the last two years, they want something new. We just do the show we want to do, we invite people to tape it. If it gets out there, that's great; that's the point, to get the music out there. We have enough faith in enough people that they'll buy the record, buy a T-shirt, a book or whatever. We have to look at the business and make a living from this, but you have to have a leap of faith that it'll work out."

Downloading is the medium of the age it seems, and 'Blue Eyed Saviour' is the kind of song that might have attracted plenty of that, given that it is a fine pop song in the classic lineage.

"People are all about downloading individual songs now, but there aren't so many of those classic pop songs around any more, which is weird. It fits in the classic verse–bridge–chorus idea, which is a very English pop thing which I've always admired. Fifteen years before, that could have been the single. Now, there are no singles. The companies still talk about having one, because they think it focuses the radio station that's not going to play your song anyway, so they focus on what they're not going to play! It frustrates me: they produce promos, which fans then buy on eBay, because the guy at the radio station doesn't want it!

"CDs did change the way people looked at putting things out. You had more space, and now downloads I guess are changing it, too. People are talking about the death of the album, and yet *Paths* was as album-like a record as you can find. I suppose, over time, as the downloaders of today become the artists of tomorrow, they might not even think about albums. They might only think of singles or individual little statements. I can see that happening.

"It's very immediate, that's great. We have our own studio, so I can write a song today about last night's hockey game; we can go in tomorrow and it's out there for download the next day. That's kinda neat rather than having to wait three years for each 'statement'.

"I guess this record is swimming against the tide. It's not like we did it intentionally, like, 'Downloading's coming, let's make a real album instead!' It was just the shape it took. In the writing process it was a very theme-driven record. It's the first record for a while where all of them have been specifically written for the album. It was all written in a three-month period, with that theme of family and the outer world creeping in on that anxiety. And it was intentional. I sat down very consciously determined to write about that. That's given it that strong album feel and the connection between the songs."

Nothing gives the record its power more than 'Follower 2', a song that might yet prove to be the finest in the Junkies' canon. More than any song on the album, it slips and slides across the generations, reaching out to the future, casting back for the past, the ages distinct yet indistinguishable across a sinuous lyric. 'Follower 2' is a centrepiece, tracing the evolution from father to son, to son becoming father, scraps from Michael's childhood, inklings from his future, one relationship becoming the other.

"That's the nice thing about songs: you bring your own stuff to it," Mike enthuses. "In 'Follower 2', the song is about my relationship with my father, mine to my son, and vice versa. 'Can't bear to hear him breathing, knowing what's to come' – that line was written about my son. You watch him lying in bed, just breathing, and it's like, 'He's 6 years old, he has no cares in the world other than his little 6-year-old cares', but not really, and you think, 'Fuck, you're 6, and I know all the crap you're going to go through – who knows what else happens in the world.' That is something I find hard to get to grips with. I sort of realized after the fact that it can be taken the other way, for me thinking about my father, or any of us thinking that, knowing that it's the end that has to come sometime."

That was how I heard those lines, coming just a couple of years after my dad had succumbed to cancer, dying on a morphine drip, breathing racked with the pneumonia that attends these moments, a parasite eating its way through what remains of the will to survive. It's the kind of song that can reduce anyone to tears. Even though that wasn't what Mike intended, he can see how it's applicable.

"'Follower 2' is my favourite lyric on the record. It's hard to listen to it even now, because of the theme, which is good in a way, but it's not going to get any easier in the future – hopefully the distant future. I'm really proud of that song and that dichotomy of whether you're talking about the son or the father; I like the way that flows. Originally, that second half of the verse, initially the lyric was 'My son lies breathing' and I got rid of that because I didn't want it to be so pointed. I wanted it so that you were thinking, which generation was it about?

"I love the way that song turned out: the string arrangement is great, Margo's delivery is right there. That was the last song she did and it took her a while to get it. Once the strings went on, she went back and sang it then and it fell into place."

"'Follower 2' is a great song to sing," says Margo. "It has really strong images about my dad and, when he's gone, that will make me so sad. But the writing is so great. 'Sneaking peeks' – I can see us as little kids, on the stairs in the house, with Mike and Cali trying to see through the banisters to see our parents in the den! The whole thing is so full of pictures from our childhood. Luckily I was brought up during the era of Women's Lib in the 1970s. Fishing was only for the boys until I came along, but I wasn't having that! Of course, my brothers hated me for going on the fishing trip, but, having gone – that whole getting up in the dark, the sun's coming up, waiting for the fish – I loved it. None of the boys would be in my boat. The only person in my boat was my dad. Even my uncle was part of that whole male thing, off somewhere else. And the weird thing is, Dad's sister was a great fisherwoman, so it's not like they had no idea! She was allowed to fish – what about me!?"

From casting lines to casting strings, the arrangement on "Follower 2" is sumptuous, made by those adornments.

"The strings are cinematic and, when we were mastering it, we took a chunk of the strings and put them on the front," says Mike. "I was trying to describe to Peter Moore, who was mastering it, what I wanted – that I wanted it laid back in the distance – and he said, 'Yeah, like an old movie soundtrack!' Which it is, really. The way the strings pick out the 'rains falls down', it's literal, but it works, it's very cool.

"I'd heard lots of demos on synths and things from Henry, so I knew where he was going with it. That's the job of producing: to not just hear it as you're given it, but to hear it in your head in context: 'I'll take that out, move that round', whatever. To me, part of the fun is that extrapolating. We've got this. 'Now what happens if I take that and put it next to this? And what if we bring this guy in to do something?' I like that: getting people to bring their vision to it and trying to assemble it. Especially with the strings – that was a great challenge. The complexity of arranging that is so far beyond me that it was fun to have somebody else come in and then to communicate with each other. It's like a 3D jigsaw, I guess, and then you go and mix it, which is a whole other thing, bringing a whole other level to what you've done. It doesn't always work; sometimes people can destroy it. And then you start again!

Good mixers are like musicians: they bring another perspective and open things up."

The music, the playing, the arrangement, all come together in a perfect storm on this rainswept song, all coalescing around the refrain, "Here you will always be", a line which is the cornerstone of the record.

"It is," agrees Mike. "That was taken from a Seamus Heaney poem. I took a whole bunch of books with me when I was writing, because you lose touch over time with that stuff that you used to read a lot of. When do I have time to read poetry?! So it was nice to take advantage of that opportunity. I'd already decided on the theme I was going to pursue, and I came across that Heaney poem, 'Follower', as I was reading. It's a beautiful poem, and initially I tried to write the song just using the poem as lyrics, but it didn't work, so I kept those two lines to build around, the same idea, and I guess that sums up the record and the way family goes down through the ages. It's him reflecting on following his father – his father was a farmer, and he's following him with the plough in the fields, trying to keep up – and then the final turnaround is his father behind him, trying to keep up."

"Here you will always be" is also about the time when his father won't be there at all, not physically. But always there in your mind, your soul, the face that looks back at you when you shave, the one whose phrases and sayings you still trot out, the one responsible for who you are, what you are, how you are.

"You can't escape it. You find yourself saying things to the kids that your dad said to you, having the same pet peeves and stuff. It drives me nuts. Dad used to get pissed off if we went in his office and took anything like a pen or a stapler or whatever. We could never see what was the big deal. But now, I understand that, because I'm in my office, I need to work, and it's, 'Where's my fucking stapler?'! I gotta spend ten minutes walking over the house to find it and it drives me nuts! Fine, take it, but put it back! It's frightening, but it's kind of comforting, too, in a weird way."

There's nothing comfortable about the maelstrom that opens up a song called "Mountain", a chaotic collage of music and sound that sounds nothing like any previous material from the Junkies, a swirl of cloud that obscures the peak, rendering it tantalizingly distant, a bit like the solutions to all the everyday problems that beset us in life. It's a musical thunderstorm, raging, rumbling, flashing light momentarily to illuminate the gloom, then gradually passing away to leave moments of peace, perhaps clarity, as it slips by, only for another to follow in behind.

"That track is bass and drums, and vocals," says Mike, "and everything else is incidental stuff – some strings, my dad talking, some weird floaty synth stuff, some piano, noises, a guitar track on the end. It's just interesting to see how it works.

"From the very beginning, when I got Al's bass part, I wanted to build something round it that was a kind of aural montage. The initial thought was to give everybody a couple of tracks – not just the band, but to Jeff Bird, to whoever – and not even give them an idea of what to play; just give them the bassline and tell them to add something. Al and Pete did their section; I had the song, the melody for the chorus; and we built the secondary bass part on that. Al found the weird synthy parts, Henry took it away to add ideas, I put some backwards guitar parts on, and it started to become this much bigger thing. I gave it to Joby and he figured it out, distinguishing things, floating the strings, bringing things in and out. It's really interesting to listen to – it achieved what we wanted."

Propelled along on a lolloping bass groove from Alan underscored by noises, outbursts, disembodied voices, in some senses it's their version of 'A Day in the Life': order out of chaos, huge ambition, monstrous imagination, a willingness to experiment and throw out the conventional and just see how the cards fall. And that includes getting someone in to read from a book – Mike, Margo and Pete's father, as it happens.

"The idea for 'Mountain' was weird," notes Margo. "We were at the point where I was thinking about backup vocals. Before we'd started, I had a lot of ideas for this record, but as we got more into it and more music was put on it, I decided I really didn't want to do any. It didn't need it – maybe a word or line here and there. To me, it's like an instrument part: you add it because it makes sense, not just because you can do it. But I did hear something in my head for 'Mountain': I wanted to talk the song, not sing it. So I talked with Mike and he was interested in the idea, but he came back to me and said, 'Rather than you talk, let's have somebody else do it.'"

"My dad being on the record was one of those little conceptual things that just fell into place," adds Mike. "We hadn't planned it, but with 'Mountain' there are tons of elements on there, it's a soundscape.

Margo was putting some vocals down one day and she said she felt she wanted to put a secondary vocal down, like a talking vocal. That was weird, because I'd been thinking of having conversation underneath it, but I hadn't figured what I wanted, I wanted narration more than random conversation.

"It looked like we might have my voice on, because it's difficult to get someone in to say something, to record it, so we thought it needed to be a bit more structured. Margo suggested I read something from Dad's book and, from that, it was just obvious we should get him to do it and it's perfect. It just spiralled that way. It made total sense in the context of the themes of the record for him to be on it, to be reading his autobiography – that was cool. He had two passes at it and it was fun to do that. It worked really well.

"The part he's reading is an incident with my mother, this nice little Christmas story, so the fact he's there, he's reading a story about his relationships, which is what the record is about. It's a neat conceptual thing that made a lot of sense."

Margo adds that, "Just from a personal thing, having Dad reading his book on tape, that's fantastic. My husband's dad was a journalist, so there's a lot of him talking on tape and it's amazing to hear it – suddenly he's there with you. Especially without video, I find it more powerful with just the voice. There's not much of that with Dad before this, so it's great to have. There's a lot of me, there'll be plenty of Mike, because of all the interviews we do, even Pete talks sometimes! That book my dad did, it's a huge gift he gave us."

The song also presents us with the phrase "How did this mountain get so high", a guttural scream of frustration about just how life mounts up in front of you and the sheer scale of what you have to get through every day, Margo wailing the words into the abyss. My dad had a variation on the theme from his RAF days – "These bloody mountains would be fine if only they'd built them flat." Given his involvement in the aviation industry, I thought it might have been a phrase Mike had picked up from his dad, but apparently it was one freshly minted in the writing sessions.

"I brought that phrase to the session. It had been in my head and I wanted something to come from that, because it's just that sense of exasperation about where we are at this point. It sort of brought all the themes together: 'There's just too much to do!'"

"Step by step, we take on weight", a powerful invocation of growing up, of ageing, of taking on the family and its responsibilities. "Secure the good, leave the rot behind" – the real trick of bringing up a family, learning from the past, forging the future, trying to find the calm in the eye of the storm rather than being thrown to the four winds by the force of the blast, the swirl and fury of the music making 'Mountain' almost harrowing. Most times, that would be the perfect conclusion to a record. But this was not most records. Here, the last song was actually 'My Only Guarantee', like the end of a whodunnit, pulling the rug out from underneath you.

"The parents did it," laughs Mike. "It was my intention that the record would build to that, that was always going to be the last song. It was supposed to have that sense of self-realization. The other songs, it's the writer, the character, the parent, whoever, working through these scenes or experiences and coming to the realization that it's the parents' fault! And now you're a parent, so you can't absolve yourself of the guilt, because now you're doing it.

"I love watching them grow and develop, being baffled by them, but it's frustrating and maddening, too. When you get down to it, 'My Only Guarantee' is about that. I've come to the realization that, no matter how hard I try, how good a parent I am, whatever that means, ultimately I'm gonna fuck you up because that's how it is – a version of that Larkin poem. This lack of control is healthy if you're trying to create and make sense, which is a big part of art: trying to figure it all out. If your life is in control – no kids, money, no pressures – what's to figure out?! You don't truly grow up, really, until you have responsibilities. Maybe that's why people put it off and put it off, have them later, and why we have such an infantile culture.

"And sure, there is an anger at mortality, I guess. 'A bigger lie I've never told' – that's in there because, although you say you'll always be there for your kids, of course you won't be, because we all go sometime. And there's an anger that you won't be here to see how things turn out. That's the frustrating thing about having kids, especially if you have them later: I won't be able to see all the things that are going to happen. I'm curious about that stuff, how will they turn out. It feels like a rip-off! That's definitely in there.

"That kind of links with the 'Here you will always be' line from 'Follower 2'; it comes back in 'My Only Guarantee', that I'm always going to be in you somewhere, even when I'm gone. When I say that 'I will fuck you up', it's not all a negative thing. It's just recognition that that is how it is. You do imitate your dad's traits, his expressions, and there's no escaping that. I am in you, I'm always going to be in there for always and you're going to have to figure it out for yourself which bit is good, what you need, what you don't, whether you can shake it off. Hopefully I'm giving you a lot of good stuff – that's my intention – but it's going to screw you up. Somewhere along the line, you're going to wonder, 'Why do I hate doing this?' 'Why do I act like this in this situation?' That's the reality. I'm in the mix along with your other experiences, what you choose to do with your life, the other people you meet, but, because I was there at the start, that's probably a bigger input than anything."

The closing song also hints at the simmering tension that's to come as the children age, the bubbling undercurrent that neither generation wants to give voice to, but knows it will, the "After all I've done for you"/"I didn't ask to be born" argument. That sentiment spins off from one of the album's most telling, poignant lyrics, one that speaks to any parent out there – "What wears most is the constancy".

"It's Margo's favourite, too," says Mike. "Absolutely, you've gotta be a parent to understand that. It never stops, physically, emotionally, mentally."

As the songwriter, did he never worry that, when they turn teenager, and have those raging hormones tumbling out of their mouths every time they open them, they might throw lines like "A bigger burden I could not drag" back at him?

"I don't worry about it. One of the singers in the choir is a friend of my daughter and she wanted to hear it as soon as we had it. I watched her as she was listening to it to see if she picked up on the language – the swearing isn't such a big deal, I try not to swear in front of the kids, but we all do. But she didn't really seem to hear it. She will get it one day. And then I'll tell her, at least I warned her!

"I think a father can accept it more easily that you can't always do the right thing, or that, however hard you try, things go wrong. I think women want everything to be perfect for their children and the idea that it's not is maybe harder to accept, so it was probably hard for Margo to sing, though I know she accepts the idea behind it. I think becoming a mother later on, with the job she has, having to go away from home a lot, it's always preying on her mind a lot, anyways. But, as a parent, you also have to do what you do as a person aside from that, aside from being Mom or Dad, but that's one of the conflicts we all have as parents, I guess. As the narrator of the record, she had to sing it, though initially we were going to get the choir to sing 'I will fuck you up'. Which doesn't make any sense! I don't know why we thought that!"

Alan agrees that was a change that had to be made: "Originally, the kids were supposed to sing the 'I will fuck you up' line, and they agreed they'd do it. One day, I was sitting at home and I thought, 'That really doesn't really make sense for the kids to be singing that.' In the narrative, that's not what they're saying. So I called Mike and said we should get Margo to sing it. And then we talked some more, because we weren't sure we wanted Margo singing that line, because it's a big statement. Margo's like the narrator on that story, and you've got to stay with the story right through. If it only makes sense for her to sing it, then she has to sing it and we'll deal with what comes. I think she sang it really well, it's a tough line to sing, but she really got it. For a woman, a mother, to sing that sentiment is tough, and we had to go through it a few times to get the right tone. It won't be a live number, that's for sure! For the record, though, it's the perfect closer."

Margo, on the other hand, is someone who has turned singing that word into an art form all its own. "I love singing 'fuck'! I love that song, too – all the sentiments that are in it are so real. To me, it's not the kids that are a burden, it's the responsibility. That's what the song is about: about parenting today. It's really hard, it's relentless, it's always at the front of your mind. And you can never understand it until you become a parent. If I could give a gift to a couple when they're making a decision on having children, I would love to have them feel that responsibility. It's not a question of babysitting for a week, because you hand the kid back and you don't have to be responsible for his life. There's still this overwhelming need to know where he is, has he eaten, what is he doing? There's no release from that; that's being a parent, and it takes a lot of energy. And then the bigger picture – 'Am I messing him up by dragging him around on the bus!?' But everybody has that question in some form. 'Should I go back to work or will that screw her up?'; 'Should he be in this school or that one?'; 'Should I let her go out with that boy or not?'

"At the end, 'My Only Guarantee' kind of explains the record. I love the fact that it's so honest, that you own up to not being perfect (which you're not allowed to do in our culture), that you're doing your best and it is what it is. The reaction we get from people is fascinating. Some go, 'Oh, yeah. God, that's totally how it is.' It's not just how they feel, but what they know; that, no matter what they do, they are going to fuck their kids up. There's nobody you meet at 45 or 50 who isn't screwed up to some degree or other. I don't know anybody who is perfectly normal! That's life.

"But then we get people who take offence at it, it's almost an insult. I don't understand that, because that sentiment is such a gift if you accept the idea. 'I'm going to do my best, God knows I am, but sorry!' It's not a 'get out of jail free' card, like you don't have to try, but it takes a little bit of the pressure off, that you don't have to angst over every single detail, like should they have chocolate today or not? It's not all a major event, which is what parenting today has become."

'My Only Guarantee' is the only logical end to a journey begun on 'Brand New World', just as *Dark Side of the Moon* was always building to 'Eclipse'. That Pink Floyd record is the closest comparison I can find in the rock canon to *At the End of Paths Taken*, in terms of the heartfelt nature of the subject matter, the narrative arc, the use of the studio to conjure sounds and noises that aren't necessarily what we'd think of as music but which propel the story on. It is also the sound of a band in perfect harmony, all four at the peak of their powers at the same moment, singing from the same hymn sheet, as Margo agrees.

"You love everything you put out – otherwise you don't put it out – but with *At the End of Paths Taken*, even more so, on every level. Over the years I've looked on records as being Pete's record where he really shines, or the one where Al is strong, or I'm really happy with my vocals, or Mike's writing is especially good, or whatever. But this one, everything shines. Making it was fun. Making them always has different sorts of memories. *Lay It Down* was fun – I remember loving that whole experience. *One Soul Now* was a very difficult time for all sorts of reasons. This one, it was great from the moment we started on it, the playing has been easy, it's fresh, it's exciting, it's new. *Early 21st Century Blues* was a different side of us, it was great to play with John again, but, above that, it just showed a band that can play together – after twenty years, you better be able to do that! But, these songs,

Mike first handed them to me as poems. No music, nothing. This is something that evolved from nowhere.

"In a way, it is a concept record. It's not a story, but it certainly has a theme. It's something that people of our age group are dealing with – parents, children, family. For us, three of us have the same parents, we are all familiar with each other's children, they're all similar ages, so we're going through that parenting thing at the same time; when they're together, it is this small mess of chaotic madness! We're all sitting there exhausted, these ageing parents, and my mom's sitting there saying, 'You should all have teenagers by now!'"

"Calling something a concept record comes with a lot of baggage from the 1970s," cautions Alan, conceding that "it is a little like that: it has a theme that goes through it, at least, and 'My Only Guarantee' brings it to a conclusion. It's not just the themes, but the way the record builds, because 'Brand New World' had to be the first track, not just because of the lyric, but the music. It's the introduction to the way the music changed. When we had it finished up, we all said that had to be the first thing on the record; it eases people into it, it starts like something off *Early 21st Century Blues*, then goes off into this whole other thing halfway through. I really like the whole progression on the record."

Mike: "It is a concept record of sorts, or a theme record, anyway. The lyrics do cover a certain area and that gives you a lot of scope rather than writing ten or eleven individual songs. As a writer, you have that much more time to work with your subject – you don't have to rethink the theme every time, you just have different perspectives on that idea. I enjoyed that approach; it made it more focused.

"Even coming to the title, it's different. People could interpret it in different ways; they could even think it was about the band – it isn't! The title does sound final, but hopefully the end of one thing is the beginning of another. Either that, or you're at the end of a path and you don't go any further! I liked the fact that, depending on your perspective, you could grab the title any way you want."

The job then was to take the album on the road, something they did with a string of spellbinding shows, the core four and Jeff Bird making the new material soar in spite of losing all the studio enhancements that had made it such a dense and enveloping record. But the Junkies are one of those rare entities that can succeed onstage and in the studio because, like those in whose line they follow, they understand what it's all about. Dylan (as so often) put it best when he said, "Most performers try to put themselves across. I didn't care about that – it was about putting the song across."

"That's interesting – for sure, that's what it's about for us," says Mike.

And yet there's such personality onstage, too?

"That's good. I hope that attaches to the song somehow – that's how it comes across – but, live, people are using their eyes as well as their ears, so there had to be something for them to look at. Early on with *Trinity Session, Caution Horses, Black Eyed Man*, we spent a lot of money on carrying a lighting rig, a show. The music was there, but we wanted people to have a visual thing almost to trance them out, so the music could come over them. Less and less we need that, because now people know what they're coming to, they've heard us before, they're coming to see us rather than just going to see a band. It's nice to have those extras and, on a bigger tour, we would have a lighting guy with us, but it's about the music, the songs. I think more and more people like to see the way we interact, because they're familiar with us, they know that that happens.

"You know what, I guess that's enough."

MUSHROOM BURGERS

To all you unwary vegetarians travelling to the United States, I give you this warning: a mushroom burger is not a burger made from mushrooms, but a huge hamburger with a huger mushroom stuck on top.

I discovered this in Somerville, Massachusetts, when searching for pre-gig food with Mike and John. Walking through town, past the record store that specializes in action-figure dolls of the Pope, we came across a diner that looked the real deal, out there on the main street, but fashioned to look like a dining car from the golden age. OK, the chrome age, if you're going to be pedantic.

We order, listen to the greatest hits of prog rock on the radio – who knew Yes would be so popular round here? Mike and John discuss the set list. Food arrives and I'm confronted by this huge slab of cow. Being English, I ignore the problem, shift the meat to one side and eat the rest. Being Canadian, they approve.

"I thought it was pretty strange when you ordered it," says Mike, a little late in the day, before explaining that, round these parts, pretty much everything you eat is meat. Has Massachusetts never heard of The Smiths?

John suppresses his own laughter and tries to offer me some surplus fries and salad. Mike takes pictures to record the confusion.

I guess this is why John works in charity consulting and Mike writes songs.

CHAPTER 24

Strange taste on my tongue

At the end of paths taken ... what comes next? After the way *Early 21st Century Blues* had gone back to their roots, was almost a summation of a career, the arrival of *At the End of Paths Taken* presented a band wearied by the years – aren't we all? – yet also reinvigorated. Did I mention that Cowboy Junkies is all about a duality of concepts?

This was a band that had taken stock of its accomplishments, had looked into the future and set its face against the cold, evening wind blowing through the music industry, a gale making it ever more difficult to survive financially in that business, harder than ever to say something of substance. And, as they did, there was a phrase upon the collective lips, the phrase they've quietly applied to these last many years: "Fuck you." For they truly are the last of the great punk bands.

"That's good," says Mike. "I'd like to think people see us that way – we've always considered ourselves as a punk band. Those are our roots, especially in the way we approach our music and our business. It's always been a DIY thing as far as we can make it, and nowadays it has to be that way, anyway. Our attitude is, you make music, you put out a record, you go on tour and try to reach individual people, and that's it. We know what we want to do, we put it out – that's really all there is to it."

It was an ethic that was going to come right into play as the band looked at the landscape ahead of them as we edged towards the second decade of the twenty-first century, as they were about to go right back to those roots, standing completely alone for the first time since they'd signed up to BMG. Even though they had left Geffen ten years earlier, there had still been "company" involvement in the shape of their distribution.

"The business side of things does have an impact – not in terms of the music itself, but just around what it's possible to do," says Mike. "After *Paths*, we had come to the end of another set of contracts and we were detaching ourselves with the various entities that we'd been involved with in the early 2000s. People like Rounder, Cooking Vinyl.

"All of that meant we had to look at how we approached things again, so we started to think about what we did in future as far as making new music went. There's always that question hanging there: 'Do we even release records any more?' But we always come back to the idea that that's what we are about; we'll release them until there's no way of doing that any longer."

It was a genuine question, though, for the music industry had shifted on its axis since the days of *Trinity Session*, such that physical product was becoming considerably less lucrative, downloading individual songs rather than albums was on the rise, and file stealing – I know, "sharing" sounds nicer, but did anybody really ask permission? – was cutting a huge hole in the money that musicians had previously relied on to pay their bills. If that wasn't challenging enough, something called streaming was coming along, Spotify and others starting to make a mark as a music library where you could have access to the world's music for next to nothing. And if *you* weren't paying much, the musicians were getting less.

"It's interesting that music is being reduced into smaller and smaller parcels, one song even, where people are watching box sets of TV series, people are still writing long novels," Mike notes, with some exasperation. "People are getting away from the ninety-minute movie and going into the ten-hour TV series instead. But the music business doesn't seem to want to have that side of it, except in the repackaging of old albums with outtakes and B-sides, those Dylan and Beatles boxes and that kind of thing.

"It's such a weird business. They totally lost control of it back when CDs came in. Everything was pushed purely towards profit, they lost the artistic thread, they lost the point of view of the fan, it all came down to numbers. I don't know why music did that where other forms didn't – not to the same extent. They're not sacrificing the actual art form, which the music business has. And then they did it again with streaming, because they're making money there, so let's push everything into that, forget the indies, forget the new artists, let's just deal with the handful of artists we can get a billion streams from. Unless you're Taylor Swift or someone like that, there's no money in streaming, because you have to have million upon million of them before you see any return. And, in ten years, they'll wonder why there's nobody new coming up any more – because nobody new can afford to put the time and creative energy into it when there's no useful outlet and no money coming in. It's so short-sighted; it frustrates me all the time."

The economics of that are rarely exposed, but they are instructive. If we're being generous to them, a streaming company will, on average, pay the rights holder something like $0.005 (a half-cent!) per stream. If, just for the sake of argument, we ignore all the ancillary payments to publishers, record companies, the tax office, etc. and say it all goes to the band, then if you would like to buy Cowboy Junkies a cola, you're going to have to stream *The Caution Horses* fifty or sixty times, in its entirety, start to finish. Even then, they'd have to buy the four straws themselves.

So, in a world like that, where everything is pushing you to go down the digital route, to release one or two songs at a time, what's a band to do? Release a box set of four albums inside eighteen months, then chuck in an album of extras on top. Obviously.

The concept that eventually became *The Nomad Series* took a while to come together, such that none of the band have quite the same story on when it truly crystallized. "We just got to the normal point of it being a couple of years since the previous record, and we got to discussing what the next one was going to be," recalls Margo. "There were a lot of ideas, I do remember that. There was talk of maybe doing a covers record, maybe of Townes' songs. We were talking about working with Vic Chesnutt on a record, but then Vic died.

"Then we wanted to maybe do something that reflected the stage version of the band a bit more – that jamming, psychedelic thing which maybe people don't know about unless they've seen us a few times, and we knew we'd have to set up in a more live way to do that properly.

"As well as that, Mike had already written some songs, we'd played some of them live, they were more reminiscent of what we did earlier in our career, and so we thought about putting out that sparser kind of record. We had all these things going around in our heads, we weren't short of ideas, but we hadn't really come to any decision, because they were all pretty different, they didn't fit together as a single record."

"As we were finishing touring with *Paths*, I was writing songs, we were playing some new ones live," notes Mike. "I was still very much in that mindset where I write songs, we record, we tour, take a break and then we do it again. But it hit me that I didn't quite know what to do with those songs at that point. I was writing without really having a focus. The songs were fine, but there wasn't really an album there at that point, it was just the start of a process.

"Then, in late 2008, we had this opportunity to go to China and live there for three months. My wife had the chance to teach there and, because our two daughters were adopted from there, it was a chance to take them back and try and find out some more things about their circumstances. Incidental to that, it was also a chance to get into a completely different headspace, a different way of thinking and looking at stuff.

"When we came back, I started to reassess what songs I already had and what to do with them. I felt like I needed a new challenge – the band, too – and, instead of just writing a new record for the sake of writing a new record, I wanted it to be different. I wanted to create the record that became *Renmin Park*. I didn't know what that was, exactly, but I knew I wanted to express that experience through the music."

'Different' was one way of putting it, for events and experiences in China had seeped into Mike's way of thinking and, suddenly, there was a whole new idea to put into the pot for the upcoming record.

"When Mike got back from China, he started talking about some new ideas for the next record," remembers Alan. "The three of us were like, 'What???' We just couldn't relate to it, because we didn't have those experiences there. Mike was saying he wanted to incorporate street sounds and have the whole thing sound like his experience in China. We were trying to figure that out, because we weren't there, we didn't know what that meant. It took us a while to wrap our heads around what it was going to sound like.

"Once we agreed to start to move that forward, Mike sent me a lot of the sounds he had from China, the street stuff, the soundscape, the ambient noises. There were maybe fifteen of those things that I focused on. I started working with Joby Baker again, because Mike was looking for me to send him a bunch of rhythm tracks for him to write around – bass, drums, keyboards, whatever. That went really well. Joby was very quick at isolating what was going to work and what was needed.

"We did a load of stuff, way more than we needed, and that was what started us thinking maybe we could do a double album. We had a lot of stuff there and Mike had a lot of lyrics and was thinking he could maybe put a larger story around it. He already had a few thematic things ready anyhow, and, as the music started coming in from my end, he started expanding his ideas on other things he'd written about and looking at how that could also be on the record. That discussion went back and forth between us all for a while and that idea about a double album was around, but that became a struggle – Mike was a bit worried about diluting the element about China.

"The next thing that happened during that early recording period was that Vic Chesnutt died, Christmas Day 2009. That made it pretty obvious that we should do a record of Vic's songs, so that fused together the earlier ideas of a covers album and the thing we'd wanted to do with Vic. That was where we started to think, 'OK, this isn't a double album about the China experience, this is something we can really expand out, we can make the China record, add an album of Vic's songs.' We'd been talking about doing a record of that psychedelic, jammy side of the band that we always had fun doing, so that fit in, that was another component. You get that far, let's do *four* records! It made sense to do something that was a bit more of a return to the more acoustic Junkies sound to complete the cycle, all around the world for us, covering all the kinds of things we do and adding some new elements too, which is where the 'Nomad' title came in.

"It was an interesting challenge. Not just the sheer amount of music, but to make each album distinct from the others while still keeping the four-album set coherent. That was what really sold us on it in the end, the concept of having four very distinct records, released individually – four albums is more than most bands have released this century. That's how I sit back and sum it up now, but it was something that evolved more slowly than that and went in different directions to ultimately reach that conclusion."

"Normally, you couldn't even think of doing something like that, four totally different records making up one set," admits Margo. "But one of the biggest revelations of going independent was having that freedom to do what we wanted to do, whenever we wanted to do it, how we wanted to do it. Nobody was going to say, 'That's too country', 'That doesn't sound like you', 'It's not this', 'It's not that', so we decided we would use that freedom."

Without that contractual freedom, there's no way *The Nomad Series* would have got off the ground, as Mike readily agrees. "We weren't going to sign any more deals, we were set up to do it completely on our own, focus on our own audience, and that gave us that chance to figure out something pretty different. It was interesting: after twenty years or more inside the business, 'Let's just do what we want, like we used to do.' The music, the packaging, the artistic decisions, the only restriction was our imagination. That was freeing, and we then took on this ultra-ambitious project that made it even freer in a weird way. 'Who cares – let's do it, let's put them out! It's cheap, we have our own studio, we're doing the writing, recording, producing, most of the playing. Let's just try this crazy thing.'

"It was pretty ambitious, especially these days, but we were beholden to absolutely nobody, there were no restraints on us, so why not celebrate that? Even though the associations with Rounder and the others were pretty loose, we'd basically call them up and say, 'We've got a new record, here you go', there's no way we'd call them up and say, 'Here's four new records that are coming in the next two years.' They couldn't have dealt with that; they'd have pretty much shelved it, given them cursory releases. If you are dealing with companies in that way, however good they are, you are always beholden to them to some degree, there are always compromises that you have to make. You can't do four records, you can't have four-colour sleeves.

"I guess it was an analogue idea in a digital world, because that was the time when people were releasing songs, not albums. That was kind of a joke at our own expense: right at the point where everybody says the album is dead, we're going to put four of them out! We're quietly proud of that attitude to things, but the truth is, that's what we do. Whenever we get down to starting a new project, we go full circle and always come back to the idea that we have to do what we want, what makes us feel good. The idea that the music business is going to dictate how we release our records, the format, the contents, there's no way that will ever happen. We will play along with it so that the music gets heard, but that's going to be as much on our terms as possible. It has to be our statement in the context we want to make it.

"It's interesting that vinyl has started to come back again. The idea of it saving the industry and making money, that's been very overblown, but from an artistic point of view it's really fun to have that again, it's cool to see that big record cover again. I really love that as a music fan and a consumer, so it's great to be able to put those out again. Maybe that played into it, too, just the idea of having this set of four vinyl records was exciting. I love them artistically and, for the enjoyment of the music, they make you sit and listen in a different way to digital music – even CDs."

"Music has long been a product like everything else," says Margo with a resigned shrug. "When we were at the point when we quit Geffen, it was already going that way, but now it's completely like that. Even if we'd stayed on those big labels – and I doubt they'd have wanted us, anyway – we wouldn't have survived as a band, we'd have become frustrated and angry, so leaving Geffen was liberating, and then it was the same feeling when the distribution deals ended after *Paths*.

"One of the things that helped us make that transition so easily was that, when we started playing our music about one hundred years ago, I don't think we ever felt we were going to be rich and famous out of it. That was never a motivation. We just wanted to play our music. That's what we did and what we still do, so in a sense it's not that big a change. And now, with streaming and downloads, it's hard to sell music and make money from it – playing live is more where you do that – and, again, that's what we've always done. We just ache a little more now!

"But, from the start, I haven't really cared if anybody listens. I'm very glad they do and I'm very grateful to the people who support us. It pays my bills, it takes me to places I'd have never been to otherwise, it's given me a life I never thought I'd have. That's amazing. But when you just go back to what the music is, we started to do it because we loved making music together, and that's still the heart of it.

"If it gets overlooked, too bad, we're still going to go out and play the songs! When I say onstage we sell records one at a time, we do, we always have. We weren't a band that had that huge hit single and that big moment. Even *Trinity Session* took a long time to sell its copies.

477

Sitting here now, I think that's a gift. I think that gave us the longevity we're still enjoying. So that meant, when we came up with this crazy idea of doing a four-record set, we were doing it for ourselves above anything else.

"What was important was that we put some limits on it. Doing it all over eighteen months wasn't so much for the challenge of it, it was more that it needed a time frame or we'd be doing it forever. I think, because we grew up with bands who did that kind of thing, not necessarily all as one piece, but putting out a lot of records in a short space of time, we didn't think of it as that different. You go back to the 1960s and the 1970s and bands were regularly putting out a couple of albums a year and doing it in the way they wanted to do it. Now, it all seems so constrained, there's none of that ambition."

Ambition was the keynote, according to Alan. That was what got the creative juices flowing. "The most interesting thing about it is that, twenty-five years into our career, or whatever it was then, we weren't afraid to do that. 'We can do this, and we can do it inside two years.' That really got us going. 'We'll show them! We're old but we can do this!' And music can still do this, too.

"Music hasn't had that scale of ambition for a long time. Music seems to have been getting smaller and sales of records have got smaller with it. There's the issue with attention span at the younger end of the audience and at the older end – it's about the amount of time you have free to give to music. TV shows, movies: people can experience those things together; listening to music is maybe more something you go away and do on your own. Finding that time is hard. But, once we got to that point, this big idea really got us excited."

There was also a streak of sensible pragmatism running through the *Nomad* concept, though. If Mike's bandmates had found his initial *Renmin Park* idea pretty far out there, he was sharp enough to realize that the wider public was likely to find it yet more bewildering, given they'd have less understanding of Mike's family pilgrimage back to his daughters' roots and the way in which it completely informed and infused a record that was the most esoteric of their career to date – their most inscrutable, not just lyrically but musically, too.

"Getting the idea for what *Renmin Park* was going to be like might have been the real spur for the whole *Nomad Series* idea, because I knew that one couldn't be the Junkies record that we based the next period on, that we created and took on the road for the next two years. It's not like the albums we'd made in the past. It was much too outside of things as an idea, it wasn't so performance-friendly in some ways and it was very personal, too, very me.

"*Renmin Park* was very focused on my experiences and blatantly so, and also a lot of it is rooted in a country that a lot of our audience won't have visited and maybe don't know too much about, so it was a little more alien in that sense. I really wanted us to make that record as a band record, but at the same time I realized that we couldn't just let it sit there and eat up a couple of years, the way records normally do. We needed to follow it up with something else more quickly than we would normally do, and, given we had all those other ideas that we'd been kicking around before I went away, we felt that that could work.

"From there, we decided that we were going to work on the records in the studio one at a time, like we normally would – I was writing in advance, so the songs would be ready – but, as far as recording and production went, they were separate studio projects."

And so the band threw their energies into what became *Renmin Park*. That in itself delayed the process for, as Mike says, "I didn't really do any songwriting at all while we were in China. I thought a lot instead. Once I got a sense for doing something, Pete sent me a recorder out because the music and the sounds I was hearing around us set me thinking I could use that. I did all the field recordings, the soundscape stuff that you hear on it, but no writing in that usual sense.

"I really got away from music, but fell in love with music again in a weird way because of this very natural, Chinese folk music, the different styles of it. What was strange was that, in such an alien place, the folk music was so familiar – that really struck me. I guess it's the instrumentation: a lot of their stringed instruments are very banjo- or mandolin-like; fiddles too, obviously. Some of the regional stuff we came across, if you didn't listen to the language, you just listen for the melody and the lilt, you could be in Ireland or the Appalachians, it is so familiar. That was cool, too. I love the way that draws the world together. My wife and I were in Morocco more recently and it was the same thing there. The local music, gnawa, is just so blues. It's Son House. It's phenomenal how, across all these distances, the traditional musics have such similar elements to them – it all comes back to the same spot eventually. We all still gravitate towards that sound and melody. There's something very basic there.

"As well as that, I really got into sound again, because there was so much going on. I got very inspired by what I was hearing, and so, when we got back, it really triggered things, took me out of my regular routine that I get in when I come to write a new record. I guess it was starting in a different place. I had a lot of interesting aural ideas to work from; I was trying to understand how to distil them and use them in our music.

"I got Joby involved again, because he'd been good at working with sounds on *Paths* and I wanted Al to get involved with him, too, to give it a musical element. I gathered up a lot of that material and I really threw it in Joby's lap, asked him to build some loops incorporating what I had. Al put some basslines in there, and I was able to write around that.

"That was probably half the songs. It frees me up, gets me out of my standard situation, sitting down with a blank sheet of paper and my acoustic guitar. I've been doing that for a long time, so you tend to go back to patterns, and that helped break them down, the same way that working with those weird, open tunings did on *Paths*.

"To be somewhere totally foreign, to have reference points, ideas, the metaphors I was able to build on, locations coming in from another part of the world – that was really liberating, too. Most of the material comes from that period, those influences and that experience. I jotted down a lot of ideas and thoughts from what I was seeing. I had that to look at when I got back, and it all just felt very fresh.

"Because it was so alien and you had none of your normal things to fall back on, because you stand out so much, it does give you an opportunity to reassess yourself, too. I found it really invigorating on that level and also because it's a very vital country, very alive. Just walking in the streets there, there's an energy and a pace to it, it's amazing; you do feel part of it, carried along. It's a very transforming energy. Everything there is constantly changing: tearing things down, building things up. It never stops, going towards God knows what in the end, but it is intoxicating. I don't think anyone knows where that ends – it's exciting and very scary at the same time. The government still wants to control everything, but good luck with that!

"Looking back, it was just three months there, but it could have been three years, because it was so intense. Every day was an adventure because everything was difficult. Just going to the grocery store was difficult. Trying to negotiate your way through a regular day was full of things you have to deal with, when, at home, it's so simple. Having the kids there, too, watching them dealing with it, it was a huge experience. As a writer, all of that input was great for me because, suddenly, I'd got a whole lot of fresh stimulus, things I could incorporate into what I was writing along with my regular themes – as Al says, 'rivers and birds'! They're still there, too, the Yangtze, the swans!"

Renmin Park is the most atypical album of the Junkies' career. No, it's not as if they'd suddenly chosen to become a speed metal band, but this was a record rooted in experiences that were very personal to its lyricist and less immediately communal in nature as far as the audience was concerned. Part travelogue, part familial journey into the heart of his daughters' roots, on the face of it Mike's preoccupations were very much on a micro level this time around. Sonically, too, this was very different territory – from the military band with which things open, through to the surprisingly musical failed phone connection at the end.

It's hard to argue against the fact that this is their least accessible piece, even Margo saying, "It's not easy for people to get into, it's an unsettling record. The way that it starts with that weird marching band, which is totally offputting and goes on forever, it doesn't make it easy for the audience." Throughout, the songs are coloured by found sound, recorded by Mike in China, then spliced and diced in Vancouver by Alan and Joby, infusing the record with a patina from the other side of the world that drifts from the unfamiliar, through the unsettling and on to the downright frightening. Comfortable, easy listening this is not.

Yet, like many a good "concept album", and there are some good ones, it's a record that repays repeated and concentrated plays. Once the strangeness turns familiar, opening the songs up and allowing you to burrow inside, there is some of Mike's rawest imagery to be uncovered, while the playing from the band – and the additional musicians – is often exceptional, underscoring just how seriously they took the project. That's especially important, because they could easily have found themselves less invested in these recordings, for it's a record unlike all their others. In many respects, it's Mike's solo album.

"Totally, it is," agrees Margo. "That was a story that was completely his experience, and that's unlike anything we've done before, because, while the songs we've done in the past might be personal, the themes are universal, too. This one was about a place that the rest of us had no clue about at that time.

"I approached that record completely differently, because it might as well have been all in a foreign language, because I had no way into it. The way I sing, the way I approach it, is by making it personal. Even if I haven't had that experience, I make it like a movie and I get into the song that way. I'm not a technical singer, I can't treat it as an exercise. But, with those songs, there was nothing there that even let me begin to try to make a movie. I had nothing. Nothing. I got so lost that, at one point, I even went down to Chinatown in Toronto and walked around there, just to try and get some feel for it. That was a dumb experiment – it was just Toronto!

"Normally, Mike will give me a song and we'll often work it out acoustically, then we go to Pete and Al and flesh it out. It often changes a lot, but I get my first interpretation in that intimate setting – an acoustic guitar, the basic melody and the words. But, for *Renmin Park*, it wasn't that kind of record, there were all these loops and sounds being done somewhere else. So I asked Mike for all the words, no music, and I just read them as poetry.

"Gradually I got into them that way, not even thinking about how I was going to sing it, but just reacting to the words. How did they move me? I got really familiar with them that way. Then I got the music and there's nothing really happening there melody-wise. It was music that was unfamiliar to me – the loops, not the kind of stuff I would put on my stereo – so again it was just trying to find a way of fitting into what Mike and Al had been doing with those sounds.

"At that point it wasn't about emotion or expression, it was finding a melody, still about, 'How do I get into this song?' Once I'd found that part of the jigsaw, I could go back to thinking, 'OK, what's my movie?' Even through all that process, I still don't feel that that album is as personally sung as something like *Demons* – that was so personal, I felt like I was going to have a nervous breakdown! – but, like anything that doesn't come so easily, something you think you maybe can't do, if you do get through it, you're more proud of it. Now, if I hear some of the songs back, I'm really proud of them."

It's pieced together very intelligently, every effort made to guide listeners into the record, jarring as it might be at times. After that opening blast of martial music, followed by something more intimate from Jingjiang, where Mike and his family stayed, the first song, "Renmin Park", is very much a traditional Junkies sound, and deliberately so, according to Mike.

"We didn't want to completely abandon who we are and just do something totally foreign. We like what we do, the audience likes it. If you go too far down a path, you can alienate people very quickly and then they miss what you're doing, so it was important there were entry points to the record that were familiar. We didn't want to alienate listeners who weren't immediately adventurous. People get frightened by that – they just want to put a record on and listen to it, enjoy it. They don't necessarily want to have to analyse it and work out what's going on. We gave them reasons to stick around and listen to more traditional elements, and to give the record time for the more experimental things to grow on them, for them to fall into it. We felt we could play both sides of the street, make a really interesting record that sounded very different but still be a Junkies record. Margo's voice is always going to ground it in that territory, anyway, but over the years we've realized that, even with all the other things going on, the four of us have a sound that's ours and that is central to what we do."

The careful way in which the audience is led into the record is exemplified by the next pair of songs. No, 'Sir Francis Bacon at the Net' does not have that immediately identifiable Junkies sound, yet there are precedents even for something that is further out there. The "found sounds" build on the collage that formed such a part of 'Mountain' on *At the End of Paths Taken*, while Mike's vocal recalls the "Creepy Man" from 'It Doesn't Really Matter Anyway' from the same record, bringing you up short with a gasp when Margo's voice does finally come in. Then, in its wake, 'Stranger Here' sees them adopting that breezy West Coast style they can do so effortlessly, with some showcase playing from the band, Pete driving it along, Alan in prime form, Margo wringing the neck of the chorus and Mike tearing into one of those angry dog solos. It's classic Cowboy Junkies, single material as good as anything they've ever sent out into a world that nowadays has unaccountably decided it'll only play that kind of stuff on radio if it was recorded before 1972. Conceptually, those two songs sit side by side, for all their musical differences, setting the tone for a record about being a stranger in a strange land and the difficulties that brings on every level, as well as the way in which it can open your eyes, not just to that other culture but to yourself.

"We were in a pretty small town by their standards – less than one million! – very unsophisticated, very few English speakers at all there. Those who did, they gravitated towards us. Patty was teaching English at the high school, it was known we were there, so we were invited out to a lot of teas and dinners so that the locals could get to know us and practise their English, too.

"As a culture it was such a strange mix of extremes – from the incredibly harsh to the extremely friendly and helpful. We grew to love the place, because it is so unfathomable. The people, on a personal, one-to-one level, were so kind and so welcoming, they were just beautiful, and they made our stay so much easier than it might have been. And, at the same time, as a society it's horrible, it's nasty, uncaring, all out for themselves, it was a complete paradox. People who didn't even know you would invite you into their homes and feed you, but God help you if you're in a bus line – they'll belt you in the stomach to get in front of you! The mass society is vicious, but individually they are so fantastic.

"It speaks to humanity, I guess, where if you break us down to an individual level, the human aspect of us, we're all the same, we all care about the person next to us. And yet, the culture you are put into, it has such a power to it that, however that acts, people flow with it on the mass level. That is a scary thing, as we saw in the last century and again now. It is very hard, very tough there. I guess that comes from their recent history, that's how they are as a societal force, but scratch below the surface and they're fantastic. That's the truth to different degrees everywhere. The hope is in the individual people, but when they act as a mass, once you give people a flag, look out!"

As the Junkies audience en masse, we can look at all of that on an intellectual level and take from it what we will, but for Mike, these are concepts that hit him in the gut, not simply because he'd been there, but because that culture could have been the one which, but for pure chance, would have steamrolled the two young girls who became his daughters. Had he and his wife chosen to adopt three months earlier or three months later, two different children would have gone on to live lives in Canada, and those who became their girls would have remained in China. That's maybe a thought best left in those dark, untouched crevices of the soul that we all have. But, when you're a songwriter, those are the places you have to visit regularly.

"Life is so fucking weird, isn't it?" Mike says. "That those two children should have been abandoned and gone through those things, and then they end up as part of our lives. What are the chances of that? What did they go through, how did they survive it, to then go halfway across the world and have lives somewhere else? It is such a weird thing.

"A lot of the album is about the society over there, but it's also about our daughters, who we adopted from there and the world they might have grown up in. While we were there, we went back to the cities where they came from and visited the orphanages, trying to make contact with as many people who knew them when they were there.

"Our youngest daughter, we actually made contact with the family who fostered her and knew her for her first year, and that was a phenomenal experience. They were so excited to see her. They were a loving family – you could just tell how natural it was how, how excited they were, and you could just feel then how well she'd been taken care of.

"Then we went to the orphanage where our oldest daughter came from and that was the exact opposite. It was just horrible, cold, alien. They barely had any records to look at; we came up with nothing. A really sterile, nasty place. 'A Few Bags of Grain' is based around that whole idea of the one-child policy that made mothers give up children and the routes they can take from there. 'Little Dark Heart' is in that vein, too.

"Those songs are more particularly focused on that aspect of it, but there's a lot of references to the process within the whole record – me trying to figure the whole thing out from my perspective as an adult and a parent, and then from their perspective as children. The trip was trying to process that idea of where the kids came from, but also having them face that reality too, and that was hard: that, for the first six months or a year of their lives, we have no clue what happened, who they were, where they were. I think facing that was ultimately very healthy for them, coming to grips with where they're from and who they are, in that sense.

"For us as parents, you feel good about giving them the opportunities that we have in adopting them, but it's always more complicated than

485

that! You look at the poverty they came from and you think automatically that, Sure, we brought them to a better place, but then, at the same time, you realize that we also took them away from something, too, because it is such a different culture. If they were still there, they'd be ostracized – the girls who are not adopted generally don't have very good lives there, they suffer from the class system – but, at the same time, they've left behind a pretty vital culture, the place they were born. How do you judge? Maybe they'd have led the revolution – who knows? Though I don't think that would be a job with great prospects there ..." The "simple truth crushed beneath the leather boot" of "Cicadas" underlines those prospects.

Musically, 'Little Dark Heart' is, appropriately enough, a slow, sad waltz, the lines "One is left in a ditch by the highway / The other 'neath the tax bureau gate" just heartbreaking. With that in mind, the musical imagery on 'A Few Bags of Grain' is equally apposite, those background industrial noises redolent of a policy where human life could not be seen as cheaper, people as machines, dispensable. Yet, within, there is always that Junkies kernel of hope: "She leaves her there sleeping, / hoping that she's dreaming / about a life worth more than a few bags of grain". Alan's contribution to this piece is immense, his writing contribution becoming ever more integral to the band and its sound.

'A Good Heart' also exemplifies that, from its clattering drum and bass start, moving into his bass as lead instrument. The song has a great rhythm track, but it's an eerie, discomforting listen, showing just how the unfamiliar can knock us off balance, even if we don't know if it's benign or threatening. Those background Chinese voices, especially when they are isolated at the end, are pretty spooky to Western ears, the confusion brought about in the listener by incomprehension. It sounds so harsh, but for all we know they might just be shouting out dance moves in school or training drills on the athletics track. More than perhaps any other song on the album, it sums up the sensory assault that a visitor to China has to come to terms with.

The line "Is it the trigger or the breach?" is a pivotal one in that song, as Mike explains. "That has a lot of levels and that's a part of China, too. It's that thing about it being exciting, but you're not sure why. Is it because I could easily get run over if I step off the kerb here, or is it exciting because there are so many possibilities and you feel that energy? You can't pin it down, but there's definitely excitement."

"It is very uncomfortable to listen to that song," says Margo. "To our ears, theirs is a very harsh-sounding language, there are rough edges to it. My memory is that, when I was recording, I didn't have the complete version of the track; a lot of it was layered in afterwards. I'd worked with the loops, but a lot of the soundscape, the grinding noises, that was put in later, which was good, because that would have been really confusing for me!

"Now, having been to China several times since then, it makes more sense to me, because, as a country, I do find it forbidding, harsh and cruel, too. My limited experience is that everybody is fighting for an inch. That's not a criticism – they have to do that; there are just so many people in the cities fighting for space. But, coming from the West, it's hard to be there and to see your fellow human beings having this intensity, pushing and shoving and making sure nobody takes their spot. We come from a part of the world where there are a lot of spots to choose from. It isn't like that there, and it is hard for us to understand that. You try to be empathetic and compassionate towards it, but it is jarring, it is harsh and I think that was the intention of starting the album with the marching band, with feeding in the voices and the sounds. Throughout the record, there's the buzzing of bees and industrial noises and that's the country. You don't relax in China, that's for sure. I'd been in countries where I was the only white person, where I'd stood out that way. I understood that feeling, but this was more than that. China has an edge that other places don't. You feel more alien there, you know you are being watched, you're under surveillance. The other side of it is that, when you get one-to-one with people, they're just like the rest of us: they're helpful, they can be so generous with what they have, which often isn't much, but the culture is very different to anything else I've come across."

Mike's personal experience of the country was the sole reference point at that time, but even he concedes that it was hard to get to grips with it over the three months his family spent there. "The language barrier made things hard, and I can't say I made too many really close connections. A couple of people took us under their wing and were instrumental in making it an amazing time for us. They were able to translate, introduce us to things we'd never have seen otherwise.

"I was very lucky to run into a young guy, Eric Chen, who spoke phenomenal English, but he'd learned it all from watching gangster movies! He'd say 'motherfucker' a lot, without really knowing what he was saying! But he was a huge music fan and introduced me to tons of Chinese music, a lot of contemporary stuff, which was great, and to one artist in particular, Zuoxiao Zuzhou, who ended up singing on the record. He took me to a few local shows, too, some of which were horrible, but that's fine, too.

"The folk stuff, I tended to find that myself by just wandering through parks, because Eric was, 'What do you want to listen to that for?' I'm sure he'd had all that traditional stuff rammed down his throat when he was growing up, but to me that was really interesting. In the parks, there was always somebody playing something or a group singing. There was this little pavilion where some old folks used to gather, I guess it was a club, and they would sing Peking opera, basically. I would sit in the back, they'd smile at me and nod, and for an hour they'd take it in turns to get up and play something. It was amazing to be there for that – very intense.

"I felt that adding a couple of songs from China made sense on the record, but we needed to be sure they were songs that we could get into as a band, whether that was structurally or lyrically, melodically. 'I Cannot Sit Sadly by Your Side' was a waltz, so that's right up our alley, and to me it's got a very Leonard Cohen-y vibe, it was easy for us to do. 'My Fall', it's got that bass groove happening, that 'Common Disaster' feel to it. We took a lot of the ideas from the original – the album it's from is a very cool-sounding record.

"Lyrically, Eric translated it for me, I took the translation and worked around the words a little bit to have a little bit more meaning for us. So it's not a direct read of it lyrically, just because I wanted them to be relevant to us and the rest of the record. It's hard translating Chinese into English – the idioms, they just don't go together – so I had to work on them so they made sense and fit the music."

Ironically, 'My Fall' is probably the most conventional song on the record, a very Western pop sound which in itself is a nod to the way in which culture, and music, can still be a tool to unite us wherever in the world we come from, just like it was 1967 all over again. 'I Cannot Sit Sadly by Your Side' is sonically a descendant of *At the End of Paths Taken*, playing particularly to Pete's strengths. But, if those two covers had some familiar staging posts, 'A Walk in the Park' was a completely different challenge for the listener, Zuoxiao Zuzhou singing his own song in his own language. Who else would put this on their record, a reminder that Cowboy Junkies are, at heart, a very experimental, risk-taking unit? Yet nobody seems to get it.

"People miss that willingness we have to put something on a record that's pretty unusual, totally they do," says Mike with a hint of frustration. "We're still the *Trinity Session* group to a lot of people, whatever it is we put out. That was the idea with not just that song, but with the whole *Nomad Series*: to try and distil each record into some of the things they know about Cowboy Junkies, but also some of those things they don't. I just love that song – it's so outside! Zuoxiao Zuzhou is quite a big star in China now. Pretty controversial, too: he's friends with Ai Weiwei. Al and Joby put this piece of music together, and then I just sent it across to him to work on it the way I had with their other pieces. I said, 'Just do what you want with it.' He wrote the lyrics and recorded them and sent it back and we added that whole weird ending to it with the national anthem being sung and all of that stuff. That was the most exciting song to do, because that was truly the age of the internet! Here's somebody 7,000 miles away or whatever. We don't speak the same language, yet we are able to record together. That's pretty amazing.

"In itself, that's interesting because there's never been a time when we've been so accessible to one another, wherever we are, and yet we seem to understand each other less and less. The whole experience just shows the difference between the macro and the micro. The micro, as people, we're OK, but when it gets to the macro side, that tries to fuck the micro all the time. You just hope that eventually all those micro relationships win out, but that's not the way it works usually!"

'A Walk in the Park' is also notable for an unhinged guitar solo at the end that sounds like the frustrations of three months all unleashed – "You might not understand what I'm saying, but listen to how I feel." It's also a very effective juxtaposition of the modern sound of electricity against a language that seems so ancient to our ears.

'Renmin Park (Revisited)' features Mike's lead vocal, perhaps a tacit acceptance that this was very much his record, before the album closes with 'Coda', a final musing over the difficulties in communication between our cultures. And then it's over. Like it or not, *Renmin Park* was anything but a standard Cowboy Junkies record, whatever that might be. Unless you read the reviews …

"It was surprising to get reviews of that as 'the same old Junkies', because there's nothing on *Renmin Park* that's really the same old Junkies!" says Alan. "I thought there would be a reaction to it, but there was really nothing much. There was more reaction in China. There was some resonance for it there, partly because Zuoxiao Zuzhou is a pretty big pop star over there, so his audience were interested in it.

"We played a couple of festival shows over there because of the record, and that was pretty amazing. We played the Great Wall Festival and they bill it as having the Great Wall behind the stage. Sounded pretty cool, but it turned out to be ninety miles outside Beijing, took five hours to get there because of the traffic. It's a beautiful setting, a hillside, surrounded by mountains, but the Wall is way up, snaking through the mountains, so it's not what you imagine.

"It was a three-day festival and the stage was the biggest I'd ever seen in my life – half a football pitch, just huge, cut into this hillside, an enormous bunker underneath with the dressing rooms, huge lights, PA. The stage was divided into two by a curtain so they could have a band playing out front and the next band would be setting up behind. As soon as the first band finishes, they roll their gear away, roll the next band forward and they're playing straight away. They had that figured out!

"It was a hundred degrees, no shade on the hillside, and we were playing the last slot on the Sunday, the third day. By then, it went from having 25,000 people on the hill to a few hundred. Nobody was left, they were all escaping the heat and starting that five-hour drive back to the city. We're getting ready to play, there's nobody there, but the promoter comes into the dressing room, all excited. 'Ten million people are watching!' He pointed to the broadcast trucks. And that was what the festival was really for: the TV audience, that was all they cared about, that's where the money was. I guess it was the biggest audience we'd played to.

"Then, going back, we were stuck in the traffic. The trucks in front, they just stopped, the drivers got out, they set up tables and chairs by the side of the road, started playing cards, because they knew nothing was moving for an hour. The local villagers all came onto the road to sell drinks and food. One of the guys said, 'This is nothing. We've had jams on this route that last five days.' An eight-lane highway. That's a lot of traffic."

Renmin Park is a record that stands apart from all the others in their career. The mix of sounds, of cultures, from ancient folkways through to modern industrial noise, they all make for an absorbing tapestry of sound, a backdrop to a lyrical story perhaps more heartfelt than ever. If you want a record to dig into, one to explore, to challenge and confound, *Renmin Park* repays the effort.

One down, three to go …

CHAPTER 25

No guarantee of happy endings

With *Renmin Park* and all its new ideas and unconventional sounds brought safely into harbour, the second *Nomad* record looked considerably more like home turf for Cowboy Junkies. Right from the off, they'd been peerless interpreters of other people's songs, and so a record of cover versions was the kind of thing that came naturally, as Mike concedes.

"When we announced the *Nomad* project, we didn't really know how it was going to shape up. We knew one would be a covers album, because it's such a big part of what we do, but we wanted to have some concept behind that rather than a collection of songs.

"Making a covers record was important as part of the whole process. It gave us the space to go and make the other two. Personally, it helped me, because I didn't have to write anything, it gave me the breathing space to put things together for the other records. Basically, the demos are already there, the originals are the demos in a way, even though we then changed things around in the arrangements. Margo could take those away and work out what she was going to do with them rather than waiting for me to give her things.

"Mentally, too, for me it's so much easier just to focus on production and playing. But I think it was refreshing for all of us in a way, to have a different focus to work on rather than it being our material – it cleans the mind a little bit, I guess. It meant we weren't going straight into another Junkies record of new material after *Renmin Park*. There wasn't a hangover in that sense; a bit of time passed, and that benefited the other two records."

Alan is in agreement on that score, adding, "I think the idea of a covers record was the key to us being able to do the four records, because the material was there, we could put our stamp on it, but we always knew where we were going. In that sense, it was kind of effortless – not that we didn't work hard to make a good record, but we'd got the template, it took less shaping and thinking through than when you're making a record from scratch."

"The question was what the concept was going to be, how were we going to approach it?" explains Mike. "We had talked about a Townes record, but that's been done a few times, but then we heard that Vic Chesnutt had died and it became pretty obvious that week that we'd found our new record, that was the way to go, life dictated where we went with it. We had already talked about making a record with him, we knew each other pretty well, we were fans and it seemed right that we should record a tribute to him and give the whole album over to his songs rather than picking from different writers. We had our own attachment to the songs, to Vic. We had good motives for doing them, it was a valid record, so that was where we started work on what became *Demons*.

"We knew that there was a very intense cult following of people who just love what he does. We had to try and put that to one side, we couldn't worry about whether we would offend them with the way we did the songs, or second-guessing what they would or wouldn't want to hear, what instrumentation Vic might have chosen or avoided. We had to let that go pretty quickly or we wouldn't have done anything."

Other opinions are available, such as Margo's. "If *Renmin Park* was hard to conquer because it was just so strange, I think on *Demons* I did the best singing I've ever done, maybe, because I really needed to. Going into it, I was really nervous about making that record. Really nervous. Vic's fans are serious fans – you don't mess with Vic! For us to take on a whole album of his stuff, that was daunting. My personality is such that I don't like to upset people, where Mike is more, 'We'll do what we want to do and if they don't like it, tough.' But he's not the one at the front of the stage!"

"It was a very intense record, because Vic had just died and it was pretty hard going through those songs at that point," Mike admits. "We

493

really threw ourselves into it, we recorded a lot of songs for that one, some of which came out later on the extras collection, some we never quite finished. There were so many great songs to pick from that it was hard to figure out exactly what we wanted to do. A lot of Margo's best performances across the four records are on *Demons*, I think. I was really pleased we made that record, although the way of it coming about was so sad. A lot of those songs still feature in our live set.

"Vic was a very unusual, unique writer, so some of the songs are odd structurally and melodically. Certainly they're odd lyrically; they weren't down Margo's alley in that sense. His approach is often very ironic – they're cheeky, lots of humour – so she had to figure out where to come at those songs from."

"In the past, when we've done covers, it's been one, maybe two, songs from a particular writer or artist at a time, so to do fifteen of them all together, that was a totally different discipline," explains Margo. "We'd never done that before. Once we got into it, it actually helped, because bands, singers, if they're good and if they've been around a while, they've got their own thing, their style. There are variations in that, but you know what they are, what they do. In doing so many songs together, you can find what that thing is and grab hold of it, use it. The first time, you're wandering around in the dark, but do five or six and you really get the feel.

"We did so many of them, more than could fit on *Demons*, because we wanted to do it right, we wanted to find those songs that we could best connect with in our own way and that would stand up, rather than just redoing Vic. I didn't know it at the time, but I've found out that was a really good way of working, of doing the covers. I'd like to do that again, I'd like to do a cover album of Townes, maybe, for the same reason. You do enough of them in a short time together, you get into the head a little bit, in a different way than you do by listening – there's just another entrance point that opens up."

Warming to that theme, Mike notes, "We all knew Vic was pretty idiosyncratic as a writer, but when you actually get to work at the songs, rather than just listen to them, when you start to take them apart to arrange them, they were full of quirks and surprises all the time. Then they took on different, or more powerful, meanings, too, because of the circumstances, so 'See You Around' suddenly became very personal, 'Flirted with You All My Life' became very prescient. They were pretty hard to work on. I always knew he was a great writer, but getting so closely into the detail you appreciate that some of his wordplay is just so fantastic as you go deeper into them. Most of them, you don't really know what he's singing about – yet you do."

Demons is a record that has perhaps improved with distance for, just as recording them so soon after his death was pretty intense, listening to them at that time was sometimes tough too. 'Flirted with You All My Life' was especially raw and it's only the passing of the years that has helped it reveal itself as a beautiful reading of the song, an agonizing lyric cased in a breezy musicality that lifts the whole with that unusual but effective juxtaposition.

Alan explains, "*Demons* was a nice change as far as doing covers is concerned, because the music wasn't really there on his records; it's not so important, it's all about the words and his voice. We had a lot of freedom to develop the music, because we were really just working from lyrics and a vocal melody. We could just invent something that we felt worked with those, which was real fun to do. When we do covers, we try to stay true to the song; you try to extract what's awesome about it but, at the same time, do it differently. For the Vic record, that was completely different: we just ignored the music pretty much, because the strength is in the words. His stuff lends itself to being covered, because the music kind of doesn't exist anyway, it's just a guy singing, so from that there are so many possibilities. We'd done some of his songs before, we'd toured with him, he played with us on the *Trinity Revisited* thing, so we had a handle on him. It was good fun to do it – there wasn't any agonizing over it, it was natural."

Of course, while the band had a certain freedom with the music thanks to the nature of the songs, for the singer it was a little different. "With Vic, it's all about the words, because if I thought Mike was wordy, oh my God! It doesn't rhyme – why can't these people write anything that rhymes, either of them?!

"If I'm truthful, I wasn't sure I could handle that kind of material. It's very dark and sure, we do dark, but not that dark! And he'd just died. It wasn't as if it was ten years ago, it was recent and it was raw, so there was an added responsibility. Obviously, as a fan, I was already familiar with the songs, so that gave me a head start. The boys recorded all the music and then I went in to do the vocals, just Mike and me. We just literally locked ourselves in for a couple of days. Saying I wanted to

495

just get it done isn't right – that sounds throwaway, which it definitely wasn't – but I felt that if I was going to go down that dark hole with that material, I wanted to stay there until I was finished … and I didn't want to stay there too long!

"It was an interesting experience, because those songs do take you to the darkest of places, yet, by the end of the day, it was so cathartic. It was like having therapy, I felt so great. It was partly that I felt I was doing good work and also that I felt Vic would be happy with it. I knew he liked us, he liked my style of singing, so that helped – it felt like he was on my side. Then, when the album was finished, I knew we'd got it right, I knew his fans would love it, and they did. That's probably among the biggest compliments we've had in our career. It was intended as a tribute to him and it stands up as that, so I was really delighted with that.

"Part of doing a cover is not getting sucked into the original too much: you want to keep some of it, but you don't want to just stay there, you want to give it something of your own. With Vic, the fact that he wasn't a melodic singer made it a little bit easier for me, because he wasn't using melody in his voice to promote the song, so that left a gap for me, that's what I brought to it.

"Vic would say that he couldn't sing, not in the way people usually mean that phrase. He had a voice all his own and it worked with that material and so you have to find a way of dealing with that. When I introduce one of his songs onstage, I try to promote him and his records, because I think people should go and buy them. But I tell them that when they first hear him, don't turn it off, because it will seem really weird, his style is so strange. Keep listening to the words, keep trying and it'll come to you, you'll figure it out. It worked for me. I was always a fan anyway, but doing *Demons*, living with those songs, I felt it brought me closer to Vic, which was also a nice thing."

The process of getting it together was relatively simple, according to Mike. "We all picked our favourite songs and started to work through them, and we went through them pretty quickly, getting our arrangements together, then we started to narrow them down to what was going to work on the album. That was the important thing. We wanted it to sound like an album even though they were songs from different parts of his career; we wanted to make it so that it hung together, instrumentally, the approach, the production. The band became the glue that made it cohesive, and it became our record at that point."

That's an interesting observation, because *Demons* isn't unlike records like *The Caution Horses* in that it's one where the core four are the foundation stone, but the musical flourishes that colour it often come from outside musicians, such as the horn section on 'Strange Language', Jeff Bird's mandolin, the various keyboards played by Joby Baker. With those additions, although the songs can be emotionally bleak, the record is somehow celebratory, too.

"We wanted to bring a particular attitude to it that suited Vic," recalls Mike. "His music covered a lot of ground, it wasn't often polished. Ramshackle is a good description, not pejoratively but as a positive. He did do things that were more produced and I don't think that was necessarily his strongest suit. A lot of his records were very loose, and I think that ramshackle was the way to go for him – it suited him and the songs. We wanted to have a little bit of that in our recordings, we recorded pretty quickly because we wanted to make sure there was that spirit there, that idea of, 'It worked. Who cares if it makes sense musically – it sounds cool.' That approach definitely came from Vic.

"The thing about Vic, he didn't take any shit! He'd roll out onstage in his wheelchair and, if he felt like fucking with the audience, he'd fuck with the audience! He was never afraid, or at least he never showed it if he was, certainly not in a public space. It was, 'Here I am, like it or don't.' His voice was a tough instrument, anyway, but if he wanted to make it even nastier, he would. There were some shows he'd do and I'd watch and think, 'My God, you're not even trying to help them!' And then there were others where there was just this beautiful, operatic voice soaring through the hall, then other nights he was doing this nails-on-a-chalk-board thing. He was a very interesting guy in that way. He didn't take any prisoners, I guess."

There were no nails on a chalk board on this recording, for *Demons* should serve as a Vic Chesnutt primer for the uninitiated. It was a great way to get inside the lyrics of a songwriter all his own via a voice with all the intensity, but rather more instant appeal, than his own. The songs are done justice, and Margo, in particular, could be justifiably proud of the outcome. Just as *Renmin Park* was Mike's record as a writer, *Demons* was hers as a singer.

Sing in My Meadow, number three in the *Nomad* sequence, was a record that belonged to the players, including the welcome addition of Jeff Bird, for this was Cowboy Junkies cutting loose and giving us that full-on, acid-blues side of their repertoire that had hitherto been largely absent on record but was such a highlight of the live shows.

"To record, that came together pretty quickly, off the floor in the studio, just a couple of run-throughs and then go for it," recalls Alan. "It was nice to have that looser record to make after the first two, which were pretty focused in their different ways. This one was blowing off some steam, really fun to do, not something we analysed too much, but something that we've learned how to do over the years, something that's been a big part of the live show. We've been recording long enough now that we have the technique to just set up and go – we don't have to spend too long in setting up to get that sound. We don't need to spend six hours getting a drum sound. It was great to have Jeff on it, too. It shows how important he is to us as a live band, but also that thing he has going with Mike is something that is pretty specific to us. The way Jeff's electric mandolin works with Mike's playing is unusual and it was good to get some of that on record."

Jeff did play a huge part on the recording, though he had his own take on just whether they should be making a record at all. "I jokingly say – though I do kind of believe it – that recording is fundamentally wrong to begin with! Recording is kind of like painting: you put something down, you step back to look and then you go with it, rub it out, whatever. It takes away something, it sucks something out of it, although that's a player's perspective, I guess, just because the playback is never the way it felt or sounded in the moment. What's happening to me as I'm playing, what I'm hearing and responding to, is not what's going down on that tape, I've learned that over the years from listening to live recordings. There are shows where you remember hating it, you're struggling, but you hear it back, sounds great. Then you get the night when it's going great: 'We're Gods, we can do no wrong.' Sometimes you play that back and it's, 'Holy smokes, that's terrible!'

"I do like that *Sing in My Meadow* record, it's very representative of the live show. Fundamentally, I think the best place to start is with some kind of live interaction going on between players. I just produced a record for a couple of women and they had this mindset that they should do it in small sections and piece it together, everything gets done 'later'. Every time we came to do something, it was, 'Are these the final takes or are we doing that later?' Well, if you do a good job now, we don't have to do anything later! It was driving me crazy, so I gave them this mantra back: 'There is no later, there's only now!' My attitude is to start recording from the moment you start playing anything, but they had it in their heads that you couldn't possibly get the finished thing like that. Well, why not? Sometimes you get a great performance that way and, if you're not tuned in and recording, you lose that.

"For me, that is the essence of what recording is, trying to capture performances, moments, that magic – and that arrives when you least expect it. All these years later, I still don't know how you get that, other than by recording it all in the hope it's there! Sometimes it arrives in that first experimental take, sometimes it comes from doing a lot of takes. But personally, my favourite way of recording is doing everything live off the floor. I've no problem editing or adding after the fact, but have that basis there first, and that's why I like that record. Apart from 'Hunted', they were new songs, we hadn't played them, but we've all played together so long, it clicks pretty easily, and it was fun to do. It isn't the same as playing live in front of an audience, because with the record there is a safety net, whereas at a show there is the element of danger, but that keeps it fresh."

For Margo, not having that audience in front of her was, paradoxically, inhibiting when it came to making *Sing in My Meadow*. "Capturing that side of us on record is harder – it never sounds quite the same; maybe music like that isn't meant to be captured, it's meant to be there and gone. I need to be in front of an audience for that; I can't really let go in the studio the way I can onstage. For some reason, there I can strip away my conservative nature, inhibitions, whatever it is, and go to those places I don't go to every day – and I don't want to! But, on this one, I think we did as good a job of it as you can.

"Of the four records in *Nomad*, I'm proud of it, but it's the one I go back to least because I know how much better it sounds really live, in the hall or the theatre. That's true of all our records in a different way. I can't listen to any of our records the way fans do, because I'm always critiquing it, I know what we were after and where we hit it and where we didn't, whereas fans buy the record and that's all they know, that finished product. And then, later, you play one of the records and you think, 'Remember that time in Italy when we really got it? I wish we had that version instead of this!' I don't ever regret anything we recorded, because at the time we did the best we could. Every record is always the best we can do at that moment. Would I do them that way now? Probably not, but that doesn't make them any less valid. They reflect what we were at the time.

"Saying that, making it was just a blast. It was great: turn up and play! It wasn't the way we planned it – we'll do these two really tight albums and then do a jammy record and release our souls! It was just how they fell, but it was just fun – this is what we do for kicks. That playing off of each other is just what we love. That feeds us too, but doing it live is one thing, that comes in the moment, the crowd – all of that. It was never quite the same for me in the studio."

Perhaps that sums up the intrinsic difference between being out front and negotiating the way the evening is going with the paying crowd and being at the back, pumping out the music. As Pete notes, the view on the project from the drum stool was very much in keeping with Jeff's. "I still like first takes, I still think you get a lot of the best stuff when it's fresh. I really like sitting in the studio with Mike, Al and Margo – Jeff on that record, too – working on stuff. It's like being back in the basement playing together all those years ago.

"I think that comes from confidence. When you're playing as much as we do, when you're improving, you can see it coming before it happens, you can see that next level. I'm not so busy just playing, so now I can step outside of that, see where we're going and play off that, like a hockey player can see not just where the puck is now, but where it's going to be in three or four seconds' time, and anticipate it. 'This would sound good with this thing that Al's about to do', and you do it."

"It's such an important part of what we do, especially live, and something that we love doing, especially the musicians, we're waiting for those moments where we can turn up and fuck around a bit!" admits Mike. "We approached it pretty much as we do onstage: Jeff came in, the five of us set up in our studio and the songs were all done live, off the floor. Margo redid a few vocals later, but the music was just us playing.

"Until we did the songs, only Margo had heard them before – except 'Hunted', obviously. We had two or three days in the studio just running through them, getting one ready, then onto the next one. They were really simple songs as far as the structure goes, so it was, 'Let's play.' I really love this record: it captures that part of us really well, and

500

it's also a side of us that people don't know so well. We really tried not to overthink it, not to make it too complicated. It's not a technical process, except inasmuch as getting the setup right. It's really about capturing energy, not controlling it or pushing it in any direction, but just going with it. Some of the sounds might not be the best sounds, but it has that edge to it; you get the idea that you're sitting in a room with five people, that's the key."

Sing in My Meadow is essentially a live record without the audience – "Play loud!" as the stickers used to say – but as a collection it surely made more sense to a North American audience who see the band regularly than to a European audience who necessarily follow more through the records. In that sense, it was a revelation – but not just to Europeans, as it turned out.

"It was to me too," admits Alan. "I was in a guitar store not long ago and there was this crazy music playing. I thought, 'This is really cool, who's this?' Just this weird feedback, no singing at that point, I really liked it. I just thought it was one of those jam bands. It went on for five minutes or something, and then Margo comes in. I couldn't believe it! I was surprised how extreme it sounded."

That is nowhere more obvious than in the one old song on the album, the reworking of 'Hunted', which now captures all the deranged menace that the song deserves, driven by Pete's drumming, with Margo now finding the vocal performance that eluded her twenty years earlier.

"That was one of the reasons we wanted to do it," she says. "It's one of those songs that, when I first got it, I probably went at it with as much courage as I could at that time – when I was maybe 30 – but, over the years, I've found my way further and further into the deeper side of that song. I've wanted to redo that song for a long time and *Sing in My Meadow* gave us the perfect opportunity, because when we do it live it's a song that's really grown."

"It fitted this project perfectly," agrees Mike. "It's one of those songs that has got so much better with age and with playing it more and more. I listen to the version on *Pale Sun* now and it doesn't have nearly the nastiness that it needs. This album gave us the opportunity to go and redo it, and we went for the screaming version of it. It's very much about the interplay between the five of us. It showcases what we have as a band when we play live. It's one of our real strengths.

501

"At this point in our career, we marvel at that. We've been playing together as a band for thirty-five years now and that is rare – it doesn't happen any longer. We have literally done thousands of shows, but each night something new happens. Even if we think it wasn't a great show, it doesn't catch fire the way we want, we're still listening to each other, playing to each other, still trying to interact, and how often does that happen? People are listening to the computer, to the click track or the backing track, whatever they're playing to. We had a front-of-house guy with us and we got to one venue and he was asked about the computer setup. 'No, man. This is the last band in the world that tours without computers!' I guess that's something! It seems everyone is triggering something from somewhere, but with us it's a blank slate. Every night, we go wherever we want to go with it and I think that's what people react to, even if they don't realize it, because we are giving them something most bands don't."

'Hunted' certainly does that, because the band cooks up a storm throughout as Margo really lets rip on the vocal. Pete is like a runaway train, the interplay between Mike and Jeff is telepathic, that electric mandolin such a signature sound of the live band, and Alan holds it all down at the bottom of the mix. That hooked-up sound of a real band playing together then spills over into 'A Bride's Price', which is a very different kind of song, loping, restrained, with Alan's subterranean bassline – another example of his and Mike's burgeoning writing partnership – rumbling away in the ether, Mike's guitar meandering this way and that, the style reminiscent in some ways of *Whites Off Earth Now!!*

It's a great vehicle for storytelling, that swampy, psychedelic blues, so much so that it's surprising so few artists go down that road, maybe Nick Cave and the Bad Seeds the other obvious exponents of the style these days. "For those of us who love it, the live show with that type of music is just the best," agrees Mike. "It gets so intense, so organic. It reaches down to the heart of who we all are – swampy blues people!"

'It's Heavy Down Here' has a similar feel, but this is the Junkies at their slowest, most intense, heaviest, a hymn to exasperation that has the texture of the *One Soul Now* period. The song is happy to sit in a mood and just stay there, wallowing in it the way The Cure could early on in their career, around the time of *Faith*, though, as Mike reveals, the inspiration for it was rather more recent.

"It's a song that reflects back to *Demons*. It's a very Vic kind of song, about the South – I could have seen him doing it. We've never played it since we did it for the record, but I really love that song. We captured the energy in the room and then I worked it a little bit in the mix, because I figured it could use a little bit more. My vocal was added in later, too."

'It's Heavy Down Here' has a spooky element and, while less obviously about the ensemble playing the way 'Hunted' or some of the other songs are when the fireworks are flashing, it's still the kind of thing they do live where they stay with a groove and see where it goes. It's demanding of the listener (because it's almost funereal), there are no easy hooks or melodies to hum, but if you want an example of the European influence on the band, dating back to Joy Division et al., you can find it here.

If you want something a little more immediate, 'Late Night Radio' offers that, for it has a warmth and tenderness to it, understandable when Mike says, "That song is my childhood right there. What I loved was it was so random: you turned the dial and you came across something from God knows where, you had no idea what it was, some of it was terrible and some of it grabbed you, and you found something new that became important to you. Now, with smartphones and all of that, you just tune straight into what you already know and you don't get those possibilities.

"That has made it tough for bands that aren't always out there in the mainstream, because people don't find things by accident any more, not the way they did. You can't find the way out to people, because radio is so formatted; streaming services just suggest you listen to something exactly the same as the thing you just listened to. That accident of hearing a band you'd never heard before and finding a new favourite song from it, that's a lot less likely now."

That loss is captured by Jeff's beautiful mandolin solo, conjuring up the atmosphere that listening in the dark could create before cleverly dying away, like a radio frequency slowly drifting out, back in the days of analogue.

"It's a true story. As a kid, I would listen to radio late at night," says Mike. "There was a little bit of music sometimes, all these amazing stations you used to be able to pick up from all over the States at night. I just loved it. You could hear anything: baseball games, religious shows, music, even the conspiracy theories were just about aliens then, not politics! It's a nostalgic song because, back then, listening to late-night radio used to be a comfort, but now it's a nightmare. I used to love it, but I can't stand it any longer. Even sports radio, I just want to numb out and listen to somebody talk about the hockey game, but you're just yelling at me, there's confrontation – it's painful to listen." The airwaves are now full of shrill, mad voices, gone are the warm tones of professional broadcasters who could fill your night with just the sound of their voice, never mind what they were saying ...

Back to the bigger themes, and the title track, 'Sing in My Meadow' takes on them all, big on the idea of sin, of doubt, of love. Nothing like giving your singer the easy stuff to work through.

"I know!" says Margo. "Can you talk to him about it for me? The first song he gave me where I thought, 'I can't do this, I don't have the personality, the experience' was 'Murder, Tonight, in the Trailer Park'. That was the first real ugly, gutsy, messed-up song and, ever since then, he's given me stuff that's got worse and worse, so I'm getting good at it! I don't think he's going to stop now!

"Even something like 'Fairytale' on *The Wilderness*, my son Eddie was about 8 when we were doing that song and I was playing it a lot at home to find my way into it. So he learned it and he'd be singing it at school: 'I'm sick of the blood, I'm sick of the bleeding.' I got a call from the principal – she hated me anyway, she thought I was the worst mother ever: 'This is inappropriate for an 8-year-old!' She should hear some of the others!

"I think my skill as a singer is that, when Mike writes those words, I can find a way where I can understand those thoughts. I'm human. I'm lucky, I have a very nice life, thank you, but that doesn't mean I don't have those darker thoughts too, sometimes. Being able to express that onstage and in the studio, that makes me very lucky, because that's a safe place to do it from. I think it confuses people that we can do songs like that and then I'll tell a stupid story onstage straight afterwards, but I think we all have those deep sides and we all have those lighter parts. They're both true."

There's a highly charged vocal to the album closer, 'I Move On', which Mike describes as "middle-age frustration set to music! It's just a big howl, Jeff's harmonica on it is just amazing, just sounds like Miles Davis in his prime on that. It was all supposed to get easier as you got older, but it didn't. Lots of lies we get told when we're young, that's one of them! I'm telling them my kids now. 'Don't worry, once you get through high school it gets easier.'" Where's the Rockwell painting, the quiet contentment and the time to go fishing every day that we were promised? There's a restless rage to the playing that matches the vocal, an "Is this it?" fury, a raw open wound. Don't play this with the lights off.

That Jeff's harmonica is just as potent a weapon as the electric mandolin in this setting is also illustrated on the album opener, 'Continental Drift', a song that has echoes of 'Cutting Board Blues' about it. Jeff's playing is such a focal point, emotive, creating the sense of confusion that Margo rails against, spitting out the words with a sneer. In that, it also calls to mind 'Murder, Tonight, in the Trailer Park', not from *Black Eyed Man*, but the twenty-first-century live version which, like 'Hunted', has come of age in its raucous, acid-blues form.

'3rd Crusade' contains suffused rage of a different sort, the sort that would crop up again on *All That Reckoning* further down the line. Looking at the way the West has made a habit of plundering the Middle East through the centuries, and the way in which that has stoked the fire of injustice which the West then refuses to acknowledge, it asks a very simple question. Wouldn't the world be a whole lot better if we all knew and understood some more history?

"I always loved history as a kid, I studied it in school," explains Mike. "It's amazing – if you study any little thing, the minutest little bit of history, you go, 'Oh my God, again? And again?'! It's freaky the way it repeats the same mistakes and things all over again. The only thing that changes is the names."

From time immemorial, the elites have looked to divide the poor by using fear, racism, jingoism and all those other tools in the populist handbook, when the real enemy of the poor isn't the other, the black, the Muslim, the Jew, the whatever. It's those rich guys who want you to beat one another up while fighting over scraps, rather than come around their houses looking for a more equal share of that huge pie they've got locked up out the back. If you're looking for a concise summing-up of the modern world, you won't do much better than the chorus:

> I've been told that you've been bold
> believing in the shit that you've been sold
> and I hear that you fear the way a simple
> damn dream can disappear.

"I don't think people hear that in the chorus, but it is exactly that. We play it in the States and I don't think people hear it as a hidden insult to their politics! But, again, it goes back to some of those things on *Renmin Park* about the Chinese people. We travel so much in the States and so many of the people there are just great, so open and welcoming, wonderful people, and then you look at their government and what happens in their name, and the two just don't fit. Same in the UK now.

"These guys in charge with these amazing, privileged backgrounds, inherited money, and yet the normal working people think they share their concerns and are going to look after them? You really think this guy gives a fuck about you? Doesn't that seem kind of unlikely? I really don't get it.

"That side of politics all around the world, I just don't understand. I could sort of respect it if the thought was, He's not going to look after us, but at least he'll fuck up the guys at the top who have been screwing us. But I don't think it goes that far, and it certainly isn't true. It just seems to be a belief in fairytales. Really, you think Trump is an OK guy, that this guy is going to help you? But that's where we're at: allowing the rich people to divide the rest of us while they run away with the money! They've figured it out."

After a record that was restless and fuelled by the adrenalin of live performance, to complete the quartet came *The Wilderness*, a record that was maybe a reward to the long-term llamas who had busily worked their way through three very different Junkies albums, different not just from one another but from what had gone before. For the finale, as Alan points out, things were a lot more familiar, the core four the co-stars of this production.

"*Wilderness* is more the kind of thing people think of as a Junkies record, just to come full circle with the project. There's only so much we can do: we're limited musicians, we are how we sound."

For Margo, it was also a record that fitted like a glove. "If we've played songs live before we record them, it is so much easier. I find that onstage I'm much freer, I don't know why, but it means I can play with a song, try things, find what works. If I can get a song before recording and work on it in front of an audience, I can get deeper into the song quicker. If we do it in the studio first, I work hard, I do them the best I can, but often we'll be on the road playing them and, six months on, the light bulb will go off: 'Oh, now I know what that's about!'"

Although it was fourth in the series, *The Wilderness* was the record that might have been made back in 2010 ... had they still been tied into recording contracts, had Mike's family not gone to China, had they just looked at one another and burst out laughing after somebody had suggested the crazy idea of doing a four-album box set. Instead, it was another two years before it came out and ended the series.

"A lot of it was written after making *Paths*," recalls Mike. "I was working towards the next record and then the whole trip to China happened and that whole rethink of how we were going to do things when we got back. We'd played a lot of them live by then. I liked the songs, but it didn't feel like a record, it didn't make sense, I didn't know what it was. I like to work with a theme or concept around a record, and that can come up front or the songs sometimes suggest it themselves as I go along. That wasn't really happening, so being able to put them aside and think about them some more while we got on with the rest of the *Nomad* stuff was helpful. And then the fact that they were individual songs started to make more sense in the bigger picture of the four records. These were the folk songs, the story songs – that side of our personality, representations of that, the kind of area that we're probably best known for, I guess. They didn't necessarily have to cling together as an album in themselves, but they made sense in the wider context of *Nomad* being about all the facets of who we are and what we do. Then there's a few of them in there that reflect back on the history of the band, too. When I was writing some of them, I was thinking, 'OK, what if I wrote a bunch of songs that were almost answers to songs I'd written twenty years earlier?' That was too much of a construct in the end, but that's there in part and, again, that fits into the idea of *Nomad* covering all the elements of what we are."

One of the songs that survived that initial plan was 'The Confession of Georgie E', the sequel to 'Murder, Tonight, in the Trailer Park'. Not that Mike told Margo that ... "No, of course not! He never tells me anything. Even where we're going! That was a hard one to get into, it's a difficult song, and now, I think I could do it better, I didn't find enough. It was a missed opportunity – that happens on records, you can't always get it how you want it."

"Structurally, it would work well on *Pale Sun*," according to Mike. "But, lyrically, it's the answer to 'Who did the murder in the trailer park?' It's Georgie E's confession. I like it, but at the same time it's an exercise, too. 'I'm going to write a song that is outside my regular pattern.' Having the idea of linking it back to a song from twenty years ago, it's working around certain parameters I set myself. Often you throw those ones out because they don't work on their own, but they give you ideas for other things, they're a staging post on the journey that opens something else up. It's hard to understand how I kept writing it – it's one of those puzzle songs. Even chordwise, harmonically, it's different for me. There are none of my go-to things on there, but I liked it when it was done."

Digging up old characters and names has been something that pops up quite a lot in Cowboy Junkies songs – was Suzie in 'Renmin Park' the same Suzie from 'Oregon Hill', the characters relocated to a love story on the other side of the world? That also cropped up in a song that ended up on the *Extras* disc at the end of the project, 'The Girl Behind the Man Behind the Gun'. Was the woman who stops in with Jen for the gossip the same one who, twenty years earlier, forgot to close the blinds the night before she saw Jenny with a black eye in 'Sun Comes Up, It's Tuesday Morning'? If you know Robert Altman's movie *Short Cuts*, where he somehow spliced together a number of Raymond Carver's short stories to make one long piece, it's not hard to imagine there's something similar to be done with the songs of Cowboy Junkies. If you're reading this in Hollywood …

One of the earliest songs was 'Angels in the Wilderness', which went through a lot of changes from its early incarnation on the road, going from something relatively breezy to a piece more contemplative, so beautifully delicate that it almost evaporates in front of you as you listen. "I really love this song," says Mike, "but we can't seem to get a live version of it any more. We lost it somewhere and maybe that's why. I think the version that ended up on the record was an earlier take on it when were in rehearsal mode, and I ended up going back to that and reworking it for the album. It's a weightier thing on the record.

"It's very heavily influenced by Marilynne Robinson, a Christian writer, actually, and she wrote a book called *Gilead*. A very intense book, it's so dense, the title comes from the text and the song is basically inspired by that. The book is about a dying man who writes a letter to his son who he had very late in life – the son is 7 or 8. You gain all this knowledge, experience, hopefully wisdom. Your understanding grows, and, as it does, you realize that it is a tough world out there. The book is a lot about that fear from being a parent of growing children and letting them into the world, but knowing that's what has to happen, on a prayer or a dream or whatever. You just hope there are angels in the wilderness that protect them."

It's as heavy a song as there is in the canon – unsurprisingly, given the source – for not only is the book infused with that fear of leaving behind a child, it's dripping in the guilt of a good man who can't help but resent the idea of his young wife finding herself a new, young husband once he passes, giving his son a new father. "I'll give you my love and watch the bitterness grow" is a line which, as they used to say, says a mouthful, the recognition that love for someone can border upon obsession, often so close to tipping over into something less savoury, more controlling, more angry, when things don't go as you want. "Oh yeah, this is a heavy song!" laughs Mike.

The line "Fly forgotten like a dream" comes, essentially, from the hymn 'Oh God, Our Help in Ages Past', a line quoted in *Gilead*, though in the book it goes on to say, "Our dreams are forgotten long before we are." That's a sentiment that worms its way into 'Fairytale', sick of "the effort it takes / to keep on dreaming / about better days, and better ways / of living".

"Isn't that beautiful?" marvels Margo. "That's one of my favourites – I think that's one of the best Mike's ever written. I think Townes was touching his shoulder there, some of those lines. The chorus, bringing in the idea of the fairytale and the little princess, I think it's great. The thing about Mike when he writes those songs, 'Shining Teeth' is another, there are these beautiful lines that he puts together that have so much power and emotion with such simple words, something so human that connects us all together."

"The chorus is really the fairytale that you tell your kids," says Mike, "but it's also what you kind of hope for, whether we admit or not; we want things to be that simple. But they aren't!"

'Fairytale' is, to a degree, a follow on from *At the End of Paths Taken* insofar as it is a meditation on the future, the need to stay hopeful given that you are sending your children into that world, your investment in that future, yet your faith in it is being battered every day simply by turning on the news or going out on the street. The recognition that "One wrong move and it's a long way down", encapsulates the fear that is used to control us, to keep us looking at our feet and to toe the line.

Yet the chorus – and the future for those children – is the thing that makes the trials visited on us by the verses worth the effort. As Margo said when the Junkies were inducted into the Canadian Music Industry Hall of Fame in 2015, "If you want to find the happiness in our songs, it's there, but you have to work at it."

'Staring Man', like 'Fairytale' a song that has echoes of *The Caution Horses* in structure and instrumentation, has some of those twenty-first-century blues, too, that sense of panic and of loss, of yourself, if nothing else. "Every night you check your desire to run", just like waking at 4 a.m. to find your heart is missing, as in 'Brand New World' on *At the End of Paths Taken*.

"I think we all try and set up these defences to keep us healthy and happy, but they are the things that ultimately destroy you," argues Mike. "Because, in trying to keep the negative out, you don't let the positive in, or the person in. It's cutting yourself off, not even recognizing yourself in the mirror – you don't even want to let the person looking back at you in."

It was clearly something very much on Mike's mind at the time, because the questioning on 'Staring Man' was not dissimilar to 'I Move On', if a little less angry. In that one, he spoke of "Trying to find answers / without digging in the dirt", followed up in 'Fairytale' with "We'll stumble on the truth / Probably fail to recognize it / as we're digging at its roots". Sounds like an admonition to self?

"It is a reminder to myself, but we all do that, don't we? You look back at things and wonder how it was possible that you didn't see it when it was staring you in the face. You're digging in the roots, you can't miss it, and you do. Happens to all of us all the time."

'Staring Man', and its question of whether what you see in the mirror is really you, is the real you, the thing you never let anyone see, maybe not even yourself sometimes – these have long been lyrical preoccupations, which in itself is paradoxical.

"It's always complicated because I write songs, I put thoughts and ideas out there. They don't have to be autobiographical, but they are the things that interest me enough to write about. But I have the advantage that Margo sings them! I think I'm lucky in that I can get as honest and down to the bone as I want, but I know I'm not going to be the one singing it – it's gone away from me by then. I'm not that sort of person. I don't put myself out there, but I can use the artifice of art to do it."

That dichotomy cropped up in 'Idle Tales' in the lines, "She stands upon an empty stage / with a song she was born to sing / She's on the road again". Mike shies away from the idea of that being specific to his sister. "It doesn't have to be as literal as that. It's about expressing oneself: you're always having to do it again, you're always on the road again in that sense, always going back to the beginning. If you were meant to express yourself, not even artistically, that's the thing you return to every time."

Other recurring themes are the myths and legends that keep us going, touched on in a number of songs across the *Nomad* project. "That's one of the tropes I keep going back to – some of it's my Catholicism hammered into me as a kid! Actually, I went to an Easter Mass, mainly for the music, but I stuck around for the sermon, and she was talking about the women who went to the tomb after the Crucifixion, and the song just took off from there. The whole idea about myth, fate, knowledge, all the stories we tell each other and how those things can determine our whole lives as individuals and the histories of our cultures. It's not just Christian tales. Every culture has its versions."

'I Let Him In' "deals with a lot of the stuff I write about all the time," admits Mike. "It was a good fit lyrically for this record, reflecting back to 'Staring Man' and 'Damaged from the Start', even 'Idle Tales' in a way. It connects them all up. But I don't really know the song. I wrote it, we recorded it, we were happy with it and we moved on. It's never come back as a live song, I don't know it intimately in that way." The phrase "You whispered those foolish incantations / So I let her in" is classic Junkies. To let her/him in is to risk fear and pain and disaster. But, like Woody Allen said, we need the eggs.

'Damaged from the Start', a kind of coda to 'My Only Guarantee', such that it's no longer 'I Will Fuck You Up' but an admission that we come ready fucked up from the factory, plays the same emotional terrain as 'I Let Him In', as Mike explains. "Every relationship you come to, it has its two sides and we are all coming at it from some place of damage, however you want to define that. I don't know what a non-damaged person is. Even if your life is absolutely perfect, you're still fucked. Relationships are so funny, because you have two people coming from their different backgrounds and experiences and you're trying to make this new thing happen together and you both come it at with parts broken or missing or whatever. How's that ever going to work?!"

Again in the mode of harking back, 'We Are the Selfish Ones' has much in common with 'Good Friday' – quite deliberately, according to Mike. "When we were working it up to play it live, I did say to the band that they should think of it in terms of 'Good Friday' – it does have that same kind of structure, that build. Like 'Good Friday', it's that moment in time, just sitting, staring and having that momentary epiphany … I find I have these moments when I'm out in nature by myself, where all of a sudden you feel connected to everything, 'Wow, holy shit.' You just get these brief moments of clarity; it all suddenly makes sense and then, immediately, it's gone. Those are beautiful, amazing moments. And the idea that we are the selfish ones, the lucky ones, the needed ones, I'm in a position where I can take those moments and express it. That's my life – what an amazing, phenomenal thing that is, and you always have to remind yourself of that." As Jaro said earlier, "The grace of God is showering upon us all the time, but we aren't aware of it. Our minds are in the physical world, and we don't see that everything is connected to everything." That guy knows his stuff.

The album's opener is a song alone, 'Unanswered Letter (For JB)', achingly painful, posing the question, "What if we can't get words from home – what's going to save us then?" The taut, tense opening is a demanding opening to an album, underlining the faith the band have in their fans to stick with it. Even so, it's a relief when the band kicks in and releases the tension.

"That was written for a friend of mine who hung himself," reveals Mike. "I'd worked with him, we'd released a couple of records, recorded with him, he'd toured with us. He went out to the West Coast and you lose track, you lose touch, that's life, right? One day, he literally walked out of the house, into the woods, and hung himself. When I heard about it, I couldn't even begin to imagine the scenario and what being in that place is like. His parents are back here in Toronto, the funeral was here. They were talking about it, not blaming themselves, but just wishing that he had contacted them, that he'd talked to them, which must always be the response for people left like that – certainly a parent."

It's a song yearning for simplicity, to find a life like that of "That blackbird clucking / Songs he knows nothing about / That bird returning / To a home that makes him sing out". Of course, blackbirds get eaten by cats, so simplicity isn't everything.

At the other end of the spectrum is the song that closes not just *The Wilderness* but *The Nomad Series* proper. 'Fuck, I Hate the Cold' is the light note at the conclusion of four pretty intense albums, but, as Mike says, "It needed it. We argued a lot about whether we should include it. My feeling was we'd asked people to go through four pretty heavy albums, we'd better give them something at the end of it all! It's great live when we tour in winter, I like the song, but I guess it fits the record, too, in that this is my life in the cold in Montreal, Toronto and London, as well as on tour sometimes. It's a true story, and that it has a little lightness to wrap up the whole morbid affair is good, too." If ever a song and a performance said, "Hey, we did it! Pass me a beer!", this is it.

In the final analysis, *The Wilderness* is a fine record, but their instinct that it was not the follow-up to *At the End of Paths Taken* was correct. Had it been that and in this form, while it's a collection of beautiful songs that the fanbase would have loved, it would have been a retrograde step off the back of its predecessor. It doesn't have the cohesion of *Paths* – nor of things like *Open* and even *Early 21st Century Blues*, for that matter. Essentially, these are "just" songs that don't quite knit together other than as a good record, but these days, Cowboy Junkies are shooting for more than that – in that regard, *Renmin Park* was a more obvious successor, an absolute triumph on its own terms but still problematic in its own way, given it was such a left-field record. But, in placing *The Wilderness* as the full stop on *Nomad*, releasing it in March 2012 instead of June 2010, it makes much better sense, touching on and collecting together some of the themes of its three predecessors. It's the final chapter that ties things up.

When you've put together a four-album set, the question is, "Is that it?" Well, no, you can always make it a five-album set by rounding up the additional tracks recorded for the project. More than a ragbag of odds and ends, this particular "extras" selection did make sense, not least because it concentrated very much on more songs from the Vic Chesnutt project.

"More than half were Vic songs and we wanted to put them out," explains Mike. "They could easily have been on *Demons*, but once we'd committed to it being a vinyl package as well as a CD one, we didn't want to make *Demons* a double album, we didn't want to have it any longer than it was, especially as it was midway through the four-album cycle.

"As well as that, at the end, having put the records out separately, we wanted to put out the complete set, too, as part of the catalogue. So then you get into the business side of it. If you bring it out as a collection, some fans will maybe want to buy it in that packaging anyway, because they're completists, so at least adding an extra album by collecting up all those extras is giving them something new. At the same time, you're almost forcing fans who wouldn't get it, because they already had the records, to buy the set anyway because it has these new songs on it. It's an awkward situation; it's one of those business compromises that you end up having to make. I understand that it can frustrate fans, but it's a no-win situation really.

"The songs we did put on *Extras* all had a certain relevance to them within the project. These ones were just left off because of the length of the records – we had too many songs. In the past, they would probably have been B-sides of singles, but there are no singles in that way now, so this, and then the extra disc on *Notes Falling Slow* a couple of years later, made sense, to collect up things we liked but couldn't find a home for, for one reason or another. They're part of the larger whole, the larger story if you're into the band in that way. I used to love B-sides, that one new track you got, usually the songs the band wanted you to hear more than the record company did!

"I guess those things are probably for the uber-fans. It's changed now, the way those things are put out – they're value-added things on albums rather than one-offs on B-sides and, for me, they've lost the appeal that way, because there's too much of it. Because it goes on the end of the album, you get five or six more songs, you can't focus on it and it takes away from the 'real' album. I'm not really attracted to it when they put out three versions of 'Kashmir', either, I'm not interested. I want to hear the one that Led Zeppelin chose as the right one. But some people love that; that's why we did those 'Anatomy' records a while back, and it's good to cater for those fans, too.

"I'm pleased we put them out. I really like 'Demons' as a song but we never quite got a version of it that really worked, but I really love the lyric. 'Marathon' and 'Guilty by Association' are great songs of Vic's, but we didn't elevate them. 'My Boy Burns' was a very important song for me when I wrote it – it was for my son – but it didn't come off how I hoped it would. That's why they missed the 'main albums', if you like, but at the same time there's good reasons to have them out there for people that really like what we do and like to dig into it."

'My Boy Burns' builds on the first verse of 'My Little Basquiat' from *At the End of Paths Taken*, a father's sense of wonder at the talents and the drive that bubble away in his son as he grows up and starts to find his own path, doing so with that ferocious intensity and energy that only the young possess. But, if that song is referring backwards, the song 'Demons' is a hint of what's to come, something of a forerunner of 'Nose Before Ear' on *All That Reckoning*, the line "You take away my demons / You take away my peace" in that same mould. The wry juxtaposition of habit and religion – a broken leg that prevented the protagonist kneeling by his bed and praying as a 12-year-old only to find that skipping prayers made no difference – is a typically Junkies idea, not so far away from 'Idle Tales' (though that is a better executed recording, perhaps explaining why 'Demons' was consigned to *Extras*).

There was a potential Junkies classic on there, though, in 'The Girl Behind the Man Behind the Gun', another song played live prior to the start of the *Nomad* project. It opens with a quote taken from Norman Mailer's *The Big Empty*: "We are not living with a guarantee of the happy ending. Anyone who purveys such a notion is not working for humanity, but against it. I would go so far as to say that."

"That quote really sums everything up. It's very true," says Mike. "It sums up our whole catalogue, really. I think a lot of the characters that are in our songs, that sums up their lives; there's no guarantee of a happy ending. I like that idea and I especially like the fact that he goes on to say that, not only is there no guarantee, but anybody who tells you otherwise is working against humanity. That is just so true. That's the big lie and that screws up so many people.

"I think that's where Western society, especially in America, does this weird balancing act. The American Dream when it began was based on a happy ending, but to get there you worked hard at it, you scraped and you clawed, you looked out for your neighbour, too. It wasn't just about getting ahead – it was about bringing everybody up, everyone getting there together, which was healthier. That part seems to have gone.

"Now it's, 'Hey, you're in America, you're in the West, everything's OK, you're bound to be happy.' That's not just individuals, but the whole country. All the entertainment programmes, all the big hit records, it's all geared to that. One big happy-fest. Not that life should be depressing, but there's more to it than that. It isn't that easy, it doesn't happen for so many people, and through no fault of their own. That idea is working against humanity, because people walk around thinking that they're the only one that it isn't working out for, and you see how dangerous that is with the amount of misery and violence there is in that society."

Looking back across the whole *Nomad Series*, it was a monumental undertaking, but one pulled off successfully. Inevitably, there were moments of inconsistency in there, as you would expect from any band putting out three hours of new music inside two years – pushing four hours, if you included *Extras* – but, across it all, not only was the standard of material and performance extremely high, the Junkies achieved that while simultaneously breaking plenty of new ground, as well as staying true to many of their touchstones. It was a high-wire act that saw them safely across from one side to the other.

"A lot of this project just came together so beautifully, almost with a life of its own," reflects Mike. "The artwork worked so well, too – that really gave it an identity. Enrique Celaya is a guy we've done things with in the past and he really wanted to do something with us for a record. The name of the project, *The Nomad Series*, that came from an exhibit of his, *Nomad*, that I saw well before we started to work on the records. I started talking to him about what he could do when the project was starting to take shape, and then I suddenly remembered that exhibit and it was just so obvious. 'If you're into giving us those for this, they're perfect!' The idea of the seasons, the cycles, the same figure in the forefront of it all, it's weird that it just fell together so perfectly. It capped it all off.

"You do worry that there's just too much there for people to assimilate but, then again, so what, really? A lot of good songs maybe got lost because of the sheer volume of it, but people can go back to them, they're there to be found. It was too much to control, for sure, but we knew that from the beginning, we knew we couldn't promote them all properly or tour them all properly, but that's fine. We were working so hard on the next one that we didn't really focus on the one we'd just put out!

"The whole project was just something so grand, so epic, it's a capping-off of a period, the end of one era and the start of something else, the start of a new era without record company associations. The problem was, because we were just starting, we didn't have the things in place to promote it. If we were doing it now, we're better set up for it as our own record company, our own promotion people, but then it was more haphazard. We didn't want to get caught up in that, we just wanted to make the music and put it on our shelf! It's something we really wanted to do; it became a real obsession and ultimately became something we're very proud of. Then there was the book, too, which had the artwork, some diaries, some photographs – it was a really cool thing that we were very proud of. Then there's the vinyl box, the CD set: it's a huge project – we felt really proud of it in the end. It turned out great.

"It was a statement: 'This is what music can do.' It used to do it, but now that ambition isn't there any longer. You wouldn't be surprised to see *Game of Thrones* come out in a huge box set with all the books and posters and all of that, so why can't music do that?"

No reason at all.

CHAPTER 26

If you're looking for an education

With Cowboy Junkies now focused on operating as a wholly independent unit, as well as putting together *The Nomad Series* they needed to take care of business, and that included looking carefully at just where they would be recording in future.

"By the time we'd finished *Nomad*, we definitely needed a new studio," admits Alan. "We'd been using the Clubhouse for about ten years, we'd recorded everything from *One Soul Now* onwards there, pretty much, and it was just getting way too cramped as we brought in more equipment. I think maybe the lease was coming up for renewal, too, so it made sense to move."

"The Clubhouse was a very small place and it got smaller and smaller, darker and darker, stickier and stickier as the years went by. It was getting pretty nasty!" remembers Mike. "We'd been wanting to buy a place for a long time, because we rented the old place. We wanted to keep it relatively close to where we live, but the longer we waited, the more expensive Toronto was getting, and so it was starting to look impossible. But then, by pure luck, Josh Finlayson from the Skydiggers drove by this building near his house and he called me to say, 'If you're still looking, you should check this out.'

"It had two rentable apartments in it, it had a big building at the back ready to be turned into a studio. We just knew that was it – if we didn't buy that place, we might as well forget it, because it was perfectly laid out for what we wanted to do. So we bought it and Pete went to work on it for about a year. There's a big space in the back and he built a studio inside that, he fixed up the apartments to rent out, then we moved everything across. We call it The Hangar and it's not only been great for us, it's opened a few other things up in terms of production, because it's a lot more welcoming than the old place. We didn't invite people in there that we didn't know!"

Having got his hands pretty dirty in constructing the place, it's little wonder that Pete is a big fan of having the studio on tap. "It's been great having The Hangar. It's been good for Mike, I think, to have a second thing to focus on instead of all the energy going into Cowboy Junkies. Nowadays, I play with him a lot, along with Josh of the Skydiggers on bass – we're the house band, that's a lot of fun. And I think that's been good for our relationship, too, having something away from Cowboy Junkies, where the focus is on working for the good of somebody else's songs rather than being concentrated on what is more Mike's vision. I think that's helped with the band, too, us working on ideas and new experiences that we can then bring to the next record."

"It's meant I've been able to do some production over the last few years," says Mike. "But that's not easy these days, because the industry money for independent artists is disappearing, there's not much money around to go into studios, and lots of people just figure they'll make music on their laptops at home. That can be a hard sell sometimes, to convince people of the value of a studio. I don't hustle for work, that's not my style, but I'm still pretty busy – stuff comes and finds me."

One of those things had found him and the rest of the band a few years earlier in the shape of a project by Scott Garbe which ultimately became *The Kennedy Suite*. A musical on the Kennedy assassination might not seem the obvious feelgood hit of the year, but it was an absorbing piece of work that the Junkies worked at, on and off, over seven years, from Clubhouse to Hangar.

"That's an interesting story in itself," says Alan. "This schoolteacher arriving with these songs he'd written over twenty years about the assassination."

"It was a great perspective on it. I thought the Kennedy piece was a great idea," adds Jeff, who was also involved in it with his other band The Potion Kings. "It's based on a picture book that Scott had in his house when he was a kid, and he wrote the songs based on specific pictures in there. So, for instance, the song 'The Dallas Youth Auxiliary' is just taken from a picture of these three girls at the railings at the airport, shrieking at Kennedy like he's a movie star. He created that song from that and he did that with the whole narrative. What was it like being the motorcycle cop that's riding with him when he gets shot? They were really interesting angles to look at that day from."

"It was a very, very long process to make," recalls Mike. "I got involved around the time I was writing for *Paths Taken*, so from there to release was about seven years. Josh from the Skydiggers brought it to me from this guy he knew, Scott Garbe. Josh gave me the demo package to listen to – it was already a really well-thought-out idea at that point – just to see if I was interested in working on it, and I loved it right from the start.

"Scott is an interesting guy, an English teacher, he puts on plays himself, a very straight guy, but a real Kennedy assassination freak – he's read all the books and watched the documentaries. It's not like he's writing all the time, this was it. He says, 'It's my *To Kill a Mockingbird*, I wrote one thing!' But I just thought the writing was so clever, that was what drew me to it. A lot of times with things that have a really clever concept, they get let down by the individual songs, they tend to be not that great. But, with this, they were so good and such a great mix of historical facts, conspiracy theories, so much humour too, real black, black humour, really funny, which is pretty weird, given the subject matter! It's a great song cycle, the songs all reflect back on each other, and there are some beautiful moments, too – beautiful songs, touching songs, too.

"The most beautiful song is 'Take Heart'. Reid Jamieson did that one in the end: the motorcycle cop following the procession, thinking about his life, which has gone to hell, but 'everything will be redeemed if I can just make sure the Kennedys are safe'. And he's turning into the Plaza thirty seconds before the President gets his head blown off. We know what's waiting for him and that all his hopes are going to disappear. It's such a devastating song, and yet the assassination hasn't even happened yet. It's really intelligent writing.

"I started working on it with Pete, with Andy and Josh from the Skydiggers. This was around 2006, 2007, we started going through the songs, no real idea of where we were going to take it or what to do with it, and then we reached a dead end with it just because time ran out.

We got into releasing and touring *Paths Taken*, then *Nomad* followed on from that. All sorts of day-to-day things took over.

"We'd come back and hack away at it every now and then, we'd do something with it and it evolved into this big collaborative project – the idea of different singers on different songs came through and we started to build it up. That became really time-consuming to get different people involved, matching schedules and things, so it went through these periods where nothing happened for a year and then there'd be a burst of activity!

"The casting of the songs was an interesting part of it. Scott already had people in mind for some of them, so we tried that first. Some said 'yes', others didn't; some we just couldn't schedule. Some of them were really obvious, but a few of them we really did have to search around, because it was important to get the right voice. The opening song, the band was great, The Screwed are a punk band so it fit right in, but their singer couldn't pull off that whole 'Roger Daltrey screaming from the mountain-top' thing. It's pretty hard to find a voice like that. There haven't been too many since The Who – it's a one-in-a-million voice. In the end, Hawksley Workman came in and did a pretty good approximation of it. There are a few like that where we couldn't quite get the vocal as I imagined it, and so that changed the direction of the song a little bit.

"When we finished with the *Nomad* stuff, we'd got The Hangar ready, so I wanted a project to work on there to bed everything in anyway, and it was great for me to be able to focus just on production and arranging without doing any writing. We knew the fiftieth anniversary of the assassination was looming then too, so we realized pretty much, 'If we don't finish it for that, we never will!' In the end, we did a full press on getting everybody involved to come and finish up their parts, and completed the record and put together a really nice package that Pete was heavily involved with. It was a great package in the end, it really captured it. He did a great job."

Pete's artwork is very much in the vein of the songs, a clever collage, drawing together all kinds of disparate elements to make sense of each of them, all the songs getting their own specific treatment. "Working on that was great. I love graphic novels and, really, that was a chance to do one. The songs are all pretty descriptive, so that was the template and, from there, putting together the collages was a really interesting thing to do. We had the standard CD and then we did a version with an A4 package with the collages as bigger photographs, and that worked really well for the detail.

"Those things are so important for graphics; the same with the quality of the printing. With *All That Reckoning*, we had it printed in Canada and they did a horrible, horrible job – nobody cared, to the point where it was black, you can't see the image. Then we got an English pressing and it was great. The promoter in Germany when we played there in 2019, he was doing the concert posters and he took the care to get a high enough resolution file of the image to use – it took him an age, but he cared enough to do a good job. You don't get too much of that any longer. Most people are, 'Oh, it'll do, whatever!' So often in the modern world, we lose quality in the pursuit of money and that's a really sad loss. So it was nice to be able to work on something that was all about the detail and to be able to see that through to the end.

"That collage style works well on computer, the cutting and pasting – I've got a couple of sketching programs but I don't find sketching works on computer. I'm not schooled in that, I'm not schooled in art, but I like to visit galleries and museums, I pick up on things that interest me, and I guess some of those things get incorporated. It's a little bit the same way we come at the music – we're not trained in that sense. It has its downside; sometimes I'd like a little more technique to be able to do what I can see in my head! There's a lot to be said for schooling, but you can be overschooled, too: a lot of the time, you get these great technicians and there's no feel or heart in what they do. I'm trying to develop a style for the iPad, because that makes it all so much quicker. I'd like to do a graphic novel and that's so much work, so, to be able to automate some of it through the computer, that would be great. I'm still always doing some artwork when I get the time, for fun, my own amusement, and I've stockpiled a lot of things now. That's something I'll do more of later, when I can't do construction any longer!"

Pete's collage-style artwork was echoed in the songs themselves, using archive audio from the time, including a chilling interview with Abraham Zapruder, the man who took that famous film footage, talking about "shooting" his movie as Kennedy went by – pretty strange terminology in the circumstances, exemplifying the shock that everyone was in at the time.

"Using those sound clips gives the whole thing a real different quality," agrees Mike. "Scott really had the idea of the historical clips to move the story along, he knew exactly what he wanted to use, and they were so effective. The Bobby Kennedy eulogy at his brother's funeral is so powerful, then it segues into the crowd when he was shot and the woman is screaming, it's so intense. It's amazing what happened across those five years: the Kennedy brothers, Martin Luther King – we think we're in a troubled period now! If any of that stuff happened now, we'd be living in a police state. They would clamp down on everything, the whole world would change: don't put your head up or you're dead. It would be terrifying.

"In a weird way, it manages to give you a different perspective on events, which, after fifty years of it being one of the most talked events in history, is pretty amazing. It's a fascinating subject – I got sucked into it, too. I'd meet with Scott and talk about the songs and then inevitably get into the assassination story and all the nooks and crannies; he gave me a few fascinating books about it. Scott isn't a conspiracy theorist, he believes Oswald did it – that's the conclusion he's come to. He looks at it as a wider thing: from the angle of the Kennedys' relationship, their life together, who they were at that point; from how the country related to them. He sees it as a bigger thing, too, which comes through in the epilogue, 'The White Man in Decline'. He sees the assassination as the beginning of the end for the United States as a guiding light in the world. He has a very interesting take on the whole thing.

"It's interesting, too, that we were making this through the Obama years, the 'new Kennedy'. Obviously, we were listening back to a lot of Kennedy's speeches as we put the thing together. It's amazing how inspiring he was and Obama was trying to tap into that same sort of thing, but now where are we? I have those Kennedy speeches going round in my head every time this orange guy in the White House opens his mouth or his Twitter account. How is it possible we went from Kennedy to Trump? Talk about your white man in decline! It's interesting, though, how Trump is the reaction to Obama in the way that ultimately, after LBJ, Nixon was the reaction to Kennedy. Those guys, hearing anything inspiring, it makes them nervous!"

Finally completed, the album came out on Latent with the Junkies' imprint, though, as Mike makes clear, "It's not a Cowboy Junkies record, that was never really the idea, but obviously in terms of marketing it and helping to sell it, having our name on it as 'Cowboy Junkies presents' made a bit more sense. It's easier for people to focus on one act and, in putting it out on our label, you're looking for every advantage you can get in that sense.

"We did a couple of nights of *The Kennedy Suite* at a very nice theatre in Toronto. Everybody came who was involved in it, so it was a huge production number: fifty musicians and singers, there was film projection, a really big show. And that was it! It was a lot of effort over a long period, but we did it because we all loved it. I was intrigued by it, the writing was so great, it was just a fun, inspiring project, something with no real endgame other than to do it and get it out there."

Reflecting on the show, Alan notes, "I think it works better as a stage thing, almost like a musical. Working with so many people was hard to put together, a lot of work, and the problem with that is that you don't get a feel that you're playing. It's a production line backstage: 'OK, you're on next!' You play one song and you're off. If you're used to playing as a band, playing your set, that feels strange, although I was on with Pete most of the time as the house rhythm section. But, with all the film and the staging, the show kind of made more sense than the record."

That's something that Cookie Bob Helm agrees with, because (naturally) he made it to the Winter Garden Theater to catch both nights. "I was in the sixth row on the first night, in full view of all the projected images. Perhaps because I never watch TV, moving images are more of a novelty to me than to the average person, and I found myself drawn into the story they told, while giving less attention to the music being performed than I normally would. The second night I was in an opera box close to the stage, and could only see fragments of the images, so that focused my attention on the musicianship. That allowed me to zero in on Scott's lyrical content, with the added benefit of being able to watch the musicians at a much closer range than I'm accustomed – there was no taping, so I wasn't by the mixing desk at the back, for a change.

"The first night, the show seemed very quickly paced, with multiple images and soundbites competing for your attention between the songs. The fact that most of the uptempo, rocking songs were found near the beginning of the performance added to my initial impression that there was more going on than I was able to process. The second night, I found much more enjoyable, as I knew what to expect and had the visuals and story from the first night in the back of my head. Being up close allowed me to see the performers' facial expressions and subtle body language that helped them convey the characters they were presenting.

"The Junkies did their piece, 'Disintegrating'. For Margo, trying to channel Jackie Kennedy's thoughts and emotions can't have been easy – even for a veteran of Michael Timmins' sad songs – and the emotional difficulty of doing so was evident on her face."

"I love that song," says Margo. "That plane ride home that she took after Dallas. We tend to skip over the fact that there was a wife who was sitting in a car and her husband's brains were on her lap and then she had to go home to tell her children. Just the thoughts that would have been flying through her mind, I can't even begin to imagine that. That gets ignored – it's all about who shot him and who was behind it, was it really Oswald? But my God, that woman was there in the middle of this thing. That song was right up my alley; it was great to do. It was really well-written from the woman's perspective, the woman's way of thinking, the doubts and insecurities. It was a great project, I loved the record. I just thought everybody involved brought so much to it in their different ways."

After the show received great acclaim, "A few people from the theatre world got involved with it," says Mike. "They were really keen on trying to give it a bigger life. We spent some time trying to get a producer involved to try and mount it somehow, at least take it to arts festivals, but it's never gone anywhere yet. People tend to love it, but these musicals can take years to get off the ground – you really have to make a full commitment to them and that's not something we can do. Maybe for the sixtieth anniversary!"

There was a little more business to take care of in the aftermath of the end of their assorted contracts, for it meant the back catalogue needed a little curating, as Mike explains. "We'd got the control of the masters back for *Open*, *One Soul Now* and *Paths Taken*, so we wanted to put them out on Latent to keep them out there and available. It made sense to put them together in a package, so it was the same kind of thing as when we put *The Nomad Series* together as a CD box: do we put anything else with it? We had a number of songs around from that period that hadn't made it onto the records, so, like the *Extras* CD with *Nomad*, it made sense to gather them all up on *Notes Falling Slow*. I don't see that record as any great addition to the collection, it is what it is. Again, they're what would have been B-sides, but I know that a lot of the fans who follow us closely wanted them out there, so we put it together.

"With all of them, there was that temptation to put them on the records they were written for, just because you can. When CD came about, there was a real tendency to put seventy minutes on there just because the space was available, just pile it in there! I think, over time, people have come to the conclusion that that's a lot of music to absorb in one sitting for a new record and it is very hard to keep up the quality over that length of time. That's a good thing about the re-emergence of vinyl, too: you've got to keep within those constraints, so it's back to forty-five-minute albums again. We've violated the rule, but I think ten or eleven songs is the maximum number, even if they're short. You're asking people to take in ten or eleven different concepts, and that's a lot, so I really try to keep it down. Nobody writes fourteen great songs in one sitting!"

It's an awkward collection, not one to be considered an album proper, for it's a set that lacks the kind of dynamic range which allows you to sit and listen from start to finish. It's a very restrained collection musically, definitely from the slow, stately end of the repertoire. That isn't to denigrate the quality of the songs individually, but as a collection it's too much of one thing to work as a cohesive whole, not that that was ever the point.

What is interesting is that, when you look at the albums they were slated for – 'Shrike' and 'So They Say' for *At the End of Paths Taken*, for instance – however good they might be, you just can't see how they would have worked with the whole, what they might have replaced. It's all down to taste, but even if you might think 'Shrike' is a better song than, say, 'Someday Soon' or 'Cutting Board Blues', swap them out and the album as a whole becomes definitely weaker.

"I really like 'Shrike' as a stand-alone song," says Mike. "We were playing it live; that was going on *Paths Taken* right up to the end. But when the album took its true shape at the end of the process, it just didn't make sense on there, it didn't fit. Sometimes you have to do that – it's not always necessarily the worst song that you drop, but conceptually it doesn't work with the others. And *Paths Taken* was a very conceptual record, so I didn't really want to destroy that balance by just throwing a song in there because we liked it."

'Morning Cried', written for *One Soul Now*, was a similar victim of the cut, understandably, given the way it has so much common ground with the darker, first half of *Open*. It's a great song, the swirling guitar figure speaking of confusion, being in a whirlpool, falling, but it was territory already covered, as things moved on for the next record. The acoustic delicacy of 'Cold Evening Wind' is especially beautiful, the lyric "Don't travel in a line if you're looking for an education" leaps out of 'Three Wishes'. Each can state its case as being worthy of attention, but, of all the songs on the collection, it's 'Ikea Parking Lot' that stands out. It muses on the banality of catastrophe. You're sitting in a car on a nothing kind of day and, suddenly, a nuclear bomb drops on you. Just you – the rest of the people around you are fine.

"It's a pretty heavy song as far as the subject matter goes. I like those songs with those mundane moments that speak volumes, and visiting Ikea is about as mundane as you can get! I just liked the juxtaposition of the people, the car, Ikea, the parking lot and this huge scene happening. But it suffered, because it is such a heavy song. How do you sequence that in an album? How would it have got on *One Soul Now*? It's pretty hard to see what comes before or after that, isn't it?"

ANOTHER 200 MORE MILES ...

Thirty-five years on the road, it's no wonder that Cowboy Junkies have gone through a number of different touring phases through that time, different kinds of shows, different modes of travel, different attitudes.

The earlier chapters in the book have talked of those early days criss-crossing the United States in the station wagon, then to the record-company-supported tours after *Trinity Session* broke big and into the brand-new world of post-Geffen life. But nothing stays still for a touring band and, as we end the second decade of the twentieth century, the Junkies find themselves in a new travelling mindset, embracing essential change as, like the rest of us, they come to terms with the passing of the years.

"You go through different doors in life," explains Pete. "When we were young, we did the long trips across the States, stopped when we wanted, took in some sights, then played a show and slept on somebody's floor – you only want to do that in your twenties! Life was more comfortable, maybe, in the 1990s, when the record companies were behind us, though it was pretty hectic at times. Then we had that period after we went independent again when we lived, ate and slept pretty much on the tour bus. That was fun for a while but, again, you get to your fifties and the appeal of that goes away. You're on top of each other, you park up at the clubs and the theatres, which are often in the grossest places, you can't go to the bathroom, you get that road film of dirt on you and you're just desperate for that hotel stop to get in the shower or, better yet, actually have a night in a bed!

"At that stage, it was starting to get hard. We got to a place where we just couldn't do it that way any longer. It was like being in a science experiment, getting in those little coffins to sleep. If you just grind, grind, grind and stay in lousy places, you get knocked out by it and you can't do that if you want to do another ten or fifteen years of this! And you have to have days free, too. If we do a run of six straight days in the States, that's tiring for all of us, but, for Marg, her voice can't take it. But that's the Timmins family thing: you just put your head down and go! Don't bang your head against the wall, but if you think you can push through it, do it! Your arm's not broken, it's just sprained! I guess we've all learned a bit about that and I think we've made some good changes."

"I think we've done pretty well the last few years in figuring out the best ways to travel, especially in the States, where the distances can be brutal," agrees Alan. "The booking agents and management have worked out the easiest routes for us, so there are no crazy drives any more, which means we can stay in hotels. It's meant playing in a lot of towns we've never been in before, they're kind of a staging post on the way, but we can still play 500-seat theatres in new places and that's fun, too, to play places we haven't played before. It's whittled down the travel and, as you get older, you need that."

Occasionally, while they're out on the road, they even get to see a spectacular live show rather than be playing in one. "Because of the way we've changed things, we just played a tour that was just in California in 2019, fifteen shows. It was a great tour, but at the last show, at the Fonda Theatre on Hollywood Boulevard, the building next to it caught fire, the Hollywood Hemp Museum. They had to evacuate the theatre at the end of our first set with the smoke pouring in. It was a real blaze. We stood on the street and it was amazing watching the firefighters putting it out, coming in full tilt, cutting through the concrete with these huge circular saws to get in and then just attacking the fire, with no idea what they're going to face. Then they got the rest of the gear in there to put the fire out and, twenty-one minutes later, done. The most amazing SWAT team I've ever seen, quite a show. All our crowd was there watching it. I said to them, 'You can't complain missing the second set because do you know how much a ticket to this show would cost?!' Could be a new Pink Floyd show – set the theatre on fire, watch it burn down, man!"

The opportunity to see the Junkies in Europe, while more frequent now, is still a comparative rarity, but that gap between shows allows you to reappraise them each time. The takeaway from the 2019 shows was that Cowboy Junkies have never looked greater than the sum of the parts than now, a band who are all on the same page and producing some of the most stellar live moments of a career that has been full of them.

"I agree with you," says Margo. "I think part of it is … It's like a marriage: it starts out with passion and excitement and everything is new and thrilling. Then you go through that middle part where you either survive or you break up, because you realize how much work is involved in it all and you wonder if there might be something else – is this really it? Individuals go through their crises and that puts the marriage in crisis, and a band is the same. Not that it's ever so traumatic as a marriage can be, but it's the same kind of dynamic. But, if you come through it, you come out stronger, with the demons gone and a focus on the things that matter.

"It was harder when we had our young babies, a really hard time sometimes. My baby is now 16 – it's much easier for me to tour now than it was ten, twelve years ago. It was just killing me to be on the road then: my head would be here for the show, but my heart was always at home. I was always feeling guilty, always worrying about what was happening back home, but I had responsibilities to the band and to myself, because I still needed that thing of being onstage. I was split in two where, now, I'm totally here. Eddie is with us when he can be, he loves it, he's a total road dog – why wouldn't he be? He's a real crew guy, he knows the job, he does his thing, we hang out together sometimes, he has his uncles around him, but he realizes we're working, where, when he was younger, and he came out with us, of course he couldn't understand that, so that made it difficult even when he was with me. And if he stays home when we're touring because it's school time, he's about to get his licence. He can drive himself to school soon; I won't even have to organize that! So much has become easier, and that reflects on how the band is.

"We've all changed. I'm not as whiny or as demanding, not as needy as I used to be! Which is weird, because I'm older and physically it's harder and it's not great going in a stinky club sometimes, but if I have to do that, OK, let's do it, where, years ago, that would really bring me down. Now, they don't affect me. As you get older, you get more stoical maybe: 'This is what I have to do, so let's get on with it.' I know I'll have a good time onstage tonight and then, tomorrow, I'll be somewhere else. And, because that has gone, what you're left with is the music and that makes it all more fun. You know what: I've whined enough and I'm tired now!

"I think in our different ways, that's true of all of us: we are all contributing more and more. Mike is much looser now, 100 per cent, and that's a big change, because he used to get off the stage and be critical, where now he's much cooler about it, good show, bad show, could have been better, whatever. That doesn't mean that we let go of the quality control. If a song was bad last night, we'll work on it the next day in the soundcheck and fix it. We still want to do a great show and get it right, but there's more acceptance that you can't be perfect every night. Now we can laugh about it – you got yourself a singer who can't remember the words! Too late to worry about that now!"

"It could be that we are even more a band now; everybody has more responsibilities across it," says Pete. "Again, the family thing helps, because we've all known each other forever, we all know each other's moods as people and as players. 'OK, Mike's in this mood, we're going to rock; Mike's in that mood, it's going to be a low-key vibe. Al's tired tonight, he's going to be a bit behind, I'll pull it along.' And they know the same about me. Like a good sports team, the sum of the parts creates something bigger. That's why those supergroups usually don't work, because they're not listening to each other, they're doing their own things.

"And Margo is right, Mike is more open. He always used to be really driven and focused – 'We have to get there, do the show, get to the next place' – and I guess that was how it had to be when we first went independent, because who knew how that would work out? But now, it's more about the quality of life: let's enjoy the travelling as much as we can, as well as the show. We drive shorter distances, we stay in hotels and not on the bus, get a proper sleep, get away from each other, then meet up again the next day and you're feeling ready to go again. That's great – it's a big change in the dynamic of the band. We all want to go home with a dollar in our pocket after a tour, but it's more relaxed now.

"I think that's also because we are also in easier places personally, because the kids are grown up, late teenagers and older – they're doing their own things now. Ed's the youngest, but he's on the road now with us when he can be, he's in the crew and that's great: it's a breath of fresh air, that energy, it's great for Margo to have him out with us so much. For all of us, things are looser. Sue can come on the road with me now our kids are grown up. We'll rent a car and drive between gigs. Al drives himself a lot of times. He loves to drive: he'll rent a car and drive from Vancouver to Cleveland to start a tour, and he'll go there via Santa Fe to see a friend!

"And we get to spend longer in towns, so I go and try to find something, the museums, the gallery, find out what's on in the town. I guess, as you get older, you get more focus. And you know you're getting closer to the finishing line. That's not anything imminent, but you have to think about just how many more times will we be playing in Berlin or Amsterdam or Edinburgh? So, you get there, you want to see what it's got – if it's got anything! Some places, the killer is between midday and soundcheck. If we're stuck in a crappy part of town with nothing to do, the boredom is tough. Give me a hammer, I'll fix your club up!"

"The physical part of it is so hard," says Margo, who has recently had to forfeit one of her favourite parts of life on tour to ease the burden. "We're always trying to find new ways to survive, and one of the things I've started doing, although it's making me feel a little sad, is to not go out and see the audience after shows. I found that, on tours, I was starting to get sick, only colds, but once you get one you can't shake it because of the travelling. Then you're singing through it, which I can do, but it's not as much fun, it's not great for me or for the audience. So I thought I'd try not going and seeing people after the show. I loved doing it, but it takes a lot of time. Everybody wants an autograph, a selfie, everyone has a story and that's great – I love that communication – but listening to the stories, it's draining, exhausting after a two-hour show. Ten years ago, it wasn't, but it is now. So I've stopped doing that, and it drives me crazy because I know people bring things for me to sign, but since I did it, I haven't got a cold, so it's working. I have to pay attention to those things now that I'm older. All these things add up. I don't go out to eat before a show, we don't go out after a show, I try and get the right amount of rest, all those things matter more. But it's worth it because I need these shows more than I ever did.

"That's what I love about touring – it forces you to be in the moment all the time, good and bad. The playing, I won't say it's easier, because that suggests you're not trying, and we are, we are as focused as we've always been. But, after so many years, it's become as natural as breathing. I love that feeling onstage, this thing that we are and that we create. It feeds me and I think the boys feel the same. I need that. As you get older, there's less in the world that gives you that thrill. When I'm onstage, it's a place of contentment. I'll keep doing it until I fall off the stage and die!

"You know, I would love to see us play, I would love to be out in the crowd. I don't mean watching a video, that's something else, but to be out there and see it objectively, without it being me staring at me on a film – which I hate! I say this in all modesty, but there must be something that we're offering that makes people keep on coming back. Genuinely, I don't know what we give them or how good we might be. We just do what we do.

"I do think we are unusual nowadays, I don't think bands play live in that way now, where it really is in the moment, where there's no click track, where the set list gets changed around every night, where the songs are what they are that night and then are maybe something else next week. That's what people heard in *Trinity* all those years ago. That was just what happened between those musicians in that room on that day. I like to think ours is a human show. It's about a connection, not about lights and fireworks. It's us and the audience and whatever happens between us in those two hours."

Often inside those two hours, they'll play '200 More Miles' with its lyric "They say that I am crazy / My life wasting on this road".

"When I sing that line now, it's nice to have the answer. Turns out they were wrong!"

CHAPTER 27

Unburden your hearts

If the band had managed to adapt their touring routines and schedules to great effect, making life on the road altogether more attractive, just like everything in life, there was a downside, at least initially. Like pretty well every other act in the world, to a greater or lesser extent, for years Cowboy Junkies had been locked in to the record–tour–record–tour cycle with, if they were lucky, a spell off the road after the tour to rest, recuperate, and then get a new album together to start it all off again.

Such breaks aren't just necessary in the sense of creating time and space in which to work, but they also act as an opportunity to get away from the music for a spell, clear the head and come back refreshed and keen to do that work. But, in their new way of working, if the Junkies had more breaks, they tended to be shorter ones and, in true Bob Dylan style, there was something of the never-ending tour about it all. For Mike in particular, it meant he was only just finishing decompressing from the last tour of duty when it was time to go off on the next, giving him no itch to scratch. How can I miss you if you don't go away?

"Getting ready to write what became *All That Reckoning* crept up gradually. *Notes Falling Slow* had been out a while, we'd been touring that, and the rest of the band were beginning to drop hints: 'Any new songs to play?'! It was weird – I really had no desire to start writing a record at that point. Because of the way we were touring, we were always working in short bursts, then going again, so I was maybe getting enough Cowboy Junkies through that. I was doing quite a bit of production work, too, so my time was pretty much full of making music. I didn't really have a spell away from it.

"I think I was a little bit disillusioned with the music world, too. I wasn't sure that I wanted to participate in it with the way it is now. Live, we do our own thing, we play our shows our way and it's just about us and the audience. Putting out a record, even on your own label, there's a certain amount of required involvement with the music business, and I didn't have too much enthusiasm for that, because it's just got worse over the last ten years with the changes in technology.

"I really can't stand streaming, especially. That record companies are pushing that is incredible. Never mind downloads, streaming is another 1,000 miles down the road away from valuing your product. This constant devaluation of what you are trying to sell, no wonder people don't want to buy – that was one of the triggers for *Nomad*, having that big, physical product that was worth buying. But the companies, they're not selling music any more, they've gone into the data business and they don't care what that data is as long as they're selling some of it. On top of that, it's a horrible way to listen to music. It's a great discovery tool – if you hear of a new band and want to check them out, it's fine. I'll do that and, if I like it, I'll buy the vinyl because that then gets me to sit and listen to it properly. But now people just have it streaming all the time; doesn't matter what it is, they're not even paying attention, it's just digital noise. So my disillusion and disgust with it has been growing and I didn't really want to go and tangle with it again.

"But there was a bit of pressure from the band, because this is what we do, we make records. So I thought, 'OK, let's see if I can still do this.' But I still didn't really have the desire to do it. Normally, I get this bubbling feeling, where I know there's something that wants to come out; I need to go and start writing. That method has always served me – something comes. But I didn't have that this time, so it was a case of sitting down with a piece of paper and deciding, 'Now, I will create!' A few things started to trickle up once I started that process, but I wasn't sure if they were good or not. Part of the reticence was just the thought of going through the whole process again – not just the writing but the recording, producing, mixing, the whole huge organization of it all, the responsibility that goes with that. It didn't seem so appealing at that stage!

"What was great this time around is that it was a real band thing – everybody stepped up and contributed, not just musically, but to all the elements around it. That was really helpful. Pete has done a lot of great work on the album designs for a while now and he took charge of that. It works really well. It's a nice echo of the *Nomad* idea, with the use of the one image of the child through everything and having all these other things going on around it.

"Pete has a great eye for that kind of thing. He came up with a few ideas and then produced what became the cover image, which was perfect. Once we had that, it was obvious to keep that child through everything and build up the collages around him. Having Pete doing the artwork was one less thing to worry about and that was great.

"I think you can tell on the record that this really was a band effort: there are a lot of dimensions to it because there are a lot of people stepping up and giving their input and doing it consistently. That's the big thing. It's great to get involved, but you have to stay involved, you have to see it through the ongoing process. Making a record is a lot of work and a part of that is just keeping the momentum going. There have been times in the past where it's been down to me to keep that going myself, but this record, there was a really steady contribution from everyone and that was great."

"Maybe that has come about since we went totally independent and all had to focus on keeping the band moving," muses Pete. "When we had BMG or Geffen, you ride along on this big, fat wave without thinking, but for twenty years or something now, but then, especially after *Paths*, we've had to focus on it ourselves – what are we going to do, where are we going to go? It suits us.

"Having Al writing more is a big step forward. It freshens things up after so long, gives it a new approach. He brought some really layered stuff to Mike for *Reckoning*, he had lots of things on there that Mike then worked through, kept what excited him, took off some of the things that didn't work with what he was writing, and that gives him a new angle to come at songwriting.

"We came into *All That Reckoning* really ready for it and it made for a great album. That comes back to us all having bigger roles now, more time to do that maybe, as well as Mike feeling happier about that. I really don't feel as if we are running out of energy or ideas; it feels fresh."

That freshness is key, because any recording project so far down the line in a career must be looking over its shoulder at what has come before, wanting to both live up to past glories but also to escape their shadow. You could argue that there has always been a thematic element to their albums as far back as you want to go, but the inescapable truth is that they have become increasingly so. That's why *The Wilderness* on its own, in some form or another, wouldn't have been a sufficiently satisfying follow-up to *At the End of Paths Taken*. And, this time, they were following up a four-album set that had covered all the band's bases. Having done that, it's even harder, yet also more important, to find something new to say.

"I do like the records to have a unifying sense or a concept to them," says Mike. "At the start, I think that was my problem. I didn't know what I should be writing about. I've written so much about interpersonal relationships, and I knew that would still be part of the equation, but I'd done that sculpture many, many times. I didn't feel inspired by simply doing that, I wanted another angle, so I was reaching for different ideas."

According to Alan, those ideas came from a source beneath the forty-fifth parallel. "After doing the *Nomad* records, the Kennedy thing was a nice holding project to work on, that ate up some time, and I think it created some ideas, too. We talked about what was next after that, but Mike really wasn't driving it the way he would normally. Then Trump arrived – that really got him going. That was something to write about!"

"At one point, I had come round to the view that, if I was going to write about personal things, then I was going to really, really get to the bone now! But that still wasn't enough – I still needed another take on it. Then the US election started to happen, the rules of things started to change very quickly. Trump won and all of that started to creep into the writing, too. I'm not really that type of writer, but that social stuff had an impact because it was such a big thing, even more so than when Bush was president. I started to realize that the personal and the social are really the same thing; the crumbling of expectations socially and politically has its echoes in the way expectations of personal relationships crumble. Age began to come into it, as well. As people, we reach this point where we think, 'What the fuck? Things didn't get easier after all!' I think we've reached that point as a society, too. All of that came together in a weird collision. A few of the songs which I had thought were purely personal began to take on this weird political tinge, as well, and vice versa.

"I wrote 'Mountain Stream' first of all, finished it, listened to it the next day and thought, 'OK, that works. It's a good song, it has a lot of meaning, a lot of levels.' That was the point where I started to find the direction for the record. I'd got into William Blake's poetry and I started pushing that direction and, lyrically and poetically, that opened it up for me. When I wrote that one, I knew I was onto something – it was the point where I saw what the record could be, speaking to those two sides, personal and political. It just needed somebody who was born 250 years ago to lead me there! From there, I wanted it to be more direct as a record. There are a few allegories in there like 'Mountain Stream', but, from the personal side, I wanted to make it very straight, I didn't want there to be any mistaking it for what it was. I wanted to bare a few things, that was the intention and that was probably why I didn't want to get started, because I didn't really want to lay those things bare. Once I got moving on the writing, I quickly came to the conclusion that I had to let all this out.

"That was the lyrical side of it, but musically I had also got to the point where I started to put some pressure on Al. 'If you want me to do this, if you can get me some basslines and stuff, that'll kick-start the process for me.' That gives me a template where I can sit and listen and find a place to jump off from, rather than having that blank piece of paper, which is hard. Al started to feed me some basslines, he really got into it and sent me tons of different ideas, mainly just on bass but some a bit more developed – keyboards, too. That was more fun for me, that began to get me moving and it started to create momentum. It got things moving musically."

Alan has always been Mike's main sounding board in terms of the direction and the conceptual thinking behind the group, but he has become increasingly important to the band as a writer from *At the End of Paths Taken* onwards. His work with Joby Baker on the soundscapes on *Renmin Park* had been crucial and, encouraged by that, *All That Reckoning* saw him producing more musical ideas – providing the genesis for about half of the record.

"I think sending Mike those ideas, it makes it easier for him," says Alan. "For sure, it's changed the sound of the band a little bit, and that started happening back on *Paths Taken*. We were twenty-five years in then, so that was a good thing for us, because it isn't easy to change your sound unless you're someone like Bowie, where change is hard-wired in, it defines what you are. You were expecting it with him, you were waiting for the next incarnation – that was part of what he was. For us, we haven't ever forced anything, the changes have happened pretty naturally. We might choose to be more acoustic on this record or do the psychedelic thing more, but they're elements of what we are anyway. But, if you add another voice to the writing, inevitably it will mix things up a little bit.

"I have a studio at home now where I can get stuff together over time. I was reading a Neil Young interview a while back and he said the best thing about having your own studio was that, because you can't control ideas, they come to you whenever – you could be sleeping, watching TV, eating – but if you can record at home, you can get in the studio right away and get it down while it's still there and fresh in your head. That was my goal, that was what I was aiming for and it's great to have that now, because I can pop down to the studio in the middle of whatever I'm doing if an idea comes into my head. We can be having dinner: 'I'll be back in a minute – just got to do this!' It really works. When you can catch that initial thought, it makes a huge difference. And, because I'm doing more writing, I think my playing is a little different, too. When you write it yourself, when you play it, you know where it began, maybe you understand it a little better. Who knows – it's just a song, right? But it really doesn't become anything until we're all in on it."

Perhaps it's a good thing for the band that it's only now that Alan is emerging as a writer, for – who knows – having another writer in the earlier days might have led to the clash of egos that have beset many a group down the years. According to Margo, though, that was never likely to have happened.

"Al is brilliant in so many ways, but he needs prodding. A lot of prodding! If there's been a missed opportunity in this band over the years it's that – in not drawing more from Al when maybe we could have. Mike and Al's relationship is such that Mike isn't going to push Al. He's always allowed him space, where he's pushed me and he's pushed Pete. He's the big brother – he can kick us around a little!

"In a way, I think Al has missed out through that, because Al is that kind of guy. He needs pushing before he'll offer something. That's not a failing, it's just his personality. It's a shame, because he is so sharp, he's brilliant, he has so many interests and such a breadth of things to bring to it all, and maybe we have missed out on that.

"The way I see it, from where I am, Al is vulnerable and Mike is a pretty massive character and a massive talent to come up against. Mike has always been able to listen to whatever anyone has to say, he's very open in that sense, but you've first got to be brave enough to go up and say, 'I've got an idea.' That's not so easy, and Mike maybe doesn't know how hard that has been for Al through the years. For me, it's just whether I'm in the mood or not! But Al has been producing a lot more music over the last few records, going back to *Paths*, I guess, and when he comes up with something it's always worth listening to. Always. It's great for us because, after twenty-five, thirty, thirty-five years or whatever, a new input is exciting, because it changes the character of it all."

"Al was huge on *All That Reckoning*," agrees Mike. "He goes through phases of being involved and not, that's Al. But, for this one, he was extremely involved, and the more enthusiastic I got about what he was sending, the more excited he got. He had a certain amount of ownership of the songs – he definitely kept me in line as far as the production went and he had tons of ideas.

"Another big change for us is that, in the last few years, he's been getting into keyboards, synths and things, which are really cool; he's got a great aesthetic for that stuff. Once we got the songs down, we sat for many days in the studio going through keyboard sounds, discussing stuff, trying things out, and so there's a lot of that on the record. Al likes those early 1970s sounds, which brings us something new. He's not a keyboard player, so he comes by it all organically, finding a sound he likes, one or two notes and that's it. It's not overdone. It doesn't go overwhelming things – it's simple, but it's really so effective because of that. It's a big addition because, although it's using those sounds from forty or fifty years ago, weirdly, it gives the record a more modern sound."

"Those keyboard sounds do give it a different texture," adds Alan. "Mike's been collecting them: he's got a Farfisa, a Rhodes, Vox, a great-sounding piano – I love that piano. I've been doing a lot of stuff on that for what will be on the next record. Mike came to me recently and said he wanted to do a really long song, fifteen minutes or something. I'd been listening to early Genesis non-stop for about two months for some reason at that point – he didn't know that – so he caught me at the right moment!

"Those classic analogue keyboard sounds, they create a mood straight away. My approach is definitely that classic rock thing, but also very much Brian Eno. I've been listening to him for so long, since 1972 probably. I think I've heard everything he's ever done. I use *Before and After Science* a lot as something to listen to before I do a keyboard part – there's just so much in there. There's something about the sensibility he has, that melodic thing, but, on top of that, his choices of sounds are amazing. You can get a million sounds out of a synthesizer, but he has the ability to find the exact, perfect thing. I don't consider what I do as playing – it's about finding sounds, finding the right character, so it's in that same kind of area as Eno." That's especially true in a song like 'When We Arrive', full of little keyboard accents that make such an impact out of their minimalism.

Pete heard all Alan's contributions and recalls the level of enthusiasm brought to the project by his colleague in the rhythm section: "It was an interesting process, because Al came up with some wacky stuff and Mike had to strip it back a little bit. Mike has to look not just at the record, but us being able to take the songs on the road without taking half a dozen guys in sports suits with us to play keyboards!"

Alan's involvement in the project really did go from start to finish, as Mike explains. "When it came to mixing, he was back home in Vancouver, but I would send him the mixes and he'd come back with thoughts and directions, which were great. It was really good for me because, when you're making a record, you can get really lost in it and lose perspective, so to have someone else listening and critiquing it was great. He's always been there for that, to a certain extent, but this time it was really, really hands-on, really involved. It kept me focused."

'Focused' is very much the word for *All That Reckoning* for, although it has two targets, the personal and the social, both come under a forensic gaze. The warning that this is going to be a heavy record comes from the outset, the sombre, powerful bass that ushers things in on the title track setting an unmistakable tone of contemplation about the things that really matter. But what, exactly, are those things?

"It's funny – so many people see that as a political statement, yet, to me, it's the most personal song I've ever written!" laughs Mike. "That's pretty interesting – I guess the angry version that we put on at the end is the political one and part one the personal. That is that duality of the whole record and that's how we decided to put it on at the start and the end. Sometimes the impetus for doing that isn't anything more than we like both versions, but there has to be a reason to put both on, which there was for 'Renmin Park' and 'Come Calling' and now for 'All That Reckoning'. They are very different readings of the same lyric. They give you a different attitude: it can be a very angry song or it can be very wistful and introspective. The album is like that, too – the political and the personal – so it totally made sense to use both."

The opener is full of sadness and resignation, the same kind of love gone cold combined with a desperate desire to rekindle the flame theme that characterized 'Bread and Wine'.

"That's my constant struggle in all my songs. That, to me, is the constant battle, right? To be able to constantly revisit, reinvigorate, to reassess and improve, to bring things forward. As we get older and go through different life experiences, things change. It's so hard for people to change and so hard for two people to change together, because different experiences obviously affect you in different ways. You each come out of a new experience (whether it be positive or negative), changed and you have to turn and face each other and say, 'OK, where are we now, how do we relate to each other after this?' And things get taken for granted and, after years and decades of that, it's not unusual to end up in places where you don't recognize each other and you have to reassess and reinvent.

"On a personal level, that's what that song is about, at this age and this relationship, not just to one another but to yourself, as well. It's asking, 'Who am I here?' Because we do that pretty rarely. You just go about your life, you have your day, and then the next and then the next, and there's no time to stop and suddenly you're 60 and 'Who the fuck am I?' It's a really healthy thing to do – something we don't do very often and we tend not to do it very well, either. It's a hard thing to do, so that, even when we think we're doing it, we're usually kidding ourselves. It's a difficult process to go through. Then that goes into the political, because societies need to do that, too, and maybe we are going through that now. You can see the upheaval that brings with it, so many influences pulling in so many different directions, and who knows where we're going to end up with that now?"

The questions that 'All That Reckoning' asks as a song were just as valid thirty years ago, on both levels. But we live in a very different world now, where TV is no longer the only drug of the nation but just one of a host of flashing lights that mesmerize us, courtesy of our smartphones and our constant connection to a digital world of a billion diversions from the daily grind. It can be fun, but it has also accelerated the collapse of attention spans on anything that deserves it. Let's face it, society doesn't really do serious any longer.

"I think that's the problem. Triviality hopefully hasn't finally triumphed – hopefully it's a temporary thing, but refusing to look at the big issues, having this celebrity culture and all the superficiality that goes with it, is so dangerous. Having real, honest discussions is a serious business. It's hard to do and you can't do that on Twitter. If you can be flippant and cynical and ironic, it's a lot easier than looking at the real issues. That is a huge problem that confronts us all right now, especially when you have people leading it who don't have the intellectual capacity to deal with it, anyway. They're not about to engage in that discussion, because they can't, they're not capable. So people use Twitter and Facebook because there's no room on there for serious discussion. All you can do is make a joke or throw an insult, and that gets enough coverage to save them having to really explain themselves."

'All That Reckoning' ends on a very hopeful note – "I wake with my heart so full of you" – the positive that is so often overlooked in the Junkies' work.

"It is a very intense song but, ultimately, it ends on a very high note," agrees Mike. "It's about that cycle, going through the process and coming out the other end in a very positive light and that is a hugely important part of it. It's not about going through it and getting lost – it's about coming through for the better."

The difference between the personal and the political is all there in those two versions: that you come to resolution on a one-to-one basis with calm reflection and consideration, but that, if we are going to resolve this unholy political mess that we are getting into all around the world, we are going to have to rage and rage again against the dying of the postwar enlightenment. That's all there in 'Part 2', the roaring sound of electricity with all that paradoxical *Sing in My Meadow* loose focus, the declaration that we're not going to take it any more. Maybe Peter Finch should be screaming the chorus from out of a window.

"These are scary days," says Mike. "You look at this record and then you look back at *Early 21st Century Blues*, at *Paths*, to some extent.

There's a darkness in some of the songs on those records that reflected those times, but here, in 2019, the state of the world and the people running it, those look like the good old days when Dubya was president! We joke about it now: 'He was a pretty decent guy!' On this record, that line in there, 'Welcome to the age of dissolution', I'd written that years ago, when I was writing *Renmin Park*, and it didn't go anywhere because it didn't mean anything at the time, but eight or nine years later, 'Oh, right. I get it now – this is it!'"

That line opens the album's second track, 'When We Arrive', and rarely has such a sad, frightening sentiment ever sounded quite so beguiling as it does when Margo sings it. But the singer is every bit as worried as the writer about just where the world is going, so much so that she took action of her own.

"We lived in Toronto and the mayor there was a terrible person, cutting this and that, an awful man. Eddie was in school there, he was 11 at the time, and he came home one day wanting to know what crack was. I asked him where he heard that and he told me, 'Oh, the mayor is a crackhead, everyone knows.' And that was it: 'OK, we're out of this town!' I was not going to raise him in the city any longer. We went to the country – it was just too ugly, and I knew it was going to get uglier. But now the President of the United States is a nightmare and you can't escape him, and more and more leaders are going that way.

"If we don't have decency, how do we raise our children? How can we tell our children that it's wrong to lie, to bully anyone or to speak badly about other people, and then you have the guy in the White House tweeting out these vicious attacks all the time? And kids are constantly on their phones – and they have to have them, so you can keep in touch and check they're safe – but they are seeing and reading this stuff all the time. There's nothing that they miss. How do we teach decency and values in that world?

"There is no sense of shame any longer and winning at all costs is the only thing that matters. Kids are growing up in this world and I hate to think what the future will look like because of that. I can still teach Eddie what I consider to be decent values, because that's how I live my life, but there is so much other stuff out there. It goes deeper than that, too, this fascination with celebrity, people being famous for doing nothing. When I grew up, at least your heroes knew how to play guitar! They could write a good song, work hard on the road – now you get ten million followers for doing your hair on YouTube. I guess we all sound pretty grumpy now, but I do worry about the world he's growing up into."

The line "Everything unsure, everything unstable" cuts to the core of it, especially significant, perhaps, to those of us who grew up in the warmth of the postwar consensus and its seemingly dependable institutions where, even if you didn't like who was in charge, there was always a feeling that they were trying to act for the best. "Maybe that was naïve," agrees Margo, "but I think it was pretty much true. But there's no sense of that now, none at all. Now they're all out to get you!"

"We've totally lost that respect for those institutions," adds Mike. "And the real worry is I don't know how we get that back. My kids, they look at politics like it's a joke, they just have no belief in it. And not in a cynical way, but in a realistic way. 'Why should we believe in that – you really think the government gives a damn about you?' That's horrible to hear, but it makes perfect sense, too. I don't know how we recover that ground, especially when the leaders are the ones who are constantly leading the condemnation, 'drain the swamp', attacking the Justice Department or whatever. We are in this weird place of not just instability in politics but in everything. There's instability in what we're supposed to believe in."

"Welcome to the world of self-delusion" really is a line for our times, one that seems to nail the cancer that is eating away at the world, explaining exactly where we are both personally and politically, where people can go into huge debt just to populate their Instagram story with exotic holiday photographs or fill their Twitter timeline with pictures of the kids who barely speak to them, where we can just turn our back on what leaders do or don't do in our name, pretend that climate change just means nicer barbecue weather and, anyway, isn't this cat video funny? This is a world where all of us have fallen asleep at the wheel and where the consequences of that could not be more deadly.

"We were in Germany in the summer of 2019," recalls Margo. "We went to Nuremberg, the stadium where they had those rallies, while we were travelling through, and it all feels just a little bit too close for comfort now. There's no way you can stand on that podium and think 'Never again', the way you maybe could have done ten years ago. It can happen again so easily, and it could happen tomorrow. Just the day after we were there, Trump was saying that he was going to have immigrants' homes raided. Even to mutter those words, to make that threat, whether you mean to do it or not, where are we going? They're not going after the crime lords, the drug barons – it's the children, the grandmothers, the soft targets. He's a typical bully. I found it really frightening, upsetting, to stand there at Nuremburg. And I know people who believe in Trump. The attitude he breeds is, 'I'm OK, I don't care about the rest.'

"Going back to some of the things in *Renmin Park*, and now some of the ideas on *Reckoning*, there's a thread there. We've never had such an opportunity as people to really know one another across the world as we do now, and to realize how, basically, we are all so similar. Yet, at the same time, there are people at the top who are desperate to stop that happening and who want to turn us against one another. We're going backwards. We've got this guy in the White House who is clearly ill. If I could be compassionate enough, I'd be sad for him, but I can't manage that, because of what he's doing. But he must be a very lonely, scared person, and the rest of us are suffering."

I've long thought that the only thing that was necessary for the 1930s to happen all over again was for enough people who lived through its horrors to die and so no longer be there to act as our conscience. It seems we've reached that tipping point.

"It's very frightening. There are so many parallels now," notes Mike. "You know, 'Trump is just a buffoon, he'll be gone soon.' That's how they saw Hitler, Mussolini. There is so much self-fantasy going on, people able to believe anything of themselves and of the world around them: 'My little corner is fine.' Climate change is the most obvious example of that: 'I'm fine, the icecap isn't melting here.' But personally it's true, too. In the past, most people didn't want to do things they would be ashamed of, but shame doesn't seem to be a motivating force any longer, because the news cycle is so fast: it's forgotten forty-eight hours later and it's somebody else's turn. And, with Facebook, we all have our own news cycle now, we are all stars of our own world, our own TV show, and that world moves just as fast. Shame is dead."

In that world, "To search for a common ground" seems a forlorn hope but, "Even in that song, it's about 'Let's be holding hands when we arrive.' That's the ultimate message. We're in the middle of the shitstorm now, and we're all going to do a lot of weird things and we might get lost and lose touch with each other … but, in the end, whenever we get to wherever the hell we're going, let's be holding hands, let's make sure we still care about each other. It's a very positive message."

'The Things We Do to Each Other' builds from a pulse throb, another of Alan's co-writes that is grounded in "a really cool bassline", according to Mike. "It does have a Lou Reed groove to it. There's a pop attitude towards it because of that. It's a one-idea song, but I think it's a strong idea."

That idea is the manipulation of fear for your own ends. Politically, it's about Trump, Bannon, Farage, all unleashing those forces, but, as the lyric admonishes, "You can control hate / but only for so long / And when you lose control / ooooh maaaan …"

"That is what I find so frightening in politics now, the irresponsibility of the leadership. Do you not understand the power you have? Although, maybe they do. Again, it's a reflection of the 1930s: 'Let's get this cyclone going and we'll still be standing when it's finished and then we'll start our new world.'"

The opening line, "Fear is not so far from hate", is one that should be chiselled onto the front of every government building in the world as both ideal and warning. We are still only eighty years away from President Franklin D. Roosevelt's famous "four freedoms" speech of January 1941, and yet it could be 1,000 years distant, so far have so many world leaders fallen from those aspirations of freedom of speech, of worship, from want and, above all, from fear. Instead, fear, particularly economic fear and the fear of anything foreign, is now the currency of the day, the thing that's driving us towards the precipice. It's the easiest way of capturing the attention of a population that would simply rather watch *The X Factor*. If you terrify them, they'll pay attention and you can mobilize them. If you can create a bogeyman, then you can persuade enough people to persecute them in order to protect themselves. It's like Winston screaming, "Do it to Julia!" in *1984*. Except now we vote for the rats.

"The record seems to have caught a mood," says Pete. "It got great press, we've had good crowds in the States, then, coming over to Europe, the Paradiso in Amsterdam was full, jammed to the rafters, we got good crowds in Germany, in the UK, sellouts pretty much. I think, in scary times like these, people turn to music and now, people our age, they just want to turn the damn phone off, get away from Netflix and go for something that's human, that's personal. We're good at that.

"It's being honest, being in the moment; it's not about being cool, it's about presenting ourselves and the songs in the way we feel about them that night. I think people recognize that, especially at this moment in a time with so much posing, so much that's false, the whole celebrity

TV thing. Kids now just want to be rich, because that's what they see as the thing to shoot for. We wanted to be musicians, actors, hockey players. YouTube stars? What's that? What does he do? Is he a juggler, skateboarder? Does he set himself on fire? No, he's a YouTube star. But I feel for kids: they do something dumb and it's on Instagram and they're being shamed for it around the world in five minutes. Or you become a star for being an idiot. Or maybe president!

"I feel like the songs on this record really speak about this moment. When we play 'The Things We Do to Each Other', it's like a gospel song – it should have a choir! It's a pretty simple idea: we should just stop hurting each other, having scapegoats. People are tuning into that."

After such a ferocious opening salvo, lyrically at least, 'Wooden Stairs' is a little more opaque. Sonically, it's a piece reminiscent of 'Lay It Down', perhaps because of the "kind of weird, spacey tuning I used on that," as Mike concedes. "Within *Reckoning* it makes sense, but, of all of the songs, lyrically it doesn't belong so much on the record. It does in that it is a baring of one's soul, but it's more of a reflection. I guess it's about now, in that it's looking back at what could have been, how you got here and where you might have been if you'd taken different paths. To me, it's not as direct as some of the other songs. But it worked on other levels, so we kept it."

For all those protests, 'Wooden Stairs' does chime with later songs on the album in its consideration of the duality of things that aren't meant to be: does that set you free to go down another path or are you handcuffed by the failure and choose frustration instead? "It's a very human thing not to accept things as they are. We are always looking for other things that could have been."

Following on from that is 'Sing Me a Song', another choice between the paths. Do you give in to the rage, or do you embrace or change the mess? It's the first real release of the tension on the record, a crunching classic rock anthem, some "rock god" guitar shapes thrown by Aaron Goldstein on lead. "I love singing that one," says Margo, whose vocal features some great production touches, too. "It speaks to my heart about what is going on nowadays. I love how the verses are looking to find that decency, love, joy that we share as humans and then it goes to the chorus, which is about all the crap that increasingly comes into our lives to blind us to the things that we really should be focusing on."

"It is one of those A/B songs where the A section is one thing and the B section is something completely different," agrees Mike. "The

A is 'sing me a song', 'tell me a tale', 'unburden your hearts', that's the preaching side to it, the positive side; and then the B section is about as dark as it gets. Those A sections are the larger view and then the B is individual things, just little snippets of real people in real pain. It does have an element of 'Wooden Stairs' there."

It's hard not to see the A section as Kennedy's America, given the band's involvement in *The Kennedy Suite*, and the B section as Trump. "I didn't necessarily think in those terms when I was writing it, but that's what it is. In the Kennedy era, that was how you got elected: you went out there and inspired people, asked people to sing a song of love, to unburden their hearts, showed leadership. It was a rallying cry – everyone coming together in something positive. Now, it's all about individuals sinking into their own morass and looking for something to get angry about, finding someone to blame, point fingers at. It's only just over a decade since Obama first got elected, but now, so soon after, we're in a time where hope isn't a currency any longer."

And, if you're looking for the personal element, what about, "Prayer looked more like grief"? Whatever our own personal thoughts on religion and if there is someone out there, I think we could all admit that a lot of the true believers don't seem especially happy with it, but seem to be in torment instead. "It is hard to distinguish, sometimes! I guess that's my Catholic upbringing again. You're supposed to be grieving at the loss and torture of your saviour and yet that's what saved the world. What a combination."

'Sing Me a Song' is another where Alan's writing contribution is apparent, meaning that the album is pretty front-loaded that way. "It just seemed to make sense like that," says Mike. "Those were the songs we all felt that had something different to them, along with the more traditional Junkies element, too. We're always fighting that thing, we didn't want people to just put it on and say, 'Oh, it's another Cowboy Junkies record.' We wanted people to feel there was something different happening from the start and we thought those songs had a different vibe to them and would make people think about it a bit more. Who knows? You can only try!"

Although they are very different musically, 'Sing Me a Song' leads the listener perfectly logically into 'Mountain Stream' and its traditional opening guitar figure, familiar ground at last. But, just as the lyric moves you around, so too does the music, Bill Dillon's backwards guitar very unsettling underneath the main thrust.

"This was the one that kicked off the process for me, the great example of the duality of the personal and the social. I used the poem 'The Angel' by William Blake for part of it, but my part of it is very personal. OK, it's an allegory song, so I'm hiding behind that a little bit, but it's about somebody thinking they have it all but realizing the things they think they possess are irrelevant and what they're ignoring are the things that matter. 'You don't know what you've got till it's gone', as they say. That's the personal element, but that really reflects too on the social and political side, as well, that whole idea of kings and queens and kingdoms.

"Maybe it harks back a little bit to the ideas on *Open*. I never do it consciously – I don't want to sit down and try and recreate something, because I want to do something new and not repeat things – but at the same time, your preoccupations in life tend to stay the same. We all tend to harp on about the same things, and that idea of being open, not shutting off, to me, that is a big part of being alive, a big part of my life, and something a lot of us struggle with. So that will recur and be cyclical, like it does in one's life. That's what this record is about on the personal side: trying to find a way through those layers and open yourself up to what's real. Often, we think we're open and we're really not – it's so, so hard."

The work of Blake echoed down the centuries and on into the next song, 'Missing Children', too. It also reinforced just how important routine, place and opportunity are to the writing process – all things that never get any easier to find.

"Getting the time and the space to write is hard. The business takes up a lot of time – family, three kids – it's not something that I can just do easily at home. I was lucky that a number of friends helped out. My wife, Patty, and her brother have a cabin in the Adirondacks in upstate New York – it's really beautiful there; mountains, water, lots of lakes – so I was there a bit. Then I went north of Toronto; Pete's mother-in-law has a place that I borrowed a few times; David Houghton has a place I used, too. The isolation is the main thing. The Adirondacks especially is just beautiful and that's where you'd want to put your writer in a film! But, really, it's just about getting away from the phone calls and the computer and the daily responsibilities. It's getting that space to just get on with it without having to keep stopping to do something else.

"So, when I went away to write, as usual I took some books of poetry with me, because I want to get into that rhythm of words, how they're used and get back to that, just the beauty of language and its power. In the year or so leading up to that, I had kept on coming across Blake in different contexts, be it a book, an introduction to a book, a quote on a programme or something, and was always really struck by him. I was going through my notebooks to look for ideas and I kept on coming across all these Blake quotes and so it was obvious I needed to take his work with me. Sitting down and really reading them, I realized they're songs, they're written like songs, and there's even speculation that that's what they were intended for – he wrote them and went to the pub and sang them. They have this great pace and rhythm to them. I read and reread them, absorbed them. He was all about duality, innocence and experience and all of that, so that fed into it, too, the allegories he was using.

"I just loved that poem, 'The Tyger', that juxtaposition. I got into reading it and it is so intense, the words they just tumble, they pour out of that poem, they're like a rap song. Is there anything more beautiful than a tiger; then, is there anything more terrifying? If you're on one side of the bars, it's amazing; if you're on the other side, your brain would freeze! That's the ultimate duality, and relationships, the emotions, they can be that way, too.

"I had this other piece that I'd carried with me for years actually, called 'Missing Children'. It was a stanza basically, I didn't know what to do with it. That finally found its home – it became the opening verse and it carried the idea of the innocence of children, then the horror of a missing child or the death of a child. That then kind of fell naturally into the Blake piece."

If the playing on 'Missing Children' is another highlight, Margo's vocal is one of the best of her career to date, choked on disgust on the "We only see them briefly" opening segment, then in full roar in the tiger section. "There are so many components to a good song, and that one has them all. It's another of Mike's very best lyrics. How does he write about such a terrible, terrible thing, the worst thing that could happen to a person, and put it into a song without it being melodramatic or over the top?"

The contrasts are vivid, coruscating. How could the same god make a tiger so beautiful yet so deadly, how then could that same god create the lamb as its prey, or the child and the killer, the predator? And, maybe more disturbing yet, how could we create a world in which a missing child is beamed onto our TV screens on the news for "perhaps just one edition" before being forgotten in the tumble of newer stories within a day, an hour? How could we create a world in which, if we don't like hearing about the child that's been killed, we can press a button and get a Coke ad or a game show instead? "We only see them briefly / Then reach to change the station". Those look like pretty screwed-up priorities, don't they?

"That's how it is now, you can just make everything go away, you can stop having to care about it by pressing a button. But also, the 24-7 news, we're talking now just a couple of days after the suicide bombings in churches in Sri Lanka at Easter, where 300 people died [on 21 April 2019]. They had to create new graveyards to cope with it all. Think about that. But that's already old news, it happened, let's move on, onto the next thing. We've lost all perspective, all context, all empathy, with anything outside our own little realm. Even that's hard, but in the wider world there's none.

"The perfect example is reporting on 'hundreds of refugees coming across the border' from wherever to wherever. That's how they've framed the conversation, these people coming to take something away from us. But they're not going across the border because they want to buy Pepsi, they're crossing because they're being chased from their homes, they're being tortured and murdered. But it gets reported as if it's some random choice that people have taken! Never mind the part that we in the West fucked up their countries in the first place!"

That reaches back to a theme looked at on '3rd Crusade' on *Sing in My Meadow*, but adding to that is the superficiality of our concentration these days and that triumph of triviality noted in 'When We Arrive'. It's all around us, the drive to prevent us concentrating on anything – more ads per TV hour, more jump cuts in every scene, music streaming where we give a song seven seconds before it's "click", five seconds, "click", ten seconds, "click". No wonder we seem so incapable of handling the big issues of politics any longer: when did you ever hear of a goldfish coming up with a theory of relativity?

The volume is dialled down again for 'Shining Teeth', but not the intensity. Featuring yet more beautiful bass from Alan, it's another song of contemplation, but contemplation from a ledge pretty deep down near the bottom of the well. Escaping from domestic warfare, down to the river to "Focus on my retrieve, work on my reprieve", or to "Wash the blood away", speaks of trying to hold together a long-term relationship of any kind in the face of potential disaster. Words spoken, better left unsaid …

"I wrote it on a personal level but I realized that, in the context of the other songs, it could be taken more widely than that, which was good," says Mike. "Margo explains it onstage as a song that you can't understand unless you've been in a relationship for decades. The song is taken from not a particularly good place in that relationship, but it still exists. It goes up and down, up and down, and the song takes place when it's really down. And those are increasingly unusual because, now, things break down pretty quickly. If it's going wrong, people are gone – another anachronism!" If you're talking anachronisms, then it's almost an allegory for the place of the Junkies in the modern musical landscape, too, an entity that keeps on fighting for its music to be heard at a time when everything is set against it. Now, that is a real complaint ripe for laying at the door of mainstream media. Never mind fake news, could we stop with the fake people?

"The last song that I wrote for the record was 'Nose Before Ear'," says Mike of the next piece on the album. "It made the cut because we just liked the vibe of it. Lyrically, it's full-on allegory, it's not very direct, unlike a lot of the others. It's about reaching a certain point in life and thinking, 'What?' 'Nose before ear' means just one step at a time, keeping this constant motion forward. 'A man and his life and his race to the finish' is what it's about. This weird idea that we are always pushing forward, trying to get to the end. Well, the end is death! What's the hurry? I find that more and more with myself. Stop. Take a day off. Go fishing. Who cares – what's the huge rush to get to tomorrow?"

Once more, it's a song about being open, and the way in which so many people try to get to the end without pain, without living or suffering.

"'What we love will kill us; that which won't don't thrill us.' That's exactly that, the idea that the pain and the danger and the excitement is what attracts us, but repels us too, the yin–yang of living. We're all trying to get through it as easily as possible, but you don't really want to do that either, because it's boring and the other way is where you're going to experience life. That's the part we like, but which also frightens us." The song has some of that spooky 'Simon Keeper' vibe from *One Soul Now*: the eerie guitar bubbling low in the mix, deeply unsettling; a haunting organ part from Jesse O'Brien; the song rising and falling on some great touches from Pete, not just that main military beat but the cymbal work too, underlining his view that this is a band album, top to bottom. It is, and it's all the stronger for that.

After the second version of 'All That Reckoning', just like *At the End of Paths Taken*, this was an album that needed the right kind of closer. It found it in the unusual form of 'The Possessed'. After all, although the devil has the best tunes, they're not often played on ukulele. "My daughter got into it, so I decided I'd get one too, so we could play together, and then, of course, I really got into playing it. It's just a really nice instrument to have lying around. I took it with me for a writing session, because part of the process is trying to trick yourself into doing something different. I don't really know the instrument fully, so I just find my way round it and I came up with this cool little riff and I built it from there."

It is the perfect closer, an update of 'Misguided Angel' in some ways, realization that the angel isn't misguided but truly devilish, but choosing to run straight into his arms anyway, because that's where the excitement is. Will we ever learn?

"I like how that ends the record," says Mike. "It doesn't pass judgement, it doesn't say do or don't, it just says this is what happens if you're lucky – or unlucky! The devil can be anything – a person, a lifestyle, a burden, whatever. You have to find that thing that brings you alive. The record needed a little epilogue, the same way *Paths* did. I think, when you have a strongly thematic record, it needs something, not to tie it up really, but just a final breath. Something simple, concise. As soon as we recorded it, it was always going to be the last song."

"It's the only way to finish the record, the same as 'My Only Guarantee' was on *Paths*. It sums it all up," says Margo. "I keep asking Mike to do that one live. I think he's afraid of the ukulele!" I have a vision of the four musicians forming up in a crescent behind Margo, all playing the uke. "Oh, Pete would do it, for sure!"

And so it goes on. More travelling, more shows to play and, in the fullness of time, more records. Promise?

"I don't feel any sense of it coming to an end," says Margo. "Right now, we're in a really good space. I was talking to Mike about it: 'Does it feel to you like we're getting more attention again, more coverage, better crowds, all of that?' And he feels it, too."

Maybe that's symptomatic of the times – that they're delivering something human, something grounded, something that many of us desperately need, just as we did back in the days of *The Trinity Session*?

"Maybe that's true. Back then, it was Michael Jackson's *Thriller*, these overproduced, zillion-dollar records made in huge studios, hundreds of tracks of recording for each song, where, with *Trinity*, it was, 'Here we are, "hello".' I don't know what it is, but I certainly feel it. It's another chapter for us and, right now, I just know that it's a really good chapter."

CHAPTER 28

Music is the drug

Way back in the eye of the storm that *The Trinity Session* briefly concocted, when Cowboy Junkies were momentarily ubiquitous, Mike recalls an interview with the English music press which turned out to be remarkably prescient. "We did a piece with *Melody Maker* and the guy came over to spend a couple of days with us. He said, 'You could be playing this music twenty or thirty years from now.' It didn't strike me at the time – because we were in our late twenties or something, you don't think that far ahead – but you know, you don't ever look too old to play our kind of music! I guess he was saying we were playing old people's music when we were still kids!"

Alan takes up the theme: "We think of ourselves as artists rather than as a band, and I guess people expect bands to break up when they're young. But you wouldn't have expected John Lee Hooker to stop playing music when he was 50 or 60. Why would we stop? We still have ideas, things to say, things to do."

The ticking of the clock – does that thing move faster as you get older? – is certainly something that has motivated them over recent times, their main songwriter in particular. "I guess as time goes on you do feel an urge to get more things done. You sometimes think, 'Why not just do nothing for a year?' But it just seems unimaginable. And you have less time to do anything, anyway, because time goes so fast, you've got other things to do with your life. I don't really have any free time between work and family.

"It's very rare I'll just sit around – I can't remember the last time I had an afternoon where I sat around doing nothing. You try and cram twenty minutes' reading in at night before you fall asleep, it's crazy. Time seems very compressed, and as you get older you get more of a sense of time ending, that finite sense to life. If you've got a lot to say, better start saying it!"

Speaking with the pride of a big brother, John makes it very clear that Cowboy Junkies not only have plenty more to say, but that our culture desperately needs to hear it.

"The culture of the last thirty years has changed so much. It's very much about simplicity, big statements, big money, fearful rather than hopeful, very reductive, but that hasn't affected their approach, their music at all. The lyric, and even the music, the way it's played, it addresses the listeners at almost a subconscious level.

"The moralistic side of a lot of the writing has to do with the eternal verities. The music can be very ethereal, neither this nor that. It's not the early psychedelic stuff, though there are echoes of that in it; it's not whatever the record companies today are asking for, it exists outside those things. There's a real subconscious element, a river that flows underground."

Jeff, as ever, has a philosophical take on it. "The culture has changed fundamentally in the years we've been doing this and, if *Trinity Session* were to come out now, you wonder how it would fare. Timing is very much involved in those kinds of things. I think it was helped then because the whole New Age music had been going on for a few years before, so people were getting used to the value of quieter and gentler music, it was becoming part of pop culture that it was OK to listen to meditative music.

"People aren't taught to listen for nuance and subtlety any more. I don't think it's their fault, but these days you are bombarded with sound, there's so much trying to get your attention that there's a war going on, and so the mainstream has become very obvious. But I'm always encouraged that people do dig deeper. It's not that many, but I'm not sure it ever was.

"I realized early on when I started playing that people aren't as interested in music as I am – there are people who are mad about their cars, where I couldn't care less as long it goes! It was kind of a relief to come to that realization. A lot of people I work with, including Cowboy Junkies to a degree, have an attitude that, if people don't like what they're doing, they're wrong. You need a bit of that to survive – it's a good defence mechanism when you're just starting out before you grow in self-confidence!

"But I just stopped being mad about it a long time ago. I'm glad for those that like it and you're not going to win the rest over by telling them they're stupid! They just like different things; there's nothing wrong in that. We've been doing this a long time – we're older, so we're pretty relaxed about it now. This is what we do. If you like it, great. If not, your choice. We're pretty clear that we do what we want, so people have to take it or leave it, and that's fine. But we're going to keep on giving it to them!"

The Chinese philosopher Mencius wrote, "The sole concern of learning is to seek one's original heart." The material that Cowboy Junkies have thus far left behind is all about that, about looking to change the signal-to-noise ratio, about trying to find your way beyond the chaos, the sheets of volume, the colour, the blaring, never-ending demands and trying to find the kernel of truth, of self, that lies buried beneath the rubble of trying to live a life in a 24-7-365 society that just never takes a breath and doesn't want you to, either.

In a world that is terrified of confronting them, it is a courageous artist who deals only in questions. But it's also an honest one. And a necessary one, because we have yet to devise anything better than art for winkling out the most subtle and intriguing moral questions. Maybe the point of all art, maybe of life itself, is simply to ask better questions?

"We're proud of what we've achieved," says Pete. "We haven't become our own tribute band and just settled for pushing what we did years ago. I think we're always learning. We listen to whatever's out there – new music and old, whatever we can find. We're still discovering stuff from all kinds of genres. We're still inspired by one another. We're still asking the questions. We don't present the answers, because *we* don't know either."

There is a quiet pride in their achievements from Margo, too, but perhaps from a different perspective. "To be around as long as we have and still to make records we feel so strongly about is great. The band is as tight as it ever was on all levels, musically, emotionally, physically –

there's no cracks showing, besides age! It still keeps getting better and better onstage; playing live is the heart of this band. And, as hard as it is, physically and emotionally, in terms of being away from home, all I have to do is get onstage for one second and it's, 'OK, I'm not giving this up. How do I make it work?'

"If there was no more Cowboy Junkies, I could give up singing. I don't think that would be a problem; I don't have to sing. But, as long as the Junkies are together, there's so much pleasure in it. Sure, there are nights I come off the stage and it's been hell, frustrating. But, even those nights, I can think that, at least I did that song well. But you're always searching for that night when you do all of them well, when we're all in the same groove, and then it's amazing. I can't give that up.

"My degree is in social work, so obviously I want to make the world feel a little bit better somehow, and this is the way I do it. It blows my mind that I've landed into doing something that makes people happy. Most of all, that's what makes me proud of what we've done."

"There are two kind of parts to being in the band," says Mike. "There's doing the work – writing, recording, making the records – and then there's the part where, when that's over, you put the record out and let the people decide if they like it or not.

"From being on the inside, the part I like best is developing a song from where it starts, through the rest of the band coming in and adding to it, until it finally gets to a place where you go, 'Yeah! Got it! Let's move on to something else.' It's an amazing process, but we never take it for granted, and that's one of the reasons we still love being in the band. We're still in awe of that process, we're always surprised by what comes out of it, the fact that it produces something emotive or evocative, and that's something you don't tire of.

"You always go into sessions wondering if it will happen. Thankfully, it's always worked so far, and that's always a relief, but we're overjoyed by it, too – you remember that's why you do it. Then, when you take it on the road, when you talk to fans, when people tell you what it is that they get out of the music, that's great. That's one of the reasons we like to maintain contact with our audience: to get that feedback from people who put their money on the line.

"We find it phenomenal that people pay to come to a show or buy a record, and that's a very big deal to us. Margo has always done the most of that, but she brings it back to us, talks about it, and it does make you realize that there is worth to what we do. No matter how many records we do or don't sell, as long as we touch the fans, and as long as we get that feedback from real people, it keeps making you want to go on and do more.

"As fans ourselves, that's what we get from music. When we go to see Springsteen or buy a Dylan record or go see a great show, it's just so moving, and to be able to extrapolate that and think, 'My God, we're having the same effect on some people who come to watch us!' That's an amazing thing, and it's very addictive."

I mentioned earlier that maybe the best art is about asking the right questions, better questions. If that's the case, then maybe I should pose one to end with, occasioned by listening to that imperial run of records from *At the End of Paths Taken* through to *All That Reckoning*. After all these years, are Cowboy Junkies now really hitting their stride?

Why not? We expect novelists, filmmakers, playwrights to all get better as they mature, grow older, accumulate wisdom or, at least, experience. It's only rock music where this slavish devotion to youth, and the idiotic notion that, in almost all cases, musicians are bankrupt after their first flush, holds sway. But if you are serious about your work, if you are intelligent writers and performers, shouldn't you be getting better at it the more of it that you do?

"As a band, I think we're better now than we've ever been," says Pete. "I don't know how it happens, I guess experience is huge like in any job, but you go through doors and you come to a different place in your playing, in what you're doing. I think doing *Nomad* showed us that you get more creative and you get more done the busier you are. When you're digging to survive, you get more creative."

In the end, you come to one final Cowboy Junkies paradox. There is album after album, song after song examining the concept of loss, of struggle, of families collapsing, of betrayal – OK, there are a couple of sweet songs in there too. If you look hard enough. But that is the bulk of the subject matter and yet Mike, Margo, Pete and Alan all have solid family lives that they go back to after each and every trek. Maybe that's why the songs, however dark, almost always come back to hope. That being so, where the hell do all those words that Margo sings come from?

"You're right: the fact that all four of us and our parents stayed married is a miracle in itself. Maybe the distance we get from touring helps. When we go away, you have the chance to come back fresh to your family every time. But, you know, it's the Catholic Church, I tell ya! It's the sense of guilt, of responsibility. I have a huge sense of responsibility – that's my driving force. It drives my wife nuts. I can't escape it. It's a positive thing, but a lot of negatives come with it, because you can't get out from underneath it.

"So, part of my thinking, my writing, is a sense of responsibility and the flipside of that is betrayal, I guess. I don't really know why it's all in there. It feeds into that idea of chance, too. That always kind of fascinates me. What's round the corner? You set yourself up to be responsible for those around you, you try to move in a certain direction, thinking you're juggling all the balls, but you know you're not; you just pretend you are. Any second now, one of them might fall and set everything crumbling from there.

"So, I guess it's that anxiety, that fear – that's probably what informs the songs. I don't know why. My psychologist must have the answer. You're not my psychologist, are you?"

Lie down on the couch, Mr Timmins. Tell me about your childhood …

ACKNOWLEDGEMENTS

From original idea to finished manuscript is a long, long journey, especially in this case – about sixteen years and thousands of miles. Along the way, many people have helped, so it's time for the "without whom" list.

Above all, of course, I owe Cowboy Junkies a huge debt. From the moment I sent my initial email to put the idea to them, their commitment to the cause has been incredible. From welcoming me onto the tour bus for the first time back in 2005 to sitting in cafés and pubs in Holmfirth in 2019 doing those final interviews, they – and, at times, their families too – have put up with me and my questions with warmth, generosity, good humour and infinite patience. To Mike, Alan, Margo, Pete, Jeff too, a mere thank you is hopelessly inadequate, but it's the only phrase we've come up with across these thousands of years, so it's all I have to offer.

That thank you extends to John Timmins, also on that tour bus back in 2005, unfailingly helpful when the last thing he probably needed on his first trip out on the road was somebody asking questions all the damn time.

Generosity of spirit seems to be the attribute that most surrounds Cowboy Junkies, whether that's because they inspire it in others or because they just find the right people, I'll leave you to decide. But so many of their collaborators gave freely of their precious time and were always willing to take just one more request.

In their different ways, meetings with Peter Moore and Jaro Czerwinec were unforgettable and their recollections were beyond illuminating. Again, thank you is not enough. David Houghton, Jim Powers, John Leckie, Linford Detweiler, Tim Easton and Luka Bloom

ACKNOWLEDGEMENTS

were all willing interviewees, even if we never got to meet. The time they gave over the phone or via email all added to the scope of the project and I'm grateful to them all.

Blair Woods helped organise things seamlessly and was a fine travelling companion, including the drive of the twenty-five ten-minute sleeps through jet lag – he was driving the truck, I was sleeping – and getting locked out in Santa Fe.

I came across countless members of the crew at different periods and every one of them was helpful and welcoming when they had better things to do. John Farnsworth ultimately did a fine job of speaking on behalf of them all in this book, so my thanks go to them all through him.

A number of the llamas were important to the story too, chief amongst them the legendary Cookie Bob Helm, who not only contributed interviews and insight but did plenty of the driving on the 2007 trip. I regularly came across Crazy Ed Casey too, another with plenty of rare stories to offer, as did Ken Hoehlin. Via the wonders of email, Jason Lent, Jason Gonulsen and Keith Bergendorff all offered huge assistance without which this book would not be the same.

Have Not Been the Same: The CanRock Renaissance 1985–1995 by Michael Barclay, Ian A.D. Jack and Jason Schneider, published by ECW Press, was an invaluable source of information on the music scene in Canada as Cowboy Junkies were taking their early steps.

And finally, thanks to publishing guru and all-round spiritual adviser Anthony Keates for finding this book a home and to David Barraclough at Omnibus for agreeing to take it on. Nikky Twyman took on the considerable task of wrestling an unwieldy manuscript through the copy-editing phase and Imogen Gordon Clark then saw it through to the book you have in your hands now. My thanks to them and to all the unnamed designers, printers and sales people that have also played their part. I salute you.

Cowboy Junkies also allowed me to quote extensively from their songs, so my heartfelt thanks again go to them. All their lyrics have been reproduced with the kind permission of publisher Paz Junk Music Inc, except where noted.

200 More Miles, 'Cause Cheap Is How I Feel, Where Are You Tonight, Escape Is So Simple, Rock and Bird, This Street That Man This Life, The Last Spike, Townes' Blues, Southern Rain, Oregon Hill,

Black Eyed Man, A Horse in the Country, Crescent Moon, Pale Sun, Anniversary Song, Ring on the Sill, Seven Years, A Common Disaster, Something More Besides You, Now I Know, Bea's Song (River Song Trilogy Part II), Lonely Sinking Feeling, New Dawn Coming, I Did It All for You, Close My Eyes, Bread and Wine, Upon Still Waters, Dark Hole Again, Thousand Year Prayer, Small Swift Birds, Beneath the Gate, The Slide, One Soul Now, My Wild Child, Notes Falling Slow, This World Dreams Of, December Skies, Brand New World, Still Lost, Cutting Board Blues, Spiral Down, Someday Soon, Blue Eyed Saviour, Follower 2, My Only Guarantee, Little Dark Heart, I Move On, Fairytale, Angels in the Wilderness, Idle Tales, I Let Him In, Unanswered Letter (For JB), Demons, Three Wishes, Missing Children, Shining Teeth, Nose Before Ear
By Michael Timmins

To Love Is to Bury, Witches
By Michael & Margo Timmins

It Doesn't Really Matter Anyway, Mountain, 3rd Crusade, All That Reckoning, When We Arrive, The Things We Do to Each Other, Sing Me a Song
By Michael Timmins & Alan Anton

Dragging Hooks (River Song Trilogy Part III)
By Michael Timmins, Alan Anton & Peter Timmins

Cicadas, A Few Bags of Grain, (You've Got to Get) A Good Heart
By Michael Timmins, Alan Anton & Joby Baker

Staring Man
By Michael Timmins & Elizabeth Bishop

Someone Out There
By Michael Timmins & Greg Clarke
Published by Paz Junk Music & Greg Clarke

Miles from Our Home
By Michael Timmins, Greg Clarke & Brodie Lodge
Published by Paz Junk Music, Greg Clarke & Bug Music